HOLLAND'S
GRIMOIRE
OF
MAGICKAL
CORRESPONDENCES

A Ritual Handbook

By

Eileen Holland

NEW PAGE BOOKS
A division of The Career Press, Inc.
Franklin Lakes, NJ

HOLLAND'S GRIMOIRE OF MAGICKAL CORRESPONDENCES
EDITED BY GINA TALUCCI
TYPESET BY EILEEN DOW MUNSON
Cover design by Jean William Naumann
Printed in the U.S.A. by Book-mart Press

To order this title, please call toll-free 1-800-CAREER-1 (NJ and Canada: 201-848-0310) to order using VISA or MasterCard, or for further information on books from Career Press.

The Career Press, Inc., 3 Tice Road, PO Box 687,
Franklin Lakes, NJ 07417
www.careerpress.com
www.newpagebooks.com

Library of Congress Cataloging-in-Publication Data
Holland, Eileen
    Holland's grimoire of magickal correspondences / by Eileen Holland.
        p. cm.
    Includes bibliographical references.
    ISBN 1-56414-831-9 (pbk.)
        1. Witchcraft. 2. Magic. 3. Ritual. I. Title: Grimoire of magickal correspondences. II. Title.

BF1566.H64 2006
133.4'3--dc22   2005049134

This book is written with thanks to the many Witches and other magickal adepts who have so generously shared with me information about the ways they and their traditions practice magick.

Thanks also goes to: the wonderful Witches on the OpenSesame e-list, especially those who made suggestions about topics to include in this book; the agricultural college in Shibin el-Kom, Egypt, for allowing me access to their library and botanical garden; the New York City Public Library and the British Council Library in Cairo for stocking curious old books in which a Witch could find forgotten things; Starhawk, whose book *The Spiral Dance* first turned me on to correspondences; and Steven Jobs, for Mac computers.

Blessed be those who share knowledge,
Eileen Holland

Contents

Introduction

Shall we write about the things not to be spoken of?
Shall we divulge the things not to be divulged?
Shall we pronounce the things not to be pronounced?
—Emperor Julian (Flavius Claudius Julianus),
Hymn to the Mother of the Gods [1]

Holland's Grimoire of Magickal Correspondences had its genesis in Egypt, where I was living when I first went looking for the Mother in the ancient names of plants. I began to write my personal Book of Shadows. The information I gathered rapidly over spilled that book, even though I used tiny handwriting, so it was with great relief that I got my first computer when I moved back to New York City. I spent the next decade transferring the correspondences to the computer (and to the more powerful custom built one that replaced it), while continuing to research and add to the correspondences.

I originally began to collect and catalog magickal correspondences for myself, and for my own practice of the Craft. I make extensive use of them when I write spells, design rituals, make charms, and create magickal recipes. Correspondences are a profound source of inspiration for me. They trigger my creative imagination.

It would be a selfish waste to accumulate knowledge and keep it all to oneself, so I have written this book. Different practitioners work magick differently. Some have no need for correspondences, but those who work as I do will find *Holland's Grimoire* indispensable.

There are those who have criticized me for my books and Website because they say that I reveal too much, that I make public things which are best kept secret. Obviously, I disagree with that. I am a priestess of Thoth, the Egyptian god of magick, writing, communication, and much more. One of the things he has dominion over is openness in magick. His temples in ancient Egypt are said to have contained books of magick which anyone who had need could consult. I believe strongly in this. It's why I write about magick, why my Website is called Open, Sesame. I believe in the saying, "the best way to guard the Mysteries is to reveal them." In my view, knowledge that

---

[1] Betz, Hans Deiter (editor). *The Greek Magical Papyri in Translation, Including the Demotic Spells* (Chicago: University of Chicago Press, 1992) p. frontispiece.

is kept secret is knowledge that is likely to be lost. As a Wiccan who bides the Rede of "harm none," I am of course concerned that some may misuse the information in this book to do harm. But as a Wiccan priestess I have, of course, also taken steps to make sure that those who do so will learn very hard lessons about the Law of Three: everything that we put forth comes back to us three times.

Writing this book has been a sheer pleasure for me, so much so that I have been reluctant to finish it. But in a sense it will never be finished, because there are always more correspondences to be discovered. Runes, chakras, tarot cards, and Sabbats are among the categories which there was no room to include here.

I hope that you will enjoy using this book as much as I have enjoyed researching and writing it. I hope that you will be scribbling notes in the margins and end papers, that you will make *Holland's Grimoire* into your grimoire.

Using This Book

Holland's Grimoire of Magickal Correspondences is intended for experienced practitioners of magick. I am a practical Taurus who likes to write useful books, so it is organized alphabetically by intent, from *Ability* to *Zodiac*. You have only to look up entries which relate to the subject of your spell or working, and you will find many correspondences for it.

This book is also cross-referenced (as much as is possible without making it too repetitive) because I find this helpful in my own work. I like specifics. If I wanted to create a banishing spell, I would base it on the general correspondences for banishing. But if I wanted to incorporate the banishment of specific things into the spell, such as spirits or negative energy, I would need more information. That is exactly what *Holland's Grimoire* provides: both general and specific correspondences, organized by intent.

Directly below an intent you will find its basic correspondences. Some topics have limited ones, while others have many. Basic correspondences, wherever they apply, are organized as follows:

Planet(s)/Moon Phase(s)/
Element(s)/Direction(s)/Time(s)/
Day(s)/Month(s)/Season(s)/
Astrological Sign(s)

Here is an example of that, from the entry for *Healing*:

Sun/Earth/Full Moon/Waxing
Moon/Earth/Air/Fire/Water/
North/Monday/Tuesday/
Sunday/Aquarius/Scorpio

The Sun and Moon are included with the planets. Earth is both a planet and an Element, so it may be listed as either. Where appropriate, it is listed as both in an entry.

The body of the entry for each topic is divided into as many of these categories as applies to it: Tool, Method, Color, Charm, Number, Letter, Animal, Stone, Metal, Potion, Stone, Oil, Fungus, Plant, Goddess, God, and Evocation. Some of these categories are self-evident, but others require explanation.

Tool

A tool is a manual implement, something that is used to accomplish a task. In the Craft tools include athames, bells, besoms, broomsticks, candles, cauldrons, censers, chalices, cords, drums, gongs, knives, mirrors, pentacles, pentagrams, rattles, scourges, staves, swords, and wands. Divination tools such as crystal balls, pendulums, and scrying bowls are also employed.

You can, of course, use any tool you prefer for any working. Those given here are the traditional ones, or those which contemporary practitioners have found to be effective for a particular purpose.

Method

A method is a technique or procedure, a way to achieve a desired result. Simple magickal techniques include anointing, asperging, chanting, dancing, drumming, smudging, and sweeping. Dream work, evocation, invocation, meditation, and visualization are examples of other popular methods. Gestures, affirmations, incantations, and offerings are also widely used. Every type of divination has magickal applications. Even mundane practices such as cleaning, bathing, and playing or listening to music can be used to work magick.

Astral projection, binding, cloaking, trance states, and shapeshifting are examples of more advanced procedures. Specific types of magick, such as candle magick, knot magick, and footprint magick, can be used effectively to achieve results. Practices from other disciplines, faiths, and traditions may require special study, but they can also be used for magick. Examples of this include feng shui, martial arts, tantra, yoga, and Kabbalah.

This is an inclusive book. Several of the methods given here, although used by some Witches, Shamans, and other practitioners, are dangerous and definitely not recommended. These methods include fasting, ingesting any type of drugs, using Ouija boards, and holding séances. The use of any intoxicant, even wine, can be dangerous. Flying ointments are hazardous if they contain the traditional toxic ingredients. Some methods, such as sensory deprivation, trance possession, hypnosis, and spirit possession, should not be attempted without special training.

Methods of working magick are limited only by human ingenuity. Many different ones are given in this book. Make use of those with which you feel comfortable.

Charm

A charm is something that adds to the magick of a spell or ritual. Charms are myriad, encompassing many things. A typical charm is an object, such as a poppet, amulet, or talisman. Ritual garb, masks, rings, necklaces, and crowns are examples of wearable charms. Shapes can be charms, as can liquids, such as witch hazel, brine, melted snow, and holy water. A charm may be edible, such as bread or a grain cake. It can also be something that you do, such as crossing running water, going barefoot, tossing a shiny coin into a well, "riding" a broomstick through a field, or making love on the ground.

Some charms come from Nature. Animals supply many natural charms, from their feathers, shells, hair and teeth to musk and ambergris. Spiders provide webs, chickens provide eggs, and snakes provide their skins when they shed them. Bees furnish honey, royal jelly, and beeswax, which can all be used as charms. But if you care about animals you will only use charms that can be obtained without harming them, such as the shark teeth and empty seashells that wash up on beaches.

Magnets, coins, horseshoes, and images of deities are examples of manufactured charms. Handmade items such as corn dollies and pomanders can also be used as charms. So can magickal things such as spell bottles, seals, and magick powders. Traditional formulas also make great charms, such as dove's blood, Florida Water, and van. Charms are limitless, and a wide variety of them are given here.

Animal

All creatures are included under this heading: birds, reptiles, insects, and fish as well as mammals. Mythological animals, such as dragons, griffins, and basilisks, are also included.

Potion

A potion is something you can drink, such as cider, milk, or water. Alcoholic potions such as wine, mead, and wassail should only be used in moderation by those who are of legal age to drink them. Alcholic potions should be avoided altogether by those with substance abuse problems.

Tea makes great potions, whether it is brewed from black tea, green tea, or from herbs such as mint, chamomile, hibiscus, lemon balm, linden flower, or yerba maté. Ginger root and raspberry, strawberry, and blackberry leaves also provide tea that can serve as potions. Flavored teas such as cinnamon, ginseng, lemon, orange, and Earl Grey, which contains bergamot mint, can be used as potions when those plants' correspondences are desired.

To identify potions for your intent, look to the plants listed in an entry as well as the Potions category. Juice from any edible plant (such as carrots), or from edible fruits such as apples, cherries, coconuts, and pomegranates, also make great potions.

Incense

Look to the list of plants to find incense that corresponds to your intent. Plants such as benzoin, camphor, copal, dragon's blood, frankincense, mastic, myrrh, pine, and wood aloes provide resin that can be burned as incense. Plants whose dried leaves or bark can be burned as incense include cedar, cinnamon, fumitory, sage, patchouli, rosemary, sandalwood, and sweetgrass. Plants whose scents are commonly used to create incense include coconut, jasmine, rose, vanilla, and ylang-ylang.

Stone

Minerals and metallic elements, such as aluminum and antimony, have also been included here.

Oil

Different types of oils, such as food oils, essential oils, and fragrance oils, are used in magick. Look to the list of plants in an entry to find oils that correspond to your intent. Plants which provide food oils include almond, coconut, corn, hazelnut, olive, palm, peanut, safflower, sesame, sunflower, and walnut. Grocery stores and gourmet shops carry most of these items. Vitamin shops and health food stores are good sources for items such as wheat germ oil, grapeseed oil, tea tree oil, fish oil, and flax seed oil.

Essential oils are extracted from the seeds, leaves, roots, flowers, or bark of plants and are considered especially potent. Fragrance oils are synthetic ones that mimic natural scents, such as those of flowers or ambergris. They aren't considered as powerful but they are generally more affordable, and they eliminate the need to trouble animals for their body fluids.

Some oils have different names than the plants which provide them. Examples of this include palmarosa, from a grass, *and* petitgrain oil, from bitter oranges.

Fungus

The only safe mushroom or toadstool is one that is being sold as food. No mushroom or toadstool should be ingested unless you are absolutely certain of its identity. Some are so poisonous that you can be harmed merely by handling them.

Plant

Magick is practiced everywhere on this planet, so there are plants from all over the world in this book.

All known correspondences have been included in this book, but some of the plants are so poisonous that their use is strongly advised against. These include belladonna, datura, eye of Satan, hellebore, false hellebore, hemlock, henbane, mandrake, nightshade, and wolfsbane. Those names may be familiar to you as dangerous plants but even some common ones, such as wisteria and morning glory, are toxic.

Caution and common sense should always be used when working with plants. No plant should ever be ingested unless it is being sold as food or medicine. Some plants, while not poisonous, are still dangerous because of their effects on the human body. These include drug plants such as foxglove and opium poppy, and skin-irritating or allergy-provoking plants such as stinging nettle and goldenrod. If any plant is prohibited where you live, such as cannabis (marijuana), do not risk legal problems by using it in your spells.

Many plants, while otherwise safe, are dangerous to pregnant women. Herbs and oils should not be used during pregnancy without medical approval. Some plants are safe for humans but dangerous to animals, and vice versa. Any plant to which you are allergic is potentially dangerous to you, so be cautious when working with new plants and oils.

Gods and Goddesses

Included with the gods and goddesses are those who, while not technically deities, function as such in magick. These include the loas and orishas of Afro-Caribbean tradition, the bodhisattvas of Buddhism, and the spirits of Native American tradition.

A single deity may have several names, variant spellings of those names, and a multitude of titles and epithets. Effort has been made to be consistent in this book, but you will find some deities referred to in more than one way. If a deity has a title that corresponds to an intent, it is provided.

Evocation

This category is for non-divinities who may be called upon for magickal help. These include angels, heroes, demigods, nature spirits, and so on.

Protection

Protection is an enormous magickal topic. It has so many aspects that, for easy use, it has been divided into five sections for this book: Amulets, Defense, Protection, Security, and Talismans. Different traditions define these terms differently, but for the purposes of this book Amulets represent "protection against" and Talismans represent "protection for."

The correspondences in this book are drawn from many cultures, faiths, and traditions. These include Egyptian, Meso-potamian, Mayan, African, Afro-Caribbean, Norse, Slavic, Buddhist, Hindu, Shinto, Greco-Roman, Judeo-Christian, Chinese, Celtic, and Native American. Some correspondences may be familiar to you, while others may be strange or even seem contrary. I suggest that you make use of them as I do: adopt those which resonate with you, and bypass any which do not.

The one item that I have omitted from this book is bluestone, also called blue vitriol and bluestone crystal. It is electric blue, looks magickal and is sold as incense and for spells, but bluestone is actually copper sulfate. It is a carcinogen, used as a pesticide, releases poisonous fumes when burned, and is much too toxic to work with.

A Glossary including botanical, mythological, and other references can be found at *www.open-sesame.com.*

Chapter 1

Ability

(See also: Skill/s, Talent)

Animal: chimpanzee, great blue heron; God: Lugh, Herne. **Conversational ability**: *to improve in men*: Stone: lodestone. **Divination ability**: *to increase*: Stone: malachite; Plant: aspen, rowan, star anise; *for scrying*: henbane (sprinkled in cauldron), mugwort. **Executive ability**: God: Jupiter, Marduk. **Intellectual ability**: Plant: benzoin, peppermint, rosemary. **Mental ability**: Color: yellow, violet; Metal: aluminum; Stone: turquoise; Plant: corn, High John, honeysuckle, lavender, maize, willow. **Organizational ability**: Capricorn; God: Rama. **Psychic ability**: Neptune/Full Moon/Water; Color: royal blue, silver; Stone: clear quartz crystal, tourmaline; Plant: cinnamon, lavender, mace, mugwort, clary sage, water lily, yarrow; God: Marduk; Evocation: Merlin; *to awaken*: Stone: pyrite; God/dess: sea deities; *to develop*: Plant: basil; *to increase*: Method: meditation, dream work; Color: gray, lavender, purple, silver, white; Metal: silver; Stone: angelite, azurite, danburite, Goddess rock, hawk's eye, iolite, jet, malachite, moonstone, pyrite, smoky quartz, tanzanite, tiger's eye, blue topaz; Plant: acacia, Althea leaves, aniseed, catnip, cinnamon, damiana, flax, honeysuckle, jasmine, juniper berry, laurel, lotus, magnolia, mallow leaf, marigold, mimosa, peppermint, rose, saffron, star anise, thyme, wisteria, wormwood, yarrow, yew; *to stimulate*: Stone: Herkimer diamond, tanzanite, zoisite; Plant: cedar, cinnamon, jasmine, juniper, lilac, mace, mango, mastic, nutmeg, peppermint, sandalwood; *to strengthen*: Stone: moonstone; Plant: gum arabic, yarrow. **Sexual ability**: Goddess: Anath, Maeve; God: Fergus, Herne. **Spiritual ability**: Stone: pyrite; Plant: frankincense.

Ability for: (See: The Astral). **divination**: (See: Divination).

Ability to: **absorb**: Earth; Color: black. **adapt**: (See: Adaptability). **be in two places at once**: Animal: ocelot. **change**: (See: Change). **communicate powerfully**: Goddess: Oya; God: Bran. **enjoy**: Plant: daisy. **fight**: Mars; Stone: carbuncle. **finish things**: Plant: spindle tree, **hide**: Animal: mouse. **laugh**: (See: correspondences for Laughter). **look inward**: Animal: mole. **love**: Plant: rose; *fall in love*: Stone: charoite. **nurture**: Plant: wild rose. **see**: (See: Senses). **survive**: Animal: polar bear. **walk on water**: God: Poseidon. **yield**: Plant: snowdrop

Ability with: **tools**: *to increase*: Plant: lemongrass; *magickal tools*: Plant: lemon.

Abundance

(See also: Prosperity)

Jupiter/Waxing Moon/North

Color: green, orange; Charm: ankh, cornucopia, pitcher, pomander, honey, ancient mother goddess statuette; Number: 8; Animal: bee, water birds, buffalo, cow, frog, nighthawk, pig, rabbit, silkmoth, squirrel; Stone: agate, moss agate, aventurine, bloodstone, citrine, jade, malachite, peridot, smoky quartz, salt, tigereye; Potion:

mulled wine; Plant: alfalfa, almond, bilberry, blueberry, coconut, corn, date palm, fig, ear or sheaf of grain, honeysuckle, orange, palm, peach, wheat, dried figs wrapped in laurel leaves, any profusely flowering or fruiting plant; Goddess: Abundantia, Aine, Alaghom-Naom, Andarta, Anna Perenna, Anu (Goddess of Plenty), Artio, Astarte, Aveta, Bast, Blodeuwedd, Bona Dea, Buanann, Ceres, Cerridwen, Chicomecoatl, Concordia, Copia, Coventina, Damona, Danu, Dechtere, Demeter (Mother of Abundance), the Deohako, Dil, Epona, Erce, Ertha, Frigg, Gauri, Habondia (She of Abundance), Henwen, Hestia, Inanna, Isis (Lady of Abundance), Kali, Lakshmi (She of the Hundred Thousands), Magaia, Magog, Mama Allpa, the Matres, Nantosuelta, Nehalennia, Nikkal, Ops, Ops Consiva (Lady Bountiful), Oshun, the Parcae, Purandhi, Rhea, Rhiannon, Rosmerta (Great Provider), Sulis, Zaramama; God: Asar-alim-nuna, Bormo, Cernunnos, the Dagda, Easal, Ellil, Enbilulu-Gugal, Ganaskidi, Gil, Hades, Jupiter, Mahanidhi, Ollodius, Reshep, Saturn, Smertrius (The Provider), Sucellos, Svarog, Ubertas, Zeus, Zuku; Evocation: Fulla, the Rusalki. **Agricultural abundance**: Goddess: Demeter; God: Dosojin, Hou chi, Saturn. **Fast abundance**: Plant: honeysuckle. **Household abundance**: Goddess: Hestia. **Perfect abundance**: God: Enki.

To: **accept abundance**: Plant: crown of thorns, mesquite, saxifrage. **attract abundance**: Taurus; Animal: rabbit; Stone: dioptase, peridot, green tourmaline; Plant: almond, orange. **manifest abundance**: Stone: citrine; Plant: harebell. **open to abundance**: Animal: puffin.

Abuse

(See also: Protection, Violence)

Plant: basil.

Child abuse: *to prevent*: Goddess: Isis, Kali; *to protect against*: Goddess: Kali, Sekhmet; *to prosecute*: Goddess: Isis. **Domestic abuse**: *to be warned of the danger of*: Evocation: the Domovoi (by pulling a woman's hair); *to recover from*: Goddess: Juno.

Abuse of: power: Number: 8; *to avoid*: Animal: horse. **sex**: *to recover from*: Plant: chaste tree. **women**: (See: Women).

To: **avenge abuse**: Goddess: the Crone; God: Bran, Hephaestus. **protect against abuse**: Color: black; Stone: jasper, lapis lazuli, obsidian, smoky quartz; Plant: dragon's blood, frankincense, laurel, saffron; **recover from abuse**: Plant: onion; Goddess: Rhiannon.

Acceptance

Earth/Air

Color: green, pink; Charm: heart; Stone: rose quartz; Plant: blueberry, clover, holy thorn, iris, moss, mulberry; Goddess: the Great Mother, Nemesis.

Self-acceptance: (See: Inner Work).

To **accept**: **abundance**: (See: Abundance). **an animal**: Goddess: the Mother. **a challenge**: Goddess: Atalanta, Macha; God: Anansi. **change**: (See: Change). **a child with an unusual appearance**: Goddess: Isis, Walutahanga. **circumstances/situations**: (See: Situations). **compromise**: Goddess: Ceres, Demeter, Persephone; God: Hades, Pluto. **your dark side**: Color: black. **death as part of the spiral of life**: (See: Death). **freedom**: Plant: saxifrage. **gifts**: the Matres. **happiness**: Plant: zinnia. **help**: Plant: spirea; *spiritual aid*: Plant: angelica. **an illness or disability**: Evocation: Chiron (The Wounded Healer). **loss**: *to learn to accept*: Plant: cypress. Goddess: Nanna. **love**: (See: Love). **others**: Stone: apatite, green jacinth; *to be selective in accepting new* *people*: Animal: wolf. **power**: Stone: tiger-eye. **reality**: Stone: aragonite; Goddess: Luonnotar. **your sexuality**: Stone: ruby. **something that is hard to take**: Plant: mustard. **spirituality**: Plant: Jacob's ladder. **transformation**: Plant: mallow. **twists of fate**: Animal: coyote; God: Loki.

Accidents

Leo/Scorpio

Car accidents: *to protect against*: Color: red, white; Charm: cat's claw; Plant: cat's claw, eye of Satan (placed in trunk or engine compartment), wormwood (hung from rear view mirror). **Horseback riding accidents**: *to protect against*: Stone: turquoise. **Violent accidents**: *to protect against*: Stone: coral.

To: help children after accidents: Plant: sweet potato. **make up for accidental harm**: Plant: hyacinth. **protect against accidents**: Color: purple. Stone: aquamarine, bloodstone, chalcedony, jade, sugilite, turquoise; Plant: feverfew, gravel root, juniper, rattlesnake root, tulip, wormwood; Goddess: Tarri Penu. **recover from accidents**: Plant: catnip.

Accomplishment

(See also: Harvest, Success)

Color: purple; Charm: circle; Number: 4, 7, 8, 9, 22; Animal: bluebird, firefly, moose; Potion: wine; Goddess: Demeter, Gauri, Isis, the Mother; God: Dionysus, Janus, Promitor, Vishnu.

All-accomplishing wisdom: North.

To: finish what you begin: Plant: spindle tree; *to learn to finish what you begin*: Animal: gazelle. **transform jealousy into accomplishment**: Color: green.

Achievement

(See: Accomplishment, Success)

Acquisition

(See also: Theft)

Taurus

Charm: beryl engraved with a crow that has a crab beneath its feet; Animal: magpie, squirrel, pack rat; Stone: beryl.

To acquire: credit/a loan: Plant: petunia. **glory**: Plant: juniper. **a job/raise**: (See: Employment). **magical tools**: God: Mannan. **material objects**: Plant: vervain. **needed rain**: Goddess: Aryong-Jong, Atlacoya; *for agriculture*: Goddess: Auxesia; God: Freyr; *food needed to sustain life*: Goddess: Uke Mochi. **real estate**: Goddess: Acca Larentia, Gefion; God: Poseidon; **wealth**: (See: Wealth). **what you need**: Full Moon; Stone: moonstone; Plant: sage; Goddess: Diana, Hecate, Rhiannon; God: Obatala. **what you want**: Animal: octopus; Plant: ladies thumb. **wisdom**: (See: Wisdom).

To learn that it isn't worth it to acquire things via theft: Goddess: Maeve.

Action

(See also: Activation, Energy, Manifestation, Movement, Opening, Progress)

Mars/Sun/Full Moon/Fire/Sunday/Tuesday/Aries

Color: green, orange, red, yellow; Number: 1, 3, 5; Animal: caribou, condor, tiger; Stone: red agate; Plant: laurel, lemon, maize, yarrow; Goddess: Anath, Angenoria, Nemesis, Sekhmet; God: Savitar, Serapis, Zeus.

Aggressive action: Mars; Animal: cobra, hippopotamus; **Assertive action**: Mars; Animal: osprey; Goddess: Anath, the Morrigan; God: Ares, Mars. **Confident action**: Plant: thistle. **Correct action**: Animal: wolf. **Covert action**: Night; Goddess: Furina. **Creative action**: Plant: broom.

Decisive action: Goddess: Ishtar. **Dynamic action**: Number: 3. **Fast action**: Color: magenta; Plant: cinnamon. **Focused action**: Plant: geranium, reed. **Government action**: Goddess: Minerva. **Harmonious action**: Color: blue; Plant: bluebell. **Immediate action**: Color: magenta; Goddess: Kali; **Independent action**: Goddess: Kamacharini; God: Poseidon. **Intelligent action**: Color: orange. **Mental action**: Wednesday; God: Baile. **Physical action**: Tuesday; Stone: almandine, rhodochrosite. **Positive action**: Stone: jade; Plant: apple; *to use to climb out of situational depression*: Goddess: Ceres, Demeter. **Ruinous action**: Goddess: Ate. **Virtuous action**: Stone: jade.

Purity of action: Plant: gardenia.

To: enable action: Goddess: Kali, Shakti. **encourage action** (make things happen): Fire; Animal: wolf; Plant: cedar, juniper berry, peppermint, thistle; Goddess: Angenoria; God: Savitar. **think before you act**: Goddess: Providentia.

Actions

Foolish actions: Plant: columbine, jonquil; Goddess: Ate; Evocation: Epimetheus; *to protect against*: Stone: chrysolite. **Government actions**: Goddess: Minerva. **Human actions**: Goddess: Pinga. **Negative actions**: *to wash away*: Water; Goddess: Ganga. **Obnoxious actions**: *to stop*: Plant: cucumber.

Actions of others: *to disrupt*: Plant: black mustard seed; *to limit*: Saturn/Saturday; Color: black. **Sex act**: (See: Sex). **Acts of passion**: *to protect against*: Plant: white heather.

To: act with respect: Plant: linden. **be responsible for the consequences of your actions**: Goddess: Greine. **ensure that criminals/wrongdoers pay for their actions**: Goddess: Isis.

Activation

(See also: Awakening, Beginning, Opening)

Sun/Fire

Tool: bell, censer, chime, gong; Method: breath work, libation; Goddess: Shakti; Plant: eucalyptus, mistletoe.

Bio-activation: Plant: globe artichoke. **Self-activation**: Plant: ephedra.

To activate: **chakras**: (See: Chakras). **change**: Stone: solidified lava. **crystals**: Sun/Moon; Charm: Austrian crystal (place natural crystals in the rainbows created by these artificial ones). **fertility**: (See: Fertility). **gods**: Goddess: Durga, Shakti; *the healing powers of Coventina*: Charm: toss a shiny coin into a well. **imagination**: Stone: aventurine. **immune system**: Plant: ginseng. **love**: Stone: rhodochrosite, rhodonite. **the mind**: Plant: thyme. **potential**: (See: Potential). **power**: (See: Power). **spells**: Color: yellow. **spleen**: Stone: hematite. **will**: Plant: ephedra. **yin**: Plant: rose.

Activity

Sun/Fire/Air

Color: green, red, yellow; Number: 3, 5; Animal: shark.

Human activities: *to record*: Goddess: Belit-Seri. **Intellectual activities**: Plant: redwood; Goddess: the Muses, Vidya-Lakshmi; God: Mitra, Ptah. **Sexual activity**: Animal: moth. **Youthful activity**: Goddess: Juventas. **Activities which require intelligence**: Goddess: Minerva.

To: disrupt the activities of others: Plant: black mustard seed. **organize an activity**: Plant: daisy. **take pleasure in activity**: Animal: wolf.

Adaptability

(See also: Flexibility)

Color: green, orange, peach; Number: 2; Animal: alligator, caracara, chameleon, dingo, eagle, eel, hyena, kite, shark, bull shark, water spider; Stone: sandstone; Plant: heather, tarragon, thyme.

Advancement

(See: Progress)

Adversity

(See also: Fortune, Problems, Uncrossing)

Animal: albatross, dragon; God: Ordog, Ponos.

Cheerfulness in adversity: Plant: chrysanthemum. **Courage to face adversity**: Plant: thistle. **Energy in adversity**: Plant: chamomile. **Fidelity in adversity**: Plant: wallflower. **Friendship in adversity**: Plant: ivy, pine, snowdrop. **Help in adversity**: Stone: black agate with white veins. **Hope in adversity**: Plant: Norway spruce. **Solace in adversity**: Plant: fire thorn. **Strength in adversity**: Animal: polar bear, tiger; Goddess: Isis.

To: avert adversity: Plant: High John. **overcome adversity**: Animal: pelican; Stone: carbuncle, onyx; Plant: birch, cottonwood, High John, poplar; Goddess: Inanna, Green Tara; God: Ganesha, Orunmila. **withstand adversity**: Plant: Japanese black pine, Japanese red pine.

Advice

(See also: Guidance)

Leo

Animal: great blue heron; Goddess: Freya, Neith.

Agricultural advice: God: Bres. **Business advice**: God: Xaman Ek (Guide of Merchants). **Good advice**: Goddess: Athena, the Crone, Fortuna, Freya, Inanna,

Ishtar, Juno Moneta, Ma'at, Mary (Our Lady of Good Counsel), Metis, Minerva, Neith, Oshun, Themis, Yemaya; God: Anubis, Aranuna (Counselor of Ea), Asar-alim, Consus, Ea, Kinma, Mimir, Thoth, Zeus (Lord of Counsel); Evocation: Anael, ancestors, angels, Merlin, Raphael, spirits, spirit guides; *sage advice in wartime*: Goddess: Athena.

To advise the dead: God: Jizo Bosatsu.

Affection

(See also: Favor, Friendship, Love, Romance)

Venus/Water/Taurus

Tool: chalice; Color: pink, red, rose; Number: 6, 7; Charm: heart; Plant: carnation, pink carnation, gillyflower, honeysuckle, jasmine, jonquil, morning glory, parsley (wreath), pear, prince's feather, rose, mossy saxifrage, sorrel, wallflower; Goddess: Agwe, Aphrodite, Philotes, Rati, Sjofn; God: Wadd.

Deep affection: Plant: white jasmine. **Endearing affection**: Plant: gorse. **Enduring affection**: Plant: wallflower; *after death*: Plant: carob tree. **Generous affection**: Plant: honeysuckle. **Maternal affection**: Animal: deer; Plant: cinquefoil, sorrel; Goddess: all prehistoric Mother goddesses. **Paternal affection**: Plant: sorrel. **Physical affection**: Animal: cat, owl. **Pure affection**: Plant: pink carnation. **Sacred affection**: Plant: marigold. **Tender affection**: Plant: pink convolvulus. **True affection**: Plant: parsley wreath. **Unchanging affection**: arbor vitae. **Return of affection**: Color: orange; Plant: jonquil.

To: attract affection: Venus; Color: pink; Plant: rose, sweetpea. **request affection**: Plant: hyacinth. **retain your husband's affection after your infidelity**: Evocation: Helen of Troy.

Afterlife

(See also: The Dead, Death, Otherworld, Reincarnation, Underworld)

West

Animal: heron, scorpion, sea birds, snake, spider, swan, wolf; Plant: acacia, pomegranate; Goddess: Cliodna, Demeter, Epona, Gaia, Hathor, Isis Amenti, Ituana, Pana, Persephone; God: Andjety, Dionysus, Osiris, Ptah-Seker-Ausar, Serapis.

Guidance in the afterlife: Goddess: Nehalennia, Nephthys; God: Anubis, Hermes Psychopompos. **Happy afterlife**: Plant: marigold; God: Charun. **Help in the afterlife**: Goddess: Pana; God: Thoth; *for children*: Goddess: Holda. **Initiation into the afterlife**: Goddess: Arianrhod; God: Februus. **Protection in the afterlife**: Goddess: Aericura, Heretkau. **Safety in the afterlife**: God: Bes. **Transition to the afterlife**: Animal: dolphin, hawk, jackal, all scavengers and carrion eaters; Plant: holy basil, myrtle, quince, wormwood (burned); Goddess: Aphrodite, Arianrhod, Corra, Culsa, Epona, Hathor, Ixtab (suicides and the hanged), Niamh (heroes), Neith, Nephthys, Nut, Selqet, Oya; God: Anguta, Anubis, Charon, Don, Februus, Gwynn, Hermes, Mithras, Ogma, Psychopompus, Pushan, Sucellos, Taxet (for those who die violently); Evocation: the Bardo, Charon, King Arthur, the Valkyries (for brave warriors slain in battle); *peaceful transition*: Plant: marjoram; *safe transition*: Goddess: Hathor; God: Anubis, Bes, Donn, Mithras; *successful transition*: Goddess: Corra; *to ease transition*: Stone: amazonite, Apache tear, fossil, hematite, jet, malachite, moonstone, obsidian, rose quartz, topaz; Plant: holy basil; Goddess: Kali Ma. **Virility in the afterlife**: God: Babi.

To have: a physical body in the afterlife: Charm: tet amulet. **sex in the afterlife**: Animal: cat; Stone: lapis lazuli. **To: move freely in the afterlife**: Charm: tet amulet. **use your mouth in the afterlife**: Tool: ur hekau; God: Wepwawet (Opener of the Way); *to drink*: Goddess: Nut, Tefnut; *to eat and drink*: God: Ptah.

Aggression

(See also: Aggressiveness, Battle, War)

Mars/Fire/East/Tuesday

Animal: alligator, barracuda, beta fish, crocodile, male gorilla, shark, squid, wolf, wolverine, all predators; Goddess: Cybele, Epona, Ishtar (Queen of Attack), the Morrigan; God: Ares, Baal.

Nocturnal attack: *to protect against*: Charm: sleep with the light on; close doors and windows and plug up all of the holes and other entry points in the bedroom; cross arms and legs while sleeping; Metal: steel; Plant: eye of Satan seeds (near the bed, or in the corners of the bedroom). **Psychic attack**: *to avert*: Stone: chalcedony; Plant: garlic, fennel; *to protect against*: Stone: black onyx; Plant: garlic, eye of Satan, yarrow; Goddess: the Crone; *against psychic vampirism*: Plant: garlic (kept near the bed); *to return*: Tool: mirror; Stone: carnelian; *to stop*: Color: black; Stone: obsidian; Plant: patchouli.

To: calm aggression: Plant: cedar. **know when to attack**: Animal: wolf. **lessen aggression**: Stone: bloodstone, rose quartz. **protect against aggression**: Animal: armadillo, dog, porcupine, skunk, wolverine; Plant: spearmint; *against attack on your luck*: (See: Luck).

Aggressiveness

(See also: Assertiveness)

Mars/Fire

Color: red; Animal: blue jay, boar, hippopotamus, penguin, wasp, woodpecker; Plant: asafetida, chili pepper, all plants with very strong smells; Goddess: Bast, Durga, Ishtar, Kali, Sekhmet; God: Ares, Baal, Marduk, Mars.

Sexual aggressiveness: Goddess: Isis, Kali; God: Pan; **Verbal aggressiveness**: Plant: snapdragon.

Aggressive action: Mars; Animal: cobra, hippopotamus. **Aggressive defense**: (See: Defense). **Aggressive magick**: (See: Magick).

To: lessen aggressiveness: Plant: cedar, lily. **make aggressive moves**: Animal: great blue heron.

Agreement

Number: 2; Plant: corn straw.

Balanced agreement: Goddess: Justitia.

Disagreement
(See also: Quarrels)

Plant: broken corn straw; Goddess: Eris; God: Stribog.

To: hear both sides in a disagreement: God: Forseti. **mediate/arbitrate a disagreement**: Goddess: Calliope, Dike, Shapash; God: Forseti (The Great Arbiter). **open a way for settling a disagreement**: God: Banaded. **settle a disagreement**: Stone: moonstone; Goddess: Zemlya; God: Mercury.

Agreements
(See: Contracts)

Agriculture
(See also: Gardening, Harvest)

Sun/Saturn/Earth/August

Stone: bloodstone; Goddess: Aine, Akka, Ala, Asase Yaa, Ashnan, Athana Lindia, Auxesia, Bo Dhu, Brigid, Campestres, Ceres, Chicomecoatl, Dea Dia, Demeter, the Deohako, Emutet, Epona, Erce, Fauna, Fura-Chogue, Gefion, Hathor, Horta, Hostilina, Hou-tu, Isis (Mother of Wheat, Lady of Green Crops, Mother of the Ears of Corn, Fructifier), Itzpapalotl, Iyatiku, Kupole, Mama Allpa, Marica, Mayahuel, Nikkal, Nu-Kua, Onatha, Ops, Rauni, Sekhet, Vacuna, Xilonen, Xochiquetzal, Yolkai Estan, Zemlya; God: Agrotes, Ahmakiq, Amaethon, Asharu, Azacca, Balarama, Bres, Coniraya, Dagon, Damuzi, Desojin, Ea, Enbilulu-Gugal, Enki, Enkimdu, Faunus, Fu Hsi, Gucumatz, Hou-chi, Inti, Kamapua, Loco, Lupercus, Mac Cecht, Marduk, Min, Ogun, Osiris, Picus, Poseidon, Saturn, Shen-nung, Sirsir, Sucellos, Sukuna-Biko, Susanowu, Telepinu, Thor, Tirawa, Tlaloc, Ubertas, Uwolowu, Volos, Xipe Totec, Yanauluha, Zaka; Evocation: the Rusalki.

Agricultural advice: God: Bres. **Agricultural cycles**: God: Baal, Yarillo. **Agricultural fertility**: God: Thor. **Agricultural growth**: (See: Growth). **Agricultural production**: Goddess: Demeter; *to manage the productivity of farmland*: God: Enki. **Agricultural prosperity**: (See: Prosperity). **Agricultural vitality**: (See: Vitality). **Agricultural wealth**: Ubertas. **Animal husbandry**: Color: brown; Goddess: Brigid, Demeter; God: Amaethon, Enki, Kupalo, Liber, Pryderi, Saturn, Serapis, Volos, Yanauluha; *to bless cattle*: Plant: hellebore; **Beekeeping**: Goddess: Isis (Lady of the House of Bees), Mellona; God: Aristaios; *to protect beekeepers*: God: Aristaios.

Crops: *fertility of crops*: Charm (to mix with seeds when planting, or sprinkle in field before planting): pork, red hair, ashes from Midsummer bonfires, grain from the last sheaf harvested the previous year; Stone: agate, moss agate; Goddess: Ashnan, Athana Lindia, Corn Mother, Demeter, Durga, Eshara, Habondia, Tellus Mater, Al-Uzzah; God: Mac Cecht, Tammuz, Thor;

Evocation: Corn Spirit; *fertility of fields*: Charm: "ride" a broomstick through the field; Goddess: Holda, Ishtar; *fertility of grain*: Goddess: Ceres, Demeter; God: Damuzi, Tammuz; *fertility of trees and vines*: Charm: fumigation at Midsummer with incense of wild thyme; Plant: vervain root; God: Telepinu; Goddess: the Alaferhviae; *fertility of apple trees*: Goddess: Pomona; *fertility of orchard trees*: Charm: hang images of Dionysus or fertility goddesses from them; *good crops*: Color: green; Omen: wolf running through a field with its tail held high; Potion: apple cider, wassail; Goddess: Ops; God: Baal, Janus, Marduk, Maximon, Ngendei, Sodza; Evocation: corn spirit, the Rusalki; *healthy crops*: Plant: vervain; God: Lactanus; *to help crops to ripen*: God: Promitor; *to prevent the blight of crops*: Stone: coral; Charm: coals from fire festival bonfires; *to protect crops*: Tool: broomstick (for "flying"); Stone: coral (powdered and mixed with seeds to protect against blight, caterpillars, locusts and storms); Plant: fennel stalk (to battle the forces that would do crops harm), African marigold (to repel weeds and insects); God: Ahmakiq, Azaca, Faunus, Svantovit; *from heavy storms*: Goddess: Diana *to protect barley*: God: Jehovah.

Farms: Goddess: Aine; *family farms*: Goddess: Zeme Pati. **Farmers**: God: Chibchacum, Dan Petro, Saturn, Thor. **Farm animals**: (See: Animals). **Fertilization**: God: Obarator. **Fertilizer**: God: Picus (manure), Stercullus.

Harvest: (See: Harvest). **Harvesting**: God: Messor.

Irrigation farming: Water; God: Epadun (Irrigator of Heaven and Earth, Lord Who Sprinkles the Fields), Marduk, Neptune, Osiris.

Plowing: Goddess: Anath, Gefion, Sita; God: Amaethon, Epadun, Imporcitor; *plowing under*: God: Redarator.

Pruning: God: Esus, Priapus; Goddess: Puta.

Seed production: God: Obarator.

Sowing: God: Insitor, Saturn; *to know where and when to plant*: God: Enki, Zulum.

Viniculture: God: Aristaeus, Dionysus, Osiris.

To bless: apple trees: Charm: smoke from Midsummer fires; Potion: wassail. **a field**: Charm: sprinkle ashes from a Sabbat bonfire in it; walk deocil naked to circle it at dawn. Goddess: Aine

To: benefit from agriculture: Animal: bluebird. **bring rain needed for agriculture**: Goddess: Auxesia; God: Freyr; **celebrate agriculture as a Female Mystery**: Plant: flax; Goddess: Demeter, Ganija; **learn how to farm**: Goddess: Demeter; God: Bres, Glooskap, Hu, Itzamna, Osiris, Saturnus; **protect agriculture**: Aphrodite of the Gardens, Ashnan (Protectress of the Grain), Pales (flocks and herds), Pomona (orchards); Aristaios (herds), Bhumiya (fields), Saturn (the sower and the seed), Tanu'ta (plants), Vertumnus (orchards).

Aid
(See: Assistance)

Alchemy
(See also: Transmutation)

Earth/Air/Fire/Water/North

Color: cobalt blue, silver, violet; Number: 22; Metal: antimony, bronze, gold, mercury, silver; Stone: cinnabar, diamond; Plant: lady's mantle; Goddess: Isis, Sekhmet; God: Lucifero, Thoth; Evocation: Hermes Trismegistus, Mary the Egyptian, Nicolas Flamel, Lao Tse.

Alertness
(See also: Awareness)

Full Moon

Color: yellow; Animal: hawk, rabbit; Stone: carnelian, moonstone, yellow zircon; Plant: almond, bergamot, peppermint; Goddess: Sarasvati; God: Horned God.

Alert mind: (See: The Mind). **Alertness to danger**: Animal: griffin. **Alertness to opportunities**: Animal: jackal.

Ambition

(See also: Career, Goals, Progress)

Saturn/Fire/Sunday/Aries/Capricorn

Number: 1, 3, 8; Color: dark green, indigo, orange, purple, bright red, silver; Animal: fire dragon; Metal: silver; Stone: garnet; Plant: hollyhock, hydrangea, mountain laurel; Goddess: Inanna, Ishtar, Isis; God: Zeus.

Female ambition: Plant: white hollyhock; Goddess: Durga. **Heroic ambition**: Plant: laurel. **Scholarly ambition**: Plant: hollyhock.

To: **counter ambition**: Color: green. **help a child achieve an ambition**: Goddess: Isis; Evocation: Nessa.

Amulets

(See also: Defense, Protection, Talismans)

To protect against: **abuse**: (See: Abuse). **accidents**: (See: Accidents). **aggression**: (See: Aggression). **aggravation**: Animal: ladybug. **air pollution**: Stone: zircon. **allergies**: Plant: coltsfoot. **Alzheimer's**: (See: Diseases/Disorders). **anger**: Stone: carnelian. Plant: juniper. **anemia**: Stone: garnet. **angina**: Plant: hawthorn berry. **animals**: (See: Animals). **arthritis/rheumatism**: Charm: steel ring; Plant: willow bark; **attack**: (See: Aggression).

Bad luck: (See: Luck). **Black magick**: (See: Magick). **Blight of crops**: (See: Agriculture). **Boils**: Plant: henbane. **Bullets**: Plant: amaranth. **Burglars**: (See: Thieves, Theft).

Catastrophe: God: Fudo-Myoo. **Cattle diseases**: (See: Diseases/Disorders). **Chaos**: God: Agayu. **Colds/flu**: (See: Diseases/Disorders). **Colic**: (See: Diseases/Disorders). **Confusion**: Plant: pennyroyal. **Convulsions**: Plant: peony root. **Cough**: Plant: black hellebore root, ginseng root, laurel.

Danger: (See: Danger). **Darkness**: (See: Darkness). **Death**: (See: Death). **Deceit**: Plant: snapdragon. **Deities**: God: Brihaspati; *against Lilith*: Charm: demon bowl; Plant: caraway. **Delusion**: Stone: peridot; Plant: nettle with yarrow. **Demons**: (See: Demons). **Depression**: (See: Depression). **Devils**: Stone: aquamarine; Plant: avens, fennel, St. John's Wort, vervain. **Disaster**: Plant: English ivy; Goddess: Auchimolgen; *natural disasters*: God: Avalokiteshvara, (Merciful Lord). **Diseases/disorders**: (See: Disease, Illness). **Disharmony**: (See: Harmony). **Disturbances**: Stone: emerald. **Dreams**: (See: Dreams). **Drunkenness**: Stone: amethyst.

Emotions: (See: Emotions); *emotional drainage*: Stone: obsidian; Plant: garlic, yarrow; *emotional tension*: Plant: yarrow; *emotional upset from past life work*: Plant: eucalyptus. **Enchantment**: (See: Enchantment). **Enemies/enmity**: (See: Enmity). **Envy**: (See: Envy). **Epidemics**: (See: Diseases/Disorders). **Epilepsy**: (See: Diseases/Disorders). **Evil**: (See: Evil). **Execution**: Goddess: Durga. **Eye diseases/problems**: Stone: emerald, jade; Plant: bistort root.

Fairies: (See: Fairies). **False friends**: Plant: bistort root. **Famine**: Goddess: the Mares, Raksha Kali. **Fantasy**: Plant: nettles with yarrow. **Fascination**: (See: Fascination). **Fatigue**: (See: Fatigue). **Fear/s**: (See: Fear). **Fire**: Color: red; Stone: bloodstone, garnet, lodestone, ruby, red tourmaline; Plant: houseleek, mistletoe, St. John's Wort (hung in window); Goddess: Brigid, Kwan Yin; God: Fudo-Myoo, Kakakl; *forest fires*: Goddess: Durga. **Fluid retention/edema**:

Stone: jasper. **Foolishness/foolish actions**: Stone: chrysolite. **Forces**: (See: Forces).

Ghosts: Metal: iron; Plant: juniper, mugwort, St. John's Wort, rosemary with garlic and sea salt. **Glandular diseases**: (See: Diseases/Disorders). **Goblins**: Plant: rue. **Government investigation**: Plant: tansy. **Guests**: God: Zeus.

Harm: Plant: clove, juniper; *physical harm*: Plant: heliotrope; Goddess: Kwan Yin; *spiritual harm*: Goddess: Kwan Yin; *harm from others*: Goddess: Isis; **Headache**: (See: Pain). **Heartbreak**: Plant: bistort root. **Hernia**: Plant: green fig wood (as firewood). **Hexes**: (See: Hexes). **Hysteria**: Plant: cuckoo flower, pennyroyal.

Ignorance: Goddess: Durga. **Illusions**: (See: Illusions). **Impotence**: Plant: dragon's blood. **Imprisonment**: Goddess: Durga. **Imps**: Plant: St. John's Wort. **Incantations**: Stone: coral. **Incubi**: Plant: eye of Satan, peony seeds. **Infection**: (See: Diseases/Disorders). **Injury**: *by others*: Plant: daffodil root (carried at night). **Insects**: (See: Animals). **Insomnia**: Stone: topaz. **Intoxication**: Stone: amethyst; Plant: linden bark. **The invisible**: Stone: jade.

Jealousy: (See: Jealousy).

Kidney disease/infection/stones: (See: Diseases/Disorders).

Lightning: (See: Lightning). **Liver disease**: Plant: garlic, **Lower forces**: Animal: jackal.

Magick: (See: Magick). **Manipulation**: Animal: alligator, crocodile; Stone: beryl. **Mechanical problems**: Charm: cat's claw (this should only be one that a cat loses naturally, or substitute the herb cat's claw). **Misfortune**: (See: Fortune). **Monsters**: Plant: garlic.

Negative energy: (See: Energy). **Negativity**: (See: Negativity). **Nightmares**: (See: Nightmares). **Night terrors**: Stone: chrysolite set in gold.

Other women: Plant: skullcap. **Overindulgence**: Stone: amethyst.

Pain: (See: Pain). **Parkinson's disease**: (See: Diseases/Disorders). **Passion**: (See: Passion). **Pestilence**: Stone: diamond, zircon. Plant: angelica. **Poison/toxins**: Stone: agate, amber, carnelian, coral, garnet, ruby, sapphire, zircon; Plant: bistort, black hellebore root; **Possession**: Stone: agate, leopardskin agate, jet. **Poverty**: Plant: alfalfa, carob. **Psychics**: *to protect your thoughts from*: Stone: carnelian. **Psychic attack**: Plant: rowan; Evocation: Towiscara. **Psychic vampirism**: Plant: garlic (kept near the bed).

Quarrels: Plant: cat's claw.

Retribution/revenge: Color: black.

Seasickness: Stone: beryl; Plant: feverfew, pennyroyal. **Self-destruction**: Plant: bistort, rowan, snowdrop. **Shipwreck**: Charm: wren feather; Plant: garlic. **Skin disease/disorders**: Stone: carnelian; Plant: aloe, vervain. **Sorcery**: Stone: agate, leopardskin agate, amber, sapphire; Plant: asphodel, horehound; God: Famien; **Spells**: (See: Spells); **Spirits**: (See: Spirits). **The state**: God: Amun (Protector of Commoners). **Stomach ache**: Plant: basil, rhubarb root, black spruce. **Stomach disease/problems**: Stone: white coral (necklace); Plant: pomegranate blossom. **Storms**: (See: Storms). **Strangers**: God: Zeus. **Stress**: Stone: lepidolite; Plant: ginseng. **Strife**: Plant: gardenia. **Stupidity**: Stone: emerald. **Sunstroke**: Potion: water. Plant: mugwort.

Tempests: (See: Storms). **Temptation**: Plant: vervain. **Terrorism**: Goddess: Mary. **Theft/thieves**: (See: Thieves). **Thoughts**: (See: Thoughts). **Throat infections/sore throat**: Charm: amber necklace. **Thunderstorms**: (See: Storms). **Trouble**: Plant: southernwood. **Tumors**: hydrangea root, mandrake root. **Twists of fate**: God: Sucellos.

Unethical dealings: God: Zulum. **Unhappiness**: Stone: peridot.

Vertigo/dizziness: Plant: woody nightshade. **Vibrations**: (See: Vibrations). **Violence**: (See: Violence). **Viruses**: Stone: salt; Plant: Echinacea. **Visions**: (See: Visions). **The visible**: Stone: jade.

War: Goddess: Kwan Yin; God: Kuan-Ti. **Warts**: Plant: beans. **Water**: Stone: lodestone; Plant: alder; Goddess: Kwan Yin; *drowning*: Animal: fish; Stone: aquamarine, Ionian gneiss, leopard skin jasper; Plant: ash, driftwood, garlic, petrified wood; *floods*: Goddess: Raksha-Kali; God: Sao Ching Niang Niang. **Bad weather**: (See: Storms, Weather). **Wind**: Plant: holly. **Witchcraft**: (See: Witchcraft). **Witches**: (See: Witches).

Anger

Mars/Fire/Aries

Color: black, red, greenish-yellow; Plant: catnip root, gorse, peony, red pepper, wormwood; Goddess: Durga, Hera, Nemesis, Oshun, Sekhmet; God: Aegir, Mars, Nergal.

Male anger: *to deal with*: Plant: saffron, snake cereus; Goddess: Kamrusepas.

Angry passion: Mars; Letter: Z; God: Ares, Mars. **Angry spirits**: *to placate*: Plant: rice, sesame seed.

Anger management: (See: Management).

To: avert anger: Stone: moss agate, emerald. **banish anger**: Stone: bloodstone; Goddess: Durga; **calm anger**: Charm: sea shells; Stone: blue lace agate, amethyst, angelite, carnelian, chrysoprase, emerald, fluorite, garnet, lignite, peridot, sugilite, topaz; Plant: benzoin, chamomile, lavender, madwort, saffron, valerian, willowherb, ylang-ylang. **Clear angry vibrations**: Tool: besom; Plant: elecampane. **Control anger**:

Color: yellow. **Learn not to anger the gods**: Goddess: Atalanta. **Learn not to misdirect your anger**: Goddess: Medea, Pasiphaë. **Overcome anger**: Plant: holly. **Placate anger**: Stone: carnelian; Goddess: Hannahannas. **Protect against anger**: Stone: carnelian; Plant: juniper. **Provoke anger**: Plant: powdered vervain root. **Release anger**: Color: blue, violet; Stone: carnelian, chrysocolla, sapphire, blue topaz; Plant: fuchsia, violet; Goddess: Oenone. **Strengthen anger**: Color: red. **Transform anger into wisdom**: Color: blue. **Treat health problems caused by anger**: Stone: sodalite.

Animals

(See also: Hunting)

Earth

Color: red; Charm: ambergris, civet, musk; Plant: arrowroot, calamus, catnip, deerstongue, juniper, motherwort, St. John's Wort, wormwood; Goddess: Artemis (Mistress of Animals), Bubona, Bugady Musun, Diana (Lady of the Animals), Zonget, Zvoruna; God: Cernunnos (Lord of Animals), Hurukan, Jaguar, T'ai-Yueh-Ta-Ti, Tuan Mac Carrell.

Black animals: Goddess: Kali. **Cloven-hoofed animals**: Goddess: Phoebe; God: Pan; **Domestic/farm animals**: Goddess: Ajyst, Damona; God: Kupalo; *fertility of*: Goddess: Epona, Vitsa Kuva (Cattleyard Lady); *fertility of cattle*: Evocation: Green George; *healthy milk production in cows*: Plant: wreathes of cowslip; *to protect domestic animals*: Goddess: Lahar; God: Krukis; *to protect cattle*: Plant: hellebore, pear tree; Goddess: Belenus, Disani, Pales, Sekhet-Hor; God: Geus Urvan; *to protect cows*: Plant: trailing pearlwort; Goddess: Lamaria; *to protect livestock*: God: Pales; *to protect sheep*: Goddess: Pales; God:

Belenus. **Flock animals**: *fertility of*: Goddess: Brigid, Ishtar; *to protect*: Plant: ivy; God: Volos. **Forest animals**: Goddess: Arduinna, Artio, Flidais; God: Cernunnos; *to protect*: Goddess: Caipora (rain forest animals), Mielikki; God: Wai. **Healthy animals**: Goddess: Brigid. **Herd animals**: Goddess: Fauna; God: Volos; *domestic herd animals*: Goddess: Lahar; *fertility of*: Plant: *Juniperus excelsa*; Goddess: Brigid, Habondia; *welfare of*: Goddess: Brigantia; *to protect*: Plant: ivy; God: Aristaios, Faunus, Volos. **Horned animals**: God: Cernunnos; *wild horned animals*: Goddess: Dali. **Power/totem animals**: *to attune to*: Stone: labradorite. **Red animals**: God: Set. **White animals**: Goddess: Juno. **Wild animals**: Goddess: Artemis (Lady of the Wild Things), Cailleach, Diana, Flidais, Vesna; God: Cernunnos, the Horned God (Lord of Animals), Ogun, Volos; *reproduction of*: Goddess: Cybele; *to protect*: Goddess: Artemis, Mielikki; *to avert/protect against*: Plant: avens, juniper, mugwort, mullein; Goddess: Durga; *to avert snakes*: Plant: adder's tongue, lemongrass, plantain; *to protect*: Goddess: Ah Wink Ir Masa, Cailleach, Flidais, Mielikki; God: Cernunnos; Evocation: Brown Man of the Muirs. **Young animals**: Goddess: Diana.

Animal calls: God: Robin. **Animal guides**: (See: Guidance, Spirits). **Animal husbandry**: (See: Agriculture). **Animal magick**: (See: Magick). **Animal passion**: Animal: cat; Goddess: Bast. **Animal sacrifice**: God: Rudra. **Animal suckling**: Goddess: Rumina.

Fertility of animals: Goddess: Artemis, Catheña, Ostara; God: Damuzi, Enten, Min, Tammuz, Telepinu; *of fish*: Goddess: Hat Mehit; *to overcome animal infertility*: Plant: mistletoe. **Fertilization/impregnation of animals**: Goddess: Fortuna; God: Tate. **Kindness to animals**: Goddess: Kwan Yin; Evocation: St. Francis of Assisi. **Knowledge of animals**: Animal: cougar, turtle.

To: **communicate with animals**: Goddess: Rhiannon; God: Thoth; Evocation: Melampus. **Heal animals**: Color: brown; Plant: blackberry, black hellebore, coriander, lemon balm, myrrh, orris root, rosemary, sandalwood. **Heal animal bites**: Stone: emerald (venomous beasts); God: Thoth (scorpion sting). **Protect animals**: Color: brown. Goddess: Artemis, Bubona, Bugady Musun, Cally Berry, Diana, Diana Tabiti, Rhiannon; God: Ah Cancum, Ah Tabai, Kurupira, Rudra, T'ai-Yueh-Ta-Ti, Tanu'ta; *birds*: Goddess: Coventina; God: Makemake; *bears*: Goddess: Artio; *boars*: Goddess: Arduinna; *cats*: Goddess: Bast, Sekhmet; God: Ra; *deer*: God: Zip; *horses*: Goddess: Epona, Dusk Zorya; Evocation: the vasily; *while being shod*: Plant: mouse-eared hawkweed; *sheep*: Goddess: Pales; *stags*: God: Silvanus Callirius; *from hunters*: Goddess: Caipora; God: Leshy; *from mistreatment*: Goddess: Pinga; Plant: avens, briar rose; God: Harpa-khered, Sukuna-Hikona.

Protect against animals: Stone: serpentary (venomous creatures); God: Bes, Harpa-khered, Sukuna-Hikona; *against insects*: Stone: red agate, obsidian, serpentary; Plant: vervain; God: Sukuna-Hikona; *scorpions*: God: Bes, Geb, Nehebu-Kau; *against reptiles*: Stone: serpentine; *crocodiles*: Stone: pyrite; Goddess: Buk; *snakes*: Stone: obsidian, sard; Plant: bistort root, centaury, onion, plantain leaf, vervain; Goddess: Janguli, Manasa; God: Bes, Horon, Nehebu-Kau, Ningirama. **Understand animals**: Plant: cloth of gold, fern seed (gathered on Midsummer eve); Evocation: Melampus. **Work with animals**: Earth; Color: brown; Plant: coltsfoot; *animal guides*: (See: Guidance); *dragons*: Plant: bistort, dragon's blood.

Anointing

(See: Blessing, Consecration)

Anxiety

(See also: Emotions, Fear/s, Mood, Stress)

Moon/Earth

Number: 6; Animal: rabbit; Plant: aspen, columbine; God: Pothos, Pryderi.

To: avert anxiety: Plant: pennyroyal. **banish anxiety**: Stone: chrysoprase; Plant: garlic, peony; God: Asar-alim-nuna. **calm anxiety**: Color: pink, rose; Charm: circlet of beads (for handling), witch hazel; Stone: agate, amazonite, amethyst, angelite, azurite, barite, chrysocolla, hematite, howlite, malachite, smithsonite; Oil: neroli, petitgrain; Potion: absinthe (dangerous, not recommended); Plant: benzoin, bergamot, betony, birch, cedar, chamomile, cypress, date, frankincense, geranium, black hellebore, jasmine, lavender, lemon balm, lime, mimosa, mint, orange, passionflower, primrose, rosemary, sage, clary sage, sandalwood, spruce, valerian, verbena, witch hazel, wolfsbane, wormwood, ylang-ylang; *about mundane things*: Color: yellow. **overcome anxiety**: Goddess: Green Tara. **release anxiety**: Stone: azurite, kyanite, malachite; Plant: castor bean (oil), sycamore.

Arguments

(See: Quarrels)

Assertiveness

(See also: Aggressiveness)

Mars/Aries/Tuesday

Color: red; Animal: copperhead, great blue heron, starling, sparrow, spider; Plant: basil, bergamot, cypress; Goddess: Inanna, Oya; God: Ares, Mars.

Assertive action: (See: Action). **Assertive defense**: Animal: long-eared owl. **To learn to assert yourself**: Stone: angelite, danburite; Plant: apple.

Assistance

(See also: Advice, Support, correspondences for whatever you need help with, such as Love, Goals, Inner Work, Success, and so on.)

Number: 2; Goddess: Ashtartu, Isis, Kwan Yin, Tara.

Emotional assistance: Plant: gardenia. **Magickal assistance**: Goddess: Ashtartu. **Spiritual assistance**: Charm: star; Animal: duck; Plant: pine, poppy, spearmint, wisteria; *to accept*: Plant: angelica. **Unique assistance**: Animal: salamander. **Unexpected assistance**: Animal: angelfish.

Helpful people: Color: yellow; Animal: otter. **Helpful spirits**: *to invite*: Plant: holly leaf.

Assistance at crossroads: God: Orunmila.

Assistance during: adversity: Stone: black agate with white veins. **pregnancy**: (See: Pregnancy). **times of danger**: (See: Danger). **times of need**: (See: Need).

Assistance in: achieving goals: God: Ogun. **achieving success**: Plant: sandalwood. **the afterlife**: (See: Afterlife). **battle**: God: Apollo Boedromios. **childbirth**: (See: Childbirth). **finding love**: Plant: jasmine. **making decisions**: (See: Decisions). **making dreams come true**: Plant: chamomile, huckleberry leaf. **making it through your darkest hours**: (See: Darkness). **making wishes come true**: (See: Wishes). **the Otherworld**: Animal: otter. **personal evolution**: Plant: lavender.

Assistance with: business: Color: orange. **communication**: Plant: linden. **creation**: God: Loki, Ocasta, Vili. **divination**: Plant: fir bough (burned); Goddess: Ertha. **family matters**: Plant: Low John, maple. **pathworking**: Stone: amethyst. **rebirth**: Goddess: Nephthys. **strange situations**: Plant: dill, High John. **stress of air travel**:

Stone: hematite. **troubled mind**: Stone: jasper; Plant: madwort, wolfbane.

To: **accept assistance**: Plant: spirea; **overcome your reluctance to ask for help**: Plant: bergamot; Stone: turquoise.

To assist: **babies**: *to sleep*: Charm: owl feather (in bed). **children**: (See: Children). **crops**: (See: Agriculture). **flow**: *of kundalini*: Stone: jet; *of physical energy*: Stone: blue lace agate, tiger's eye; Plant: sycamore. **forest travelers**: God: Byelobog. **a garden/plants to grow**: (See: Growth). **lovers**: Stone: moonstone. **the mentally ill**: God: Shiva. **newborns**: *into the light*: Goddess: Candelifera. **someone who is ill**: Animal: dog, goose. **spirits**: (See: Spirits). **students**: Plant: peach tree leaf. **warriors**: *to escape from enemies*: Plant: vervain. **working class people**: Goddess: Acca Larentia.

To get assistance from: **fairies**: Plant: fairy wand, hazelnut. **spirits**: Color: blue; Plant: lemon, mint. **the Universe**: Plant: High John with galangal.

The Astral

Air/Water

Color: violet; Stone: celestite.

Astral body: Color: yellow; Plant: lavender; *to align astral bodies*: Stone: amazonite; Plant: ginger. **Astral plane**: God: Cernunnos, Hu Gadarn; Evocation: Yesod; *to contact*: Plant: frankincense; *etheric plane*: Moon; *first astral plane*: Earth; *second astral plane*: Mars; *third astral plane*: Venus; *fourth astral plane*: Saturn; *fifth astral plane*: Mercury; *sixth astral plane*: Jupiter; *seventh astral plane*: Sun. **Astral power**: Stone: meteorite.

Astral projection/travel: Air/Monday; Color: blue, gold, purple, violet, white, yellow; Tool: scourge; Method: trance; Charm: ankh, flying ointment (dangerous and strongly advised against if it contains the traditional toxic ingredients); Animal: crane, heron, owl; Stone: amethyst, ametrine, apophyllite, azurite, calcite, celestite, fluorite, hematite, iolite, malachite, meteorite, moldovite, opal, clear quartz crystal, sapphire, tourmilated quartz, tourmaline, turquoise; Plant: ash, belladonna, benzoin, celery, cinnamon, cinquefoil, datura, dittany, gardenia, geranium, ginger, hemlock, hellebore, henbane, jasmine, mandrake, mugwort, narcissus, wild parsnip, parsley, plane tree, poplar leaves, potato, opium poppy, orris root, sandalwood, wolfsbane; Goddess: Isis, Luaths Lurgann, Nut, Oshun, Pelé; God: Anubis, Khnum, Ochosi; Evocation: dryads, Gabriel; *protection during*: Animal: jackal; Stone: red jasper, moldovite; God: Anubis; Plant: comfrey, ti; *safe astral travel*: Plant: cinnamon; *to increase ability for astral projection*: Color: yellow; Stone: moldovite (held, or under pillow).

Astral strength: Plant: frankincense, myrrh. **Astral vision**: Stone: carnelian, clear quartz crystal. **Astral work**: Plant: frankincense, galangal, rowan.

Astrology
(See: Zodiac)

Attachment

Animal: mussel; Plant: harebell, jasmine, thornless rose, all climbing plants.

Attachment to the home: Animal: cat; Plant: ivy. **To transform attachment into discernment**: Color: red.

Attachments

Emotional attachments: *to release*: Plant: hawthorn. **Karmic attachments**: Stone: tiger's eye; *to release*: Stone: hawk's eye. **Negative attachments**: *to release*: Stone: moldovite, sugilite; Plant: bunchberry.

To: clear attachments: Stone: calcite. **release attachments**: Plant: bloodroot, bunchberry, raspberry; Goddess: Bandhananashini (Detacher of Attachments); *release the need for attachments*: Plant: raspberry.

Attack

(See: Aggression, Battle, Protection)

Attraction

Sun/Venus/Waxing Moon/Sunday/Libra

Color: gold, orange, pink, yellow; Charm: honey, magnet, musk, orange feather, orange flower water, talisman; Number: 4, 5; Stone: hematite, lodestone, tourmaline; Metal: silver; Plant: bayberry, cinnamon, frangipani, ginseng, High John, jasmine, linden, orange blossom, orris root, patchouli, spikenard, strawberry, sweet pea, wisteria; Evocation: the rusalki.

Fatal attraction: God: Angus. **Sexual attraction**: Plant: cherry bark, orris root; God: Krishna; *mutual*: Plant: magnolia. **Spiritual attraction**: Plant: sweetgrass.

To attract: abundance: (See: Abundance). **affection**: (See: Affection). **attention**: Plant: chamomile, ylang-ylang; *the attention of the one you want*: Charm: daisy chain (worn in the hair), milk in which cowslip blossoms have been infused (to wash face, not to drink as a potion); Plant: marjoram; *sexual attention*: (See: Sex). **beauty**: Stone: turquoise; Plant: maidenhair fern; **blessings**: (See: Blessings). **business**: (See: Business). **butterflies**: Plant: bloodflower, butterfly bush, ivy, milkweed, viper's bugloss. **calm**: Plant: yarrow. **confidence**: Plant: frangipani, rose, yarrow. **contentment**: Plant: apple. **courage**: Plant: yarrow. **customers**: (See: Business). **deities**: (See: The Divine). **desire**: (See: Desire). **the one you desire**: (See: Desire). **doves**: Plant: vervain. **elves**: Plant: rosemary. **energy**: (See: Energy). **fairies**: (See: Fairies). **favors**: Stone: tourmaline. **fertility**: Color: green, emerald green. **fidelity**: Stone: amber, rose quartz; Plant: basil. **friends/friendship**: (See: Friendship). **goodness/good things**: Color: orange; Stone: lodestone; Plant: papaya; **happiness**: (See: Happiness). **harmony**: Plant: basil, lilac. **higher influences**: Color: gold. **good health**: (See: Health). **a home**: Animal: rabbit. **hope**: Stone: moonstone. **honor**: Plant: frankincense, myrrh. **honors**: Metal: gold. **hope**: Stone: moonstone. **influence**: (See: Influence). **inspiration**: (See: Inspiration). **joy**: Plant: lemon. **lightning**: (See: Lightning). **love**: (See: Love); *loving relationships*: Color: pink. **a lover**: (See: Lovers). **loyalty**: Plant: sweet pea; *loyal friends*: Stone: tourmaline. **good luck/fortune**: (See: Fortune, Luck). **a mate**: (See: Marriage). **men**: (See: Men). **money**: (See: Money). **the opposite sex**: Plant: allspice, clove, frangipani, honeysuckle, lovage, orris root. **peace**: (See: Peace). **people**: Plant: azalea, vanilla. **popularity**: Color: green; Plant: angelica, passionflower. **positive energy**: Plant: lemon, wisteria, ylang-ylang. **possessions**: Stone: garnet; Plant: lavender. **power**: (See: Power). **prestige**: Plant: High John. **prosperity**: (See: Prosperity). **protection**: (See: Protection). **the return of a lover**: Plant: damiana, dragon's blood, pineapple. **romance**: (See: Romance). **security**: Plant: cinnamon, vetiver. **sexual attention**: (See: Sex). **spirits**: (See: Spirits). **spirit guides**: (See: Guidance). **a spouse**: Plant: olive. **strength**: Plant: wood aloes. **success**: (See: Success). **trust**: Plant: frangipani. **vibrations**: (See: Vibrations). **wealth**: (See: Wealth). **well-being**: Plant: sage. **wisdom**: Stone: sodalite. Plant: hyacinth. **women**: (See: Women). **yang**: Sun; Metal: gold; Plant: dragon's blood. **yin**: Moon; Metal: silver.

To increase attraction: Color: red.

Attractiveness

(See also: Beauty, Charisma)

Venus

Color: peach, pink; Number: 3; Stone: amber; Plant: iris, jasmine, lemon verbena, parsley, rose.

Female attractiveness: Charm: orange flower water (in bath); Plant (in bath): orange blossom, raspberry leaf. **Male attractiveness**: Stone: black agate with white veins (worn). **Sexual attractiveness**: Charm: musk; *female*: Plant: rose hips, ylang-ylang; *male*: Plant: acorn (carried).

Auras

Stone: rose quartz, rhodochrosite.

Healthy aura: Color: orange; Plant: jasmine, myrrh. **Auric balance**: (See: Balance).

To: align the aura with the body: Stone: brown tourmaline. **clear the aura**: Stone: amethyst, calcite, labradorite, sunstone; Plant: citronella. **enlarge the aura**: Plant: saffron. **perceive auras**: Animal: copperhead. **prevent energy leaks in the aura**: Stone: labradorite. **protect the aura**: Stone: aquamarine, labradorite; Plant: citronella, clove, fern. **purify the aura**: Charm: lead crystal; Stone: citrine, iolite, labradorite, lapis lazuli, schist, selenite, brown tourmaline; Plant: citronella, clove, fennel, juniper berry, pine, vetiver. **seal the aura**: Plant: aloe vera, vetiver. **strengthen the aura**: Stone: garnet, iolite; Plant: vetiver.

Authority

(See also: Command, Control, Mastery, Power)

Jupiter/Saturn/Fire/Sunday/Leo

Tool: hazel rod, scourge; Color: orange, purple; Charm: crook and flail, scepter; Number: 8; Animal: great blue heron, lion; Metal: gold; God: Baal, Ea, El, Jupiter, Marduk, Odin, Zanahary, Zeus.

Spiritual authority: Charm: lotus throne; Plant: lotus; Goddess: Lakshmi; Evocation: Amergin.

Authority over others: Number: 3; God: Nergal. **Obedience to authority**: God: Mithras.

For: charm and elegance when asking a favor of authority: Plant: cinquefoil. **intercession with authority**: Goddess: Anunitu.

To: delegate authority: God: Ea; *delegate it wisely*: God: Enki. **gain favor with those in authority**: (See: Favor). **hide from authority**: Stone: lodestone.

Averting

(See also: Banishing, Protection)

Saturday

Color: black; Stone: bloodstone; Plant: angelica, horse chestnut, citronella, lilac, mustard seed (under doorway), oregano, black pepper.

To avert: aches and pains: Plant: horse chestnut. **adversity**: Plant: High John. **anger**: Stone: moss agate, emerald. **animals**: (See: Animals). **anxiety**: Plant: pennyroyal. **arthritis/ rheumatism**: Plant: hazel, nutmeg. **bad weather**: Plant: clove, garlic (hung up outdoors). **black magick**: (See: Magick). **bladder disease/infection**: Plant: cranberry, rose hip. **burglars**: (See: Thieves). **calamity**: Stone: diamond. **cancer**: Plant: garlic, gum tragacanth. **childhood illnesses**: Stone: jade. **conflict**: God: Kuan-Ti. **danger**: (See: Danger). **darkness**: Sun; God: Mithras. **death**: God: Haoma. **demons**: (See: Demons). **depression**: (See: Depression). **discord**: Stone: diamond. **diseases**: (See: Disease). **earthquakes**: Goddess: Bona Dea. **enchantment**: Charm: fat of a wolf.

Stone: diamond. **enemies**: Color: dark gray. Stone: green beryl. **envy**: (See: Envy). **epidemics**: Goddess: Mary. **evil**: (See: Evil, Home). **evil spirits**: (See: Spirits). **fairies**: (See: Fairies). **fear**: (See: Fear). **fever**: (See: Illness). **ghosts**: Stone: diamond. Plant: black beans (spit at them), garlic and rosemary with sea salt, nettle. **harmful people from the family**: Plant: marjoram. **hexes**: (See: Hexes). **illness**: (See: Illness). **illusions**: Stone: brown chalcedony, diamond. **impurity**: Goddess: Cerridwen. **incubi**: Plant: vervain. **infectious/contagious disease**: Plant: bachelor's buttons, cornflower, thyme. **inflammation/inflammatory diseases**: Stone: fluorite, garnet. **invaders**: Goddess: Banba, Fotia and Eriu. **jealousy**: (See: Jealousy). **Lilith** *(succubi/nocturnal emissions)*: Plant: artichoke. **lust**: (See: Lust). **mental illness**: (See: Illness). **misfortune**: (See: Fortune). **monsters**: Plant: High John, moonwort; God: Glooskap. **negativity**: (See: Negativity). **negative energy**: (See: Energy). **negative forces**: Plant: clove. **negative influences**: (See: Influences). **negative thought forms**: Color: black; Plant: geranium. **nightmares**: (See: Nightmares). **obstacles**: God: Ganesha. **panic**: Stone: diamond. **people**: (See: People). **psychic attack**: Stone: chalcedony; Plant: garlic, fennel. **respiratory diseases/disorder/infections**: Plant: Echinacea. **sleepwalking**: Stone: diamond. **snakes**: Plant: adder's tongue, lemongrass, plantain. **sorrow**: Stone: diamond, ruby. **spells**: (See: Spells). **spirits**: (See: Spirits). **storms**: (See: Storms). **succubi**: Plant: eye of Satan, vervain. **thoughts**: (See: Thoughts). **trouble**: Plant: white mustard seed (carried). **troublemakers**: (See: People). **visitors**: Charm: Go Away Powder. Plant: coriander, mugwort. **witchcraft**: Plant: dill seed. **witches**: (See: Witches). **wounds**: Plant: yerba santa.

Awakening

(See also: Activation, Beginning, Opening)

Sun/Rising Sun/East/Spring/Dawn

Animal: baboon, rooster, wren; Stone: clear quartz crystal; Plant: cayenne pepper; Goddess: the Great Goddess, Sekhmet (Awakener).

New awakenings: Plant: cherry. **Spiritual awakening**: Color: pink, rose, white; Stone: fluorite, quartz crystals, rose quartz; Plant: silverweed, snowdrop.

To awaken: desire: Stone: pearl; Goddess: Eos. **eroticism**: Plant: tuberose. **fertility**: (See: Fertility). **higher consciousness**: (See: Consciousness). **your inner healer**: Plant: eucalyptus. **inner knowledge**: Stone: iolite. **inner self**: Charm: rainbow. **joy**: Stone: kunzite; Plant: tangerine. **kundalini energy**: God: Dionysus. **the life force**: Plant: pine. **the mind**: Stone: chrysoprase; Plant: benzoin, peppermint. **past life memories**: Plant: camphor, lemon balm. **psychic ability**: (See: Ability). **psychic awareness**: (See: Awareness). **psychic mind**: Plant: lemongrass. **sensitivity**: Animal: cricket. **sensuality**: Plant: rose, vetiver. **sexuality**: Plant: ylang-ylang; *sacred sexuality*: Plant: sandalwood. **sexual energy**: Plant: patchouli. **spiritual gifts**: Animal: firefly. **understanding**: Sun.

Awareness

(See also: Alertness, Consciousness, Perception)

Tool: censer; Method: meditation, scent, yoga; Color: turquoise; Stone: obsidian; Animal: hawk; Plant: anise, ash, dandelion, honeysuckle, lime, oak; Goddess: Sekhmet (The Aware), Vör.

Artistic awareness: Goddess: Hathor. **Conscious awareness**: Animal: owl; Stone: azurite, barite, Herkimer diamond, quartz crystal; Plant: tamarack; Goddess: Alaghom-Naom; *to bring dreams to*: Stone: Herkimer diamond. **Cosmic awareness**: Plant: birch. **Discriminating awareness**: West. **Emotional awareness**: Plant: dandelion. **Inner awareness**: Stone: amethyst, clear quartz crystal; *to change*: Plant: grass of Parnassus, milkweed. **Mental awareness**: Color: yellow; Stone: yellow quartz; Plant: carnation. **Psychic awareness**: Moon; Color: blue, purple, silver, bluish silver, violet, yellow; Charm: blue feather; Stone: amethyst, ametrine, avalonite, calcite, celestite, citrine, hematite, picture jasper, lapis lazuli, moonstone; Oil: neroli; Plant: acacia, anise, betony (burned), borage, camphor, celery, cinnamon, citron, clove, deerstongue, flax, frankincense, galangal, heather, heliotrope, honeysuckle, iris, lemongrass, lotus, mace, marigold, mugwort, mullein, myrrh, nutmeg, peppermint, queen of the night, rose, sandalwood, star anise, sumbul, thyme, tuberose, yarrow, yerba santa; *to awaken*: Plant: mugwort; *to increase*: Saturn; Metal: silver; Stone: beryl, emerald, lapis lazuli; Plant: dragon's blood, heather; *to stimulate*: Stone: lapis lazuli,

sapphire; Plant: lemongrass. **Self-awareness**: Animal: chimpanzee, dolphin; Plant: camellia, Jacob's ladder, silverweed, tamarack. **Sensory awareness**: Stone: hematite, ruby. **Social awareness**: Uranus. **Spiritual awareness**: Stone: amber, amethyst, lapis lazuli, tanzanite; Plant: silver fir, forget-me-not, myrrh; *to increase*: Stone: amber, amethyst.

Growth of awareness: Stone: picture jasper.

Awareness of: ancestors: Charm: ancestral altar; Plant: cypress, plumeria; **the Earth**: Plant: tulip; **light**: Plant: bergamot; **other realms**: Plant: mushroom; **tone**: Animal: dolphin.

To: become aware of subtle energy: Method: meditation; Plant: lady's slipper, myrrh. **change awareness**: Tool: censer; Stone: staurolite; **increase awareness**: Stone: picture jasper, lapis lazuli; Fungus: mushroom; Plant: daisy, lavender, snowdrop. **open awareness**: Plant: lady's slipper, lotus, reindeer moss. **reach other planes of awareness**: Plant: yarrow. **stimulate awareness**: Plant: freesia.

Chapter 2

Babies

(See also: Childbirth, Children, Pregnancy)

[Note: Nothing should be given to a baby to chew, drink, or ingest except on the advice of a pediatrician. Do not place herbs or anything else that might cause an allergic reaction on or near a baby.]

Plant: baby's breath; Goddess: Hathor.

Boy babies: *omen of*: Plant: plentiful nut harvest; *to speed healing after circumcision*: Goddess: Weri Kumbaba. **Dead baby**: *to grieve for*: Goddess: La Llorona (The Weeping Woman), Mary (Lady of Sorrows). **Healthy baby**: Goddess: Juno, Juno Lucina; *healthy newborn*: Goddess: Juno, Juno Lucina. **Infant**: *to protect*: Goddess: Potnia, Volumna. **Newborn**: *to bless*: Charm: bread (so the child will never know hunger), gold or money (so the child will never know want); Stone: salt; Plant: frankincense, myrrh; Goddess: the Seven Hathors; *to bless new mother and baby*: Plant: fir needles; *to determine the personality of*: Method: astrology; Goddess: Renenet; *to name*: Goddess: Renenet; *to find the right name for*: Goddess: Frigg; *to predict its fortune/fate/future*: Method: astrology; Plant: apple tree, clove tree or coconut palm (planted when the baby is born); Goddess: Candelifera, Carmentia, Renenet, Rozanica, the Seven Hathors; *to protect*: Charm: blue bead, hand of Fatimah; Stone: mother of pearl; Plant: clover, fava bean, fenugreek; Goddess: Deverra, Intercidona, Juno, Laima, Volumna; God: Bes, Pilumnus, Vagitanus; *to protect the eyesight of*: Goddess: Lucina; *to protect the first cry of*: God: Vagitanus. **Premature baby**: *to care for*: Animal: kangaroo, koala, all female marsupials. **Unborn baby**: Goddess: Waldmichen; *to avert jealousy from*: Plant: squaw vine (in the bath); *to bond with*: Plant: forget-me-not; *to know the future of*: Goddess: Aegeria; *to protect*: Goddess: Decima, Yemaya, Yemaya Olokun; God: Acat; *to strengthen the bones of*: Goddess: Ossipago; *healthy unborn child*: Goddess: Alemona.

To: **bless a baby/child**: Goddess: Freya, Isis. **help a baby sleep**: Charm: owl feather (in bed). **nourish a baby**: Goddess: Edusa, Potnia, Rumina; *breast-feeding*: Stone: white chalcedony; Plant: alder, anise, basil, caraway, wild carrot, catnip, devil's bit scabious, dill, dittany, fenugreek, holy thistle, hops, lettuce, licorice, nettle, sage, Venus hair fern, viper's bugloss, willow, wintergreen, yohimbine; Goddess: Atchet, Ishtar (Mother of the Fruitful Breast), Isis, Mary, Rumina; *to increase lactation*: Color: white; Charm: clear quartz crystal steeped in honey(used as a charm, not to ingest); Stone: chalcedony; Plant: alder, anise, basil, borage, dandelion, devil's bit scabious, fennel, fenugreek, holy thistle, hops, lettuce, licorice, nettle, sage, Venus hair fern, viper's bugloss, willow, wintergreen, yohimbine; *to reduce lactation*: Plant: catsfoot, hemlock, mint, parsley, reed, walnut; *to let infants drink safely*: Goddess: Potnia.

Protect babies: Goddess: Volumna; Plant: chick pea, clove, clover, dill, fenugreek, grain, lentil, rice; *from evil*: Charm: blue bead, hand of Fatimah amulet; Plant: birch wood, hawthorn leaf; *from evil spirits*: Charm: birch wood cradle; *from fairies*: (See: Fairies); *protect the nursery*: Goddess: Cunina, Volumna. **Take care of a baby**: Goddess: Zorya; *for teething*: marshmallow root, orris root; *for colic*: Plant (tea): dill seed; aniseed and caraway seed with mint.

Balance

(See also: Stability)

Water/North/West/Night/Libra/Gemini

Charm: orange feather, honey, scales, twins, eggs stood upon their ends; Color: brown, gray, green, indigo, orange, pink, white; Animal: bass, cougar, dolphin, eagle, elephant, macaw, porpoise, spider, swan; Number: 2, 6; Metal: gold; Stone: agate, tree agate, amazonite, amethyst, aventurine, chrysocolla, citrine, emerald, fluorite, garnet, hematite, Herkimer diamond, brown or green jasper, obsidian, onyx, peridot, clear quartz crystal, smoky quartz, rhodochrosite, rhodonite, sodalite, staurolite, tigereye, topaz, tourmaline, green or watermelon tourmaline, turquoise; Oil: palmarosa; Plant: angelica, anise, avocado, basil, begonia, benzoin, bergamot, carnation, cat's claw, cedar, chamomile, cherry, cinnamon, coconut, comfrey, corn, enchanter's nightshade, eucalyptus, fig, frankincense, geranium, harebell, holly, honeysuckle, hops, hyssop, jasmine, lavender, lemon, lemongrass, lilac, maple, meadowsweet, mullein, myrrh, orange, patchouli, peach, pine, redwood, rose, rosewood, sage, sandalwood, spikenard, spruce, tuberose, vervain, vetiver, woodruff, yarrow, ylang-ylang; Goddess: Kishi-Mojin, Libra, Ma'at, Nemesis, Themis, Unk, Yemaya; God: Cernunnos, Horned God, Inyan, Nagi, Osiris, Shango, Shiva, Thoth (He Who Balances), Orunmila, Vishnu.

Auric balance: Stone: ametrine, citrine, iolite, jasper, labradorite, quartz, tourmaline; Plant: amber. **Creative/practical balance**: Animal: sea turtle. **Ecological balance**: Goddess: Sedna (sea and marine life); God: Cernunnos (animals and woodlands), Nergal. **Emotional balance**: Color: blue, green; Stone: agate, moss agate, chrysocolla, chrysoprase, emerald, garnet, hematite, jade, jasper, jet, malachite, moonstone, onyx, opal, rose quartz, rhodonite, sodalite, sugilite; Plant: anise, benzoin, bleeding heart, jasmine, lavender, orchid, rosemary, vanilla; *to balance will/emotion*: Color: gold, yellow; *to balance emotional energy*: Stone: moss agate; *to balance emotions in a friendship/relationship*: Stone: rose quartz; *to balance mind/emotions*: Stone: calcite, pink calcite; Plant: clary sage; *to balance mind/body/emotions*: Goddess: Unk; *to balance mind/spirit/emotions*: Stone: garnet; *mind/body/spirit*: Stone: emerald, hematite. **Fire/water balance**: Potion: liquor (in moderation). **Inner balance**: Moon; Stone: hanging rock; Plant: cinnamon, delphinium, tulip. **Karmic balance**: Color: indigo; Stone: amethyst, beryl, turquoise; Goddess: Kwan Yin. **Mental balance**: Metal: Apache gold (iron ore); Stone: agate, tree agate, bloodstone, chiastolite, citrine, fluorite, hematite, rhodochrosite, ruby, sodalite, blue topaz, tourmaline; Plant: aloe, cedar, cherry blossom, clove, coconut, passion flower, clary sage; *mind/body balance*: Stone: peridot; Plant: geranium; *mind/body/emotions balance*: Goddess: Unk; *mind/body/spirit balance*: Number: 3; Stone: emerald, hematite; *mind/spirit balance*: Stone: pearl. **Moral balance**: God: Vishnu. **Natural balance**: Goddess: Angerona. **Perfect balance**: Color: white.

Physical balance: Color: green; Animal: kangaroo; Metal: copper; Stone: green aventurine, chrysocolla, emerald, watermelon tourmaline, wulfenite; Plant: cinnamon, morning glory, pine, spearmint. **Positive/negative balance**: (See: Positiveness). **Psychic balance**: Plant: red clover. **Spiritual balance**: Method: knot magick; Charm: triskelion; Stone: agate, emerald; Plant: cumin, lotus, passionflower, vetiver; God: Byelobog/Chernobog; *emotional/ spiritual balance*: Stone: garnet; *physical/ spiritual balance*: Stone: black moss agate, apophyllite, malachite; *to balance: mind/ body/spirit*: Stone: emerald, hematite; *mind/ spirit/emotions*: Stone: garnet; *the spiritual with the mundane*: Color: indigo; Stone: ametrine, jade; Plant: cumin, lavender. **Yin/ yang balance**: (See Yang, Yin); *to balance yang*: Plant: banana, holly, sunflower; *to balance yin*: Plant: patchouli, quince.

Balanced agreement: Goddess: Justitia.

Balance in: communication: Stone: chrysocolla. **love**: Stone: rhodochrosite; Plant: ylang-ylang.

To balance: breathing: Air; Animal: dolphin; Plant: ylang-ylang. **career/work and family life**: Plant: pomegranate. **chakras**: (See: Chakras). **darkness and light**: (See: Darkness). **ego**: Plant: lotus, peppermint, sunflower. **energy**: (See: Energy). **gains and losses**: Goddess: Nemesis. **hormones**: Stone: fluorite, jasper, moonstone; Plant: burdock, evening primrose, geranium, clary sage, vetiver; *female hormones*: Stone: moonstone; Plant: black cohosh, soybean. **intent**: Animal: cougar, mountain lion, puma. Plant: holly. **joys and sorrows**: Plant: bleeding heart; Goddess: Nemesis. **left brain/right brain**: (See: The Body). **male/female**: Animal: bass, slug, snail. **opposites**: Animal: carp. **positive and negative forces**: (See: Forces). **power**: Animal: cougar, mountain lion, puma. **risk and safety**: Animal: coyote.

stress: Stone: jasper; Plant: orchid, vanilla. **the number of human males and females**: Goddess: Juksakka. **yourself**: Animal: crocodile.

To: appreciate balance: Animal: deer. **increase balance**: Stone: chrysoprase. **restore balance and cosmic order**: Goddess: Durga.

Imbalance

Moon

Color: gray; Metal: silver.

To balance an imbalance: Stone: watermelon tourmaline.

Banishing

(See also: Amulets, Averting, Clearing)

Saturn/Setting Sun/Waning Moon/Saturday

Tool: inverted pentacle; Color: black, green, magenta, purple; Charm: brimstone; Stone: aventurine, bloodstone, pumice, salt, black salt, sulfur; Plant: agrimony, alder, angelica, asafetida, avens, basil, bat nut, black beans, betony, blackthorn, buckthorn, cactus, camphor, cayenne pepper, cedar, clove, clover, comfrey, copal, cumin, cypress, devil's bit scabious, dragon's blood, elecampane, elder, fern, frankincense, fumitory, galangal, garlic, heliotrope, horehound, horse chestnut, horseradish, hyssop, juniper (as incense), juniper berry, laurel, lilac, logwood, mallow, mandrake, mint, mistletoe, mugwort, mullein, myrrh, nettle, onion, patchouli, peach, peony, black peppercorn, peppermint, pine, rose, rosemary, rue, sagebrush, sandalwood, St. John's Wort, snapdragon, Solomon's seal, star anise, tamarisk, thistle, tobacco, vervain, blue vervain, vetiver, violet, witch grass, yarrow; Goddess: Banba, Carman, Durga, Hastebaad, Kupala, the Morrigan, Dawn Zorya, Dusk Zorya; God: Astalluhi, Hanuman, Kephera, Khonsu.

To banish: addictions: Waning Moon; Stone: amethyst. **anxiety:** (See: Anxiety). **darkness:** (See: Darkness). **demons:** (See: Demons). **depression:** (See: Depression). **desire:** (See: Desire). **disharmony:** Plant: betony. **envy:** Stone: chrysoprase. **evil:** (See: Evil). **fatigue:** Plant: rosemary. **fear:** (See: Fear). **foolishness:** Stone: coral. **greed:** Stone: chrysoprase; God: Krishna. **hardship:** Goddess: Kwan Yin. **illness:** (See: Illness). **laziness:** Stone: beryl. **negativity:** (See: Negativity). **negative emotions:** (See: Emotions). **negative energy:** (See: Energy). **phobias:** Stone: aquamarine. **rain:** Animal: burrowing owl. **spirits:** (See: Spirits). **stupidity:** Stone: beryl. **unwanted people:** Charm: Go Away Powder, Hot Foot Powder.

Barriers

(See also: Averting, Blockages, Limits, Obstacles)

Stone: salt; Plant: cactus, dragon's blood, sage, wormwood, all spiny and thorny plants.

To bar: fairies: (See: Fairies). **ghosts and spirits:** (See: Spirits). **to break gender barriers:** Goddess: Atalanta.

To remove: emotional barriers: Plant: bleeding heart. **mental barriers:** Animal: orca; Stone: pink tourmaline.

Battle

(See also: Aggression, Defense, Overcoming, War)

Mars/Fire/Autumn

Color: red; Animal: crow, dog, elephant, raven, wolverine; Metal: iron, steel; Stone: brown agate; Plant: alder (also called battle witch), ash; Goddess: Aeron, Anahita, Anath, Aphrodite, Agasaya (The Shrieker), Agrona, the Alaisiagae, Alecto, Alfhild, Ambika, Andraste, Aoife, Arinna, Artemis, Ashtoreth, Astarte, Ashtartu Takhazi

(Athtart of the Battle), Athene, Badb (Crow of Battle), Banba, Bellona, Brigid, Queen Brigantia, Cathubodua, Crove Dairg, Cymidei Cymeinfoll, Danu, Devi, Durga, Elphame, Epona, Estiu, Fea, Freya, Greine, Gullveig, Inanna, Ishtar (Lady of Battle), Isis, Kali, Litavis, Lot, Macha, Maeve, Minerva, the Morrigan (Battle Raven, Goddess of Battles), Muireartach, Neith, Nematona, Oya, Pallas Athene, Rhiannon, Scathach, Sekhmet, Sin, Tiamat, Ushas, Al-Uzzah, Zorya; God: Ashur, Astabis, Baal, Belatucadros, Bishamon, Bran the Blessed, Brenos, Camulos, Cocidius, the Dagda, Ek Chua, Enos, Gwydion, Hachiman, Indra, Jarovit, Kamapua, Karttikeya, Kibuka, Ku, Kuan Ti, Laran, Llasar Llaesgyfnewid, Lugh, Marduk, Mars, Mars Caturix (King of Combat), Nergal, Ninurta, Odin, Ogun, Osiris in Battle, Patollo, Perun, Suwaliyattas, Teutates (Battle King), Thor, Tonatiuh, Triglav, Tu, Zaba; Evocation: Michael.

Hand-to-hand combat: Goddess: Ishtar (Queen of Attack and Hand-to-Hand Combat); God: Thor. **Personal combat:** God: Thor; Evocation: Achilles, Aigiarm, Penthesilea. **Single combat:** Goddess: Aoife, Durga, Scathach; God: Asaruludu, Baal, Marduk; Evocation: Androdameia, Cuchulain.

Battle charges: Goddess: Neith. **Battle cries:** Goddess: Scathach. **Battle madness:** Fungus: fly agaric; Goddess: Fea, the Morrigan, Nemain, Sekhmet; God: Modi. **Battle skills:** Goddess: Scathach, Uathach.

Courage in battle: Goddess: Athena. **Good fortune in battle:** Stone: opal. **Help in battle:** God: Apollo Boedromios. **Inspiration in battle:** God: Odin. **Invincibility in battle:** Goddess: Andraste, the Morrigan, Scathach. **Leadership in battle:** Goddess: Banba; God: Odin; Evocation: Quingu. **Power in battle:** Animal: eagle; Fungus: fly agaric. **Protection in battle**: Stone: tigereye (engraved as a talisman); Plant: spearmint; Goddess: the Crone, Sangramarakshika (Protectress in War); God: Reshep. **Strategy in battle**: Animal: praying mantis. **Victory in battle**: Charm: conch shell; Stone: brown agate; Goddess: Aerten, Andraste, the Morrigan, Badb, Devi, Ishtar (Lady of Battles and Victory), Nike, Sangramajayaprada (Granter of Victory in War); God: Odin, Savitri, Stribog, Tyr.

Ecstasy of battle: Goddess: Anath, the Morrigan, Sekhmet. God: Odin. **Oracles of battle**: Goddess: Inanna.

To battle: black magick: God: Väinämöinen. **chaos**: God: Baal, Marduk. **dark powers**: (See: Power). **demons**: Goddess: (See: Demons). **evil**: (See: Evil). **evil spirits**: Plant: fennel stalk. **foreign powers**: God: Teshub. **giants**: God: Thor. **greed**: God: Gwydion. **small minds**: God: Gwydion, Pan.

To: gain favor in battle: Goddess: Andraste. **influence the outcome of a battle**: Goddess: Aerten, Badb, Fea, the Morrigan, Nemain; God: Odin. **prevent blood loss in battle**: Color: red. **staunch/treat wounds in battle**: Stone: bloodstone; Plant: burnet, yarrow. **summon spirits to battle**: Plant: rowan (bonfire).

attlefields

Animal: raven; Goddess: Bellona, the Morrigan; God: Odin.

Battlefield magick: (See: Magick).

eauty

(See also: Attractiveness)

Venus/New Moon/Full Moon/Friday/Spring

Color: light blue, green, pink; Charm: ambergris, dew collected on May Morning (May 1); Animal: hummingbird, swan; Stone: amber, chalcedony, Herkimer diamond, jasper, red jasper, opal, tigereye, topaz, zircon, orange zircon; Plant: almond, aloe, amaryllis, apple, aloe, avocado, calla lily, catnip, chamomile, clover, cowslip, elder, flax, gardenia, ginger, ginseng, golden seal, hazel, hibiscus, holly, honeysuckle, jasmine, lavender, lemon verbena, lilac, lily, maidenhair fern, orange blossom (in the bath), orchid, rose, red rose, strawberry, violet, weeping willow, yerba santa; Goddess: Aega, Alcmene, Aphrodite (Queen of Beauty), Arianrhod, Athene, Branwen, Brigid, Chalchihuitlcue, the Charites, Cliodna, Clothra, Diana, Donagh, Eithne, Emer, Erzuli, Finncaev, Freya, Hathor (The Beautiful Face in the Boat of Millions of Years), Hebe, Hora, Lada, Lady of the Lake, Lakshmi, Mylitta, Niamh, Oshun, Philyra, Qadesh, Sarah, Sarasvati, Semiramis, Tsilah, Tureann, Tyche, Uma, Venus, Xochiquetzal, Zorya; God: Angus, Apollo, Baldur, Mitra, Nuadha, Xipe Totec; Evocation: Deirdre, Helen of Troy.

Capricious beauty: Plant: lady's slipper, musk rose. **Female beauty**: Animal: swan; Plant: calla lily, *Justitia*, orchid; Goddess: Aphrodite, Lakshmi, Liban, Venus; *to maintain*: Plant: silverweed. **Ill-natured beauty**: Plant: citron. **Inner beauty**: Stone: geode, opal; Plant: agave, columbine, daffodil, hyacinth, iris, orchid, rose; *ability to see*: Goddess: Psyche. **Lasting beauty**: Plant: gillyflower. **Lost beauty**: Plant: goldenrod; Goddess: Medusa. **Male beauty**: God: Adonis, Apollo, Attis, Krishna; Evocation: Ampelus, Hyacinthus. **Modest beauty**: Plant: painted trillium. **Physical beauty**: Color: pink; Plant: orchid; Goddess: Aega, Aphrodite, Vapurda (Granter of Beautiful Appearance); God: Angus. **Spiritual beauty**: Plant: cherry blossom. **Sweet beauty**: Plant: baby's breath. **Transient beauty**: Plant: night-blooming Cereus. **True beauty**: Plant: lilac. **Unconscious beauty**: Plant: red daisy, burgundy rose.

Youthful beauty: Stone: alexandrite; Plant: clover, elder, lemon verbena; Goddess: Chalchihuitlcue, Hebe; God: Angus.

Beautiful dreams: Plant: mistletoe. **Beautiful eyes**: (See: The Body). **Beautiful life**: Plant: apple; Goddess: the Graces. **Beautiful mind**: Plant: clematis, kennedia, rosemary. **Beautiful voice**: (See: Speech).

To: attract beauty: Stone: turquoise; Plant: maidenhair fern. **encourage beauty**: Stone: red jasper. **increase/enhance beauty**: Charm: rosewater (in bath); Stone: amber, amethyst, rhodochrosite, tiger's eye, orange zircon; Potion: rose petal tea; Plant: pink rose. **keep beauty**: Color: yellow; God: Gwydion. **manifest beauty**: Plant: agave, cactus. **open to beauty**: Stone: blue apatite. **protect beauty**: Stone: jasper. **recognize/ appreciate beauty**: Stone: kunzite; Plant: columbine, rose. **sacrifice beauty**: Goddess: Triduana.

Beginning

(See also: Activation, Awakening, Birth, Creation, Ending, Opening)

New Moon/Waxing Moon/East/Dawn/ Spring/Aries

Color: white; Number: 1; Tool: bell, gong; Charm: conch shell; Plant: birch; Goddess: Chalchihuitlcue, Eos, Sadarnuna; God: Ganesha (Lord of Beginnings), Janus.

Auspicious/bright/good beginning: Sun/ Venus/Dawn; Goddess: Albina, Aurora, Aya, Bast, Candelifera, Chasca, Dilbah, Dolya, Eos, Isis, Marici, Mater Matuta, Tefnut, Ushas, Xoli-Kaltes, Zorya, Dawn Zorya; God: Auilix, Ganesha, Janus, Shahar, Tlahuizcalpantecuhtli; *to make a good start in a new job*: God: Janus. **Cyclical re-beginning**: New Moon/Spring; Number: 10; Goddess: Ostara, Persephone. **New beginnings**: Number: 1; Animal: tadpole; Stone: moonstone; Oil: new mown hay; Plant: birch, elder, freesia; Goddess: Aurora, Cessair, Coventina, Juno, the Maiden; God: Ganesha, Janus, Kephera; *endings that lead to new beginnings*: God: Saturn; *seeds of a new beginning*: Number: 9. **Spiritual beginnings**: Stone: iolite.

To begin: again/make a fresh start: Stone: blue lace agate; Plant: birch, pine; God: Hoder. **a new enterprise**: Aries; God: Ganesha. **gossip**: Plant: clove. **a journey**: God: Freyr. **in a new school**: God: Ganesha, Janus.

To decide where to begin: Plant: verbena.

Benevolence

(See: Kindness)

Bereavement

(See: Grief)

Bewitching

(See: Enchantment)

Binding

(See also: Limits)

Saturn/Waning Moon/Saturday

Tool: cord, inverted pentacle; Method: gravity; Color: black; Charm: black thread, chain, knot, lead plate, linen thread, poppet, spider web, vinegar, apple cider vinegar; Animal: spider; Metal: lead; Stone: geode, jet, lodestone, obsidian, onyx; Potion: absinthe (dangerous, not recommended); Plant: apple, bindweed, calamus, cayenne, comfrey, cypress, dragon's blood, High John, knotweed, flax, pine, black pepper, periwinkle vine, pine, rowan, wormwood; Goddess: Isis, Juno Covella (binder with cords), Linda (The Binder with Linen Thread), Selqet; God: Ea, Hephaestus, Jupiter Stator, Marutakku, Nergal, Ninurta, Odin, Varuna, Vulcan.

Binding oath: God: Horcus.

To bind: the body: Stone: coral, sard. **energy**: Color: black. **evil**: Plant: angelica, mandrake. **lovers**: (See: Lovers). **minds**: (See: The Mind). **negative forces**: Saturn/ Saturday; Color: black. **slander/defamation**: Plant: clove. **someone to you**: Stone: salt; Plant: jasmine, white rose, rosemary. **spells**: (See: Spells). **weather**: God: Baal.

To bind together: Plant: white rose, rosemary, willow; Goddess: Ananke.

Unbinding

Uranus/Waxing Moon/Full Moon

Color: black; Goddess: Aditi (The Unfettered); God: Hephaestus, Teshub, Varuna, Vulcan.

To unbind minds: God: Odin.

Birth

(See also: Beginning, Childbirth, Life, Rebirth)

Mars/Moon/New Moon/Waxing Moon/ Earth/Spring/Aries

Color: black, red; Number 3; Letter: A; Animal: crocodile, fish; Plant: apple (male birth tree), birch, dittany, elder, fir, silver fir, holy thorn, Low John, palm tree, pear (female birth tree), pine, watermelon; Goddess: Ani, Arianrhod, Bast, Demeter, Flora, Freya, Ishtar, Meshkent, Sekhmet, Smyrna, Teteoinnan (Grandmother of Birth); God: Uwolowu, Yum Caz.

Birthstones: (See: Zodiac). **Birth and death**: Plant: elder.

Bitterness

Fire/Water

Charm: brimstone, brine; Stone: sea salt, sulfur; Plant: bitter almond, cypress, myrrh, rue, spikenard, wormwood; Goddess: Krivda; Evocation: Bitter Man.

Bitter thoughts: Plant: deadly nightshade. **Bitter truth**: Plant: savory.

To: clear bitterness: Plant: borage. **heal bitterness**: Stone: moss agate.

Blessing

(See also: Consecration)

Method: anointing, asperging, smudging; Charm: Florida Water, holy water, vervain water; Stone: jasper; Oil: palmarosa; Plant: acacia, carnation, chamomile, cypress, elder, fennel, frankincense, hyssop, jasmine, Joshua tree, lily of the valley, lotus, mint, mistletoe, myrrh, plane leaves, rose, rosemary, rue, vervain; Goddess: Coatlicue, Fortuna, Freya, Hecate, Isis, Sheela-na-gig; God: Apollo, Obatala, Satyanarayana.

To bless: alcoholic beverages: God: Accasbel. **apple trees**: (See: Agriculture). **a baby/child**: (See: Babies). **cattle**: Plant: hellebore. **a field**: (See: Agriculture). **a garden**: Charm: make love in it. **a grove**: Goddess: Nematona. **a home**: (See: The Home). **keys**: Charm: throw them into a fire. **a marriage**: (See: Marriage). **merchants/ shopkeepers**: God: Mercury. **a new mother**: Plant: fir needles. **people as they arrive or depart**: God: Janus. **a season**: God: Freyr. **seekers**: Goddess: Kali. **sexual union**: Goddess: Shekinah. **a son with virtue and character**: God: Ganesha. **those in need**: Goddess: Lakshmi; God: Ganesha. **tools**: God: Credne; *wands*: God: Baile. **a wedding ceremony**: (See: Weddings).

Blessings

Tool: pentacle; Color: white; Charm: white feather; Stone: lodestone, pearl (worn when asking blessings of Isis); Plant: daisy, elder, frankincense, holy thistle, lemon, mistletoe, mugwort, peach, pomegranate, rice, walnut tree, all citrus fruits; Goddess: Aakuluujjusi, Abhijit, Abnoba, Aericura,

Alavina, Ancasta, Ancomna, Andarta, Anna Livia, Antu, Asase Yaa, Astraea, Aveta, Boudina, Caiva, Cuda, Damkina, Dea Nutrix, Estsanatlehi, Felicitas, Fortuna, Galata, Gaomei, Gatumdug, Ghldeptis, the Great Mother, Grund, Habondia, Hannahannas, Ida, Isis, Iztaccihuatl, Juventas, Magog, the Matronaea, Mut, Nantosuelta, Nehalennia, Pandora, Samhain, Sedna, Sheela-na-gig, Vagdavercustis, Yemaya, Yhi; God: Damballah, El; Evocation: the Apsaras, fairies.

Fairy blessings: Plant: daisy (at Midsummer), elecampane; *to attract fairy blessings or gifts*: Plant: elecampane root, primrose (spray or garland over the door), rose petals, rowan (planted near the house); *to open to fairy blessings*: Plant: primrose. **Financial blessings/rewards**: Color: purple; Stone: sardonyx; Goddess: Benzaiten, Lennaxidaq. **Harvest blessings:** Plant: wheat. **Lunar blessings**: Moon; Plant: willow. **Shared blessings**: Animal: turkey. **Solar blessings**: Sun; Color: gold, yellow; Plant: sunflower. **Spiritual blessings**: Color: blue, lavender, white; Stone: amethyst, lapis lazuli, moldovite, clear quartz crystal, blue topaz; Plant: frankincense, High John, lotus, sweetgrass; *to attract*: Plant: High John, sweetgrass; *to the home*: (See: The Home).

Blessings in marriage: Plant: yarrow; Goddess: Shekinah.

To: attract blessings: Charm: Glory Water; Plant: acacia, acorn, bayberry, daisy (worn at Midsummer); Goddess: the Matres. **double blessings**: Stone: serpentine.

Blockages
(See also: Barriers, Obstacles)

Number: 4.

Communication blocks: *to open*: Color: blue.

Creative blocks: *to overcome*: Moon; Plant: licorice; *to unblock creative expression*: Plant: holy thorn, spikenard, sunflower (See also: Creativity, Inspiration). **Emotional blocks**: *to open*: Stone: blue lace agate, bloodstone, kunzite, blue tourmaline; Plant: cedar, myrrh, oleander. **Mental blocks**: *to clear*: Color: yellow; Plant: apple, cedar, harebell. **Psychic blocks**: *to open*: Stone: lapis lazuli. **Sexual blocks**: *to unblock sexuality*: Plant: hibiscus; *to unblock female sexual energy*: (See: Yin); *to unblock male sexual energy*: Plant: wild oat, yohimbine; God: Min. **Spiritual blocks**: *to remove*: Plant: grass of Parnassus, myrrh.

To: clear blockages: Charm: tet amulet; Stone: azurite, carnelian, peridot, smoky quartz; Plant: cedar, sycamore. **release blockages**: Plant: horsetail. **unblock energy**: (See: Energy). **unblock fear**: (See: Fear).

The Body
(See also: Chakras, Diseases/Disorders, Healing, Health, Illness, Pain, The Physical, Senses)

[NOTE: All correspondences are given here as charms. Some of the plants are poisonous, and nothing is meant to be ingested. Magick is a supplement to medical care, not a substitute for it. In most cases, incense should not be burned near someone who is ill.]

Waxing Moon/Earth/Water/North

Plant: patchouli.

Abdomen: Jupiter; Stone: smoky quartz; Plant: asoka tree, chaste tree, gentian, silverweed, spruce, yohimbine; Goddess: Oshun; *to protect*: Goddess: Oshun; *abdominal pain*: (See: Pain).

Adrenaline: Plant: borage.

Ankles: Aquarius.

Appendix: Stone: chrysolite.

Appetite: Animal: barracuda, bear; *to improve*: Plant: alfalfa, aniseed, cannabis, ginseng, goldenseal, gum tragacanth, clary sage; *to increase*: Plant: broomrape, calamus, cannabis, caraway, carrot, catnip, chamomile, cornflower, dandelion, dittany, gentian, holly, bitter orange, periwinkle, star thistle, sweet cicely; *to stimulate*: Plant: angelica, anise, broomrape, calamus, cayenne, chamomile, clove, cornflower, cuckoo flower, dandelion, gentian, ginger, holly, holy thistle, horehound, iris, juniper, masterwort, bitter orange, paprika, periwinkle, potentilla, quince, saffron, scallion, star thistle, tarragon, thyme, wood sorrel, wormwood; *to suppress*: Plant: fennel, patchouli; *good appetite*: Plant: aniseed, barberry, cannabis, gentian; *sexual appetite*: (See: Libido).

Arms: Gemini; Goddess: Neith.

Back: Sun/Leo; Plant: petrified wood; *lower back*: Libra; *back pain, sciatic pain*: (See: Pain).

Bile: *to stimulate*: Plant: buckthorn, dandelion, garlic, gentian, purslane, St. John's Wort, tamarind.

Bladder: Water; Stone: topaz; Plant: agrimony, asparagus, basil, belladonna, couch grass, cranberry, fennel, horsetail, huckleberry, hydrangea, kelp, lemon balm, marshmallow, silkweed, uva ursi; *to strengthen*: Stone: jasper; *bladder pain*: (See: Pain).

Blood: Uranus/Jupiter/Water/Aquarius; Color: red; Stone: bloodstone, carnelian, hematite, lodestone; Potion: pomegranate juice, red wine; Plant: anemone, bloodroot, burdock, dragon's blood, herb robert, holy thistle, oregano, pomegranate, red rose, silverweed, tormentil, viper's bugloss, yarrow; God: Skan; *coagulation of*: Plant: ginkgo, moon cereus, yarrow; *to dissolve blood clots*: Plant: figwort; *flow of*: Plant: barberry, thistle, yarrow, yohimbine; *to donate*: God: Ganesha; *to purify*: Color: red; Stone: amethyst, bloodstone, hematite, jasper; Plant: alfalfa, burdock, asparagus, celery seed, clover, daisy, damiana, dandelion, devil's claw, Echinacea root, elder berry, eyebright, garlic, gotu kola, hops, hydrangea, indigo, juniper, kelp, nettle, sarsaparilla, wallflower, yarrow, yucca; *to strengthen*: Color: red; Metal: iron; Stone: amethyst, bloodstone, coral, garnet, hematite, red jasper, kyanite, malachite; Plant: horsetail; *blood magic*: (See: Magick); *womb blood*: Goddess: Addamu.

Blood vessels: Fire; Charm: witch hazel; Stone: fluorite; Plant: butcher's broom, caper, cayenne, cypress, daisy, ephedra, fir, ginseng, groundsel, hawthorn berry, horse chestnut, dead nettle, ivy, linden, mistletoe, motherwort, olive, pheasant's eye, St. John's Wort, shepherd's purse, *to relax*: Plant: linden, mistletoe, olive.

Body fluids: Water; Stone: moonstone; Goddess: Anahita.

Bones: Saturn/Earth/Water/Capricorn; Color: white; Animal: coral; Stone: calcite, lapis lazuli, topaz with tourmaline; Plant: comfrey, spurge laurel, water buttercup; God: Obatala; *to repair breaks in*: Color: white; Plant: bear's breech, comfrey, dragon's blood, elm, royal fern, heliotrope, holly, Solomon's seal; God: Khnum; *to strengthen*: Stone: fluorite, onyx; *arms or legs*: God: Khnum; *bones of babies in the womb*: Goddess: Ossipago; *bone pain*: (See: Pain).

Bone marrow: Sun; Stone: amber, chalcedony; *to strengthen*: Stone: black onyx.

Brain: Sun/Mercury/Moon/Water; Metal: copper, silver; Stone: coral; Plant: belladonna, datura, ginkgo, henbane, marjoram, oats, wild lettuce; God: Chio Yuan-Tzu, Obatala; *to clear*: Plant: basil, lavender; *to improve function of*: Charm: vulture crown; Stone: obsidian; Plant: ginkgo, gotu kola, heliconia, thistle; *to open*: Plant: juniper, laurel; *to protect*: Plant: lemon balm; *to quiet*: Stone: jacinth; Plant: lotus, wormwood; *to stimulate*: Plant: ginseng, mint, peppermint, saffron; *to strengthen*: Color: violet; Stone: jasper; Plant: cowslip, dill, eyebright, germander, ginkgo, gotu kola, juniper berry, lemon balm, lily of the valley, rosemary; *right brain*: Metal: silver; *to balance left brain/right brain*: Stone: moss agate, malachite; Plant: honeysuckle (See also: Intelligence, The Mind, Thought).

Breasts: Moon/Cancer; Goddess: Bast.

Breast milk: Goddess: Anahita (See: Babies).

Buttocks: Venus.

Calves: Aquarius; God: Ptah.

Cervix: Stone: zoisite.

Chest: Cancer; Plant: borage, black cohosh, comfrey, everlasting, fir, ginger, horseradish, horsetail, hyssop, Iceland moss, iris, juniper, licorice, marshmallow, marjoram, mastic, milkweed, great mullein, mustard seed, myrtle, rue, stinging nettle, poppy, apothecary's rose, Venus hair fern, violet; *chest pain*: Plant: myrtle.

Circulatory system: Water/Aquarius; Stone: bloodstone, citrine, garnet, hematite, ruby, yellow topaz; Plant: alfalfa, asparagus, barberry, bayberry, bilberry, butcher's broom, cayenne, chamomile, chickweed, black cohosh, couch grass, damiana, dandelion, yellow dock, dong quai, ephedra, eyebright, feverfew, garlic, ginger, ginkgo, ginseng, goldenseal, gotu kola, hawthorn berry, holy thistle, wild lettuce, lobelia, peppermint, milk thistle, raspberry, wild thyme, willow, wild yam, yarrow; *to improve*: Stone: pyrite, ruby; Plant: clove, garlic, ginkgo, linden, St. John's Wort, yarrow; *to open*: Plant: mugwort; *to stimulate*: Oil: neroli; Plant: basil, catnip, ephedra, fennel, ginger, ginkgo, laurel, lavender, lemon balm, mint, peppermint, sage, tansy, vetiver, yerba maté; *to strengthen*: Stone: pyrite.

Digestive system: Jupiter; Stone: blue lace agate, citrine, howlite, yellow jade, jasper, peridot, tigereye; Plant: alfalfa, algae, aloe, asparagus, barberry, bayberry, betel, betony, burnet, carline thistle, cascara sagrada, catnip, cayenne, chamomile, chickweed, clove, clover, blue cohosh, comfrey, cow parsnip, cuckoo flower, damiana, dandelion, yellow dock, Echinacea, elecampane, eyebright, fennel, fenugreek, feverfew, fir, garlic, gentian, germander, ginger, goldenseal, gum tragacanth, hawthorn berry, hibiscus, holy thistle, hops, horehound, horsetail, horseradish, hydrangea, hyssop, juniper berry, kelp, laurel, lettuce, licorice, linden, lobelia, loquat, lovage, marjoram, marshmallow, masterwort, milk thistle, mint, mullein, mustard seed, nettle, oak, onion, bitter orange, oregano, papaya, paprika, parsley, peppermint, potentilla, psyllium, raspberry, safflower, saffron, sage, clary sage, samphire, sarsaparilla, selfheal, senna, St. John's Wort, strawberry, summer savory, tansy, tea tree, thyme, turmeric, black walnut, wintergreen, yam, yarrow, yucca; *to balance*: Stone: topaz; Potion: chamomile tea with milk; Plant: hops; *to cleanse*: Plant: chicory; *to stimulate*: Plant: angelica, aniseed, bael tree, betel palm, broomrape, calamus, caraway seed, centaury, chamomile, cherry, clove, corn, cornflower, eucalyptus, gentian, ginger, goldenseal, holly, holy thistle, horseradish, lemon, linden flower, mistletoe, bitter orange, periwinkle, sage, star thistle, thyme, yarrow; *to soothe*: Plant: oregano; *to strengthen*: Plant: celery, garlic mustard, horehound, horseradish, lemon, nasturtium, orange.

Ears: Air/Water; *inner ear*: Stone: rhodonite; *left ear*: Mars; *earache*: (See: Pain); *hearing*: (See: Senses).

Endocrine system: Metal: boron; Stone: magnetite, sodalite; Plant: carrot seed, fo-ti-teng.

Eyes: Sun/Moon; Stone: amethyst, aquamarine, aventurine, optical calcite, emerald, jade, lapis lazuli, snowflake obsidian, opal, peridot, rhodochrosite; Plant: belladonna, chamomile, chickweed, daisy, elder, eyebright, fluellen, fumitory, grass of Parnassus, juniper, knapweed, licorice, maple, marigold, marsh mallow, nasturtium, potato, purslane, raspberry, rosemary, rue, strawberry, tormentil, vine; Goddess: Hathor; God: Chu Ying, Ming Shang; *to clear*: Stone: black onyx; Plant: clary sage, goldenseal; *to soothe*: Color: green; Plant: anise, potato; *to strengthen*: Color: green; Stone: green aventurine, chrysoprase, emerald, green jade, lapis lazuli, peridot, turquoise; Plant: clove, eyebright, juniper berry; *beautiful eyes*: Animal: all felines; Stone: tigereye; Plant: belladonna, striped tulip; *evil eye*: (See: Evil); *inner eye*: (See: Vision); *left eyes of women*: Sun; *right eyes of men*: Sun; *third eye*: (See: Chakras); *eye pain*: (See: Pain); *eyesight*: (See: Senses).

Face: Aries; God: Ra.

Feet: Pisces; God: Ptah.

Gallbladder: Saturn/Mars; Stone: orange calcite; Plant: agrimony, barberry, burdock, celandine, costmary, yellow dock, dragon's gall, madder, parsley, peppermint, pine, sage, clary sage, wormwood; *to protect*: God: Qebsennuf.

Genitals: Scorpio; Plant: damiana; *female*: Venus/Moon; *male*: Mars/Pluto.

Glands: Moon/Jupiter; Charm: lead crystal; Stone: aquamarine, beryl; Plant: anise, belladonna, burdock, cascara sagrada, red clover, blue cohosh, coriander, dandelion, yellow dock, ephedra, ginseng, goldenseal, holy thistle, juniper, kelp, licorice, nettle, black walnut, wild yam; *to stimulate*: Plant: anise, barberry; *lymph glands*: Stone: tourmaline; Plant: male fern, watercress; *mammary glands*: Plant: anise; *pineal gland*: Color: purple; Animal: butterfly; Metal: copper; Stone: sugilite; *pituitary gland*: Jupiter/Saturn; Metal: copper; Stone: garnet, sapphire, sugilite; Plant: parsley; *prostate gland*: Stone: chrysoprase; Plant: aloe, wintergreen; *reproductive glands*: Pluto/Saturn/Scorpio; *salivary glands*: Plant: white clover; *sweat glands*: Plant: elder, hyssop; *swollen glands*: Stone: amber; Plant: alder, horsetail, yarrow; *thymus gland*: Plant: thyme; *to strengthen*: blue quartz.

Hands: Mercury/Gemini; *thumb*: Venus.

Head: Moon/Aries; Color: white; Plant: betony, lotus, valerian; Stone: amber; God: Horus; *headache*: (See: Pain).

Heart: Sun/Venus/Leo/Fire; Color: green, pink, red; Metal: gold; Stone: bloodstone, rose quartz; Plant: asparagus, chili pepper, cinnamon, dandelion, foxglove, lichen, oleander, rose, tansy, tuberose, valerian; God: Horus, Ptah; *to balance*: Stone: aventurine; *to calm/soothe/quiet*: Stone: aquamarine, garnet; Plant: fo-ti, yarrow; *to open*: Stone: amethyst, emerald, labradorite, moonstone, peridot, ruby; Plant: azalea, bergamot, bleeding heart, forget-me-not, geranium, lemon balm, wild rose, tuberose; *to protect*: God: Duamutef; *to purify*: Plant: white lily; *to stimulate*: Plant: adonis, foxglove, ginseng, St. John's Wort; *to strengthen*: Color: deep blue; Stone: black agate with white veins, amethyst, jacinth, lapis lazuli, lodestone, sapphire; Metal: gold; Plant: broom, butterbur, marigold, mustard, red or white rose, saffron, walnut (See: Chakras, Emotions, Heartbreak, Love).

Hips: Sagittarius; Plant: petrified wood.

Hormones: *female hormones*: Plant: anise, willow; *to balance*: Stone: moonstone; Plant: black cohosh, soybean; *to stimulate*: Plant: sage.

Immune system: Stone: blue apatite, barite; Plant: devil's claw, gum tragacanth, rose hips, sage, sarsaparilla, yerba santa; *to stimulate*: Charm: lead crystal; Plant: Echinacea, ginseng, gum tragacanth, horseradish, lavender, lemon, licorice, oregano, sage, St. John's Wort, savory, tea tree, thyme; *to strengthen*: Stone: golden beryl, ruby, quartz; Plant: Echinacea, garlic, juniper berry.

Intestines: Moon/West/Virgo; Stone: amber; Plant: agrimony, aloe, amaranth, ambergris, angelica, anise, avens, belladonna, betel nut, bitter orange, blueberry, cascara sagrada, chamomile, dog's mercury, fenugreek, flax, garlic, loquat, marshmallow, nutmeg, pennyroyal, peppermint, plantain, potentilla, slippery elm, spearmint, stinging nettle, black nightshade; *to protect*: Goddess: Selqet; God: Qebehsenuef; *to purify*: Plant: aniseed, basil, chamomile, cucumber seed, garlic, groundsel, horehound, Iceland moss, knapweed, lavender cotton, loosestrife, male fern, mugwort, pumpkin seed, rue, southernwood, St. John's Wort, stonecrop, tarragon, black walnut, wormwood, yarrow; *small intestines*: Fire; *to protect*: God: Hapy; *large intestines*: *to protect*: God: Imsety.

Joints: Sun; Plant: comfrey, garlic, germander, ginseng, horsetail, marjoram, pennyroyal, pine, rosemary, savory, valerian, yucca; *joint pain*: (See: Diseases/Disorders, Pain).

Kidneys: Mars/Venus/Water/Libra; Stone: bloodstone, green calcite, jade, quartz crystal, smoky quartz, rhodochrosite, topaz; Plant: agrimony, barberry, blueberry, burdock, burnet saxifrage, centaury, chickweed, couch grass, dandelion, eucalyptus, fennel, fenugreek, finger grass, groundsel, heather, horsetail, huckleberry, juniper, marsh mallow, meadowsweet, myrtle; *to cleanse*: Plant: goldenrod, strawberry; *to improve function of*: Plant: ginger;

to stimulate: Plant: angelica, goldenrod, marshmallow; *kidney pain*: (See: Pain).

Knees: Capricorn.

Larynx: Stone: morganite, turquoise; Plant: chamomile, horseradish, licorice, mustard, peppermint (See also: Speech).

Legs: Goddess: Neith, Selqet.

Lips: God: Ptah.

Liver: Jupiter/Venus/Moon/South/Sagittarius; Animal: dragon, tiger; Stone: aquamarine, beryl, bloodstone, topaz, zircon; Plant: acorn, angelica, avens, barberry, butternut, celandine, celery, centaury, chestnut, chickweed, chicory, comfrey, costmary, cucumber, dandelion, yellow dock, dog rose, dragon's gall, fenugreek, fumitory, grape, groundsel, hart's tongue, hops, horehound, licorice, liverwort, madder, peppermint, stinging nettle, pellitory, restharrow, rock samphire, sage, spindle tree, spruce, strawberry, thyme, toadflax, vervain, woody nightshade, wormwood, yarrow; *to cleanse of toxins*: Stone: amethyst; Plant: agrimony, black alder, goldenrod, indigo; *to improve function of*: Stone: emerald; Plant: dong quai, elecampane, gentian, ginseng, wormwood; *to open*: Plant: agrimony, angelica, celery, gentian, hops, maple, restharrow, rock samphire, toadflax; *to protect*: Plant: globe artichoke, milk thistle; God: Qebsennuf; *to soothe*: Plant: licorice; *to stimulate*: Plant: goldenrod; *to strengthen*: Stone: azurite, iolite, jade, jasper, malachite; Plant: agrimony, black alder, maple, rose.

Lungs: Mercury/Jupiter/Air/North/Gemini; Animal: tiger; Stone: amethyst; Plant: honeysuckle, lungwort, nasturtium, bloodroot, Solomon's seal, yarrow; *to clear*: Plant: coltsfoot; *to protect*: God: Duamutef; *to strengthen*: Plant: hazelnut, thyme; *to open breathing*: Air; Plant: eucalyptus, laurel.

Lymphatic system: Uranus/Water/Pisces; Plant: barberry, red clover, lemon, red root, tangerine.

Menopause: Waning Moon; Stone: moonstone; Plant: aloe vera, anise, bergamot, black cohosh, cypress, evening primrose, fennel, grapefruit, hawthorn, mugwort, passionflower, clary sage, soybean; Goddess: the Crone.

Menstruation: Moon/Full Moon; Color: red; Stone: bloodstone, carnelian, chrysoprase, coral, garnet, malachite, moonstone, ruby; Plant: agrimony, angelica, bergamot, bistort, butterbur, red clover, black cohosh, blue cohosh, damiana, dong quai, dragon's blood, licorice, motherwort, oats, oregano, parsley, pennyroyal, raspberry, safflower, sage, turmeric; Goddess: Adamu, Sarasvati; Evocation: Satan; *to stimulate*: Plant: anemone, angelica, butterbur, cabbage, catnip, celery, centaury, chamomile, cotton seed, dog's mercury, fennel, feverfew, groundsel, horehound, hyssop, ivy, lavender, lavender cotton, white lily, lovage, madder root, marigold, masterwort, motherwort, mugwort, pennyroyal, savin, southernwood, tarragon, toadflax, wormwood, yarrow, yohimbine; *menstrual cramps/pain*: (See: Pain).

Metabolism: *to control*: Animal: polar bear; *to stimulate*: Plant: calamus, ginseng, pansy, St. John's Wort; *slow metabolism*: Pisces.

Mouth: Earth; Stone: beryl; God: Khonsu, Ptah; *to open*: Tool: ur hekau; God: Anubis; Charm: green scarab set in gold and placed over the heart; Plant: palm tree; God: Anubis, Ptah, Wepwawet.

Muscles: Mars/Earth; Plant: belladonna, paprika, queen of the night; *to relax*: Stone: smithsonite; Plant: birch, caraway, chamomile, dandelion, lemon, madder root, sage, scullcap, thyme, valerian; *to soothe*: Plant: eucalyptus, paprika; *to strengthen*: Plant: Chinese lantern, spearmint, wild cherry; *muscle pain*: (See: Pain); *muscle problems*: (See: Diseases/Disorders); *to relax internal muscles*: Plant: madder root; *to relax muscle spasms*: Plant: celandine.

Neck: Taurus; Animal: giraffe, swan; Stone: amethyst, chrysocolla, chrysoprase, dolomite, fluorite; Plant: bryony, mustard, oregano; Goddess: Uatchet; *neck pain*: (See: Pain).

Nerves: Mercury/Neptune/Virgo/Gemini; *to calm*: Plant: barberry, chamomile, evening primrose, safflower; *to soothe*: Stone: red agate; Plant: cannabis, chamomile, heliotrope, lemon balm, narcissus, passionflower, scullcap; *to quiet*: Plant: borage, chamomile, lemongrass; *to stimulate*: Plant: peppermint; *neurological pain*: (See: Pain).

Nervous system: Virgo; Metal: copper; Stone: blue lace agate, yellow carnelian, chrysocolla, chrysoprase, galena, jasper, morganite, peridot, yellow topaz, black or green tourmaline; Plant: belladonna, betel, betony, catnip, chamomile, black cohosh, damiana, ephedra, feverfew, ginkgo, gotu kola, hepatica, hound's tongue, lobelia, marjoram, mistletoe, oats, oleander, passionflower, rose, rue, sage, scullcap, silkweed, valerian, vervain, willow, wormwood, yohimbine; *to balance*: Plant: passionflower; *to quiet*: Plant: passionflower, sandalwood, valerian; *to stimulate*: Plant: ginseng, rosemary, wolfsbane; *neurological pain*: (See: Pain).

Nose: God: Thoth.

Organs: Goddess: Carna; *to protect*: Goddess: Carna; *to regenerate*: Stone: moonstone, peridot.

Ovaries: Stone: chrysoprase, smoky quartz; Plant: licorice, St. John's Wort.

Pancreas: Moon/Earth; Stone: alexandrite, amethyst, green calcite, citrine, smoky quartz, rhodochrosite; Plant: barberry, cassia, iris, licorice; *to soothe*: Plant: licorice; *to stimulate*: Plant: cassia.

Pelvis: Venus; Stone: jade; Plant: daisy, motherwort, myrtle; *to relax*: Plant: Low John.

Pulse: Stone: hematite, jasper; Plant: pheasant's eye.

Reproductive system: Pluto; Charm: musk; Stone: green gypsum; Plant: dragon's blood, ginger, nutmeg, pennyroyal, tuberose, turmeric, black willow; *to strengthen*: Metal: copper; *female reproductive system*: Plant: black cohosh, dong quai, raspberry, rose, southernwood, tarragon, white dead nettle, wormwood; Goddess: Diana; *reproductive/sex organs*: Scorpio; Color: pink; Stone: kunzite, morganite, rose quartz, pink tourmaline; Plant: cannabis, chaste tree, damiana; *to protect*: God: Prajapati; *to strengthen*: Plant: quince; *to protect female reproductive organs*: Goddess: Diana.

Respiratory system: Mercury/Air; Stone: turquoise; Plant: blood root, cannabis, chickweed, black cohosh, comfrey, Echinacea, elder, elecampane, ephedra, fennel, fenugreek, garden cress, garlic, gum tragacanth, horseradish, marshmallow, yohimbine.

Ribs: Jupiter.

Saliva: Water; Stone: onyx.

Semen: Moon; Animal: slug; Goddess: Anahita; God: Enki; *to purify*: Goddess: Anahita; *sperm*: Jupiter; Plant: mistletoe berry.

Shins: Aquarius.

Shoulders: Gemini; Stone: chrysoprase; God: Set.

Side: *left side of women*: Moon; *right side of men*: Moon.

Sinuses: Air; Stone: amethyst, rhodochrosite; Plant: belladonna, marjoram, marshmallow, myrrh; *to open*: Plant: eucalyptus, horseradish; *sinus pain*: (See: Pain).

Skin: Saturn/Capricorn; Stone: agate; Plant: belladonna, cocoa (butter), oleander, vervain, petrified wood; *to soothe*: Plant: almond, aloe vera, bergamot, burdock, comfrey, ladies' bedstraw, laurel, sage, Solomon's seal, tea tree; *to stimulate growth of*: Plant: comfrey.

Solar plexus: Stone: leopardskin jasper, malachite, tigereye (See also: Chakras).

Spine: Leo; Charm: tet amulet; Stone: bloodstone, Herkimer diamond; Plant: barberry, cow parsnip, ginseng, henbane, lilac, valerian, yohimbine.

Spleen: Metal: lead; Stone: fluorite, jade; Plant: black alder, angelica, barberry, celery, fumitory, woody nightshade, pellitory, restharrow, rock samphire, spleenwort, vervain; *to activate*: Stone: hematite; *to open*: Plant: angelica, celery, hops, maple, restharrow, rock samphire; *to strengthen*: Stone: alexandrite, bloodstone, green calcite, chalcedony, lapis lazuli, rhodochrosite.

Stomach: Venus/Moon/Earth/Water/East/Cancer; Stone: aquamarine, beryl, yellow carnelian, chrysocolla, citrine, white coral, jade, jasper; Plant: hops, peppermint, rosemary, slippery elm, turmeric, vervain; *to protect*: God: Duamutef, Imsety; *to strengthen*: Charm: jasper necklace; Plant: sage; *stomach ache/pain*: (See: Pain).

Testicles: Mars; Stone: alexandrite, chrysoprase, smoky quartz, zoisite; Plant: celery seed, fennel, mugwort.

Teeth: Saturn/Earth/Capricorn; Color: ivory, white; Stone: aquamarine, calcite, fluorite, topaz with tourmaline; Plant: dragon's blood; Goddess: Selqet; God: Obatala, Ptah; *toothache, teething pain*: (See: Pain).

Thighs: Mercury/Sagittarius.

Throat: Venus/Taurus; Charm: honey; Animal: warbling birds; Plant: betony, bugle, gentian, marsh mallow, mustard, slippery elm, tea tree; Goddess: Mert; *infections/sore throat*: (See: Disease).

Thyroid: Stone: chrysoprase, galena, lapis lazuli, morganite, blue tourmaline; Oil: palmarosa; Plant: ephedra, iris, kelp, walnut; *to balance*: chili pepper; *to stimulate*: Plant: ginseng.

Tongue: Mercury/Fire; Animal: frog, toad; Plant: bryony, calamus, dandelion, houseleek, lemon; Goddess: Ma'at; God: Hermes, Al Lisan, Ptah, Thoth.

Urinary system/tract: Plant: ambrosia, asparagus, barberry, blackthorn, burdock, butcher's broom, cannabis, chamomile, chickweed, red clover, comfrey, elecampane, fennel, fenugreek, gotu kola, gum tragacanth, holy thistle, hops, horsetail, hydrangea, juniper berry, nettle, parsley, raspberry, safflower, saw palmetto, uva ursi, white dead nettle; *to clear/cleanse*: Stone: jade; Plant: asparagus, celery seed, chicory, couch grass, cranberry, fennel seed, gorse, groundsel, hops, horsetail, madder, mugwort, restharrow, shepherd's purse, spleenwort, uva ursi, vervain; *to open*: Plant: couch grass, mugwort; *to soothe*: Plant: columbine, horsetail, marsh mallow, meadowsweet, mullein; *to stimulate*: Plant: asparagus, dandelion, juniper berry, pheasant's eye, silkweed, stinging nettle, uva ursi, watermelon.

Vascular system: Water; Plant: belladonna, bloodroot, butcher's broom, Echinacea, garlic, ginkgo, goldenseal, horse chestnut. **Veins**: Color: blue; Plant: chickweed, knapweed, valerian; *to relax*: Plant: witch hazel.

Womb/uterus: Venus/Moon/Water; Stone: amber, geode; Plant: ash, bayberry, burdock, dong quai, elecampane, groundsel, heliotrope, Low John, motherwort, parsley, raspberry, rue, shepherd's purse, vervain; Goddess: Anahita, Astarte (She of the Womb), Ninhursag (The Womb Goddess), Sheela-na-gig; *to open*: Plant: blackberry; Goddess: Diana (Opener of the Womb), Ishtar; God: Wepwawet; *to protect*: Goddess: Oshun; *to purify*: Tool: censer (by stepping over smoke); Plant: feverfew; Goddess: Anahita; *to stimulate*: Plant: broom, goldenseal, senna; *to stimulate contractions*: Plant: broom, cotton, pennyroyal; *to strengthen*: Plant: feverfew; Goddess: Anahita; *to shape a fetus in*: God: Khnum, Obatala; *womb blood*: Goddess: Addamu.

To: bind the body: Stone: coral, sard. **control the body**: Plant: comfrey. **enforce your right of ownership of your own body**: Goddess: Vashti. **enjoy your body**: Animal: cat, dolphin, swan; Plant: African marigold, elder. **get in touch with your body**: Plant: patchouli. **protect the body**: Stone: ruby. **serve the Goddess with the altar of your body**: Goddess: White Shell Woman. **soothe the body**: Stone: rhodochrosite. Plant: flax. **strengthen the body**: Stone: malachite.

Boundaries

(See: Limits)

Bravery

(See: Courage)

Building

Saturn/Earth

Color: brown; Number: 4, 22; Animal: carpenter ant, beaver, bee, muskrat, wasp; Stone: granite, marble; Plant: bamboo; Goddess: Sesheta (Lady of Builders, Foremost of Builders); God: Ea, Gilma, Imhotep, Kothar-wa-Khasis, Mushdamma (Great Builder of Enlil), Ptah (The Builder), Yvastar (Divine Builder).

To build: boats: God: Kan, Tanemahuta. **bridges**: Number: 22; Animal: army ant. **dams/earthworks**: God: Ptah. **permanent things**: God: Gilma. **with stone**:

Goddess: Cybele. **strong foundations**: God: Lugalabdubur. **temples**: God: Janus. **towers/skyscrapers**: Goddess: Cybele.

Business

(See also: Finance, Money, Real Estate)

Mercury/Jupiter/Earth/Wednesday

Color: green; Charm: money purse, wallet; Stone: bloodstone, emerald, lodestone; Plant: borage, cinnamon, lemon balm, lilac, marigold, oakmoss; Goddess: Demeter, Dharani, Hecate, Hera, Juno, Lakshmi, Mgasiras, Minerva, Olwen, Ops, Oya, Pusya, Sri, Ushas, Yaparamma; God: Cernunnos, Dionysus Plutodotes, Ek Chua, Ganesha, Hermes, Inari, Lugh, Mercury, Osiris, Quetzalcoatl, Shango, Sukuna-Hikona, Thoth, Vertumnus, Veles, Volos, Yacatecuhtli, Zulum.

Flourishing business: Plant: sage. **New business**: Aries; Goddess: Jana; God: Ganesha, Janus. **Strong business**: Plant: High John.

Businesses: curio shops: God: Kuan Kung. **pawnshops**: God: Kuan Kung. **restaurants**: God: Kuan Kung. **seaside businesses**: God: Njord. **profit**: Plant: cabbage; Goddess: Habondia, Minerva; God: Ebisu, Mammon, Mercury, Ts'ai-Shen; *to increase*: Plant: goldenseal. **trade**: God: Sukuna-Hikona.

Business advice: God: Xaman Ek (Guide of Merchants). **Business assistance**: Color: orange. **Business development**: Plant: mistletoe. **Business goals**: Color: orange. **Business**

people: (See: People). **Business progress**: Color: royal blue, purple. **Business prosperity**: (See: Prosperity). **Business security**: (See: Security). **Business success**: (See: Success). **Business transactions**: Mercury; Color: orange; God: Hermes, Mercury; *to get a bargain*: Evocation: Herakles Melkarth; *to make a good deal*: Stone: jade. **Business travel**: (See: Travel, Travelers).

For: effective advertising: Stone: emerald. **good luck in business**: Color: gold, green; Metal: gold; Plant: bamboo, frankincense, mint, peony; God: Hotei, Maximon.

To: attract business: Color: green; Stone: lodestone; Plant: basil, benzoin, lavender, mistletoe. **attract customers**: Stone: lodestone; Plant: citronella, lavender, mint, mistletoe, Irish moss, peony, yellow dock. **banish spirits from places of business**: (See: Spirits). **become expert in business**: Stone: amethyst. **erase business mistakes**: Plant: pine (especially oil, added to wash water, laundry soap, and so on). **Expand a business**: Sagittarius; Stone: bloodstone, lodestone; Plant: bayberry, cinnamon, ylang-ylang. **Increase business**: Charm: Kananga Water; Plant: bayberry, cinnamon, High John, mint, mistletoe, vetiver, ylang-ylang. **Increase revenue**: Stone: bloodstone (kept in the cash register), emerald; Plant: allspice, bayberry, Irish moss. **Make wise business decisions**: Stone: jade (held in the hand). **Open a business or other enterprise**: Goddess: Jana; God: Ganesha, Janus; *open a tavern*: God: Accasbel.

Chapter 3

Calling
(See: Summoning)

Calm
(See also: Peace, Tranquility)

Moon/Water/Spring

Method: meditation; Color: pale aqua, blue, light blue, sea green, pale to medium pink, white; Charm: bee pollen, beeswax, honey, orange flower water, royal jelly, silver ring; Animal: koala; Stone: red agate, amazonite, amber, amethyst, angelite, Apache tear, aquamarine, avalonite, azurite, pink calcite, emerald, fluorite, hematite, jet, kunzite, lepidolite, malachite, morganite, moonstone, clear quartz crystal, rose quartz, rhodonite, pink sapphire, tourmaline, pink tourmaline; Oil: neroli; Plant: amber, aster, azalea, benzoin, camellia, cannabis, carnation, castor bean, cedar, chamomile (in the bath), red clover, cypress, daisy, fir, geranium, jasmine, juniper, kava kava, laurel, lavender, lily of the valley, linden, marjoram, mimosa, myrrh, narcissus, nettle, black nightshade, nutmeg, orange, passionflower, pine, purslane, rosewood, rue, clary sage, sandalwood, spruce, tangerine, thyme, valerian, verbena, vetiver, ylang-ylang; Goddess: Alcyone, Mary (Our Lady of Infinite Calm); God: Shiva.

Emotional calm: Color: blue, pink; Stone: blue lace agate, aquamarine, blue or green aventurine, celestite, chalcedony, chrysocolla, hematite, kyanite, lapis lazuli, moonstone, morganite, peridot, rhodochrosite, rose quartz, sapphire, sodalite, tigereye, blue topaz, blue tourmaline; Plant: benzoin, bistort root (kept near the heart), chamomile, clove, geranium, lavender, masterwort, nettle, orange, rue, vervain. **Inner calm**: Plant: lavender; *to calm inner conflicts*: Stone: sodalite. **Physical calm**: Color: blue, light blue; Stone: agate, celestite, topaz, blue topaz; Plant: chamomile, nutmeg; *to calm the heart*: Stone: lepidolite; *to calm the nerves*: Stone: aquamarine, amazonite, peridot; Plant: basil, lavender, mint, pennyroyal, spearmint.

Calm atmosphere/home: (See: The Home). **Calm after a storm**: Charm: rainbow; Goddess: Rauni. **Calm communication**: Plant: cosmos. **Calm judgment**: Color: white. **Calm mind**: (See: The Mind).

To: **attract calm**: Plant: yarrow. **bring calm**: God: Njord. **calmly face danger**: Stone: amethyst.

To calm: **aggression**: Plant: cedar. **anger**: (See: Anger). **anxiety**: (See: Anxiety). **emotions**: Color: green; Plant: lily; Stone: amazonite, green aventurine, fluorite, garnet, moonstone, tigereye; Plant: borage, chamomile, lemon balm, lemongrass, lily, mistletoe, orange, passionflower, rose, tarragon, vanilla; *negative emotions*: Stone: lepidolite; *emotional chaos*: Stone: amazonite; *emotional problems*: Stone: amethyst, aquamarine. **fear**: (See: Fear). **hysteria**: Plant: hyssop, pennyroyal. **the sea**: Goddess: Amphitrite, Isis; God: Triton; *stormy seas*:

Plant: ginger; Goddess: Amphitrite; *waves*: God: Triton. **storms**: (See: Storms). **a violent temper**: Plant: chamomile, honeysuckle, saffron. **the wind**: Plant: broom (added to a fire).

areer

(See also: Employment, Job, Status, Work)

Sun/Earth

Goddess: Inanna.

Career progress: Goddess: Inanna.

To: balance career and family life: Plant: pomegranate. **change career**: Stone: aventurine. **have a good career despite a physical disability**: God: Vulcan.

entering

Saturn/Earth/Center

Tool: cauldron; Method: meditation; Color: brown, white, yellow; Stone: amazonite, andalusite, Apache tears, aragonite, calcite, pink calcite, hematite, Herkimer diamond, brown jasper, kunzite, obsidian, onyx, phantom, smoky quartz, brown zircon; Oil: elemi, palmarosa; Plant: cedar, chamomile, cypress, elder, juniper, myrrh, oakmoss, patchouli, pine, clary sage, sandalwood, saxifrage, sweetgrass, vervain, water lily; Goddess: Bo Find, Gula; God: Legba, Ometeotl (He Who Is At The Center), Mahapratisara, Vairochana.

Mental centering: Plant: red clover.

To center: emotions: Plant: tuberose. **energy**: Plant: pomegranate.

ertainty

(See also: Doubt)

Full Moon

Plant: angelica, canavalia.

To know with certainty that springtime will always follow winter: Goddess: Persephone, Proserpine.

hakras

Stone: sugilite, turquoise; Plant: lilac, lotus, sandalwood.

Brow (6th) chakra (third eye): Color: blue, silvery blue, indigo, purple, red, violet; Animal: falcon; Stone: amethyst, azurite, iolite, lapis lazuli, sapphire, sodalite, tanzanite; Oil: elemi; Plant: frankincense; *to activate*: Charm: pyramid; Stone: agate, amethyst, azurite, lapis lazuli, sodalite; Plant: flowers, especially honeysuckle; *to open*: Method: meditation, psychotropic drugs (dangerous, not recommended); Charm: bindi, pyramid; Color: purple, indigo; Animal: cat, jaguar, leopard, panther, vulture; Stone: blue lace agate, amethyst, azurite, bismuth, chrysocolla, hematite, iolite, jade, violet jade, lepidolite, moldovite, clear quartz crystal, sapphire, star sapphire, tanzanite; Plant: ambergris, deerstongue, eyebright, frankincense, honeysuckle, lime, lotus, mimosa, mugwort, nutmeg, sandalwood, patchouli, star anise; Goddess: Kali; God: Maa-hes, Shiva; *to stimulate*: Color: blue, indigo, red; Stone: tanzanite; Plant: myrrh.

Crown (7th) chakra: Tool: crystal ball; Color: gold, purple, silver, violet, white; Animal: butterfly; Stone: amethyst, citrine, fluorite, clear quartz crystal, smoky quartz, sugilite, tanzanite, tigereye; Plant: dragon's blood, lotus, rose; *to activate*: Stone: amethyst, quartz, sugilite; Plant: honeysuckle, lavender; *to balance*: Stone: amethyst; *to open*: Stone: sugilite; Plant: amber, frankincense, honeysuckle, lime, tuberose; *to stimulate*: Stone: tanzanite; Plant: myrrh.

Heart (4th) chakra: Air/Center; Color: green, sea green, pink; Charm: crescent, orange flower water; Stone: moss agate, amazonite, aventurine, chrysoprase, dioptase, emerald, jade, malachite, peridot, rose quartz, rhodochrosite, ruby, green tourmaline; Plant: lavender, orange blossom, rose, sesame seed, ylang-ylang; *to activate*: Color: green; Stone: aquamarine, aventurine, emerald, jade, malachite, peridot, rose quartz; Plant: gentian; all green trees and plants; *to open*: Stone: rose quartz; Plant: freesia, jasmine; *to stimulate*: Color: red; Stone: aquamarine; Plant: cyclamen, frangipani, freesia, gardenia, spikenard.

Root (1st) chakra (base chakra): Earth; Charm: civet, musk, square; Color: black, red; Stone: blue lace agate, bloodstone, coral, garnet, hematite, red jasper, black obsidian, smoky quartz, tiger's eye, ruby, black tourmaline; Plant: Adam and Eve root, ginger, patchouli, sesame (See also: Kundalini); *to activate*: Stone: bloodstone, garnet, hematite, obsidian, smoky quartz, ruby, black tourmaline; *to open*: Plant: poinsettia, tomato; *to stabilize*: Stone: black obsidian; *to stimulate*: Charm: musk; Plant: frangipani.

Sacral (2nd) chakra (belly/spleen/sexual chakra): Water; Charm: circle; Color: orange, peach; Stone: amber, orange calcite, carnelian, citrine, coral, orange jasper, malachite, fire opal, rhodochrosite, tigereye; Plant: allspice, patchouli, clary sage, sandalwood, ylang-ylang; *to activate*: Color: red; Stone: carnelian, fluorite, moonstone, onyx; Plant: orange; *to open*: Stone: sugilite; *to stimulate*: musk; *to strengthen*: Plant: pennyroyal.

Solar plexus (3rd) chakra (stomach chakra): Sun/Fire; Charm: triangle; Color: yellow; Stone: amber, citrine, malachite, sulfur, topaz; Plant: cinnamon, lemon, mandarin orange; all yellow flowers, foods and plants; *to activate*: Charm: sunbathing; Stone: amber, citrine, sulfur, tigereye, topaz; *to strengthen*: Plant: pennyroyal.

Throat (5th) chakra: Water/Ether; Charm: star; Color: blue, turquoise; Animal: bear, robin; Stone: blue lace agate, aquamarine, celestite, chrysocolla, blue onyx, sapphire, tanzanite, blue topaz, blue tourmaline, turquoise; Plant: chamomile, myrrh; *to activate*: Color: blue; Stone: blue lace agate, aquamarine, celestite, lapis lazuli, blue topaz, turquoise; Plant: citronella, laurel; *to open*: Color: blue; Stone: blue lace agate, lapis lazuli, sodalite; *to stimulate*: Plant: violet.

To: activate chakras: Stone: quartz crystal. **balance chakras**: Stone: bloodstone, prehnite, quartz crystal, ruby. Plant: clove, lotus, poinsettia, thyme. **clear chakras**: Stone: amethyst, clear quartz crystal. **energize chakras**: Sun; Stone: sunstone. **open chakras**: Stone: fluorite, kyanite, clear quartz crystal; Plant: damiana, pineapple, sandalwood. **purify chakras**: Stone: quartz crystal; Plant: patchouli, sweetgrass. **strengthen chakras**: Stone: turquoise. **unite chakras**: Stone: rose quartz, smoky quartz; Plant: hibiscus.

Change

(See also: Changes, Passage, Transformation, Transition)

Mercury/Moon/Water/South

Color: black, blue, red, white; Charm: melted snow or ice; Number: 5; Animal: butterfly, chameleon, chimpanzee, dolphin, dragon, moth, porpoise, snake; Number: 2, 5, 7; Metal: mercury; Stone: malachite; Plant: honeysuckle, pimpernel, yarrow; Goddess: Estsanatlehi, Kali, Lakshmi, Persephone, Rhiannon, the Triple Goddess, Xochiquetzal.

Aggressive change: Animal: copperhead. **Major change**: Animal: butterfly. **Orderly change**: God: Vertumnus (The Changer). **Profound change**: God: Osiris. **Social change**: Goddess: Dakini. **Changeable disposition**: Plant: rye.

Ability to change: Moon/Water/ Gemini; Color: dark blue; God: Loki. **Courage to change**: Stone: hessonite. **Fear of change**: Number: 5. **Forces of change**: Goddess: Oya. **Something is about to change**: Plant: anise. **Winds of change**: Goddess: Oya. **Willingness to change**: Moon/Water; Metal: mercury; God: Enki.

Changing of the seasons: Goddess: Al Uzza, Keiva; God: the Dagda, Janus, Vertumnus.

To: accept change: Animal: butterfly; Stone: sandstone; Plant: sweet woodruff; *to learn to accept change*: Goddess: Demeter. **adjust to change**: Stone: garnet. **activate change**: Stone: solidified lava. **force change**: Goddess: Oya. **manifest change**: Color: orange, red; Stone: ruby; Plant: dragon's blood; Goddess: Tiamat; God: Tate. **resist change**: Plant: stonecrop. **take advantage of change**: Animal: wolf.

To change: awareness: Tool: censer; Stone: staurolite. **consciousness**: Animal: raven. **an environment**: Animal: monkey. **form**: (See: Shapeshifting, Transmutation). **gender**: Deity: Ganga, Inari, Kwan Yin; God/dess: Inari. **job/career**: Stone: aventurine. **minds/attitudes/ways of thinking**: Color: green; Stone: kyanite, lepidolite; Plant: licorice, squill. **a negative into a positive**: (See: Negativity). **a pattern**: Stone: azurite; *a family/hereditary pattern*: Plant: morning glory. **perception**: (See: Perception). **a person**: Goddess: Artemis, Cavillaca, Circe; God: Ares, Gwydion, Jupiter, Quetzalcoatl, Zeus. **plans**: Color: orange. **a situation**: Stone: malachite, turquoise. **the weather**: God: Perun. **the world**: God: Osiris. **your life**: (See: Life). **your luck**: (See: Luck). **your mind**: God: Ra. **yourself**: Color: orange. Animal: butterfly, frog, octopus; *make positive changes in yourself or your life*: Goddess: Isis.

Changeability
Moon/Water/Gemini

Color: dark blue, indigo; Metal: mercury.

Changes
(See also: Change, Passage, Transformation, Transition)

Uranus/Moon/Scorpio

Tool: wand; Color: black; Charm: black feather; Plant: dragon's blood, lady's mantle, peppermint, woodruff; Goddess: Xochiquetzal, Yolkai Estsan; God: Gwydion.

Anticipated changes: Goddess: the Maiden. **Inner changes**: Stone: coral; Plant: grass of Parnassus. **Major changes**: Stone: sugilite. **Needed changes**: *to bring*: Plant: hawthorn berry; *to make*: Plant: nasturtium; *to make needed changes in thinking*: Stone: lepidolite. **Positive changes**: Waxing Moon; Color: red; Animal: bluebird; Charm: red feather; Plant: violet; Goddess: Isis; *omen of*: Animal: chameleon; *to make in yourself or your life*: Goddess: Isis. **Rapid changes**: Color: magenta; Animal: komodo dragon; *to adapt to*: Animal: octopus. **Subtle changes**: *to detect*: Animal: salmon. **Sudden changes**: Uranus; Color: orange, yellow; Stone: citrine, topaz. **Unexpected changes**: God: Coyote, Loki. **Weather changes**: Plant: yarrow.

To: make changes: Animal: komodo dragon; Plant: heliconia; Goddess: Oya; God: Gwydion; *make mental changes*: Stone: lepidolite. **trust changes**: Animal: wooly caterpillar. **understand changes**: Stone: peridot.

Chaos
(See also: Confusion, Order)

Water

Number: 2; Animal: dragon, scorpion, wolf; Plant: May flowers; Goddess: Discordia, Oya, Tiamat (Dragoness of Chaos); God: Agayu, Chaos, Chernobog, Loki, Set.

Emotional chaos: *to calm*: Stone: amazonite; *to recognize*: Stone: clear quartz crystal. **Primeval chaos**: Goddess: Nammu, Nun; God: Anzu, Apsu, Chaos, Mbombo, Nun, Yamm.

Chaos magic: (See: Magick).

To: battle chaos: God: Baal, Marduk. **create order from chaos**: (See: Order). **defeat chaos**: Plant: lavender yarrow; Goddess: Isis; God: Marduk (Breaker of Chaos), Sirsir. **find your way through chaos**: Animal: jaguar. **prevent chaos**: Charm: clean house; God: Ea. **protect against chaos**: Stone: emerald; God: Agayu. **understand chaos**: Animal: jaguar.

Charisma

(See also: Attractiveness)

Sun/Sunday/Sagittarius

Color: gold, purple, yellow; Charm: musk; Number: 3; Stone: peridot; Metal: gold; Plant: buttercup, devil's claw, musk rose; God: Osiris; Evocation: May King.

Charity

(See also: Generosity)

Aquarius

Charm: orange flower water; Color: green, red; Stone: jet, pearl, rose quartz; Plant: grape, Jacob's ladder, orange blossom, turnip; Goddess: Acca Larentia, Hestia, Lakshmi, Mary (Our Lady of Charity), Oshun; Evocation: Charissa.

To: reward charity: God: Zeus. **teach charity**: Goddess: Nzambi; God: Odin.

Charm

(See: Charisma)

Cheerfulness

(See also: Happiness, Mood)

Sun/Fire

Color: yellow; Animal: chickadee, cricket, meadowlark, pig; Stone: carnelian, citrine, ruby, tourmaline; Plant: daisy, sunflower, zinnia; Goddess: Prassana, Sekhmet (Lady of Cheerfulness), Suprasanna (always smiling and cheerful).

Cheerfulness in adversity: Plant: chrysanthemum.

To: cheer: Stone: tigereye, turquoise, zircon; Plant: basil, cherry blossom, orange; Goddess: Baubo. **make cheerful**: Stone: fluorite, ruby, sardonyx; Plant: motherwort.

Childbirth

(See also: Pain: labor pain, Pregnancy, Babies)

Moon/Water/Aries

Color: blue, red; Animal: stork; Stone: ammonite, chrysocolla, geode, hematite, malachite, pumice, rose quartz, rutilated quartz, sard; Plant: date palm, elm, sweet corn, tansy; Goddess: Abnoba, Acna, Acuecueyotl, the Afliae, the Ahinehiae, the Ahueccaniae, Akhushtal, the Alaferhviae, the Alagabiabus, the Alaisiagae, the Albiahenae, Antevorta, Aveta (The Midwife), Arianrhod, Artemis, Aruru, Averruncus, Bast, Brigid, Candelifera, Carmenta, Chakwaina Okya, Cihuacoatl, Cihuacoatl, Comitia, Diana, Dolya, Eileithyia, Eingana, Ethausva, the Euthungae, Freya, the Friagabiae, Frigg, the Gavasiae, the Hamavehae, Hathor, Haumea, Hecate, Heqet, Hera, Ix Chel, Juksakka, Kishi-Mojin, the Kotharot, Kwan Yin, the Lanehiae, Lucina (She Who Brings To Light), the Maluisae, Mami, the Marsacae, Mary, Mater Matuta, Mokosh, Mylitta, Ninmah, Nintu, Opet, Ops, Pi-Hsai

Yuan Chin, Pukkeenegak, Sarakka, Sasthi, the Sasuratum, the Seubis, Sheng Mu, Smyrna, Teteoinnan, Thalna, Tonantzin, Toci, Tzu-Ku-Shen, Xmucane, Xochiquetzal, the Xulsigiae, Yemaya; God: Bes, Khnum.

Easy childbirth: Stone: lodestone; Goddess: Freya; *for a quick delivery*: Plant: columbine, laurel; *to ease childbirth*: Stone: bloodstone, coral, jasper, red jasper, moonstone; Plant: cyclamen, hyacinth; Goddess: Rauni, Taweret; God: Perun. **Healthy childbirth**: Plant: nuts. **Safe childbirth**: Charm: hexagon; Goddess: Ajyst, Anahita, Averruncus, Brigid, Coventina, Isis (Divine Midwife), Juno Lucina, Rauni, Taweret; *to reduce the dangers of childbirth*: Stone: clear quartz crystal. **Successful childbirth**: Goddess: Bride, Egeria.

Help in childbirth: Stone: malachite; Plant: jasmine; Goddess: Athirat, Brigid, Eileithyia (She Who Aids Women in Labor), Frigg, Lucina, Mayahuel, Sarakka, Selqet; God: Ah Cuxtal; *help in the final stage of childbirth*: Goddess: Hecate, Heqet; *midwifing*: Goddess: Aveta (The Midwife), Mokosh.

To: encourage labor: Stone: lapis lazuli; Plant: blue cohosh. **mourn children who die at birth**: Goddess: Cihuacoatl, La Llorona (The Weeping Woman). **protect women in childbirth**: Goddess: Artemis, Hathor, Laima, Nekhebet, Opet, Pi-Hsai Yuan Chin, Yama; God: Bes, Jizo Bosatsu. **reduce the dangers of childbirth**: (See: Danger).

Childhood

(See also: Youth)

Plant: buttercup, primrose.

Bad childhood: *to overcome*: Plant: valerian; Goddess: Atalanta; *to recover from*: Color: pink; Stone: pink calcite, rose quartz. **Childhood illnesses**: (See: Illnesses). **Children's sleep**: Goddess: Cuba.

Childishness

(See also: Maturity/Immaturity)

Aries

Color: coral, pink.

To finally grow up: Goddess: Athena; Plant: bracken.

Children

Water

Stone: lapis lazuli; Goddess: Abeona, Artemis, Hathor (Mother of Children), Iyatiku, Xochiquetzal; God: Jizo Bosatsu, T'ai-Yueh-Ta-Ti.

Dead children: Goddess: La Llorona; Evocation: Erathipa; *to grieve for*: Animal: nightingale; Goddess: La Llorona (The Weeping Woman), Mary (Lady of Sorrows). **Happy children**: Plant: vervain; Goddess: Sasthi; *to protect the happiness and welfare of children*: Goddess: Sasthi; *to make children happy and apt to learn*: Plant: vervain. **Healthy children**: Stone: coral; Goddess: Jezanna; God: Hiruku, Tvashtri. **Inner child**: (See: Inner Work). **Missing children**: *to find a stolen child*: Goddess: Cairene, Hecate; Evocation: King Arthur; *safe return of a lost, stolen, or kidnapped child*: Plant: mullein; Goddess: Ceres, Demeter, Modron; Evocation: King Arthur; *to help lost children*: Goddess: Cairene; *to help a child find his/her way safely home*: Goddess: Persephone, Prosperina; *to prevent abduction by fairies*: Plant: ash berry, mistletoe, plantain. **Needy children**: *to protect*: Goddess: Akonadi. **Sick/distressed children**: *to comfort children in crisis*: Goddess: Yemaya; *to end fear of the dark*: Stone: chalcedony; *to help children after accidents or trauma*: Plant: sweet potato; *to increase a child's emotional security*: Charm: teddy bear; Potion: chamomile tea; *for a seriously ill child*: Goddess:

Cairene. **Small/young children**: Color: white; God: Legba; Plant: clover; Goddess: Artemis; *to protect*: Plant: fava bean; Goddess: Artemis, Kwan Yin, Yemaya; God: Legba; *to teach to speak*: God: Fabulinus. **School children**: Goddess: Adeona. **Special needs children**: *autistic children*: God: Thoth; *hyperactive children*: Charm: chamomile syrup; *to parent children with special needs*: Goddess: Angerboda, Isis. **Strong children**: Plant: hazel nut. **Your child/ren**: *to protect*: Stone: coral.

Child abuse: (See: Abuse). **Compassion for those who lose children**: (See: Compassion). **Generosity to children**: God: Ixtlilton. **Good luck for children**: Plant: wintergreen. **Grief for children**: (See: Grief). **Parent/child harmony**: (See: Harmony). **Safe passage for children**: Goddess: Adeona.

To: accept a child with an unusual appearance: Goddess: Isis, Walutahanga. **bless children**: Goddess: Freya, Isis. **communicate with children**: Plant: zinnia. **control children**: Plant: primrose. **defend children**: Goddess: Boldogasszony, Caireen, Isis. **discover whether a child is bewitched**: (See: Enchantment). **end fascination in children**: Charm: sweep the face gently with a pine bough. **entertain children**: God: Bes. **help a child**: *to achieve his/her ambitions*: Goddess: Isis; Evocation: Nessa; *to find his/her way safely home*: Goddess: Persephone, Prosperina; *to grow*: Goddess: Althea (She Who Makes Things Grow), Blodeuwedd; *to learn*: Plant: lemon verbena, vervain; *to recover*: *from accidents*: Plant: sweet potato; *from nightmares*: (See: Nightmares). **nourish children**: Goddess: Edusa. **protect children**: Moon; Animal: bear, cheetah, musk ox; Stone: agate, alum, amber, coral, malachite; Metal: gold, silver; Plant: angelica, dill, flax, Putranjiva seed; Goddess: Artemis, Athirat, Bast, Boldogasszony, Brigid, Cairene,

Hariti, Hecate, Isis, Kishi-Mojin, Sasthi, Sekhmet (The Great Cow Who Protects Her Child), Ursula, Yashoda; God: Acat, Bes, Chang Hsien (Protector of Children), Jizo; Evocation: Hariti; *in bathtubs/showers*: Goddess: La Sirene; *from bad influences*: Stone: citrine; *from danger*: Stone: coral; *from evil spirits*: Plant: dill; *from fairies*: (See: Fairies); *from falling*: Stone: agate; *against fascination*: (See: Fascination); *against illness*: Plant: caraway seed; *in rivers*: God: Sobek; *against witchcraft*: Stone: amber; *from Witches*: Plant: caraway seeds (under the bed); *when they leave home*: Goddess: Abeona; *while sleeping*: Plant: garlic; Goddess: Cardea; *from the Night Hag*: Plant: hawthorn; *from the Night Mare*: Stone: leopardskin jasper, malachite; Plant: chamomile; *protect orphans*: God: Zeus; *protect small/young children*: Plant: fava bean; Goddess: Kwan Yin, Yemaya; God: Legba; *protect teenagers*: Stone: citrine; *protect unwed girls*: Goddess: Gefion. **raise children**: Plant: quince; Goddess: Althea; *raise a foster child*: Goddess: Isis. **save a child's life**: Goddess: Isis; God: Maximon, Thoth. **strengthen the mother/child bond**: Animal: orangutan; Plant: linden tree. **take care of children**: Goddess: Renenet. **teach children**: Goddess: Emanjah; *to sing and dance*: Goddess: Ahnt Kai'; **train a child for public life**: Goddess: Isis.

Civilization

(See also: Culture)

Saturn

Goddess: Bast, Demeter, Isis, Mawu, Nü-Kua, Semiramis, Vegoia; God: Enki, Marduk, Ogun, Osiris, Quetzalcoatl, Saturn; Evocation: the Wawalag Sisters.

Civilized behavior: Goddess: Fura-Chogue. **Civilizing influence**: Evocation: Kekrops, the Oannes.

Clairaudience

(See also: Psychism)

Animal: lemur; Stone: apatite, diamond, Herkimer diamond, fire opal; Plant: snapdragon.

Clairvoyance

(See also: Intuition, Psychism)

Air/Water/East/Scorpio

Color: white, purple, silver, yellow; Animal: kite; Number: 7; Metal: peacock ore; Stone: apatite, azurite, chrysoprase, diamond, halite, Herkimer diamond, green jasper, jet, malachite, moonstone, obsidian, opal, peridot; Plant: acacia, alfalfa, anise, arrowroot, basil, bistort, cannabis, cedar, cinnamon, clove, dandelion, dittany, eyebright, frankincense, hazel, heliotrope, hibiscus, honeysuckle, laurel, lavender, lemongrass, lilac, marigold, moonwort, mugwort, nutmeg, oakmoss, patchouli, rose, rowan, saffron, sandalwood, sage, thyme, wormwood, yarrow; Evocation: Amphiarus.

Clairvoyant dreams: Plant: marigold (in dream pillows).

Clarification

Method: tarot; Animal: bittern.

Dream clarification: Stone: turquoise; Plant: orchid, vanilla. **Emotional clarification**: Plant: rose.

Clarity

Air/North

Color: blue, clear, silver, violet, white, yellow; Charm: Eye of Horus, van van; Animal: fox; Stone: amazonite, amber, aventurine, jade, kyanite, lapis lazuli, clear quartz crystal, selenite, sulfur, tigereye, blue topaz, blue tourmaline, turquoise; Plant: azalea, bayberry, camphor, cedar, cypress, dandelion, everlasting, eyebright, frankincense, gotu kola, grape, heather, horehound, hyssop, iris, jasmine, laurel, lavender, lemon, lemon balm, lemongrass, lime, mint, peppermint, periwinkle, pomegranate, raspberry, rue, sage, clary sage, sandalwood, spruce, sunflower, tangerine, black tea, walnut, evergreens, all citrus fruits; God: Obatala, Thoth; Goddess: Sheela-na-gig.

Emotional clarity: Animal: duck; Stone: hematite, pearl, tigereye; Plant: basil, bunchberry, orange, passionflower, white rose. **Inner clarity**: Stone: labradorite, selenite; Plant: dandelion, clary sage, spearmint. **Intellectual clarity**: Plant: lemon. **Intellectual clarity**: Plant: angel trumpet, lemon. **Spiritual clarity**: Stone: malachite.

Clear communication: (See: Communication). **Clear expression**: (See: Expression). **Clear focus**: Stone: kyanite; Plant: lavender, persimmon. **Clear insight**: Stone: tourmaline. **Clear light**: Color: indigo; God: Apollo, Vindonnus. **Clear mind**: (See: The Mind). **Clear perception**: Plant: alder, thoroughwort. **Clear perspective**: Plant: birch. **Clear sight**: Color: clear, indigo; Plant: birch. **Clear speech**: Stone: celestite; Plant: laurel. **Clear thinking**: (See: Thought). **Clear vision**: (See: Vision).

Clarity leading to wisdom: New Moon. **Clarity in romantic relationships**: Plant: papaya. **To increase clarity**: Stone: tigereye; Plant: dandelion, horehound, lavender. **To make clear choices**: Plant: pomegranate. **To make dark energies clear**: God: Inyan.

Clearing

(See also: Banishing, Purification)

Fire/Air/Water

Tool: besom, censer; Method: sweeping; Charm: wind; Stone: lodestone, meteorite, moldovite, sea salt, black tourmaline; Plant: benzoin, fir, geranium, heather, jasmine, magnolia, sage, sweetgrass, tea tree, vervain; Goddess: Tlaelquarni; God: Vayu.

Emotional clearing: Stone: malachite; Plant: amaryllis, rue. **Physical clearing**: Tool: besom; Plant mullein.

To clear: the air after a quarrel: (See: Quarrels). **attachments**: Stone: calcite. **the aura**: (See: Auras). **blockages**: (See: Blockages). **chakras**: (See: Chakras). **darkness**: Goddess: Kali. **disharmony**: (See: Harmony). **energy**: (See: Energy). **entities**: Method: asperging, smudging; Charm: Florida Water; Stone: calcite; Plant: eye of Satan. **evil**: (See: Evil). **fear**: (See: Fear). **the heart**: Plant: burnet. **the home**: (See: The Home). **illusions**: (See: Illusions). **the mind**: (See: The Mind). **negativity**: (See: Negativity). **nightmares**: (See: Nightmares). **the obsolete**: Goddess: Kali. **obstacles**: (See: Obstacles). **the old in order to make room for the new**: God: Zeus. **the past**: Plant: birch. **a path/road**: (See: Pathworking). **problems**: Charm: machete; God: Ogun. **spirits**: (See: Spirits). **storms**: God: Vayu. **vibrations**: (See: Vibrations).

Cleverness

(See also: Cunning, Ingenuity, Intelligence)

Mercury

Animal: coyote, fox, goanna, monkey, wolverine; Stone: emerald; Goddess: Eileithyia, Ishtar, Isis; God: Al-Hanishah, Anansi, Bel (Cleverest of the Clever), Ea, Enki, Heimdall, Hermes, Kothar-wa-Khasis, Loki; Evocation: Vasilisa.

Clever solutions: (See: Solutions).

Cloaking

(See also: Deceit, Invisibility)

Charm: fog, magick powder, mist; Animal: fox, grouper, octopus, squid, walking stick; Goddess: Ayauhteotl, Greine, Nephthys, Zorya; God: Angus.

Comfort

(See also: Soothing)

Earth/Taurus

Color: yellow; Number: 6; Animal: cat; Metal: gold; Stone: agate, calcite, dioptase, emerald; Plant: amber, clove, fir, gardenia, red-flowered geranium, marigold, marjoram, myrrh, white oak, papaya, pear, rosemary, sage, tuberose; Goddess: Anu, Bast, the Great Mother, Yemaya; God: Borvo, Jizo Bosatsu.

To comfort: Plant: benzoin, cedar, cypress, evergreens, fir, frankincense, gardenia, red geranium, vanilla; Goddess: Kwan Yin. **children in crisis**: Goddess: Yemaya. **grief**: (See: Grief). **the heart**: Stone: blue chrysocolla, rose quartz; Plant: burnet, lemon balm. **the recently deceased**: Goddess: Hathor. **the dying**: Goddess: Danu. **nerves**: Plant: mint. **the sick**: Goddess: Shekinah. **women in distress**: Stone: jasper.

Command

(See also: Authority, Control, Mastery)

Tool: wand; Color: purple; Charm: ambergris; Plant: dittany, brown mustard seed, orris root; Goddess: Aeval, Aoife, Hecate, Kali, Nemesis, Sekhmet, Venus; God: Marduk, Neptune, Odin, Poseidon, Tirawa, Zeus.

Divine commands: Animal: owl; Goddess: Iris. **Effective command**: God: Enki. **To command**: **Earth elementals**: Goddess: Frigg. **winds**: God: Lugal-dim-er-ankia.

Communication

(See also: Contact, Eloquence, Expression, Messages, Speech)

Mercury/Air/Fire/Earth/Wednesday/Gemini

Color: blue, orange, peach, yellow; Number: 3, 5; Metal: silver; Animal: ape, dolphin, monkey, carrier pigeon, whale; Stone: black agate, blue lace agate, amazonite, amethyst, apatite, aquamarine, azurite, celestite, chrysocolla, danburite, lapis lazuli, quartz, morganite, moonstone, selenite, blue topaz, turquoise; Plant: allspice, almond, broom, buttercup, yellow carnation, chamomile, garlic, geranium, marigold, rosemary, sycamore; Goddess: Bharati, Fama, Gna, Iris, Nidaba, Pairikas, Rosmerta, Waramurungundji; God: Al Lisan (the Tongue), Al-Shafi, Amergin, Arawn, Corvus, Goidel, Hashye-Altye, Hermes, Hermod, Ikto, Legba, Mercury, Nabu, Ogma, Thoth (Lord of Divine Words), Turms.

Authoritative communication: God: Hu. **Calm communication**: Plant: cosmos. **Clear communication**: Stone: aquamarine, tanzanite, turquoise; Plant: dandelion. **Cordial communication**: Plant: linden, marigold. **Divine communication**: (See: Oracles). **Dream communication**: God: Hypnos. **Internal communication**: Plant: horsetail; Plant: dandelion. **Loving communication**: Stone: kunzite; Plant: chamomile. **Meaningful communication**: Stone: blue lace agate; Metal: peacock ore. **Nonverbal communication** (body language): Animal: squid. **Oracular communication**: God: Apollo. **Oral communication**: (See: Speech). **Peaceful communication**: Stone: blue lace agate, amazonite; Plant: marigold. **Plant communication**: Animal: leopard. **Public communication**: Stone: amazonite, yellow carnelian; Plant: trumpet vine. **Receptive communication**: (See: Senses: listening). **Written communication**: Plant: papyrus; Goddess: Belit-Seri, Nisaba, Rosmerta; God: Nabu, Ogma.

Balance in communication: Stone: chrysocolla. **Sensitivity in communication**: Plant: marigold. **Clarity of body-mind communication**: Plant: dandelion. **Good communication in relationships**: (See:

Relationships). **Ability to communicate powerfully**: Goddess: Oya; God: Bran. **Sensitivity in communication**: Animal: catfish; Plant: marigold.

To communicate: limits: Plant: briar, cactus, nettle, thorn. **universal law**: Stone: azurite. **visions**: Stone: tanzanite.

To communicate in: the dark: (See: Darkness). **in good faith**: Goddess: Fides.

To communicate with: animals: (See: Animals). **children**: Plant: zinnia. **the dead**: (See: The Dead). **entities**: Tool: mirror; Charm: dreams. **higher beings**: Plant: orris root.

To communicate between: levels of consciousness: Plant: horsetail. **the sacred and the secular**: God: Legba. **spirit guides**: Goddess: the Crone. **to open: communication**: God: Ba Neb Tetet. **communication blockages**: Color: blue; Stone: lodestone. **lines of communication**: Charm: dinosaur bone; Plant: white violet. **the way for communication**: Charm: dinosaur bone; Stone: blue lace agate; Plant: horsetail, violet. **worlds/realms**: Stone: fluorite, topaz; God: Legba.

To: assist communication: Plant: linden; Goddess: Fama. **improve communication skills**: Plant: papyrus. **reestablish communication**: Plant: broom; Goddess: Hebat. **unite speech with communication**: God: Al-Shafi. **withhold communication**: Number: 3.

Community
(See also: People)

Color: green; Animal: ant, bee, gorilla, wolf.

Prosperous community: Goddess: Athana Lindia. **Community life**: Goddess: Vesta. **Community power**: Animal: ant, bee, goose. **Community work**: Goddess: Ala.

To: protect the community: God: Lubangala. **Serve the community**: Metal: peacock ore.

Compassion

(See also: Kindness, Mercy)

Venus/Water/West/Aquarius/Pisces

Charm: heart; Number: 4, 6, 9, 33; Color: aqua, green, pink, red, white; Stone: aquamarine, celestite, chrysoprase, garnet, jade, green jasper, red jasper, kunzite, moonstone, rose quartz, ruby, tourmaline, green tourmaline, turquoise; Plant: allspice, almond, bleeding heart, calla lily, centaury, cherry tree, elder, gardenia, holy thorn, jade plant, lotus, mesquite, potato, rhododendron, tarragon; Goddess: Amaterasu, the Crone, Ishtar, Iyatiku, Kali (Treasure House of Compassion), Kishi-Mojin, Kwan Yin (Hearer of Cries, Lady of Compassion), the Great Mother, the Ocean Mother, Mary, Melusine, Sekhmet, Shekinah, Tara (The Compassionate One), Yemaya (Compassionate One); God: Apollo, Bres, Dayakara, Dayanidhi, El (The Compassionate), Kephera, Marduk, Mithras, Obatala, Shiva, Varuna; Evocation: Chiron.

Compassion for: emotional problems: Stone: green jasper. **the mentally ill**: Stone: green jasper. **the recently deceased**: God: Anubis. **those who lose children**: Goddess: Ceres, Demeter, Modron. **those in need**: God: Shiva. **young men**: God: Mardu.

Commerce

(See: Business)

Concentration

(See also: Focus, Thought)

Air

Tool: candle, cauldron; Color: brown, yellow, violet, white; Number: 4; Animal: leopard; Stone: amethyst, carnelian, emerald, fluorite, hematite, malachite, pyrite, clear quartz crystal, ruby, blue topaz; Oil: petitgrain; Plant: air fern, basil, benzoin, bergamot, broom, buckthorn, cardamom, cascara sagrada (as potpourri), cedar, celery seeds, cinnamon, coffee, cypress, frankincense, garlic, iris, lavender, lemon balm, lemongrass, lilac, marjoram, mastic, mint, narcissus, nutmeg, parsley, persimmon, rosemary, sage, sandalwood, scullcap, spikenard.

Concentration in psychic work: (See: Work). **Power of concentration**: Color: brown, violet, white, yellow. **To increase concentration**: Stone: pyrite; Plant: cassia, cinnamon, hibiscus, mint, verbena.

Conception

(See also: Fertility, Pregnancy)

Artificial insemination: Animal: salamander. **Magickal conception**: Goddess: Arianrhod, Isis. **Miraculous conception**: Plant: hawthorn; Goddess: Mary.

To conceive: Tool: goatskin scourge, pussy willow scourge; Color: green; Stone: emerald, peridot, green tourmaline; Plant: almond, bistort, carrot seed, yellow dock, hawthorn blossom, lettuce, mandrake, mistletoe, pomegranate, pussy willow, sage, sunflower seed, watermelon; Goddess: Ahurani, Astarte (Conceiving Womb), Diana, Hathor (Mother of Children), Heqet, Hestia, Kishi-Mojin, the Kotharat, Kuan Yin, Libera, Lucina, Sasthi, Sinivali, Yemaya; God: Khonsu, Wepwawet; *or beget*: Plant: mistletoe; Goddess: Anahita, Juno Populonia, Sarasvati; *at an advanced age*: Goddess: Sarah; *in an unusual way*: Goddess: Dechtere, Isis, Marjatta, Mary, Nana, Nephthys, Sheng-Mu.

Confidence

Sun/Fire/Sunday/Capricorn/Leo

Color: royal blue, gold, peach, yellow; Charm: musk; Animal: bluebird, butterfly, cougar, elephant, mountain lion, puma, seahorse; Metal: gold; Stone: carbuncle, carnelian, blue chrysocolla, diamond, garnet, jade, larimar, moonstone, opal, rhodonite, tiger's eye; Oil: neroli, palmarosa, petitgrain; Plant: basil, benzoin, bergamot, camellia, caraway, cardamom, carnation, cedar, cypress, ephedra, fern, fig, geranium, hepatica, lime, liverwort, myrrh, nettle, orange, passion flower, sweet pea, clary sage, tamarack, thyme, turmeric; God: Bacchus, Balder, Lugh.

Self-confidence: Fire; Color: orange, purple; Charm: musk; Animal: cougar, tiger; Stone: agate, aventurine, bloodstone, orange calcite, carbuncle, carnelian, chrysocolla, citrine, diamond, garnet, lodestone, rose quartz, rhodonite, ruby, tiger's eye, tourmaline; Plant: amber, camellia, cypress, dragon's blood, heather, rosemary, sweet pea, tamarack, yarrow. **Spiritual confidence**: Plant: passionflower, reed.

Confident action: Plant: thistle. **To: appear confident**: Stone: rhodonite. **attract confidence**: Plant: frangipani, rose, yarrow. **gain someone's confidence**: Color: yellow.

Overconfidence
Animal: gazelle.

onfusion
(See also: Chaos)

Color: black, gray, silver; Number: 2; Animal: bobwhite, platypus; Goddess: Discordia; God: Al Balal, Loki, Maui.

Emotional confusion: *to overcome*: Stone: sodalite; Plant: passionflower. **Mental confusion**: Evocation: the Rakshasa; *to overcome*: Plant: birch, goldenrod, thoroughwort. **Sexual confusion**: *to overcome*: Plant: coconut.

To confuse: Plant: poppy seed. **enemies**: Plant: blueberry. **travelers**: Evocation: Pooka; *forest travelers*: Evocation: dames vertes.

To: overcome confusion: Stone: azurite, rhodonite, sodalite; Plant: broom, daisy, foxglove, High John. **prevent confusion from spirit contact**: Color: black. **protect against confusion**: Plant: pennyroyal.

onjuring
(See: Magick, Spells, Witchcraft)

onnection
(See also: Contact, Family, Friends, Marriage, Relationships, Union)

Venus

Animal: condor; Stone: obsidian, ruby; Metal: copper; Plant: bird of paradise, mariposa lily, enchanted nightshade, rose hip.

Cosmic connection: Stone: jade, lapis lazuli, prase. **Emotional connection**: Plant: water lily; *to connect body/mind/emotions*: Stone: moonstone. **Spiritual connection**: Stone: amethyst, rhodochrosite; Plant: maize, peach, silverweed, thistle; *material/spiritual*: Number: 5; Animal: eagle, wolverine; Plant: sea pink; *mental/spiritual*: Stone: pearl; *mundane/spiritual*: Stone: jade; Plant: lavender; *physical/spiritual*: Animal: cat, ocelot, swan; Stone: jet.

To connect: ancient/modern: Plant: horsetail. **body/mind/spirit**: Charm: triangle; Number: 3. **chakras**: Stone: rhodochrosite. **higher/lower consciousness**: Stone: topaz. **humans/deities**: Animal: bear, all animals. Stone: azurite, malachite. **human intelligence/animal intelligence**: Animal: dolphin. **humans/spirits**: Animal: all animals. **inner self/outer world**: Plant: ash. **past/future**: Animal: spider. **past life/current life**: Animal: spider.

To connect with: elements: Stone: labradorite. **higher realms**: Stone: zoisite. **inner levels**: Stone: alexandrite. **inner self**: Plant: Japanese maple. **kindred spirits**: Stone: alexandrite. **Nature**: Plant: petrified wood. **other planes**: Plant: narcissus, ylang-ylang; *inner planes*: Stone: obsidian. **psychic consciousness**: Plant: forget-me-not, marjoram. **spirits**: Animal: cougar. **the soul**: Stone: iolite. **universal energy**: Goddess: Isis. **the unseen**: Animal: ocelot.

Interconnection

Animal: all parasitic and symbiotic animals; Stone: all composite stones; Metal: alloys; Plant: mistletoe, reindeer moss, all parasitic and symbiotic plants.

Reconnection

Stone: kyanite, tourmaline; Plant: African violet.

Conquest

(See: Banishing, Ending, Overcoming, Victory)

Consecration

(See also: Blessing)

Earth/Air/Fire/Water

Tool: athame, censer, pentacle; Method: anointing, asperging, smudging; Color: purple, white; Charm: holy water, honey, hyssop water, lavender flower water, ointment, rosewater, salted water, vervain water; Stone: bloodstone, obsidian, onyx, quartz crystal, salt, sea salt; Plant: acacia, alfalfa, almond, angelica, anise, arrowroot, holy basil, buckthorn, carnation, cascara sagrada, cassia, cedar, cinnamon, copal, cypress, dragon's blood, elder, eucalyptus, frankincense, galangal, gum arabic, hibiscus, High John, holly, hyssop, jasmine, lavender, lily of the valley, lotus, mimosa, mugwort, myrrh, olive, rose, rosemary, rue, sage, sandalwood, spikenard, star anise, thyme, vervain, wood aloes, yarrow.

To consecrate: an altar: Plant: acacia, benzoin, hyssop, myrrh, sandalwood, spikenard, vervain. **amulets, candles, talismans, charms, and so on**: Charm: van van; Plant: acacia, allspice, apple blossom, cedar, cinnamon, cinquefoil, coriander, dragon's blood, frankincense, High John, hyacinth, jasmine, lily of the valley, lotus, mint, myrrh, rose, rosemary, wisteria. **boundary markers**: Plant: garland of herbs or flowers; God: Terminus; **contracts**: Plant: patchouli. **magical tools**: (See: Magick). **newlyweds**: Goddess: Unxia. **a pyre**: God: Thor. **ritual objects**: Plant: copal, cypress (as incense), frankincense, myrrh.

Consciousness

(See also: Awareness, The Mind)

Sun/Moon

Color: gold, silver; Animal: jaguar; Stone: clear quartz crystal; Goddess: Mens.

Altered consciousness: Tool: censer; Method: meditation, astral projection; Animal: raven; Stone: diamond. **Collective consciousness**: *to access*: Stone: avalonlite; *to unite with*: Plant: lime. **Cosmic consciousness**: Color: white; *to access*: Stone: opal. **Emotional consciousness**: Number: 6; Metal: silver. **Group consciousness**: Plant: lime. **Higher consciousness**: *to awaken*: Plant: benzoin, cannabis, frankincense, lime, lotus, snowdrop; *to connect higher and lower consciousness*: Stone: topaz. **Infinite consciousness**: Goddess: Aditi. **Psychic consciousness**: *to connect with*: Plant: marjoram. **Pure consciousness**: God: Shiva. **Self-consciousness**: *to overcome*: Potion: elderberry wine; Plant: elder. **Social consciousness**: Number: 6. **Spiritual consciousness**: Plant: sage. **Super-consciousness**: Stone: amethyst. **Universal consciousness**: Goddess: Isis. **Victim consciousness**: *to overcome*: Plant: everlasting.

Conscious awareness: (See: Awareness). **Conscious growth**: Plant: spirea.

Conscious mind: (See: The Mind). **Conscious structure**: Number: 4. **Conscious transformation**: Stone: smoky quartz. **Conscious understanding**: *of life experiences*: Stone: ruby. **Night consciousness**: Color: black, indigo, purple; Goddess: Nephthys. **Light of consciousness**: Color: white; Plant: birch.

To: affect consciousness: Metal: copper; Stone: meteorite; God: Dionysus, Soma, Tepoztacatl. **change consciousness**: Animal: raven; Metal: copper; *to reorient afterward*: Plant: gardenia. **communicate between levels of consciousness**: Plant: horsetail. **expand consciousness**: Stone: blue lace agate, calcite, fossil; Plant: cannabis, lotus, morning glory, petrified wood; Goddess: Tara. **explore consciousness**: Animal: wolf. **lose consciousness**: Waning Moon. **open consciousness**: Color: black, gray; Stone: fossil; Plant: lotus, oak, passionflower. **raise consciousness**: Plant: frankincense, passionflower. **refocus consciousness**: Stone: clear or violet fluorite, tourmaline. **regenerate consciousness**: Stone: amethyst. **remain conscious**: Plant: black hellebore; God: Bran. **transform consciousness**: Goddess: Tara.

The Subconscious

Moon/Water

Goddess: Lilith; God: Olokun.

To: access: Method: dreams; Stone: malachite, obsidian; Plant: horsetail; Metal: silver. **enlighten**: Stone: black star sapphire. **receive messages from**: Animal: bat. **release subconscious tension**: Plant: corn, orange. **unblock subconscious fears**: Stone: citrine.

The Unconscious

Water

Color: black; Animal: lizard; Goddess: Durga, Hecate; God: Olokun.

Collective unconscious: Animal: owl; Goddess: Yemaya; *to study*: Method: mythology. **Deep unconscious**: Scorpio; Goddess: Frigg. **Unconscious beauty**: Plant: red daisy, burgundy rose. **Unconscious fear**: *to relieve*: Stone: opal; *to unblock*: Stone: citrine. **Unconscious forces**: (See: Forces). **Treasures of the unconscious mind**: Animal: dragon.

Constancy

(See also: Fidelity, Endurance, Stability)

Color: yellow; Animal: bull, cougar, mule, ox, wolf; Stone: green beryl, garnet; Plant: bluebell, hyacinth, ivy, lily of the valley, marigold, pansy, sycamore; Goddess: Lakshmi, Sita, Themis (The Steadfast One); God: Olokun; Evocation: Penelope.

Constancy of conviction: Plant: oak. **Constancy in love**: Stone: garnet. **Constancy of mind**: Stone: emerald; Plant: bunchberry.

Steadfast devotion: Goddess: Parvati. **Steadfast piety**: Plant: wild geranium. **Steadfast power**: Earth; God: Zeus.

Inconstancy

Plant: evening primrose.

Female inconstancy: Plant: hellebore.

Contact

Dream contact: *with spirits*: Charm: ice water (under the bed, with a letter in it); Plant: cowslip (under the pillow). **Negative contacts**: *to absorb the negativity*: Plant onion bulb; *to purify afterward*: Plant: eucalyptus.

To contact: Stone: Apache gold. **the cosmic mind**: Plant: birch. **deities**: Method: invocation; *Mother Earth*: Earth; Charm: soil; go barefoot, sit on the ground; Stone: all; Plant: all, but especially corn; *orishas*: God: Legba. **elves**: Plant: daffodil, foxglove, wood sorrel. **female sexuality**: Plant: hibiscus. **other planes**: Plant: alfalfa, aniseed, cascara sagrada, copal, damiana, frankincense, galangal, hibiscus, hyssop, lemongrass, oakmoss, patchouli, thyme, yarrow; **spirits/the spirit world**: (See: Spirits). **spirit guides**: (See: Guidance). **the astral plane**: Plant: frankincense. **your inner child**: Plant: zinnia. **your power animal**: (See: Animals).

Contentment

(See also: Happiness, Satisfaction)

Color: peach; Animal: cat; Stone: amethyst, carnelian; Plant: apple blossom, catnip, cow parsnip, valerian; Goddess: Allat, Felicitas; God: Hotei.

To: attract contentment: Plant: apple. **restore contentment**: Stone: geode.

Contracts

Water

Goddess: Vör; God: Arom, Berith, Mithras (Lord of the Contract).

Marriage contracts/prenuptial agreements: Goddess: Isis, Vör; God: Jupiter, Zeus Gamelios. **Social contracts**: Goddess: Themis. **Fairness in contracts**: Goddess: Aequitas. **Sanctity of contracts**: God: Mithras.

To: anoint contracts: Plant: patchouli. **enforce contracts**: God: Kinma. **sign contracts**: Vör. **witness contracts**: Goddess: Zemlya; God: Helios.

Control

(See also: Command, Discipline, Moderation, Will)

Jupiter/Scorpio

Tool: cord; Color: orange, purple; Number: 3, 22; Stone: aquamarine; Plant: bayberry, bergamot, bindweed, camphor, lime, mandrake root, oak; God: Jumala.

Breath control: Animal: dolphin. **Emotional control**: Color: orange; Stone: citrine;

Mental control: Plant: Jacob's ladder. **Self-control**: Color: black, orange; Stone: onyx, black opal, black star sapphire, sardonyx; Plant: cedar, fig tree, vervain; Goddess: Atalanta, Athene, Brigantia, Diana; God: Mithras; *of sexuality*: (See: Sexuality).

To control: anger: Color: yellow. **the body**: Plant: comfrey. **breathing**: Animal: dolphin. **children**: Plant: primrose. **darkness**: (See: Darkness). **your dark side**: Color: black. **destiny**: Goddess: the Norns. **dreams**: Animal: lizard; God: Hermes. **earthquakes**: Goddess: Coatlicue. **the Elements**: God: Don. **emotions**: Color: orange; Stone: citrine; **energy**: (See: Energy); **entities**: Tool: wand; *demons*: (See: Demons); *elementals*: Plant: alder. **fire**: Goddess: Brigid; God: Njord. **a bewitched horse**: Charm: rowan whip. **intensity**: Animal: basilisk. **people**: (See: People). **the surface of the sea**: God: Aegir. **the senses**: (See: Senses). **sexual desire**: Stone: onyx; Plant: hemlock. **a situation**: (See: Situations). **snakes**: Goddess: Visahari. **spending**: Plant: sassafras. **spirits**: (See: Spirits). **storms**: God: Mabon. **water**: Goddess: Brigid; *bodies of water*: Evocation: the Vodyanoi. **weather**: (See: Weather). **winds**: Tool: alder wood whistle; Plant: alder; Goddess: Sunna; God: Marduk, Njord.

To: keep control: Animal: gila monster; God: Shango; **learn to control your temper**: Goddess: Medea. **not allow anyone to control you**: Goddess: Durga. **overcome fear of losing control**: Stone: sandstone; Plant: bistort, daisy. **overcome the need to control others**: Plant: bistort. **release the need to control**: Plant: horsetail. **stop being a control freak**: Plant: bistort, Jacob's ladder.

The Cosmic

Stone: meteorite, moldovite; Plant: lotus; Goddess: Itzpapalotl, Jyestha, Parvati; God: Mithras, Shiva.

Cosmic awareness: Plant: birch. **Cosmic connection**: Stone: jade, prase. **Cosmic consciousness**: Color: white; *to access*: Stone: opal. **Cosmic dance**: Goddess: Eurynome, Jagadhamba; God: Dionysus, Shiva. **Cosmic energy**: (See: Energy). **Cosmic forces**: (See: Forces). **Cosmic influence**: Color: gold. **Cosmic mind**: God: Brahma; *to contact*: Plant: birch. **Cosmic order**: (See: Order). **Cosmic passion**: God: Eros. **Cosmic power**: Color: yellow, gold; God: Mithras. **Cosmic productive urge**: Goddess: Prakrta. **Cosmic truth**: Goddess: Kali. **Cosmic wisdom**: Animal: whale.

To perceive the cosmic: Method: meditation; Charm: shooting star; Animal: whale.

Counsel
(See: Advice, Guidance)

Courage
(See also: Fear)

Mars/Waxing Moon/Fire/Water/Aries/Leo/ Tuesday

Number: 1, 9; Color: brown, green, red, orange, yellow; Animal: badger, bear, boar, carp, cougar, eagle, lion, panther, rooster, tiger, wolf, wolverine; Charm: red feather, musk, van van; Metal: gold; Stone: agate, red and black agate, amber, amethyst, aquamarine, aventurine, bloodstone, carnelian, blue chalcedony, chrysoprase, diamond, garnet, hematite, Herkimer diamond, jade, jasper, labradorite, lapis lazuli, ruby, sapphire, sard, sardonyx, spinel ruby, staurolite, tigereye, topaz, turquoise, tourmaline, red tourmaline, turquoise; Oil: palmarosa; Plant: allspice, ambrosia, basil, bergamot, black cohosh, borage, cardamom, catnip, cedar, clove, coconut, columbine, dragon's blood, fennel seed, frankincense, galangal, garlic, geranium, rose geranium, ginger, heliotrope, hickory, High John, lady's mantle, lavender, mandrake, masterwort, mullein, nettle, oak, pepper, pine, poke weed, poplar, rose, rosemary, St. John's Wort, spindle tree bark, sweet pea, black tea, thistle, thyme, tonka bean, turmeric, French willow, wormwood, yarrow; Goddess: Anath, Artio, Atalanta, Athena, Bellona, Eve, Ishtar, Isis, the Morrigan, Neith, Oya, Pallas Athena, Sita, Suwa, Ursula, Zorya; God: Atlas, Mars, Mithras, Odin, Shango, Tyr, Vahagn, Wachabe (Black Bear); Evocation: Achilles, Gilgamesh, Hercules, Jason, Perseus.

Courage in: athletic competitions: Plant: mistletoe. **battle**: Goddess: Athena, Bellona. **carrying out duties**: Plant: catnip. **dangerous situations**: Plant: yarrow. **dealing with the dark side**: Plant: mullein.

Courage to: change: Stone: hessonite. **leave an unsuitable mate**: Goddess: Aine.

Courage to face: adversity: Plant: thistle. **danger**: Plant: yarrow. **death**: Animal: wolf; Goddess: Inanna, Ishtar. **deepest feelings**: West. **scary situations**: Plant: thistle. **self-expression**: Stone: amazonite. **trials and conflicts**: Color: red; Stone: carnelian, garnet.

To: attract courage: Plant: yarrow. **increase courage**: Stone: agate, leopard skin agate, bloodstone; Plant: borage, heliotrope, mandrake, rose. **inspire courage**: Stone: carnelian, tigereye. **protect the courageous**: Goddess: Athena. **reward courage**: Plant: laurel; *brave battle-slain warriors*: Goddess: the Valkyries; God: Tonatiuh; *women who die bravely in childbirth*: God: Tonatiuh. **strengthen courage**: Plant: sweet pea; *in a shy or timid person*: Stone: orange calcite, carnelian. **test courage**: Plant: edelweiss.

Court

(See also: Judgment, Justice)

Fire

Court cases: Thursday; Color: brown, green, orange, purple; Stone: amethyst, bloodstone; Plant: buckthorn, cascara sagrada, celandine, cypress, hickory, marigold, sandalwood; Goddess: Akonadi, Ananke, Aradia, Astraea, Eirene, Eunomia, Fortuna, Kadi, Megaera, the Moirae, Nanshe, Santati (Granter of Issues), Sin; God: Apollo, Baal, the Dagda, Nanna, Rhadamanthys, Shakaburu.

Protection in court or from a court case: Color: purple. **Success in court**: Color: black, green, red; Stone: aventurine, bloodstone, brown chalcedony, diamond, rose quartz; Plant: cascara sagrada, deerstongue, dill seed, galangal (chewed and spit out), High John, laurel, lovage root, marigold, mustard seed, pine nut or cone, St. John's Wort, sassafras, snakeroot, tobacco, vervain, vetiver; Goddess: Demeter Thesmophoros, Ida-Ten, Victoria; *if your cause is just*: Stone: diamond; Goddess: Justitia; *when being persecuted by an enemy*: Plant: mustard seed, pine nut or cone, tobacco.

For: **a fair judge**: Plant: patchouli, sandalwood; God: Suduk. **a sympathetic judge**: Plant: carnation, galangal.

To: **plead "not guilty"**: Cancer; Goddess: Syn. **speak well in court**: Plant: black pepper (See also: Eloquence). **swear in court**: (See: Oaths).

Creation

Sun/Full Moon/Earth/Water

Color: red, white; Charm: scarab; Number: 1; Animal: bear, bee, scarab beetle, crocodile, eagle, silkworm, spider; Plant: ash, banana, elm, fig, fir, larch, lotus, oak, pomegranate; Goddess: Aakuluujjusi, Abzu, Aditi, Ambika, Amma, Ammavaru, Amphitrite, Anath, Antu, Anzu, Ararat, Aruru, Asase Yaa, Asintmah, Astarte, Ataensic, Atanea, Aya, Bast, Ceres, Chalchihuitlcue, Coatlicue, Cura, Cymidei Cymeinfoll, Delphine (Womb of Creation), the Djanggawul Sisters, Dwyvach, Eingana (World Creator), Eka Abassi, Estsanatlehi, Eurynome, Eve, Geezhigo-Quae, Hen Wen, Gefion, Geqet, Honabe, Hou-Tu, Huruing Wuhti, Isis (Creation), Izanami, Kali, Kli, Kokyan, Luonnotar (Creatrix of the World), Mader Akka, Mama Cocha, Mami, the Ocean Mother, Mawu, the Mother, Nammu, Neith, Ninhursag, Nu Kua, Nzambi, Pah, Paiowa, Perimbó, Prakrta, Quootishooi, Ragno, Rodenica, Rukko, Sarasvati, Sekhmet, Shekinah, Somagalags, Spenta Armaiti, Sussistanako, Tethys, Tiamat, Tsichtinako, Tuli, Ukemachi, Wa, Wakini-Hai, Walo, Waramurungundji, Wari-Ma-Te-Takere, Yemaya (Womb of Creation), Yhi, Zipaltonal; God: Aguku, Akongo, Amon, Anansi, Anu, Arasy, Atum, Au-Co, Awonawilona (Creator of All), Byelobog, Biame, Brahma, Buku, Bumba, Cagn, Coniraya, Coyote, the Dagda, Daksha (Lord of Creation), Dis Pater, Ea, El, Ellil, Enki, Enlil, Gizh-numun-ab, Glooskap, Great Spirit, Gudratrigakwitl, Hurukan, Imana, Io, Ioskeha, Isten, Itzamna, Janus, Jehovah, Jumala, Kalumba, Karora, Khnum, Kolpia, Konori, Kukulcan, Ku'urkil, Kvasir, Kyala, Libanza, Lokakriti, Lother, Laulaati, Malah, Marduk, Melu, Michabo, Muluku, Mummu, Nebiru, 'Ngai, Ngendei, Nobu, North Star, Nu Kua, Numitorum, Nzambi, Obatala, Odin, Ogun, Olelbis, Oloddumare, Ometeotl, Ometecuhtli, Ophion, Ove, Perun, Phan Ku, Prajapati, Prometheus, Ptah, Quetzalcoatl, Ra, Rig, Rod (Creator of Heaven), Shiva, Suhgurim, Tangaroa, Takami-Musubi, Tamakaia, Teljavelik, Telpochtli, Tirawa, Tlaloc, Toko'yoto,

Tonacatecuhtli, Tsui' Goab, Tvashtri, Uchtsiti, Umvlinkwangi, Unkulunkulu, Unumbote, Uru'n Ajy Toyo'n (Lord Bright Creator), Tupa, Uwolowu, Vahguru, Varuna, Ve, Virachone, the White Hactin, Wuni, Yahweh, Zanahary; **Evocation**: Uru'n Ajy Toyo'n.

Continued creation: Goddess: Aditi, Venus. **Material creation**: God: Poseidon. **Re-creation**: Color: white; Charm: scarab; Number: 5; Animal: scarab beetle; God: Bes, Viracocha; *to destroy in order to recreate*: (See: Destruction). **Self-creation**: Animal: spider; Goddess: Aditi, Neith; God: Ashur, Atum, Ptah, Ra, Thoth.

New creation: Plant: hibiscus.

The mystery of creation: God: Ptah. **Destruction that leads to creation**: Water; God: Anzu, Marduk.

Creation via: dance: Goddess: Eurynome. **the spoken word**: Air; God: Ptah.

To create: bonds: Tool: cord; Charm: Celtic knot; Stone: salt; *with a cat*: Plant: catnip; *with the Goddess*: Stone: chrysoprase. **discord**: (See: Discord). **harmony**: Plant: vervain. **jealousy**: Plant: hemlock; God: Zeus. **monsters**: Plant: scorpion weed. **order from chaos**: (See: Order). **a psychic shield**: Method: visualization. **a shield of protection**: (See: Protection). **something positive from a negative situation**: Goddess: Atanea. **sacred space**: (See: The Sacred). **spells**: (See: Spells).

To: assist creation: God: Loki, Ocasta, Vili. **limit creation**: God: Nergal. **manage creation**: God: Marduk, Ruwa.

Creativity

(See also: Imagination, Ingenuity. Inspiration, Invention)

Venus/Mercury/Moon/Earth/Air/Fire/Water/South/East/Monday/Wednesday/Sunday

Tool: censer; **Color**: chartreuse, coral, green, gold, orange, pink, red, silver, turquoise, violet, white, yellow; **Charm**: blue sonata, musk, scarab; **Number**: 1, 3, 4, 6, 9, 22; **Animal**: scarlet macaw, parrot, spider, scarab beetle, turtle; **Metal**: silver; **Stone**: agate, amethyst, angelite, aventurine, green aventurine, calcite, carnelian, chrysocolla, citrine, coral, emerald, fluorite, garnet, kyanite, lapis lazuli, moonstone, obsidian, rutilated quartz, ruby, pink or green or watermelon tourmaline, turquoise; **Plant**: amber, apricot, cannabis, cardamom, carnation, chamomile, wild cherry, cinnamon, citronella, clove, daisy, elder, ginseng, hawthorn, honeysuckle, hyssop, iris, jasmine, laurel, lavender, lilac, lily, lotus, myrtle, nutmeg, orchid, orris root, peppermint, pine, pomegranate, rose, rosemary, sandalwood, savory, scullcap, storax, all seeds, squash blossom, valerian, vervain; **Goddess**: Athena, Astarte, Brigid, Carmenta, Cerridwen, Druantia, the Graces, Kali, Luonnotar, Maya, Mnemosyne, the Muses, Namagiri, Rhiannon, Rigantona, Shakti, the Triple Muse; **God**: Angus, Apollo, Bragi, Brahma, Dionysus, Ea, Enki, Genius, Goibniu, Hephaestus, Jumala, Khnum, Llma, Lugh, Marduk, Mercury, Mimir, Nudimmud, Odin, Prometheus, Ptah, Thoth, Tvashtri, Veveteotl, Weng Shiang, Zeus.

Artistic creativity: Plant: iris. **Divine creativity**: Goddess: Kali. **Female creativity**: Metal: silver; Plant: fir, pomegranate, squash blossom. **Male creativity**: Animal: seahorse; Metal: gold. **Mental creativity**: Air; Color: yellow; Plant: jasmine, yellow jasmine. **Passionate creativity**: Waxing Moon. **Personal creativity**: Color: orange. **Practical creativity**: Color: green, brown. **Sexual creativity**: Plant: apple, patchouli; God: P'an chin-Lien.

Creative action: Plant: broom. **Creative blocks**: (See: Blockages). **Creative desire**: *to stimulate*: Metal: peacock ore. **Creative dreams**: Plant: clary sage. **Creative energy**: (See: Energy). **Creative expression**: (See: Expression). **Creative focus**: Plant: iris. **Creative freedom**: Plant: iris, spikenard. **Creative genius**: Color: orange. **Creative illumination**: Color: orange; Stone: amber. **Creative insight**: Stone: aquamarine, aventurine. **Creative inspiration**: (See: Inspiration). **Creative passion**: God: Eros. **Creative potential**: Plant: milkweed. **Creative power**: (See: Power). **Creative process**: Animal: silkworm. **Creative spirit**: Animal: eagle. **Creative thinking**: (See: Thought). **Creative vision**: Goddess: Turan, Vac; God: Zeus. **Creative work**: (See: Work).

To: **increase creativity**: Charm: blue sonata; *increase creative energy*: Stone: garnet. **open creativity**: Stone: green tourmaline. **release creativity**: Plant: iris, especially wild iris. **stimulate creativity**: Color: green; Animal: salamander; Stone: agate, moss agate, green aventurine, emerald, green tourmaline; Plant: cinnamon, clove, peppermint, vervain.

Crossroads

Mercury/Wednesday/Dawn/Midnight

Color: red, black; Number: 3, 4, 9; Animal: black animals; Oil: red palm oil; Plant: dogwood, holly, huckleberry; Goddess: Daea Quadriviae, Diana Trivia (Guardian of the Crossroads), Ereshkigal, Hecate (Queen of Crossroads), Hecate Trivia (Hecate of the Three Ways), Pombagira, Tlazolteotl, the Triple Goddess; God: Bhairava, Carrefour, Cernunnos, Ghede (Guardian of Crossroads), Hermes, the Lares, Legba (Guardian of the Threshold), Maximon, Mercury, Nbumba Nzila, Sarudahiko; Evocation: Ghanta Karna, Ieles.

Crossroads in life: *for help when you reach*: God: Orunmila; *to choose your direction when you reach*: God: Janus; *to make good decisions when you reach*: Goddess: Pakshalika; God: Legba, Orunmila. **For protection at crossroads**: Goddess: the Deae Quadriviae, Diana Trivia; God: Bhairava, Hermes, the Kumado-No Kami, the Lares, Mercury.

Culture

(See also: Civilization)

Plant: acanthus; Goddess: Athena Lindia, Nu Kua; God: Bochicha.

Cunning

(See also: Cleverness)

Color: ocher; Animal: adder, boar, cougar, fox, lapwing, mouse, rat, wolf; Goddess: Anath, Frigg, Hathor, Isis, Macha, Medea, Medusa, Themis; God: Ea, Enki, Glooskap, Hermes, Loki, Mercury, Odin, O-Kuni-Nushi, Pwyll, Set; Evocation: Agamede, Cuchulain, Finn MacCool, Odysseus/Ulysses.

Mother-cunning: Animal: bear. **Wolf-cunning**: Animal: wolf; Evocation: Lycomedes.

Curses

(See: Hexes, Magick)

Cycles

Moon

Charm: spiral, spiral sea shell, wheel; Goddess: Isis; God: Cernunnos, Janus.

Agricultural cycles: God: Baal, Yarillo. **Calendar cycle**: Goddess: Goda. **Lunar cycle**: Moon; Stone: moonstone; Fungus: mushroom, toadstool; Goddess: Hecate, Phoebe. **Menstrual cycle**: Moon; Goddess:

Juno (See also: The Body: menstruation). **Natural cycles**: Goddess: Demeter; *sensitivity to*: Stone: moonstone. **Negative cycles**: *to reverse*: Charm: van van; Plant: wisteria (See also: Uncrossing).**Cycle of life**: (See: Life). **Complete cycle of manifestation**: Number: 12. **Cycle of reincarnation**: (See: Reincarnation). **Cycle of the seasons**: Goddess: Estsanatlehi. **Cyclical re-beginning**: (See: Beginning). **Ending of a cycle/era**: Plant: myrtle bough. **To release a cycle**: Color: pink.

Chapter 4

Danger

Pluto/Moon/Sagittarius

Color: red; Animal: grizzly bear, wild boar, cobra, polar bear, Portuguese man-of-war, rattlesnake, shark, black widow spider, wolf; Plant: hemlock, mandrake, peony, rhododendron; Goddess: Chalchihuitlcue, the Graeae, Lilith; God: Loki.

Hidden dangers: *to protect against*: Animal: jackal. **Physical danger**: *to protect against*: Stone: black and white banded agate, malachite. **Potential danger**: Goddess: Scylla; God: Silvanus, Yam.

Dangerous desert insects/animals: *to have power over*: Goddess: Malinalxochi. **Dangerous desires**: (See: Desires). **Dangerous dreams**: Plant: elder. **Dangerous enchantment**: (See: Enchantment). **Dangerous love**: Plant: tuberose. **Dangerous pleasures**: Plant: tuberose; **Dangerous situations**: *for courage in*: Plant: yarrow.

Dangers of: childbirth: *to protect against*: Goddess: Heqet; *to reduce*: Stone: clear quartz crystal; Goddess: Heqet; **the forest**: God: Silvanus; *to protect against*: God: Revanta. **lead or steel**: *to protect against*: Stone: lodestone.

For help: in times of danger: Goddess: Isis; God: Airsekui (Great Spirit), Vishnu. **when facing danger**: Goddess: Mal. **with imminent danger**: Plant: mugwort (as incense). Goddess: Isis, Kali Ma, Kwan Yin. **for strength and support in times of danger**: God: Vidar.

To be: alert to danger: Animal: griffin. **rescued from danger at sea**: Goddess: Andromeda, Tin Hou; God: Castor and Pollux. **warned of danger**: Animal: rattlesnake, all birds; Stone: ruby (grows pale), turquoise (grows pale or changes color); Goddess: Angerboda (The One Who Warns of Danger), Spider Woman; *of domination by others*: Stone: jade; *of domestic abuse*: Evocation: the Domovoi (pull a woman's hair).

To: avert danger: Stone: Apache tear, brown jasper, ruby, tourmaline; Oil: palmarosa; Plant: nettle (thrown into fire); *from poison*: Plant: heliotrope. **escape danger**: Goddess: Ishtar. **face danger**: *calmly*: Stone: amethyst; *with courage*: Plant: nettle (worn), yarrow. **learn the dangers of excess**: Goddess: Agave. **overcome danger**: Stone: black agate with white veins; Goddess: Green Tara, Spider Woman. **protect**: *children from danger*: Stone: coral; *newborns from danger*: Goddess: Intercidona; *an endangered relationship*: Goddess: Albina; *the home from danger*: Oil: palmarosa; Plant: houseleek, mugwort, spearmint; God: Legba; *a life in danger*: Goddess: Hlin; *a woman in imminent danger of violence*: Goddess: Kali Ma. **protect against danger/s**: Stone: coral, malachite, tigereye, topaz, turquoise; Plant: spearmint; Goddess: Hygeia, Kwan Yin; God: Fudo-Myoo; *dangerous animals/creatures*: Plant: avens, centaury, mullein; Stone: sard, serpentary; Goddess: Buk, Durga, Janguli, Manasa; God: Bes, Geb, Harpa-khered, Nehebu-Kau, Ningirama, Sukuna-Hikona.

Darkness

(See also: Light)

Saturn/Waning Moon/Dark Moon/Night/
Winter

> [Note: Darkness is equated with evil
> in some cultures, so it is best to
> know who these deities are before
> one invokes them.]

Color: black, midnight blue; Animal: bat,
cat, black cat, black jaguar, mole, owl, scorpion; Plant: queen of the night; Goddess:
the Dark Goddess, Evaki, Furina, Hecate,
Hel, Hina, Kali (The Dark One), Laylah,
Prisni, Skadi; God: Aedh, Ahriman (Prince
of Darkness), Apep, Chernobog, Erebus,
Hades, Itzcoliuhqui, Seker, Tobadzistsini,
Troyan, Tshernybog, Tuoni, Yaotl; Evocation: Nidhogge, Satan (Prince of Darkness),
Vritra.

Primeval darkness: Color: black; Goddess: Nyx. **Spiritual darkness**: *to overcome*:
God: Vishnu. **Utter darkness**: Evocation:
Afagddu.

Dark deeds: Goddess: Hecate. **Dark
forces/powers**: (See: Power). **Dark predictions**: Goddess: Cerridwen. **Dark of the
Moon**: Goddess: Hecate (Goddess of the
Dark of the Moon), Scathach. **Dark
thoughts**: Color: black; Plant: nightshade.
The dark side (of human nature, the Craft,
and so on.): Plant: white rose; *for courage
in dealing with*: Plant: mullein; *to resist*: God:
Quetzalcoatl. **Your dark side**: *to accept*:
Color: black; *to confront*: Stone: jet; *to control*: Color: black; *to understand*: Color:
black.

Fear of darkness: *to end*: Animal: crow,
jaguar, nightingale; Stone: chalcedony,
black coral; Plant: St. John's Wort; *to overcome*: Animal: mole; Plant: moss. **Freedom
from darkness**: Goddess: Yhi. **Guidance in
the dark**: Animal: crow. **Power of darkness**:

God: Apep (Lord of the Powers of Darkness), Mabon, Set. **Power of light over darkness**: (See: Light). **Victory of light over
darkness**: Animal: rooster; God: Ra. **For
help making it through your darkest hours**:
Plant: false hellebore, snowdrop; Goddess:
Isis; God: Shiva.

To: **access the dark**: Animal: owl. **avert
darkness**: Sun; God: Mithras. **balance
darkness/light**: Plant: enchanter's nightshade; God: Chernobog. **banish darkness**:
Sun/East/Dawn. Tool: candle; Color: gold,
yellow; Animal: dragon, firefly, phosphorescent sea creatures; Stone: peridot; God/
dess: all deities of the Sun and dawn, such
as the goddesses Akewa, Alectrona, Aya,
Bast, Cupra, Dilbah, Eos, Hebat, Hepat,
Isis (Goddess of the Rosy Dawn), Saule,
Sekhmet, Shapash, Sunna, Tefnut, Ushas,
Xatel-Ekwa, Yhi, Dawn Zorya; the gods
Amon, Apollo, Auilix, Hyperion, Horus,
Inti, Janus, Kephera, Ku, Lucifer (Son of
Morning), Ra, Salim, Shahar, Sol. **clear
darkness**: Stone: pearl, topaz; Goddess:
Kali. **communicate in the dark**: Animal:
hyena, phosphorescent sea creatures. **control darkness**: Goddess: Sekhmet (The One
Who Holds Back Darkness); God: Mabon.
deal with darkness: Animal: bat; God:
Hoder. **emerge from darkness into light**:
(See: Light). **find your way out of darkness**: God: Byelobog. **make dark energies
clear**: God: Inyan. **overcome darkness**: Sun/
Dawn. Animal: phosphorescent sea creatures; Plant: snowdrop; Goddess: Ahau Kin,
Amaterasu, Aurora, Isis, Mallina, Ushas,
Yhi; God: Baldur, Ra, Vishnu. **protect
against darkness**: God: Virudhaka; *against
evil that comes in darkness*: God: Ah Kin
Xoc. **protect in darkness**: Stone: black moss
agate, garnet. **replace darkness with light**:
(See: Light). **see in darkness**: Animal: cat,
bat, owl, wolf; Stone: garnet. God: Heimdall.
work with the energies of light and darkness: (See: Light).

The Dead

(See also: Afterlife, Death, Spirits, Otherworld, Underworld)

Pluto

Color: black; Stone: fossils; Plant: narcissus, oak, pomegranate, red poppy, yew; Goddess: Agaman Nibo, Ala (Queen of the Dead), Anu, Ereshkigal (Queen of the Underworld), Flora, Hathor (Queen of the Dead), Hecate, Hoatziqui (Lady of the Dead), Isis (Queen of the Dead), Nehalennia, Nephthys, Persephone, Ran, Sedna, Sekhmet (Mother of the Dead), Selqet, Tellus, Tsagaglal, the White Lady (Queen of the Dead); God: Anubis, Bile, Dis Pater, Don, Februus, Hades (Lord of the Dead), Mictlantecuhtli, Mot, Ngendei (King of the Land of the Dead), Odin, Osiris, Pluto, Tuoni, Yama.

Dead baby: (See: Babies). **Dead children**: (See: Children). **Dead hope**: Plant: bindweed. **Dead men**: God: Osiris. **Dead warriors**: (See: Warriors). **Dead women**: (See: Women). **Those who drown at sea**: Goddess: Ran.

Information about the dead: God: Baron Samedi. **Offerings to the dead**: Plant: apple, lotus, marigold. **Spirits of the dead**: Goddess: Manea; Evocation: Guédé, the Manes, the Vanths; *to communicate with*: Animal: swallow-tailed kite; *to see*: Plant: wormwood.

To: advise the dead: God: Jizo Bosatsu. **bring joy to the dead**: Plant: marigold, marjoram. **comfort the dead**: Plant: marjoram; Goddess: Hathor. **communicate with the dead**: Animal: bee; Charm: ice cold water; Plant: cowslip (under the pillow); Goddess: Flora, Hecate; God: Legba. **help the dead to reach the afterlife**: (See: Afterlife). **honor the dead**: Tool: censer. Plant: apple, basil, coca leaf, cowslip wreathes (laid on the grave at Full Moon for thirteen months), lily, rose, violet. **judge the dead**: Goddess: Ma'at; God: the Anunnaki, Anubis, Emma-o, Osiris, Rhadamanthys, Thoth; Evocation: Aati, Aeacus, Ahi, Amkhaibitu (Eater of Ghosts), Amsnef (Eater of Blood), Anaf, Anhotep, Anty, Arimabef, Basty, Fenty, Hai, Heptshet, Herfhaf, Heriuru, Hetchabehu, Kenemty, Khemy, Maa-Anuf, Maatifemkhet, Maatifemtes, Minos, Neba, Neb Heru, Neb Nebu, Nehaher, Nehebnefert, Nekhenu, Qerty, Rerty, Sekheriu, Sertiu, Setqesu (Bone-Breaker), Shetkheru, Taret, Tchesertep, Temsep, Teni; Thenemy, Thenret, Tutu, Uamemty, Uatchnesert, Usekhnemmet, Utunesert, Uturekhit. **prepare/care for the bodies of the dead**: Plant: aloe, benzoin, mint, myrrh, myrtle, rosemary, tansy; Goddess: Libitina, Nephthys; God: Anubis. **preserve the dead**: Stone: cinnabar; Plant: tansy; God: Anubis. **protect the dead**: (from evil, necromancy, and so on.): Stone: jade; Goddess: Ala, Heretkau, Heqet, Isis, Neith, Nephthys, Selqet, Shapash; God: Anubis, Bes, Lubangala, Sobek; *from demons*: (See: Demons); *from evil spirits*: Plant: elder branches (buried or cremated with them). **purify the dead**: Plant: aloe, myrrh, wood aloes; Goddess: Libitina; God: Februus. **raise/revive the dead**: Plant: dried amaranth flowers, yew; Goddess: Airmid, Ereshkigal; God: Aguku, Asclepius, Jesus. **remember the dead**: Animal: screech owl; Plant: basil, cypress, lotus, patchouli, rosemary. **summon the dead**: Plant: wormwood.

Death

(See also: Afterlife, The Dead, Grief, Life, Otherworld, Passage, Reincarnation, Transition, Underworld)

Saturn/Pluto/Waning Moon/Earth/West/Saturday/Autumn/Winter/Scorpio/Pisces

Color: black, red, dark purple, white, yellow; Charm: sickle; Letter: I, R; Animal:

boar, crow, dog, large black dog, fish, black hen, owl, barn owl, pig, polar bear, raven, scorpion, snail, swan, vulture, wolf; Metal: lead; Stone: white coral; Fungi: death cap mushroom, all poisonous mushrooms and toadstools (none of these should be ingested and some can cause harm just by touching the fungi so use extreme caution if using); Plant: acacia, alder, autumn leaves, bare branches, blackberry, cypress, elder, iris, poison hemlock, myrtle, parsley, periwinkle, pomegranate, black poplar, quince, rosemary, willow, yarrow, yew; Goddess: Alys, Anath, Ani, Annis, Anu, Arianrhod, Astarte, Athene, Athene Oncë, Averna, Baba Yaga, Badb, Car, Cerridwen, Circe, Coatlicue, the Crone, Culsa, Cyhiraeth, Daena, Dewi Shri, Durga, Echidne, Egeria, Eingana, Ereshkigal (Mistress of Death), Freya, Giltine, the Gray Ones, Habondia, the Harpies, Hathor, Hecate (Queen of Death), Hel (Queen of Death), Hera, the Hesperides, Idunn, Ina, Ishtar, Ituana, Ixtab, Iyatiku, Kali (Goddess of Death), Kalma, Kore, Latiaran, Macha (Mother of Life and Death), Manca, Marena, Mor, Morgana, the Morrigan, Nana Buruku, Nav, Nehalennia, Nephthys, Oya (Guardian of the Gates of Death), Queen of Elphame, Papa, Rhiannon, Sedna, Sekhmet (Lady of the Tomb), Sheela-na-gig, Sulis, Taranis, Tlazolteotl, Tonantzin, Tuchulcha, al-Uzzah, Una-Kuagsak, Vanth, Vedma, the White Lady, Yabme-Akka, Yuki-Onne; God: Angus (Lord of Love and Death), Anubis, Balor, Baron Samedi, Bel, Beli, Carneios, Cernunnos (Opener of the Gates of Life and Death), Chu Jung, Cizin, Cromm Cruiach (Lord of the Mound), the Dagda, Dis Pater, Don (Lord of the Underworld), Emma ten, Gwynn Ap Nudd, Hades, Holer, Horned God (Lord of Death), Hunhau, Iku, Itzcoliuhqui, Llud, Luchtain, Mabon, Masauwu, Maximon, Mela, Mictlantecuhtli, Mider, Mors, Mot,

Namtar, Nuadh, Odin, Ogun, Pluto, Reshep, Rudra, Shiva, Sucellos, Supay, Tethra, Thanatos, Varuna, Veles, Yen Wang; Evocation: Grim Reaper.

Impending death: Animal: black dog, crane, owl, deathwatch beetle; Plant: apple; Goddess: Auchimolgen (of important persons), Bean Sidhe, Cyhiraeth, the Morrigan (in battle); God: Namtar; Evocation: Achemorus (Bringer of Doom), Domovoi, Washer at the Ford. **Natural death**: Animal: bat. **Painless death**: Goddess: Artemis. **Peaceful death**: Plant: wormwood. **Quick death**: Goddess: Artemis. **Ritual death**: Animal: bat, puffer fish. **Seasonal death**: Plant: grain, holly, oak, vine; Goddess: Anieros, Axiocersa, Brigid, Cailleach, Persephone/Prosperine; God: Adonis, Attis, Baal, Baldur, Damuzi, Dionysus, Gwynn, Jesus, Mithras, Mot, Osiris, Tammuz; Evocation: Green Knight, Holly King, Linus, Lityerses, Oak King. **Sudden death**: God: Nergal; *to protect against*: Stone: topaz. **Untimely death**: *to protect a son against*: Goddess: Putrapamrityunashini. **Violent death**: Mars; Goddess: Cer; God: Moros, Nergal; *transition to the afterlife for those who die violently*: Taxet.

Death messages: (See: Messages). **Death omens**: (See: Omens). **Death rituals**: Plant: myrtle, parsley, rosemary; Goddess: Taranis; God: Cromm Cruiach, Esus, Gwynn, Sucellos. **Death spirits**: (See: Spirits). **Death-in life**: Animal: magpie, vulture; Plant: elder; Goddess: Aphrodite. **Death in war**: Goddess: the Morrigan; God: Nergal, Reshep. **Death of the sacred king**: (See: The Sacred). **Life after death**: (See: Afterlife, Reincarnation). **Life-in-death**: (See: Life).

Affection that endures after death: Plant: carob tree. **Inevitability of death**: Goddess: Atalanta; God: Hades, Pluto. **Peace in death**: Plant: cypress; God: Anubis; Evocation: Cyparissus. **Places of**

death (crematoria, morgues, mortuaries, funeral homes, and so on.): *to protect*: Goddess: Nephthys; God: Anubis. **Potential for life after death**: God: Osiris. **Power of life and death**: Plant: mistletoe; Goddess: Macha (Mother of Life and Death), Rhiannon; God: Reshep. **Power of love over death**: Goddess: Isis. **Sweetness in death**: Plant: rice. **Transformation from death to life**: God: Osiris.

To: **accept death as part of the spiral of life**: Stone: amethyst; Plant: snowdrop; Goddess: the Goddess; God: Aegir, Osiris. **avert death**: God: Haoma. **come to terms with death**: Stone: amethyst. **comfort the dying**: Goddess: Anu. **ease death**: Stone: amazonite, Apache tears, fossil, hematite, jet, malachite, moonstone, obsidian, rose quartz, topaz; Goddess: Kali Ma. **face death with courage**: Animal: wolf; Goddess: Inanna, Ishtar. **foretell death**: Animal: owl; Goddess: Cyhiraeth; Evocation: Beane Sidhe. **overcome death**: Sun; Plant: evergreens, laurel; Goddess: Isis; God: Damuzi, Jesus, Osiris, Tammuz; Evocation: Hercules/Herakles. **overcome fear of death/dying**: Animal: blue jay. Plant: St. John's Wort, snowdrop; Goddess: Kali (Remover of the Fear of Death); God: Baldur, Herakles. **understand death**: Plant: cypress.

Deceit
(See also: Cloaking, Honesty, Illusion, Treachery, Truth)

Mercury/Moon

Color: black, reddish brown, dark green, red, yellow; Animal: chimpanzee, lapwing, merlin, owl, sandpiper, all decoy predators; Metal: brass; Plant: aspen, bilberry, buttercup, cherry tree, yellow lily, snapdragon, Venus fly trap; Goddess: Apate, Eris, Fraud; God: Ictinike, Loki, Odin, Set; Evocation: Apep, Brangaube, Odysseus/Ulysses, Satan.

False accusation: Evocation: Phaedra; *to overcome*: Goddess: Auge; *to survive*: Goddess: Rhiannon. **Deceitful charms**: Plant: datura. **False friends**: *to protect against*: Plant: bistort root. **Deceitful hope**: Plant: daffodil. **False riches**: Stone: pyrite; Plant: sunflower. **False sense of security**: Animal: wolf.

To: **deceive hunters**: God: Zip. **detect deceit**: Stone: emerald; Plant: pimpernel; Goddess: Fraud. **learn to beware of deceit**: God: Hod, Osiris. **learn not to be deceived by appearances**: Animal: owl. **learn not to get stung by deceit**: Goddess: Fraud. **protect against deceit**: Plant: snapdragon. **stop lies**: Color: purple; Plant: pimpernel. **understand deceit**: Animal: alligator, crocodile.

Deception
(See: Cloaking, Deceit)

Decision/s
(See also: Decisiveness, Judgment)

Color: brown; Charm: sea shell; Stone: ametrine, aventurine, azurite (held in the hand), bloodstone, carnelian, selenite; Goddess: Ishtar; God: Mimir, Ninnuam (Decider of Decisions), Sin.

Fair judgment/decision: (See: Judgment). **Government decisions**: Goddess: Minerva. **Precise decisions**: Stone: jade. **Quick decisions**: Stone: jade. **Strong decisions**: Goddess: Lilith. **Wise decisions**: Stone: onyx; Plant: sage, Solomon's seal; *wise business decisions:* Stone: jade (held in the hand).

For help in making decisions: Animal: slug; *when you reach a crossroads in life*: God: the Quadriviae.

To: **decide guilt or innocence**: God: Enki. **decide where to begin**: Plant: verbena. **make decisions**: *and carry them out*: God:

Ziukkinna; *decisions about relationships*: Plant: apple; *decisions about rituals*: Goddess: the Kotharat; *decisions about work*: Plant: apple; *to make good decisions at crossroads*: Goddess: Pakshalika; God: Legba, Orunmila. **question decisions**: Goddess: Ninsûna.

Indecision
Libra

Goddess: Chantico.

To overcome indecision: Tool: sword; Plant: cayenne, peppermint, yucca.

Decisiveness
Aries

Plant: basil. **Decisive action**: Goddess: Ishtar.

Defense
(See also: Amulets, Battle, Protection, Security, Talismans)

Mars/Fire

Tool: shield; Color: black, silver; Animal: dog, electric eel, komodo dragon, polar bear; Plant: angelica, basil, bayberry, birch, burdock, cinnamon, cinquefoil, club moss, cranberry, cypress, dill, dragon's blood, fern, feverfew, fir, frankincense, garlic, gorse, hawthorn, hazel, heather, holly, jasmine, juniper, laurel, lily of the valley, marjoram, mistletoe, mugwort, mullein, nettle, oak, patchouli, pepper, pine, black poplar, rosemary, rowan, rue, St. John's Wort, tangerine, thistle, vervain, wormwood, yarrow; Goddess: Adrastea, Alphito-Baitule Lusia, Anahita, Boldogasszony, Frigg, Ratis, Sekhmet, the Udravarinehae; God: Ares, Krishna, Mars Alator, Mars Nodens, Thor.

Aggressive defense: Animal: damselfish, electric eel; *of the home*: Animal: osprey. **Assertive defense**: Animal: long-eared owl. **Creative defense**: Animal: moth. **Radar defense systems**: God: Lugaldurmah (Watcher of the Skies). **Self-defense**: Animal: porcupine; Stone: garnet, onyx; Plant: dragon's blood, thistle; Goddess: Scathach; God: Credne, Gwion, Llew Llaw, Jupiter Stator. **Silent defense**: Animal: long-eared owl.

To defend: blind people: Goddess: Anahita. **boundaries**: Animal: hyena. **children**: Goddess: Boldogasszony, Caireen, Isis. **deaf people**: Goddess: Anahita. **Egypt**: Goddess: Wadjet; **England**: God: Bran; Evocation: King Arthur; *London*: God: Ludd. **Ireland**: Goddess: the Morrigan; *Ulster*: Evocation: Cuchulain. **newborns**: *against evil*: Charm: hamsa hand, blue bead; Goddess: Deverra, Intercidona. **Palestine** (Gaza strip): God: Dagon. **the righteous**: Adrastea. **women**: Goddess: Boldogasszony.

To protect: the defenseless: Goddess: Demeter. **those who need defense**: Goddess: Athena.

Defensiveness
Animal: hedgehog; Plant: rowan, thistle.

Defensive magick: (See: Magick). **For defense against: evil**: (See: Evil). **witches**: Plant: rue.

Defeat
(See: Adversity, Ending, Loss, Overcoming, Victory)

Demons
Stone: onyx; Plant: coca; God: Shiva (Lord of the Demons); Evocation: the Asuras, Ravana.

Envious demons: *to protect against*: Charm: colored rice. **Forest demons**: *to protect against*: Goddess: Gramadevata. **Night demons**: *to invite*: Stone: onyx. **Underworld demons**: Goddess: Sedna; Evocation: Satan, the utukki.

To: **avert demons**: Charm: demon bowl; Plant: benzoin, peach pit, vervain; Goddess: Isis. **banish demons**: Charm: demon bowl; Stone: emerald; Plant: fumitory, mandrake, mullein; God: Bi-har-Fu-mo ta-ti (Great Ruler Who Banishes Demons); *demons that cause disease*: Plant: clove, ginger, all pungent spices. **battle demons**: Goddess: Durga (Reducer of the Number of Demons), Geshtinanna, Kali; God: Kupalo. **bind demons**: Charm: demon bowl; Goddess: Selqet. **control demons**: Charm: demon bowl; Goddess: Hecate; Evocation: Ariel. **defeat demons**: Goddess: Devi, Durga, Kali. **destroy demons**: Goddess: Ambika, Durga (Slayer of Demons), Kali; God: Krishna, Rama, Shiva (Demon-Slayer), Vishn. **evoke demons**: *for protection while evoking*: Charm: vervain crown. **face your demons**: Goddess: The Morrigan. **overcome demons**: Charm: demon bowl; Goddess: Kali; God: Agastya, Horon, Indra. **protect against demons**: Charm: demon bowl; Stone: agate, coral, turquoise; Plant: nettle, sandalwood, St. John's Wort, vervain; God: Bi-har-Fu-mo ta-ti, Famien, Horon, Kuan-yin, Shong-Kui; *against demonic possession*: Stone: diamond; *protect the dead from demons*: Stone: jade; Goddess: Ala, Heretkau, Heqet, Isis, Neith, Nephthys, Selqet, Shapash; God: Anubis, Bes, Lubangala, Sobek. **summon demons**: Plant: rowan, valerian root. **tame demons**: Plant: fern.

Depression

(See also: Happiness, Illness, Grief, Mood, Sorrow, Spirit)

[Note: Magick can be helpful with the blues, but clinical depression is a serious medical problem that requires professional medical treatment. All plants are listed here as charms. They are not meant to be taken internally, or used as an alternative to medical care.]

Mercury/Earth/Capricorn

Color: black, blue, dark blue, gray, indigo; Plant: dark geranium.

Manic-depression (bipolar disorder): God: Dionysus; *to improve*: Stone: kunzite; Plant: grapefruit, hellebore. **Post partum depression**: *to relieve*: Plant: frankincense, jasmine, vetiver. **Seasonal depression**: Sun; God: Dionysus; *to treat*: Plant: snowdrop, sunflower, water hyacinth. **Situational depression**: *after an operation*: Plant: ginseng; *to use positive action to climb out of*: Goddess: Ceres, Demeter. **Depressing dreams**: (See: Dreams).

To: **avert/protect against depression**: Stone: chrysoprase, coral, garnet, jet, malachite, olivine, sardonyx, topaz; Plant: burnet. **banish depression**: Color: dark blue; Stone: chalcedony; Plant: burnet, dead nettle, fumitory, lemon verbena. **improve depression**: Sun; Color: blue, pink, rose, yellow; Charm: gold amulet, orange flower water; Metal: gold, platinum; Stone: amber, amethyst, golden beryl, bloodstone, yellow calcite, carbuncle, carnelian, citrine, fluorite, garnet, geode, hematite, jet, kunzite, lapis lazuli, larimar, lepidolite, moonstone, peridot, rose quartz, smoky quartz, sapphire, sodalite, tigereye, black tourmaline, yellow zircon; Potion: absinthe (dangerous, not recommended); Oil: neroli, petitgrain; Plant: basil, bergamot, betony, bluebell, borage, bupleurum root, cayenne pepper, celandine, celery seed, chamomile, chaste tree, cinnamon, clover, cumin, lesser dodder, everlasting, fo-ti, frankincense, fumitory, geranium, grapefruit, hawthorn, hellebore, High John (carried), jasmine, juniper, lavender, lemon, lemon balm, marjoram, melilot, mimosa, motherwort, nasturtium, oats, orange (fruit or blossom), mandarin orange, peppermint, blue pimpernel, rosemary, sage, clary sage, spearmint, St. John's

Wort, sugar cane, thyme, valerian, lemon verbena, blue vervain, viper's bugloss, wormwood, yerba maté, ylang-ylang, zinnia; Goddess: Kali, Vajravarahi. **resist depression**: Stone: garnet. **worsen/cause depression**: Charm: barley bread; Stone: lodestone, onyx; Plant: angelica, autumn crocus, hops, sandalwood.

Desire

(See also: Libido, Lust, Passion, Satisfaction, Wishes)

Venus/Mars/Fire/Water

Plant: cactus, caper, datura, ginseng, yellow jasmine, jonquil, lily of the valley, mandrake root, orchid, periwinkle, orange or red rose, saffron, scopalia root, trailing pearlwort, wild oats; Goddess: Aine, Anath, Aphrodite, Astarte, Chandika, Harsa, Ishtar (Lady of Passion and Desire), Isis, Kamarupa, Parvati, Qadesh, Rati, Venus; God: Amour, Cernunnos, Cupid, Eros, Himeros, the Horned God, Kama, Pan, Pothos, Yarillo; Evocation: Orion.

Creative desire: *to stimulate*: Metal: peacock ore. **Divine desire**: Fire. **Ecstatic desire**: Goddess: Parvati. **Insatiable desire**: God: Shiva. **Irrational desire**: God: Eros. **Sexual desire**: Fire; Goddess: Rati; God: Eros, Himeros; *to control*: Stone: onyx; Plant: hemlock; *to quiet*: Stone: onyx; Plant: camphor, rue; *to stimulate*: Charm: musk; Stone: carnelian, diamond; Plant: cannabis, cubeb, dittany, galangal, rose hips, vanilla (See also: Lust, Passion). **Unattainable desire**: Evocation: Orion; *to stop wanting*: Plant: lily of the valley. **Uncontrolled desire**: God: Yarillo.

Desired things: Jupiter. **Desire to: help**: Color: yellow. **know**: Number: 5. **please**: Plant: daphne, mezereon.

To: attract desire: Charm: musk; Plant: High John, rose hip; Goddess: Aphrodite, Nimuë/Vivienne; God: Krishna. **attract the one you desire**: Plant: dill seed, gentian root, marjoram, trailing pearlwort. **awaken desire**: Stone: pearl; Goddess: Eos. **banish desire**: Stone: amethyst; Plant: celandine, rue; Goddess: Mohanashini. **become desirable**: Charm: musk; Stone: moonstone; Plant: rose, rose hips; Goddess: Erzulie. **be granted your desire**: Stone: aquamarine. **destroy desire**: Goddess: Mohanashini (Destroyer of Desires). **distinguish between need and desire**: Stone: tigereye. **focus desire**: Stone: topaz. **increase desire**: Plant: galangal; God: Ganesha. **overcome desire**: Color: yellow; *for revenge*: Plant: canna lily. **stimulate desire**: Stone: garnet, ruby.

Desires

(See Also: Wishes)

Base desires: *to resist*: Plant: apple. **Dangerous desires**: *to protect against*: Stone: jasper, red jasper. **Fulfill/realize/satisfy/manifest desires**: Stone: amber, lodestone, malachite, sapphire, turquoise; Plant: acacia, angelica, basil, chamomile, myrrh, Turk's cap lily, willow; Goddess: Astarte, Diana, Kilili Mushritu, Sekhmet (Satisfier of Desires).

Destiny

Method: runes; Charm: fetish, strings of palm nuts, spider web; Animal: pig, raven, spider; Plant: blackthorn, cannabis, flax, coral honeysuckle, ilex; Goddess: Acaviser, Aerten, Aida Wedo, Akohito, Allat, Alphito, Ananke, Arachne, Arianrhod, Atropos (Inflexible), the Audrinehae (The Friendly Powers of Destiny), Badb, Circe (Fate-Spinner), Clotho (Spinner), Decuma, Dolya, Dubhlaing, Durga, Fata, Fatima, Fei Cthline, Fortuna, Frigg, the Graiae, Gula, Hathor, Heimarmene, Hemsut, Holda, Inanna, Ishtar, Isis (One Above Fate),

Itzpapalotl, Lachesis (Alotter), Mal, Mammetum (Mother of Fate), Manat, Maya, Meri, Meskhenet, the Moirae (the Fates), Mokosh, Morgana, the Morrigan (Great Queen of Fate), Morta, Necessitas, Nemesis, Nona, the Norns (Skuld, Urd, Verdande), Nortia, the Parcae (the Fates), Renenet, Sesheta, Shait, Spenta Armaiti, the Telchines, Vortumna; God: Anu, Asharu, Bel, Dazhbog, Ellil, Enlil, Enki, Fa, Fu-Hsing, Hermes, Legba, Marduk (Ruler of Destinies), Nabu, Namtar (Fate Cutter), Nyame, Orunmila (Witness to Destiny in its Creation), Ptah, Shai, Sin, Sud, Tahit, T'ai-Yueh-Ta-Ti, Thoth, Wuni, Zeus, Zurvan.

New fate: Animal: black widow spider. **Personal destiny**: Charm: birth tree; Plant: coral honeysuckle, palm nuts; Goddess: Atropos, Clotho, the Fates, Laima, Larchesis, the Moirae (the Fates), the Norns, the Parcae (the Fates); God: Fa; *to know your destiny*: Method: astrology, meditation, tarot; God: Anubis; *to achieve*: Stone: labradorite; *to protect*: Goddess: Enekpe. **Spiritual destiny**: God: Jesus, Osiris.

Destiny of: babies: (See: Babies). **cities**: Goddess: Inanna. **lovers**: Goddess: Inanna; *to protect ill-fated lovers*: Goddess: Albina. **soldiers**: Goddess: Badb, the Morrigan (Choosers of the Slain).

Power of destiny: Goddess: the Audrinehae. **Impassivity of fate**: Stone: diamond. **Twists of fate**: *to accept*: Animal: coyote; God: Loki; *to protect against*: God: Sucellos.

To: alter fate: Animal: black widow spider; Goddess: Isis; God: Mithras. **control destiny**: Goddess: the Norns. **decree fate**: God: Anu. **fix fate/destinies**: Goddess: Inanna; God: Ellil, Enlil, Marduk. **know the fate of lovers**: Plant: orpane and red sage (gathered on Midsummer Eve). **obey fate**

without struggle: Virgo. **recognize destiny**: Stone: labradorite. **understand destiny**: Stone: moonstone.

Destruction

Fire/West/Scorpio

Color: red; Animal: crocodile, crow, dragon, fox, locust, mouse, termite; Plant: yew; Fungus: destroying angel, all poisonous mushrooms and toadstools; Goddess: Alphito, Anath (The Destroyer), Cailleach, Carman, Circe, Elphame, Hecate, Ix Chel, Kali (Night of Destruction), Macha, the Morrigan, Nirriti, Prakrta, Ran, Sekhmet (The Destroyer, Terrible One, Devouring One, Mistress of Terror, Destroyer By Plagues), Scathach, the White Goddess; God: Apep, Ares, Belatycadros, Chernobog, Ellil, Holer, Ina, Itzam Cab, Itzcoliuhqui, Marduk, Ogun, Pillan, Shiva (Destroyer), Susanowo, Ulu Toyo'n (Horrible Lord), Vulcan.

Self-destruction: Scorpio; Plant: tobacco; *to protect against*: Plant: bistort, rowan, snowdrop. **Sudden destruction**: Goddess the Harpies, Ix Chel.

Destruction: by fire: Goddess: Sekhmet (Destroyer by Fire); God: Kagutsuchi, Nergal, Vulcan. **of oceangoing vessels**: God: Aegir. **that leads to creation**: Water; God: Anzu, Marduk; *to recreation*: Goddess: Coatlicue, the Great Goddess; God: Shiva.

Destructive: cosmic forces: God: Shiva. **energy**: Goddess: Kali. **power**: (See: Power). **violence**: Goddess: Hathor. **winds**: Air; Charm: alder whistle; Plant: alder; God: Hurukan, Ninurta, Typhon.

To destroy: adversaries: God: Zahrim, Zulum. **crops**: God: Kamapua. **demons**: (See: Demons). **desire**: Goddess: Mohanashini (Destroyer of Desires). **disease**: (See: Disease). **enemies**: (See: Enemies). **evil**: (See:

Evil). **fascination**: Stone: carnelian. **hexes**: Plant: High John. **ignorance**: Goddess: Kali. **the indestructible**: Goddess: Inanna. **lies**: New Moon; Plant: yew. **lust**: Plant: hemlock, rue. **negativity**: Color: black; *negative energy*: Color: black; Stone: garnet. **the old**: Plant: morning glory; *in order to make way for the new*: Uranus/Water; Goddess: Kali; God: Apsu, Uranus. **rebellion**: Goddess: Sekhmet (Destroyer of Rebellion). **sex drive**: Plant: hemlock. **vermin**: Animal: cat; Plant: eucalyptus; Goddess: Bast.

To: **learn to not allow a loss to destroy you**: Goddess: Aideen, Isis. **take lesbian lovers without destroying a marriage**: Goddess: Fauna.

Determination

(See also: Will)

Mars/Leo

Color: red; Charm: musk; Number: 1; Animal: buffalo, polar bear, salmon; Plant: allspice, aspen, birch, chamomile, dragon's blood, ephedra, hibiscus, iris, laurel, mullein, white poplar, rosemary; Goddess: Isis.

Self-determination: Goddess: Atalanta.

Devotion

Color: blue, purple, yellow; Animal: dog, horse; Stone: diamond, garnet, pink tourmaline; Plant: heliotrope, honeysuckle, lavender, marigold, rose, sweet pea; Goddess: Ida, Spenta Aramaiti; God: Hanuman.

Devoted love: Plant: honeysuckle.

Devotion to: a calling/career/occupation: God: Ebisu. **a husband**: Goddess: Indrani, Isis, Sita. **a goal**: Stone: garnet. **an idea**: Color: pale blue. **parents**: Animal: stork; Goddess: Pietas. **a promise/oath**: Goddess: Gaia, Pietas.

Dignity

Jupiter

Color: indigo, lavender, purple; Animal: cat, elephant, heron, wolf; Stone: rose quartz; Plant: clove, dahlia, elm, frankincense, rose, saguaro; Goddess: Branwen; God: El, Jupiter, Osiris.

Discernment

Tool: athame; Animal: angelfish, armadillo, starfish; Plant: honeysuckle, rue, sage; God: Ganesha, Sicun.

Discriminating awareness: West. **Discernment in communication**: Animal: catfish.

Lack of discernment: Color: brown. **Wisdom of discernment**: Color: red.

Discipline

(See also: Control, Will)

Saturn

Color: black; Number: 8; Stone: hematite; Plant: basil, bodhi tree, spirea; Goddess: Athene, Disciplina, Eunomia, the Horai; God: Enlil, Mithras.

Mental discipline: Method: meditation. **Self-discipline**: Capricorn; Method: martial arts, meditation, tantra, yoga; Animal: ant; Stone: hematite; Plant: apple, silverweed; Goddess: Disciplina, Eunomia, Snotra. **Spiritual discipline**: Method: chanting, dance, meditation, yoga.

Discord

(See also: Chaos, Enmity, Harmony, Peace, Quarrels)

Mars

Color: black; Animal: hyena, squirrel; Number: 6; Goddess: Ate, Discordia, Eris.

To: **avert discord**: Stone: diamond. **battle discord**: Plant: dogwood. **clear discord**: Tool: besom. **counter discord**: Plant: gardenia, valerian. **create discord**: Charm:

Four Thieves Vinegar; Plant: hot pepper; Goddess: Discordia, Eris; *between lovers*: Stone: fire garnet; *between yourself and another*: Stone: opal (given as a gift). **release discord**: Stone: iolite; Plant: moneywort

Diseases/Disorders

(See also: The Body, Healing, Illness, Pain)

[NOTE: All correspondences are given here as charms. Some of the plants are poisonous, and nothing but potions are meant to be ingested. Magick is a supplement to medical care, not a substitute for it. In most cases, incense should not be burned near the patient.]

Color: black, greenish-yellow; Animal: fly, mosquito, rat; Plant: anemone; Goddess: Cailleach, Durga, Elphame, Hel, Mara Moru, Marena; God: Apollo, Holer, Namtar, Nanautzin, Rudra.

Acne *to improve:* Stone: amethyst; Oil: niaouli, palmarosa; Plant: agrimony, almond, aloe, barberry, bergamot, burdock, butterbur, cedar, celery, chamomile, cucumber, daisy, elecampane, garlic, horse radish, jojoba, juniper, lady's mantle, lavender, lemon, marigold, orris root (powder), patchouli, pawpaw, pea, rosemary, clary sage, sandalwood, soapwort, stinging nettle, tea tree, thyme, yarrow; barley with southernwood.

Addiction: Moon/Sagittarius; Plant: opium poppy, tobacco; *to banish*: Waning Moon; Stone: amethyst; *to overcome*: Color: purple, violet; Stone: amethyst, ametrine, calcite, citrine, coral, emerald, jet, kunzite, obsidian, rose quartz, topaz; Plant: basil, cat's claw, cedar, dragon's blood, laurel, morning glory, oat, peppermint, petrified wood, spikenard; God: Mithras; *alcoholism:* Stone: amethyst; Plant: cayenne; *nicotine addiction*: Plant: plantain, watercress; *opiate addiction*: Plant: oats, passionflower (See also: Sobriety).

AIDS: *to treat:* Stone: jasper; Plant: chicory, chrysanthemum, St. John's Wort.

Allergies: Plant: ambrosia, feverfew, goldenrod, yarrow; *to alleviate*: Color: purple, violet; Stone: amethyst, apatite, carnelian, clay, white coral, dolomite, garnet, moldovite; Oil: niaouli; Plant: aloe, comfrey, eyebright, fenugreek, galbanum, horseradish, nettle; *to protect against*: Plant: coltsfoot.

Altitude sickness: Air; *to improve*: Plant: coca leaf, wormwood.

Alzheimer's: *to cause*: Metal: aluminum; *to protect against*: Plant: garlic, onion, pennyroyal, rosemary, green tea.

Anemia: *to alleviate:* Stone: coral, garnet, kunzite, ruby, tourmaline; Plant: betony, dandelion, dong quai, ginseng, nettle, black pepper, peppermint, sage; *to cause*: Metal: copper; *to protect against*: Stone: garnet.

Anorexia: Oil: palmarosa; Plant: cannabis, centaury, gentian, thyme, wormwood, yerba mate.

Arthritis/rheumatism: *to alleviate*: Color: orange; Charm: eelskin, thermal spring; Metal: copper, gold; Stone: amber, amethyst, azurite, green calcite, carnelian, chrysocolla, dolomite, lapis lazuli, lodestone, malachite, ruby, topaz, black tourmaline; Plant: alfalfa, angelica, asparagus, balm, benzoin, bilberry, blackberry, box tree, butcher's broom, caper, castor bean, cayenne, celery seed, chamomile, charlock, chili pepper, cinnamon, clove, red clover, comfrey, coriander, cowslip, black cumin, dandelion, devil's claw, evening primrose, eucalyptus, fenugreek, feverfew, flax, fumitory, gentian, ginseng, grapevine, gravel root, hawthorn berry, heather, henbane, henna, holy thistle, iris, ironwood, ivy, juniper berry, kava kava, kelp, laurel, lavender, lemon, marjoram, marshmallow, marigold, mint, black mustard, nettle, olive, pansy, peppermint, pine, pistachio, plane tree, poplar, potato (stolen, carried), apothecary's rose, rosemary, rowan wood (carried), rue, sage, sarsaparilla, sassafras, silkweed, stinging nettle, storax, summer savory, tarragon, thyme, turmeric, vine, violet, willow, petrified wood, wood aloes, yam, yerba santa, yucca; *to avert*: Plant: hazel, nutmeg, willow shoot with five, seven, or nine knots tied in it (carried); *to protect against*: Charm: steel ring; Plant: willow bark.

Asthma: *to treat*: Color: orange, pink; Stone: amethyst, malachite, obsidian, rutilated quartz, tigereye; Plant: almond, anise, apricot, belladonna, betony, calamus, camel thorn, cannabis, carob, cedar, chicory, black cohosh, coltsfoot, cumin, black cumin, date palm, datura, elderberry, elecampane, ephedra, eucalyptus, evening primrose, fennel, feverfew, flax, garlic mustard, ginseng, hemlock, henbane, licorice root, linden, lobelia, mandrake, marsh mallow, milk thistle, mint, mullein, myrtle, nettle, oregano, parsley, passionflower, pine, red poppy, rock rose, rosemary, sage, clary sage, soapwort, sorrel, spikenard, stinging nettle, St. John's Wort, summer savory, sundew, thyme, Venus hair fern, lemon verbena, watercress, wood aloes, yerba santa.

Autism: *to improve*: Animal: dolphin; Stone: moldovite, sugilite; Charm: Blood of Thoth; God: Thoth.

Bipolar disorders: (See: Depression).

Bladder disease/infection: Water; *to improve:* Stone: amber, coral, jade, jasper; Plant: anemone, barberry, basil, blueberry, couch grass, cranberry, garlic, mallow, thyme, uva ursi, vervain; *to avert*: Plant: cranberry, rose hips; *to restore control*:

Plant: lemon balm; *bladder cancer*: Plant: dandelion; *male bladder problems*: Plant: avens, parsley.

Blood clots: Color: red; *to treat:* Stone: amethyst; Plant: figwort, horsetail, pellitory of the wall, Solomon's seal.

Blood diseases/disorders: Jupiter; Color: red; *to improve:* Stone: agate, red agate, amethyst, chrysolite, jasper, ruby; Plant: dragon's blood, purslane; *to prevent*: Charm: musk; Plant: cherry, fenugreek, gooseberry, lemon.

Blood pressure: *to affect:* Stone: aventurine, bloodstone, chrysocolla, garnet, sodalite, tourmaline; Plant: angelica, betony, dong quai, ginseng, hawthorn berry, passionflower; *high blood pressure*: Aries; Color: blue; Stone: apatite, aventurine; *to lower*: Stone: hematite; Plant: asparagus, barberry, betony, broom, couch grass, dandelion, false hellebore, garlic, hawthorn, lavender, leek, marjoram, mistletoe, oleander, olive, onion, lesser periwinkle, pulsatilla, psyllium, reed, shepherd's purse, stonecrop, string bean, vetiver, vine, ylang-ylang; *to prevent*: Plant: fenugreek; *low blood pressure*: Pisces; *to raise*: Stone: salt; Plant: celandine, ephedra, garlic, gentian, licorice, St. John's Wort, thyme.

Boils: Charm: *to treat:* rye bread, the touch of a menstruating woman; Plant: burdock, chicory, clary sage, cuckoopint, daisy, elder, fenugreek, fig, cobweb houseleek, kidneywort, madonna lily, marigold, rue, sorrel, stonecrop, viper's bugloss; *to protect against*: Plant: henbane.

Bone damage/diseases/disorders: Saturn; *to treat:* Stone: amethyst, turquoise; Plant: bear's breech, comfrey, elm, gravel root, heliotrope, holly, royal fern, Solomon's seal; God: Khnum.

Bowel diseases/disorders: Stone: golden beryl; Plant: blackthorn, bramble, cascara sagrada, chestnut, garlic, ginger, mallow, mouse-eared hawkweed, peppermint, plantain, rue, sarsaparilla, silverweed, slippery elm, Solomon's seal, sorrel, turmeric, yam.

Brain diseases/disorders: Moon; *to treat:* Metal: silver; Plant: lavender, rosemary.

Bronchitis: *to treat:* Color: black, pink; Metal: gold; Stone: lodestone, rutilated quartz; Plant: angelica, anise, balsam, benzoin, blackberry leaf, borage, bryony, cedar, celery, black cohosh, black cumin, calamus, camel thorn, cedar, chamomile, charlock, cherry, red clover, coltsfoot, comfrey, cowslip, cumin, elder, elecampane, eucalyptus, flax, frankincense, garlic, ginkgo, ginseng, heliotrope, hemlock, holly, horehound, horseradish, ipecac, laurel, licorice, marshmallow, milk thistle, milkweed, mullein, black mustard, myrtle, nasturtium, nettle, olive, orris root, pennyroyal, pine, pomegranate, reed, dog rose, rosemary, rue, sage, St. John's Wort, storax, sundew, thyme, turmeric, Venus hair fern, violet, wormwood.

Bruises: *to alleviate:* Color: any color that is close to your normal skin tone; Plant: arnica, bilberry, bistort, comfrey, daisy, elder, iris, laurel, lobelia, marigold, pellitory of the wall, pistachio, rue, Solomon's seal, tansy, turmeric, valerian, blue vervain, black walnut, woody nightshade, yarrow, yerba santa; *bone bruise:* Plant: rue.

Burns: *to treat:* Stone: chrysoprase, gem silica; Plant: aloe, balsam, bear's breech, burdock, cedar, chamomile, chickweed, comfrey, cucumber, datura, yellow dock, elder, elm, slippery elm, eucalyptus, flax, gum tragacanth, hound's tongue, lavender, lettuce, marigold, marsh mallow, mulberry, mullein, black nightshade, oats, passionflower, pellitory, plantain, raspberry, reed, sorghum, St. John's Wort, sycamore, tea tree, thyme, vervain, vetiver, witch hazel.

Cancer: Moon/Cancer; *to avert:* Plant: garlic, gum tragacanth; *to cause:* Plant: tobacco; *to treat:* Stone: jasper, moonstone, selenite; Plant: almond, aloe, apricot, benzoin, box tree, buckthorn, cantaloupe, caper, carob, castor bean, cedar, charlock, chick pea, chicory, cinnamon, red clover, cockle, cotton, dandelion, dill, fava bean, fig, flax seed, garlic, ginseng, goosegrass, gum tragacanth, henna, hops, houseleek, ivy, juniper, leek, lemon, lettuce, licorice, madonna lily, marigold, mastic, millet, mistletoe, black mustard, myrtle, narcissus, holly oak, kermes oak, oleander, olive, onion, papyrus, periwinkle, plane, pomegranate, opium poppy, reed, saffron, sorghum, sorrel, star thistle, storax, sugarcane, sycamore, walnut, watercress, water lily, wood aloes, yew; *to relieve cancer pain:* Plant: opium poppy; *bowel cancer:* Plant: rue; *breast cancer:* Plant: houseleek; *metastatic cancer:* Plant: benzoin, southernwood; *skin cancer:* Plant: violet; *cancerous growths:* Plant: wood sorrel.

Cattle diseases: *to alleviate:* Plant: herb robert; *to protect against:* Fungus: fly agaric; Plant: groundsel (gathered with the left hand while fasting), herb Robert.

Cholera: Water; Plant: bistort, gotu kola, yellow iris, reed, scullcap; *to protect against:* Stone: malachite; God: Hardaul.

Chronic diseases/disorders: Taurus; *to treat:* Plant: ginseng, oregano, savory, thyme; *chronic fatigue syndrome:* Stone: amethyst, aquamarine, aragonite, rhodochrosite, rose quartz, ruby; Plant: tansy.

Circulatory disorders: *to treat:* Plant: asparagus, chili pepper, couch grass, cypress, garlic, ginseng, bitter orange, peppermint, pine, rosemary, thyme.

Colds/flu: Venus/Air; *to protect against:* Plant: eucalyptus (under pillow), mullein (in shoe), mustard seeds (in red mojo bag), onion (peeled, to absorb germs in the air), St. John's Wort; *to treat*: Charm: honey, molasses; Color: green, orange; Metal: zinc; Stone: carnelian, yellow topaz; Oil: niaouli; Plant: angelica, aniseed, balm of Gilead, betony, borage (in bath), cajeput, caraway seed, catnip, cayenne, cedar, chamomile, charlock, cinnamon, clove, comfrey, cucumber, cypress, damiana, dong quai, Echinacea, ephedra, elder (flower or berry), eucalyptus (leaf or pod), eyebright, feverfew, flax, galbanum, garlic, ginger, heliotrope, horehound, hyssop, larch, laurel, lavender, lemon, lemon balm, licorice, linden, mallow, marjoram, mint, mugwort, mullein, black mustard, onion, oregano, orris root, pennyroyal, peppermint, pine, plantain, purslane, raspberry, rock rose, rose hips, rose of Jericho, rosemary, sage, scallion, spearmint, southernwood, styrax, sugarcane, sweetgrass, tarragon, tea tree, thyme, Venus hair fern, watercress, willow, weeping willow, wormwood, yarrow, yerba santa; *cold sores*: Stone: fluorite; Plant: rose, tea tree.

Colic: *to protect against:* Stone: malachite; Plant: white henbane root; *to treat:* Stone: coral, jade; Plant: agrimony, angelica, aniseed, barberry, basil, black cumin, buckthorn, burnet saxifrage, caraway seed, cascara sagrada, catnip, centaury, chamomile, coriander seed, dill seed, fennel seed, fumitory, galangal, ginger, groundsel, holly berry, lavender, lemon balm, lovage, marjoram, masterwort, mint, morning glory, black mustard, hedge mustard, oregano, passionflower, peppermint, rosemary, rue, senna, silverweed, sorrel, spearmint, star anise, St. John's Wort, summer savory, tarragon, turmeric, lemon verbena, walnut, yam.

Constipation: *to improve:* Color: white; Stone: golden beryl; Plant: almond, aloe, apple, basil, belladonna, bryony, buckthorn, calamus, cascara sagrada, chamomile, chestnut, chick pea, chickweed, chicory, blue cohosh, cowslip, dandelion, dittany, flax, iris, kelp, mallow, nasturtium, rosemary, sage, senna, blue vervain, violet, watercress.

Convulsions: *to improve:* Stone: amber, amethyst, carnelian, lapis lazuli, moldovite, quartz crystal; Plant: honeysuckle, horehound, iris, lavender, mistletoe, motherwort, mugwort, passionflower, scullcap, sundew, valerian; *to protect against*: Plant: peony root.

Cough: *to improve:* Color: orange; Charm: honey; Plant: acacia, agrimony, alkanet, almond, anise, apricot, bear's breech, benzoin, calamus, cannabis, catnip, cayenne, basil, beech, black cumin, bloodroot, burdock, butterbur, cajeput, carob, catsfoot, chamomile, cherry, chestnut, black cohosh, coltsfoot, cornflower, cow parsnip, cowslip, damiana, date palm, dill, dock, elderberry, elecampane, ephedra, eucalyptus, everlasting, eyebright, fennel, fenugreek, feverfew, flax, garlic, ginseng, gum tragacanth, heliotrope, holly, horehound, hound's tongue, hyssop, Iceland moss, iris, juniper berry, laurel, lavender, lettuce, licorice, lungwort, mallow, mandrake, mastic, milk thistle, mint, mullein, garlic mustard, myrrh, myrtle, onion, oregano, orris root, pansy, parsley, pellitory of the wall, peppermint, pennyroyal, pine, pistachio, plantain, opium poppy, red poppy, psyllium, pulsatilla, purslane, apothecary's rose, dog rose, rosemary, rue, sage, sandalwood, sea holly, soapwort, sorrel, spikenard, spleenwort, squill, St. John's Wort, sugarcane, sundew, sunflower, terebinth, thyme, valerian, vervain, blue vervain, violet, viper's bugloss, wall fern, wintergreen, wolfsbane, wormwood; *to protect against*: Plant: black hellebore root, ginseng root, laurel; *to soothe*: Plant: coltsfoot; *whooping cough*: Charm: bread, buried for three days and then eaten (yuck, definitely not recommended); Animal: caterpillar (live, placed in a bag and worn hung at the neck); Stone: coral; Plant: ambrosia, belladonna, bryony, cajeput, catnip, cedar, chestnut, clary sage, red clover, black cohosh, cypress, datura, elecampane, eucalyptus, evening primrose, ipecac, ivy, lobelia, moneywort, passionflower, sandalwood, sugarcane, sundew, sunflower, thyme, violet.

Cystic fibrosis: *to treat:* Plant: blue cohosh.

Diabetes: *to treat:* Stone: amethyst, ametrine, citrine; Plant: acacia, alfalfa, artichoke, blueberry, burdock, cassia, chamomile, chicory, cinnamon, dandelion, elecampane, fenugreek, garlic, ginseng, goldenseal, gum tragacanth, hawthorn, herb robert, laurel, leek, licorice, mugwort, black mulberry, onion, Madagascar periwinkle, reed, restharrow, rosemary, sage, sorghum, stinging nettle, strawberry, string bean, tormentil, watercress.

Diarrhea: Water; *to treat:* Stone: golden beryl, quartz crystal; Plant: ambrosia, avens, barberry, bayberry, betony, bistort, carrot, chamomile, cinnamon, cockleburr, black cohosh, crab apple, crown of thorns, gentian, ginger, ginseng, gum tragacanth, marsh mallow, mastic, oak bark, passionflower, plane, pulsatilla, raspberry leaf, rose hips, summer savory, water lily, wheat.

Digestive disorders/problems: *to improve:* Color: green; Stone: red coral (worn), diamond, emerald, jade, pearl, peridot; Plant: agrimony, angelica, aniseed, artichoke, red alder, ash, avens, basil, black cumin, bryony, burdock, calamus, carnation, carrot, cascara sagrada, catnip, cayenne pepper, celandine, centaury, chamomile, cherry, cinnamon, clove, club moss, dandelion, dill seed, dittany, dock, dogwood, dragon's blood, slippery elm, eucalyptus, evening primrose, fennel seed,

fir, garlic, ginger, ginseng, hellebore, hops, horehound, knapweed, lavender, lemon, lemon balm, lemongrass, lotus, goldenseal, hawthorn, milkweed, mugwort, oregano, papaya, parsley, black pepper, peppermint, pineapple, poplar, pulsatilla, rosemary, rue, sage, clary sage, spearmint, summer savory, tangerine, tarragon, thyme, valerian, lemon verbena, vervain, willow, wormwood, yarrow; *to prevent:* Plant: Echinacea.

Ear diseases/disorders: *to treat:* Plant: grapefruit, kidneywort, knotgrass, damask rose, violet; *earache:* (See: Pain); *hearing problems:* Stone: amethyst.

Epidemics: Goddess: Marena, Mary; *to avert:* Goddess: Mary; *to predict:* Plant: violet; Goddess: Bean Sidhe; *to protect against:* Charm: four thieves vinegar; Plant: angelica, cedar, pine, rosemary, saffron, sage; Goddess: Raksha Kali (The Protectress), Zemlya.

Epilepsy: Mercury/Moon; *to alleviate:* Charm: a one-year-old penny with a grain of grain and vervain that was gathered while the Sun was in Aries; Animal: mole; Stone: coral, emerald, geode, lapis lazuli; Metal: silver; Plant: anise, belladonna, calamus, cattail, cow parsnip, gotu kola, hellebore, Jacob's ladder, kidneywort, lavender, madonna lily, linden, mandrake, mistletoe, mugwort, narcissus, oats, passionflower, rose of Jericho, rosemary, rue, sage, scullcap, sorghum, spikenard, star anise, St. John's Wort, tansy, valerian, blue vervain, vetiver, violet, wormwood, yarrow; Goddess: Lilith; *to diagnose:* Stone: jet; *to predict:* Animal: dog; *to protect against:* Stone: emerald, jasper, onyx (necklace); Plant: anise, cuckoo flower, mistletoe, peony root, vervain.

Eye diseases/problems: *to improve:* Stone: aquamarine, beryl, golden beryl, emerald, green jasper, opal, sard, tigereye; Plant: cape aloe, bachelor's buttons, blueberry, burdock, cannabis, carrot, celandine, chamomile, club moss, comfrey, cornflower, dandelion, dead nettle, devil's bit scabious, eyebright, fumitory, herb robert, houseleek, horsetail, knapweed, loosestrife, Low John, parsley, plantain, polygonum root, pulsatilla, Queen Anne's lace, raspberry, dog rose, rue, toadflax, viper's bugloss, willow, witch hazel; Goddess: Sulis; God: Apollo; *to protect against*: Stone: emerald, jade; Plant: bistort root; *to relieve eyestrain*: Stone: emerald, jade, lodestone (See also: Senses, Vision).

Fibromyalgia: *to treat:* Stone: amber, amethyst, citrine, emerald, hematite, lapis lazuli, morganite, obsidian, clear quartz crystal, sodalite, tigereye.

Fluid retention/edema: Water; *to improve:* Stone: amber, jasper, jet, quartz crystal; Plant: acorn, alder, asarabacca, ash, asparagus, barberry, borage, broom, burdock, bryony, cedar, celandine, dandelion, fennel, ginger, gooseberry, grape, gum tragacanth, hawthorn, juniper, lemon, madonna lily, milk thistle, milkweed, mouse-eared hawkweed, garlic mustard, stinging nettle, woody nightshade, oleander, oregano, watercress, watermelon; *to protect against*: Stone: jasper.

Gallbladder diseases/disorders: *to treat:* Plant: barberry, celandine, costmary, elecampane, eyebright, dragon's gall, parsley, peppermint, pine, sage, wormwood; *gallstones*: Plant: barberry, caper, dandelion, mouse-eared hawkweed, parsley.

Glandular diseases: Jupiter; *to treat:* Plant: burdock, male fern; *enlarged glands*: *to treat:* Plant: alder, hemlock, pawpaw, rock rose, watercress.

Gout: *to improve:* Stone: amethyst; Plant: agrimony, angelica, asparagus, autumn crocus, barberry, bear's breech, belladonna, betony, bilberry, blackberry,

burdock, castor bean, chamomile, chicory, cotton, couch grass, cow parsnip, daisy, dandelion, elder, endive, germander, ginseng, heliotrope, henbane, horsetail, lemon, meadowsweet, mustard, woody nightshade, oak, pansy, primrose, rosemary, sassafras, soapwort, stinging nettle, tansy, tarragon, thyme, vervain, willow, wormwood, yew; *to protect against*: Stone: bloodstone; Plant: cherry, crab apple, lemon, gooseberry, strawberry.

Gum diseases/infections: *to treat:* Plant: barberry, bistort, blackberry leaf, germander, hare's foot clover, fennel, loosestrife, marsh mallow, myrrh, myrtle, peppermint, dog rose, sage, tea tree, thyme, tormentil, walnut.

Headache: (See: Pain).

Heartburn: Jupiter; *to treat:* Potion: carrot juice; Plant: caraway seed, celery, chamomile, dandelion, dogwood, ginseng, meadowsweet, rowan, wormwood, yerba mate.

Heart disease/disorder: *to treat:* Charm: musk; Stone: amethyst; Plant: borage, broom, chicory, cinnamon, black cohosh, corn, cuckoo flower, cumin, ephedra, false hellebore, flax, foxglove, ginseng, grapevine, hawthorn berry, horehound, laurel, lemon balm, lily of the valley, linden, motherwort, oats, olive, oleander, pheasant's eye, rose, scullcap, spikenard, string bean, valerian, vervain, wallflower, witch hazel; *congestive heart failure*: *to treat:* Plant: borage, corn, hollyhock.

Hernia: *to improve:* Plant: restharrow, rupturewort; *to protect against*: Plant: green fig wood (as firewood).

Herpes: *to improve:* Plant: black alder, balm, burdock, chickweed, cucumber, dragon's blood, elecampane, elm, goldenseal, houseleek, rock rose, soapwort, tea tree, vine.

High cholesterol: *to prevent*: Plant: fenugreek, maple; *to reduce*: Waning Moon; Fungus: mushroom; Plant: alfalfa, birch, carob, devil's claw, fenugreek, garlic, globe artichoke, gotu kola, bitter orange, sunflower.

HIV: *to treat*: Plant: St. John's Wort.

Hodgkin's disease: *to treat*: Plant: periwinkle.

Hypoglycemia: *to treat*: Stone: serpentine; Plant: ginseng, orange, walnut.

Infection: *to alleviate*: Stone: pearl; Oil: niaouli; Plant: balm of Gilead, barberry, burdock, chili pepper, comfrey, Echinacea, eucalyptus, frankincense, garlic, ginseng, goldenseal, gum tragacanth, horsetail, juniper berry, lavender, lemon, licorice, marsh mallow, millet, oregano, peppermint, rose hips, rosemary, sage, clary sage, star of Bethlehem, tea tree, thyme, yarrow; *to prevent*: Stone: amber; *to protect against*: Stone: garnet, pearl; Plant: angelica, dragon's blood, garlic, southernwood, thyme; *to protect the household against*: Plant: *yeast infection*: Plant: turmeric.

Infectious/contagious disease: Air; *to alleviate*: Plant: eucalyptus, marsh gentian, opium poppy; *to avert*: Plant: bachelor's buttons, cornflower, thyme; *to protect against*: Goddess: Bast.

Inflammation/inflammatory diseases: *to avert*: Stone: fluorite, garnet; *to soothe*: Plant: cypress, elder, elm, eucalyptus, silver fir, garlic, juniper, larch, laurel, lungwort, myrtle, pine, snapdragon, Solomon's seal, spruce, vervain.

Insomnia: (See: sleep disorders).

Intestinal diseases/problems: *to treat*: Stone: agate, amber; Plant: belladonna, marsh mallow.

Joint disease/problems: *to treat*: Plant: comfrey, dandelion, germander, ginseng, rosemary, summer savory (See: arthritis/rheumatism, page 77).

Kidney disease/infection: Libra/Aries; *to alleviate:* Stone: hematite, jade, green jasper; Plant: agrimony, aloe, barberry, blueberry, burdock, burnet saxifrage, centaury, chickweed, cinnamon, couch grass, cranberry, dandelion, fennel, fenugreek, finger grass, ginger, ginseng, heather, horsetail, juniper, meadowsweet, parsley, mallow, myrtle, dog rose, strawberry, uva ursi, yarrow; *to protect against*: Stone: jade; *kidney stones: to treat:* Plant: sea ambrosia, asparagus, cornsilk, dandelion, dropwort, feverfew, gooseberry, gorse, hydrangea, kidneywort, madder, masterwort, parsley, rupturewort, star thistle, uva ursi, vervain, watermelon; *to protect against*: Plant: madder root.

Leukemia: *to treat*: Plant: asparagus, Madagascar periwinkle, reed.

Liver disease: Stone: beryl; Plant: acorn, agrimony, avens, barberry, bistort, burdock, butternut, cascara sagrada, greater celandine, centaury, horse chestnut, chickweed, chicory, costmary, dandelion, dogwood, dragon's gall, groundsel, fennel, fenugreek, fumitory, gorse, grape, hart's tongue, hops, horehound, licorice, madder, milk thistle, parsley, safflower, sage, spindle tree, stinging nettle, strawberry, thyme, turmeric, vervain, wormwood; *to protect against*: Plant: garlic; *cirrhosis*: Plant: ambrosia, dandelion; *hepatitis*: Color: green; Plant: dandelion, milk thistle, turmeric, vetiver, wood aloes; *to protect against*: Plant: garlic; *jaundice*: Color: yellow; *to treat*: Stone: turquoise; Plant: boneset, butcher's broom, red clover, cockle, dandelion, yellow dock, endive, fumitory, gentian, goldenseal, gorse, hops, hyacinth, lovage, madder root, mallow, marigold, milk thistle, nettle, reed, sheep sorrel, snowdrop, star thistle, toadflax.

Lung diseases/disorders: *to treat*: Charm: musk; Stone: amethyst; Plant: angelica, borage, coltsfoot, dropwort, fenugreek, horehound, mouse-ear hawk-weed, mullein, mustard, sanicle, spearmint, sundew, thyme, Venus hair fern.

Male mood disorders: *to treat*: Plant: snake cereus.

Menstrual disorders: Moon; *to treat*: Stone: garnet; Plant: agrimony, angelica, bistort, catnip, black or blue cohosh, black cumin, bryony, cassia, chicory, cinnamon, red clover, damiana, dragon's blood, eucalyptus, fennel, feverfew, ginger, lady's mantle, lavender, lemon, Low John, meadowsweet, mistletoe, mugwort, mulberry, nettle, pomegranate, rock rose, safflower, saffron, clay sage, sandalwood, spikenard, turmeric, yam; *PMS*: Stone: moonstone; Plant: aloe vera, chamomile, blue cohosh, dong quai, fennel, geranium, grapefruit, mint, oats, passionflower, clary sage, valerian.

Migraines: (See: Pain).

Morning sickness: *to treat*: Potion: apricot nectar; Plant: ginger, peach.

Motion sickness: *to treat*: Plant: ginger, mandrake, peppermint.

Mouth diseases/infections: *to treat*: Plant: bistort, clove, sage.

Muscle problems: *to treat*: Plant: clove; *cramps/spasms*: *to alleviate*: Stone: ruby; Plant: astralagus, barberry, bilberry, black cohosh, blue cohosh, cajeput, cascara sagrada, catnip, cayenne, cedar, chamomile, red clover, cork oak, cranberry, cypress, dong quai, elder, eucalyptus, fennel seed, garlic, gotu kola, hibiscus, hops, horse chestnut (carried), horsetail, lavender, licorice, lobelia, mullein, nettle, passionflower, peppermint, lesser periwinkle, raspberry leaf, rose hip, rosemary, sage, clary sage, sandalwood, scullcap, senna, tangerine, tansy, thyme, valerian, wild yam, yarrow, yerba santa; *to prevent while swimming*: Charm: eelskin garter; *torn muscle*: *to improve*: Stone: sunstone.

Nausea: *to treat*: Stone: golden beryl; Plant: anise, apricot, cinnamon, clove, fennel, galangal, ginger, ginseng, pennyroyal, peppermint, rose petals (in conserve).

Neurological diseases/disorders: Moon; *to treat*: Color: orange, red; Stone: amethyst, aquamarine, carnelian; Plant: mistletoe, nux vomica, peppermint, petrified wood.

Nosebleed: Plant: cornflower (held until warm).

Obesity: Moon; *to reduce*: Waning Moon; Stone: apatite, golden beryl, moonstone, rose quartz; Plant: ash, birch, camel thorn, fennel, garlic, grapefruit, kelp, lemon, rosemary, thyme.

Ophthalmia: God: Yen Kuang Niang-Niang.

Parkinson's disease: *to treat*: Plant: datura, fava bean, henbane, passionflower.

Plague: *to alleviate*: Stone: garnet, topaz; *to end*: Goddess: Cailleach; *to protect against*: Charm: Four Thieves Vinegar; Stone: carnelian, diamond, zircon; Plant: angelica, asafetida, garlic, linden tree (bit of bark or leaf wrapped in a spider web and placed under a green stone in a ring), onion, rosemary, rue, vervain; God: Ayiyanayaka

Pneumonia: *to treat*: Stone: fluorite; Plant: charlock, false hellebore, fava bean, foxglove, holly, black mustard.

Prostate diseases/disorders: *to treat*: Plant: chickpea, cornsilk, flax, hemlock, hops, meadowsweet, pansy, parsley, restharrow, rupturewort, saw palmetto, stinging nettle, uva ursi, watermelon, wintergreen.

Psoriasis: *to treat*: Stone: salt; Plant: barberry, comfrey, autumn crocus, yellow dock, geranium, iris, juniper berry, milk thistle, tamarisk, tea tree.

Raynaud's disease: Plant: barberry, ginkgo.

Reproductive system diseases/disorders: Venus; Plant: ginger, mugwort, willow; *female system*: Moon; Goddess: Artemis; Plant: mugwort, raspberry leaf, southernwood, tarragon, wormwood.

Respiratory diseases/disorder/infections: Air; *to alleviate:* Stone: amber, rutilated quartz; Oil: cajeput, niaouli; Plant: angelica, balsam, barberry, betony, borage, bryony, burnet saxifrage, celandine, chamomile, elder, ephedra, eucalyptus, fennel, fig, flax, ginger, horehound, Iceland moss, lavender, lemon, licorice, maidenhair fern, marjoram, marshmallow, mustard, oregano, pine, pulsatilla, ribwort, dog rose, sage, slippery elm, St. John's Wort, sundew, tea tree, thyme, valerian; *to avert*: Plant: Echinacea.

Seasickness: *to alleviate:* Plant: citron, holy thistle, oregano, paprika, pennyroyal, wormwood; *to protect against*: Stone: beryl; Plant: feverfew, pennyroyal.

Sexual disorders: *to treat*: Color: red; Stone: diamond, all red gems and stones; *to treat male sexual disorders*: Metal: gold; Stone: lodestone.

Sinus disease/disorder: *to treat:* Stone: salt; Potion: salt water (to gargle, or for aspirating sinuses); Plant: belladonna, bistort, eucalyptus, horseradish, lavender, marsh mallow, black mustard, peppermint, rosemary, wormwood.

Skin disease/disorders: *to alleviate:* Color: pink, yellow; Charm: elder flower water, witch hazel; Stone: agate, yellow carnelian, garnet, moonstone; Oil: niaouli, palmarosa; Plant: alder, almond, aloe, apple, bistort, blackberry, burdock, butterbur, carline thistle, carrot, chamomile, red clover, club moss, coltsfoot, columbine, comfrey, cow parsnip, devil's bit scabious, dock, dragon's blood, dwarf elder, elecampane, elm, eucalyptus, eye of Satan, feverfew, figwort, flax, frangipani, fumitory, goosegrass, gotu kola,

hyssop, iris, juniper, kava kava, knotgrass, ladies bedstraw, laurel, lavender, loosestrife, lovage (in bath), mace, marigold, mezereon, milk thistle, mint (in bath), mullein, nightshade, orris root, pansy, patchouli, pea, periwinkle, white poplar, purslane, restharrow (in bath), rue, sage, clary sage, sanicle, sarsaparilla, soapwort, sorrel, spikenard, stinging nettle, stonecrop, tansy, tea tree, woad, yew; Goddess: Leuce; *to protect against*: Stone: carnelian; Plant: aloe, vervain.

Sleep disorders: *to treat*: Color: purple, violet; *fitful sleep*: Plant: scullcap; *insomnia*: Aquarius; *to alleviate:* Charm: dream pillow; Color: blue; Stone: amethyst, aventurine, blue jacinth, peridot, quartz crystal, sapphire, sodalite, zircon; Oil: petitgrain; Plant: aniseed, catnip, celery, chamomile, chicory, clary sage, columbine, ginseng, hawthorn, hops, laurel, lavender, lemon balm, lettuce, mandrake, marjoram, meadowsweet, mint, nutmeg, oats, orris root, passionflower, opium poppy, primrose, rosemary, scullcap, spearmint, spikenard, St. John's Wort, stonecrop (in a black cloth, under the pillow), tangerine, thyme, valerian, blue vervain, violet, water lily, willow, ylang-ylang; *to protect against*: Stone: topaz; *oversleeping*: *to alleviate:* Stone: amethyst; *sleepwalking*: *to alleviate:* Stone: diamond, topaz; Plant: dittany.

Spirits of disease: *to protect against*: Plant: coca leaves (burned).

Spleen diseases/disorders: *to treat:* Charm: tamarisk wood drinking cup; Stone: malachite; Plant: barberry, bird's nest fern, dandelion, fumitory, heliotrope, holly, mouse-eared hawkweed, oak, spleenwort, stinging nettle, sunflower, vervain, woad.

Stomach disease/problems: *to alleviate:* Color: yellow; Stone: yellow carnelian, jade, jasper, green jasper, jet, sunstone; Plant: alfalfa, angelica, anise, basil, caraway, chamomile, dandelion, fennel, galangal, ginger, ginseng, hops, licorice, orris root, pennyroyal, peppermint, rue, sage, summer savory, valerian, vervain; *to protect against*: Stone: white coral (necklace); Plant: pomegranate blossom.

Stroke: *to improve:* Stone: lapis lazuli; Plant: hawthorn; *to prevent*: Plant: ginkgo.

Throat infections/sore throat: Taurus; *to alleviate:* Stone: blue agate, amber, aquamarine, beryl, blue topaz; Oil: cajeput, niaouli; Plant: agrimony, alder, angelica, barberry, betony, bistort, blackberry, burdock, catnip, gum cistus, eucalyptus, hollyhock, lemon, licorice, mallow, mulberry, myrrh, olive, pine, pomegranate, rush, sage, sanicle, sycamore, tea tree, thyme; *to protect against*: Charm: amber necklace.

Tropical diseases: *to treat:* Plant: clove.

Tuberculosis: *to treat:* Plant: aloe, anemone, barley, beet, cedar, cinnamon, comfrey, date palm, garlic, ginseng, grapevine, horsetail, licorice, Low John, madder, male fern, myrtle, plantain, apothecary's rose, rue, saffron, sage, sea holly, southernwood, thyme, violet, wall fern, watercress, wheat, yerba santa.

Tumors: *to protect against:* Plant: hydrangea root, mandrake root; *to treat:* Charm: beeswax; Stone: jet; Plant: anemone, buckthorn, cattail, red clover, endive, hemlock, horsetail, houseleek, hydrangea, holly oak, plane, vervain, watercress, water lily, Madagascar periwinkle, yucca; *fibroid tumors:* Plant: ash, cayenne.

Ulcers: *to alleviate:* Stone: agate, golden beryl, chrysocolla, peridot; Plant: aloe, dragon's blood, goldenseal, pennyroyal, tea tree.

Urinary tract problems: *to alleviate:* Plant: barberry, broom, burnet saxifrage, celery seed, Chinese lantern, red clover, club moss, comfrey, couch grass, cranberry,

finger grass, flax, garlic, heather, horsetail, hydrangea, juniper berry, kava kava, ladies' bedstraw, linden, lovage, marsh mallow, nasturtium, oats, parsley, wild parsnip, psyllium, rupturewort, sea holly, uva ursa, vervain; *to prevent*: Stone: jade; Plant: cranberry.

Varicose veins: *to treat:* Stone: topaz; Plant: bilberry, butcher's broom, centaury, coltsfoot, comfrey, horse chestnut, knotgrass, marigold, mint, rosemary, witch hazel.

Venereal diseases/STD's: Venus; *to treat:* Plant: aloe, ash, burdock, cannabis, chrysanthemum, black cohosh, corn, couch grass, date palm, frankincense, mastic, millet, pansy, pine, rose, sandalwood, sarsaparilla, savin.

Vertigo/dizziness: *to alleviate:* Animal: elk; Stone: quartz crystal; Oil: neroli; Plant: acorn, burdock, mandrake, mistletoe, lemon verbena, peppermint, rosemary, rue; *to protect against*: Plant: woody nightshade (See also: Balance).

Viruses: *to alleviate:* Stone: fluorite, hematite; Oil: niaouli; Plant: golden amaranth, Echinacea, eucalyptus, frankincense, geranium, lavender, St. John's Wort, tea tree, thyme, vetiver; *to protect against*: Stone: salt; Plant: Echinacea.

Warts: Animal: toad; *to protect against*: Plant: beans; *to be rid of*: Stone: salt; Plant: apple (cut open, rubbed on wart then buried), beans, celandine, chicory, dandelion (milky sap from stem), fig (milky sap), garlic, heliotrope, houseleek, lemon, mandrake, marigold, mercury, pea pod, stonecrop, tea tree, thyme, tormentil, willow bark.

Wasting diseases: Moon; *to alleviate:* Stone: Jasper; Plant: almond, costmary, date, peanut.

Wounds: *to improve:* Color: blue; Charm: spider web; Plant: dragon's blood, hart's tongue, lady's mantle, marigold, potentilla; *to prevent infection in:* Plant: aloe, garlic; *to stop bleeding of:* Stone: bloodstone; Fungus: puffball; Plant: bistort, blackthorn, burnet, comfrey, dragon's blood, fluellen, goldenrod, heliotrope, herb robert, horsetail, cobweb houseleek, hyssop, white dead nettle, goldenseal, kidneywort, ladies bedstraw, lady's mantle, lemon, medlar, moneywort, mouse eared hawkweed, moon cereus, mulberry, periwinkle, plantain, Solomon's seal, southernwood, St. John's Wort, stonecrop, tamarisk, willowherb, witch hazel, yarrow, yerba santa

To: absorb disease: Charm: Midsummer bonfire; Stone: hematite, lodestone; Plant: ash, garlic, onion. **avert disease**: Stone: bloodstone, malachite; Plant: garlic, eucalyptus, hemlock (grown near house), black pepper, onion (hung in sickroom), rosemary, rue, thyme, turmeric; Goddess: Sekhmet; Evocation: Alauwaimis. **banish demons that cause disease**: Plant: clover, ginger, all pungent spices. **cause disease**: Animal: dragon, rat; Plant: elder grove, sesame; Goddess: Gula; God: Reshep. **cure disease**: Plant: mistletoe; Goddess: Gula, Isis, Sekhmet, Tatevali; God: Hatdastsisi. **destroy disease**: Fire; Goddess: Brigid, Cailleach, Sekhmet. **diagnose disease**: Method: divination, dream incubation; Plant: coca leaves. **end disease**: Waning Moon. **prevent disease**: Metal copper (worn on left side of body); *prevent the spread of disease*: Goddess: Salus. **protect against disease/disorders**: Sun; Charm: glass ring; Metal: copper; Stone: red agate, amethyst, carnelian, coral, Herkimer diamond, sapphire; Plant: clove, hemlock, juniper berry, laurel, mistletoe, mugwort, woody nightshade, onion, rosemary, rue, southernwood, willow; Goddess: Bast, Gula

Bau (Great Physician), Ix Chel, the Mares (the Mothers), Medusa, Pattinidevi, Sekhmet, Tarri Penu; God: the Adityas, Hatdastsisi, Jizo Bosatsu, Sha'taqat; *diseases caused by witchcraft*: God: Hayenezgani. **purify disease**: Plant: Echinacea, tomato, yucca root. **remove disease**: Charm: magnet; Stone: lodestone. **treat disease**: Plant: ginseng, mistletoe, pennyroyal, rue (See also: Healing).

Disorder
(See: Chaos)

Disputes
(See: Agreement, Quarrels)

Divination
(See also: Foretelling, Oracles, Prophecy, Psychism)

Mercury/Moon/Waning Moon/Full Moon/ Air/Water/Fire/East/Wednesday

Color: black, gold, purple, silver, violet, white, yellow; Tool: crystal ball, pendulum, scrying bowl or mirror, wand; Method: I Ching, runes, scrying, tarot; Metal: gold, lead, silver, tin; Animal: armadillo, chicken, lynx, rabbit, slug, wren; Stone: amethyst, azurite, flint, fluorite, hematite, red jasper, jet, lapis lazuli, mica, moonstone, mother of pearl, obsidian, pyrite, clear quartz crystal, tiger's eye, topaz; Plant: acacia, alder, amber, angelica, aniseed, apple, ash, banana, basil, birch, bistort, broom, camphor, cardamom, cascarilla, cassia, catsfoot, cedar, cherry, cinnamon, cinquefoil, clove, coca leaf, copal, cypress, dandelion, datura, dittany, dodder, dogwood, eyebright, fig, fir, silver fir, frankincense, ginseng, goldenrod, hazel, hibiscus, High John, honeysuckle, horse chestnut, ivy, juniper, kelp, laurel (as incense), lavender, lemon, lemongrass, lettuce, lilac, linden bark, maize, mandrake, marigold, meadowsweet, mistletoe, moonwort, morning glory, mugwort, mullein, myrrh, narcissus, nutmeg, oakmoss, orange, orris root, palm kernel, pansy, patchouli, peppermint, pomegranate, poplar, pussy willow, rose, rowan, rue, sage, clary sage, sandalwood, St. John's Wort, spindle tree, strawberry, black tea, thyme, tuberose, vervain, willow, wisteria, woodruff, wormwood, yarrow, yew; Goddess: Andraste, Ariadne, Astarte, Brigid, Carmenta, Cerridwen, Cethlion, Cihuacoatl, Corra, Coventina, Cyhiraeth, Delphine, Dione, Egeria, Ertha, Feithline, Fortuna, Freya, Gaia, Gwendydd, Hecate, Ida, Inanna, Ishtar, Isis, Kali, Kwan Yin, Mari, Masaya, Mawu, Mokosh, Namagiri, Nemglan, Nephthys, Oya, Philyra, Rodenica, Shaushka, Teteoinnan, Uzumi, Vortumna. Zemlya; God: Aktab Kutbay, Anubis, Apollo, Arawn, Asharu, Bannik, Evander, Finn Mac Cool, Hermes, Hoenir, Hubal, Ifa, Maximon, Mercury, Nemglan, Neptune, Odin, Ogma, Orunmila, Phoebus Apollo, Poseidon, Shamash, Svantovit, Tages, Thoth; Evocation: Chiron, Merlin.

Love divination: Charm: ointment of honey with marjoram, marigold, thyme and wormwood; Potion: honey and vinegar with marigold, thyme, marjoram and wormwood; Plant: birch, hazelnut, marjoram, mullein, orpane with red sage, rose, yarrow. **Medical divination**: Plant: alder; Goddess: the Crone, Teteoinnan. **Water divination**: Plant: ash, hazel. **Weather divination**: Plant: yarrow.

Divination tools: Moon; Plant: mugwort; *to increase the power of*: Potion: mugwort tea; *of tarot cards*: Color: black; Stone: amethyst, quartz crystals.

Divination by: arrows: God: Hubal. **dice**: God: Mercury. **the flight of birds**: Animal: crane, crow; Evocation: Romulus. **pebbles**: God: Hermes. **smoke**: Tool: censer; Plant: jasmine, rose, poppy seeds.

scrying: Tool: bowl, cauldron, mirror; Stone: obsidian, pyrite. **the sound of birds**: Animal: wren. **the sound of rustling leaves**: Plant: oak, willow; Goddess: Dione. **divination in trance work**: Plant: nutmeg (as incense). **power of divination**: Charm: cowrie shell; Plant: mugwort, yarrow.

To: increase divination ability (See: Ability). **prepare for divination**: Plant: anise (in bath).

The Divine

Color: red, white; Charm: ankh, rain water; Animal: eagle, hawk; Metal: copper; Plant: angelica, apple, carnation, cedar, coca, hyssop, lotus, rowan berry.

Divine accolade: Plant: laurel. **Divine commands**: Animal: owl; Goddess: Iris. **Divine communication**: (See: Oracles). **Divine creativity**: Goddess: Kali. **Divine desire**: Fire. **Divine energy**: (See: Energy). **Divine favor**: Goddess: Anumati. **Divine fire**: God: Agni. **Divine grace**: Plant: lotus; Goddess: Mary; Evocation: Hanael. **Divine happiness**: Goddess: Lakshmi. **Divine inspiration**: (See: Inspiration). **Divine intelligence**: God: Thoth. **Divine judgment**: (See: Judgment). **Divine justice**: (See: Justice). **Divine law**: God: Dharma; *to keep*: God: Enki. **Divine light**: Color: white; Goddess: Uma; God: Svarog. **Divine love**: (See: Love). **Divine madness**: God: Dionysus. **Divine messages**: (See: Messages). **Divine motherhood**: Goddess: Isis, Modron. **Divine order**: (See: Order). **Divine power**: (See: Power). **Divine protection**: (See: Protection). **Divine revelation**: Stone: jacinth. **Divine truth**: Plant: lotus. **Divine union**: Goddess: Parvati. **Divine vengeance**: (See: Revenge). **Divine will**: (See: Will). **Divine wisdom**: Color: blue, clear, white; Goddess: Lakshmi, Tara. **Divine words**: Goddess: Isis, Mary, Tara; God: Obatala, Thoth (Lord of Divine Words).

To: attract deities: Tool: censer; *gods*: Sun; Color: gold, golden-yellow; *the Goddess*: Moon; Color: silver, gray; *the influence of the Goddess*: Color: silver; Metal: silver; *Lakshmi*: Charm: tiny lanterns, hung like stars; *Venus*: Color: emerald green. **bridge the human and the divine**: God: Lugh; Evocation: Apis bull. **honor deities**: Tool: censer; Method: libation, offerings; *the Goddess*: Color: silver; Charm: silver crescent moon; *the Crone*: Waning Moon; Plant: comfrey. **protect deities**: Evocation: Michael. **recognize divine influence**: Goddess: Mawu.

Divining

(See: Dowsing)

Domination

(See also: Aggressiveness, Control, Power)

Tool: scourge; Plant: beech, calamus root, quassia bark.

For a woman to dominate the home: Plant: rosemary.

To: attract a dominant lover: Plant: safflower with snakeroot (burned). **be warned of danger of domination by others**: Stone: jade. **dominate enemies**: Plant: poppy seed. **escape domination**: Plant: chickweed. **not allow yourself to be dominated**: Goddess: Durga. **recover from domination**: Plant: lilac.

Doubt

(See also: Certainty)

Dark Moon

Color: brown; Number: 7; Stone: staurolite; Plant: evening primrose; God: Ahriman.

To: overcome doubt: Plant: aspen. **relieve doubt**: Stone: amethyst, carnelian, tigereye; Plant: azalea, mullein. **understand doubt**: Plant: alder.

Dowsing

Earth

Dowsing rods: Plant (forked branches): hazel, peach, rowan, willow, witch hazel.

To divine: gems/minerals: Stone: flint. **gold**: Tool: witch hazel rod; Stone: flint. **hidden things**: Tool: hazel rod. **metal**: Tool: rowan rod. **buried treasure**: Tool: hazel rod; Stone: flint. **water**: Tool: hazel rod, willow rod, witch hazel rod; Stone: flint.

Dreams

(See also: Nightmares, Sleep)

Neptune/Moon/Water/West/Monday/Night/Winter

Color: blue, gray, lavender, silver, yellow; Charm: musk, well; Number: 2; Animal: bear, lizard, polar bear, swan; Metal: silver, steel; Stone: amethyst, azurite, hematite, Herkimer diamond, jade, blue quartz, sapphire, blue tourmaline; Plant: anise, ash leaf, bergamot, catnip, chamomile, cinnamon, dandelion root, datura, eucalyptus, holly, jasmine, juniper, kava kava, laurel, wild lettuce, lotus, marigold, mistletoe, motherwort, mugwort, passionflower, black pepper, royal fern, saffron (as incense), clary sage, sandalwood, southernwood, tangerine, blue tansy, tarragon, lemon verbena, willow, wormwood, yarrow, ylang-ylang; Goddess: Caer, Erzulie, Gatumdug, Hecate, Huitaca, Isis, Kali, Nephthys, Niorun, Rhiannon, Tana, Yemaya (Mother of Dreams and Secrets), Yemaya Olokun; God: Epos, Hermes, Hypnos, Moeuhane, Morpheus, Oneicopompus, the Oneroi, Somnus; Evocation: Queen Mab.

Bad/upsetting dreams: Stone: onyx; God: Phobetor; Evocation: Mara, the Mare; *to protect against*: Charm: dream catcher; Color: white; Stone: moonstone, clear quartz crystal; Potion: chamomile tea (drunk at bedtime); Plant: anise (under the pillow), heavenly bamboo (grown in bedroom), betony, peony seeds, rosemary; *to stop*: Stone: fluorite. **Beautiful dreams**: Plant: mistletoe. **Clairvoyant dreams**: Plant: marigold (in dream pillows). **Creative dreams**: Plant: clary sage. **Dangerous dreams**: Plant: elder. **Deep dreams**: Pluto; Plant: vetiver. **Depressing dreams**: *to protect against*: Plant: peony (root or flower). **Erotic dreams**: Plant: heather; Goddess: Lilith; Evocation: incubi, succubi; *to prevent*: Plant: horse mint, pansy, purslane seeds. **Fairy dreams**: Plant: apple blossom, clover, lilac, peony, primrose, violet. **Financial dreams**: Color: green; Stone: emerald. **Healing dreams**: Method: dream incubation; Goddess: Damona, Isis; God: Asclepius, Nodens; *dream oracles related to healing*: God: Asclepius. **Inspirational dreams**: Animal: all nocturnal creatures. **Lucid dreaming**: Animal: grebe, water spider (See also: The Astral: astral projection/travel). **Peaceful dreams**: Stone: amethyst, chrysocolla; Plant: chamomile, jasmine, St. John's Wort. **Pleasant dreams**: Plant: holly berry, jasmine, mimosa. **Prophetic dreams**: Moon; Charm: dream pillow; Color: blue, orange, silver; Stone: amethyst, azurite, lodestone, moonstone, sodalite; Fungus: fly agaric; Plant: acacia, agrimony, angelica, anise, bracken, buchu, camphor, carob, celery seed, lesser celandine, celery seed, cinnamon, cinquefoil, daisy, heliotrope, holly, honeysuckle, hops, ivy, jasmine, laurel, lilac, lovage, mandrake, marigold, mimosa, mistletoe, mugwort, onion, peppermint, poppy, opium poppy, purslane, rose, clary sage, sandalwood, St. John's Wort, verbena, vervain, violet, wormwood, yarrow; Goddess: Caer, Pasiphaë; God: Faunus, Oneiros, Shoney. **Psychic dreams**: Pisces; Charm: dream pillow; Color: blue, silver; Animal: crab, lizard; Stone: amethyst, jade, onyx; Metal: silver (worn, or under pillow); Plant: acacia, ash leaves (under pillow), camphor, cedar, chamomile, cinquefoil, eucalyptus, eyebright, frankincense, heliotrope, holly, jasmine, laurel, lilac, lavender and linden (in dream pillows), wild lettuce, marigold, mimosa, mistletoe, mugwort, poppy, rose, rosemary, saffron, clary sage, sandalwood, scullcap with mugwort, southernwood, tarragon, lemon verbena, wormwood, yarrow; Goddess: Caer, Circe, Niorun; God: Hypnos, Morpheus, Somnus; *to release*: Plant: heliotrope; *to stimulate*: Plant: ash leaves (under the pillow); *psychic dreams related to healing*: Goddess: Damona. **Realistic dreams**: God: Icelus. **Sad dreams**: *to banish*: Plant: peony seeds. **Strange dreams**: Stone: onyx; Fungus: fly agaric; Plant: datura; God: Phantasmos. **Vivid dreams**: Stone: amethyst; Plant: mugwort, clary sage. **Wet dreams**: *to prevent*: Plant: artichoke, horse mint (juice applied topically, patch test first), pansy, purslane seeds; Goddess: Lilith; Evocation: Succubi.

Dream clarification: (See: Clarification). **Dream communication**: God: Hypnos. **Dream contact**: (See: Contact). **Dream guidance**: (See: Guidance). **Dream interpretation**: Method: meditation, tarot; Animal: swan; Stone: kyanite, smoky quartz; Plant: mugwort; Goddess: Gatamdug, Geshtinanna, Gula-Bau, Nanshe; Evocation: Ninsûn. **Dream magick**: (See: Magick). **Dream messages**: (See: Messages). **Dream oracles**: (See: Oracles) **Dreamtime**: (See: Time)/ **Dream visions**: (See: Visions). **Dream visitation**: *to prevent*: Goddess: Lilith; Evocation: incubi, succubi; *to prevent*: Plant: eye of Satan (near the bed), peony seeds. **Dream work**: (See: Work). **Dream world**: Animal: crab; *wisdom of the dream world*: Animal: owl.

Freedom to dream: Plant: hops.

To dream of: **animals**: God: Icelus. **fairies**: Plant: peony; *fairyland*: Plant: elder (slept beneath). **the location of stolen goods**: Plant: marigold (under pillow). **lucky numbers**: Plant: huckleberry leaf, marigold. **people**: God: Icelus. **the thief who stole from you**: Plant (under pillow): heliotrope, marigold. **your future spouse**: Plant: Adam and Eve root (under pillow), yarrow (in dream pillow). **your lover**: (See: Lovers).

To: **bring dreams to conscious awareness**: Stone: Herkimer diamond. **control dreams**: Animal: lizard; God: Hermes. **facilitate dreams**: Stone: labradorite, rutilated quartz, turquoise; Plant: garlic, wild lettuce. **help dreams come true**: Animal: loon; Plant: chamomile, huckleberry leaf. **improve the quality of dreams**: Plant: vervain (in dream pillow). **increase dreams**: Plant: datura, nutmeg; *induce dreams*: Stone: citrine, garnet; Plant: datura. **induce dreams for psychic work**: Plant: wild lettuce; Goddess: Nephthys. **intensify dreams**: Animal: grebe; Stone: Herkimer diamond. **learn to respect dreams**: Animal: lizard. **manifest dreams**: Stone: sapphire; Plant: chamomile. **protect dreams**: God: Morpheus. **realize dreams**: Stone: turquoise. **remember dreams**: Method: dream journal; Charm: dream pillow; Animal: lizard; Stone: garnet, jade, labradorite; Plant: caraway, comfrey, mimosa, mugwort, rosemary; Goddess: Isis, Mawu. **share dreams**: Stone: turquoise. **stop dreams**: Stone: jade; Plant: lemon verbena; *of yourself*: Plant: yarrow (under pillow).

Duality

(See also: Polarity, Yang, Yin)

Gemini

Number: 2; Metal: mercury; Goddess: Ishtar, Kali; God: Dionysus, Mithras, Ometeotl, Sobek.

Chapter 5

Ecstasy

(See also: Joy, Pleasure, Satisfaction)

Neptune/Fire/Water

Method: dance, drugs (dangerous, not recommended), fasting, flagellation, orgasm, orgiastic sex (not recommended), psychic union, trance, trance possession; Charm: fairy music; Animal: jaguar; Color: white (white hot); Stone: diamond; Potion: wine; Plant: coca, ephedra, gardenia, ivy, maguey, snakeplant; Goddess: Anath, Kali; God: Bacchus, the Horned God, Liber, Od, Shiva.

Mutual ecstasy: God: Krishna. **Passionate ecstasy**: Goddess: Anath. **Regenerative ecstasy**: Goddess: the Morrigan. **Religious ecstasy**: Goddess: Agave, Cybele, Hathor; God: Dionysus, Soma; Evocation: the Maenads. **Sexual ecstasy**: Goddess: Anath. **Spiritual ecstasy**: Stone: diamond; Goddess: the Great Mother.

Ecstatic celebration: God: Bacchus, Dionysus. **Ecstatic desire**: Goddess: Parvati. **Ecstatic experiences**: Goddess: Kali, Sekhmet (Giver of Ecstasies).

Ecstasy of: battle: (See: Battle). **war**: Goddess: Anath.

Eloquence

(See also: Communication, Expression, Speech)

Mercury/Air

Charm: sit beneath willow trees; Color: orange; Animal: nightingale; Metal: quicksilver; Stone: agate, amazonite, carnelian, celestite, chalcedony, chrysoprase, emerald, jasper, sardonyx, turquoise; Plant: aspen, dahlia, fennel, hazel, yellow jasmine, lavender, lily, lotus, crepe myrtle, valerian, water lily, willow; Goddess: Benzaiten, Brigid, Calliope (beautiful voice), Don, Hera, Oya, Sarasvati, Sarasvati Vagdevi, Vac; God: Arawn, Baile, Balder, Bragi, Don, Forseti, Hermes, Lugh, Mercury, Nabu, Ogma (The Honey-Mouthed), Volos; Evocation: Hercules, Hiawatha, Orpheus.

Emotions

(See also: Anger, Cheerfulness, Grief, Happiness, Joy, Love, Mood, Sorrow, and so on.)

Moon/Full Moon/Water/West/Friday/Scorpio/Cancer/Gemini

Tool: cauldron, chalice; Color: pink, red; Number: 6; Charm: heart; Animal: muskrat, stork, swan; Stone: bloodstone, garnet, moonstone, rose quartz, ruby, spinel ruby, red or pink tourmaline; Plant: costmary, lilac.

Abstract emotions: Venus. **Deep, unexpressed emotions**: Number: 9. **Heartfelt emotions**: Color: pink. **Intense emotions**: Neptune; Animal: macaw; Plant: cannabis; *to release*: Method: breath work; Animal: dolphin; *to lessen over-intense emotions*: Stone: fluorite. **Negative emotions**: Moon; *to banish*: Waning Moon; Charm: brimstone (as incense); Color: blue, pink; Metal:

silver; Stone: blue lace agate, blue aventurine, celestite, chrysocolla, lapis lazuli, peridot, sapphire, blue topaz, blue tourmaline; *to calm*: Stone: lepidolite; *to overcome*: Color: pink; Stone: Apache tear, blue aventurine, pearl, smoky quartz; *to transform into positive emotions*: Plant: juniper berry. **Positive emotions**: *to inspire*: Plant: pine. **Repressed emotions**: *to release*: Plant: fuschia, onion.

Emotional awareness: Plant: dandelion. **Emotional balance**: (See: Balance). **Emotional barriers**: *to remove*: Plant: bleeding heart. **Emotional blocks**: (See: Blockages). **Emotional calm**: (See: Calm). **Emotional chaos**: (See: Chaos). **Emotional clarification**: Plant: rose. **Emotional clarity**: (See: Clarity). **Emotional clearing**: Stone: malachite; Plant: amaryllis, rue. **Emotional comfort**: Stone: rose quartz; Plant: clove. **Emotional commitment**: Number: 2. **Emotional conflict**: *to resolve*: Plant: yerba maté. **Emotional confusion**: *to overcome*: Stone: sodalite. **Emotional connection**: (See: Connection). **Emotional consciousness**: Number: 6. **Emotional control**: Color: orange; Stone: citrine.

Emotional dependence: *to end*: Plant: scarlet pimpernel. **Emotional depth**: Water; Stone: green tourmaline; Plant: tuberose; God: Neptune. **Emotional detachment**: Virgo; Stone: fluorite, sodalite; Plant: lemon, hawthorn, yarrow. **Emotional drainage**: *to protect against:* Stone: obsidian; Plant: garlic, yarrow. **Emotional empowerment**: Stone: azurite, malachite. **Emotional expression**: (See: Expression). **Emotional extremes**: Number: 9. **Emotional fear**: *to unblock*: Plant: red clover. **Emotional freedom**: Plant: snapdragon. **Emotional healing**: (See: Healing). **Emotional intelligence**: (See: Intelligence). **Emotional liberation**: (See: Liberation). **Emotional love**: (See: Love). **Emotional maturity**: Color: deep blue. **Emotional needs**: (See: Need). **Emotional pain**: (See: Pain). **Emotional passion**: Mars/Aries; Color: red, purple. **Emotional peace**: Plant: amber. **Emotional perception**: Water. **Emotional problems**: (See: Problems). **Emotional protection**: (See: Protection). **Emotional purification**: Water; Plant: lotus, water hyacinth.

Emotional recovery: Stone: emerald. **Emotional redirection**: Stone: tourmaline. **Emotional release**: (See: Release). **Emotional renewal**: Plant: calla lily, carnation. **Emotional security**: (See: Security). **Emotional scars**: *to prevent*: Stone: tektite. **Emotional shield**: Stone: pyrite. **Emotional stability**: (See: Stability). **Emotional strength**: (See: Strength). **Emotional stress**: (See: Stress). **Emotional support**: (See: Support). **Emotional tension**: (See: Tension). **Emotional thawing**: Fire; Plant: sandalwood; Stone: rock salt; Plant: nettle. **Emotional transformation**: Stone: obsidian. **Emotional trauma**: (See: Trauma). **Emotional upliftment**: Stone: chrysocolla, chrysoprase, jet, lapis lazuli; Plant: bergamot, hyacinth, rosemary, water hyacinth. **Emotional upset from past life work**: *to protect against:* Plant: eucalyptus.

To: connect body/mind/emotions: Stone: moonstone. **protect emotions**: Animal: snail; Stone: ruby. **understand emotions**: Plant: fuchsia.

Empathy
(See also: Compassion, Sympathy)

Waxing Moon/Water

Charm: heart; Number: 2; Animal: armadillo, koala, otter; Plant: birch, mugwort.

Empathic intuition: North.

Employment
(See also: Career, Work, Workers)

Earth

Color: green; Stone: tigereye; Plant: lucky hand, pecan; God: Bladud, Lu Hsing.

Steady employment: Color: green.

To: change jobs: Stone: aventurine. **get a job**: New Moon; Color: green; Animal: dog, elephant; Stone: lodestone, green lodestone; Charm: magnet; Plant: devil's shoestring, gravel root, heliotrope, High John, laurel, lavender; *in sales*: God: Mercury; *a good job*: Plant: Job's tears. **get a raise**: Plant: gravel root. **have a good start in a new job**: God: Janus. **keep a job**: Plant: devil's shoestring. **transfer from one department, job, or organization to another**: God: Janus.

Empowerment

(See also: Inner Work, Power)

Tool: athame, censer; Method: invocation, visualization; Stone: tigereye; Plant: benzoin, High John, redwood, thistle; Goddess: Hecate, the Morrigan.

Emotional empowerment: Stone: azurite, malachite. **Sexual empowerment**: Stone: lava. **Self-empowerment**: Method: affirmation; Animal: jaguar; Plant: loosestrife; Goddess: Diana, Eve, Lakshmi, Sekhmet.

To empower: amulets: Tool: athame; Plant: dragon's blood, vervain. **curses**: Goddess: Sulis. **spells**: (See: Spells). **to neutralize an empowered object**: Stone: salt.

Enchantment

(See also: Fascination, Illusion, Magick)

Moon

Color: silver, white; Stone: opal, quartz crystal; Animal: cat, hummingbird, swan; Plant: enchanter's nightshade, fern, hawthorn, holly, sorrel leaf, vervain (Herb of Enchantment), willow (Tree of Enchantment); Goddess: Angtia, Carmen, Circe, Don (The Enchanter), Fata-Morgana, Freya, Hecate, Ina, Isis (Great Enchantress, Mighty One of Enchantments), Lady of the Lake, Luna, the Maiden, Morgan le Fay, Morgen, Nimuë, Oshun, Phaedra, Rhiannon, Sekhmet (Lady of Enchantments, Mighty One of Enchantments), Selene, the Telchines (The Enchanters), Vivienne; God: Gwydion, Math ap Mathonwy; Evocation: Caelia, dryads, fairies, Merlin, mermaids, the Rusalki, sirens, Taliesin.

Dangerous enchantment: Fungus: fairy ring of mushrooms or toadstools; Plant: field of bluebells; Evocation: fairies. **Fairy enchantment**: *to release*: Plant: foxglove leaf. **Female enchantment**: Letter: S; Number: 7.

Enchanting music: Charm: flute, harp; Plant: apple bough; Goddess: Hathor; Evocation: fairies. **Enchanted sleep**: Plant: field of bluebells, yew; Evocation: fairies.

Freedom from enchantment: Stone: sapphire. **Plants potent for enchantment**: God: Tellus.

To enchant: locks: Plant: vervain. **weapons**: Goddess: Morgan le Fay.

To: avert enchantment: Charm: fat of a wolf; Stone: diamond. **control a bewitched horse**: Charm: rowan whip. **discover whether a child is bewitched**: Charm: In strict silence place three acorns in a basin of water under the child in its cradle. If they sink, the child is bewitched. **overcome enchantment**: Stone: sapphire; Plant: scarlet pimpernel; *overcome fairy enchantments*: Plant: foxglove; *overcome love enchantments*: Plant: poppy. **protect against enchantment**: Stone: olivine, peridot; Plant: aspen, rowan. **turn an enchantment back upon its maker**: Charm: mirror; Stone: diamond, red jasper; Plant: agrimony (burned), galangal (chewed and spit out), Low John, nettle, nutmeg.

Encouragement

Color: orange, peach, red; Animal: boar; Plant: bergamot, cedar, heather, linden, sycamore, woodruff.

To encourage: action: (See: Action). **beauty**: Stone: red jasper. **calmness**: Animal: buffalo. **fun**: Color: orange. **goodness**: Stone: diamond, yellow jacinth, sapphire. **kinship**: Animal: wolf. **love**: (See: Love). **peace**: (See: Peace). **protection**: Plant: linden. **revelation of secrets**: (See: Secrecy). **a wedding**: (See: Weddings).

Endings

(See also: Banishing, Beginnings Overcoming)

Saturn/Setting Sun/Waning Moon/West/ Winter/Pisces

Number: 3, 13; Plant: boxwood, comfrey, elder, myrrh, rosemary, slippery elm; Goddess: the Crone, the Goddess, Hecate, Jana; God: Janus.

Endings that lead to new beginnings: God: Saturn. **Ending of a cycle/era**: Plant: myrtle bough.

Bitter end: Plant: wormwood. **Gentle endings**: Goddess: Yuki Onne. **Happy endings**: Goddess: Mary (Our Lady of Happy Endings); *a happy ending after a difficult beginning*: Charm: rainbow; Goddess: Caer. **Untimely end**: God: Balder.

To end: an age: Goddess: Badb, Kali; God: Kalki Avatara. **bad luck**: Color: purple; Potion: wassail. **cannibalism**: Goddess: Isis. **codependency**: Goddess: Kali. **chronic illness**: Waning Moon; Plant: violet. **crossed conditions**: (See: Uncrossing). **disease**: Waning Moon. **drought**: Goddess: Atlacoya, Auxesia, Dodola, Juturna, Sao-Ts'ing Niang; God: Ryujin, Varuna. **emotional dependence**: Plant: scarlet pimpernel. **a fallow period**: Color: white, gray; Goddess: the Wave Maidens. **fascination**: (See: Fascination). **fear of the dark**: (See: Darkness).

habits: (See: Habits). **interference in a relationship**: (See: Relationships). **loneliness**: (See: Loneliness). **a losing streak**: Plant: alkanet. **love**: (See: Love). **misfortune**: (See: Fortune). **mood swings**: (See: Mood). **negative patterns**: (See: Negativity). **negative situations**: (See: Situations). **nervousness**: Plant: garlic. **night terrors**: Plant: St. John's Wort. **obsession**: (See: Obsession). **oppression**: Goddess: Durga. **plague**: Goddess: Cailleach. **problems**: (See: Problems). **a relationship**: (See: Relationships). **quarrels**: (See: Quarrels). **strife**: Plant: valerian. **suffering**: Goddess: Kali, Kwan Yin. **war**: Tool: cauldron; Color: white; God: Guan Di. **winter**: Goddess: Uzume; God: Kokopeli.

Endurance

(See also: Longevity, Stamina, Strength)

Mars/Saturn/Earth/Thursday/Taurus

Charm: tet amulet; Animal: alligator, badger, buffalo, carp, crocodile, horse, shark, wolf, wolverine; Stone: garnet, jade, meteor, moldovite, sodalite; Plant: box tree, cactus, ginkgo, gotu kola, hand of Maryam, hickory, licorice, oak, black pepper, pine, rose of Jericho, sycamore, yucca; Goddess: Isis, Pandora; God: Lisa, Thor; Evocation: Boudicca, Chiron, the Fisher King.

Physical endurance: Plant: ginseng. **Spiritual endurance**: Plant: poplar.

Enduring affection: (See: Affection). **Enduring grief**: Plant: red anemone. **Enduring life**: (See: Life).

Endurance in love: Stone: emerald; Plant: gorse, marigold. **Endurance upon one's path**: Color: indigo; Animal: elk. **Endurance in pregnancy**: Animal: elephant; Goddess: Luonnotar. **Endurance during travel**: Animal: monarch butterfly, hummingbird. **Strength through persistence and endurance**: Saturn.

To test endurance: Plant: wormwood.

Energy

(See also: Action, Fatigue, Power, Strength)

Sun/Full Moon/Fire/South/Aries/Leo/Sagittarius

Color: green, red, magenta, orange, silver, yellow; Number: 5; Tool: sword; Charm: red feather, musk; Animal: electric eel, horse, jaguar, lion, tiger; Stone: agate, banded agate, moss agate, red agate, beryl, calcite, orange calcite, carnelian, chalcedony, garnet, hematite, red jasper, kyanite, quartz, rutilated quartz, rhodochrosite, ruby, spinel ruby, selenite, sodalite, sunstone, tigereye, topaz, tourmaline, red tourmaline, volcanic ash, red zircon; Plant: allspice, anemone, bayberry, bergamot, caraway, carnation, cinnamon, cinquefoil, clove, dragon's blood, elder flower, fennel, fir, frankincense, galangal, ginger, ginseng, gorse, gotu kola, hawthorn berry (as incense), holly, horehound, laurel, lemon, lime, lotus, lovage, mango, marigold, mistletoe, nettle, oak, patchouli, peppermint, pine, pineapple, primrose, rose hips, rosemary, sassafras, St. John's Wort, sycamore, thyme, vanilla, verbena, vervain, wisteria, ylang-ylang; Goddess: Anath, Fatimah, Inanna, Kali, Ninshubur, Shakti; God: Ganesha, Luchtaine, Mars, Poseidon, Shiva. Evocation: Orion.

Cosmic energy: Goddess: Durga, Jagadhamba, Jyestha, Parvati, Shakti; *to open to*: Plant: yarrow; Stone: moldovite; *female cosmic energy*: Goddess: Jagad-Yoni, Lilith, Shakti. **Creative energy**: Fire/Aries/Leo/Sagittarius; Animal: hippopotamus; Stone: garnet; Plant: iris, orris root; God: Kephera, Luchtaine, Ptah; *to awaken*: Animal: frog, spider; *to increase*: Stone: garnet; *female creative energy*: Metal: silver; *male creative energy*: Metal: gold. **Destructive energy**: Goddess: Kali. **Divine energy**: Sun; Plant: lotus; Goddess: Shakti; God: Somhlth. **Dragon energy**: Earth/Air/Fire/Water; Animal: basilisk, dragon, komodo dragon; Plant: basil, bistort, dragon's blood, hyssop (as incense). **Earth energy**: Earth; Method: geomancy; Charm: ley line; Color: brown, green, blue; Animal: dragon, mole, turtle; Stone: red jasper, smoky quartz; Plant: cedar, patchouli; *to ground*: Color: black. **Electrical energy**: Charm: lightning; Animal: electric eel, firefly. **Emotional energy**: *to balance*: Stone: moss agate, labradorite, topaz. **Fairy energy**: *to attract*: Plant: foxglove. **Female energy**: (See: Yin). **Fire energy**: Fire; Goddess: Pelé; God: Vulcan; *to balance*: Plant: firethorn. **Healing energy**: Sun/Earth/Scorpio; Animal: dolphin, whale; Stone: rhodonite, sunstone; Plant: catnip, cinnamon, eucalyptus, lady's slipper, sandalwood, black tea; *to channel*: Scorpio. **High energy**: Color: magenta, red. **Kinetic energy**: God: Shiva; **Kundalini energy**: Stone: carnelian, lava; Animal: bobcat, fox, red-tailed hawk, panther, snake; God: Ganesha; *to assist the flow of*: Stone: jet; *to awaken*: Animal: eel; God: Dionysus; *to channel*: Stone: garnet. **Latent energy**: Stone: geode; Plant: lotus. **Love energy**: Stone: beryl, garnet; *to attract*: Color: pink. **Lunar energy**: Moon; Color: silver, white; Number: 3; Stone: moonstone, selenite; Plant: myrrh, queen of the night; God/dess: all Moon deities; *to open to*: Plant: queen of the night. **Magickal energy**: Stone: citrine, garnet, malachite; Plant: carnation, galangal, laurel, nutmeg, orange. **Magnetic energy**: Stone: lodestone, topaz. **Male energy**: (See Yang). **Negative energy**: God: Cythrawl, Set; *to absorb*: Color: black; Charm: egg; Stone: hematite, quartz crystal, salt, tourmaline, black tourmaline; Plant: onion; *to avert*: Color: black; Stone: garnet; Plant: clove, geranium, patchouli, thyme, yarrow; *to banish*: Stone: amethyst; Plant: agrimony, laurel, pine, star anise; *to clear*: Water; Tool: besom, censer; Method:

asperging, smudging, sweeping; Charm: brimstone, egg; Animal: frog; Color: black, gray, silver; Metal: silver; Stone: agate, bloodstone, geode, obsidian, snowflake obsidian, peridot, quartz crystal, smoky quartz, black or green tourmaline; Plant: anise, benzoin, clove, dill, eucalyptus, frankincense, hawthorn, juniper (wood, needles or berries), laurel, myrrh, onion, patchouli, sage, sweetgrass, vervain, vetiver, yarrow; God: Maximon; *to clear after a quarrel*: Plant: copal, eucalyptus; *to clear when strong or resistant*: Charm: brimstone; *to consume*: Color: black; Stone: smoky quartz, tourmaline; Goddess: Tlazolteotl (Eater of Filth); *to counteract*: Color: indigo, gray; *to destroy*: Color: black; Stone: garnet; *to neutralize*: Color: gray; *to protect against*: Color: black; Animal: butterfly; Stone: garnet, pyrite, quartz crystal, selenite; Plant: sunflower, yarrow; *to protect fairies against*: Plant: elder; *to reverse/return to its sender:* Charm: mirror; Stone: red jasper, schist; Plant: pine (See also: Uncrossing); *to transform into positive energy*: (See: Transformation). **Nervous energy**: *to end*: Plant: burdock. **Organic energy**: Earth; Color: brown, green; Stone: agate, moss agate, amber; God: Green Man; Evocation: devas, nature spirits. **Physical energy**: Mars; Color: red; Stone: banded agate, orange calcite, carnelian, garnet, Herkimer diamond, quartz, obsidian, tigereye, red tourmaline; Plant: allspice, camphor, carnation, garlic, geranium, ginseng, lemongrass, orange, pennyroyal, petrified wood, rosemary, saffron; *to assist the flow of*: Stone: blue lace agate, tigereye; Plant: sycamore; *to balance*: Stone: red agate, coral; *to increase*: Stone: rhodochrosite, sunstone, tigereye; Plant: allspice, guarana seed; *to increase during illness*: Stone: sunstone, tigereye; *to restore*: Stone: agate, banded agate, carnelian, moonstone, tigereye, topaz; Plant: carnation. **Positive energy**: Mars/Sun; Tool:

pentacle; Color: white; Animal: oriole; Stone: amber; Plant: dill, sunflower; Goddess: Bast, Isis; God: Balder, Ra; *to attract*: Plant: lemon, wisteria, ylang-ylang; *to stimulate*: Stone: quartz crystal. **Productive energy**: Charm: phallus; Plant: bamboo, all trees. **Projective energy**: Sun, Mars. Tool: wand; Color: orange, red; Metal: aluminum, antimony, brass, gold, mercury, steel, tin; Stone: black, brown or banded agate, amber, Apache tear, aventurine, bloodstone, orange calcite, carnelian, citrine, diamond, flint, fluorite, garnet, hematite, red or leopardskin jasper, meteorite, obsidian, onyx, opal, pyrite, rhodochrosite, ruby, serpentine, staurolite, sunstone, tigereye, topaz, red tourmaline, zircon. **Protective energy**: Earth; Stone: amethyst, Apache tear. **Psychic energy**: Neptune/Full Moon/Water/Pisces/Scorpio/Cancer; Charm: willow water; Animal: swift, turtle; Stone: quartz crystal; Plant: geranium, mugwort, thyme, willow, yerba maté; God: Ganesha; *flow of*: Stone: garnet; *to amplify*: Stone: clear quartz crystal; *to attract*: Color: silver; *energy in psychic work*: Plant: ginseng, yerba maté; *energy for visualization*: Plant: ginseng. **Receptive energy**: Moon/Venus/Water/Earth; Tool: cauldron; Color: black, blue, clear, green, red, white; Metal: copper, lead, mercury, silver; Stone: green, moss, black and white, or blue lace agate, alum, amazonite, amethyst, aquamarine, azurite, beryl, clear or blue or green calcite, chalcedony, chrysoprase, coral, emerald, geode, Goddess rock, jade, brown or green jasper, jet, lapis lazuli, lodestone, malachite, moldovite, moonstone, mother-of-pearl, opal, pearl, peridot, quartz crystal, rose quartz, salt, staurolite, sapphire, pink or blue or green tourmaline, turquoise; Plant: mariposa lily, petrified wood. **Ritual energy**: Stone: garnet; Plant: cinnamon. **Sexual energy**: Sun/Venus/Mars; Method: tantra; Color: red; Charm: musk; Stone:

carnelian, citrine, Herkimer diamond, jade, jasper, obsidian, ruby, sunstone, volcanic ash, zircon, yellow zircon; Plant: banana, bean, caper, black cohosh, damiana, oak, olive, patchouli; Goddess: Anath; God: Ammon; *to awaken*: Plant: patchouli; *to balance*: Stone: smoky quartz; Plant: balm of Gilead; *to increase*: Stone: staurolite, sunstone, zircon, yellow zircon; *to manifest*: Method: tantra; *to restore*: Plant: balsam poplar; *female sexual energy*: *to unblock*: Plant: hibiscus, queen of the night, rose with hibiscus; *male sexual energy*: God: Hermes; *to balance*: Plant: banana; *to restore*: Plant: horny goatweed, yohimbine; *to synchronize*: Plant: balm of Gilead. **Solar energy**: Sun; Color: gold, yellow; Stone: amber, sunstone; Plant: frankincense, heliotrope, sunflower; God/dess: all Sun deities; *to manifest*: God: Kephera. **Spiritual energy**: Stone: celestite, phantom; Plant: yarrow; *to control*: Plant: mandrake; *to ground*: Stone: charoite, snowflake obsidian, onyx; Plant: myrrh. **Subtle energy**: Water; *to become aware of*: Method: meditation; Plant: lady's slipper, myrrh. **Trickster-energy**: Mercury/June/Gemini; Animal: blue jay, coyote, fox, lapwing, monkey, rabbit, raven, wolverine; Plant: High John the Conqueror root; Goddess: Frigg, Gefion, Inanna, Isis, Sheela-na-gig; God: Abarta, Anansi, Angus, Blue jay, the Dagda, Ea, Enki, Eros, Hermes, Italapas, Kokopeli, Konira Viracocha, Krishna, Kutnahin, Legba, Loki, Master Rabbit, Maximon, Maui, Mercury, Michabo (Great Hare), Prometheus, Raven, Tezcatlipoca, Ueuecoyotl (Coyote); Evocation: Br'er Rabbit, High John the Conqueror, leprechauns, the Manitou, Reynard the Fox, Sun Hou-Tzu, Ulysses/Odysseus. **Universal energy**: Stone: clear quartz crystal; *to attract*: Stone: hematite; *to connect with*: Goddess: Isis. **Vibrant energy**: Color: magenta; Plant: ginseng. **Vibrational energy**: Method: chanting; Animal: nightingale, whale, all songbirds. **Water energy**: Water; Animal: duck, fish, whale; God: Neptune, Poseidon.

Energy leaks: *to close*: Animal: whale; *to prevent in the aura*: Stone: labradorite. **Energy shield**: Stone: onyx.

Energy in: **adversity**: Plant: chamomile. **psychic work**: Plant: ginseng, yerba maté.

To: **absorb energy**: Stone: quartz crystal. **attract energy**: Plant: ylang-ylang. **attune to the energy of others**: Stone: turquoise. **balance energy**: Color: blue, purple; Number: 2; Stone: amethyst, barite, chrysocolla, garnet, jet, malachite, blue opal, rhodonite, sapphire, tanzanite, blue or watermelon tourmaline; Plant: cinnamon, eucalyptus, fairy duster, pineapple, ylang-ylang; Goddess: Hanwi; *in the home*: Animal: goldfish; *balance/manage energy flow*: Stone: barite, jet; **bind energy**: Color: black; **center energy**: Plant: pomegranate. **clear energy**: Fire; Plant: fireweed. **collect energy**: Plant: gorse. **conduct energy**: Metal: silver; Stone: amber, jet; *collect scattered energy*: Stone: Apache tear. **conserve energy**: Animal: gyrfalcon; Stone: barite; Plant: spleenwort. **contain energy**: Tool: cord; Charm: magick Circle. **control energy**: Plant: dragon's blood. **focus energy**: Tool: wand; Metal: copper; Stone: amber, crystal point; Plant: Aaron's rod, lady's slipper. **ground energy**: Earth; Stone: carnelian, fluorite; Plant: angelica; *ground Earth energy*: Color: black; Stone: onyx, black opal. **increase energy**: Stone: banded agate, amber, fossil, ruby, sunstone; Plant: betel nut, carnation, coca, ephedra, garlic, ginkgo, grapefruit, horehound; Goddess: Hebe; *of stones*: Stone: phenacite. **manifest energy**: Stone: hematite, obsidian, sugilite; Plant: geranium; *as physical movement*: Stone: celestite; God: Skan. **protect one's energy**: Plant: tuberose, violet. **raise energy**: Color: pink; Plant: cinnamon. **release energy**:

Stone: lava, volcanic rock; Plant: grass of Parnassus. **renew/restore energy**: Fire; Stone: agate, moss agate; Plant: asarabacca, carnation, damiana, grapefruit, marigold, rosemary, snowdrop, spearmint, thyme, vanilla; *the flow of energy*: Stone: manganite. **send energy**: Stone: moss agate, beryl, quartz crystal. **stimulate energy**: Stone: bloodstone; Plant: carnation. **store energy**: Tool: cord; Method: knot magick; Animal: bear, magpie, all hibernating mammals; Stone: crystal; Plant: gorse, lady's slipper. **strengthen energy**: Plant: gum tragacanth, yarrow. **synthesize energy**: Plant: laurel. **transform energy**: Charm: volcano; Stone: amethyst, obsidian; Plant: geranium; *into matter*: Plant: geranium; *transform substance into energy*: Goddess: Annapurna; *transform negative energy into positive energy*: Color: purple; Stone: amber, hawk's eye, green tourmaline, unakite, zoisite; Plant: amber, honesty. **unblock energy**: Metal: zinc; Stone: Herkimer diamond, zincite; Plant: horsetail, orchid, vanilla. **understand energy**: Animal: mole. **use energy to fight**: Mars. **use energy wisely**: Animal: albatross, elk, spider. **work with energy**: Stone: fluorite; Goddess: Ignirtoq, Ninsubur; *with the energies of light and darkness*: (See: Light).

Enlightenment
(See also: Illumination, Wisdom)

Sun

Tool: scourge; Method: meditation, yoga; Color: white, purple; Animal: dragon, owl; Stone: amethyst; Plant: bodhi tree, lotus, wisteria; Goddess: Badb, Bast, Diana, Eve, Idunn, Kwan Yin, Mary, Sekhmet (Enlightener), Sarasvati, Tara, Vidya-Lakshmi; God: Fugen Bosatsu, Osiris; Evocation: the Buddha.

Spiritual enlightenment: Color: white; God: Hurukan. **Power of enlightenment**: Goddess: Sapas.

To enlighten: **the subconscious**: Stone: black star sapphire. **a violent person**: Goddess: Diana.

To: protect the enlightened: Evocation: Ista Devata. **speed enlightenment**: Plant: lotus.

Enmity
(See also: Battle, Discord, Quarrels, War)

Mars/Leo

Color: black; Animal: snake; Goddess: Inanna.

Omen of an enemy: Animal: toad. **Strength against enemies**: Stone: diamond. **Success in court when being persecuted by an enemy**: Plant: mustard seed, pine nut or cone, tobacco. **Victory over enemies**: Stone: amethyst.

To: avert enemies: Color: dark gray; Stone: green beryl. **be without enemies**: Goddess: Kwan Yin. **bind enemies**: Color: black. **calm fears of enemies**: Stone: bloodstone. **counter an enemy**: Color: black; Charm: Four Thieves Vinegar, van van; Stone: sulfur; Plant: chicory, comfrey, mullein, black mustard seed, safflower, witch grass, wormwood; Goddess: Medb. **defeat enemies**: Goddess: Anath. **destroy enemies**: Plant: safflower; Goddess: Kali, Sekhmet (The Eye of Ra Who Burns the Enemy), Ushas; *instant destruction of enemies*: God: Sobek. **dominate enemies**: Plant: poppy seed. **drive enemies away**: Color: red; Charm: Go Away Powder, Hot Foot Powder; Plant: bittersweet, knotweed; God: Maximon. **earn the enmity of fairies**: Plant: primrose (if neglected and allowed to die). **escape enemies**: Plant: vervain. **frighten enemies**: Animal: boar; Stone: banded red agate; Goddess: Badb. **locate an enemy**: God: Ochosi (Tracker of Enemies). **make lightning strike an enemy**: God: Shango. **make trouble for enemies**: Plant: Guinea pepper (on doorstep). **outwit enemies**: Animal: fox, wolf. **overcome enemies**: Tuesday; Charm: labrys; Animal: mole; Stone: bloodstone, diamond (on left hand or arm), fossil ammonite, salt, sapphire, sulfur; Plant: celandine, Guinea pepper, galangal, High John; Goddess: Aerten, Andraste, Diana, Ekajata, Luaths Lurgann, Macha, Medb, the Morrigan, Rhiannon, Sekhmet (She Who Overcomes All Enemies), Sin, Ugra-Tara; God: Baal, Finn Mac Cool, Ptah; Evocation: St. Barbara. **pacify enemies**: Stone: sapphire. **protect against enemies**: Charm: eye of Horus; Animal: cat, cobra; Stone: lodestone; Plant: bat nut; God: Anhur, Onuris, Thor; *protect the state/government officials against enemies*: Evocation: Emperor Kuan. **protect against enmity**: Charm: open eye, witch's bottle. **punish enemies**: Goddess: Ushas. **release enmity**: Color: black. **stand up to enemies**: Stone: diamond. **turn an enemy into a friend**: Plant: tonka bean. **weaken enemies**: Stone: green beryl; Plant: poppy seed; Goddess: Medb.

Enjoyment
(See: Pleasure)

Enthusiasm
(See: Zeal)

Envy
(See also: Jealousy)

Moon/North

Color: green; Plant: African marigold, briar, blackberry, crane's bill; Goddess: Aoife, Prosperine; God: Phthonus, Poseidon, Set; Evocation: Aglaurus.

Fatal envy: *to protect against*: Plant: garlic.

Envious demons: *to protect against*: Charm: colored rice. **Envious thoughts**: *to stop*: Stone: agate.

To: avert envy: Plant: garlic; Goddess: Tara; *avert envious people*: Plant: garlic (hung over doorway). **banish envy**: Stone: chrysoprase. **lessen envy**: Plant: holly. **protect against envy**: Color: black; Stone: carnelian, sapphire; Plant: garlic (hung in home or boat); God: Maximon. **release envy**: Stone: carnelian.

Equilibrium
(See: Balance)

Escape
(See also: Freedom, Liberation)

Air

Method: cloaking, shapeshifting; Animal: orangutan; Plant: celandine, ephedra, pine cone; Goddess: Amaterasu, Greine; God: Proteus, Väinämöinen.

To escape: a bad marriage: (See: Marriage). **confinement**: Goddess: Branwen, Cliodna, Isis. **the cycle of reincarnation**: Evocation: the Buddha. **danger**: Goddess: Ishtar. **enemies**: Plant: vervain. **a natural disaster**: Evocation: Dwyvach, Noah, Utnapishtim. **a negative situation**: Plant: celandine, ephedra. **notice**: Animal: chameleon, sandpiper, walking stick, wolf. **poverty**: Goddess: Acca Larentia. **religious persecution**: Goddess: Dahut. **sexual assault**: (See: Sex: sex crimes). **a stalker**: Evocation: Arethusa. **your body**: Color: purple; Animal: eagle (See also: The Astral: astral projection).

Escapism
Number: 7. **To overcome escapism**: Plant: birch.

Ethics
Sun

Goddess: Durga, Themis; God: Mithras, Obatala, Ogun.

Work ethic: Animal: ant, beaver, bee.

Ethical conduct: Goddess: Kwan Yin; God: Sharma, Mithras, Varuna. **Ethical guidance**: God: Obatala; Evocation: ancestors. **Ethical knowledge**: God: Al Da'ya.

To: protect against unethical dealings: God: Zulum. **understand ethics**: Animal: crow, puma.

Evil

(See also: Negativity)

Number: 2, 7; Animal: dragon, shrew; Plant: blackthorn, parsley, black pepper, valerian; Goddess: Ate, Dunawali, Itzpapalotl, Kali, Louhi, Nirriti, Tiamat; God: Ahriman (Prince of Darkness), Apep (Evil-Doer), Bolverk (Evil-Doer), Chernobog (The Black God), Erra, Evening Star, Gunab, Guruhi, Kava, Loki, Malsum, Mot (Prince Evil), Ordog, Set, Sousson-Pannan, Tutu (Doubly Evil One), Xolotl, Zu; Evocation: Cacus (The Evil One), frost giants, Hahgwehdaetgh, Ildabaoth, Ocasta, the Rakshasa, Satan, Tau, Towiscara, Uar (The Cruel).

Evil circumstances: *to clear*: Plant: gravel root. **Evil creatures**: *to protect against*: Plant: ash. **Evil deeds**: *to protect against*: Plant: vervain, dill, trefoil and St. John's Wort (dried or dried powder to be mixed together and used as a charm, or fresh herbs to be plaited or mixed together and used as a charm). **Evil that comes in darkness**: God: Ah Kin. **Evildoers**: *to destroy*: God: Anu, Kalki; *to punish*: Goddess: the Erinyes, Sekhmet; God: Byelobog, Perun, Pu'gu, Vishnu. **Evil entities**: *to banish*: Method: asperging, smudging; Charm: Florida Water, rosewater; Plant: dragon's blood, elder, fumitory, pine; *to destroy*: God: Hino; *to protect against*: Plant: ash, basil (as incense), caraway, clove, eye of Satan, fern frond (burned), mint (as incense). **Evil eye**:

Stone: opal; God: Balor of the Evil Eye; *to avert*: Color: bright blue; Charm: blue bead, coral hand, coral horn, hamsa hand, right hand print, hand of Fatimah, Eye of Horus; Plant: aniseed, eye of Satan, hyssop (in the bath), periwinkle, rue, sage; *to banish*: Plant: basil; *to detect*: Animal: rabbit, turkey; *to protect against*: Color: bright blue, red; Charm: blue beads, cowrie shell, hamsa hand, Hand of Fatimah, Eye of Horus, porcupine quill, a quill filled with mercury (sealed at both ends and bound to the body—dangerously toxic, strongly advised against); Stone: amethyst, chalcedony, chiastolite, coral, malachite, marble, tigereye; Plant: anise, ash key, eye of Satan, figwort, garlic, rue, sage, vervain, last sheaf of harvested grain (bound with bamboo and hung up); God: Balor of the Evil Eye. **Evil forces**: (See: Forces). **Evil that comes in darkness**: *to protect against*: God: Ah Kin. **Evil gossip**: *to protect against*: Stone: beryl. **Evil human handiwork**: *to avert*: Plant: cinquefoil. **Evil influences**: Fungus: toadstool; *to banish*: Plant: white clover; *to counteract*: Plant: myrrh; *to protect against*: Plant: fern (collected at midnight on Beltane eve), hawthorn, meadowsweet, periwinkle, rosemary, St. John's Wort; Goddess: Bast; *to protect the home from*: Plant: asphodel (planted near gate), meadowsweet garland (hung indoors). **Evil intentions of others**: *to protect against*: Plant: cedar. **Evil omens**: *to remove threats from*: Goddess: Ereshkigal. **Evil people**: (See: People). **Evil spells**: (See: Hexes). **Evil spirits**: (See: Spirits). **Evil thoughts**: (See: Thoughts).

Defense against evil: Plant: dill, peony wood, St. John's Wort, trefoil, vervain; God: Shango. **knowledge of evil**: Plant: apple, apricot, fig. **power over evil**: Goddess: Isis.

To: **absorb evil**: Charm: egg; Animal: cat; Stone: turquoise (worn); Plant: onion, pumpkin. **avert evil**: Saturday; Color: black, purple; Charm: jade crab, silver crescent, scarab; Stone: jet; Plant: angelica (sprinkled at the four corners), basil, bat nut, boldo leaf, chili powder (burned), cumin seed, devil's shoestring, elder leaves (hung over the door, especially at Beltane), ephedra, frankincense, garlic (burned, especially on Fridays), hemlock (grown near house), honeysuckle, laurel, lilac, myrrh, nettle, patchouli, pomegranate tree (grown near entrance), rosemary, vervain, willow, yew; Goddess: Alcyone (The Princess Who Averts Evil), Hecate, Sekhmet (The One Before Whom Evil Trembles); God: Bes, Khonsu, Osiris. **banish evil**: Waning Moon; Color: black, purple; Tool: besom, censer, sistrum; Method: asperging, smudging, sweeping; Stone: emerald; Plant: angelica, anise leaves, clove, comfrey, dragon's blood, fern fronds (burned), garlic, gravel root, mistletoe, myrrh, black peppercorns; Goddess: Hathor; *charms that banish evil*: God: Tuku. **battle evil**: Color: red; Plant: fennel stalk; Goddess: Bast, Inanna; God: Perun, Ra, Väinämöinen; Evocation: Bechuille. **bind evil**: Plant: angelica, mandrake. **clear evil**: Color: white; Tool: besom; Charm: brimstone (burned), egg (to absorb it, then be discarded or offered to Hecate at a crossroad); Stone: meteorite, quartz crystal; Plant: acacia, garlic, gum arabic, hyssop, wild olive, onion, pennyroyal (sprinkled), black pepper, peppermint, spikenard; Goddess: Kupala. **counteract evil**: Plant: scarlet pimpernel. **destroy evil**: Goddess: Durga, Isis; God: Anu, Glooskap, Nayenezgani, Rama, Sin, Sobek, Tobadzistsini. **detect evil**: Sun; Stone: emerald, ruby; Plant: clover; God: Sin. **draw off evil**: Stone: turquoise (worn). **free from evil**: Color: black. **frighten evil away**: Tool: rattle; Charm: mask; God: Bes. **hide from evil**: Plant: pine; Goddess: Buto. **neutralize evil**: Color: gray; Stone: salt (thrown into fire). **oppose evil**: God: Mithras. **overcome evil**: Plant: mandrake root; God: Enki, Ra. **prevent evil from entering the house**: (See: The Home). **protect against evil**: Color: white; Charm: ambergris; Animal: heron; Charm: broom tea (asperged); Stone: alum, coral, jet, lodestone, peridot, tigereye, tourmaline; Plant: amber, angelica, balm of Gilead, basil, holy basil, bat nut, birch, blackberry (leaf or fruit), burdock root, carob, cascara sagrada, daffodil, devil's shoestring, elder, frankincense, garlic, ginger, ginseng root, gum arabic, hemlock, juniper, laurel, mistletoe, mullein, myrrh, wild olive, peony, pomegranate tree, rosemary, St. John's Wort, vervain, willow; Goddess: Alcyone, Auchimolgen, Bast, T'ao Hua Hsiennui; God: Bes, Indra, Jizo Bosatsu, Osiris Un-neffer; *protect babies from evil*: (See: Babies); *protect a car from evil*: Plant: eye of Satan (in trunk), plantain (hung in car); *protect cattle from evil*: Plant: black hellebore (waved over them); *from the evil eye*: Plant: woody nightshade; *protect a house from evil*: Charm: broom tea (asperged); Plant: birch tree (planted in the yard), white daffodils (planted in the yard), yellow daffodils (grown indoors), elder (grown near entrance or planted as a hedge around property), ferns (grown near house), hemlock (planted in the yard), holly (grown in the yard), ivy (grown on or near house), pomegranate tree (planted near the door), yucca; God: Men Shen; *evil magick/spells/witchcraft*: (See: Hexes); *evil psychic forces*: Plant: rowan; Evocation: Towiscara. **punish evil**: Goddess: the Erinyes, Sekhmet; God: Byelobog, Glooskap, Perun, Pu'gu, Vishnu. **purify evil**: Charm: brimstone (as incense), egg (to absorb it, then be discarded or left at a crossroad as an offering to Hecate); Stone: quartz crystal, cluster of crystals; Plant: acacia, angelica, gum arabic, camphor, hawthorn, laurel, onion, yucca root. **release evil**: Plant: myrrh. **remove evil**: Goddess: Kupala; *from the home*: Plant: pennyroyal (strewn in the house). **return evil to its sender/source**: Crescent Moon; Charm: silver crescent, black and white feather, mirror; Stone: black and white stone; Plant: Low John, nettle, blackberry leaf, black peppercorn. **unite against evil**: Plant: scarlet verbena.

Exams

(See: Tests)

Exhaustion

(See: Fatigue)

Exorcism

(See: Banishing)

Expression

(See also: Communication, Eloquence, Speech)

Number: 3; Color: blue; Animal: ape, monkey; Stone: lapis lazuli, blue tourmaline; Plant: cosmos, snapdragon, sunflower.

Clear expression: Plant: cosmos, devil's club, lotus, violet; Goddess: Sarasvati. **Creative expression**: Color: blue; Animal: black widow spider; Stone: agate, amazonite, howlite, ruby. Plant: holy thorn, iris, snapdragon; *to unblock*: Plant: holy thorn, spikenard, sunflower. **Emotional expression**: Water/Cancer/Scorpio/Pisces; Color: orange; Animal: horned toad; Plant: fir, Japanese maple, pine, snapdragon, sunflower; *emotions that are deeply felt but not expressed*: Number: 9. **Full expression**: Plant: laurel. **Self-expression**: Color: aqua, orange; Stone: blue lace agate, celestite, chrysocolla, lapis lazuli; Plant: broom, citronella, orchid, moss, sunflower; *courage in*: Stone: amazonite; *to open*: Stone: blue lace agate. **Sexual expression**: Plant: apple. **spiritual expression**: Plant: fir, laurel, pine, sunflower.

Authenticity of expression: Color: blue. **Strength of expression**: Stone: chrysocolla. Goddess: Isis.

To express: grief: (See: Grief). **joy**: Method: dance; Plant: almond, sunflower. **yourself**: *calmly*: Plant: snapdragon; *peacefully*: Stone: blue lace agate; *strongly*: Plant: sunflower.

Chapter 6

Fairies

Air/Earth

Color: green, yellow; Charm: dew from toadstools in fairy rings, honey; Animal: frog, mouse, pig, rabbit, seal, snake; Stone: emerald, quartz crystal, staurolite; Potion: elderberry wine, milk; Fungus: all toadstools, but especially "fairy rings" of toadstools; Plant: apple bark (burned), blackberry, blackthorn, bluebell, cowslip, daisy, fairy flax, foxglove, hawthorn, hazel, pink hollyhock, laurel, mistletoe, ancient hollow oak trees, primrose, rose petals, rosemary, rue, wild thyme, wood sorrel, vervain, violet, yarrow; Goddess: Aeval, Aine, Airmid, Albina, the Apsaras, Caer, Cyhiraeth, Queen of Elphame, Eri, Feithline, Finnine, Greine, Maeve, Morgan le Fay, the Morrigan, Rodenica, Sin, Waldmichen; God: Addanc, Angus, Credne, the Dagda, Leshy, Shoney, Wayland (Prince of Fairies); Evocation: Donagh, dryads, Finvarra, Gwynn ap Nudd (King of the Fairies), hamadryads, Heliconian, Iubdan of the Faylinn, Queen Mab, Melia, Mustard-seed, Oberon, Puck, Shiri Bagerthum (King of the Fairies), the sidhe, Summer, Titania, Vila.

Fairy blessings: (See: Blessings). **Fairy dreams**: (See: Dreams). **Fairy enchantment**: *to release*: Plant: foxglove leaf. **Fairy Magic**: (See: Magick). **Fairy realm**: *to guard the entryway to*: Animal: turtle. **Fairy voices**: Air; Plant: willow (the sound of wind in).

To: **attract fairies**: Charm: honey, milk, bright shiny objects; Stone: crystals, emerald, jade, peridot; Fungus: toadstool; Plant: alder, ambrosia, apple tree (bark or fruit peel), ash, aster, birch, blackberry, blackthorn, bluebell, butterfly bush, butterfly weed, cinquefoil, clover, cosmos, cowslip, daisy, Shasta daisy, elder, elderberries (as incense), elecampane, fern, foxglove, hawthorn (tree, bark, berries or blossoms), hazel, heather, holly berries, hollyhock, horsemint, lavender, lilac, lily of the valley, oak, pansy, petunia, primrose, rose, rosemary, rowan, St. John's Wort, strawberry, thyme (sprinkled on door and window sills), verbena, vervain, willow, yarrow, zinnia; *fairy energy*: Plant: foxglove; *fairy gifts*: Plant: elecampane root, primrose (spray or garland over the door), rose petals, rowan (planted near the house). **avert fairies**: Charm: bells, gong, wind chimes; Metal: iron; Plant: morning glory, trailing pearlwort, rue, tomato; *avert malicious fairies*: Plant: rosemary. **bar fairies**: Metal: iron; Plant: primrose petals (scattered outside the door). **be abducted by fairies**: Plant: hawthorn. **be protected by fairies**: Plant: rowan (planted near the house). **break fairy spells**: Plant: four leaf clover. **dream of fairies**: Plant: peony; *fairyland*: Plant: elder (slept beneath). **earn the enmity of fairies**: Plant: primrose (if neglected and allowed to die). **enter the fairy realm**: God: Angus. **evoke fairies**: Plant: daffodil. **find fairy gold/treasures**: Plant: cowslip, fern seed, forget-me-not. **get help from fairies**: Plant: fairy wand, hazelnut. **make contact with fairies**: Plant: daffodil; Goddess: Elphame, Sionnan; Evocation: MacKay. **open to fairies/fairy magic, gifts, treasure**: Plant: forget-me-not, primrose. **overcome fairy magic**: Plant: four leaf clover, daisy; *overcome fairy enchantments*: Plant: foxglove. **prevent abduction by fairies**: Plant: ash berry, daisy, mistletoe, plantain. **protect fairies**: Plant: elder. **protect against fairies**: Metal: iron, steel; Plant: alder, ash, four leaf clover, forget-me-not, trailing pearlwort, St. John's Wort; *protect babies from fairies*: Plant: ash berries (in the crib), plantain; *protect cattle from fairies*: Plant: rowan (as incense); *protect children from fairies*: (See: Children); *protect the family from fairies*: Plant: trailing pearlwort (grown or placed near the door). **see fairies**: Charm: sleep on a fairy mound; Potion: elderberry wine; Plant: four leaf clover, harebell, primrose, wild thyme; seven grains of wheat with a four leaf clover; groves of oak, ash and hawthorn trees; Goddess: Aine. **work with fairies**: Plant: daisy, grapevine, mandrake; *with sea fairies*: Goddess: Domnu, Muireartach.

⬚airness

Air

Goddess: Genetaska, Ma'at; God: Obatala, Shango.

Fair dealing: Goddess: Fides, Inanna; God: Aequitas. **Fair fight**: God: Yudistira. **Fair judge**: Plant: patchouli, sandalwood. **Fair judgment/decision**: (See: Judgment). **Fair justice**: Goddess: Calladice. **Fair trial**: God: Obatala. **Fair victory**: God: Ares.

Fairness in: contracts: Goddess: Aequitas. **negotiations**: Goddess: Aequitas.

Unfairness

God: Plutos; Plant: briar rose.

Unfair situations: (See: Situations). **Unfair treatment**: God: Pluto. **To: punish unfairness**: God: Obatala, Zeus. **escape an unfair situation**: Plant: celandine.

⬚aith

Fire/South

Color: green, yellow; Animal: painted turtle; Number: 7; Stone: diamond, garnet, pearl, sapphire; Plant: apple, iris, white mustard seed; Goddess: Pistis Sophia, Shekinah, Sraddha; God: Hanuman.

Inner faith: Color: green.

To: inspire faith: Stone: amazonite. **marry outside your faith**: Goddess: Eri. **restore faith**: Stone: rose quartz; Plant: thistle; God: Shiva; *in yourself*: Plant: heather. **show faith in the future**: Charm: plant a tree.

⬚aithlessness

Number: 7; Animal: owl; Stone: opal.

⬚alsehood

(See: Deceit)

⬚ame

Color: silver; Stone: heliotrope, green beryl; Plant: crown of amaranth flowers, trumpet flower; Goddess: Ayauhteotl, Fama, Lakshmi, Pheme, Ushas; God: Lu Pan, Zeus; Evocation: Cuchulain.

Good fame: Plant: apple blossom; Goddess: Tyche. **Literary fame**: Animal: carp.

⬚amily

(See also: The Home)

Moon/Monday/Cancer

Number: 6; Animal: boar, cat, dog; Goddess: Disani, Enekpe, Hestia, Luaths Lurgann, Nonadieve; God: Rod, Semargl.

Fruitful family: Plant: olive. **Happy family**: Plant: basil; Goddess: Sif. **Healthy family**: Goddess: Jara. **Peaceful family**: Plant: rose; Goddess: Chantico. **Royal family**: Stone: lapis lazuli; *life and vitality of a royal family*: God: Telepinu; *to protect the British royal family*: God: Bran. **Secure family**: Plant: olive. **Strong family**: Animal: lion; Plant: bloodroot.

Family farms: Goddess: Zeme Pati. **Family harmony**: Goddess: Verplace. **Family issues**: *to work on*: Animal: baboon. **Family life**: Goddess: Hestia, Vesta; *to balance work and*: Plant: pomegranate; *to protect*: Goddess: Cardea. **Family line**: God: Rod. **Family loyalty**: Goddess: Airmid, the Furies. **Family luck**: (See: Luck). **Family matters**: Number: 6; *help in family matters*: Plant: Low John. **Family omens**: (See: Omens). **Family/hereditary pattern**: *to change*: Plant: morning glory. **Family problems**: *to end*: Plant: pennyroyal. **Family prosperity**: (See: Prosperity). **Family quarrels**: (See: Quarrels) **Family records/history**: Goddess: Saga. **Family relations**: Stone: moonstone; *good family relations*: Goddess: Verplace; *to strengthen*: Plant: bloodroot. **Family ties**: Animal: gibbon; Goddess: Gwendydd. **Family union/unity/togetherness**: (See: Union). **Family values**: Animal: bee, grosbeak, wolf, all hive and pack animals. **Family vitality**: Goddess: Frigg.

For: support when your family objects to your choice of mate: Goddess: Lofn. **the well-being of the family**: Goddess: Frigg; God: the Penates.

To: avert harmful people from the family: Plant: marjoram. **deal with stress of family**: Plant: rose. **found a family**: Goddess: Chien-Ti. **learn respect for family members**: Plant: bloodroot. **meet family responsibilities**: Goddess: Pietas. **obtain fairy blessings for the family**: Plant: rowan tree (in yard or garden). **protect the family**: Animal: boar, dog, monkey, wolf; Plant: motherwort; Goddess: the Afliae, the Ahinehiae, the Ahueccaniae, the Alaferhviae, the Alagabiabus, the Alaisiagae, the Albiahenae, Cardea, Disani, the Euthungae, the Friagabiae, the Gavasiae, the Hamavehae, the Lanehiae, the Maluisae, the Marsacae, the Seubis, the Xulsigiae; God: Bes, Kuladevata, Lar, Nang Lha, the Penates, Rama, Tsao-chü; *from fairies*: Plant: trailing pearlwort (grown or placed near the door).

Farming
(See: Agriculture)

Fascination
(See also: Enchantment, Illusion, Obsession)

Moon

Stone: jacinth; Plant: carnation, fern, moonwort, orange rose; Goddess: Ashtaroth, Diana; Evocation: fairies.

To: destroy fascination: Stone: carnelian. **end fascination**: Charm: split an oak and pass yourself through it; *in children*: Charm: sweep the face gently with a pine bough. **protect against fascination**: Stone: beryl, carnelian, coral; Plant: horehound, hyssop, lily, madwort (hung up in the house), kernel of the fruit of a palm tree.

Fate
(See: Destiny)

Fatigue
(See also: Energy, Strength)

Mental fatigue: *to overcome*: Plant: eucalyptus, ginseng, black pepper, peppermint, blue vervain. **Physical fatigue**: *to overcome*: Plant: ginseng, lemon, paprika, clary sage, thyme. **Chronic fatigue syndrome**: (See: Diseases/Disorders).

To: banish fatigue: Plant: rosemary. **protect against fatigue**: Plant: garlic, mugwort (worn), pennyroyal (in shoe), southernwood, tarragon. **reduce/relieve fatigue**: Color: orange, red; Stone: moss agate, golden beryl, smoky quartz, tourmaline; Plant: basil, calamus, chestnut, coca leaf, dong quai, ephedra, eucalyptus, evening primrose, geranium, guarana seed, gum tragacanth, lavender, lemon, lemongrass, mercury, oats, pansy (in bath), peppermint, pulsatilla, rosemary, rush, sage, clary sage, sorrel, spearmint, sycamore, tea tree, valerian, yerba maté. **release fatigue**: Plant: marjoram.

Favor

(See also: Affection)

Jupiter

Animal: kite; Plant: chicory, crown of amaranth flowers; Goddess: Concordia, Hecate, the Morrigan.

Bridal favor: Plant: ivy-leaved geranium, meadowsweet. **Divine favor**: Goddess: Anumati. **Judicial favor**: Stone: hematite; Plant: galangal. **Popular favor**: Plant: rock rose. **Royal favor**: Stone: hematite, sapphire, topaz.

Favorable legal judgment: Stone: garnet. **Favorable winds**: Plant: dandelion (buried or planted at NW corner of the house).

To gain favor: in battle: Goddess: Andraste. **of the one you love**: Goddess: Benzaiten.

To gain favor with: those in authority/power: Stone: agate, hematite; *princes*: Stone: sapphire, topaz. **Cybele**: Stone: jet (worn). **fertility and vegetation deities**: Color: green; Stone: moss agate. **the Goddess of Love**: Plant: myrtle. **Saule**: Animal: green snake.

Favors

Stone: lodestone; Plant: chicory, sycamore; Goddess: Isis (The One Whose Favors are Great); God: Maximon, Nergal.

For: charm and elegance when asking a favor of authority: Plant: cinquefoil. **women to gain favors**: Goddess: Kwan Yin.

To: attract favors: Stone: tourmaline. **gain favors**: Plant: cinquefoil; *from Allat*: Stone: large white granite rock (circled naked, while invoking her); *from Isis*: Stone: pearl (worn); *from powerful people*: Stone: agate (worn or carried); Plant: chicory (juice rubbed on body—patch test on skin first, and instead use to anoint candles if you are allergic).

Fear/s

(See also: Anxiety, Courage)

Mercury/Water

Color: black; Number: 7; Animal: rabbit; Goddess: Angerona, the Erinyes, Kali, Pallor, Pavor; God: Deimos, Phobos, Rakh, Svarog (Fear Lord).

Deepest fears: *to face*: Plant: false hellebore, spikenard; Goddess: Kupala. **Emotional fear**: *to unblock*: Plant: red clover. **Foolish fears**: *to overcome*: Stone: emerald. **Innermost fears**: *to confront*: Goddess: Kupala. **Subconscious/unconscious fears**: *to relieve*: Stone: opal; *to unblock*: Stone: citrine.

Fear of: the dark: (See: Darkness). **change**: Number: 5. **enemies**: *to calm*: Stone: bloodstone.

To: avert fear: Stone: citrine, chrysocolla, pearl, sapphire; Plant: nettle with yarrow. **banish fear**: Stone: amazonite, chalcedony, emerald; Goddess: Bhayanashini (Remover of Fear), Kwan Yin; *from children*: Stone: lapis lazuli (worn). **calm fear/s**: Stone: amethyst; Plant: frankincense, lavender, scullcap. **calmly face fear**: Plant: red clover. **clear fear**: Stone: amazonite, bloodstone, geode; Goddess: Durga, Kali. **face fear**: Animal: lizard. Plant: red clover, false hellebore. **overcome fears**: Color: brown, indigo, red, yellow; Animal: crayfish; Stone: agate, amazonite, amber, aquamarine, green calcite, chalcedony, charoite, citrine (worn at night), diamond, emerald, jasper, jet, obsidian, peridot, ruby, rutilated quartz, sodalite; Plant: allspice, aspen, cinnamon, dragon's gall, black pepper, primrose, sage, scorpion weed, thistle, wild garlic, wolfsbane, yarrow; Goddess: Dakshina Kalika, Durga (Remover of Fear), Juno, Kali, Kwan Yin, Green Tara; *overcome fearfulness*: Animal: rabbit; Stone: sunstone.

To overcome fear of: **abandonment**: Plant: raspberry. **aging**: Plant: mallow; God: Govannon. **the dark**: Animal: mole; Plant: moss. **death/dying**: (See: Death). **deep meditation**: Stone: azurite, malachite. **drowning**: Animal: seal. **failure**: Plant: laurel. **freedom**: Color: orange; Plant: moss. **loss**: Plant: sumach; *losing control*: (See: Control). **obscurity**: Plant: St. John's Wort. **poverty**: Plant: harebell. **public speaking**: Stone: carnelian; Plant: trumpet vine. **rejection**: Plant: holy thorn. **responsibility**: Animal: mountain lion. **risk**: Plant: laurel. **touch**: Plant: avocado. **the unknown**: Animal: eagle; Stone: black coral.

To: **protect against fear/s**: Stone: carnelian, coral, sapphire; Plant: daffodil root (carried at night), nettles with yarrow; Goddess: Tara. **provoke fear**: Night; Charm: bells, mask, rattle; Animal: alligator, crocodile, owl, polar bear, rattlesnake, shark; Stone: banded red agate, Apache tear, onyx with white veins; Plant: centaury; Goddess: Auchimolgen, Coatlicue, Kali, Matangi, Scathach (She Who Strikes Fear), Sekhmet

(She Who Inspires Great Fear); God: South Star; Evocation: the Rakshasa. **strike enemies with fear**: Stone: banded red agate; Goddess: Badb. **release fear**: Animal: bat; Stone: carnelian, emerald; Plant: enchanter's nightshade, fig, forget-me-not, wild garlic, raspberry leaf. **relieve/diminish fear**: Water; Stone: ammonite fossil, amazonite, beryl, chrysocolla, jasper, smoky quartz, sapphire, sodalite, tiger's eye, topaz, tourmaline; Plant: fig, rose geranium, thistle. **unblock fear**: Stone: opal; Plant: fig.

Fearlessness

Aries/Sagittarius

Animal: blue jay, butterfly, crow, eagle, polar bear, skunk; Plant: morning glory; Goddess: Brigantia, Ishtar, Oya; God: Shiva. **Fearlessness in hunting**: Goddess: Banka-Mundi. **Freedom from fears**: Plant: St. John's Wort.

Femininity

(See: Yin)

Fertility

(See also: Conception, Growth, Pregnancy)

Venus/Sun/Moon/Full Moon/Earth/Water/South/Spring/Friday

Tool: broomstick, cauldron, rattle; Color: dark blue, green, emerald green, spring green, red; Charm: babies, cornucopia, earth dug up by the horns of a bull or a wild boar, earth from a prostitute's doorway, fish, flowers, grain, harvest basket, menstrual blood, musk, poppet of the mummified Osiris, semen, yoni; Number: 7, 8; Animal: bluebird, boar, carp, cattle, dove, dragon, fish, frog, goat, horse, silkmoth, parrot, pig, pigeon, snake, turtle; Stone: amazonite, amethyst, carnelian, emerald, garnet, jade, green jasper, geode, malachite, onyx, rose quartz, zoisite; Potion: coconut milk; Fungus: fly agaric; Oil: palmarosa; Plant: acorns (especially those gathered at night), alfalfa, almond, aniseed, apple, banana, basil, bistort, bodhi tree, cabbage, carnation, carrot seed, celery seed, chickweed, coconut, coriander, cuckoo flower, cucumber, cyclamen, daffodil, date palm, yellow dock, fennel, fig, gentian, geranium, rose geranium, ginseng, grapevine, hawthorn, hay, hazel nut, hellebore, horsetail, juniper berry, lemon balm, lettuce, lotus, ivy, lavender, mandrake, American mandrake, mistletoe, motherwort, mugwort, mustard seed, myrtle, narcissus, nuts, oak, olive, orange peel/blossom, papyrus, parsley, patchouli, peach, pine cones and nuts, pomegranate, poppy seeds, pussy willow, rice, rose, sage, clary sage, St. John's Wort (gathered naked on Midsummer Eve), sunflower seeds, all seeds, vervain, violet, walnut, wheat, willow, yarrow; Goddess: Abnoba, Abundantia, Aditi, the Afliae, the Ahinehiae, the Ahueccaniae, Ahurani, Aima, Aine, Ala, the Alaferhviae, the Alagabiabus, the Alaisiagae, the Albiahenae, Albina, Allat, Althaea, Ama-No-Uzume, Amaterasu, Amauntet, Anaitis, Anahita, Anath, Andarta, Annapurna, Anne, Anumati, Aphrodite, Araugelensis, Arianrhod, Artemis, Artio, Asase Yaa, Asherali, Astarte, Ashtoreth, Atargatis, Atete, Athirat, Auxesia, Baalith, Banba, Banda, Bast, Bendis, Berecyntia, Benzaiten, Bhu-Devi, Blodeuwedd, Bo Fina, Boldogasszony, Bona Dea, Brigid, Brimo. Campestres, Caolinn, Catheña, Ceres, Cerridwen, Chalchihuitlcue, Chantico, the Charites, Chicomecoatl, Cinteotl, Clothru, Coatlicue, Cocomama, Copper Woman, Cotys, Coventina, Cupra, Cybele, Damara, Damia, Damona, Danu, Dea Nutrix, Demeter (Mother of Abundance and Fertility), Derceto, Diana, Dil, Dione, Disani, Divona, Dizelle, the Djanggawul Sisters, Druantia, Durga, Dzidzileyla, Egeria, Eileithyia, Epona, Erce, Erigone, Eriu, Ertha, Erzulie, Estsanatlehi, the Euthungae, Fana, Faumea, Fauna, Faustitas, Fecunditas, Felicitas, Feronia, Fjorgyn, Flora, Fortuna, Freya, the Friagabiae, Frigg, Fulla, Ganga, Gatumdig, the Gavasiae, Gefion, Gerd, Goda, Greine, Hathor, the Hamavehae, Haumea, Hecate, Hera, Hina, Horta, Hou-Tu, the Hyades, Ibla, Idunn, Ilamatecuhtli, Inghean Bhuidhe, Inanna, Ishtar, Isis, Ix Chel, Juno, Juno Februa, Kali, Kapo, Keiva, Kilili-Mushritu, Kishi-Mojin, Kore, Kostroma, the Kotharot, Kwan Yin, Lada, Lailah, Laima, Lakshmi, the Lanehiae, Lassair, Latis, Latona, Leto, Libera, Lilith, Lono, Lupa, Ma, Macha, Maeve, Magaia, Magog, Maia, the Maluisae, Mama Allpa, Manasa, Mari, the Marsacae, Mater Matuta, Mati Syra Zemlya, Mawu, Mayahuel, Medb, Melusine, Minerva, Modron, Mokosh, Mut, Mylitta, Nanna, Nantosuelta, Nehalennia, Neith, Nemetona, the Nemausicae, Nerio, Nerthus, Ninhursag, Nissaba, Opet, Ops, Ortha, Oshun, Ostara, Oya, Pachamama, Paraskiva, Parvati, Persephone, Pidray, Pomona, Prithivi, Qadesh, Raka, Rati, Renenet, Rhea, Rhiannon, Rosmerta, Sarah, Sarasvati, Sashti, Satis, Saule, Sekhmet, Selqet, Sessrumnir, the Seubis, Sheela-na-gig, Sif, Sirona, Smyrna, Spenta Armaiti, Sulis, the Suleviae, Tanith, Taweret, Tellus, Thoueris, Tlazolteotl, Turan, Uke-Mochi, Uzumi, Al-Uzzah, Ved-Ava, Venus, Vesta, Vortumna, Wari Ma-Te-Takere, White Shell Woman, Xochiquetzal, the Xulsigiae, Yemaya, Zemyna; God: Acat, Adad, Alisanos, Ammon-Ra, Amun, An, Anu, Aparajita, Apollo, Ashur, Baal, Bacchus, Bel, Bes, Bhumiya, Bres, Cernunnos, Chac, Chango, Chandra, Cinteotl, Cronos, the Dagda, Dagon, Damuzi, Dianus, Dionysus, Dis Pater, Dushares, Dylan, Ea, Enki, Esus, Faunus, Frey, Ghede, Gil (Furnisher of

Seed), Hanuman, Hermes, Herne, Horned God, Ialonus, Idath, Indra, Ing, Itzamna, Jaguar, Krishna, Leucetius, Liber, Llma, Lupercus, Lutinus, Mabon, Marduk, Mars Ollodius, Maximon, Menu, Min, Mithras, Net, Nemglan, Ninib, Njord, Odin, Ogma, Osiris, Pales, Pam, Perkunas, Perun, Phoebus Apollo, Pluto, Poseidon, Potrimpo, Priapus, Ptah, Pushan, Quetzalcoatl, Reshep, Rod, Saturn, Serapis, al-Shafi, Shango, Shiva, Sokar (He Who Causes to be Fertile), Sulpa'e, Tammuz, Tane, Taranis, Teutates, Teyrnon, Tlaloc, Ullr, Uranus, Xipe Totec, Yarillo, Zeus Chronius.

Female fertility: Moon; Charm: cowrie shell; Animal: cow; Stone: garnet; Plant: Greek juniper, lady's mantle, mandrake, American mandrake, mustard seed, poppy seed; Goddess: Athtartu, Bona Dea, Catheña, Maan-Emo, Sita; God: Obatala. **Human fertility**: Stone: geode; Plant: rice; Goddess: Tonantzin; *to strengthen*: Metal: copper. **Male fertility**: Animal: ram; Plant: mistletoe, oak; Goddess: Catheña; God: Enki, Gil (Furnisher of Seed), Min, Shango; *to increase*: Plant: ashwagandha, saw palmetto; God: Herne.

Fertilization: Animal: bee, moth; Goddess: Fortuna; God: Obarator, Picus, Stercullus. **Fertilizing power**: (See: Power).

Fertile garden: Stone: agate, moss agate; Goddess: Horta. **Fertility rituals**: Goddess: Yemaya. **Fertility wishes**: Plant: sunflower seed, watermelon; Goddess: Libera.

Fertility of: animals: (See: Animals). **crops**: (See: Agriculture). **land**: (See: Land). **Nature/ the Earth/the natural world**: (See: Nature). **plants**: Sun/Earth/Water; Stone: agate; Goddess: Atargatis, Lakshmi; God: Damuzi, Green Man, Ialonus, Ih P'en, Tammuz; Evocation: Simargl; *to increase*: Stone: agate.

To: **activate fertility**: Sun/Moon/Water; *of land*: Charm: Great Rite; *of Nature*: God: Krishna. **attract fertility**: Color: green, emerald green. **awaken fertility**: Spring; Plant: patchouli (as incense); *of the Earth in springtime*: Goddess: Greine. **gain favor with fertility deities**: Color: green; Stone: moss agate. **increase fertility**: Color: green; Stone: emerald, jade; Goddess: Inanna; Evocation: Amatheon. **restore fertility**: Goddess: Hannahannas.

Infertility
Animal: dragon, mule; Stone: carnelian; Plant: walnut; God: Mot, Set; Stone: carnelian; Plant: lettuce, mandrake, veronica; Goddess: Isis, Yemoja.

To overcome infertility: Plant: lettuce, mandrake, pomegranate, tamarisk, veronica; Goddess: Isis, Yemoja; *animal infertility*: Plant: mistletoe; *female infertility*: Charm: roll on the ground beneath an apple tree; Plant: catnip; Goddess: Isis, Kwan Yin, Yemaya; God: Obatala; *male infertility*: God: Enki.

Fever
(See: Illness)

Fidelity
(See also: Loyalty)

Thursday

Charm: menstrual blood, poppet; Color: blue (true blue), pink, white; Animal: boar, buffalo, dog, goose, horse, otter, turtledove, wolf; Stone: amethyst, aphrodite, diamond, emerald, garnet, Herkimer diamond, lapis lazuli, pair of lodestones, morganite, rhodonite, rose quartz, topaz; Potion: rose petal or linden flower tea with lemon; Plant: Adam and Eve root (one carried by each partner), basil, blackthorn, caraway seed, cedar, chickweed, chili pepper, clover, red clover, coriander seed, cumin seed, damiana, dragon's blood, elder, hebe, heliotrope, honeysuckle, ivy, laurel, lavender, lemon peel or blossom, lemongrass, licorice, lime, linden, magnolia leaf or blossom, marigold, myrtle, narcissus, nutmeg, olive, orange, pikaki, pine, rhubarb, rose, rosemary, rye, scullcap, senna (in the bath), spikenard, slippery elm, spikenard, pair of unicorn roots, veronica, giant vetch, blue violet, yarrow, yerba maté; Goddess: Aphrodite, Chup-Kamui, Fauna, Fides, Hera, Sif, Sita, Vara; God: Hades, Hanuman; Evocation: Penelope.

Female fidelity: Animal: emu; Plant: veronica. **Male fidelity**: Animal: kangaroo; Plant: ivy; *to maintain*: Plant: basil (powdered).

Fidelity in: adversity: Plant: wallflower. **established relationships**: Stone: rose quartz. **love**: Plant: lemon, lime, senna. **marriage**: (See: Marriage). **misfortune**: Plant: wallflower.

To: attract fidelity: Stone: amber, rose quartz; Plant: basil. **maintain fidelity**: Plant: magnolia.

Infidelity

Animal: cat; Plant: yellow rose; Goddess: Aphrodite, Blodeuwedd, Guinevere, Ishtar; God: Zeus; Evocation: Daphnis, Jason.

To: expose infidelity: Stone: blue lodestone, turquoise; God: Hephaestus, Vulcan. **get a husband to forgive your infidelity**: Stone: lodestone; Evocation: Helen of Troy.

⊞inances

(See also: Business, Money, Prosperity, Wealth)

Mercury/Earth

Color: gold, green; Plant: honeysuckle, vetiver; God: Njord.

Financial blessings/rewards: (See: Blessings). **Financial dreams**: Color: green; Stone: emerald. **Financial gain**: Color: gold, purple; Plant: fumitory, hyssop, blue iris. **Financial goals**: *to attain*: Color: gold, green; Goddess: Lakshmi; *to manifest*: Plant: lavender. **Financial problems**: *to end*: Waning Moon. **Financial protection**: Animal: sand dollar; Stone: jet. **Financial ruin**: *to prevent*: Stone: tigereye. **Financial success**: (See: Success). **Financial transactions**: God: Hermes; *success in*: Stone: tigereye. **Financial wishes**: Plant: cinnamon, cinquefoil, honeysuckle; Goddess: Lakshmi.

To control spending: Plant: sassafras.

⊞lexibility

(See also: Adaptability)

Water

Animal: cheetah, kite; Stone: coral, selenite, topaz; Plant: bamboo, lilac, heather, honeysuckle, papyrus, rhododendron, rubber tree, spruce, willow.

Mental flexibility: Stone: sodalite; Plant: heather, rhubarb, saxifrage, strawberry, willow. **Flexibility in working toward goals**: Plant: papyrus.

Inflexibility

Earth

Charm: square.

⊞ocus

(See also: Concentration, Thought)

Tool: prism, all tools and props; Method: meditation; Charm: musk; Animal: cat, cheetah, mouse; Stone: fluorite, hematite, red jasper, kyanite, lepidolite, pearl, quartz crystal, topaz; Plant: ash, birch, grapefruit, honeysuckle, lemon, lime, myrrh, orange, orchid, sandalwood, vanilla, verbena.

Clear focus: Stone: kyanite; Plant: lavender, persimmon. **Creative focus**: Plant: iris. **Intense focus**: Animal: cheetah. **Mental focus**: Stone: clear calcite, citrine; Plant: eucalyptus.

Focused action: Plant: geranium, reed. **Focused light**: (See: Light). **Focused meditation**: Animal: cat.

To focus: desire: Stone: topaz. **energy**: (See: Energy). **healing**: Stone: lodestone. **telepathy**: Color: red; Stone: ruby, red tourmaline.

To: focus on reality: Stone: hematite. **refocus**: Stone: amazonite; Plant: hops; *refocus consciousness*: Stone: clear or violet fluorite, tourmaline. **unfocus**: Tool: crystal ball; Stone: bloodstone, hematite, snowflake obsidian.

Foolishness

Animal: ostrich; Plant: pomegranate.

Foolish actions: (See: Actions). **Foolish fears**: *to overcome*: Stone: emerald. **Foolish progress**: God: Baal. **Foolish thoughts**: *to avert*: Stone: ruby.

To: banish foolishness: Stone: coral, olivine (set in gold). **make a fool of someone**: Animal: fox; God: Loki. **play the fool**: Evocation: High John the Conqueror. **protect against foolishness**: Stone: chrysolite.

Force

Sun/Mars/Fire

Color: red; Number: 5; Animal: jaguar; Plant: cayenne; Goddess: Aetna, Bia, Pelé, Sekhmet, Shakti, Taweret; God: Ares, Hades, Mars, Pluto.

Creative force: Plant: lavender; Goddess: the Goddess, Mut; God: Glooskap, Oloddumare, Shiva; *to control*: Animal: komodo dragon; *to protect*: Animal: basilisk. **Destructive force**: Goddess: Bia; God: Malsum, Pillan, Shiva. **Divine force**:

Number: 22; Goddess: Hathor; God: Yahweh. **Driving force**: Color: rose. **Life force**: Sun/Earth/Spring; Animal: hawk; Stone: quartz crystal; Plant: citronella, hot pepper; Goddess: Aine, Vidya Lakshmi, Yemaya, Yum; God: Frey, Varuna; *to attune with*: Plant: damiana; *to awaken*: Plant: pine; *to disseminate*: God: Tate; *to manifest*: Evocation: plant devas; *to renew*: Plant: gorse; *to strengthen*: Plant: citronella. **Physical force**: Goddess: Macha. **Seminal force**: God: Min. **Undue force**: Number: 1. **Universal healing force**: *to get in touch with*: Aquarius. **Vital force**: Goddess: Ishtar (See also: Vitality).

To force: change: Goddess: Oya. **justice**: Evocation: Biadike.

To get your way by force: Goddess: Sekhmet (The One Who Takes Possession by Force); God: Pluto.

Forces

Astrological forces: God: Mithras. **Cosmic forces**: *to unite*: God: Min; *destructive cosmic forces*: God: Shiva; *productive cosmic forces*: Goddess: Prakrta; God: Shiva. **Dark forces/powers**: (See: Power). **Elemental forces**: Earth/Air/Fire/Water; Goddess: Erzulie; Evocation: elementals. **Evil forces**: *to banish*: Charm: curry powder; *to destroy*: Goddess: Durga; *to protect against*: Plant: juniper; *against evil psychic forces*: Plant: rowan; Evocation: Towiscara. **Natural forces**: Goddess: Dhat-Badan, Kali, Mother Nature; God: Grand Bois, Green Man, Helios; Evocation: nature spirits; *to exist peacefully with*: Plant: reindeer moss. **Negative forces**: *to avert*: Plant: clove; *to banish*: Waning Moon/Saturday; Charm: brimstone; Plant: clove; *to bind*: Saturn/Saturday; Color: black; *to protect against*: Plant: dragon's blood; *to balance positive and negative forces*: Libra; Stone: fluorite, malachite, tourmaline; God: Mithras; *negative unconscious forces*: *to overcome*: Plant:

bloodroot. **Opposing forces**: *to banish*: Plant: clove (burned); *to battle*: God: Ra. **Psychic forces**: *to protect against evil psychic forces*: Plant: rowan; Evocation: Towiscara. **Spiritual forces**: Animal: firefly.

Forces of change: Goddess: Oya. **To battle forces that would do crops harm**: Plant: fennel stalk.

Foresight

Plant: holly; Goddess: the Afliae, the Ahinehiae, the Ahueccaniae, the Alaferhviae, the Alagabiabus, the Alaisiagae, the Albiahenae, Cessair, the Euthungae, Freya, the Friagabiae, Frigg, the Gavasiae, Gullveig, the Hamavehae, the Lanehiae, the Maluisae, the Marsacae, the Seubis, the Xulsigiae.

Foretelling

(See: Divination, Prophecy)

Forethought

Stone: peridot; Goddess: Providentia; Evocation: Utnapishtim.

Forgiveness

Color: blue; Animal: dove; Stone: Apache tear, rhodochrosite; Plant: bleeding heart, rowan, tuberose; Goddess: Ishtar (Forgiver of Sins), Isis, Khama, Mary, Mawu, Pales; God: El, Ganesha, Vishnu.

Forgiveness after penitence: God: Apollo.

To: forgive yourself: Stone: angelite, blue topaz; Plant: geranium, rowan, wormwood. **get a husband to forgive your infidelity**: Stone: lodestone; Evocation: Helen of Troy.

Fortune

(See also: Destiny, Luck)

Sun

Color: gold, orange; Plant: bayberry, bergamot, cedar, chamomile, cinnamon, cinquefoil, laurel, lemon balm, lotus, mint, nutmeg, orange peel, star anise, vervain, violet, woodruff, yellow dock; Goddess: Abhijit, the Amfratninae, Anuradha, Asvayujau, Benzaiten, Chala, Coatlicue, Fortuna, Juno Moneta, Kichohu, the Muses, Renenet, the Seven Hathors, Tyche; God: Agathadaimon, Daikoku, Hermes, Patollo, T'ai-Yueh-Ta-Ti, Tamon.

Good fortune: Jupiter; Number: 1, 2, 3, 4, 5, 6, 7, 9; Color: blue, brown, gold, green; Animal: pair of cranes; Charm: anchor, fairy ring of mushrooms; Stone: alexandrite, green aventurine, carnelian, chrysoprase, garnet, jacinth, jasper, malachite, moonstone, onyx, ruby, turquoise (given with love); Plant: amber, ash leaves, banyan, bayberry, birch, cedar, chamomile, cinnamon, cinquefoil, coca leaves, cumin, dill, yellow dock, honeysuckle, jasmine, laurel, lotus, mint, mistletoe, myrtle, nutmeg, peony, pomegranate, rose, sweet pea, vanilla, vervain, violet, wintergreen, wisteria; Invoke: Dama, the Pa hsien (the Eight Immortals); Goddess: Abhijit, the Afliae, the Ahinehiae, the Ahueccaniae, the Alaferhviae, the Alagabiabus, the Alaisiagae, the Albiahenae, Atargatis, Benten, Diana, Dolya, the Euthungae, Erzulie, Freya, the Friagabiae, Felicitas, the Gavasiae, Habondia, the Hamavehae, Isis, Juno Fortuna, Kajata, Laima, Lakshmi (Abode of Fortune), the Lanehiae, the Maluisae, the Marsacae, Nortia, Pachamama, Renenet, Al-Rusa, Saubhagya Bhuvanesvari (buddha of good fortune), the Seubis, Sheng-Mu, Shri Devi (Good Fortune), Taweret, Ukat, Venus, Venus Felix, the Xulsigiae; God: Bishamon, Bonus Eventus, Cernunnos, Ekkekko, El, Ganesha, Gonaqade't, Hotei, Li T'ieh Kuat, Patollo.

Good fortune for: newborns: Goddess: Pi-Hsai Yuan Chin. **new homes**: Plant: coca leaf; Goddess: Pachamama. **the young**: Plant: clover.

Good fortune in: battle: Stone: opal. **hunting**: Goddess: Pinga. **legal matters**: Stone: chalcedony. **a woman's good fortune in marriage**: God: Bhaga.

To: attract good fortune: Waxing Moon; Color: green; Charm: jump over a Sabbat bonfire; Stone: alexandrite, amazonite, jade, jasper, lodestone; Plant: allspice, almond, basil, bayberry, bistort, catnip, cinnamon, frankincense, ginseng, High John, horse chestnut, myrtle, olive, poppy seed, strawberry, vanilla, wisteria, wood aloes. **revoke good fortune**: God: Patollo. **transform a nightmare into good fortune**: Evocation: the Baku.

Fortunes of war: God: Nergal.

To: improve fortune: Goddess: Gefion. **increase fortune**: Plant: cumin. **predict a newborn's fortune**: (See: Babies). **reverse fortune**: Waning Moon. **send good or bad fortune**: God: Brianan.

Misfortune

(See also: Adversity, Luck, Problems, Uncrossing)

Moon

Color: dark blue; Number: 5; Animal: dragon; Stone: opal, tourmaline, green turquoise; Plant: basil, datura, white rose, wormwood; Goddess: Ardra, Aslesa, Beda, Bestalannitsa (Luckless), Bharani, Chitra, Dhanistha, Nedolya, Nelaima, Pelé; God: Mait' Carrefour, Chernogolov, Kafour Legba, Moros, Odin, Patollo, Xolotl; Evocation: the Rakshasa.

Fidelity in misfortune: Plant: wallflower. **Unfortunate love**: Plant: devil's bit scabious.

To: avert misfortune: Charm: throwing yourself down in front of a whirlwind (dangerous, not recommended); Plant: houseleek, sage; God: Bes. **end misfortune**: Charm: blue star (especially a blue pentacle drawn on the forehead); Plant: parsley, star anise; God: Patoll. **protect against misfortune**: Plant: cedar, mandrake, mistletoe, sage; God: Bes, Sucellos. **understand misfortune**: God: Horus.

Freedom

(See also: Escape, Independence, Liberation)

Uranus/Air/Sunday/Aquarius

Color: blue, clear, red; Number: 5; Animal: butterfly, dolphin, elk, fish, owl, porpoise, all birds; Stone: amethyst, rose quartz; Plant: calla lily, mariposa lily, rue, water willow; Goddess: Aeval, Artemis, Athene, Isis, Libera, Libertas, Lady Liberty; God: Aeolus, the Horned God, Liber, Pan.

Creative freedom: Plant: iris, spikenard. **Emotional freedom**: Plant: snapdragon. **Female freedom**: Goddess: Minerva, Yemaya. **Inner freedom**: Plant: hawthorn, Japanese maple. **Mental freedom**: Plant: dandelion, sandalwood. **Personal freedom**: Plant: bird of paradise. **Sexual freedom**: Plant: hibiscus; Goddess: Anath, Aphrodite, Arianrhod, Freya, Frigg, Inanna, Ishtar, Lilith, Qadesh, Uathach, Xochiquetzal; God: Pan; Evocation: Aisha Qandisha, Guinevere.

Carefree life: Animal: dragonfly. **Power of Fire to free Earth from Water**: Plant: alder. **Sense of freedom**: Stone: ruby, sugilite; Plant: geranium; God: Hermes. **Urge to be free**: Uranus.

Free love: Goddess: Milda. **Free sexuality**: Stone: onyx. **Free will**: (See: Will).

Freedom from: bounds: Goddess: Aditi (The Unfettered) (See also: Binding/ Unbinding). **captivity**: Stone: sapphire. **the cycle of reincarnation**: Goddess: Lakshmi. **darkness**: Goddess: Yhi. **enchantment**: Stone: sapphire; evil: (See: Evil). **fears**: Plant: St. John's Wort. **guilt**: Animal: cheetah, puma; God: Dionysus Liber. **influence**: Plant: hawthorn. **jealousy**: Animal: otter. **a negative past life**: Plant: African tulip tree. **obsessions**: Plant: frankincense. **pain**: Goddess: Kwan Yin. **the past**: Plant: sandalwood. **problems**: Goddess: Aditi (The Unfettered); *emotional problems*: Plant: lavender. **routine**: God: Loki. **tension**: Plant: dandelion, fireweed, passionfruit.

Freedom to: dream: Plant: hops. **leave**: Plant: purple African violet. **freedom of movement**: (See: Movement).

To free: emotions: Plant: fuchsia. **the imagination**: Plant: cannabis. **the mind**: Animal: dolphin, whale; Plant: sandalwood.

To: accept freedom: Plant: saxifrage. **limit freedom**: Saturn/Saturday. **overcome fear of freedom**: Color: orange; Plant: moss. **protect freedom**: Goddess: Lady Liberty; God: Zeus Eluetherious. **set yourself free**: Goddess: Kali.

Friendliness

Sagittarius

Color: pink, yellow; Animal: otter; Stone: sapphire; Plant: white jasmine, mistletoe; Goddess: Surabhi; God: Balder.

Friendly conversation: Color: pink, rose.

Friends

(See also: Friendship)

Goddess: Sif.

Absent friends: Plant: zinnia; *to honor*: Charm: toss a floral wreath into a river. **True friends**: God: Thor.

To: attract friends: Color: pink; Stone: moss agate, chrysoprase, lodestone, red lodestone, pink tourmaline; Plant: angelica, pink carnation, citronella, frangipani, gardenia, gravel root, lilac, papaya, passion flower, strawberry, sweet pea, yarrow; God: Eros; *to the home*: Plant: citronella, frangipani; *attract loyal friends*: Stone: tourmaline; *attract new friends*: Stone: turquoise. **incite quarrels between friends**: Stone: salt. **keep friends**: Stone: moss agate; *keep in touch with friends*: Stone: garnet. **make friends**: Stone: moss agate; Plant: catnip, holythorn, two nuts in one kernel; *with animals*: Color: brown; Evocation: Enkidu. **mourn the loss of a friend**: Plant: red anemone; Evocation: Gilgamesh. **reconcile differences between friends**: Stone: green beryl. **turn an enemy into a friend**: Plant: tonka bean.

Friendship

(See also: Affection, Friendliness, Friends, Loneliness, Relationships)

Sun/Venus/Waxing Moon/Water/Friday/ Sunday/Aquarius/Leo

Number: 3, 6; Color: blue, gold, pink, rose, violet, yellow; Charm: hand, hand print, lavender flower water, rosewater, triskelion; Animal: cat, dog; Stone: alabaster, agate, aventurine, chrysoprase, quartz crystal cluster, lapis lazuli, lodestone, moonstone, rose quartz, sapphire, tourmaline, turquoise; Potion: apple juice, passionflower juice; Plant: acacia, aloe, allspice, apple blossom or fruit, bluebell, carnation, pink carnation, catnip, clover, daffodil, gardenia, geranium, honeysuckle, ivy, lavender, lemon, lime, love seed, passionflower, blue periwinkle, pine, rose, pink rose, yellow rose, rosemary, strawberry, sweet pea; Goddess: Amphityonis, Isis, Maitri, Philotes, Sif; God: Arawn and Pwyll, Eros,

Gucumatz and Hurukan, Hanuman and Rama, Mitra, Zeus; Evocation: Gilgamesh and Enkidu.

Deep friendship: Plant: acacia flower. **Eternal friendship**: Stone: beryl; Plant: sweet woodruff. **Happy friendship**: Stone: rose quartz; Plant: sweet pea. **Intimate friendship**: Color: blue; God: Mitra. **New friendship**: New Moon; Plant: primrose. **True friendship**: Color: blue (true blue); Stone: garnet; Plant: oakleaf geranium; Goddess: Maiden. **Unchanging friendship**: Plant: arbor vitae. **Universal friendship**: Aquarius. **Warm friendship**: Plant: basil.

Friendship in adversity: Plant: ivy, pine, snowdrop. **Friendship between nations**: Goddess: Amphityonis. **Stoicism in friendship**: Plant: box tree.

To: balance the emotions in a friendship: Stone: rose quartz. **end a friendship**: Goddess: the Crone. **influence a friendship**: Color: brown. **strengthen friendship**: Stone: emerald; Plant: macadamia nut; God: Arawn. **sustain friendship**: Plant: clove.

Fulfillment

(See: Satisfaction)

Chapter 7

Gambling

Mercury

Goddess: Fata, Tlazolteotl; God: Macuilxochitl.

Gambling luck/success: Color: green, red; Animal: bat, black cat; Charm: alligator tooth, badger tooth, nutmeg filled with mercury (very dangerous, not recommended), the shed skin of a snake; Stone: amazonite, aventurine, green aventurine, green jade, lodestone, tigereye; Plant: anise (especially oil, to anoint money), bergamot, chamomile (especially cool tea, to wash hands) cinnamon (especially oil, to anoint hands—best mixed with a carrier oil such as olive oil or mineral oil; patch test skin first, and use instead to anoint amulets or candles if you are allergic), fig frankincense, lily of the valley, mimosa, myrrh, patchouli, rose, sandalwood, vanilla; *to protect against attack of your luck*: (See: Luck).

Games of chance: *for manual dexterity in*: Plant: High John; *for success in*: Stone: lodestone; Plant: laurel.

To: **dream of lucky numbers**: Plant: huckleberry leaf, marigold. **end a losing streak**: Plant: alkanet. **keep your winnings**: Plant: comfrey. **win the lottery**: Goddess: Fortuna.

Gardeners

(See: People)

Gardening

(See also: Agriculture, Growth)

Sun/Venus/Moon/Earth

Color: brown, florals, green; Stone: agate, moss agate, Herkimer diamond, jade, jasper, malachite, moonstone; Plant: apple, grape; Goddess: Antheia, Aphrodite of the Gardens, Flora, the Mother, Pomona, Rhea, Venus (Venus of the Vine), Vortumna; God: Dinditane, Ialonus, Priapus, Reshep of the Garden, Vertumnus.

Fertile garden: Stone: agate, moss agate; Goddess: Horta. **Healthy garden**: Color: green; Stone: moss agate, jade.

To: **bless a garden**: Charm: make love in it. **help a garden grow**: (See: Growth). **prepare a garden for winter**: Goddess: the Crone. **protect a garden**: Stone: ruby (buried); Plant: elder; Goddess: Aphrodite of the Gardens, Pomona, Venus; God: Vertumnus; Evocation: Ladon.

Generosity

(See also: Charity, Greed, Hospitality, Selfishness)

Jupiter

Color: green, pink; Number: 9; Animal: buffalo, gorilla, woodpecker; Plant: apple, heather, honeysuckle, orange tree, primrose; Goddess: Bast, Benzaiten, Empanada, Erzulie, Estsanatlehi, Fatimah, Gefion, Habondia (Queen of Generosity), Kwan

Yin, Lakshmi, Liberalitas, Oshun, Saule, Yemaya; God: Bres, Legba, Njord, Shiva; Evocation: Hiawatha.

Generous affection: Plant: honeysuckle. **Generosity to children**: God: Ixtlilton.

Gentleness

Water/North/South/Spring/Aquarius

Color: indigo, pink, yellow, pastels; Number: 2; Animal: deer, gorilla, rabbit; Stone: kunzite, lapis lazuli, pearl, rose quartz; Plant: camellia, celery, chamomile, hyacinth, lavender, love-lies-bleeding, motherwort, pink rose, sycamore; Goddess: Fair Maiden, Isis (Gentle Lady), Nanna, Yemaya; God: Dogoda, Kephera.

Gentle endings: Goddess: Yuki-Onne. **Gentle persuasion**: Color: yellow; Number: 2. **Gentle protection**: God: Rudra. **Gentle strength**: (See: Strength). **Gentle striving in relation to a secret hope**: Metal: tin. **Gentle touch**: Animal: deer; Plant: ladies slipper. **Gentle wisdom**: God: Nereus.

Ghosts

(See: Spirits)

Glamours/Glamoury

(See: Illusion)

Goals

Sun/West

Higher goals: *to achieve*: Animal: ladybug.

Good luck with goals: Stone: fluorite. **Help in achieving goals**: God: Ogun. **Motivation toward goals**: Stone: sapphire. **Patience in working toward goals**: Stone: garnet. **Perseverance to achieve goals**: Stone: garnet.

To: achieve/attain goals: Saturn/Full Moon; Method: candle magick, spells, visualization; Animal: gazelle, salamander; Metal: copper; Stone: garnet, turquoise; Plant: beech, High John; *business/career goals*: Color: orange; *financial goals*: Color: gold, green; Plant: lavender; Goddess: Lakshmi; *material goals*: Goddess: Lakshmi. **clear obstacles to goals**: Stone: malachite; God: Ogun. **find an alternate path to a goal**: Animal: deer, hart. **make your way toward your goal**: Invocation: river deities. **work toward goals**: Stone: garnet; *flexibility in*: Plant: papyrus.

Gossip

Leo

Animal: kookaborra, parrot; Number: 3; Plant: adder's tongue, clove, deerstongue; Goddess: Morgan le Fay, Pheme.

Evil gossip: *to protect against*: Stone: beryl.

To: protect against gossip: Method: cloaking; Stone: beryl; Plant: clove, devil's shoestring, slippery elm; Goddess: Tacita. **start gossip**: Plant: clove. **stop gossip**: Saturn; Method: binding; Color: indigo, gray, purple, white; Stone: beryl; Plant: adder's tongue, clove, dragon's blood, iris, lavender, orris root, slippery elm; Goddess: Tacita (The Silent Goddess); Evocation: St. Raymond.

Goodness

(See also: Fortune, Health, Luck)

Number: 7; Color: blue; Stone: turquoise; Plant: butterbur, heliotrope, lily, mercury, snowball; Goddess: Amaterasu, Armaita, Bast, Bona Dea (The Good Goddess), Goda the Good, Lakshmi; God: Ahura Mazda, Angatupyry, Baldur, Byelobog, Hahgwehdiyu, Hino, Mithras; Evocation: archangels, the Fisher King, Ioskeha.

Greater good: *to sacrifice for*: Animal: deer. **Knowledge of goodness**: Plant: apple, apricot, fig tree.

Good appetite: (See: The Body). **Good advice**: (See: Advice). **Good beginning/start**: (See: Beginning). **Good career**: Color: orange; *to have despite a physical disability*: God: Vulcan. **Good character**: Goddess: Fides. **Good communication in relationships**: (See: Relationships). **Good conversation**: Color: pink. **Good deal**: *to make*: Stone: jade. **Good deeds**: Goddess: Anahita. **Good education**: Plant: cherry tree. **Good eyesight**: Plant: vervain. **Good faith**: Water; Goddess: Fides; God: Jupiter. **Good fame**: Plant: apple blossom; Goddess: Tyche. **Good feelings**: *to restore after a quarrel*: Plant: bergamot, copal. **Good fishing**: Plant: hawthorn; God: Mannan; Goddess: the Matronaea. **Good fortune**: (See: Fortune). **Good harvest/crops**: (See: Agriculture, Harvest). **Good health**: (See: Health). **Good humor/spirits**: Plant: cherry blossom. **Good hunt**: God: Itzamna. **Good job**: *to find*: Plant: Job's tears. **Good judgment**: (See: Judgment). **Good luck**: (See: Luck). **Good manners**: Stone: agate; God: Orunmila. **Good marriage**: (See: Marriage). **Good memories**: Goddess: Saga. **Good mind**: Color: yellow. **Good mood**: (See: Mood). **Good nature**: Plant: great mullein. **Good neighbor**: Color: green. **Good news**: Goddess: Pheme. **Good outcome**: God: Bonus Eventus. **Good people**: (See: People). **Good relations/relationships**: (See: Relationships); **Good reputation**: Stone: beryl. **Good sex**: Plant: lemongrass. **Good sleep**: Stone: citrine, blue topaz. **Good stewardship**: God: Enki. **Good times**: God: Fufluns, Ixtlilton, Lado. **Good timing**: Stone: tigereye. **Good trip**: *good sea voyage*: Goddess: Aphrodite Euploia. **Good vibrations**: (See: Vibrations). **Good will**: Color: blue; Stone: all gems; Plant: mistletoe; Goddess: Concordia. **Good wishes**: Plant: basil, holly (wreath). **Good works**: Stone: sapphire.

To: **attract goodness/good things**: Color: orange; Stone: lodestone; Plant: papaya.

encourage goodness: Stone: diamond, yellow jacinth, sapphire. **make a good match**: Goddess: Juno Pronoba. **protect places where goodness is taught**: God: the Celestial Kings.

Grace

Animal: deer, elephant, hart, otter, stag, swan; Stone: chrysoprase, red jasper; Plant: cowslip, elm, jasmine, yellow jasmine, rose, rue, stonecrop, green tea, vervain, willow; Goddess: Epona, Mary (Mother of Grace), Nzambi; God: Marduk, Vishnu.

Divine grace: Plant: lotus, willow; Goddess: Mary (Mother of Divine Grace); Evocation: Hanael. **Grace under pressure**: Goddess: Branwen. **To recognize grace**: Plant: thistle.

Gracefulness

Animal: antelope, cat, deer, ferret, gazelle, goshawk, stingray, swan; Stone: peridot; Plant: birch, spruce, weeping willow; Goddess: Anne (The Graceful One), Chang-O, the Graces, Harini, Vidya Lakshmi; Evocation: devas, fairies.

Graciousness

Stone: lodestone; Goddess: the Goddess, the Graces, Isis, Mylitta, Sekhmet (Gracious One), Semiramis; God: Asar-alimnuna (The Gracious), Aten, El, Krishna, Osiris, Shachar, Shalim.

Gratitude
North

Color: white; Animal: deer, hart; Stone: amethyst, clear quartz crystal; Plant: agrimony, camellia, campanula, frankincense, lotus, myrrh, sage.

Deep gratitude: Plant: agrimony. **Joyful thanks**: Plant: valerian.

Ingratitude

Plant: buttercup.

Greed

(See also: Generosity)

Sun

Color: dark green; Number: 8; Animal: raven; Metal: gold; God: Hades, Yo; Evocation: Aglaurus, Balaam, Geri, Midas, Pazazu, Tantalus.

To: banish greed: Stone: chrysoprase; God: Krishna. **battle greed**: God: Gwydion. **overcome greed**: Color: green, dark green. Plant: silverweed.

Grief

(See also: Death, Heartbreak, Loss, Sorrow)

Color: black, deep purple, dark crimson; Number: 7; Animal: lamb, mourning dove; Stone: amber; Plant: aloe, red anemone, benzoin, calla lily, cyclamen, harebell, marigold, parsley, poplar, dark red rose, purple scabious, snowdrop, willow, weeping willow, yew; Goddess: Anath, Geshtinanna (The One Who Always Weeps), Gore, the Heliads, Isis, Mary, Nephthys, Nestrecha, Saitada; God: Chernobog, Mot, Penthus; Evocation: Gawaunduk, Phyllis.

Enduring grief: Plant: red anemone. **Violent grief**: Goddess: Anath. **Bereavement rituals**: Goddess: Aericura. **Extravagant mourning**: Goddess: Geshtinanna; God: Adonis, Attis, Orpheus.

Grief for: children: *dead baby*: (See: Babies); *lost child*: Goddess: Ceres, Demeter; *dead children*: Animal: nightingale; Goddess: La Llorona (The Weeping Woman), Mary (Lady of Sorrows); Evocation: Aedon, Niobe. **a friend**: Plant: red anemone; Evocation: Gilgamesh. **a loved one**: Goddess: Anath, the Heliads, Isis, Nephthys; Evocation: Galatea. **someone's absence**: Plant: zinnia.

To: comfort grief: Plant: balm of Gilead, cypress, lemon balm, marjoram; Goddess: Baubo, Hlin; God: Shiva; *grief counseling*: Goddess: Saitada. **ease grief**: Color: light pink; Stone: agate, amethyst, Apache tear, carnelian, chrysocolla, chrysoprase, fluorite, jet, onyx, opal, rose quartz, watermelon tourmaline; Oil: neroli; Plant: anemone, balm of Gilead, basil, bistort, cinquefoil, cypress, hyacinth, lavender, lemon balm, marjoram, myrrh, pitcher plant; Goddess: Hlin. **express grief**: Animal: nightingale; Oil: neroli; Plant: benzoin, hyacinth, lemon balm, rose, mimosa, vetiver; *keening in grief*: Goddess: Brigit; God: Bres; Evocation: the sirens. **get through the grieving process**: Plant: vetiver. **overcome grief**: Tool: bells; Stone: apatite, ruby, topaz, torbenite; Plant: anemone, balm of Gilead, bergamot, bistort, cinquefoil, cypress, hyacinth, lemon balm, Japanese maple, snowdrop, vetiver; Goddess: Coyolxauhqui, Isis. **protect against negative vibrations of mourners**: Plant: cypress. **understand grief**: Plant: cypress. **prevent grief**: Plant: thyme. **release grief**: Plant: Japanese maple.

Grounding

Earth/Earth

Color: brown, black, green; Charm: hug a tree, soil; Animal: baboon, earthworm, gorilla, nuthatch, ostrich, burrowing owl, tortoise, turtle, all burrowing animals, flightless and ground nesting birds; Metal: iron; Stone: agate, amethyst, Apache tear, aragonite, pink calcite, chrysocolla, emerald, fluorite, hematite, jasper, brown or red or green jasper, kunzite, moonstone, obsidian, onyx, peridot, smoky quartz, salt, rock salt, tigereye, tourmaline, green or black tourmaline, turquoise, unakite, brown zircon; Oil: elemi; Plant: amber, banyan, cedar, cypress, elm, hops, jojoba, lima bean, oakmoss, patchouli, petrified wood, pine, roots, sage, clary sage, sweetgrass, vervain, vetiver, all trees; Goddess: Acca Larentia, Aericura, Altria, Amba, Atabei, Audjal, Auxesia, Collatina, Coatlicue, Demeter, Eithinoha, Erda, Ertha, Escheman (Grandmother Earth), Eseacar, Etugen, Fir Daughter, Gaia, Grund, Hou-Tu, Hybla, Ikas, Iweridd, Iyatiku, Ki, Latiaran, Magog, Mati Syra Zemlya (Moist Mother Earth), Mother Earth, Pachamama, Tonantzin, Uchtcelbh, Urash.

Physical grounding: Stone: obsidian; Plant: all trees. **Sexual grounding**: Plant: sandalwood.

To ground: **emotions**: Plant: queen of the night. **energy**: (See: Energy). **after a ritual**: Stone: hematite, brown jasper. **during psychic work**: Animal: harrier hawk.

Growth

(See also: Fertility)

Sun/Mars/Moon/Waxing Moon/Full Moon/Water/Earth/Aries/Leo/ Sagittarius

Color: green, yellowish green, turquoise; Stone: moss agate; Plant: angelica, aniseed, heather, patchouli, wheat; Goddess: Althaea (She Who Makes Grow), Auxesia, Ceres, Cybele, Druantia, Fecunditas, Gefion, Hina, Isis, Lakshmi, Lassair, Maia, Perfubre, South Daughter, Summer Daughter, Takotsi (Our Grandmother Growth), Vaisgamta, the White Goddess; God: Ayyappan, Marduk (Lord of Growth), Osiris, Shang Te, Yum Caaz.

Agricultural growth: Stone: moss agate; Goddess: Ops, Tellus Mater; God: Amun, Lactanus, Loco; *healthy growth of crops*: Goddess: Asherah; *to help crops to grow*: Charm: "ride" a broomstick through the field; God: Telepinu; *growth of crops*: God: Ammon, Lactanus; *of grain*: Goddess: Hostilina; God: Sirsir; *of grapes*: God: Osiris; *of maize*: Goddess: Estsanatlehi. **Artistic growth**: Stone: blue topaz. **Conscious growth**:

Plant: spirea. **Emotional growth**: Color: light blue; Plant: sandalwood. **Healthy growth**: Stone: peridot. **Human growth**: Goddess: Ops. **Inner growth**: Plant: gentian, geranium, spaghnum moss. **Intellectual growth**: Stone: lapis lazuli, sapphire, black tourmaline; Plant: rosemary; Goddess: Ceibhfhionn. **New growth**: Spring; Animal: coral, robin. **Personal growth**: Stone: ruby; Plant: water lily; Goddess: Atargatis. **Physical growth**: Stone: amazonite, red calcite; *to stimulate in humans*: Charm: dinosaur bone. **Psychic growth**: Color: purple; Stone: amethyst, peridot; Plant: anise, lemongrass. **Rapid growth**: South; Goddess: Estsanatlehi, Sapas. **Regrowth**: Animal: lizard, starfish; Plant: lemon. **Spiritual growth**: Moon/Monday; Method: meditation, yoga; Color: lavender, purple, yellow; Charm: spiral, vulture goddess crown; Stone: amber, pink calcite, celestite, citrine, iolite, lapis lazuli, malachite, sugilite; Plant: fir, frankincense, lotus, myrrh, pine, sandalwood; Goddess: Padma Lakshmi; Invoke: the Dharmapatat; *to increase*: Stone: charoite, sugilite, sunstone. **Springtime growth**: Plant: bonfire of furze; Goddess: Chalchihuitlcue (Precious Green Lady).

Growing pains: *to relieve*: Plant: celery. **Growing plants**: Goddess: Demeter, Lassair. **Growing things**: Goddess: Chalchihuitlcue (Precious Green Lady), Green Tara; God: the Horned God, Osiris. **Spiral growth patterns**: Plant: ivy, vine; Goddess: Helice.

Growth of: **awareness**: Stone: picture jasper. **hair**: Plant: lavender, magnolia, yarrow. **love**: Stone: pink tourmaline. **money**: Plant: mandrake root, thyme. **plants**: Earth; Plant: lotus; Goddess: Ops, Rayste, Tellus Mater; God: Amatheon, Baal, Green Man, Loco, Mithras, Osiris; Evocation: the Rusalki; *to help plants to grow*: Stone: moss agate, green jasper; God: Asharu, Baal, Green Man; *to help a garden grow*: Sun/Earth; Charm: make love in it; Stone: agate, moss agate, crystals, Herkimer diamond, jasper; Plant: chamomile; Goddess: Blodeuwedd, Horta.

To: finally grow up: Goddess: Athena; Plant: bracken. **help a child to grow**: Goddess: Althea (She Who Makes Grow), Blodeuwedd. **understand growth as a part of the cycle of life**: (See: Life).

Guidance
(See also: Advice)

Moon/Neptune/Pole Star/Leo

Method: astrology, oracle, runes, tarot; Color: blue, dark blue; Animal: crow, dragon, jackal, slug; Number: 33; Stone: lodestone, moonstone, clear quartz crystal; Oil: palmarosa; Plant: broom, rhubarb, star of Bethlehem; Goddess: Athena, Baba Yaga, Belit-Seri, the Crone, Fortuna, Freya, Egeria, Inanna, Ishtar, Juno Moneta, Kwan Yin, Ma'at, Mary (Our Lady of Good Counsel), Metis, Minerva, Neith, Oshun, Themis, Yemaya; God: Anubis, Asar-alim, Consus, Ea, Baron Ghede, Jupiter, Kinma, Mimir, Thoth, Zeus (Lord of Counsel); Evocation: Anael, ancestors, angels, animal guides, archangels, Merlin, Pythia, Raphael, spirits, spirit guides, vila.

Dream guidance: Animal: muskrat, wolf; Plant: vervain, yarrow; Goddess: Huitaca. **Ethical guidance**: God: Obatala; Evocation: ancestors. **Inner guidance**: Stone: unakite; Plant: pine; God: Hermes. **Psychic guidance**: Stone: azurite. **Spiritual guidance**: Neptune; Color: white; Animal: burrowing owl; Stone: azurite, pearl; Plant: mint, sandalwood; Evocation: angels; *in dreams*: Plant: mint. **Grief counseling**: Goddess: Saitada.

Animal guides: Color: brown, red; Plant: sage, violet; *to work with*: Method: dream work, meditation, trance; Stone: ametrine, azurite, leopardskin agate, tanzanite;

Plant: violet. **Spirit guides**: Animal: goshawk; Stone: fluorite; *to attract*: Color: white; Stone: jade; Plant: dandelion, elecampane, lemon, lemongrass, lotus, rowan, sweetgrass, wormwood; *to communicate with*: Goddess: the Crone; *to contact*: Color: indigo, white; Animal: eagle; Stone: moss agate, kyanite, lapis, moonstone, tourmaline; Plant: honeysuckle, lotus, mugwort, sandalwood; Goddess: Ixtaccihuatl; *to understand*: Stone: morganite; *to work with*: Stone: ametrine, azurite, leopardskin agate, tanzanite; Metal: peacock ore. **Animal spirit guides**: *to contact*: Goddess: Ixtaccihuatl; *to work with*: Stone: ametrine, azurite, leopardskin agate, tanzanite.

Guidance in: adventures: Goddess: Al-Uzzah. **the afterlife**: (See: Afterlife). **the dark**: Animal: crow. **Egypt**: God: Ra (Guide of the Two Lands). **meditation**: Animal: wolf. **service**: Goddess: Frigg. **guidance on the road**: God: Janus. **guide to the Otherworld**: (See: Otherworld).

To guide: the dead: Goddess: The Bardo (Ladies Who Guide). **lost souls**: Goddess: Sedna. **merchants**: God: Xaman Ek. **newborns**: Goddess: Candelifera. **ships**: Goddess: Asherah. **travelers**: God: Puchan; Evocation: Breasal; *business travelers*: God: Yacatecuhtli. **battle-slain warriors**: Goddess: the Morrigan, Valkyries.

Guilt

Goddess: Ate.

Guilty pleasures: Goddess: Tlazolteotl.

To: determine guilt: Charm: hazel divining rod; God: Enki. **ease guilt**: Stone: jasper, watermelon tourmaline; Plant: bloodroot, sage. **end guilt**: Stone: pearl, sodalite; Goddess: Alphito-Baitule Lusia (Deliveress from Guilt); God: Dionysus Liber. **punish guilt**: Animal: white dog with red ears; Goddess: the Erinyes; Evocation: Ammut.

Chapter 8

Habits

(See also: Diseases/Disorders: Addiction, Sobriety)

Bad habits: *to break/end/overcome*: Saturn/Waning Moon; Color: indigo, purple, violet; Stone: amethyst, beryl, jet, clear quartz crystal, topaz, turquoise; Oil: new mown hay; Plant: basil, cat's claw, cedar, cypress, dragon's blood, laurel, lavender, morning glory, oat, patchouli, peppermint, rose, rosewood, spikenard. **Bad eating habits**: *to break/end/overcome*: Stone: moonstone.

Handfastings

(See: Weddings)

Happiness

(See also: Contentment, Joy, Satisfaction, Sorrow)

Venus

Color: blue, light blue, royal blue, peach, pink, gold, white, yellow; Animal: bat, bluebird, ladybug, goose, hummingbird, sparrow; Charm: Celtic knot, dried figs and dates with honey, feathers that are both brown and white, honey, horseshoe (over doorway); Stone: agate (especially blue lace, brown or moss agate), amber, amethyst, aquamarine, apophyllite, aventurine, beryl, chrysoprase, garnet (given as a gift), hematite, Herkimer diamond, malachite, moonstone, onyx, peridot, rhodonite, blue quartz, rose quartz, ruby, turquoise, yellow zircon; Oil: neroli; Plant: Adam and Eve root, amber, apple, apple blossom, aster, avocado, baby's breath, basil, bayberry, bergamot, catnip, cedar, celandine, cherry blossom, citrus fruit, clove, coriander, cyclamen, cypress, date, fig, fir, frankincense, gardenia, geranium, hawthorn, heliotrope, High John, honeysuckle, hyacinth, jasmine, juniper, laurel, lavender, lemon, lemon verbena, lilac, lily, lily of the valley, loosestrife, lotus, marigold, marjoram, meadowsweet, morning glory, motherwort, mugwort, myrrh, orange, mandarin orange, orchid, oregano, palm, patchouli, peach, purslane, quince, rose, rosemary, St. John's Wort, saffron, savory, sunflower, sweet pea, thyme, tuberose, valerian, vanilla, vervain, vetiver, yellow violet, water lily, wisteria, witch grass, yarrow, ylang-ylang, laurel with palm; Goddess: Amaterasu, Ani, Benzaiten, Chie, Cocomama, Dolya, Erzulie, Eutychia, Felicitas, Fortuna, Ganga, the Graces, Hathor, Isis, Jara, Jubchas-Guaya, Lada, Lakshmi, Marici (Sun of Happiness), Matangi, Nemesis, Oshun, Samkhat, Suntra, Tara, Ustrecha; God: Akandi, Ataksak, Balder, Byelobog, Bishamon, Daikoku, Dazhbog, Dionysus, Ekajata, Frey, Fu-hsing, Ganesha, Hotei, Kokopeli, Lado, Marduk, Omacatl, Tien Kuan, Yum Caaz.

Divine happiness: Goddess: Lakshmi. **Inner happiness**: Method: journaling; Plant: orange. **Rural happiness**: Plant yellow violet. **Youthful happiness**: Plant: spring crocus.

Happy afterlife: Plant: marigold; God: Charun, Osiris Un-Nefer. **Happy children**: (See: Children). **Happy ending**: (See: Endings). **Happy family**: Plant: basil; Goddess: Sif. **Happy friendship**: Stone: rose quartz; Plant: sweet pea. **Happy home**: (See: Home). **Happy life**: (See: Life). **Happy marriage**: (See: Marriage). **Happy memories**: Plant: rosemary. **Happy old age**: Goddess: Sekhmet (She of the Happy Old Age). **Happy omen**: Stone: jade. **Happy pregnancy**: Plant: gooseberry, squash blossom, summer savory. **Happy relationship**: (See: Relationships). **Happy thoughts**: Plant: pansy. **Happy times**: Plant: wisteria.

Happiness of children: Plant: vervain. **Happiness in love**: Plant: patchouli; God: Sasthi. **Happiness from the past**: Animal: cicada. **Return of happiness**: Plant: lily of the valley.

To: accept happiness: Plant: zinnia. **attract happiness**: Stone: garnet, rose quartz; Plant: apple, lemon, orange, sunflower, vanilla, vervain, wisteria; *happy events*: Plant: vanilla. **increase happiness**: Stone: beryl, peridot. **stimulate happiness**: Stone: amber, garnet.

Unhappiness

Color: brown, gray; Plant: rue, wormwood; Goddess: Nedolya.

Unhappy marriage: (See: Marriage).

To: end unhappiness: Plant: jasmine. **protect against unhappiness**: Stone: peridot.

Harmony

(See also: Agreement, Peace, Tranquility)

Venus/Libra

Color: aqua, blue, light blue, dark blue, green, sea green, pink, white; Number: 1, 3, 6; Animal: dolphin, dove, porpoise; Stone: amber, carnelian, celestite, coral, pink diamond, emerald, galena, kunzite, lapis lazuli, malachite, manganite, moonstone, cluster of clear quartz crystals, rose quartz, pink tourmaline; Oil: palmarosa; Plant: angelica, anise, apple blossom, basil, bayberry, bergamot, catnip, cedar, chamomile, cherry blossom, cinnamon, clove, cypress, dulse, fir, frankincense, gardenia, geranium, hibiscus, hyssop, jasmine, juniper, lavender, lemon, lilac, lily of the valley, loosestrife, lotus, magnolia, meadowsweet, motherwort, myrrh, narcissus, orange, orchid, patchouli, pineapple weed, primrose, rose, rosemary, rosewood, rowan, sage, clary sage, sandalwood, sea pink, spikenard, spruce, strawberry, sunflower, tea tree, tuberose, valerian, lemon verbena, vervain, ylang-ylang; Goddess: Athene, Concordia, Harmonia, Ishtar, Lada, Pax; God: Forseti, Kuan Ti, Mabon, Mithras, Nagi, Obatala (Bringer of Peace and Harmony).

Domestic harmony: Color: blue, green; Plant: bayberry, camphor, cumin seed, narcissus, patchouli, pine, vetiver; Goddess: Concordia, Hestia, Uma, Verplace; God: Dhatri, Unkulunkulu. **Family harmony**: Goddess: Verplace. **Group harmony**: Plant: mullein. **Inner harmony**: Color: pink; Stone: tourmaline; Plant: lotus. **Parent/child harmony**: Plant: cypress, motherwort, pineapple weed. **Sexual harmony**: Stone: garnet. **Spiritual harmony**: Plant: lotus.

Harmonious action: Color: blue; Plant: bluebell. **Harmonious home**: Plant: cumin. **Harmonious relationship**: (See: Relationships). **Harmonious surroundings**: Stone: amber, amethyst, quartz crystals, rose quartz, tiger's eye; Plant: camphor, petrified wood; God: Unkulunkulu. **Harmony in the workplace**: Animal: beaver; Plant: chamomile.

To: attract harmony: Plant: basil, lilac. **create harmony**: Plant: vervain. **restore harmony**: Charm: Celtic cross; Stone: moonstone; Plant: betony, comandra, lily of the valley, rowan.

Disharmony

(See also: Discord, Strife)

Mars/Aries

Color: black, greenish yellow; Number: 6; Stone: fire garnet, onyx, opal; Plant: blackthorn, wormwood; Goddess: Ate, Discordia, Eris; God: Ares.

To: banish disharmony: Plant: betony. **clear disharmony**: Tool: besom, censer; Method: smudging, sweeping; Stone: iolite; Plant: betony (as incense). **clear everything causing disharmony**: Stone: torbenite. **protect against disharmony**: Oil: palmarosa. Plant: geranium.

Harvest

(See also: Agriculture)

Full Moon/August/September/October

Goddess: Akka, Ala, Ambika, Artemis Tridaria, Campestres, Ceres, Delia, Demeter, Erce, Habondia, Latiaran, Mama Allpa, Modron, Morgay, Renenet, Tailtiu, Zisa; God: Adonis, Cromm Cruaich, Cronos, Damuzi, Esus, Hou-chi, Perun, Uwolowu, Volos; Evocation: Harvest May, Harvest Mother.

Bountiful harvest: Goddess: Bast, Kupole; God: Baal, Enbilulu-Gugal, Illya, Janus, Maximon, Tammuz. **Grain harvests**: Charm: last sheaf of grain in the field; Goddess: Baba, Ceres, Corn Mother, Grandmother, Old Corn Woman, Old Woman, Zitniamatka; Evocation: Corn Maiden, Lityerses, Maneros; *rye*: Goddess: Mother of Rye; *wheat*: Goddess: Mother of Wheat. **Grape harvests**: God: Accasbel.

Harvest blessings: Plant: wheat; **harvest spirit/s**: (See: Spirits). **Harvest vehicles**: God: Sarritor. **Positive omen for harvests**: Charm: spring Sabbat bonfire smoke blowing in the direction of the field; Animal: a wolf seen running through the field with his tail held high.

To: call storms that ruin harvests: Goddess: Hecate. **harvest the fruits of anything you have sown**: God: Byelobog.

Healing

(See also: The Body, Disease, Health, Illness, Recovery)

Sun/Earth/Full Moon/Waxing Moon/Earth/Air/Fire/Water/North/East/Monday/Tuesday/Sunday/Aquarius/Scorpio

Tool: rattle, ash wand, hazel wand, willow wand; Method: candle magick, galdr; Color: blue (all shades), brown, clear, gold, green, emerald green, orange, purple, red, turquoise, violet, white; Charm: bread, condor feather, musk; Number: 1, 3, 7, 9, 33; Animal: adder, boar, condor, dog, dolphin, eagle, fox, frog, hummingbird, ibis, ram, rattlesnake, raven, toad, whale, two entwined snakes; Stone: agate (especially green, black, red, moss or leopardskin agate), amber, amethyst, ametrine, aquamarine, aventurine, blue aventurine, azurite, beryl, bloodstone, calcite, blue calcite, carnelian, celestite, chrysoprase, citrine, coral, diamond, dioptase, emerald, flint, fluorite, garnet, Goddess rock, hematite, Herkimer diamond, jade, jasper (especially red, green or leopardskin jasper, jet, kunzite, lapis lazuli, lodestone, malachite, moldovite, moonstone, peridot, quartz crystal, rose quartz, ruby, sapphire, sodalite, sugilite, sulfur, tiger's eye, topaz, green tourmaline, turquoise, zircon, red zircon; Metal: brass, copper, gold, iron, peacock ore, silver, steel; Oil: palmarosa; Plant: adder's tongue, allspice, aloe, amaranth, anemone, angelica, apple, ash, balm, balm of Gilead, balsam, barley, basil, benzoin, betony, birch, bittersweet, bracken, bramble, burdock, calamus, camphor, cannabis, carnation, cassia, cedar, chamomile, wild cherry, horse chestnut, cinnamon, cinquefoil, citron, citrus, clove, clover, coffee (in bath), comfrey, coriander, cotton, cowslip, cranberry, cucumber, cypress, dandelion, dock, yellow dock, dragon's blood, elder, eucalyptus, all evergreens, everlasting, fennel, figwort, flax seed, frankincense, gardenia, garlic, geranium, red geranium, ginger, ginseng, golden seal, goat's rue, grapefruit, groundsel, hazel, heather, heliotrope, hedge woundwort, henna, honeysuckle, hops, horehound, hyssop, ivy, jasmine, Job's tears, juniper, kava kava, laurel, lavender, lemon, lemon balm, lily of the valley, lime, loranthus, lotus, mandrake (especially in a white cloth or mojo bag), marjoram, marshmallow, marsh woundwort, mesquite, milkweed, mimosa, mint, mistletoe, mugwort, mullein, mustard, myrrh, nettle, oak, oak moss, olive, onion, oregano, pawpaw, pennyroyal, pepper, peppermint, persimmon, petrified wood, pine, plantain, plum, potato, rose, rose hip, rosemary, rosemary with juniper berry, rowan, rue, saffron, sage, sandalwood, St. John's Wort, savory, saw palmetto, spearmint, spikenard, spruce, stinging nettle, tansy, tea tree, thistle, thyme, ti, valerian, vervain, blue vervain, violet, willow, wintergreen, woodruff, wood sorrel, wormwood, yarrow, yerba santa; Goddess: Achelois, Aibheaeg, Aine, Airmid, Anagtia, Anahita, Anceta, Ancomna, Angina, Angitia, Arnamentia, Artemis Caryatis, Artemis of the Thousand Breasts, Athena, Athene Hygeia, Bast, Board, Bormana, Bricta, Brigantia, Brigid, Caolainn, Carmenta, Ceadda, Ceibhfhionn, Clota, Coatlicue, Coventina, Cybele, Damona, Dazimus, Eir, Epona, Fand, Freya, Glispa, Gula, Gullveig, Habetrot, Hathor, Hebe, Hecate, Helice, Hygeia, Ina, Inanna, Ishtar, Isis (Isis Medica, Great Sorceress Who Heals), Itzpapalotl, Ivilla, Ix Chel, Kamrusepas, Kupala, Magaia, Mary, Mati Syra Zemlya, the Matronaea, Meduna, Minerva Medica, Morgan le Fay, Morgen, Nehalennia, Nephthys, Nortia, Oenone, Panacea, Philyra, Qadesh, Rosmerta, Scathach, Sekhmet (The Great One of Healing), Sequana, Sirona, Sulis, Teteoinnan, Tozi, Ushas, Vila, Yemaya; God: Ah Kin Xoc, Al-Shafi, Apollo, Apollo Grannus, Asclepius, Baal Marqod, Babalu Ayé, Bel, Borvo, Cian, the Dagda, Dian Cecht, Dionysus, Endouellicus, Eshmun, Govannon, Hastehogan, Horus, Imhotep, Itzamna, Ixtlilton, Khonsu, Khors, Legba, Lugh, Maponus, Marduk (Great Healer), Mars Ocelus, Maximon, Mercury, Nuadh, Paeon (Healer of All Ills), Rudra, Serapis, Shiva, Slaine, Suko-No-Biko, Thoth, Vishnu, Vorocius, Vu-Kutis, Yanauluha (Great Medicine Man), Zeus Nosios; Evocation: the Camenae, Chiron, the Wilden Wip.

Aggressive healing: Animal: copperhead. **Emotional healing**: Color: aqua; *after a loss*: Color: sea green, fuchsia, lavender; Stone: agate, amber, aventurine, citrine, emerald, malachite, morganite, rose quartz, sodalite; Plant: amber, balm of Gilead, bleeding heart, cyclamen, fuschia, lavender, lemon balm, orange, sweetgale, ylang-ylang; Goddess: Saitada; Evocation: mermaids; *after a relationship ends*: Plant: lemon balm, lily, rue. **Herbal healing**: Plant: herbs picked in August; Goddess: Eir. **Inner healing**: Stone: amethyst; Plant: buffalo gourd, heather, self-heal; *male inner healing*: Charm: musk. **Mental healing**: Stone: citrine. **Organic healing**: Color: red. **Physical healing**: Stone: amethyst, bloodstone, coral, jade, jasper, sodalite, sugilite, turquoise; Plant: mistletoe; God: Dian Cecht. **Psychic healing**: Color: indigo; Stone: azurite, quartz crystal; Plant: honeysuckle; Goddess: Sekhmet. **Psychological healing**: Animal: swan; Stone: amber, amethyst, ametrine, citrine, sodalite; *to open the way for*: Stone: chrysoprase; Plant: lemon balm, black hellebore, madwort; Evocation: Melampus. **Remote healing**: Metal: peacock ore; Stone: clear quartz crystal, moldovite;

for focus in: Stone: lodestone. **Self-healing**: Animal: frog; Stone: amber, hematite, green jade, moldovite; Plant: self-heal. **Sexual healing**: Venus; Color: red; Goddess: Kilili-Mushritu. **Spiritual healing**: Color: magenta; Stone: moldovite, unakite; Plant: fennel seeds; Goddess: Tara; *to protect spiritual healers*: Stone: moldovite.

Healing chants: Air; Goddess: Glispa. **Healing dreams**: (See: Dreams). **Healing energy**: (See: Energy). **Healing image spells**: Color: blue; Charm: poppet; Plant: potato, rosemary. **Healing incantations**: (See: Incantations). **Healing incense**: *to increase the magickal power of*: Plant: mesquite. **Healing plants**: *knowledge of*: (See: Knowledge). **Healing power**: (See: Power). **Healing rituals**: Goddess: Sulis. **Healing songs**: Animal: nightingale. **Healing springs**: Water; Goddess: Ceadda, Coventina, Egeria, Epona, Ianuaria, Icovellauna, Ivilla, Magaia, Meduna, Vercana, Visuna; God: Babalu Ayé. **Healing touch**: Scorpio; Animal: deer. **Healing vibrations**: (See: Vibrations). **Healing waters**: Water; Goddess: Coventina, Sulis.

Patience in healing: Animal: crane. **Strength to heal**: Plant: broom.

To heal: alienation: Plant: mariposa lilly. **animals**: Color: brown; Plant: agrimony, catnip. **animal bites**: Stone: emerald (venomous beasts). **bitterness**: Stone: moss agate. **chakras**: Stone: turquoise. **emotional pain**: (See: Pain). **emotional trauma**: (See: Trauma). **the heart**: Plant: witch hazel; *a broken heart*: (See: Heartbreak). **injuries**: Plant: clover. **jealousy**: Animal: hummingbird; Goddess: Oenone; God: Abarta. **negativity from past lives**: Stone: hawk's eye. **passion**: (See: Passion). **plants**: Color: brown; Plant: chamomile (living plant, placed near sick plants). **a relationship**: Plant: basil. **separation**: Plant: mariposa lilly. **sorrow**: Goddess: Tara. **the spirit**: (See: Spirit).

To heal: with light: Sun. **by poetic incantations at sacred wells**: Goddess: Brigid.

To: allow yourself to heal: Plant: aloe. **awaken your inner healer**: Plant: eucalyptus. **focus healing**: Stone: lodestone. **get in touch with the universal healing force**: Aquarius. **learn healing**: Goddess: Athena. **open the way for healing**: Plant: bergamot. **release healing**: Plant: elder, rosemary. **speed healing**: Mercury; Stone: green aventurine, turquoise; Plant: aloe vera, cedar, cinnamon, Echinacea, elecampane, grass of Parnassus, oregano, southernwood, thyme, crown of amaranth flowers; *after circumcision*: Goddess: Weri Kumbaba; *of wounds*: Plant: gotu kola, plantain. **stimulate healing**: Stone: bloodstone, iolite, lapis lazuli. **strengthen healing herbs**: Stone: sunstone; Plant: betony.

Health

(See also: Healing, Well-being)

Sun/New Moon/Water/Earth

Charm: Eye of Horus, blue feather, dance around a Sabbat bonfire; Color: blue, light blue, green, orange, pink, red, rose, violet; Number: 4, 6, 7, 8; Animal: serpent; Stone: agate, moss agate, amethyst, aquamarine, aventurine, brown rocks, carnelian, garnet, Goddess rock, Herkimer diamond, jade, jasper, red or green jasper, jet, pearl, peridot, ruby, salt, staurolite, sunstone, tourmaline; Metal: copper; Plant: amber, anemone, apple, ash, banana, birch, camphor, caraway, carnation, carob, cinquefoil, coriander, elder, eucalyptus, everlasting, fern, figwort, galangal, gardenia, garlic, geranium, rose geranium, ginger, ginseng, goat's rue, groundsel, guarana seed, heliotrope, honeysuckle, Iceland moss, jasmine, juniper, knotweed, larkspur, lavender, lemon, mandrake, marjoram, melon, mistletoe, mullein, myrrh, nutmeg, oak, oak moss, onion, orange, pimpernel, pine, plantain, rose, rose hips, rose of Jericho, rue, saffron, sage, St. John's Wort, sassafras, scarlet pimpernel, self-heal, sorrel, spikenard, sumbul, sunflower, tansy, thyme, violet, walnut, wintergreen, wood sorrel, yarrow, yerba mate; Goddess: Anahita, Anath, Apa, Artemis, Bast, Bormana, Brigid, Brigantia, Caedda, the Camenae, Carmenta, Carna, Coatlicue (Mother of Health), Cocomama, Danu, Demeter, Eir, Erzulie, Fand, Frigg, Ganga, Gula Bau, Hygeia (Health-Bringer), Inanna, Jaso, Kamrusepas, Kwan Yin, Liban, Mary (Health of the Afflicted), the Matronaea, Meditrina, Munthukh, Neith, Oshun, Panacea, Qadesh, Rhea, Rigantona, Salus, Saukhyada (Bestower of Well-Being), Sekhmet, Sulis, Tara, Tonantzin, Turan, Valetudo; God: Abhjnaraja, Acan Chob, Adonis, Agnitas, Ahau Chamahez, Al-Shafi, Alawaimis, Apollo, Asclepius, Asokottamasri (medicine buddha), Baal, Babalu Ayé, Basamum, Bel, Belenus, Bhaisajyagura, Bile, Binzuku, Borvo, Bran, Chic Chac Chob, Dian Cecht, Dharmakirtisagaraghosa (medicine buddha), Dhatri, Eshmun, Famien, Mars, Melkarth, Obatala, Ra, Rudra, Shen-nung, Tatanka, Tatevali, Tien Kuan, Zeus; Evocation: Chiron.

Bad health: Charm: Broken promise, stagnant water; *to protect against*: Stone: jet. **Good health**: Sun/Fire; Color: blue, green, pink, orange, rose; Charm: Eye of Horus; Animal: monkey; Stone: agate, aquamarine, carnelian, Goddess rock, peridot; Potion: apple cider, apple juice; Plant: apple, garlic, High John, lavender, mistletoe, olive, onion, papaya, peach, rosemary, sage, tarragon, wintergreen, yarrow; Goddess: Ardvi Sura Anahita, Arogyada (Granter of Good Health), Bast, Eir, Erzulie, Fand, Ganga, Hygeia (Bringer of Good Health), Meditrina, Neith, Panacea, Qadesh, Sulis; *to attract*: Stone: dioptase, jade; Animal:

rabbit; Plant: ginseng, lilac, nutmeg, orange; *to increase*: Waxing Moon; Plant: thyme; *to maintain*: Charm: gold chain (worn); Color: green, rose; Stone: green beryl, garnet, green jade; Plant: apple, aspen, eucalyptus, figwort, larch, oregano, rosemary, sage, wintergreen, yarrow; *to protect*: Stone: amber, green jasper; Plant: galangal, ginseng, tarragon; Goddess: Vyadhinashini (Vanquisher of Ailments); *to restore*: Stone: moss agate; *good health with marriage*: Goddess: Paraskeva-Platnitsa; *good health during travel*: Plant: comfrey root. **Mental health**: Stone: sugilite, tigereye, tourmaline; Plant: madwort, sage, St. John's Wort. **Physical health**: Color: green, yellow; Stone: green aventurine, bloodstone. **Public health**: Plant: birch; Goddess: Salus. **Women's health**: Goddess: Eir. **Health wishes**: Plant: cinquefoil.

Healthy animals: Goddess: Brigid; *healthy milk production in cows*: Plant: wreathes of cowslip. **Healthy attitude**: Stone: fluorite, garnet. **Healthy aura**: Color: orange; Plant: jasmine, myrrh. **Healthy baby**: (See: Babies). **Healthy childbirth**: Plant: nuts. **Healthy children**: (See: Children). **Healthy crops**: (See: Agriculture). **Healthy family**: Goddess: Jara. **Healthy garden**: Color: green; Stone: moss agate, jade. **Healthy growth**: Stone: peridot. **Healthy hair**: Stone: galena; Oil: petitgrain; Plant: ylang-ylang. **Healthy husband**: Goddess: Maha Lakshmi (Great Lakshmi). **Healthy life**: Stone: ruby. **Healthy mind**: Stone: turquoise. **Healthy pleasure**: Plant: marigold. **Healthy relationship**: (See: Relationships). **Healthy self-esteem**: Plant: red rose. **Healthy sex life**: Goddess: Parvati; God: Bes. **Healthy skin**: Plant: aloe vera, sandalwood, tea tree, ylang-ylang. **Healthy trees**: Goddess: Brigid.

To: **improve health**: Waxing Moon; Stone: green agate, garnet; Plant: ginseng, goldenseal; *of plants*: Stone: jade; Plant: chamomile, honeysuckle. **protect health**: Goddess: Danu. **treat health problems caused by anger**: Stone: sodalite.

Heartbreak

(See also: Emotions, Grief, Happiness, Loss, Sorrow)

Plant: bleeding heart; Goddess: Branwen; Evocation: Deirdre of the Sorrows.

To: **ease heartbreak**: Water; Color: red; Stone: aventurine, chrysocolla, chrysoprase, garnet, rose quartz; Plant: amaranth, balm of Gilead (carried close to the heart), cinquefoil, feverfew, gardenia, lavender, myrtle, white rose petals, rosemary, swallow wort, violet leaf (worn in shoe), yarrow; Goddess: Branwen, Oenone, Tara; Evocation: Selemnus. **protect against heartbreak**: Plant: bistort root.

Help

(See: Assistance)

Hesitation

Color: brown.

To **stop hesitation**: Animal: cormorant, all diving birds.

Hexes

(See also: Evil, Magick, Spells, Uncrossing, Witchcraft)

Moon/Earth

Tool: aspen rod, blackthorn staff; Charm: demon bowl, footprint, lead tablet, poppet, witch bottle; Color: black; Charm: footprint, hair, nail clipping; Animal: dog; Metal: lead; Stone: salt; Potion: liquor; Plant: asafetida, blackthorn, chicory, dill, elder, hyssop, kelp, black pepper, hot pepper, wormwood;

Goddess: Anath, Cailleach, Carman, Hecate, Morgan le Fay, Ninhursag, Sulis, Tellus.

To: **absorb hexes**: Plant: violet. **avert hexes**: Tool: mirror; Color: red; Charm: hex sign; Stone: jet, salt; Metal: silver; Potion: liquor; Plant: ash leaves, dragon's blood, hellebore, hyssop, rue. **clear hexes from the home**: Plant: pennyroyal (strewn indoors). **destroy hexes**: Plant: High John, horehound. **overcome/remove hexes**: Full Moon/Waning Moon; Color: black, blue, red; Tool: besom; Charm: black cat hair, broken chain, van van; Stone: salt; Plant: agrimony, ague weed, angelica, aspen, balsam, bamboo, basil, bergamot, bloodroot, cedar, chamomile, chili pepper, cinquefoil, citronella, clove, cyclamen, datura, dragon's blood, eye of Satan, galangal, gardenia, garlic, geranium, rose geranium, ginger, ginseng, High John, holy thistle, honeysuckle, horehound, huckleberry, hydrangea, hyssop, juniper, laurel, lilac, Low John, mandrake, mint, myrrh, nettle, nutmeg, orris root, palo azul, palo santo, papaya, patchouli, black pepper, hot peppers, pine, poke root, rose geranium, rosemary, rue, sandalwood, sassafras, soapwort, spindle tree, squill, sweet pea, ti, toadflax, verbena, vervain, vetiver, wintergreen, wisteria, yucca root; Goddess: Sheela-na-gig; *overcome love hexes*: Plant: dill, rose petals. **protect against hexes**: Charm: eye of Horus; Stone: emerald, jet, clear quartz crystal, onyx; Plant: angelica, ash leaves, carob, cascara sagrada, clover, devil's shoestring, dragon's blood, eye of Satan, fern, hellebore, juniper (burned), laurel, mullein, nettle, rosemary, rowan branch (hung over the doorway), rue, vetiver (burned); Goddess: Hecate; *protect a business from hexes*: Plant: marjoram. **release hexes**: Plant: basil, balsam, nutmeg. **reverse a hex (return it to its source)**: Tool: mirror; Color: red, white; Stone: red jasper; Plant: agrimony, bayberry, chestnut, citronella, galangal, Low John, nettle, nutmeg, bitter orange, pine, rue, witch grass.

The Home
(See also: Family, Land, Real Estate)

Moon/Earth/Monday/Taurus/Cancer

Color: brown, gold, orange, yellow; Number: 6; Goddess: Chantico, Ertha, Hestia, Jara, Juno, Marena, Mokosh, Nonadieve, the Suleviae, Taweret; God: Dabog, Satyanarayana. Evocation: the Kikimora.

Calm home: Color: pale blue; Stone: blue lace agate; Plant: amber, coriander, dragon's blood, narcissus, passionflower, rose, vervain, ylang-ylang; *to restore calm to the home*: Color: purple; Plant: nettle. **Happy home**: Method: hearth magick; Charm: horseshoe (over the door); Stone: blue lace agate; Plant: daisy, patchouli, vanilla, ylang-ylang; Goddess: Chantico, Verplace, Vesta; God: Bes. **Harmonious home**: Plant: cumin. **New home**: *to bless*: Color: blue; Charm: bread; Stone: coal, salt; Oil: palmarosa; *to find*: Animal: rabbit; Goddess: Hestia; *to protect*: garlic; *good fortune for*: Plant: coca leaf; Goddess: Pachamama. **Peaceful home**: Method: hearth magick; Color: pale blue; Animal: cicada; Stone: quartz crystal; Plant: basil, bayberry, bougainvillea, coriander seed, cumin seed, dragon's blood, dulse, enchanter's nightshade, eryngo, gardenia, heather, lavender, lilac, loosestrife, meadowsweet, mistletoe (hung up), olive leaf, passion flower, patchouli, peach, pennyroyal, purslane, reindeer moss, rose petals, scullcap, lemon verbena, vervain, ylang-ylang; Goddess: Chantico, Hestia, Vesta; Evocation: the Domovoi; *to return peace to a home*: Charm: rosewater; Plant: rose, **Prosperous home**: Color: green; Animal:

chicken; Stone: green calcite; Plant: alfalfa, bayberry, American mandrake; Goddess: Jara; Evocation: the Domovoi; *prosperity of the family home*: Charm: ash Yule log; God: Majas Gars. **Quiet home**: Plant: dragon's blood, patchouli, peach. **Safe home**: Goddess: Demeter; *safe house for battered women*: Goddess: Juno. **Spiritual home**: Charm: altar; Plant: African violet.

Love of home: Cancer. **Home improvements**: Animal: deer mouse; Goddess: Hestia. **Home security**: (See: Security).

House cats: Goddess: Bast. **Household spirits**: (See: Spirits). **Housekeeping**: Goddess: Brigid. **Housework**: (See: Work).

Domestic abuse/violence: (See: Violence). **Domestic arts**: Goddess: Athena, Brigid, Ix Chel, Neith. **Domestic harmony**: (See: Harmony). **Domestic life**: Goddess: Ertha, Vesta; God: Bes; *to protect*: Goddess: Neith. **Domestic matters**: Goddess: Cardea, Chantico, Dugnai, Nonadieve, Sif; God: Gucumatz; Evocation: the Kikimora. **Domestic order**: (See: Order). **Domestic pleasures**: God: Bes.

To attract: a home: Animal: rabbit. **blessings to the home**: *spiritual blessings*: Plant: anise, basil, bayberry, lavender, thyme; God: Ganesha. **friends to the home**: Plant: citronella, frangipani. **love to the home**: (See: Love). **good luck to the home**: Charm: horseshoe (hung over doorway); Animal: cicada, cricket; Plant: aloe, basil, bayberry, catnip (grown indoors or in the yard), clove; *to the household*: Animal: cricket (if found on the hearth); Plant: aloe, basil, bayberry, catnip (grown indoors, or in the yard). **money to the home**: (See: Money).

To: avert bad luck from the home: Plant: cumin. **balance energy in the home**: Animal: goldfish. **bless a home**: Charm (sprinkled): rosewater, salt and water; Stone: salt; Oil: palmarosa; Plant: dill, lavender, olive, rose, vervain. **bless keys**: Charm: throw them into a fire. **clear the home**: Tool: besom, censer; Method: asperging, sweeping, washing; Charm: floor wash, infusion of broom tops; Stone: salt; Plant: benzoin, camphor, cumin seed, hawthorn, hyssop, laurel, myrrh, pine, rose; *clear evil/hexes from the home*: Plant: pennyroyal (strewn indoors); *clear spirits from the home*: (See: Spirits). **protect the home**: (See: Security). **prevent evil from entering the house**: Plant: dogwood (rubbed on doorknobs), fennel (hung over doorways), garlic, nettle, papaya twigs (over the door), pomegranate tree (grown outside the door), rosemary (grown in the yard or near the door); *prevent evil spirits from entering*: Plant: hawthorn. **purify the home**: Charm: Kananga Water; Plant: allspice. **remove evil from the home**: Plant: pennyroyal (strewn in the house). **return home**: Plant: mugwort; Goddess: Persephone; Evocation: Odysseus.

Honesty

(See also: Deceit, Truth)

Sagittarius

Color: brown, clear; Charm: cicada in a hat; Animal: boar, kookaburra; Metal: gold; Stone: chalcedony; Plant: amber, basil, dragon's blood, High John, honesty, honeysuckle, lemongrass, mullein, rosemary, thyme; Goddess: Aequitas, Fides, Ma'at; God: Anubis, Obatala, Thoth.

Honor

Jupiter/Fire/Thursday

Color: blue, royal blue, pink, rose; Animal: crane, stork; Stone: jacinth, pearl, zircon; Plant: apple, cardinal flower, ivy, laurel, parsley, pine; Goddess: Hokmah, Maia, Majestas, Mary (Vessel of Honor), Pietas, Rhiannon; God: Fides, Jupiter, Mithras, Tyr.

Military honor: God: Honus, Tyr.

To: **attract honor**: Plant: frankincense, myrrh. **restore honor**: Goddess: Rhiannon.

To honor: **ancestors**: Tool: ancestral altar; Animal: crow, rook; Plant: cypress. **the dead**: (See: The Dead). **deities**: (See: The Divine). **parents**: Goddess: Isis, Pietas.

Honors

Color: purple, violet; Plant: juniper.

To attract honors: Metal: gold.

Hope

(See also: Optimism/Pessimism)

Uranus/Sun/Rising Sun/Aquarius

Color: blue, white; Animal: carp, firefly, heron (seeming to fly out of the sun); Charm: anchor, white feather, gray-and white-feather; Metal: gold; Stone: amazonite, opal, malachite, moonstone; Plant: almond, flowering almond, date palm, silver fir, hawthorn, pomegranate, white poplar, snowdrop, violet; Goddess: Astraea, Branwen, the Maiden, Pandora, Spes; God: Asar-alim, Cautes.

Dead hope: Plant: bindweed. **Deceitful hope**: Plant: daffodil. **Lost hope**: Plant: black poplar. **Renewed hope**: Plant: azalea, snowdrop; God: Mider. **Secret hope**: Metal: tin. **Withered hope**: Plant: garden anemone. **Hope in adversity**: Plant: Norway spruce. **Hope of immortality**: Animal: goat stag, stag. **Hope of marriage**: Plant: bachelors button, hawthorn. **Hope of rebirth/reincarnation**: (See: Reincarnation).

To attract hope: Stone: moonstone.

Hopelessness

Setting Sun

Plant: amaranth, black poplar, yew; Goddess: Louhi; God: Cautopates. **Hopeless love**: Plant: yellow tulip.

To overcome hopelessness: Goddess: Nephthys.

Hospitality
(See also: Generosity, Graciousness)

South/East

Charm: bread; Plant: lotus, oak, pineapple, tangerine; Goddess: Ertha, Estsanatlehi, Fatimah, Hestia, Nerthus, Themis; God: Aegir, Tatanka, Thor, Zeus Xenios; Evocation: Baucis.

Formal hospitality: God: Aryaman.

Inhospitality

God: Bres.

To punish inhospitality: Goddess: the Erinyes.

Hunting
(See also: Animals)

Moon/New Moon/Autumn/Tuesday/ Sagittarius

Charm: arrow, arrowhead; Animal: dog, hyena, lioness, orca, polar bear, wolf, all predators; Stone: amethyst; Plant: mistletoe, evening primrose; Goddess: Abnoba, Anath, Arduinna, Artemis (Huntress, Lady of Wild Animals), Artio, Astarte, Atalanta (Virgin Huntress), Banka Mundi, Britomartis, Carravogue, Ceres, Dali, Diana (The Huntress), Dilwica, Dziewona, Flidais, Garbh Ogh, Hastseoltoi, Hecate, Ishtar, Mielikki, Neith (The Huntress), Oya, Pinga, Poshjo-Akka, Sarama (The Huntress), Skadi, Ushas, Vesna, Zonget, Zvoruna; God: Anhur (Divine Huntsman), Apollo, Aspalis, Cernunnos (Lord of the Hunt), Cocidius, Cunomaglus (Hound Lord), Erra, Herne (The Hunter), Mixcoatl, Nergal, Ogun, Oshosi, Rundas, Silvanus, Tatanka, Tekkeitserto, Tirawa, Ullr, Vosegus, Zip; Evocation: Keevan, Orion, Sosondowah.

Bear hunting: God: Leib Olmai, Mercury Artaios. **Beaver hunting**: Animal: Great Beaver. **Boar hunting**: God: Mercury Moccus. **Good hunt**: God: Itzamna, Zip. **Good luck/fortune in hunting**: Plant: mistletoe; Goddess: Hecate, Pinga, Yamano-kami; God: Kanati (The Lucky Hunter), Lein-Olmai. **Reindeer hunting**: Plant: aspen, larch; God: Kied kie Jubmel (Lord of Herds). **Seal hunting**: *to avenge*: Evocation: selkies. **Stag hunting**: God: Silvanus Callirius (Lord of the Woodland). **Successful hunt**: Method: trance; Goddess: Hastseoltoi; God: Asdiwal, Herne; *omen of success*: Animal: buffalo.

Hunting dance: Evocation: Ocasta. **Fearlessness in hunting**: Goddess: Banka-Mundi.

To: have accurate aim: Stone: turquoise. **hunt at night**: Animal: owl, wolf. **hunt down anything/anyone**: God: Marduk. **hunt down those who deserve punishment**: Animal: white dog with red ears; Goddess: the Erinyes. **master hunting**: Animal: cougar; God: Arawn, Horned God, Tekkeitserktock. **protect hunters**: Goddess: Hastseyalti; God: Rudra. **protect animals from hunters**: Goddess: Caipora; God: Leshy.

Chapter 9

Idealism

Fire/Aquarius/Aries

Color: purple, violet; Number: 9, 11, 22; Stone: bloodstone.

Practical idealism: Color: purple. **Lofty ideals**: Plant: oak.

Idealistic love: Libra. **To hold to ideals**: Color: indigo.

Ideas

Waxing Moon/Air/Gemini

Number: 1.

Illuminating ideas: God: Shango. **New ideas**: New Moon; Stone: amethyst, pink tourmaline; Goddess: the Maiden. **Sound ideas**: God: Osiris. **Devotion to an idea**: Color: pale blue. **To turn an idea into reality**: Tool: wand.

Ignorance

(See also: Enlightenment, Knowledge, Wisdom)

Color: dark brown; Number: 7.

Ignorance that causes the cycle of reincarnation: Center.

To: choose enlightenment over ignorance: Goddess: Eve. **destroy/overcome ignorance**: Goddess: Kali; God: Gwydion, Shiva. **protect against ignorance**: Goddess: Durga; Evocation: Virudhaka.

Illness

(See also: The Body, Diseases/Disorders, Healing, Health Pain, Recovery)

[NOTE: All correspondences are given here as charms. Some of the plants are poisonous, and nothing is meant to be ingested. Magick is a supplement to medical care, not a substitute for it. In most cases, incense should not be burned near patients.]

Plant: anemone; Goddess: Coyolxauhqui, Kipu-Tytto, Marena Moru, Triduana; God: Agas, Asakku, Kanaloa, Mait' Carrefour.

Childhood illnesses: Cancer; Plant: mistletoe, saffron; *to avert*: Stone: jade. **Chronic illness**: Taurus; Number: 8; Plant: yellow gentian; *to end*: Waning Moon; Plant: violet. **Long illness**: *to recover from*: Plant: eucalyptus. **Mental illness**: Moon/Full Moon/Mercury/Water; Goddess: Aine, Lilith, Nyx; God: Dionysus, Pan the Pursuer; *to avert*: Plant: clover, St. John's Wort; *to banish*: Stone: chalcedony; *to calm*: Stone: topaz; *to cause*: Color: red; Charm: honey from box tree flowers; Plant: chili pepper, black hellebore, henbane, mandrake; Aine, Cybele, Discordia, Eris, Inanna; God: Herabe; *to diagnose*: Stone: malachite; *to protect against*: Stone: yellow chrysolite, topaz; Plant: mandrake; *to survive*: Goddess: Goleuddydd; God: Dionysus; *to treat*: Color: indigo; Charm: rye bread; Stone: amethyst, aventurine, beryl, bloodstone, chrysolite, diamond, fluorite, lapis lazuli, rhodochrosite, topaz; Plant: betony, cattail, chamomile, clover, datura, daffodil, gotu kola, black hellebore, honesty, madwort, mistletoe, rose, rue, sage, St. John's Wort; Goddess: Aine, Hera; God: Shiva; *divine madness*: God: Dionysus; *holy madness*: Goddess: Cybele; *the line between genius and madness*: Aquarius (See also: Depression). **The mentally ill**: *compassion for*: Stone: green jasper; *peace of mind for*: Plant: hyacinth; *to help*: God: Shiva (See also: Depression). **Psychosomatic illness**: Virgo/Capricorn; God: Babalu Aye; *to improve*: Plant: fuchsia, jasmine.

Fever: Mars/Fire; Color: pink; *to avert*: Stone: chrysolite, jet; Plant: beech, coriander, cypress, dogwood, yellow gentian, hazel, logwood, St. John's Wort, wormwood, yarrow; *to cause*: Plant: lily; *to protect against*: Charm: left eyetooth of a crocodile; Stone: red jasper; Plant: beech, cassia, cinnamon, cypress, endive, gentian, hazel; *to reduce*: Waning Moon; Color: indigo; Stone: agate, chrysoprase, emerald, garnet, hematite, peridot, clear quartz crystal, ruby; Plant: acacia, ash, barberry, basil, bayberry, beech, bergamot, bistort, blackthorn, borage, box tree, butchers broom, carnation, catnip, chamomile, chaste tree, cypress, date palm, dogwood, dragon's blood, Echinacea, elder, endive, eucalyptus, feverfew, frankincense, garlic, yellow gentian, ginger, ginseng, goldenseal, gotu kola, hazel, holly oak, holy thistle, juniper, kermes oak, lady's mantle, lemon balm, marigold, milk thistle, motherwort, mugwort, black mulberry, narcissus, oleaster, olive, orange, pansy, parsley, patchouli, pennyroyal, black pepper, peppermint, greater plantain, plum tree bark, poplar, putranjiva, safflower, saffron, sage, sarsaparilla, senna, sorrel, spearmint, sunflower, thyme, valerian, lemon verbena, vetiver, water lily, willow bark, wood aloes,

wormwood, yerba santa; *chills and fever*: Plant: catnip, elder, gravel root, lavender; *relapsing/recurrent fever*: Moon; Plant: dogwood, eucalyptus; *rheumatic fever*: Plant: crocus; *scarlet fever*: Plant: black cohosh; *yellow fever*: Plant: vetiver.

To: absorb illness: Stone: hematite, lodestone, moonstone; Plant: onion. **accept an illness or disability**: Evocation: Chiron (The Wounded Healer). **avert illness**: Charm: Four Thieves Vinegar; Stone: carnelian, green jasper, ruby; Plant: ash, comfrey, eucalyptus, laurel, oak, mistletoe twig, rosemary, rue, St. John's Wort, thyme, tonka bean, yerba santa; Goddess: Sekhmet; God: Perun. **banish illness**: Fire; Plant: acorn, ginger, peach branch, rosemary; Goddess: Triduana. **battle illness**: God: Bishamon. **cause illness**: Charm: fairy ring; Goddess: Ereshkigal, Gula. **cure illness**: Charm: fairy ring; Plant: four-leaf clover, myrrh; Goddess: Gula, Huchi, Morgan le Fay, Oya; God: Apollo the Physician, Damballah. **help someone who is ill**: Animal: dog, goose. **increase physical energy during illness**: Stone: sunstone, tigereye. **protect against illness**: Stone: carnelian; Plant: garlic, pine; God: Jizo Bosatsu; *protect children*: Plant: caraway seed; *protect the household*: Plant: eucalyptus, laurel, mandrake. **recover from illness**: Stone: jet; Plant: comfrey, nettles (under the bed), yucca root (as soap); *to speed recovery*: Plant: carnation, cayenne; Goddess: Oya. **remove illness**: Animal: guinea pig. **release illness**: God: Govannon. **resist illness**: Goddess: Ishtar.

▓Illumination

(See also: Enlightenment, Light, Wisdom)

Sun/Uranus/Moon/Full Moon/Dark Moon/Fire/East/Day/Sunday

Tool: candle, grimoire; Method: solar magick; Animal: coyote, firefly, glowworm, phosphorescent sea creatures; Metal: gold (given as a gift); Stone: pearl; Oil: palmarosa; Plant: cinnamon, wisteria; Goddess: Hecate, Isis, Kwan Yin, Pandia, Sekhmet (The One Who Enlightens the Land); God: Mitra, Mithras, Quetzalcoatl, Shiva, Sin (The Illuminator), Surya (Illuminator of Infinite Causes), Yarikh (Illuminator of Myriads).

Creative illumination: Color: orange; Stone: amber. **Inner illumination**: *to open to*: Animal: slug. **Spiritual illumination**: Method: candle magick; Animal: eagle; Plant: frankincense; Goddess: Tara; God: Dionysus; *sexuality as a road to*: Method: tantra; Goddess: Tara.

Illuminating ideas: God: Shango. **Wisdom leading to illumination**: Crescent Moon.

Illusion

(See also: Enchantment, Fascination, Reality, Truth)

Neptune/Moon/Air/Pisces

Method: seidr; Animal: dragonfly, spider; Plant: apple, bat nut; Goddess: Bidhgoe, Maya, Morgan le Fay, Vidya-Lakshmi; God: Dian Cecht, Gwydion, Manannan Mac Lir, Shiva; Evocation: Adekato, Cathbad, fairies, Merlin.

Visual illusions: Animal: chameleon; Goddess: Fata Morgana; Evocation: fairies; *mirages*: Goddess: Ignus Fatuus.

To: avert illusions: Stone: brown chalcedony, diamond. **clear illusions**: Charm: lead crystal; Stone: apophyllite; Plant: bladderwort. **distinguish between reality and illusion**: (See: Reality). **magnify illusions**: Stone: black obsidian. **overcome illusions**: Stone: aragonite, chalcedony; Goddess: Kali. **protect against illusions**: Stone: chalcedony, peridot; Plant: madwort. **recognize/dissolve illusion**: Color: white; Animal: dragonfly; Stone: azurite, chalcedony, jasper, clear quartz crystal; Plant: bladderwort, four-leaf clover, wolfsbane. **release illusions**: Charm: brimstone; Animal: snake; Stone: kyanite, sulfur; Plant: enchanter's nightshade, orchid.

Imagination

(See also: Creativity, Inspiration)

Air/West

Color: gray, yellow; Charm: sea shell; Number: 2, 6, 7; Animal: loon, monkey; Stone: aventurine, coral, garnet, rose quartz, sapphire; Plant: belladonna, cannabis, jasmine, lupin, clary sage.

Visionary imagination: Goddess: Turan. **Power of imagination**: Color: white. **To: activate imagination**: Stone: aventurine. **free the imagination**: Plant: cannabis.

Immortality

(See also: Fame, Longevity)

Sun

Charm: cartouche, narwhal horn, scarab, spiral, unicorn horn; Animal: cicada, crane, dragonfly, pig, scarab beetle, serpent, snake; Stone: cinnabar, jade, salt; Fungus: fly agaric; Plant: amaranth flower, globe amaranth, apple, balm of Gilead, bean plant, coriander seed, cypress, everlasting, frangipani, hazel, heather, laurel, linden, lotus, mango, Madagascar periwinkle, mistletoe, peach, pine, pomegranate, sage, sorb apple, tansy, vervain, yew; Goddess: Angerboda, Anima Mundi, Annis, Apa, Chang-O, Estsanatlehi, Hebe, Helice, the Hesperides, Hokmah, Ho Hsien-Ku, Idunn, Morgen, Xi Wang-Mu; God: Ameretat, Dushares, Nyambe, the Pa-hsien (The Eight Immortals), Sin, Soma.

Physical immortality: God: Ameretat. **Poetic immortality**: Plant: apple. **Spiritual immortality**: God: Ameretat. **Immortality

through wisdom: Plant: apple. **Hope of immortality**: Animal: goat stag, stag. **Promise of immortality**: Plant: apple, apple blossom; God: Serapis.

Immortality of: deities: Goddess: Anath, Idunn. **the soul**: Animal: birds; Goddess: Demeter; God: Dionysus, Jesus, Mithras.

Improvement

(See also: Increase)

Sun

Stone: lapis lazuli; Plant: ginger.

Home improvements: Goddess: Hestia. **Mental improvement**: Stone: fluorite; Plant: vanilla bean; **Self-improvement**: Mercury/New Moon/Wednesday; Stone: smoky quartz.

To improve: appetite: (See: The Body). **autism**: (See: Diseases/Disorders). **brain function**: (See: The Body). **circulation**: (See: The Body). **concentration**: Plant: ginkgo, ginseng, hawthorn. **depression**: (See: Depression). **communication skills**: Plant: papyrus. **eyesight**: (See: Senses). **fortune**: Goddess: Gefion. **health**: (See: Health). **hearing**: Plant: garlic, ginkgo. **karma**: Goddess: Kwan Yin. **kidney function**: Plant: ginger. **liver function**: Stone: emerald; Plant: gentian, wormwood. **an unhappy marriage**: (See: Marriage). **memory**: (See: Memory). **metabolism**: Plant: gum tragacanth. **the mind**: (See: The Mind). **mood**: (See: Mood). **negative attitude**: Plant: snowdrop, spider lily. **negative self-image**: Stone: apatite, rose quartz. **negative thoughts**: Stone: sapphire. **negotiating skills**: Plant: papyrus. **nutrition**: Stone: fluorite, turquoise; Plant: mountain grape. **personality**: Stone: zircon. **property**: Goddess: Luonnotar. **quality of dreams**: Plant: vervain (in dream pillow). **a relationship**: (See: Relationship). **self-esteem, self-image**: (See: Inner Work). **selfishness**: Stone: moonstone. **sex**: (See: Sex). **sight**: (See: Senses). **soil**: Animal: earthworm; Plant: sunflowers (grown in the soil). **speech**: Animal: dolphin; Metal: silver. **thinking**: (See: Thought). **visual perception**: Plant: clary sage, eyebright.

Impulsiveness

Fire/Aries

Color: dark blue, indigo, red; Number: 5.

Incantations

Air

Tool: bowl; Method: chanting, galdr, knot magick, weaving; Charm: bonfire, prayer beads; Stone: coral; Plant: birch, hemlock, myrrh, rowan, saffron; Goddess: Brigid, Circe, Hecate, Isis; God: Brihaspati, the Dagda, the Dactyls, Ea (Lord of Incantations), Enki, Namtillaku, Nuada, Ogma, Ptah, Thoth; Evocation: Amergin, Medea, Merlin, Picus.

Healing incantations: God: Dian Cecht; *healing via poetic incantations at sacred wells*: Goddess: Brigid. **Poetic incantations**: Goddess: Brigid.

To protect against incantations: Stone: coral.

Increase

(See also: Improvement, Intensity, Strength)

Waxing Moon/South/Spring

Number: 2, 8, 16; Color: royal blue; Plant: High John, rosemary; Goddess: Anahita, Maia; God: Al-Yazid, Al-Yusef, Apsu (Father of Increase).

Material increase: Earth; Color: brown. **Psychic increase**: Moon/Waxing Moon. **Solar increase**: Sun; Number: 8.

To increase: ability: (See: Ability). **appetite**: (See: The Body). **attraction**: Color: red. **awareness**: (See: Awareness). **beauty**: (See: Beauty). **business**: (See: Business). **circulation**: Plant: cayenne, ginger. **clarity**: (See: Clarity). **concentration**: (See: Concentration). **conviction**: God: Mars. **courage**: (See: Courage). **creativity**: (See: Creativity). **divination ability**: (See: Ability). **desire**: Plant: galangal; God: Ganesha. **dreams**: Plant: datura, nutmeg. **effectiveness of magick**: (See: Magick). **emotional security**: (See: Security). **energy**: (See: Energy). **fertility**: (See: Fertility). **fortune**: Plant: cumin. **good health**: Waxing Moon. **growth**: (See: Growth). **happiness**: Stone: beryl, peridot. **herds**: Goddess: Anahita; Plant: thyme. **influence**: Color: royal blue. **intelligence**: (See: Intelligence). **kidney function**: Plant: nettle. **lactation**: (See: Childbirth). **libido**: (See: Libido). **light**: Stone: rhodochrosite; Plant: juniper berry. **liver function**: Plant: nettle. **longevity**: (See: Longevity). **love**: Color: pink; Stone: tourmaline. **mental power(s)**: (See: Power). **magick**: (See: Magick). **money**: (See: Money). **passion**: (See: Passion). **perception**: (See: Perception). **popularity**: Tool: pentacle; Plant: cinnamon, mandrake. **power**: (See: Power). **profits**: Plant: goldenseal. **prosperity**: (See: Prosperity). **psychism**: (See: Psychism). **quality of a new project**: Stone: calcite. **resistance to stress**: Stone: hematite. **resolve**: God: Mars. **responsibilities at work**: Goddess: Inanna. **retention of information**: Stone: beryl. **revenue**: (See: Business). **sensitivity**: (See: Sensitivity). **female sensuality**: Plant: juniper berry. **sex**: Plant: mint. **sexual pleasure**: (See: Pleasure). **spirituality**: (See: Spirituality). **strength**: (See: Strength). **success**: (See: Success). **virility**: Plant: juniper berry; God: Herne. **virility**: Plant: acorn, wild celery, horny goatweed, juniper berry, ma huang, mandrake root, wild oat, snakeroot, yohimbine. **vitality**: (See: Vitality). **wealth**: (See: Wealth).

Independence

(See also: Freedom, Liberation)

Virgo

Number: 1; Color: green, purple; Animal: crane, polar bear; Stone: aventurine, dark pink tourmaline; Plant: blackthorn, oak, tarragon, thistle; Goddess: Atalanta, Diana, Frigg, Goleuddydd, Isis, Neith, Oya, Venus.

Female independence: Goddess: Eve, Kali, Lilith; Evocation: Amazons. **Independent action**: Goddess: Kamacharini; God: Poseidon. **Independent mind**: Number: 9. **To protect independence**: Stone: jade.

Influence

Jupiter/Moon/Water

Color: royal blue; Goddess: Badb, the Morrigan; Evocation: Merlin.

Civilizing influence: Evocation: Kekrops, the Oannes. **Cosmic influence**: Color: gold. **Magnetic influence**: Stone: lodestone, ruby. **Stabilizing influence**: Charm: a well-tended hearth fire.

Influence from afar: Goddess: Hecate.

To: attract influence: Color: purple; *attract higher influences*: Color: gold; *attract the influence of the Goddess*: Color: gray, silver; Metal: silver. **be less easily influenced**: Plant: pennyroyal. **increase influence**: Color: royal blue. **protect against the influence of evil spirits**: Plant: laurel. **understand influence**: Method: astrology.

To influence: elementals: *Earth elementals*: Color: brown; *Water elementals*: Color: aquamarine, blue, sea green. **a friendship**: Color: brown. **the heart**: Stone: aventurine, tanzanite; Plant: cinnamon. **the outcome of a battle**: (See: Battle). **the outcome of a trial**: Plant: galangal. **reality**: Goddess: the Norns; God: Anu. **weather**: (See correspondences for: Weather).

Influences

Negative influences: *to avert*: Plant: cinquefoil (as incense), heliotrope, ivy; *to avert negative magickal influences*: Charm: brimstone; Plant: asphodel (planted near the entry); *to banish*: Plant: cinquefoil, dragon's blood, frankincense, heliotrope; *to clear*: Tool: bell, besom; *to counter*: Color: gray; Plant: sycamore; *to neutralize*: Color: gray, silver; Metal: silver; *to protect against*: Plant: coriander seed, cypress, hyacinth, juniper berry; Goddess: Bast; *to protect children from*: Stone: citrine. **Outside influences**: Plant: blackthorn. **Unwanted influences**: *to protect against*: Stone: citrine; Plant: bayberry.

Ingenuity

(See also: Cleverness)

Plant: chamomile, clove, geranium, sequoia; God: Enki; Evocation: Daedalus, Lysippe, Odysseus.

Initiation

New Moon/East

Tool: cord, scourge; Charm: bull-roarer, egg, mask; Color: gray; Animal: crocodile, raven, snake; Plant: basil (as incense), gorse, heather, pennyroyal, wormwood; Goddess: Arianrhod, Ayizan, Baba Yaga, Blodeuwedd, Estsanatlehi, Fama (She Who Initiates), Ishtar, Isis, Julunggul, L'etsa'aplelana, Nevinbimbaau; God: Cernunnos, the Dagda, Hermes, Lugh, Thoth.

Female initiation into motherhood: Plant: pussy willow; Goddess: Libera. **Male initiation ceremonies**: Plant: datura; *initiation of males by females*: Plant: apple; Goddess: Eve. **Spiritual initiation**: Plant: snowdrop.

Initiation into: the afterlife: Goddess: Arianrhod; God: Februus. **the mysteries of love**: Venus; Letter: O.

To: attain higher degrees of initiation: God: Thoth. **protect initiates**: God: Ochosi.

Initiative

Mars/Aries

Number: 1; Metal: copper; Plant: chamomile, laurel; God: Ea.

Inner Work

Moon/West

Method: astrology, meditation; Color: pink, violet; Animal: bear, mole, polar bear; Stone: amethyst, carnelian, fluorite, fossil, moonstone, clear quartz crystal, tigereye, wulfenite; Plant: balm of Gilead, camellia; Goddess: Ista Devata; God: Tob Tob (Great Bear).

Inner awareness: (See: Awareness). **Inner balance**: (See: Balance). **Inner beauty**: (See: Beauty). **Inner calm**: (See: Calm). **Inner clarity**: (See: Clarity). **Inner changes**: Stone: coral; Plant: grass of Parnassus. **Inner child**: *to awaken*: South; *to contact*: Plant: zinnia; *to know*: Method: candle magick, meditation; Color: blue, green; *to protect*: Animal: slug, snail; Stone: coral. **Inner conflict/struggle**: *to calm*: Stone: sodalite; *to resolve*: Plant: primrose. **Inner conviction**: Stone: labradorite. **Inner development**: Plant: vine. **Inner eye**: (See: Vision). **Inner faith**: Color: green. **Inner freedom**: Plant: hawthorn, Japanese maple. **Inner growth**: Plant: gentian, geranium, spaghnum moss. **Inner guidance**: Stone: unakite; Plant: pine; God: Hermes. **Inner happiness**: Method: journaling; Plant: orange. **Inner harmony**: Color: pink; Stone: tourmaline; Plant: lotus. **Inner healing**: (See: Healing). **Inner hearing**: (See: Senses). **Inner journeys**: Stone: tanzanite. **Inner knowledge**: (See: Knowledge). **Inner law**: God: Dharma. **Inner levels**: *to connect with*: Stone: alexandrite. **Inner light**: (See: Light). **Inner life**: Color: white. **Inner opening**:

(See: Opening). **Inner peace**: (See: Peace). **Inner power**: (See: Power). **Inner purification**: (See: Purification). **Inner realms**: *to enter*: Stone: alexandrite; Plant: petrified wood. **Inner resources**: Animal: toad. **Inner restrictions**: *to deal with*: Stone: amethyst; Plant: harebell. **Inner rhythms**: Animal: seal. **Inner secrets**: Waning Moon; Stone: geode. **Inner security**: Plant: raspberry leaf (tea). **Inner self**: Plant: heather; *to connect with*: Plant: Japanese maple; *to connect with the outer world*: Plant: ash; *to get in touch with your inner male or female self*: God: Ometeotl. **Inner sight**: Color: indigo; Stone: Apache tear. **Inner signals**: *to understand*: Animal: hawk. **Inner stability**: Plant: wild rose. **Inner stillness**: Plant: bistort, primrose, stonecrop. **Inner strength**: (See: Strength). **Inner transformation**: (See: Transformation). **Inner treasures**: *to evoke*: North. **Inner truth**: (See: Truth). **Inner vision**: (See: Vision). **Inner vitality**: Stone: azurite, malachite. **Inner voice**: (See: Voice). **Inner warmth**: (See: Warmth). **Inner wisdom**: (See: Wisdom). **Inner worth**: *to appreciate*: Plant: cinquefoil.

Higher self: Stone: celestite, tourmaline; Plant: lime; *to listen to*: Stone: angelite; Plant: angelica. **Physical self**: *to know*: Plant: patchouli. **Shadow self**: Animal: owl. **True self**: Plant: birch, cinquefoil, elder, holy thorn, tamarack; Goddess: Demeter; *to be true to*: Color: purple; Animal: mountain lion; *to reveal*: paper birch.

Self-acceptance: Color: pink; Animal: skunk; Stone: apatite, pearl; Plant: African violet, azalea, bleeding heart, elder, potato, wild rose, self-heal, yellow toadflax; *to accept your dark side*: Color: black; *to accept your sexuality*: Stone: ruby. **Self-activation**: Plant: ephedra. **Self-awareness**: (See: Awareness). **Self-completeness**: Number: 1. **Self-confidence**: (See: Confidence). **Self-consciousness**: *to overcome*: Potion: elderberry wine; Plant: elder. **Self-containment**:

Animal: turtle; Goddess: Sekhmet (The Self-Contained). **Self-control**: (See: Control). **Self-creation**: (See: Creation). **Self-criticism**: Waning Moon. **Self-defense**: (See: Defense). **Self-destruction**: (See: Destruction). **Self-determination**: Goddess: Atalanta. **Self discipline**: (See: Discipline). **Self-empowerment**: (See: Empowerment). **Self-esteem**: Color: yellow; Animal: cheetah, heron, moose; Stone: moss agate, aquamarine, charoite, chrysoprase, citrine, fluorite, garnet, rhodonite, zircon; Plant: butterbur, narcissus, sunflower; Goddess: Venus; *to improve*: Charm: musk; Stone: moss agate, amethyst, charoite, citrine, garnet, rhodonite; Plant: grapefruit, jasmine; Goddess: Aphrodite; God: Balder; *healthy self esteem*: Plant: red rose. **Self-expression**: (See: Expression). **Self-fulfillment**: Animal: lion. **Self-healing**: (See: Healing). **Self-image**: Tool: mirror; *to improve*: Charm: paua shell; *to improve negative self-image*: Stone: apatite, rose quartz. **Self improvement**: (See: Improvement). **Self-indulgence**: Goddess: Erzulie, Hathor, Huitaca. **Self-knowledge**: (See: Knowledge). **Self-love**: (See: Love). **Self-nurturing**: (See: Nurture). **Self perception**: Stone: garnet. **Self-pity**: *to overcome*: Plant: rowan. **Self-realization**: Plant: everlasting, sunflower; God: O-Kuni-Nushi. **Self-reflection**: Plant: bougainvillea, delphinium, milkweed. **Self-reliance**: Animal: heron; Stone: labradorite; Plant: harebell, stonecrop; Goddess: Isis. **Self-renewal**: (See: Renewal). **Self-respect**: Animal: skunk; Stone: pink calcite. **Self sacrifice**: (See: Sacrifice). **Self-sufficiency**: South; Stone: jade; Plant: acacia. **Self-support**: (See: Support). **Self-worth**: Stone: amethyst, orange aventurine, dioptase, rhodonite; Plant: buttercup, dahlia; Goddess: Gerd.

Joy in being yourself: Stone: dioptase, ruby; Plant: mullein. **Openness to yourself and others**: (See: Openness).

To: appreciate yourself: Plant: columbine. **be less critical**: Plant: beech. **be true to oneself**: Color: purple; Animal: mountain lion. **believe in yourself**: Stone: labradorite, green tourmaline. **change yourself**: (See: Changes). **come out of your shell**: Animal: crab, crawfish, lobster, all crustaceans. **confront your innermost fears and insecurities**: Goddess: Kupala. **ease inner work**: Plant: onion. **follow your star**: Animal: starfish. **forgive yourself**: Stone: angelite, blue topaz; Plant: rowan, wormwood. **get back to your roots**: Animal: toad. **heal bitterness**: Stone: moss agate. **laugh at yourself**: Animal: coyote; Plant: valerian. **learn to assert yourself**: Stone: angelite, danburite; Plant: apple. **manage your anger**: (See: Management). **open yourself**: Stone: apatite; Plant: clary sage. **protect yourself while doing inner work**: Plant: wolfsbane. **reinvent yourself**: Goddess: Aditi. **restore faith in yourself**: Plant: heather. **sell yourself**: Color: yellow. **set yourself free**: Goddess: Kali. **stop being so hard on yourself**: Stone: pink calcite; Plant: crown of thorns. **take an inner stand**: Stone: apatite. **trust yourself**: Plant: day lily, raspberry, rose, Syrian rue.

Innocence
South/Spring

Color: white; Charm: orange flower water; Animal: white horse, lamb, white swan, unicorn; Stone: diamond, pearl; Plant: apple, white carnation, daisy, marjoram, myrtle, orange blossom, white rose, spearmint, white violet, all white flowers; Goddess: Astraea, Kore, the Maiden, Semiramis, Tyne; God: Balder; Evocation: angels.

Lost innocence: Plant: pomegranate (eaten), dried white rose; Goddess: Eve. **Sacred innocence**: Goddess: Astraea. **Stolen innocence**: Evocation: Shamhat.

Innocent joy: Animal: cicada; Plant: daisy, peony. **Innocent love**: Plant: rosebud.

Innocent simplicity: Plant: chickweed. **Innocent youth**: Plant: white lilac, white lily; God: Mabon.

To: arbitrate in matters of innocence: Goddess: Prithivi. **decide innocence or guilt**: God: Enki. **prove innocence**: Goddess: Sita. **rediscover innocence**: Plant: daisy. **remember innocence**: Plant: forget-me-not.

Insight
(See also: Intuition)

Color: lavender, violet; Number: 2, 11; Charm: dinosaur bone; Animal: coyote; Stone: chiastolite, emerald, lapis lazuli, leopardskin jasper, tanzanite, tigereye; Plant: angelica, cedar, chamomile, silver fir, forget-me-not, green apple, cedar, queen of the night, rush, sage; Goddess: Binah, Cerridwen, Deshtri, Estsanatlehi, Kwan Yin, Namagiri, Sheng Mu, Toma; God: Ahura Mazda, Amon, Gwion, Hanuman, Hermes, Marduk Gibil, Mimir, Ra, Shoney, Sia, Tenjin.

Clear insight: Stone: tourmaline. **Creative insight**: Stone: aquamarine, aventurine. **Mystical insight**: Wednesday. **Personal insight**: Plant: papaya. **Spiritual insight**: Goddess: Kwan Yin. **Subtle insight**: Stone: meteorite, moldovite. **Visionary insight**: Animal: gazelle.

Inspiration
(See also: Imagination, Creativity)

Moon/Neptune/Mercury/Waxing Moon/Nearly Full Moon/Fire/Water/East

Tool: cauldron; Color: light blue, pink, purple, silver, violet, white, yellow; Charm: blue sonata; Animal: butterfly, carp, eel, firefly; Number: 1, 5, 9, 11, 33; Stone: blue lace agate, amethyst, aquamarine, garnet, jade, opal, clear quartz, selenite, blue topaz, tourmaline, zircon; Potion: wine; Plant: acacia, angelica, balm of Gilead, benzoin, bougainvillea, cannabis, cinnamon, cinquefoil, clove, cranberry, cypress, dogbane, dragon's blood, fir, frankincense, ginger, hazel, iris, jasmine, laurel, lavender (thrown into a fire, especially at Midsummer), lily of the valley, moss, oak, green oak (added to Midsummer bonfire), orchid, reed, rose, rosemary, rowan, rue, sandalwood, tangerine (oil), vanilla, vervain, willow; Goddess: Aa (She Who Inspires), Artemis Caryatis, Badb, Bast, Benzaiten, Board, Brigid (Flame of Inspiration, Lady of Bright Inspiration), Canola, Cardea, Ceibhfhionn, Cerridwen (White Lady of Inspiration, Keeper of the Cauldron of Inspiration), Coventina, Gonlod, Gwendydd wen adlam Cerrddeu, Hokmah, Iamanja, Isis (Leader of the Muses), the Muse, Nimuë (White Lady of Day), the Ocean Mother (Muse of Inspiration), Sulis, the White Goddess, Yemaya; God: Bacchus, Dionysus, Mimir, Ogma, Soma; Evocation: Amergin.

Architectural inspiration: Goddess: Athena; Plant: acanthus, lotus. **Artistic inspiration**: Plant: iris; God: Credne. **Creative inspiration**: Moon; Color: violet, yellow; Animal: caterpillar, newt; Stone: amethyst, chrysocolla, moonstone, green tourmaline, turquoise; Plant: iris, lilac, lotus, orris root, rose, rosemary, ylang-ylang; Goddess: Benzaiten, Brigid, the Muses. **Higher/divine inspiration**: Color: blue; Stone: blue celestite, blue onyx, peridot; Plant: honeysuckle, iris; Goddess: Awen, Ceibhfhionn, the Muses. **Literary inspiration**: Goddess: Aa, Aya. **Oracular inspiration**: Plant: laurel. **Poetic inspiration**: Charm: the sound of wind in willow trees; Plant: grapevine, hazelnut, willow; Goddess: Sarasvati. **Practical inspiration**: God: Ptah. **Spiritual inspiration**: Pisces; Animal: firefly. **Sudden inspiration**: God: Zeus.

Inspiration in battle: God: Odin. **Inspirational meditation**: Color: light blue. **Inspirational speech**: Plant: trumpet vine.

To attract inspiration: Stone: tourmaline; Plant: dragon's blood, tuberose. **to inspire**: **courage**: Stone: carnelian, tigereye. **faith**: Stone: amazonite. **fear**: (See: Fear). **love**: Evocation: the Apsaras. **positive emotions**: Plant: pine.

Integration

Color: pink, purple, white; Stone: lepidolite; Plant: angelica, basil, broom, cosmos, daisy, laurel, tuberose, yarrow.

Integration with Nature: God: Ganesha.

To integrate: **emotions**: Plant: bleeding heart, fuchsia. **information**: Plant: daisy. **mind/body**: Color: purple. **old/new**: Plant: horsetail. **past life information**: (See: Past Life Work). **personal life with professional life**: Plant: quince. **spirituality with everyday life**: Plant: lavender.

Integrity

(See also: Honesty)

Animal: moose; Metal: gold; Stone: pearl; Plant: basil, silverweed, willowherb; Goddess: Fides, Haurvatat, Prithivi, Virtus; God: Mithras.

Personal integrity: Color: violet; Goddess: Fides. **Spiritual integrity**: Plant: plumeria; Goddess: Haurvatat.

Arbitration in matters of integrity: Goddess: Prithivi. **Integrity in relationships**: Stone: lapis lazuli.

Intellect

(See also: Intelligence, The Mind)

Sun/Air

Color: blue, orange, yellow; Number: 6; Stone: emerald, tigereye, topaz; Plant: balm of Gilead, lemon, rosemary, walnut; Goddess: Alaghom-Naom (Mother of Mind), Athena, Sarasvati; God: Apollo, Marduk, Osiris, Ptah, Sicun, Thoth.

Directed intellect: Number: 2. **Superior intellect**: God: Marduk Gibil.

Intellectual ability: Plant: benzoin, peppermint, rosemary. **Intellectual activities**: (See: Activity). **Intellectual clarity**: Plant: lemon. **Intellectual growth**: (See: Growth). **Intellectual knowledge**: Stone: hematite. **Intellectual power**: Color: purple; *to increase:* Plant: rosemary. **Intellectual stimulation**: (See: Stimulation). **Intellectual success**: Plant: benzoin.

To: recharge the intellect: Color: orange. **sharpen the intellect**: Stone: sapphire; God: Hermes.

Intelligence

(See also: Intellect, Knowledge, Thought, Wisdom)

Mercury/Fire

Number: 7; Color: yellow; Animal: chimpanzee, cougar, coyote, crow, dolphin, fox, octopus, orangutan; Charm: yellow feather; Stone: agate, amethyst; Plant: hazel, impatiens; Goddess: Minerva, Shait, Sheng-Mu (Mother of Perfect Intelligence), Sussistanako; God: Chango, Coeus, Enki, Fugen Bosatsu, Ganesha, Pagalguenna, Sia; Evocation: Sila.

Divine intelligence: Goddess: Yemaya; God: Thoth. **Emotional intelligence**: Animal: frog; Stone: green jasper Plant: violet. **Higher intelligence**: Goddess: Lilith. **Sudden intelligence**: Plant: spindle tree. **Power of intelligence**: Goddess: Sussistanako. **Activities which require intelligence**: Goddess: Minerva. **Intelligent action**: Color: orange.

To: collect intelligence: Animal: raven; God: Odin. **increase intelligence**: Color: yellow; Stone: aventurine, green aventurine, emerald, red jasper. **link instinct/ intelligence**: Animal: wolf.

Intensity

(See also: Increase, Strength)

Scorpio

Color: red; Number: 8; Stone: malachite, obsidian; Plant: chili pepper; Goddess: Kali.

Intense emotions: (See: Emotions). **Intense experience**: God: Shango. **Intense focus**: Animal: cheetah.

To control intensity: Animal: basilisk.

To intensify: dreams: Stone: Herkimer diamond. **physical sensation**: Goddess: Sentia. **properties of herbs**: Plant: yarrow. **sexual passion**: Plant: damiana.

Intuition

(See also: Clairvoyance, Insight, Psychism)

Jupiter/Moon/Waning Moon/Air/Water/ Fire/Monday/Aquarius/Pisces/Cancer

Tool: divination tools, wand; Color: blue, silvery blue, brown, gold, green, lavender, pink, purple, silver, violet; Charm: lightning bolt (bolt from the blue); Number: 2, 7, 11; Animal: basilisk, cougar, elephant, hare; Stone: amazonite, amethyst, azurite, green or yellow calcite, chrysolite, purple fluorite, hematite, lapis lazuli, malachite, moonstone, rhodonite, ruby, sapphire, sodalite, blue topaz, turquoise; Plant: ash, birch, broom, chamomile, clover, coconut, elm, eyebright, hazel, holly berry, honeysuckle, lavender, papaya, poppy, queen of the night, rosemary, clary sage, spruce; Goddess: Bast, Kali, Nephthys; God: Fugen Bosatsu, Jupiter, Mimir, Neptune.

Empathic intuition: North. **Practical intuition**: Stone: labradorite. **Sensitive intuition**: Animal: cricket. **Transcendent intuition**: Goddess: Prajnaparamita.

Intuitive knowledge: Uranus; Stone: sodalite. **Intuitive wisdom**: Plant: Solomon seal root.

To: **appreciate intuition**: Animal: swan. **increase/develop intuition**: Color: yellow; Goddess: the Mother. **learn to trust intuition**: Animal: cricket; Plant: pine. **open intuition**: Stone: amethyst, sapphire. **sharpen/ strengthen intuition**: Cancer; Stone: hematite; Animal: hare, rabbit; Plant: honeysuckle, yarrow; Goddess: Kali. **stimulate intuition**: Charm: sea shell; Animal: cricket; Stone: apophyllite.

Invention

(See also: Creation)

Fire

Number: 1; Goddess: Arrang Dibatu, Athene, Canola, Godasiyo, Druantia, Isis (Inventrix, Inventor of All Things), Philyra, Sarasvati, Sesheta, Whaitiri; God: Dagon, Fu Hsi, Itzamna, Kamapua, Kothar-wa-Khasis, Manabozho, Mercury, Ogma, Ptah, Teutates, Thoth, Väinämöinen.

Inventions: Goddess: Sesheta; God: Thoth.

To reinvent yourself: Goddess: Aditi.

Inventiveness

(See also: Creativity, Invention)

Aquarius

Goddess: Athena, Kokyan, Mayahuel.

Sexual inventiveness: God: P'an-Chin-Lien.

Invincibility

Sun

Stone: diamond; Metal: adamantine; Animal: brown hare, hoopoe, lion, porpoise; Plant: ash, chicory, High John with St. John's Wort, decoction of any plant found growing as a parasite on a tamarind tree; Goddess: Andraste (The Invincible One), Durga, Hecate (Invincible Queen), Scathach, Sekhmet (Invincible One); God: Abraxas, Ganesha, Goibniu, Sol Invictus.

Invincible charm: Goddess: Aphrodite.

Invincibility in battle: Goddess: Andraste, the Morrigan, Scathach.

The Invisible

God: Hades (The Unseen, The Invisible One).

To: **protect against the invisible**: Stone: jade. **see invisible fairies**: Charm: wear a four-leaf clover in your hat.

Invisibility

(See also: Cloaking)

Night Sun/Dark Moon

Color: clear, gray, white; Charm: a sardonyx engraved with a quail and a sea tench beneath its feet; Stone: bloodstone, diamond, moonstone, opal (wrapped in a laurel leaf), tigereye; Plant: crown of amaranth flowers, chicory (gathered in silence at Midsummer with a gold knife), edelweiss, fern seed (gathered on Midsummer Eve with a white cloth), hazel rod (a fathom and a half long with a green hazel twig inserted into it), heliotrope, black hellebore root, mistletoe, poppy, primrose, sunflower juice, vervain, wolfsbane; Goddess: Ayauhteotl, Dubhlaing, Greine, Nephthys; God: Angus, Hades, Mannan MacLir.

Near-invisibility: Stone: diamond, lodestone with sapphire. **Invisibility to witches**: Plant: sow thistle. **To make the invisible visible**: Plant: primrose.

Chapter 10

Jealousy

(See also: Envy)

Moon/North/Aries/Taurus/Leo/Scorpio

Color: green, dark green, greenish-yellow, yellow; Animal: snake; Stone: orange zircon; Plant: acacia, hyacinth, marigold, yellow rose; Goddess: Circe, Cybele, Erzulie Dantor, Hera, Indrani; God: Ares, Hephaestus, Jehovah, Mars, Perun, Poseidon, Rama, Set, Shiva, Vulcan, Yahweh; Evocation: Ajax, Clothru, Iki Ryo, Uchtdealbh, Verseria.

Freedom from jealousy: Animal: otter.

To: **avert jealousy**: Charm: Eye of Horus, van van; Stone: carnelian; Plant: garlic; *jealousy of the Moon goddess*: Plant: willow; *from an unborn child*: Plant: squaw vine (in the bath). **create jealousy**: Plant: hemlock; God: Zeus. **destroy jealousy**: Goddess: Durga. **ease feelings of jealousy**: Stone: carnelian; Plant: bayberry, holly, sassafras, vetiver. **heal jealousy**: Animal: hummingbird; Goddess: Oenone; God: Abarta; **learn not to be jealous**: Goddess: Volupta. **overcome/learn to overcome jealousy**: Color: green; Charm: van van; Stone: sugilite; Animal: mountain lion; Goddess: Becuma, Hera, Juno, Volupta; God: Abarta. **protect against jealousy/jealous people**: Charm: van van. Plant: garlic, plantain. **transform jealousy into accomplishment**: Color: green. **understand jealousy**: God: Abarta.

Jinxes

(See: Hexes)

Job

(See: Employment)

Joy

(See also: Contentment, Ecstasy, Happiness)

Venus/Sun/New Moon/Fire

Method: dance, music; Color: aqua, light blue, crimson, orange, peach, turquoise, yellow; Number: 11; Animal: dolphin, flying heron, hummingbird, otter; Charm: rosemary infusion, sweetmeats of figs, honey and dates; Stone: blue apatite, green apophyllite, aquamarine, green aventurine, pink calcite, carnelian, diamond, garnet, fire garnet, jasper, lapis lazuli, pale green olivine, Pecos diamond, rose quartz, rhodonite, ruby, sapphire, turquoise; Oil: palmarosa; Plant: almond, aloe, amber, anemone, anise, apple, azalea, bergamot, calla lily, calamus, catnip, elder, gardenia, gorse, grapefruit (oil), grapevine, holy thistle, honeysuckle, ivy, jasmine, laurel, lemon balm, marigold, mariposa lily, marjoram, mint, mullein, orange, mandarin orange, oregano, palm branches, pine, potentilla, rhododendron, rose of Jericho, wild rose, rosemary, saffron, star anise, strawberry, sunflower, yellow toadflax, water lily, wood sorrel; Goddess: Aglia, Amaterasu, Bast,

Chie, Devi, Estsanatlehi, Euphrosyne, Felicitas, the Graces, Hathor, Ishtar, Isis (Lady of Joy), Mawu, Oshun, Samkhat, Sekhmet (Mistress of Joy, Who Gives Joys Unwaveringly), Themis, the Textumeihae (Bringers of Joy), Uzume, Venus; God: Anandi (Bringer of Joy), Ataksak, Bacchus, Baldur, Freyr, Fu-hsing, Hotei, Kokopeli, Mitra, Omacatl, Tien Kuan, Yum Caz.

Innocent/childlike joy: Animal: cicada; Plant: daisy, peony. **Perverse joy**: God: Poseidon. **Physical joy**: Method: dance; Animal: dolphin; Plant: elder, marigold; Goddess: Chantico, Venus. **Pure joy**: Animal: hummingbird. **Renewed joy**: Plant: geranium. **Secret joy**: Stone: geode; Plant: crimson rose. **Sexual joy**: Plant: damiana; Goddess: Anath, Aphrodite, Asherah, Bast, Chantico, Qadesh, Suratamangari, Venus; God: Krishna. **Simple joy**: Plant: silverweed.

Joyous events: Goddess: Felicitas. **Joyful motherhood**: Plant: motherwort, **Joyous music**: God: Apollo. **Joyful thanks**: Plant: valerian. **Joy in being yourself**: Stone: dioptase, ruby; Plant: mullein. **Return of joy**: Plant: calla lily, toadflax.

To: **attract joy**: Plant: lemon. **awaken/open joy**: Stone: kunzite; Plant: tangerine. **balance joys and sorrows**: Plant: bleeding heart; Goddess: Nemesis. **bring joy to the dead**: Plant: marigold, marjoram. **express joy**: Method: dance; Plant: almond, sunflower. **find joy**: Animal: eagle; Stone: amber. **make joyful**: Stone: peridot; Plant: lemon balm; Goddess: Euphrosyne. **restore joy**: Plant: anemone, azalea. **share joy**: Color: orange; Animal: horse, moose; Plant: bergamot, wild rose.

Judgment

(See also: Court, Decision/s, Justice)

West

Animal: dog; Stone: jade, turquoise; Plant: hemlock; Goddess: Aeval, Danaë (She Who Judges), Ereshkigal, Le-Hev-Hev, Ma'at, Meshlent, Nana, Neith, Sekhmet (Great One in the Places of Judgment and Execution), Shait, Themis; God: Anubis, Baal, Chitragupta, Dazhbog, Dian Cecht, Emmao, Forseti, Kuan Ti (The Great Judge), Mithras, Nergal, Ninnuam (Judger of Judgments, Decider of Decisions), Osiris, Ra, Rashnu (The Just Judge), Shamash (Lord of Judgment, Judge of the World), Shiva, Thoth (Judge of Right and Truth), Tyr.

Accurate judgment: Stone: tigereye. **Calm judgment**: Color: white. **Divine judgment**: Goddess: Themis; God: Geb, Mandanu, Osiris, Thoth (Judge of the Gods). **Fair judgment**: God: Dazhbog, Forseti, Varuna; Evocation: Genetaska; *for a fair judge*: Plant: patchouli, sandalwood; God: Suduk. **Final judgment**: Goddess: Belit-Seri; God: Osiris; Evocation: Michael (Angel of the Last Judgment). **Good/sound judgment**: Color: violet; Stone: amethyst, lapis lazuli; God: Rhadamanthys, Thoth. **Moral judgment**: God: Shango. **Unbiased judgment**: Color: white. **Wise judgment**: Stone: tigereye; Goddess: Aeval.

Being judgmental: Plant: loosestrife, rowan. **Favorable legal judgment**: Stone: garnet. **For a sympathetic judge**: Plant: carnation, galangal

To: **guarantee that a judgment is executed**: God: Enki. **judge the dead**: (See: The Dead). **judge the appropriateness of revenge**: Goddess: Melusine.

Justice

(See also: Court)

Jupiter/Sun/Thursday/Libra/Pisces

Color: vibrant shades of blue, orange, purple; Charm: blindfold, scales; Stone: bloodstone, diamond, jade, rose quartz;

Plant: bayberry, cedar, chamomile, cinnamon, cinquefoil, cypress, yellow dock, frankincense, garlic, High John, honeysuckle, jasmine, *Justicia*, laurel, lotus, mint, nutmeg, pine, sandalwood, vervain, violet; Goddess: Aedon, Akonadi, Ala, Alecto, Aleitheia, Alidice, Ananke, Aradia, Arete, Astraea, Athene, Dike, the Erinyes, Eunomia, Fortuna, the Furies, the Harpies, Hokmah, the Horai, Irene, Itone, Justitia (The Scales), Kadi, Kukuri-Hime, Kwan Yin, Libra, Ma'at, Mayet, Megaera, the Moirae, Nanshe, Nekhen, Nekmet Awai, Nemesis, Nina, Ninhursag, the Norns, Nyoirin, Oya, Shapash, Sho, Sin, Themis, Victoria, Yansa, Zemlya; God: Anbay, Apollo, Byelobog, Chu Jung, the Dagda, Dazhbog, Dian Cecht, Forseti, Gibil, Horagalles, Ida-Ten, Jupiter, Jupiter Fidius, Lugalsisa, Lu-hsing, Mabon, Misharu, Nabu, Nereus, Nushku, Obatala, Odin, Ogun, Ra, Rasnu, Rhadamanthys, Sakarabru, Shango, Sin, Thor, Thoth, Tyr, Ullr, Utu, Varuna, Vishnu, Zeus; Evocation: Althaea, Andrasteia, Asmodeus, Chiron, Elektra, Michael, Uriel.

Divine justice: Goddess: Dike, Themis; God: Perun; Evocation: Tzadkiel. **Fair justice**: Goddess: Calladice. **Human justice**: Goddess: Dike. **Karmic justice**: Goddess: Nemesis. **Social justice**: Goddess: Aradia. **Spiritual justice**: Animal: crane. **Swift justice**: God: Odin. **Wide justice**: Goddess: Eurydice.

Just cause: *to prevail in court with*: Stone: diamond; Goddess: Justitia.

Do me justice: Plant: chestnut, chestnut tree. **The people's justice**: Goddess: Laodice. **Justice by force**: Evocation: Biadike. **Justice for women who die of knife wounds**: Goddess: Ma Kiela.

To: **bind justice/legal spells**: Charm: bright blue or dark blue thread; Plant: nettles, vine. **bring someone to justice**: Saturn/Saturday; *bring a thief to justice*: Method: footprint magick. **see that justice is done**: Plant: coltsfoot, tussilage; Goddess: the Mother.

Injustice
Plant: hops; **to protect against injustice**: God: Kuan Ti.

Chapter 11

Karma

(See also: Past Life Work, Reincarnation)

Pluto/Saturn/Saturday

Charm: spiral, wheel; Number: 8; Animal: bee; Stone: Apache tear; Plant: lotus; Goddess: Arianrhod, Holda, Kali, Kali Ma (Mother of Karma), Mahakali (Great Kali, The Absolute Mother of Karma), Manat; God: Brahma, T'ai-Yueh-Ta-Ti, Vishnu; Evocation: undines.

Karmic attachments: Stone: tigereye; *to release*: Stone: hawk's eye. **Karmic balance**: (See: Balance). **Karmic events**: *to reveal*: Goddess: Hecate. **Karmic justice**: Goddess: Nemesis. **Karmic law**: Plant: ash; *karmic law enforcement*: Animal: coyote. **Karmic pain**: *to relieve*: Stone: morganite. **Karmic retribution**: Goddess: Nephthys. **Karmic work**: (See: Work).

To: improve karma: Goddess: Kwan Yin. **resolve karma**: Plant: anemone, rowan.

Kindness

(See also: Charity, Compassion, Mercy)

Venus/Jupiter

Color: light blue, green, orange; Number: 6; Animal: deer, dolphin; Potion: milk; Stone: chrysoprase, jade; Plant: allspice, bleeding heart, bluebell, clover, hyacinth, potato; Goddess: Bast, Benzaiten, Gyhldeptis, Habondia, Iris, Ishtar, Isis, Juno, Kwan Yin, Lakshmi, Pandora; God: Mithras, Orunmila, Thor.

Loving kindness: Plant: bleeding heart; Goddess: Kwan Yin, Mary. **Kindness to animals**: Goddess: Kwan Yin; Evocation: St. Francis of Assisi.

To: be kind to yourself: Plant: potato. **feel kindness**: Plant: flax. **reward kindness**: Goddess: Cailleach.

Unkindness

Unkind speech: Animal: snapping turtle.

Knowledge

(See also: Intelligence, Learning, Wisdom)

Saturn/Waxing Moon/Air/South/Wednesday

Color: blue, gold, yellow; Tool: grimoire, cauldron, wand; Charm: well; Number: 7; Animal: cougar, phoenix, salmon, all fish; Stone: jade; Plant: alder, apple, apricot, aspen, balm of Gilead, banyan, benzoin, calamus, cinnamon, citronella, elder, fig, frankincense, hazel, rowan, sage, yew (Spell of Knowledge); Goddess: Anahita, Aoife, Benzaiten, Binah, Buddhi, Cerridwen, Deshtri, Druantia, Emer, Eve, Hen Wen, Hokmah (She Who Knows All), Isis, Minerva, Mokosh, Namagiri, Nehalennia, Neith, Ninsun, Oshun, Pistis Sophia, Saga, Sarasvati, Sarpanitum, Sheng Mu, Sionnan, Snotra (Master of All Knowledge), Sulis, Sulis Minerva, Toma; God: Ahura Mazda, Amon-Ra, Brahma, Asclepius, Cernunnos, the Dagda (Mighty One of Knowledge, Lord of Great Knowledge), the Dagda (Lord of Great Knowledge), Dagdae Dana

(The Red One of Great Knowledge), Ecne, Gwydion, Hanuman, Hermes, Ifa, Itzamna, Karttikeya, Kvasir, Kwai Hsing, Lugh (Master of Knowledge), Math ap Mathonwy, Mercury, Mimir, Namru, Orunmila, Ruad ro-fhessa (Red One of Great Knowledge, Lord of Perfect Knowledge), Sarvagny (The All-Knowing), Sia, Tenjin, Thoth, Yanauluha (Great Medicine Man); Evocation: Raziel, Taliesin, the Watchers.

Abstract knowledge: *to assimilate*: Stone: blue topaz. **Ancestral knowledge**: God: Damballah-Wedo. **Ancient knowledge**: Pluto; Animal: alligator, blackbird, crocodile, eagle, owl, salmon, sphinx, stag; Stone: fossil; Plant: ginkgo, giant sequoia; *secret ancient knowledge*: Animal: sphinx; God: Lugalanna, Thoth. **applied knowledge**: Stone: moonstone. **ethical knowledge**: God: Al Da'ya. **genetic knowledge contained in seeds**: Goddess: Phyllis. **inner knowledge**: Full Moon; Color: black; Plant: black ash; Metal: peacock ore; Stone: iolite, phenacite, triangular stones; God: Hades, Odin; *doorway to*: Plant: oak; *to awaken*: Stone: iolite; *to learn to trust*: Plant: heather, pine. **intellectual knowledge**: Stone: hematite. **intuitive knowledge**: Uranus; Stone: sodalite. **learned knowledge**: Goddess: Nissaba. **magickal knowledge**: Animal: eagle; Plant: dill; Goddess: Hecate, Nimuë; God: Dumduku (Possessor of the Lapis Wand, Knower of the Secret Name, Knower of the Secret Number), Leshy, Math ap Mathonwy, Thoth; Evocation: Merlin; *of the laws of magick*: God: Aranunna; *of the magickal properties of plants*: Goddess: Vedma. **mystical knowledge**: Goddess: Neith. **occult knowledge**: Animal: magpie; Plant: yew; Goddess: Brigid, Diana, Mokosh, Zemlya; God: Odin. **old knowledge**: Plant: beech; Evocation: ancestors. **omnipresent knowledge**:

Sun; God: Ra. **oracular/prophetic knowledge**: Method: astrology, palmistry, pendulum, runes, scrying, tarot; Animal: fox, all birds; Stone: mother-of-pearl; Plant: dill; Goddess: the Seven Hathors; God: Nereus; *of the destiny/fate of lovers*: Goddess: Inanna; Plant: orpane and red sage (gathered on Midsummer Eve); *the future of an unborn child*: Goddess: Aegeria; *the life span of any being*: God: Esizkur; *the past, the present, or the future*: Goddess: Cerridwen, Frigg, the Norns; God: Legba; *of your destiny*: Method: astrology, I Ching, meditation, tarot.

Past knowledge: Plant: beech. **Sacred knowledge**: North; Stone: lapis lazuli. **Secret knowledge**: Stone: lapis lazuli; Goddess: Pte San Wi, Senge Dong-ma, Sesheta; God: Dumduku (Knower of the Secret Name, Knower of the Secret Number), Marukka, Thoth; *secret knowledge systems*: Goddess: Sesheta; *secret ancient knowledge*: Charm: sphinx; God: Lugalanna, Thoth.

Self-knowledge: Full Moon; Method: journaling, meditation; Color: blue; Stone: citrine, emerald, pink tourmaline; Plant: ivy; Goddess: Demeter; God: Ganesha; *to know your destiny*: (See: Destiny); *to know your inner child*: Method: candle magick, meditation; Color: blue, green; *to know your own mind*: (See: The Mind); *to know your purpose in life*: Color: blue; *to know yourself*: Goddess: Demeter; *your physical self*: Plant: patchouli.

Spiritual knowledge: Animal: wolf. **Stolen knowledge**: Goddess: Aoife. **Superior knowledge**: Animal: cougar. **Transcendental knowledge**: Goddess: Corra, Rajarajesvari. **Universal knowledge**: Stone: lapis lazuli, clear quartz crystal. **Written knowledge**: Plant: papyrus; God: Thoth.

Branches of knowledge: God: Thoth. **Light of knowledge**: Goddess: Rohini. **Power of knowledge**: Tool: candle, grimoire; Method: candle magick. **Desire to know**: Number: 5; **Power to know**: East. **Knowledge systems**: Goddess: Sesheta.

Knowledge of: animals: Animal: cougar, turtle. **the arts**: Plant: hazel. **evil**: Plant: apple, apricot, fig tree. **fire**: Goddess: Pelé. **goodness**: Plant: apple, apricot, fig tree. **healing plants**: Goddess: Airmid, Samovila; Evocation: Alcamede, Chiron; **medicines**: Goddess: Guabonito; **poisons**: Goddess: Janguli; **science**: Plant: hazel; **the sea**: Water; Stone: coral, sea salt; Animal: dolphin, seal, whale.

To: bless those who strive for knowledge: Goddess: Kali. **gain knowledge**: Method: shapeshifting; Animal: spirit guides; Stone: tektite; Plant: hazel nut, rosemary. **overcome fear of the unknown**: Animal: eagle; Stone: black coral. **seek knowledge**: Animal: chickadee; Plant: apple; Goddess: Kali, Sionnan; God: Odin.

To know: if your lover is telling the truth: Stone: emerald. **reality**: Stone: aquamarine, moonstone; God: Brahmavid (Knower of Reality). **right from wrong**: Goddess: Melusine. **with certainty that springtime will always follow winter**: Goddess: Persephone, Prosperine. **what direction to take**: Stone: iolite. **what not to say**: North. **where and when to plant seeds/crops**: God: Enki, Zulum. **whom you will marry**: (See: Marriage).

To know when: to attack: Animal: wolf. **to lie low**: Animal: bear, squirrel; Goddess: Artio. **to leave**: Animal: butterfly. **to reserve your strength**: Animal: bear; Goddess: Artio. **someone is lying**: Plant: pimpernel.

Kundalini

Venus/Earth

Color: red; Number: 3; Animal: snake; Stone: garnet; Goddess: Kali, Kundalini, Shakti.

Kundalini energy: (See: Energy). **Kundalini power**: (See: Power).

Chapter 12

Land

(See also: Agriculture, Gardening, Nature, Real Estate)

Saturn/Earth

Color: brown, green; Goddess: Isis (Lady of the Land Matter), Mati Syra Zemlya (Moist Mother Earth), Yolkai Estsan; God: Ellil, O-Kuni-Nushi (Lord of the Land), She Chi.

Arable land: God: Baal. **Dry land**: Tuesday. **Grazing land**: God: Marduk. **Uncultivated land**: God: Silvanus. **Unspoiled land**: *to protect against development*: God: Pan, Robin.

Landmarks: God: Terminus. **Land reformation**: God: Osiris.

Fertility of land: Sun/Earth/Water; Charm: bonfire or Yule log ashes (sprinkled on ground); grain cake (as an offering); jump over a Sabbat bonfire; "ride" a broomstick through or around it, sacred marriage; Stone: agate; Goddess: Bo Dhu, Bo Find, Bo Ruadh, Creiddylad, Satis; God: Baal, Damuzi, Ialonus, Seker, Serapis, Telepinu; Evocation: Green George; *to activate*: Charm: Great Rite; *to restore*: God: Telepinu.

To: divide land: God: Itzamna. **heal land**: Goddess: Ceres, Gaia. **have dominion over land**: God: Enki. **protect land**: Plant: chamomile (planted on it); Goddess: Queen Brigantia, Nagararakshika (Protectress of Land); God: Bran; Evocation: Merlin; *from wind and weather*: Charm: bread thickly spread with honey and butter (left out as an offering); Goddess: Walpurga; God: Bran, Marutakku; Evocation: Merlin. **reclaim land from water**: God: Ea, Ptah.

Laughter

Sun/Air/Spring

Tool: small bells; Color: royal blue, yellow; Animal: dolphin, monkey, otter; Stone: rhodonite; Plant: bergamot, saffron, sunflower, zinnia; Goddess: Baubo, Chie, Felicitas, Kali, Sheela-na-gig, Uzume; God: Dionysus, Geb, Hotei, Irdlirvirissong, Lado, Loki, Pan, Thor; Evocation: the domovoi.

Healing power of laughter: Goddess: Baubo, Chie, Uzume.

To: laugh and cry at the same time: Gemini. **learn to laugh at yourself**: Animal: coyote; Plant: valerian.

Laziness

Saturn

Color: blue, brown, brownish-orange; Plant: cannabis; God: Shiva.

Mental laziness: *to overcome*: Plant: peppermint.

To: banish laziness: Stone: beryl. **overcome laziness**: Fire; Color: red; Stone: ruby; Plant: cayenne; Evocation: pixies. **punish laziness**: Goddess: Perchta.

Leadership

Jupiter/Sun/Fire/Sunday/Aries/Leo

Color: red; Charm: trilobite fossil; Number: 1; Animal: bull, condor, cougar, earth dragon, silverback gorilla, lion, mountain lion, puma, alpha wolf; Stone: ruby, blue topaz; Goddess: Arinna, Brigantia, Cessair, Domnu, Isis, Medb, Neith; God: Ambisagrus, Anhur, Asaruludu, Bran, Bres, El, Jupiter, Marduk, Odin, Yebaad, Yeba Ka, Zeus; Evocation: Cleopatra, King Arthur.

Female leadership: Goddess: Cessair, Oya. **wise leadership**: Animal: cougar, lion. **leadership in battle**: Goddess: Banba; God: Odin; Evocation: Quingu.

Legal Matters

(See: Court, Justice)

Learning

(See also: Education, Knowledge, Study, Teaching)

Mercury/Air/West

Color: yellow; Stone: aquamarine; Plant: pine, rosemary; Goddess: Airmid, Brigid, Cerridwen, Deshtri, The Maiden, Sarasvati, Sesheta, Tara; God: Ehecatl, Ganesha, Hanuman, Imhotep, Ogma, Quetzalcoatl, Saturn, Tenjin, Thoth (Lord of Books and Learning).

Quick learning: Animal: dingo. **Learned knowledge**: Goddess: Nissaba.

To learn: cloaking: Color: gray. **lessons**: Plant: juniper berry; *life lessons*: God: Legba; *the lessons of folly*: Goddess: Ate; *the lesson that beauty isn't everything*: Goddess: Donagh. **magick**: Goddess: Freya. **respect**: (See: Respect). **the Law of Three**: God: Cacus; *the lesson of the Law of Three*: Goddess: Oenone. **the dangers of excess**: Goddess: Agave. **the outcome of a pregnancy**:

Goddess: Antevorta. **the secret language of trees**: Goddess: Kupala. **trust**: (See: Trust). **the truth**: (See: Truth). **your place in society**: Animal: wolf.

To learn from: the past: Plant: honeysuckle; *past experience*: Plant: rowan; *past mistakes*: Plant: birch; God: Bres.

To learn that: grudges are toxic: Goddess: Oenone; **it isn't worth it to acquire things via theft**: Goddess: Maeve; **we are all mortal**: God: Baldur.

To learn to: accept change: Goddess: Demeter. **accept loss**: Plant: cypress. Goddess: Nanna. **appreciate the bittersweet nature of love**: Goddess: Jurata. **appreciate the magick of life**: Animal: hummingbird. **assert yourself**: Stone: angelite, danburite; Plant: apple. **be careful what you wish for**: Goddess: Caolainn, Pte San Wi. **beware of deceit**: God: Hod, Osiris. **break routines**: God: Loki. **control your temper**: Goddess: Medea. **define boundaries**: Animal: armadillo. **detect lies and treachery**: Goddess: Fraud. **finish what you begin**: Animal: gazelle. **handle your emotions in ways that cause no harm to yourself or to others**: Goddess: Phaedra. **have fun**: Goddess: Chie. **have a healthy respect for the potentially destructive power of the ocean**: Goddess: Scylla. **laugh at yourself**: Animal: coyote; Plant: valerian. **let go**: Oil: palmarosa; Goddess: Demeter. **listen**: (See: Senses). **love yourself**: (See: Love). **overcome jealousy**: (See: Jealousy). **overcome sibling rivalry**: God: Poseidon. **receive**: Plant: sycamore. **respect dreams**: Animal: lizard. **think before you act or speak**: Goddess: Providentia. **truly know yourself**: Goddess: Demeter. **trust inner knowledge**: Plant: heather, pine. **trust intuition**: Plant: pine. **use magickal power wisely**: Goddess: Arianrhod.

To learn how to: do no harm: Goddess: Kwan Yin. **farm**: (See: Agriculture). **please**

a woman sexually: God: Krishna. **stand on your own**: Animal: heron, all wading birds.

To learn not to: **allow a loss to destroy you**: Goddess: Aideen, Isis, Pattini. **anger the gods**: Goddess: Atalanta. **believe everything you hear**: Goddess: Ailinn. **be too trusting**: God: Osiris. **get stung by deceit**: Goddess: Fraud. **give your power away**: Goddess: Erzulie, Yemaya. **hold grudges**: God: Ganesha. **leave yourself open to treachery**: God: Baldur, Osiris. **misdirect your anger**: Goddess: Medea, Pasiphaë. **sacrifice yourself**: Plant: tarragon, witch hazel. **take life too seriously**: Animal: clown fish, coyote; God: Loki. **take yourself too seriously**: Animal: burrowing owl, puffin.

To learn not to be: **jealous**: Goddess: Volupta. **a sore loser**: God: Poseidon. **too difficult a taskmaster**: Goddess: Louhy. **vain**: Goddess: Ayauhteotl.

To: **give children a love for learning**: Plant: vervain. **help a child to learn**: Plant: lemon verbena, vervain.

Liberation

(See also: Escape, Freedom, Release)

Fire

Plant: hyssop, oak, St. John's Wort; Goddess: Kali, Shekinah (Liberating Angel); God: Dionysus, Mabon, Shiva, Soma.

Emotional liberation: Plant: harebell, onion, rhododendron, scarlet pimpernel. **Female liberation**: Goddess: Lilith. **Male liberation**: God: Soma; *male sexual liberation*: God: Pan. **Personal liberation**: Plant: morning glory. **Sexual liberation**: Method: tantra.

Libido

(See also: Desire, Lust, Sex, Sexuality)

Mars/Fire/Aries

Color: red; Goddess: Lilith, Macha; God: Coyote, the Dagda, Eros, Fergus, Pan, Zeus.

Female libido: Goddess: Anath, Maeve. **High libido**: Number: 4; Goddess: Achtland, Anath, Medb. **Male libido**: God: Diab, Fergus, Pan; *to control*: Plant: hemlock; *to increase*: Plant: banana, cardamom, cinnamon.

To: **destroy libido**: Plant: hemlock. **increase libido**: Stone: garnet; Plant: damiana, ginseng, mint, wild oat, patchouli, pine cone; Goddess: Venus. **restore libido**: Plant: damiana, rosewood.

Lies

(See: Deceit)

Life

(See also: Afterlife, Birth, Creation, Death, Longevity, Rebirth, Vitality)

Sun/Earth/Air/Fire/Water/East

Tool: pentacle; Color: green, red; Number: 6; Charm: ankh, scarab; Animal: buffalo, pair of fish, scarab beetle, serpent; Stone: bloodstone, ruby, salt, red tourmaline; Plant: acorn, alfalfa, apple, ash, coconut palm, elm, grain, holly, lotus, maize, mistletoe, oak leaf, palm tree, papyrus, pine, rowan, sesame, wheat, pussy willow; Goddess: Anath (Strength of life), Badb, Coatlicue, Eve, Gaia (Mother of Life), Isis (Giver of Life), Kali (Lady of Life), Kishi-Mojin, Kore, Kupala, Macha (Mother of Life and Death), Sekhmet (Strength of Life, Lady of Life); God: Acat, Ahura Mazda, Cernunnos, Dushares, Itzamna, Marduk (Master of Life), Ra, Yum Caz.

Adventurous life: Color: orange; Plant: lilac, lily of the valley, all flowers that bloom in May; Goddess: Atalanta. **Afterlife**: (See: Afterlife). **Carefree life**: Animal: dragonfly. **Clean life**: Water/Fire; Color: pink. **Contemplative life**: Color: blue. **Domestic life**: (See: Home). **Enduring life**: Charm: ankh, spiral; Plant: forsythia, lotus, snowdrop. **Eternal life**: Color: black; Charm:

ankh; Stone: salt; Plant: evergreens, everlasting, laurel, lotus, peach, sage; Goddess: Isis; God: Mithras, Osiris (Lord of Life, Lord of Eternity). **Everyday life:** *to integrate spirituality with*: Plant: lavender. **Exciting life:** Color: orange. **Family life:** (See: Family). **Happy life:** Stone: ruby; Plant: black cohosh, potentilla, squash blossom. **Healthy life:** Stone: ruby. **Inner life:** Color: white. **Long life:** (See: Longevity). **Magickal life:** Plant: mint, queen of the night; *to learn to appreciate*: Animal: hummingbird. **Marine life:** Neptune/Water; Goddess: Sedna, Yemaya; God: Djila'qons, Glaucus, Ka'cak, Kere'tkun, Neptune, Nereus, Peruten, Phorcys, Poseidon, Proteus, Tinirau. **Married life:** Plant: wall fern. **Marsh life:** God: Enki. **New life:** Color: green; Animal: silkmoth, turtle; Letter: J; Goddess: Nehalennia; God: Cernunnos, Jupiter. **New outlook on life:** Metal: peacock ore. **Organic life:** Earth; Plant: lotus. **Past life:** (See: Past Life Work). **Peaceful life:** Stone: garnet, ruby. **Personal life:** *to integrate professional life with*: Plant: quince. **Plant life:** Earth; Color: green; Stone: moss agate, amber; Goddess: Flora, Nehalennia. **Pleasant life:** Animal: otter; Metal: silver; Goddess: Isis. **Potential life:** Charm: scarab; Plant: all seeds. **Public life:** *to train a child for*: Goddess: Isis. **Quiet life:** God: Hurukan. **Sex life:** (See: Sex). **Simple life:** Waning Moon; Color: purple. **Successful life:** Plant: High John, sandalwood. **Teeming life:** Animal: frog.

Life crisis: Animal: raven. **Life force:** (See: Force). **Life lessons:** *opportunities to learn*: God: Legba; *to understand*: Charm: dinosaur bone; Stone: charoite. **Life passages:** Stone: garnet; Plant: cypress. **Life process:** Goddess: Durga. **Life span:** Animal: spider; Goddess: the Fates. **Life stages:** *to enter a new stage of life*: God: Janus.

Crossroads in life: (See: Crossroads). **Death-in-life:** (See: Death). **Life after death:** (See: Afterlife, Reincarnation). **Life and death:** Animal: rattlesnake. **Life-in-death:** Color: silver; Animal: magpie, vulture, all carrion feeders; Plant: apple, elder, holly, myrtle; Goddess: Olwen.

Breath of life: Air; Charm: ankh; Animal: dolphin; Goddess: Isis, Mayin; God: Quetzalcoatl. **Cycle of life:** Moon; Color: red; Charm: spiral, shed snake skin, Celtic knot; Animal: horse, jackal, snake, vulture, wolf, all scavengers and carrion eaters; Goddess: Anieros, Epona, Kore, Lady of the Lake, Nephthys, Sedna; God: Cernunnos, Marduk, Mider, Shiva; *cycle of a woman's life*: Number: 3; *to accept death as part of*: (See: Death); *to understand growth as a part of*: Method: knot magick; Goddess: Anieros, Axiocersa, the Proximae, the Quadriviae, the White Goddess, the Y Mamau. **Fire of life:** Goddess: Brigid; God: Agni. **Flow of life:** Charm: Celtic knot; Stone: alexandrite. **Magick of life:** *to learn to appreciate*: Animal: hummingbird. **Pattern of life:** Animal: spider. **Power of life:** Animal: pair of birds. **Renewal of life:** Animal: dove, scarab beetle. **Spiral of life:** Charm: Celtic knot, spiral; Animal: octopus; Goddess: Arianrhod, Demeter, Epona, Kali; God: Cernunnos, Osiris; Evocation: Salmon Boy. **Strength of life:** Goddess: Anath, Sekhmet. **Tree of life:** Plant: ash; Goddess: Athirat, Shekinah. **Waters of life:** Water; Goddess: Anahita, Apa, Ishtar. **Unity with life:** Stone: amazonite; Plant: enchanter's nightshade. **Zest for life:** Color: orange; God: the Dagda.

To: allow life to unfold: Plant: bistort. **change your life:** Animal: hippopotamus, snake; Charm: shed skin of a snake; Stone: moldovite; Plant: cinquefoil, hawthorn berry (as incense), heliotrope, leopardsbane, nasturtium, nutmeg, peppermint, squill; Goddess: Isis, Kali; *make positive changes in yourself or your life*: Goddess: Isis. **Clear negative people/situations from your life:**

(See: Situations). **Enjoy life**: Stone: dioptase; Plant: daisy, gorse, petrified wood; Goddess: Chie. **Fight for your life**: Goddess: Sedna. **Find your direction/purpose in life**: Color: deep blue; Stone: citrine. **Get ahead in life**: Color: white. **Improve life**: God: Glooskap. **Learn not to take life too seriously**: Animal: clown fish, coyote; God: Loki. **Live by your wits**: Animal: rabbit. **Maintain life**: God: Namtillaku. **Move forward in life**: (See: Progress). **Organize your life**: Charm: paua shell. **Participate fully in life**: Stone: flint, fluorite; Plant: damiana, jojoba, enchanter's nightshade, peppermint, rosemary. **Preserve life**: Sun; Animal: large fish; Plant: burnet. **Protect a life in danger**: Goddess: Hlin. **Save a child's life**: Goddess: Isis; God: Maximon, Thoth. **Structure life**: God: Mitra. **Sustain life**: Earth/Water; Goddess: Carna, Neith; *get the food needed to sustain life*: Goddess: Uke-Mochi. **Understand life**: Earth; Animal: owl; Stone: alexandrite, citrine, fossil, picture jasper; Plant: sage.

Light

(See also: Darkness, Enlightenment, Illumination)

Sun/Moon/Full Moon/Fire/South/Day/Sunday

Method: candle magick; Number: 7, 42; Metal: gold, silver; Stone: agate, chrysoprase, garnet, hematite, ruby; Plant: laurel, lotus; Goddess: A, Aditi (Light of Heaven), Amaterasu, Anunitu, Bast (Lady of Light), Belisama, Gerd, Hathor, Hemera, Inanna, Juno, Lucina, Selene, Uma, Yhi; God: Ahura Mazda, Apollo, Atea, Aton, Baldur, Belatucadros, Belenos (The Shining One), Byelobog, Brono, Dionysus, Heimdall, Hyperion, Itzamna, Jupiter, Khors, Lucifer, Lugh (Lord of Light), Marduk (Lord of Light), Mithras (Bringer of Light), Napi, Phanes (radiance), Qos, Ra, Shamash (Bringer of Light), Svarog (bright), Vishnu (Lord of Light), Yima.

Bright light: Goddess: Pandia. **Brilliant light**: Goddess: Aditi. **Celestial light**: Goddess: Lucina. **Clear light**: Color: indigo; God: Apollo, Vindonnus. **Daylight**: Sun; Goddess: Cupra; God: Byelobog, Brono, Eguski, Fionn. **Divine light**: Color: white; Goddess: Parvati, Uma; God: Svarog, Svantovit (Holy Light). **Firelight**: God: Agni. **Focused light**: Tool: magnifying glass, prism; Stone: clear quartz crystal. **Golden light**: Sun; Color: gold; Metal: gold; Stone: agate; Goddess: Aurora. **Green light**: Stone: alexandrite, peridot; Goddess: Tara. **Inner light**: Color: blue, dark blue; Animal: firefly, phosphorescent sea creatures; Stone: moonstone, peridot, ruby, topaz; God: Lucifero (Lord of Inner Light). **Moonlight**: Moon/Night; Color: silver; Number: 9; Stone: moonstone; Plant: jasmine, queen of the night; Goddess: Artemis, Diana, Helene (Bright Moon), Isis, Leucothea, Lucina, Phoebe, Selene; God: Khonsu, Sin. **Morning light**: Sun/East/Dawn; Goddess: Isis (Maker of the Sunrise, Mistress of the Dawn, Goddess of the Rosy Dawn); God: Lucifer (light-bearer), Phosphoros (light-bringer); *early morning light*: Dawn; Color: gold, rose; Goddess: Aurora; God: Lucifer, Mithras. **Primordial light**: God: Legba. **Sheer light**: Sun. **Starlight**: Night; Goddess: Neith, Sekhmet; God: Astraeos. **Sunlight**: Sun/Day/Sunday; Color: yellow; Number: 1; Animal: lion; Plant: laurel, sunflower; Goddess: Amaterasu, Bast, Bisal-Mariamna, Day, the Graces, Isis (Shining One, Ray of the Sun), Mitra (Goddess of Light), Sekhmet (The One Who Shines in the Sky); God: Apollo, Aten, Eguski, Freyr, Helios, Mithras (Light of Heaven, Light of the World, Lord of Heavenly Light), Ra, Shu; *fertilizing power of*: God: Amun, Mithras, Ra. **Torchlight**: Goddess: Hecate; God: Mithras (Torch of

Light). **Twilight**: Water/West; Color: blue, indigo; Animal: fox; Goddess: Sandhya, Twilight Zorya; God: Dellingr. **White light**: Color: white; Stone: scolectite.

Light of: consciousness: Color: white; Plant: birch. **knowledge**: Goddess: Rohini. **life**: Fire. **perfection**: Color: white. **reason**: Color: white. **wisdom**: Goddess: Parvati.

Power of light: Sun/Moon; Method: candle magick; *over darkness*: Tool: black candle; Animal: firefly, all phosphorescent sea creatures; Stone: peridot, black star sapphire.

To: balance darkness/light: Plant: enchanter's nightshade; God: Chernobog. **bring into the light**: Goddess: Lucina (She Who Brings to Light); *help newborns into the light*: Goddess: Candelifera. **emerge from darkness into light**: Animal: crow; Stone: black star sapphire; Goddess: Lucina. **find light in darkness**: Animal: cricket. **heal with light**: Sun. **help spirits reach the light**: (See: Spirits). **increase light**: Stone: rhodochrosite; Plant: juniper berry. **light the way**: God: Ishum. **lighten up**: Plant: elder, lemon, snowdrop; Goddess: Baubo. **open to light**: Stone: apophyllite, peach calcite; Plant: fir cone, grapefruit, grass of Parnassus, lilac; Goddess: Yhi. **replace darkness with light**: Animal: firefly; Stone: black star sapphire; God: Asar-alim. **walk in the light**: Animal: deer. **work with the energies of light and darkness**: Color: gray; Stone: smoky quartz; Goddess: Hanwi (Grandmother Moon), Hecate.

Lightness

Air

Lightness of being: Symbol: balloon; Animal: butterfly, hummingbird; Plant: daisy, dragon's gall, larkspur, zinnia. **Lightheartedness**: Animal: hummingbird; Plant: shamrock, thyme; Goddess: Thalia.

Lightning

(See also: Storms, Weather)

Fire/Air

Goddess: Begoe, Fulgora, Ignirtoq, Inanna, Isis, Kadlu, Mary, Oya, Pelé, Rainha Barba; God: Apep, Baal, Bel, Chac, Jupiter, Marduk, Perun, Shango, Shiva, Summanus, Thor, Tlaloc, Tupan, Ukko, Zahrim (Lord of Lightning), Zeus.

To: attract lightning: Charm: lightning rod; Stone: lodestone; Plant: ash tree, oak tree; God: Jupiter Fulgurator (Sender of Lightning). **make lightning strike an enemy**: God: Shango. **protect against lightning**: Animal: kingfisher (dried body); Stone: diamond (powdered), garnet, ruby, zircon; Plant: elder, hawthorn, hazel, holly branch, houseleek, laurel, mint, mistletoe, mountain mahogany, rowan, St. John's Wort; Goddess: Brigid; *to protect homes from lightning*: Charm: mistletoe broom (hung in the house); Plant: hawthorn (growing near the house), houseleek (especially if growing on the roof), mugwort (hung in the house); Goddess: Fulgora. **treat victims of lightning strikes**: Charm: rose oil with purslane juice.

Limitation

(See also: Barriers, Binding, Freedom)

Saturn/Saturday

Color: black; Number: 4; Stone: black salt; Plant: bonsai tree; God: Mercury, Terminus.

To: communicate limits: Plant: briar, cactus, nettle, thorn. **guard boundaries**: Animal: muskrat; God: Kumado-No-Kami, Terminus (Guardian of Boundaries). **measure boundaries**: Goddess: Zemlya. **overcome limitations**: Animal: dragonfly, snake; Stone: alexandrite; Plant: date palm; *refuse to be bound by traditional female roles*: Goddess: Arianrhod; *freedom from bounds*: Goddess: Aditi (The Unfettered). **recognize**

limitations: Stone: hematite. **set limits or fix boundaries**: Tool: athame, cord; Charm: image of Mercury; Goddess: Sesheta, Vegois; God: Terminus. **transcend boundaries/limitations**: Animal: condor; Goddess: Isis; *sexual boundaries*: God: Dionysus, Hermes, Pan.

To **limit**: **actions of others**: Saturn/Saturday; Color: black. **creation**: God: Nergal. **freedom**: Saturn/Saturday.

ogic

Air/Virgo/Tuesday

Color: yellow; Stone: sodalite; God: Thoth.

Logical analysis: Prattisamvit. **Logical inference**: Goddess: Skuld. **Logical mind**: Animal: crane, heron. **To see things logically**: Stone: fluorite.

oneliness

(See also: Friends, Friendship, Relationships)

Dark Moon

Color: blue, gray; Number: 8; Plant: stonecrop.

To: **ease loneliness**: Stone: chrysoprase; Plant: hyacinth, lavender, lemon, marjoram, sesame seed, sumac, sunflower, toadflax; Goddess: Yhi. **end loneliness**: Waning Moon; Stone: rose quartz; Plant: cinquefoil; God: Brahma, Cupid, Wak. **protect the lonely**: God: Shiva.

ongevity

(See also: Endurance, Immortality, Life, Vitality, Youth)

Saturn

Color: brown, green; Charm: jade scarab; Animal: carp, crane, crow, dove, eagle, elephant, komodo dragon, macaw, parrot, phoenix, swan, tortoise, all long-lived animals; Metal: gold; Stone: agate, moss agate, green beryl, bloodstone, carnelian, coral, fossil, jade, jasper, moonstone, pearl; Plant: aloe, angelica (especially the root), avocado, bamboo, cedar, black cohosh, coriander, cypress, everlasting, fennel, fig, fo-ti, ginseng, gotu kola, linden, lavender, lemon, lemon balm, lilac, linden, lotus, maple, marigold, mistletoe, mullein, oak, onion, date palm, peach, pine, rosemary, sage, sarsaparilla, giant sequoia, sorb apple, tansy, tonka bean, tulip, valerian, petrified wood, yarrow; Goddess: Apa, Ayurda (Granter of Longevity), Freya, Ishtar, Setlocenia (She of the Long Life), Takotsi (Grandmother Growth), White Tara, Tou Mu, Ushas, Xi Wang Mu; God: Fugen Bosatsu, Fukurokuju, Junrojin, Pan, Shiva, Shouhsing, Shou-Lao, T'ai-Yüeh Ta-ti; Evocation: Winonah.

Husband's longevity: Goddess: Maha Lakshmi. **Long marriage**: Stone: citrine; Plant: laurel, orange blossom.

To: **know the life span of any being**: God: Esizkur. **make a spell last a long time**: Charm: lead tablet, sands of time; Stone: amber, fossil; Plant: everlasting.

oss

(See also: Grief, Sorrow, Theft)

Waning Moon

Color: black; Plant: devil's bit scabious.

Blood loss: *to prevent in battle*: Color: red; *to treat*: Plant: comfrey, horsetail, witch hazel. **Memory loss**: (See: Memory). **Personal loss**: Number: 9. **Weight loss**: Waning Moon; Method: visualization; Stone: topaz; Plant: fennel, grapefruit, jasmine.

Lost beauty: Plant: goldenrod; Goddess: Medusa. **Lost children**: (See: Children). **Lost deities**: *to restore*: God: Namtillaku. **Lost hope**: Plant: black poplar. **Lost innocence**: Plant: pomegranate (eaten), dried white rose. **Lost love**: (See: Love). **Lost**

manhood: (See: Men). **Lost people**: (See: People). **Lost property/objects**: Air; *to locate*: Color: brown; Plant: morning glory; *to recover*: Stone: ametrine, charoite, hematite, kyanite, moldovite, phenacite, tiger's eye; *to replace*: God: Punarvasu; *to prevent loss of property*: Plant: comfrey. **Lost senses**: (See: Senses). **Lost souls**: Animal: raven; *to guide*: Goddess: Sedna. **Lost vision**: *to restore*: (See: Vision). **Lost wealth**: *to restore*: Stone: tiger's eye. **Lost youth**: *to restore*: Plant: anise.

Comfort when suffering a loss: Color: black; Stone: agate; Plant: balm of Gilead, cypress, myrrh, willow; Goddess: Hina. **Emotional healing after a loss**: (See: Healing). **Strength after loss**: Plant: cypress.

To: balance gains/losses: Goddess: Nemesis. **deal with loss**: Plant: currant, reindeer moss, ylang-ylang; Evocation: Orion. **end a losing streak**: Plant: alkanet. **keep magickal tools from getting lost**: Plant: caraway seed. **learn to accept loss**: Plant: cypress; Goddess: Nanna. **learn to not allow a loss to destroy you**: Goddess: Aideen, Isis, Pattini. **learn not to be a sore loser**: God: Poseidon. **lose consciousness**: Waning Moon. **mourn the loss of a friend**: Plant: red anemone; Evocation: Gilgamesh. **overcome fear of losing control**: (See: Control). **overcome fear of loss of freedom**: Plant: sumach. **regenerate losses**: Animal: lizard. **survive the loss of a spouse**: Goddess: Isis.

Love

Venus/Mercury/Moon/Waxing Moon/Full Moon/Earth/Water/Fire/South/West/ Friday/Monday/Libra/Capricorn

Tool: apple wood wand, willow wand; Color: green, emerald green, pink, deep pink, red, rose, white; Charm: ambergris, civet, cowrie shell, dove's blood, ginger cooked or steeped in maple syrup, heart, honey, two knots, lavender flower water, musk, orange flower water, peacock feather, rosewater, sugar; Number: 2, 3, 5, 6, 7; Letter: O; Animal: carp, deer, dove, horse, hummingbird, lynx, swallow, partridge, pigeon, wryneck, pairs of birds; Metal: copper, pink gold, platinum, silver; Stone: agate, green or red agate, alexandrite, amber, amethyst, aphrodite, beryl, bloodstone, calcite, pink calcite, chrysocolla, coral, diamond, pink diamond, dioptase, emerald, garnet, jade, jasper, pink jasper, kunzite, lapis lazuli, lepidolite, red lodestone, pairs of lodestones, malachite, moonstone, morganite, olivine, opal, pearl, rose quartz, rhodochrosite, rhodonite, ruby, sapphire, pink sapphire, sard, topaz, tourmaline, pink or blue or watermelon tourmaline, turquoise, zircon; Potion: absinthe (dangerous, not recommended); red wine with rose petals, coriander seeds or balm of Gilead; apple cider; herbs of love mulled in apple cider; Plant: acacia flowers, Adam and Eve root, almond, aloe, amber, aniseed, apple (fruit, wood or blossom), apricot, aster, avens, avocado, bachelor's buttons, balm of Gilead, barley, basil, beans, red beans, pink beans, beet, benzoin, betony, birch, bleeding heart, bloodroot, Brazil nut, burdock, calamus, cannabis, caper, caraway seed, cardamom, carnation, cascara, sagrada, cassia, catnip, cedar, chamomile, cherry, chestnut, chickweed, chili pepper, red chrysanthemum, cinnamon, cinquefoil, clove, clover, red clover, coconut, black cohosh, coltsfoot, columbine, copal, coriander, corn, cornflower, couch grass, autumn crocus, cubeb, cuckoo flower, cumin, Cupid's dart, cyclamen, daffodil, daisy, damiana, deerstongue, devil's bit scabious, dill, dodder, dogbane, dragon's blood, dutchman's breeches, elder, elder berry, elecampane, elm, endive, eryngo, fern, feverfew, fig, frangipani, frankincense, freesia, galangal, gardenia, gentian, geranium, white geranium, ginger, ginseng, grains of paradise, gravel root, gum arabic, haw-thorn, heather, heliotrope, hemp, hibiscus, High John, hollyhock, honeysuckle, house-leek, hyacinth, iris, ivy, English ivy, jasmine, juniper, kava kava, kelp, ladies bedstraw, lady's mantle, lavender, leek, lemon, lemon balm, lettuce, licorice, lilac, lily of the val-ley, lime, linden, liverwort, lotus, lobelia, lovage, love grass, love seed, mace, madonna lily, magnolia, maidenhair fern, maize, male fern, mallow, mandrake, maple, marigold, marjoram, marsh mallow, marigold, mas-tic, meadowsweet, milkweed, mimosa, mint, mistletoe, moneywort, moonwort, motherwort, mugwort, mustard seed, myrrh, myrtle, narcissus, nuts, nutmeg, ole-ander, orange, orchid, purple orchis, orris root, pansy, papaya, patchouli, peach, pea, peach, pear, pennyroyal, peppermint, peri-winkle, Madagascar periwinkle, pimento, plum, plumeria, pomegranate, poppy, opium poppy, prickly ash, primrose, purslane, quassia, quince, raspberry, rose, rose geranium, rose hips, rosemary, rue, rye, saffron, sage, sandalwood, sarsaparilla, savory, scullcap, sea holly, senna, sorrel, southernwood, spearmint, spider lily, spi-derwort, spikenard, St. John's Wort, stephanotis, strawberry, sugar cane, sumbul, sweet pea, sweet william, sycamore, tamarind, tansy, thyme, tomato, tonka bean, tormentil, trillium, tuberose, tulip, valerian, vanilla, Venus fly trap, verbena, lemon ver-bena, vervain, blue vervain, vetiver, violet, violet with lavender, water lily, willow, witch grass, wood aloes, woodruff, wormwood, yarrow, yerba maté, ylang-ylang, yohimbine; Goddess: Aegea, Aeval, Aideen, Aileen, Aine, Akka, Allat, Amaterasu, Anahita, Anath, Ani, Antheia, Aphrodite, Artemis, Asherah, Asherali, Ashtoreth, Astarte, Astrilde, Atargatis, Baalith, Belili, Belit Ilani, Benzaiten, Blathnat, Blodeuwedd, Branwen, Brigid, Britomartis, Catheña, Chalchihuitlcue, Ch'i Ku-Niang, Creiddylad, Cytherea, Devana, Diana, Dictynna, Didilia, Dione, Esmeralda, Erzulie, Fides, Finncaev, Flora, Freya, Frigg, Gaia, Geshtinanna, Goda, Guinevere, Hathor, Hecate, Hera, Holda, Ibla, Inanna, Io, Ishhara, Ishtar (Great Goddess of Love and War), Isis (Lady of Love), Juno, Kali, Kurukulla, Kwan Yin, Lada, Lady of the Lake, Lakshmi (Mother of Love), Lofn, Luna, Maia, Menglod, Milda, Mlukuh, Mylitta, Myrrha, Nanna, Neith, Niamh, Olwen, Oshun, Ostara, Psyche, Qadesh, Rati, Rauni, Rhea, Al-Sarah, Satis, Sekhmet (Lady of Love), Semiramis, Shakti, Shekinah, Sjofna, Syria Dea, Tanith, Tara, Tlazolteotl, Turan, Uma, Unxia, Urvasi, al-Uzzah, Vara, Venus, Vidya-Lakshmi, Xochiquetzal, Yaoji, Yemaya, Yolkai Estsan, Yum, Zorya; God: Adonis, Ah Kin Xoc, Aizen Myo-o, Amon-Ra, Amor, Ananga, Angus (Lord of Love and Death), Anteros, Attis, Arunis, Baile, Cernunnos, Cian, Cupid, Damuzi, Dhatri, Dulha Deo, Dwyn, Ericepaius, Eros, Faunus, Fu-hsing, Ghede, Haoma, Hymen, Kama, Krishna (Lord of Love), Lel, Manmatha, Maximon, Mitra, Pan, Phanes, Pothos, Rimmon, Robin Hood, Shakarabru, Soma, Tammuz, Tatanka, Vishnu, Wadd, Xipe Totec, Yarillo; Evocation: Anael (Angel of the Star of Love), Diarmuid of the Love Spot, Evander, Galatea, Io, Rosamund.

Absent love: Plant: myrtle. **All-consuming love:** Goddess: Ishtar; Plant: Syrian mal-low. **All-or-nothing love:** Number: 4. **Ardent love:** Plant: double-blossom red carnation. **Brotherly love:** Plant: honey-suckle, virgin's bower; God: Mithras, Pachacamac. **Carnal love:** Goddess: Aphrodite Porne, Aphrodite Pandemos; God: Kama, Yarillo. **Dangerous love:** Plant: tuberose; Goddess: Ishtar; Evoca-tion: Dahut. **Deep love:** Plant: carnation. **Devoted love:** Plant: honeysuckle. **Divine love:** Color: cobalt blue; Stone: amethyst;

unconditional divine love: Stone: jade; Goddess: Kali. **Earthy love**: Taurus. **Elevated love**: Stone: tourmaline. **Emotional love**: Color: pink, rose, wine; Stone: amethyst, rose quartz; Plant: lilac; Goddess: Radha; *to attract*: Stone: amber; Plant: white lily. **Endless love**: Plant: Japanese maple. **Enduring love**: Plant: camellia. **Erotic love**: Goddess: Isis. **Estranged love**: Plant: lotus; *to reconcile*: Plant: balm of Gilead. **Eternal love**: Charm: Celtic knot. **Fatal love**: Goddess: Inanna, Ishtar; God: Angus. **Filial love**: Plant: virgin's bower. **Forbidden love**: Goddess: Diana, Ishtar, Lofn. **Forsaken love**: Plant: willow. **Fraternal love**: God: Pwyll Pen Annwn. **Free love**: Goddess: Milda (See also: Sex). **Homosexual love**: Color: any shade of purple, especially lavender; Animal: eel; Oil: Oil of Malabar, palmarosa; Plant: lavender, violet, oil grasses: vetiver root, citronella grass, camel grass, lemon grass, ginger grass. **Hopeless love**: Plant: yellow tulip. **Idealistic love**: Libra. **Impersonal love**: Number: 9. **Infinite love**: God: Vishnu. **Innocent love**: Plant: rosebud. **Lost love**: Goddess: Freya, Jurata; *to regain*: Plant: star anise, violet leaf. **Manly love**: Plant: live oak. **Married love**: Venus; Animal: turtledove; Stone: beryl, green beryl, geode, clear quartz crystal; Plant: ivy, linden, periwinkle, pomegranate, rosebuds, rosemary; Goddess: Gaia, Hera, Isis, Juno, Selqet; *to preserve*: Stone: green beryl. **Maternal love**: Cancer; Stone: mother-of-pearl; Plant: moss, quince; Goddess: Ceres, Demeter, Eileithyia, Gnowee, Isis, Mary. **Mature love**: Color: blue. **Mutual love**: God: Anteros. **New love**: Waxing Moon; Animal: swallow; Stone: rhodochrosite; Goddess: the Maiden; *to attract*: Color: orange, pink; Stone: turquoise; Plant: asphodel, balm of Gilead, gardenia. **Obsessive love**: Goddess: Ishtar; Evocation: Dala Kumara, Merlin. **Passionate love**: Color: red; Goddess: Arami, Cybele, Februata,

Hathor, Ishtar, Lalita; God: Bes, Eros; *to attract*: Plant: red rose petals; *to excite*: Goddess: Lofn. **Paternal love**: Cancer. **Perfect love**: God: Marduk. **Physical love**: Venus; Goddess: Circe, Fand, Frigg, Liban, Tlazolteotl, Venus; God: Cernunnos, the Horned God, Shiva; *to attract*: Plant: caraway, juniper berry; *to combine with spiritual love*: Plant: jasmine; *violently physical love*: Goddess: Ishtar. **Platonic love**: Virgo; Plant: acacia. **Profane love**: Goddess: Venus. **Pure love**: Plant: red carnation, rose, rosebud. **Respectful love**: Plant: lavender. **Romantic love**: Libra; Color: pink; Stone: rose quartz; Plant: pink or white rose; Goddess: Erzulie, Isis (Lady of Romance); God: Kama; *to attract*: Plant: pink rose bud, white rose bud. **Secret love**: Plant: yellow acacia, honey flower, crimson rose; Goddess: Diana; *to protect*: Goddess: Diana. **Secure love**: Stone: emerald; Plant: olive. **Self-love**: Color: pink, rose; Stone: aquamarine, pink calcite, danburite, feldspar, green gypsum, hiddenite, kunzite, lepidolite, rose quartz, rhodochrosite, rhodonite, ruby, pink tourmaline, turquoise; Plant: butterbur, carnation, milk thistle, sage; *unconditional self-love*: Stone: rose quartz; Plant: pink azalea; *to learn to love yourself*: Stone: fresh water pearl, rose quartz; Plant: milk thistle. **Sensual love**: Taurus; Color: scarlet; Goddess: Sarasvati. **Sexual love**: Venus/Fire/Scorpio; Color: red; Stone: ruby; Charm: musk; Plant: jasmine; Goddess: Aphrodite, Arami, Astarte, Dubhlaing, Fand, Freya, Hathor, Heqet, Indrani, Lalita, Liban, Pertunda, Philotes, Qadesh, Rati, Tlazolteotl, Venus; God: Bes, Cernunnos, Cupid, Eros, Kama, Min, Pan, Shiva, Yarillo; *to attract*: Potion: rose hips steeped in red wine; *to protect in marriage*: Goddess: Cloacina. **Silent love**: Plant: primrose. **Sisterly love**: Goddess: Geshtinanna. **Slighted love**: Plant: yellow chrysanthemum; *to avenge*: God: Anteros.

Sorrowful love: Plant: basil. **Spiritual love**: Stone: emerald; Plant: jasmine, white rose; Goddess: Aphrodite Urania, Charitë; *to attract*: Stone: lapis lazuli. **Spurned love**: Evocation: Phaedra. **Stolen love**: God: Angus; Evocation: Paris. **Sweet love**: Charm: honey; Plant: honey flower, jasmine, sugar cane. **Tough love**: Goddess: Althaea, Isis. **True love**: Color: pink; Stone: amethyst, moonstone; Potion: white rose petals steeped in white wine; Plant: Adam and Eve root, birch bark, forget-me-not, four leaf clover, gardenia, jasmine, lavender, lily of the valley, Low John, patchouli, rose, pink rose, white rose, rosemary, ylang-ylang; God: Cupid; *to attract*: Stone: amethyst, aphrodite, emerald; Plant: gardenia, white lily, rose, pink or white rose petals; *to find your true love*: Goddess: Ailinn, Pele. **Unconditional love**: Animal: deer, dog, your familiar; Stone: kunzite, rose quartz, rhodonite; Plant: aster, harebell, pikaki, primrose, rose, red rose, white rose; *to attract*: Plant: amber. **Unfading love**: Plant: globe amaranth. **Unfortunate love**: Plant: devil's bit scabious. **Universal love**: Color: pink; Charm: attar of roses; Stone: amazonite, rose quartz, sugilite; Plant: holy thorn, white rose. **Unrequited love**: Color: yellow; Plant: daffodil, yellow tulip; Evocation: Clytie. **Wanton love**: Goddess: Arianrhod. **Woman's love**: Plant: pink carnation; Goddess: Aphrodite. **Young love**: Plant: marjoram, southernwood; Goddess: Venus; God: Angus, Chama, Yarillo.

Loving: Color: pink, rose; Stone: charoite, sphaerocobaltite; Plant: basil. **Loving communication**: Stone: kunzite; Plant: chamomile. **Loving kindness**: Plant: bleeding heart; Goddess: Kwan Yin, Mary. **Loving vibrations**: Stone: rhodochrosite, rose quartz; Plant: rose.

Love affairs: Plant: cardamom; Goddess: Aphrodite, Venus. **Love amulets**: *to increase the power of*: Plant: coltsfoot. **Love divination**: See: Divination). **Love energy**: (See: Energy). **Love at first sight**: Charm: lightning bolt; God: Zeus. **Love poems**: Goddess: Erato. **Love potions**: Moon/Water; Tool: cauldron, chalice; Charm (to be added to potions in minute amounts): dew from a fairy ring, maple syrup (in which ginger has been cooked or steeped, then thinned with spring water), rosewater; Stone: lodestone; Potion: rose petals or balm of Gilead steeped in red wine; herbs of love mulled in apple cider; any of the following kinds of tea, with honey or sugar: ginger, jasmine, linden, mint, raspberry, rose, strawberry leaf, yerba mate; Fungus: stinkhorn; Plant: cinnamon, coriander seeds, Cupid's dart, lemon balm, lovage, pansy, periwinkle, rose, savory, vervain, violet; Goddess: Yaoji. **Love purification**: Plant: valerian. **Love songs**: Goddess: Erato. **Love spells**: (See: Spells). **Love wishes**: Plant: catnip, cinquefoil, ginger, juniper.

Love of: deities: Stone: rhodochrosite. **Nature**: Plant: magnolia. **Water**: Cancer; Animal: all marine life; Plant: willow.

Ability to love: Plant: rose; *ability to fall in love*: Stone: charoite. **Receptivity to love**: Plant: linden flower. **Bittersweetness of love**: Charm: mermaid; Goddess: Jurata. **Bonds of love**: Plant: honeysuckle. **Declaration of love**: Color: red; Plant: red rose, red tulip. **Growth of love**: Stone: pink tourmaline. **Mysteries of love**: *initiation into*: Venus; Letter: O. **Power of love**: Venus; Animal: pairs of birds; Stone: uncut emerald; Plant: carnation; *over death*: Goddess: Isis; *transformational power of love*: Plant: holy thorn; Goddess: Latis. **Return of love**: Plant: ambrosia, toadflax; God: Anteros.

Balance in love: Stone: rhodochrosite; Plant: ylang-ylang. **Choice in love**: Plant: apple blossom. **Constancy in love**: Stone: garnet. **Cruelty in love**: Plant: marigold. **Endurance in love**: Stone: emerald; Plant:

gorse, marigold. **Fidelity in love**: Plant: lemon, lime, senna. **Luck in love**: *bad*: Stone: onyx; *good*: Charm: eating the last slice of bread when offered it; Stone: fluorite, moonstone; Plant: cowslip, jasmine, Low John, rose. **Gullibility in love**: Number: 3. **Happiness in love**: Plant: patchouli; Goddess: Sasthi. **Success in love**: Animal: carp; Stone: azurite, emerald, lapis lazuli; Plant: ginger, red or pink or orange rose; Goddess: Unxia, Urvasi. **Transformation through love**: Plant: holy thorn; Goddess: Latis.

To: **accept love**: Stone: apatite, aphrodite, malachite, fresh water pearl, rose quartz. **activate love**: Stone: rhodochrosite, rhodonite. **attract love**: New Moon; Color: pink, green, emerald green, orange, red; Charm: civet; Animal: rabbit; Metal: copper, silver; Stone: amber, beryl, chrysocolla, pink diamond, dioptase, emerald, jade, kunzite, lapis lazuli, lodestone, red lodestone, two lodestones, moonstone, morganite, pearl, rose quartz, rhodochrosite, topaz, blue or pink or watermelon tourmaline, turquoise, yellow zircon; Oil: palmarosa; Plant: amber, asphodel, basil, catnip, cedar, chamomile (in bath), cherry, chickweed, cinnamon, clove, red clover, copal, coriander seed, dragon's blood, elecampane, gardenia, gentian, ginseng, hibiscus, High John, pink hyacinth, jasmine, juniper berry, lavender, licorice, white lily, lovage root, Low John, lucky hand root, mandrake, mint, mistletoe, myrtle, orris root, patchouli, poppy seeds, prickly ash (fruit of the tree), red rose, rose buds or petals, southernwood, strawberry, vanilla, lemon verbena, vetiver, willow, wood aloes, yarrow; Goddess: Aphrodite, Isis, Nimuë/Vivienne; God: Krishna; *to the home*: Plant: frangipani, lavender, patchouli, rose, southernwood; *from a man*: Plant: lavender, orris root; *from the opposite sex*: Plant: mullein; *from a woman*: Plant: henbane; *for males to attract love from females*: Plant: henbane, High John; *attract the one you love*: Charm: milk infused with cowslip blossoms (for washing the face or hair, not for ingesting); (See also: Attraction). **control love**: God: Tatanka. **encourage love**: Plant: jasmine, meadowsweet, papaya, peppermint, raspberry, strawberry; *encourage love for learning in children*: Plant: vervain. **end love**: Color: red with black; Plant: parsley (cut with a knife). **enhance love**: Stone: diamond, rose quartz; Plant: papaya (eaten by both partners together); *enhance the ability to love*: Stone: charoite. **fall in love**: Plant: apple (eaten by both people together); Goddess: Aphrodite; God: Cupid, Zeus. **find love**: Color: green, red; Stone: morganite, rhodochrosite; Plant: orris root; *find higher love*: Stone: rose quartz. **gain love**: Charm: two nuts in one shell; Plant: mistletoe, peach (eaten by both people together) or pear (eaten by both people together); Goddess: Benzaiten. **gain the favor of**: *the Goddess of Love*: Plant: myrtle; *the one you love*: Goddess: Benzaiten. **give love**: Stone: aphrodite, malachite; Goddess: Aphrodite. **grieve for a loved one**: (See: Grief). **increase love**: Color: pink; Stone: tourmaline. **increase the power of love amulets**: Plant: coltsfoot. **influence the heart**: aventurine, tanzanite; Plant: cinnamon. **inspire love**: Evocation: the Apsaras. **interfere with love**: Color: black; Stone: onyx. **keep love**: Method: binding, knot magick; Color: red; Plant: coriander, orris root. **keep someone from leaving**: Plant: caraway. **maintain love**: Stone: morganite. **manifest love**: Stone: amethyst, sugilite; *manifest the transformational power of love*: Goddess: Latis. **open to love**: Stone: apatite, emerald, labradorite, moonstone, rose quartz, pink tourmaline; Plant: azalea, mariposa lily, linden, lotus; *open the heart*: Stone: emerald, labradorite, moonstone, ruby; Plant: azalea, bergamot, bleeding heart, forget-me-not, geranium, lemon balm, wild rose, tuberose. **preserve love**: Stone: emerald; Plant: mistletoe. **protect love**: Goddess: Hathor; Evocation: the Apsaras. **receive love**: Stone: kunzite. **refuse love**: Plant: laurel. **restore love**: Plant: canna lily. **return love**: Plant: ambrosia; God: Anteros. **send love**: Stone: amazonite. **stimulate love**: Stone: rose quartz; Plant: cherry, white lily. **strengthen love**: Color: pink; Stone: pink diamond, kunzite, morganite, rose quartz, pink tourmaline; Plant: cinnamon, ylang-ylang. **take great risks for love**: Goddess: Jurata. **uncross love**: Plant: dill. **understand love**: Stone: green gypsum, rubiolite.

Lovers

(See also: Sex)

Venus/Full Moon

Goddess: Luna, Myrrha, Selene, Venus; God: Cupid, Krishna (The Divine Lover).

Arbitration between lovers: Goddess: Isis. **Peace between lovers**: Stone: sapphire; Goddess: Juno. **Happiness between lovers**: Stone: sapphire.

To: attract a lover: Stone: moonstone; Oil: palmarosa; Plant: caraway, chamomile (in the bath), chickweed, citronella, clove, black cohosh root, damiana, frangipani, juniper berry, lovage root, orris root, patchouli, rose hips, sweet pea, violet leaf; *a female lover*: Plant: fig; *a male lover*: Plant: banana; *the return of a lover*: Plant: damiana, dragon's blood, pineapple; *for a male to attract a lover*: Plant: holly. **bind lovers**: Charm: ring; Plant: apricot, jasmine; Goddess: Aphrodite (She Who Binds Hearts Together). **create discord between lovers**: Stone: fire garnet. Plant: vervain root (powdered). **dream of your lover**: Charm: vinegar with honey, wormwood, marigold flowers, thyme and marjoram (as a charm, not to be ingested); Plant: poppy. **end a lovers' quarrel**: Plant: geranium. **enforce the promises of lovers**: Goddess: Vara. **get a lover**: Plant: chamomile, cuckoo flower, dandelion seed head. **get over a lover**: Plant: camphor. **help lovers**: Stone: moonstone. **keep a lover**: Stone: rhodonite. **keep a lover faithful**: Plant: cedar, clover, coriander seed, cumin seed, rosemary. **keep a lover interested**: Plant: catnip, lime. **know the destiny/fate of lovers**: Goddess: Inanna; Plant: orpane and red sage (gathered on Midsummer Eve). **know if your lover is telling the truth**: Stone: emerald. **make a lover more passionate**: Charm: ambergris; Plant: apricot, cardamom. **protect lovers**: God: Angus, Baile; *protect ill-fated lovers*: Goddess: Albina. **punish a heartless lover**: Goddess: Nemesis. **reconcile lovers**: Goddess: Psyche; *quarreling lovers*: Stone: diamond; Plant: valerian root; *lovers whose families parted them*: Goddess: Lofn. **release a lover**: Plant: camphor, sesame. **take a lover or lovers**: Goddess: Aphrodite, Cliodna, Freya, Guinevere, Ishtar, Venus. God: Indra; *take lesbian lovers without destroying a marriage*: Goddess: Fauna.

Loyalty

(See also: Constancy, Fidelity)

Thursday/Leo/Scorpio

Color: blue (true blue), royal blue, red; Animal: dog, horse, penguin, wolf; Number: 4; Stone: garnet, kyanite, moonstone; Plant: laurel, lime, rosemary; Goddess: Luaths Lurgann, Sekhmet (Loyal One), Sigyn; God: Fides, Hanuman, Mithras, Pwyll Pen Annwn; Evocation: Brangaine, Enkidu.

Family loyalty: Goddess: Airmid, the Furies.

To: attract loyalty: Plant: sweet pea; *attract loyal friends*: Stone: tourmaline. **influence loyalty**: Plant: sweet pea. **strengthen loyalty**: Stone: lodestone, red or green lodestone.

Luck

(See also: Fortune)

Jupiter/Waxing Moon/Thursday

Color: dark blue, green, orange, purple; Charm: fairy ring; Animal: dragon; Number: 6; Stone: obsidian, opal, pyrite, sapphire, staurolite; Plant: allspice, ash leaf, cabbage, caraway, catnip, red clover, devil's shoestring, ginseng, heather, white heather, grains of paradise, holly berry, kava kava, lady's mantle, lavender, lilac, linden, mace, mint, narcissus, nettle, nutmeg, oak moss, olive, orange, patchouli, poppy seed, rose hip, rosemary, spikenard, white rose, rue, strawberry leaf, vetiver, violet leaf, water lily; Goddess: Benzaiten, Caipora, Cerridwen, Chala, Dolya, Fortuna (Lady Luck), Hecate, Kichohu, Lakshmi, Lennaxidaq, Manat, the Muses, Tyche, Ustrecha; God: Amaethon, Byelobog, Bishamon, Cernunnos, Daikoku, Fukurokuju, Hotei, Meni, Odin, Tamon, Xolotl; Evocation: Azazel.

Bad luck: Number: 4, 13; Charm: bread (if thrown away, or if the last piece is taken without offering it to others), breaking a mirror, haggling over the price of a magickal tool, harming a lark, killing a wren or disturbing its nest, opening an umbrella indoors, viewing the Moon through glass, walking beneath a ladder; Animal: albatross, black cat (if it crosses your path), cricket (if harmed), ladybug (if killed); Stone: any flawed gemstone (if worn), salt (if spilled), tourmaline; Plant: apple tree (if all of its apples are harvested), aspen, basil, blackthorn, broom (if used for sweeping while it is blooming), coca leaf, elder (if harmed, cut down, used for fire wood, brought into the house, or has its twigs broken), grain (if not well-sprouted by Summer Solstice), grass (if a fairy ring of trampled grass is interfered with), harebell, hawthorn, houseleek (if blooming or

uprooted), oak tree (if cut down), parsley, sage (if grown alone, or planted by yourself in your garden), tamarisk; Goddess: Bestalannitsa, Nedolya; God: Mait' Carrefour, Ueuecoyotl, Xolotl; *for the household*: Evocation: Domovoy; *in love*: Stone: onyx; *in marriage*: Stone: onyx; *for non witches*: Number: 13; *to avert*: Charm: garland of mugwort from Midsummer celebrations; *to avert from the home*: Plant: cumin; *to end*: Color: purple; Potion: wassail; *to protect against*: Charm: ambergris; Plant: coca leaf, mugwort; God: Sucellos; *to reverse*: God: Orunmila. **continuing luck**: Plant: banyan tree. **family luck**: Plant: St. John's Wort (root, dug up at sunrise on Beltane morning). **gambling luck**: (See: Gambling). **good luck**: Color: green, orange, red, silver; Charm: anil, stone arrowhead, four-leaf clover, jade crab, corn dolly, horseshoe, rabbit's foot, rose leaves or petals thrown into fire, solar cross fashioned from two hazel twigs with red or green thread to bind it, wheat cake, Yule log; Number: 3; Animal: bat, caterpillar, cricket (when singing), ladybug (landing on you), robin, sow (with piglets, if they cross your path), toad; Metal: copper, tin; Stone: alexandrite, amber, Apache tear, aventurine, green or orange aventurine, chalcedony, chrysoprase, citrine, emerald (especially when worn on Friday), garnet, jade, dark green jade, green jasper, red jasper, jet, lepidolite, lodestone, malachite, moonstone, olivine, pearl, pyrite, smoky quartz, sapphire, sardonyx, staurolite, tigereye, topaz, turquoise; Potion: wassail; Plant: acorn, allspice, aloe, aniseed, apple (especially when eaten on Samhain), ash leaves (especially leaves with symmetrical edges), bamboo, banyan tree, basil, bayberry, bean, blackberry, bluebell, cabbage, calamus, caper, cascara sagrada, cedar, chamomile, Chinaberry, chestnut, cinchona, cinnamon, cinquefoil, clover, four-leaf clover, coconut, cotton, daffodil, daisy (especially when worn at Summer Solstice), devil's shoestring, dill, yellow dock, dragon's blood, eye of Satan, fern, frankincense, galangal, ginger, goldenrod, grain (if well-sprouted by Summer Solstice), hazel, heather, white heather, heliotrope, High John, holly (wreath or bough), honeysuckle, huckleberry, iris, Irish moss, ivy (crown or garland), jasmine, Job's tears (seven of them), kava kava, lavender, lemongrass, linden, lotus, Low John, lucky hand root, maize, male fern, meadowsweet, mint, mistletoe, moss, mustard seed, myrrh, myrtle (grown indoors), nuts (especially two nuts in a single shell), nutmeg, oak, oakmoss, olive, orange, nine peas in a single pea pod, peach, peony, peppermint, persimmon, pineapple, pomegranate, poppy, purslane, rose, rose bud, rosemary, rosewood, rowan, sandalwood, snakeroot, shamrock, spearmint, spikenard, St. John's flower, St. John's Wort, star anise, straw, strawberry, sumbul, thyme, tonka bean, vanilla, vervain root, vetiver, violet (leaf or flower), wheat, woodrose, yarrow; Goddess: the Amfratninae, Benzaiten, Dolya, Felicitas, Gefion, Kishijoten, Kupala, Lakshmi, Ukat, Ustrecha; God: Byelobog, Bishamon, Bonus Eventus, Daikoku, Fu-hsing (Lucky Star), Fukurojuku, Ganesha, Hanuman, Hotei, Jorojin, Jukurokujin, Junrojin, Ketha, Koto-Shiro-Nushi, Kupallo, Maximon, Mercury, Patollo, Ptah, Shango, Sors, Thor, Ueuecoyotl; Evocation: Arkan Sonney, leprechauns; *to attract*: Plant: cinnamon, High John, nutmeg.

Good luck for: brides: Stone: moonstone (when given by groom); Plant: vervain. **children**: Plant: wintergreen. **family undertakings**: Plant: St. John's Wort (root, gathered before sunrise on Beltane morning). **females**: Metal: silver; Stone: green aventurine; Plant: ivy. **gamblers**: (See: Gambling). **Geminis**: Stone: pearl. **the home**: (See: The Home). **hunters**: (See: Hunting). **Libras**: Stone: opal. **males**: Plant: holly. **newborns**: God: Perun. **newlyweds**: Plant: hazel fruits or nuts, ivy with holly; God: Perun. **sailors**: Charm: carved masthead figure; Goddess: Hecate. **Scorpios**: Stone: opal. **witches**: Number: 13. **woodspeople**: Goddess: Yama.

Good luck in: business: (See: Business). **love**: (See: Love). **marriage**: (See: Marriage). **good luck with: goals**: Stone: fluorite. **money**: (See: Money). **success**: Stone: fluorite.

To attract good luck: Waxing Moon; Color: green; Charm: jasper arrowhead; Stone: alexandrite, amazonite, jade, jasper, brown jasper, lodestone, sunstone; Plant: allspice, aloe, basil, bayberry, bistort, catnip, cinnamon, frankincense, ginseng, High John, horse chestnut, hyacinth, Job's tears, myrtle, nutmeg, olive, poppy seeds, strawberry, vanilla, wisteria, wood aloes; God: Hotei. **quick luck**: Color: gold, red, red with green, yellow; Metal: mercury (toxic, not recommended); Charm: nutmegs filled with mercury (dangerous, not recommended); Plant: alkanet, allspice, cinnamon, cinquefoil, coconut, mustard seed, tonka bean, vanilla, verbena, wintergreen, wisteria.

Luck during travel: Plant: lucky hand root, sea holly. **Luck wishes**: Plant: hazel.

To: change your luck: Color: orange, hot pink; Charm: clean house, change name, rearrange furniture; Plant: dragon's blood. **dream of lucky numbers**: Plant: huckleberry leaf, marigold. **obtain money by chance/luck**: Goddess: Fortuna. **protect against attack on your luck**: Plant: agar agar, alfalfa, alkanet, angelica root, anise, arrowroot, blue bonnet, carnation, chamomile, cinnamon, cinquefoil, devil's shoestring, galangal, ginger, High John, Irish moss, jasmine, laurel, lemon, lucky hand, whole nutmeg, orris root, peony root, rose, star anise, tonka bean, vetiver; Goddess: Anath, Fata, Tlazolteotl; God: Thoth; Evocation: the Apsaras.

Lust

(See also: Desire, Libido, Passion, Sex)

Venus/Mars/Fire/May/Capricorn/Scorpio/ Taurus/Aries

Metal: tin; Color: red; Animal: boar, goat, serpent, wolf; Stone: carnelian, garnet; Potion: cardamom-spiced coffee with sugar, tea from an herb of lust with sugar; Plant: artichoke, avocado, bishop's weed, caper, caraway, cardamom, carrot seed, cattail, celery seed, cinnamon, clove, black cohosh, couch grass, cuckoopint, cyclamen, daisy, damiana, deerstongue, devil's bit scabious, dill, dragon's blood, dulse, endive, galangal, garlic, ginger, ginseng, grains of paradise, High John, hibiscus, lemongrass, licorice, maguey, mastic, mint, mustard seed, myrrh, nettle, olive, onion, parsley, patchouli, peppermint, pear, black pepper, peppermint, periwinkle, poppy seed, radish, rosemary, saffron, sea holly, sesame seed, southernwood, sugarcane, tea tree, tuberose, vanilla, violet, witch grass, yerba maté, ylang-ylang; Goddess: Aeval, Anath, Cliodna, Flidais, Ichpuchtli, Ishtar, Juno Caprotina, Kilili-Mushritu (She Who Leans Out Invitingly), Maeve, Pelé, Qedrin, Rangta, Sekhmet, Sjofna, Tlazolteotl; God: Apollo, Dionysus, Fergus, Ghede, the Horned God, Maximon, Pan, Ueuecoyotl, Zeus.

Blood lust: Mars; Goddess: Anath. **Female lust**: Goddess: Arani; God: Supai; Evocation: Lilith, succubi; *to arouse*: Charm: knotted whip under the mattress; Plant: cinnamon. **Male lust**: Charm: phallus; Plant: cardamom, celery, yohimbine; God: Min, Pan, Priapus; Evocation: incubi, satyrs; *to arouse*: Plant: cinnamon, lavender. **Selfish lust**: Plant: African marigold.

Lust at first sight: God: Zeus. **Lust for power**: Evocation: Nimrod.

To: arouse lust: Tool: scourge; Method: massage; Stone: carnelian, ruby; Metal: lead; Plant: artichoke, avocado, bishop's weed, cannabis, chamomile (oil, worn), cinnamon, garlic, ginseng, jasmine, licorice, mustard, nettle, parsnip, patchouli, peanut, clary sage, spearmint, violet with lavender; Goddess: Sjofna; God: Eros. **attract lust**: Plant: High John, rose hips. **avert lust**: Stone: emerald, ruby; Plant: marjoram, rue. **destroy lust**: Plant: hemlock, rue. **reduce lust**: Stone: onyx; Plant: rue. **release lust**: Plant: garlic. **restrain/overcome/ repel lust**: Saturn; Stone: emerald, ruby; Plant: marjoram, rue. **satisfy lust**: Venus; Plant: peach. **stop lustful thoughts**: Plant: hemlock.

Luxury

Taurus

Number: 6; Animal: cat, silkworm; Stone: emerald; Potion: absinthe (dangerous, not recommended); Plant: chestnut tree, pecan; Goddess: Bast, Erzulie, Oshun; God: Enbilulu-Gugal; Evocation: Asmodeus.

To repress luxury: Stone: green beryl.

Chapter 13

Magick

(See also: Enchantment, Hexes, Spells, Uncrossing, Witchcraft)

Mercury/Moon/Full Moon/Fire/North/Cancer

Color: black, all colors; Animal: baboon, boar, butterfly, coyote, crane, crow, white dog with red ears, fox, frog, heron, ibis, jaguar, merlin, owl, raven, spider, black widow spider; Stone: amber, diamond, leopardskin jasper, jet, lodestone, obsidian, pearl, quartz crystal, star sapphire, staurolite, tanzanite; Metal: electrum, gold, lead, mercury (toxic, not recommended), silver; Plant: amber, ammoniac gum (as incense), apple, benzoin, blackthorn, carnation, cascarilla, cinnamon, cinquefoil, dragon's blood, elder, eucalyptus, eye of Satan, frankincense, garlic, ginger, ginseng, goldenseal, hawthorn, hazel, hellebore, High John, Job's tears, laurel, mandrake, mastic, mistletoe, mugwort, mullein, nettle, oakmoss, purple orchis, papaya, patchouli, rosemary, rowan, rue, sage, sandalwood, St. John's Wort, sunflower, tangerine, vanilla, vervain, vetiver, willow; Goddess: Adsagsona (Weaver of Spells), the Ahueccaniae, Aradia, Arianrhod, Ayizan, Baba Yaga, Cerridwen, Chlaus Haistic, Chun T'i, Circe, Coyolxauhqui, Danu, Diana (Queen of Witches), Dubhlaing, Durga Mahamaya (Great Sorceress), Eriu, Ertha, Etain, Eterna, Fodla, Freya, Frigg, Gullveig, Habondia, Hecate (Mistress of Magick), Heqet (Great Magician), Herodias, Holda, Isis (Great Magician, Lady of Spells, Mistress of Magic), Jezi-Baba, Kali Mahamaya (Great Sorceress), Kamrusepas (Goddess of Spells), Kupala, Kwan Yin, Maeve, Maia (Grandmother of Magick), Margawse, Mari, Medusa, Morgan le Fay, the Morrigan, Nanna, Neith, Nemain, Nephthys, Nerthus, Nimuë, Noctiluca, Oya, Pasiphaë, Pelé, Rangda, Renenet, Rhiannon, Sarasvati, Schathach, Sekhmet (Great One of Magic, Mighty One of Enchantments), Selene, Selqet, Skadi, Spider Woman, Unial, Vedma, Xi Wang Mu, Xochiquetzal, Yolkai Estsan; God: Amaethon, Amon, Anubis, Carrefour, Cernunnos, Coyote, the Dagda, Dian Cecht, Dis Pater, Dumduku (Possessor of the Lapis Wand), Dylan, Ea, Enki, Gwydion, Hermes, Hermes Trismegistus (Thrice Great Hermes), Horus, Ilmarinen, Jaguar, Khenti-Amenti, Kothar-wa Khasis, Legba (Great Sorcerer, Lord of Magicians), Leshy, Loki, Lugh, Mannan Mac Lir, Marduk (Great Sorcerer), Math ap Mathonwy, Maximon, Mercury, Mithras, Nuadh, Nudimmud, Odin, Ogma, Proteus, Shango, Shiva, Tagni, Tezcatlipoca, Thoth, Tsui' Goab, Veles, Volos; Evocation: Bechuille, Cessair, Fintan, Hellawes, Hercules the Dactyl, Medea, Medusa, Merlin, Taliesin, Vila, Vilmeth and Vidolf, Wilden Wip, Witch of Endor.

Aggressive magick: Mars; Tool: sword; Charm: demon bowl, poppet, spell bottle; Animal: blue jay, crow, raven; Metal: lead;

Plant: alder; Goddess: Cybele, Durga; God: Ares, Baal, Karttikeya, Lugalabdubur (Vanquisher).

Angel magick: Color: light blue, pale pink, white, pastels; Animal: angelfish; Stone: blue lace agate, amethyst, angelite, aquamarine, celestite, moonstone, morganite, obsidian, quartz crystal; Plant: angelica, basil, begonia, datura, dong quai, flax, frankincense, honeysuckle, iris, marigold, moonwort, myrrh, pink rose, sandalwood, snowdrop, violet; Goddess: Mary (Queen of Angels), Shekinah, Pistis Sophia; Evocation: aeons, angels, archangels, archons, cherubim, elohim, Gabriel, guardian angels, Metatron, Michael, Raphael, seraphim, Uriel.

Animal magick: Earth; Color: brown; Animal: your familiar; Plant: catnip, coltsfoot, dragon's blood, myrrh, yarrow; Goddess: Arduinna, Artio, Cally Berry, Estiu, Flidais, Inanna, Samovila; God: Tuan MacCarell; Evocation: animal guides; *bird magick*: Charm: naturally shed feathers; Animal: all birds; Goddess: Estiu, Le Tkakawash, Rhiannon, Zonget; God: Nemglan; *butterfly magick*: Air; Animal: butterfly (in any stage of development); Plant: butterfly weed, mariposa lily; *cat magick*: Earth/Leo; Charm: civet, naturally shed cat fur, teeth and whiskers; Animal: cat, civet cat, jaguar, leopard, lion, lynx, ocelot, panther, puma, mountain lion, tiger, all felines; Stone: tiger's eye; Plant: catnip; Goddess: Bast, Lady Civet Cat, Freya; God: Shu, Ra (Great Cat of Heliopolis); *horse magick*: Earth/Sagittarius; Charm: horse hair, horse shoe; Animal: all horses; Goddess: Epona, Freya, Rhiannon; God: Epos, Poseidon Hippios (Lords of Horses); Evocation: amazons, centaurs; *snake magick*: Earth/Water; Charm: shed snake skin; Animal: all snakes; Goddess: Corchen, Echidne, Eingana, Melusine, Renenet; God: Great Rainbow Snake, Raja Naga.

Battlefield magick: Mars; Animal: raven; Goddess: Badb, the Morrigan, Nemain, Schathach; God: Odin; Evocation: Merlin.

Black magick: Color: black, deep purple; Charm: fingernails, hair, poppet, lead tablet, wax tablet; Animal: black rooster; Plant: asafetida (as incense), blackthorn, henbane, kelp, mandrake, mullein (as incense), yew; Goddess: Maman Brigitte, Carman, Circe, Hecate, Kali, Louhi, Skadi, Tlazolteotl; God: Apep, Apollo, Malsum, Set; Evocation: Curaton, the Rakshasas, Satan; *to avert*: Tool: mirror; Charm: Eye of Horus, hex sign, witch ball; Color: black; Plant: eye of Satan; *to avert from the home*: Plant: dill seed; *to battle*: God: Väinämöinen; *to overcome*: Color: black; *to protect against*: Color: black; Stone: amber, chalcedony, jet, malachite, black onyx, clear quartz crystal, wonderstone; Plant: eye of Satan, hellebore, High John, juniper (as incense), rosemary, rowan branch (hung over the doorway), St. John's bread, vetiver (as incense); Goddess: Hecate; *to protect the home from*: Plant: marjoram, St. John's Wort.

Blood magick: Color: red; Charm: blood; Potion: apple cider (as substitute for blood); Goddess: Macha.

Calendar magick: Moon; Charm: calendar; Animal: hare, wolf; Goddess: Aditi, Cardea, Goda, Mama Quilla; God: Janus, Quetzalcoatl, Sin (Lord of the Calendar), Xiuhtecuhtli.

Candle magick: Fire; Tool: candle; Color: as appropriate to the spell; Goddess: Brigid, Candelifera, Lucina.

Ceremonial magick: Tool: athame, censer, pentagram, sword; Method: astrology, evocation, incantation, invocation, libation, lustration; Charm: altar, ritual garb, seals; Color: as appropriate to the working; Stone: as appropriate to the working;

Plant: frankincense, rowan; God: Thoth; Evocation: angels, demons, salamander.

Chaos magick: Animal: dragon; Goddess: Nunet, Oya, Tiamat (Dragoness of Chaos); God: Anzu, Chaos, Loki, Nun, Set, Yamm; Evocation: demons, djinn, Satan; *to overcome*: Plant: lotus; Goddess: Isis; God: Baal, Marduk (Breaker of Chaos), Ptah.

Cord magick: Tool: cord (traditionally nine feet long); Color: as appropriate to the working; Goddess: Eingana, Sesheta, Tlazolteotl.

Crone magick: Waning Moon/Autumn/Winter; Tool: cauldron; Color: black; Animal: crow, black dog, raven, sow; Plant: autumn leaves, bare branches, dried flowers; Goddess: Annis, Atropos, Baba Yaga, Badb, Bronach, Cailleach, Carravogue, Elle, the Erinyes, the Graiae, Greine, Hecate, the Fates, Kali, Lassair, Latiaran, Macha, Masaya, the Morrigan, Nemain, Nicevenn, the Norns, Sedna, Oya, Scotia, the White Goddess.

Defensive magick: Mars/Fire; Tool: mirror; Method: binding, cloaking; Charm: fire wheel, poppet; Color: red; Metal: brass, gold, iron, lead; Stone: jade, red jasper, onyx, sapphire; Plant: arnica, basil, bayberry, carnation, red carnation, cinnamon, citronella, cypress, dragon's blood, frankincense, jasmine, juniper, laurel, lilac, lily of the valley, lotus, marjoram, nettle, patchouli, pine, rose thorn, sandalwood, sesame (oil), thistle, vervain, violet, black willow, yarrow; Goddess: Alphito, Anahita, Aoife, Banba, Caireen, Eriu, Fodla, Hecate, Ratis, Schathach, Sekhmet; God: Lugalabdubur (Vanquisher), Perun; *for protection while working defensive magick*: Stone: jade.

Dragon magick: Mars/Air/Fire/Earth/Water/ East/Spring; Color: green; Animal: dragons; Plant: bistort, dragon's blood; Goddess: Cailleach, Ishtar, Tiamat; God:

Dewi, Raja Naga (King of the Sea Serpents), Ryujin; Evocation: Medea (Dragon Queen).

Dream magick: Moon/Water; Plant: cinnamon, holly, huckleberry; Goddess: Caer, Gatumdug, Hecate, Isis, Nephthys, Niorun, Rhiannon, Tana, Yemaya Olokun; God: Epos, Hermes, Oneicopompus.

Elemental magick: Waxing Moon/Earth/Air/Fire/Water; Tool: pentacle; Animal: dragon; Stone: staurolite; Goddess: Domnu, Isis; God: Sobek, Zurvan; Evocation: devas, fairies, all elementals; *to command*: Goddess: Frigg; *to evoke*: Plant: foxglove; *Air spells/magick*: Mercury/Jupiter/Air/East/Dawn/Spring/Gemini/Libra/Aquarius; Tool: athame, censer, sword, whistle; Color: blue, pale blue, sky blue, clear, lavender, orange, pastels, purple, silver, white, yellow, bright yellow; Charm: ambergris, bellows, blue circle, fan, feather, flute, perfume, van van; Stone: aventurine, jade, mottled jasper, lapis lazuli, clear quartz crystal, topaz; Animal: dolphin, dove, dragon, eagle, hawk, owl, sphinx, all birds and flying insects; Metal: aluminum, mercury, silver, tin; Fungus: fly agaric, puffball; Oil: neroli; Plant: acacia agrimony, almond, aloe, anise, crab apple, anemone, angelica, anise, asafetida, aspen, azalea, baby's breath, bamboo, banyan, bayberry, beans, beech, benzoin, bergamot, birch, blue bonnet, bodhi tree, borage, bracken, Brazil nut, bromeliad, broom, camphor, caraway, cedar, chicory, citron, citronella, all citrus, clover, comfrey, dandelion, dock, elecampane, elder, endive, epiphytic plants such as bird's nest fern, eucalyptus, eyebright, fenugreek, fern, balsam fir, fluffy seed heads, frankincense, freesia, fumitory, galbanum, white geranium, goldenrod, gourd, grapefruit, gum arabic, hazel, heather, honeysuckle, hops, horehound, houseleek, jasmine, lavender, lemongrass, lilac, lily of the valley, lime, linden, mace, maple, marjoram, mastic, meadowsweet, mint, mistletoe, mugwort, mulberry, myrrh, nutmeg, parsley, pecan, peppermint, pimpernel, pine, plants and trees with aerial roots or which provide incense, pansy, parsley, pennyroyal, pine, pistachio, poplar, primrose, rice, sage, sandalwood, shamrock, slippery elm, snowdrop, star anise, storax, spores, storax, sweetgrass, thyme, lemon verbena, vervain, violet, wall fern, winged seed pods, wood aloes, wormwood, yarrow; Goddess: Aditi, Aerope, Agasaya, Aima, Aine, Allat, Anath, Aphrodite, Aradia, Arianrhod, Cardea, Cybele, Domnu, Don, Durga, Estsanatlehi, Freya, Frigg, Hathor, Hera, Iris, Isis (Mistress of the Sky), Juno, Lilith, Maman Brigette, Mary, Nut, Oya, Rauni, Sekhmet, Semiramis, Sesheta, Tanith, Urana, Ushas, Vajravaraki (Wanderer of the Air); God: Adad, Aeulus, Aether, Amon (The Invisible One), Anu, Aquilo, Arilma, Baal (Rider of the Clouds), Boreas, Ellil, Enlil, Favonius, Great Spirit, Horus, Hurukan, Indra, Jumala, Jupiter, Kephera, Krishna, Llma, Marduk, Mercury, Mithras, Njord, Odin, Orunmila, Perun, Poseidon, Ra, Quetzalcoatl, Shiva, Stribog, Teshub, Thor, Thoth, Tyr, Ukko, Uranus, Vayu, Volturnus, Yao, Zephyrus, Zeus, Zurvan; Evocation: angels, Ariel, Cloud Vila, elves, fairies, Finvarra, Gabriel, Hresvelgr, the lilitu, Michael, Orion, Pegasus, Raphael, spirits, sprites, sylphs, undines. *Earth spells/magick*: Waxing Moon/Earth/North/Winter/Midnight/Taurus/Virgo/Capricorn; Color: black, brown, green, yellow; Tool: beeswax candle, pentacle; Charm: ambergris, clay, honey, mud, musk, pottery, soil, yellow square; Animal: bison, buffalo, bull, cattle, earth dragon, earthworm, goat, jaguar, mole, earth-dwelling snake, sphinx, stag, tortoise, wolf, all burrowing creatures; Stone: all, but especially agate, moss agate, black and white agate, alum, amazonite, bloodstone, green calcite,

carnelian, chrysoprase, emerald, brown or green jasper, jet, black opal, peridot, quartz crystal, smoky quartz, salt, rock salt, tiger's eye, black or green tourmaline; Metal: coal, lead, mercury (toxic, not recommended); Fungus: mushroom; Plant: all, but especially acorn, Adam and Eve root, adonis, alfalfa, allspice, amaranth, amber, apple, asafetida, aspen, balm of Gilead, banyan, barley, bayberry, beet, benzoin, bergamot, bistort, blessed thistle, buckwheat, burdock, caraway seed, carrot, cedar, chamomile, cinquefoil, clover, comfrey, corn, cotton, cowslip, cypress, elecampane, elm, slippery elm, fennel, fern, frankincense, fumitory, ginseng, all grain, gravel root, heliotrope, High John, honeysuckle, hops, horehound, ivy, jasmine, licorice, magnolia, maize, mandrake, mastic, millet, motherwort, mugwort, narcissus, oak, oakmoss, oats, oleander, patchouli, pea, pennyroyal, petrified wood, pine, red poppy, potato, primrose, redwood, rhubarb, rice, roots, root vegetables, rue, rye, sage, sagebrush, shepherd's purse, Solomon seal, Spanish moss, storax, strawberry, tarragon, tulip, turnip, lemon verbena, vervain, vetiver, wheat, wormwood, yarrow, yerba santa; Goddess: Acca Larentia, Aericura, Aditi, Aeval, Akka, Ala, Alaghom-Naom, Altria, Amba, Anath, Ararat, Audjal, Auxesia, Axo-Mama, Berecyntia, Bona Dea, Califia, Carravogue, Cathubodia, Ceres, Cerridwen, Coatlicue, Collatina, the Comedovae, Corchen, Cybele, Damkina (Lady of the Earth), Danu, Delphine, Demeter (Queen of the Fruitful Earth), Durga, Eithinoha, Erce, Ertha, Escheman (Grandmother Earth), Estsanatlehi, Eve, Fana, Fauna, Fjorgyn, Flora, Gaia, Gerd, Habondia, Hebat, Hou Tu, Iweridd, Joerd, Kalikamata (Black Earth Mother), Ki, Kumbhamata, Maeve, Magog, Maka, Makkuth, Mami, Mati Syra Zemlya (Moist

Mother Earth), Mokosh, Mother Earth, Mother Nature, Nanna, Nerthus, Ninhursag, Nokomis, Onatha, Ops, Parvati (Lady of the Mountain), Pazardzik, Persephone, Pomona, Prithivi, Prosperine, Rhea, Rhiannon, Al-Sarah, Sarpanitum, Sequana, Sheela-na-gig, Sita, Tellus, Terra, Themis, Tonantzin, Urash, Usert, Vasudharini, Yolkai Estan, Zemyna; God: Achilles, Adonis, Arawn, Atlas, Attis, Baal (Lord of Earth), Bacchus, Cernunnos, Dagon, the Dagda, Damuzi, Dionysus, Enki, Enlil, Geb, Green Man, Horned God, Marduk, Maruka, Osiris, Pacha Camac, Pan, Robin Goodfellow, Saturn, Serapis, Shango, T´ai-Yüeh Ta-ti, Tammuz, Tatanka, Tatenen (Exalted Earth), Tepeyollotl, Ti Kuan (Official of Earth), Unkulunkulu, Vertumnus, Zeus Chronius or Green Zeus; Evocation: ´Aretsaya biti Ya´abdar, Ariel, devas, dryads, gnomes, hamadryads, nature spirits, Uriel; *Fire spells/magick*: Sun/Mars/Jupiter/Fire/South/ Summer/Noon /Aries/Leo/Sagittarius; Tool: athame, censer, sword, wand; Color: crimson, gold, orange, hot pink, red, white; Method: candle magick; Charm: anvil, bellows, bonfire, brimstone, civet, crucible, fire wheel, forge, hearth, star, red triangle, witch hazel; Animal: dragon, firebird, horse, lion, phoenix, salamander, snake; Metal: brass, gold, iron, steel; Stone: amethyst, Apache tear, orange calcite, carnelian, citrine, coal, diamond, flint, fire garnet, hematite, red jasper, lava, meteorite, obsidian, fire opal, pyrite, rhodochrosite, tigereye; Potion: absinthe (dangerous, not recommended), orange pekoe tea, Strega liqueur; Plant: acacia, alder, allspice, almond tree in bloom, amaranth, anemone, angelica, asafetida, ash, asphodel, basil, bergamot, betony, bramble, cactus, cardamom, carnation, cascara sagrada, cashew, cassia, cattail, cedar, celandine, celery, chestnut, chili pepper, chrysanthemum, cinnamon, cinquefoil, clove, copal, coriander, cranberry, cumin, damiana, dandelion, dill, dittany, dragon's blood, evergreens, eye of Satan, fennel, fig, fire thorn, fireweed, flame tree, flax, frankincense, galangal, garlic, gentian, ginger, ginseng, golden seal, hawthorn, heliotrope, hibiscus, High John, holly, hollyhock, horseradish, hyssop, iris, jalapeño, juniper, laurel, leek, licorice, mandrake, marigold, milk thistle, mullein, mustard, nettle, nutmeg, oak, olive, onion, orange (fruit or blossom), mandarin orange, orris root, pennyroyal, peony, pepper, hot peppers, peppermint, pine, pineapple, pomegranate, red poppy, primrose, radish, rose, rosemary, rowan, rue, saffron, St. John's Wort, sassafras, sesame, sunflower, tangerine, tea, thistle, thyme, tobacco, tuberose, vanilla, vervain, walnut, witch hazel, wormwood, yohimbine, yucca; Goddess: Aetna, Aibheaeg, Arrang Dibatu, Ashtoreth, Astarte, Ayabe, Ayida Wedo, Bast, Belisama, Berecyntia, Brigid, Caca, Chantico, Chiconahui, Chuginadak, Coatlicue, Coyolxauhqui, Darago, Dzalarhons, Ebhlinne, Fuji, Gabija, Greine, Hestia, Huchi, Isis, Kali, Kupala, Latiaran, Loo-Wit, Mahuika, Masaya, Oya, Pelé, Sekhmet, Vesta; God: Agni (The Divine Fire), ´Ailaau (Forest Eater), Aodh, Ard Greimme, Atar (Fire of the Sky), Baal, Bel, Belchans, Belenus, Bile, Cearas, Chu Jung, the Dagda, Gerra, Govannon, Hastsezini, Heimdall, Hephaestus, Horus, Huehueteotl, Hurukan, Ilmarinen, Ishum, Jupiter, Kagutsuchi, Kaponis, Logi, Loki, Lugh, Marduk Gibil, Masubi, Maui, Mithras, Mulciber (The Smelter), Nairyosangha, Njord, Nushku, Ogun, Paiva, Podaga, Shango, Shiva, Sogbo, Surya, Svarog, Svantovit, Svarozic, Tatevali, Tcolawitze, Tirawa, Tohil, Tsao Chun (Lord of the Hearth), Uwolowu, Vishnu, Vulcan, Xiuhtecuhtli (Lord of Fire); Evocation: djinn, Ariel, Lonomakua (Keeper of the

Flame), Michael, Prometheus, Pyrrha (The Red One), Raphael, seraphs, Uriel; *Water spells/magick*: Neptune/Venus/Moon/Saturn/Water/West/Twilight/Autumn/Aquarius/Pisces/Cancer/Scorpio; Tool: bowl, cauldron, chalice; Method: asperging, libation, lustration; Charm: ambergris, silver crescent, holy water, ice, mist, rain, tears, inverted triangle; Color: aqua, black, blue, clear, green, sea green, ultramarine, white; Animal: diving birds, sea birds, wading birds, crab, crocodile, dolphin, fish, frog, sea gull, porpoise, salamander, sea serpent, scorpion, water snake, all marine life, all marsh, pond, lake, swamp and river creatures; Metal: copper, mercury (toxic, not recommended), silver; Stone: blue lace agate, amethyst, aquamarine, azurite, beryl, blue or clear or pink calcite, chrysocolla, coral, geode, jade, lodestone, mother-of-pearl, water opal, pearl, fresh water pearl, clear quartz crystal, river rocks, sapphire, sea salt, blue tourmaline, blue topaz; Fungus: all; Potion: water; Plant: Adam and Eve root, aloe, amber, apple, apricot, aromatic rush roots, ash, aster, avocado, balm of Gilead, banana, bat nut, belladonna, birch, blackberry, buckthorn, burdock, cabbage, calamus, camellia, camphor, cannabis, cantaloupe, caper, cardamom, cascarilla, catnip, cattail, chamomile, cherry, chickweed, clover, coconut, coltsfoot, comfrey, coriander, cowslip, cucumber, cyclamen, daffodil, daisy, datura, driftwood, gray dulse, elder, elecampane, elm, eryngo, eucalyptus, fern, foxglove, frangipani, gardenia, geranium, rose geranium, gourd, grape, gravel root, heather, hellebore, hemlock, henbane, hibiscus, hops, hyacinth, iris, ivy, jasmine, kava kava, kelp, lemon, lemon balm, lettuce, licorice, lilac, lily, lime, linden, lobelia, lotus, lovage, Low John, meadowsweet, mesquite, mimosa, morning glory, moss, mustard, myrrh, myrtle, narcissus, orange, orchid, orris root, papaya, papyrus, passionflower, peach, pear, periwinkle, persimmon, peyote cactus, pitcher plant, plumeria, poplar, poppy, raspberry, reeds, rice, rose, red rose, white rose, rosemary, rushes, sandalwood, scullcap, spearmint, spikenard, star anise, strawberry, sweet pea, tamarisk, tamarind, tansy, thyme, tomato, tonka bean, valerian, vanilla, vervain, violet, watercress, watermelon, water lily, willow, weeping willow, wintergreen, wisteria, wolfsbane, wood aloes, yarrow, yew, ylang-ylang, all plants that grow in or near water; Goddess: Adamisil Wedo, Adsulatta, the Ahinehiae, the Ahueccaniae, Ahurani, Aibheaeg, Anahita (Great Goddess of Waters), Ancomna, Anna Livia, Anuqet, Apa, Arnamentia, Ashiakle, Asima Si, Atargatis, Axona, Ayida Wedo, Belisama, Benzaiten, Boann, Bormana, Bricta, Brigantia, Brigid, Caedda, Caolainn, Carmentis, Chalchihuitlcue, Cliodna, Clota, Coventina, Cyhiraeth, Danu, Devona, Dubh Lacha, Egeria, Feng-po-po, Fland, Ganga, Icovellauna, Ilmatar, Ina, Inanna, Ivilla, Jamaina, Jurata, Juturna, Korrigan, Kupala, Lady of the Lake, Laga, Laha, Latis, Logia, Luandinha, Luonnotar (The Water Mother), Magaia, Mama Cocha (Mother Sea), Mama Watta, Marina, Meduna, Mehet-Weret (Great Celestial Water), Mokosh, Morgen, Murigen, Nagera, Naitienae, Nammu, Nantosuelta, Nehalennia, the Nemausicae, Nina, Oba, Oshun, Pressina, Ran, Ritona, Rosmerta, Sarasvati (Flowing Water), Sarpanitum, Satis, Sequana, Sionnan, Sirona, Sulis, Tefnut, Tiamat, Toci, Ved-Ava (Water Mother), Veden Emo (Mother of the Water), Visuna, the Wave Maidens, the Xulsigiae, Yemaya; God: Aegir, Apsu, Borvo, Condatis Dylan, Ea (Lord of the House of Water), Enbilulu, Enlil, Enki, Glaucus, Hapi, Itzamna, Llyr, Mannan mac

Lir, Mars Condatis, Mimir, Naki, Nechtan, Neptune, Nethuns, Njord, Nu, Nuadh, Shoney, Shui Kuan (Official of Water), Tethra, Tlaloc, Vu-Kutis, Yamm; Evocation: Arduisher (Giver of Living Waters), Ariel, Daeira, Gabriel, Ganymede, Kelpie, Kludde, merfolk, Michael, naiads, nereids, oceanids, Raphael, sirens, undines, water sprites, and nymphs of rivers, fountains, waterfalls, and so on. (See also: ice magick, river spells, sea spells.)

Elfen magick: Charm: tinkling silver bells; Oil: palmarosa; Fungus: toadstools; Plant: buckthorn, daisy, elecampane, rose geranium, rosemary, lavender, blue violet; Goddess: Perchta (Elf Woman), Wanne Thekla; Evocation: Argante; *to make contact with elves*: Plant: daffodil, foxglove, wood sorrel.

Fairy magick: Color: green; Plant: apple bark or fruit, bluebell, cowslip, daffodil, daisy, elecampane root, foxglove, primrose, rose petals, violet, wild thyme (gathered from fairy mounds), wood sorrel, ylang-ylang; Goddess: Aeval, Aine, Albina, Almha, Cyhiraeth, Eri, Feithline, Finnine, Greine, Rodenica; God: Addanc, Angus, the Dagda, Gwynn ap Nudd, Iubdan, Shoney; Evocation: Donagh; *to neutralize*: Charm: turn your coat or cloak inside out; *to open to*: Plant: forget-me-not, primrose; *to overcome*: Plant: four leaf clover, daisy; *to protect against*: Plant: rowan, St. John's Wort.

Female magick: Moon; Color: silver; Animal: fox; Metal: silver; Plant: queen of the night.

Finger magick: Method: gesture; Plant: finger grass; God: the Dactyls; Evocation: Herakles Dactyl.

Flower magick: Earth/Spring/May; Charm: hexagon; Plant: all flowers; Goddess: Aphrodite Antheia (Aphrodite of the Flowers), Blodeuwedd, Creiddylad, Feronia, Flora, Idunn, Inghean Bhuidhe,

Olwen, Venus, Xochiquetzal (Flower Mistress); God: Dionysus Antheus (Dionysus of the Flowers), Xochipilli; Evocation: Clytie, Hyacinthus, Narcissus.

Garden magick: (Use correspondences for: Gardening).

Hearth magick: Fire; Tool: cauldron; Charm: Yule log; Goddess: Athena, Ayabe, Brigid (Lady of the Hearth), Caca, Chantico (Lady of the Hearth), Chiconahui, Ertha, Fornax, Hestia, Kikimora, Vesta; God: the Penates, Thor, Tsao-chun (Lord of the Hearth), Zeus; Evocation: firedrake, hearth kamis, salamander, Swarowicz.

Herbal magick: Earth; Color: green; Plant: all herbs, but especially those with healing properties; Goddess: Airmid, Europa, Greine, Kupala, Morgen, Tellus, Vedma, Venus; God: Asharu.

High magick (See: ceremonial magick).

Ice magick: Water/Winter; Charm: freezer, ice; Goddess: Caca.

Image magick: Metal: aluminum; Plant: apple, roots: bryony, ginger, ginseng, mandrake, American mandrake, potato, sweet potato; Goddess: Cura, Fornax, Isis, Ruko; God: Ea, Enki Mummu, Khnum, Maximon, Ogmio, Ptah; *healing image spells*: (See: Spells).

Incantatory magick: Tool: bowl; Method: incantation, prayer beads; Plant: hemlock, yarrow; God: Brihaspati, Ea (Lord of Incantations).

Knot magick: Earth; Tool: cord; Animal: spider; Goddess: Anath, Ariadne, Arianrhod, Asintmah, Atropos, Bertha, Bil, Brigid, Chibirias, Clotho, Freya, Frigg, Habetrot, Holda, Isis (Lady of the Shuttle), Ix Chel, Ix Zacal Nok (Lady Cloth Weaver), Minerva, Neith, Nona, the Norns, Penelopeia, Perchta, Potnia, Rana Nedia, the Ratheihiae, Spider Grandmother,

Sussistanako (Spider Woman), Tonantzin, Waka-Hiru-Me, Walpurga, Xochiquetzal, Yolkai Estsan.

Lunar magick: Moon/Full Moon/Water/Night/Monday/Cancer; Tool: willow wand; Color: silver, white; Number: 3, 9, 13, 369; Animal: white bull, cat, cow, crab, dog, dolphin, hare, ibis, moth, owl, rabbit, scarab, vixen, wolf, all nocturnal animals; Metal: silver; Stone: sea green beryl, moonstone, mother-of-pearl, pearl, clear quartz crystal, selenite; Fungus: mushroom; Plant: acanthus, adder's tongue, agave, cabbage, camphor, white carnation, coconut, cucumber, gray dulse, ginger, ginseng, honesty, ice plant, iris, jasmine, lemon, lettuce, lotus, melons, madonna lily, melon, mimosa, moon cereus, moonwort, poppy, pumpkin, queen of the night, white rose, clary sage, sandalwood, sea holly, watercress, water lily, willow, all night-blooming trees and flowers; Goddess: A, Aa, Aine, Albion, Alcmene, Allat, Alphito, Anumati, Anunitu, Arianrhod, Artemis, Asherali, Ashima, Auchimolgen, Aya, Bast (in cat form), Belili, Bendis, Blodeuwedd, Britomartis, Brizo, Calliope, Cameira, Candi, Car, Cerridwen, Chang-O (Queen Moon), Circe, Coatlicue, Coyolxauhqui, Danu, Dewi Shri, Eurynome, Diana, Dictynna, Europa, Fatima, Frigg, Hianuwele, Hanwi (Grandmother Moon), Hecate, Hecate Selene (Far-Shooting Moon), Helene (Bright Moon), Helice, Hina, the Hyades, Ialysa, Ina, Inanna (Queen Moon), Io, Iole, Ishhara, Ishtar, Isis, Ix Chel, Jana, Jezanna, Juno Levannah, Libya, Linda, Losna, Luna, Luonnotar, Lupa, Manasa-Devi, Mama Quilla (Mother Moon), Mardoll, Mawu, Nanna, Nimuë, Ngame, Pah, Pasiphaë, Perimbó, Phoebe, Phoenissa, Rhiannon, Selene, Sheng Mu, Stheino, Tanith, Ursula, Wahini-Hai (The Moon), Yolkai Estsan, Zarpanit, Zirna; God: Ashimbabbar, Chandra, Car, El, Eterah, Ge, Helenus, Kashku, Khonsu, Mah, Mawu, Menu, Myesyats, Nanna, Nyamiabe, Pah, Phorcys, Poré, Porphyrion, Shiva, Shiva Somantha (Lord of the Moon), Sin, Soma, Thoth, Tsukiyomi, Varuna, Yarikh; Evocation: Phaedra; *to counter*: Plant: garlic, onion, squill, willow; *to open to*: Moon; Plant: queen of the night; *to protect against*: Plant: Aaron's rod, garlic, moly, onion, squill.

Male magick: Sun; Color: gold; Metal: gold; Plant: pine.

Manipulative magick: Goddess: Diana.

Mirror magick: Venus/Water; Tool: mirror; Stone: obsidian, pyrite; Plant: eyebright, clary sage; God: Tsuki-Yomi.

Music magick: Air; Charm: drum, flute, all musical instruments; Goddess: Caer, Canola, Glispa; God: Angus, Donn, Gwydion; *magickal wind instruments*: Plant: alder.

Natural magick: Earth; Animal: heron; Stone: all; Plant: all, pine (incense); Goddess: Mother Earth; Evocation: nature spirits.

Night magick: Moon/Night; Color: black, midnight blue; Animal: bat, cat, firefly, jaguar, nightingale, owl, birds that sing at night, all nocturnal animals; Stone: clusters of crystals, moonstone, pearl, peridot; Plant: jasmine, orange blossom, queen of the night, tuberose, night-blooming plants and trees; Goddess: Achlys, Anniki, Diana (Queen of the Night), Europa, Evaki, Furina, Hecate (Queen of the Night), Kali (Absolute Night), Mawu, the Morrigan, Nephthys, Niorun, Nott, Nut, Nyx, Oshun, Ratri, Tlazolteotl, Midnight Zorya; God: Marduk (Master of the Night), Nergal (Lord Who Prowls By Night).

Psi-magick: Stone: quartz crystals; Plant: mugwort; Goddess: Dakini; God: Shiva, Thoth.

Religious/sacred magick: Number: 9; Plant: benzoin, cinnamon, frankincense, myrrh; God: Brihaspati.

Rock magick: Earth; Stone: all; Goddess: Califia, Chalchihuitlcue (Precious Jewel Lady); God: Alisanos, Inyan.

Rune magick: Earth; Method/Charm: runes; Plant: bracken; Goddess: the Norns; God: Freyr, Odin.

Seasonal magick: Sun/Earth; Goddess: Aestas, Anieros, Axiocersa, Beiwe, Brigid, Cailleach, Lassair, Rhea, Summer Daughter, Tamar, Themis, Al-Uzzah.

Seed magick: Earth; Plant: all seeds; God: Gil, Saturn.

Sex magick: Venus/Mars/Full Moon/ Fire/Friday/Taurus/Leo/Scorpio; Color: red; Animal: goat, dove, sparrow, sphinx; Charm: ambergris, civet, musk, sugar; Stone: pair of lodestones, rose quartz; Oil: neroli; Plant: ambrosia, avocado, bishop's weed, caper, caraway, cardamom (especially oil, worn as perfume), carline thistle, carrot, celery, cinnamon, clove, coriander, cow parsnip, cyclamen, damiana, devil's bit scabious, dill, gray dulse, endive, eryngo, fig, galangal, garden cress, garlic, ginger, ginseng, henbane, jasmine, kelp, licorice, lovage, Low John, mandrake (root or stem), mistletoe berry, myrrh, nasturtium, nut grass, olive, orris root, patchouli, pear, periwinkle, purslane, radish, rose (without thorns), saffron, red sandalwood, savory, saw palmetto, Solomon's seal, southernwood, sugar cane, vanilla, vervain, violet, watercress, wood aloes, wormwood, yerba maté, yohimbine; Goddess: Achtland, Aeval, Ailinn, Anath, Aphrodite, Arani, Asherah, Astarte, Ashtoreth, Bast, Ceile De, Cotytto, Cytherea, Dahut, Dione, Erato, Erzulie, Freya, Frigg, Harsa, Hathor, Inanna, Ishtar, Isis (Lady of Love and Magic), Isis Shentet (Isis in the Bedchamber), Ix Chel, Juno Caprotina (Juno of the Goats), Juno Februa, Kali, Kilili-Mushritu (She Who Leans Out Invitingly), Lilith, Lofn, Lupa, Macha, Maeve, Medb, Modron, the Morrigan, Mylitta, Naamah, Oshun, Pales, Qadesh, Sekhmet, Selqet, Shakti, Sheela-na-Gig, Sjofna, Sphinx, Tlazolteotl, Turan, Venus, Voluptas, Xochiquetzal; God: Angus, Bacchus, Cernunnos, Chango Macho, Cupid, Dianus, Dionysus, Eros, Faunus, Hermes, Kama, Krishna (Lord of Love), Linga, Lupercus, Manmatha, Mars, Maximon, Menu, Min, Neptune, Pales, Pan, Poseidon, Priapus, Robin, Set, Shango, Shiva, Svarog, Susanowa, Te Tuna (Phallus), Ueuecoyotl, Yarillo; Evocation: Aisha Qandisha, Anael, the Apsaras, Ardat Lili, Azazel, Hercules, satyrs; *female sex magick*: Venus; Plant: cinnamon, fig, vanilla; Goddess: Aeval, Bast; *gay sex magick*: Color: lavender, violet; Plant: citronella, pansy, vetiver; God: Eros; Evocation: Ganymede; *male sex magick*: Mars; Plant: asparagus, caper, carrot, celery, dragon's blood, ginseng, High John, lettuce, parsnip, sarsaparilla, yohimbine; God: Backlum Chaam, Cernunnos, Min, Pan, Priapus.

Solar magick: Sun/Day/Sunday; Tool: ash wand; Animal: lion, phoenix; Charm: honey; Goddess: Adsulatta, Aega, Aimend, Akewa, Alectrona, Allat, Amaterasu, Arinna, Asva, Aya, Bast (in lion form), Chup-Kamui, Coatlicue, Eos, Gnowee, Greine (House of the Sun), Hebat, Hsi-Ho, Igaehindvo, Li, Mallina, Mor, Saule, Sekhmet, Selqet, Shapash, Sunna, Tamar, Teteoinnan, Walo, Yhi; God: Amon, Anubis, Aodh, Apollo, Baldur, Belenus, Bladud, Dabog, Dyaus, Gwawl, Helios, Hyperion, Inti, Khors, Maui, Ogma (Sun Face), Ra, Sabazius, Sol, Surya, Uttu.

Spiritual magick: Plant: cinnamon, frankincense.

Trance magick: (See correspondences for: Trance).

Tree magick: Earth; Color: green; Plant: all trees; Goddess: Edinkira, Druantia (fir trees), Fir Daughter, (forest trees), Jarina, Medeine of the Trees (forest trees), Pomona (apple trees).

Triple magick: Moon; Number: 3; Plant: elder.

Voice magick: Mercury/Air/Taurus; Charm: honey; Animal: nightingale, whale; Plant: licorice; Goddess: Isis (Lady of Words of Power); God: Biale, Odin, Thoth; Evocation: fairies, sirens.

Water magick: (See: Elements).

Weather magick: (See correspondences for: Weather).

White magick: Color: white; Plant: hawthorn, hazel; Goddess: Isis.

Wild magick: Color: red; God: Dionysus, Pan; Plant: May flowers.

Magickal arts: Goddess: Gefion, Gullveig. **Magickal assistance**: Goddess: Ashtartu. **Magickal boats**: Water; Goddess: Becuma. **Magick books**: God: Thoth; *to guard magickal writings*: Animal: sphinx; God: Tao-chün.

Magickal charms: Method: astrology; Stone: coral, all gems; Plant: myrtle wood, oak gall, rowan; *to protect against*: Color: black; Plant: rowan; *to increase the power of amulets*: Plant: lemongrass; *of love amulets*: Plant: coltsfoot. **Magickal children**: *to bear*: Goddess: Aine. **Magick circles**: Fungus: fairy mushroom; Evocation: Vila; *to cast*: Tool: sword, wand; Method: invocation; Stone: clear quartz crystal; Plant (as rod or wand for drawing the circle): hazel, rowan, willow; God/dess: Lords of the Watchtowers; *to protect*: Animal: musk ox; Plant: turmeric (sprinkled). **Magical conception**: Goddess: Arianrhod, Isis. **Magickal creatures**: *to see*: Plant: marigold.

Magickal devotion: deep blue. **Magickal dye**: Plant: alder, saffron. **Magickal empowerment**: Goddess: Hecate. **Magickal energy**: (See: Energy). **Magick fire**: Potion: Strega liqueur; Plant: rowan; cedar and juniper with sandalwood. **Magickal food**: Animal: pig; Goddess: Idunn. **Magick hoops**: Plant: trefoil with vervain and dill; vervain, dill, trefoil and St. John's Wort; dandelion, marigold, milkwort and butterwort; woodbine with ivy and rowan. **Magickal incense mixtures**: *to strengthen*: Plant: dragon's blood, frankincense. **Negative magickal influences**: *to avert*: Charm: brimstone; Plant: asphodel (planted near the entry). **Magickal ink**: Plant: dragon's blood (with lampblack). **Magickal knowledge**: (See: Knowledge). **Magickal life**: (See: Life). **Magick mists**: Plant: willow; Goddess: the Telchines; God: Indra; Evocation: fairies. **Magickal/Craft names**: *to find*: Goddess: Angerona; God: Arawn. **Magickal oils**: Water; *to increase the power of*: Method: astrology; Charm: ambergris; Plant: bergamot, High John. **Magickal path**: Color: indigo. **Magickal potions**: Moon/Water; Tool: cauldron, chalice; Goddess: Cerridwen, Meng Po-Niang. **Magickal power**: (See: Power). **Magickal powders**: Earth. **Magickal quest**: Color: indigo. **Magical relationship**: Animal: one's familiar. **Magickal rituals**: Tool: wand; Color: green; Metal: gold; Plant: hyssop; Goddess: Kamrusepas. **Magickal secrets**: Goddess: Diana. **Magickal skill**: (See: Skill/s). **Magickal strength**: Stone: amber; Plant: ash. **Magickal success**: Plant: benzoin, ginger. **Magickal support**: Color: black. **Magickal tools**: God: Goibniu, Luchtain; Plant: birch, cypress, elder, hawthorn, hazel, holly; *to acquire*: God: Mannan; *to anoint/consecrate*: Plant: acacia, caraway, catnip (infusion or incense), frankincense, myrrh; *to increase ability with*: Plant: lemon; *to prevent getting lost*: Plant: caraway seed;

to purify: Plant: mullein, rue; *athame*: Waning Moon; Plant: ginger; *censer*: Plant: acacia, myrrh, rose geranium, spikenard; *sword*: God: Tyr; *wand*: God: Baile; Plant: almond, ash, cedar, elder, elm, hazel, maple, great mullein, oak, peach, willow; *divination tools*: Moon; Plant: mugwort. **Magickal understanding**: Color: violet. **Magickal visions**: Stone: green beryl, jasper. **Magickal vows**: *to keep*: Goddess: Aine. **Magickal weapons**: God: Kothar-wa-Khasis, Luchtar, Odin, Tsohanoai. **Magical workings**: *to strengthen*: Stone: garnet.

Mystery of magick: God: Mithras. **Openness in magick**: God: Thoth. **Unpredictable results in magick**: Color: red.

To: absorb magick: Plant: rowan. **be invulnerable to magick**: Goddess: Aoife. **counter magick**: Plant: eye of Satan, rue. **contemplate magick**: Color: gray, silver. **increase the effectiveness of magick**: Tool: candle; Stone: amber, bloodstone, rutilated quartz; Plant: benzoin, galangal, lavender. **learn magick**: Goddess: Freya. **learn to appreciate the magick of life**: Animal: hummingbird. **make magick flow**: Plant: sandalwood. **neutralize magick**: Color: indigo. **prepare mentally to work magick**: Potion: chamomile tea. **purify in preparation for magick**: Water; Stone: aquamarine, sapphire; Charm: infusion of chamomile (in the bath), infusion of rosemary (to wash hands). **protect against magick**: Plant: mugwort, rue; Goddess: Hecate; *against magickal charms*: Plant: rowan. **release magick**: Plant: enchanter's nightshade. **return magick to its sender**: Charm: mirror; Stone: red jasper. **see magical creatures**: Plant: marigold. **teach magick**: Goddess: Aradia, Selene; God: Amaethon; Evocation: Merlin, the vili. **understand magick**: Stone: sugilite; Plant: dill.

Magicians

(See also: Witches)

Moon

Goddess: Asherah, Selene; God: Carrefour, the Dagda, Enki (Master of Magicians), Legba (Lord of Magicians), Tezcatlipoca, Thoth, Xolotl.

Management

Charm: trilobite fossil; God: Marduk, Thoth.

Management skills: God: Enki.

Anger management: Metal: silver; Stone: moss agate, carnelian, emerald, garnet, kunzite, topaz; Plant: toadflax; *to learn not to anger the gods*: Goddess: Atalanta; *to learn not to misdirect your anger*: Goddess: Medea, Pasiphaë. **Pain management**: Goddess: Achelois; God: Achelous. **Time management**: Animal: tiger; Plant: morning glory; God: Thoth.

To manage: clerical staff: God: Thoth. **creation**: God: Marduk, Ruwa. **energy flow**: Stone: barite, jet. **productivity of farmland**: God: Enki. **wealth**: (See: Wealth).

Manifestation

Full Moon/Earth/Capricorn

Tool: rattle, wand; Number: 3, 4; Animal: butterfly, jaguar, snake, spider; Metal: iron; Stone: amber, amethyst, carnelian, emerald, garnet, lepidolite, obsidian, tanzanite, tourmaline, turquoise; Plant: balm of Gilead, camphor, dittany, fuchsia, lavender, laurel, mastic, myrrh, patchouli, sandalwood, Turk's cap lily, vervain (as incense); Goddess: Arachne, Ariadne, Asherah, Binah, Demeter, Eve, Sussistanako; God: Anu, Ea, Ellil, Enlil, Orunmila, Phanes (Manifestor), Ptah, Skan.

Complete cycle of manifestation: Number: 12. **Personal manifestation**: Stone: chalcanthite, tourmaline, blue tourmaline. **Psychic manifestation**: Color: purple, violet; Stone: blue lace agate. **Physical manifestation**: Earth; Number: 4. **Spiritual manifestation**: Color: blue; Stone: blue agate, turquoise.

Manifest power: Plant: red rose.

To manifest: abundance: Stone: citrine; Plant: harebell. **beauty**: Plant: agave, cactus. **change**: (See: Change). **a deity**: Method: trance possession. **desires**: (See: Desires). **dreams**: Stone: sapphire; Plant: chamomile. **energy**: (See: Energy). **financial goals**: Plant: lavender. **the life force**: Evocation: plant devas. **love**: Stone: amethyst, sugilite; *the transformational power of love*: Goddess: Latis. **money**: Plant: lavender. **potential**: Earth/North; Goddess: Urd. **power**: *inner power*: Stone: carnelian, citrine; *personal power*: Stone: citrine. **prosperity**: Plant: vetiver. **results**: Plant: patchouli. **spirits**: (See: Spirits). **spirituality/spiritual qualities on the physical plane**: Stone: turquoise. **strength**: Plant: agave. **thoughts**: Plant: Turk's cap lily; Goddess: Yhi; God: Io. **wealth**: Plant: cactus. **words into deeds**: Air; Method: breath work; God: Anu, Ea, Ellil; **will**: Stone: tanzanite.

To speed manifestation: Stone: garnet.

To unmanifest: Number: 0; *unmanifest spirits*: Plant: asafetida (thrown into fire).

Marriage

(See also: Relationships, Union, Weddings)

Tool: broom (for jumping over), chalice; Color: green, lavender, pink, red; Charm: orange flower water; Animal: carp; Stone: beryl, green beryl; Plant: cyclamen, gardenia, hawthorn, ivy, lavender, linden, myrtle, orange blossom, peach, rosemary, saffron, verbena, vervain, violet, yarrow; Goddess: Al-Uzza, Aphrodite, Benzaiten, Brigid, Chalchihuitlcue, Didilia, Erzuli, Freya, Frigg, Hathor, Hera, Hulda, Ishtar, Isis, Jugalis, Juno, Juno Pronoba, Kilya, Kumbhamata, Lada, Lofn, Oshun, Parvati, Mama Quilla, Selqet, Vesta, Xochiquetzal, Yolkai Estsan; God: Ah Kin Xoc, Bes, Bhaga, Dulha Deo, Gekka-O, Hymen, Lado, Lel, Svarog, Xpiyacoc.

Bad marriage: *to escape*: Goddess: Branwen, Leucothea; Evocation: Deirdre of the Sorrows, Dido. **Forbidden marriage**: Goddess: Lofn. **Fruitful marriage**: Plant: dong quai, nuts, rice; Goddess: Xochiquetzal; God: Thor. **Good marriage**: Stone: green beryl; *to preserve*: Plant: lemon verbena. **Happy marriage**: Animal: duck; Stone: aquamarine, beryl, citrine, obsidian, onyx, rhodonite, sardonyx; Plant: Adam and Eve root, pink carnation, red clover, cyclamen, hawthorn, lady's mantle, laurel, magnolia, marjoram, mistletoe, orange blossom, pussy willow, vanilla, violet, yarrow; Goddess: Conciliatrix, Freya, Indrani, Lada; God: Lado; **Long marriage**: Stone: citrine; Plant: laurel, orange blossom. **Peaceful marriage**: Plant: violet (oil, in bath); Goddess: Lada. **prosperous marriage**: Plant: red clover; Goddess: Juno. **sacred marriage**: Plant: anise; Deities: Aphrodite and Adonis, Astarte and Melkarth, Basilissa and Dionysus, Gerd and Freyr, Hera and Zeus, Inanna and Damuzi, Ishtar and Tammuz, Isis and Osiris, Juno and Jupiter, Venus and Adonis. **stable marriage**: Goddess: Vesta. **temporary/trial marriage**: Plant: yarrow; Goddess: Taillte; God: Llew. **unhappy marriage**: Stone: onyx; Goddess: Lilith; *to improve*: Color: pink; Stone: amethyst, lapis lazuli; Plant: apple blossom, pink rose, sandalwood, lemon verbena.

Marriage arrangers: Goddess: Nu Wa. **Marriage bed**: Goddess: Pertunda. **Marriage contracts/prenuptial agreements**: (See: Contracts). **Married life**: Plant: wall fern. **Married love**: (See: Love). **Marriage oaths/vows**: Goddess: Vör; God: Hymen. **Marriage plans/preparations**: Plant: orange blossom; Goddess: Unxia. **Marriage problems**: *to end*: Plant: pennyroyal, ylang-ylang. **Marriage proposals**: Charm: orange flower water; Plant: deerstongue, mandrake, orange blossom. **Marriage rites**: Goddess: Demeter, Unxia. **Marriage songs**: Goddess: Erato. **Marriage ties**: Plant: ivy. **Married women**: (See: Women).

Bad luck in marriage: Stone: onyx. **Blessings in marriage**: Plant: yarrow; Goddess: Shekinah. **Fidelity in marriage**: Stone: sardonyx; Plant: lavender, yarrow; Goddess: Hera, Pattinidevi, Sif, Sita, Tenye Te'en. **Good fortune in marriage**: Plant: nuts; *for women*: God: Bhaga. **Good luck in marriage**: Stone: moonstone (if given by bride to groom); Plant: hazel. **Good health with marriage**: Goddess: Paraskeva-Platnitsa. **Hope of marriage**: Plant: bachelors button, hawthorn. **Quarrels in marriage**: Plant: lemon verbena; *to end*: Goddess: Conciliatrix, Juno, Sjofna; *to settle*: Goddess: Juno Viriplaca. **Reconciliation in marriage**: Stone: beryl, lodestone. **Sanctity of marriage**: Goddess: Aphrodite.

To: attract a mate: Stone: moonstone; Plant: Guinea pepper, olive; *attract a loving mate*: Stone: rhodonite; *attract a wife*: Stone: emerald. **bless a marriage**: Goddess: Juno, Shekinah; *bless a new marriage*: Goddess: Arianrhod, Juno; God: Ganesha, Janus, Puchan. **enforce marriage vows**: Goddess: Vör. **find a spouse**: Plant: queen's root; *find a husband*: Goddess: Hathor; God: Haoma; *find a wife*: God: Ah Kin. **interfere with a marriage**: Stone: onyx.

know whom you will marry: Tool: mirror (for scrying by candlelight at midnight on Samhain); Plant: hemp seed (to plant at midnight), rose; Goddess: Ch'i Ku-Niang. **make a happier second marriage**: Goddess: Skadi. **make a good match**: Goddess: Juno Pronoba. **marry outside your faith**: Goddess: Eri. **marry a very strong woman**: God: Nergal. **protect marriage**: Metal: silver; Goddess: Juno, Neith, Vör; *protect a married couple's bedroom*: God: Bes; *protect a married couple's bed*: Goddess: the Kotharot; *protect sex/sexual love in marriage*: Goddess: Cloacina. **refuse to marry for wealth**: Goddess: Kwan Yin. **stop interference in a marriage**: Color: indigo; Stone: moonstone; Plant: frangipani, laurel, pine. **strengthen a marriage**: Animal: cockatoo. **survive the loss of a spouse**: Goddess: Isis. **survive marriage to an unsuitable mate**: Goddess: Aphrodite, Venus. **take a lesbian lover without destroying a marriage**: Goddess: Fauna.

Masculinity
(See: Yang)

Mastery
(See also: Ability, Authority, Command, Control, Skill/s)

Color: purple; Animal: jaguar; Plant: agave, High John, patchouli; God: Baal, Lugh, Marduk.

To learn not to be too difficult a taskmaster: Goddess: Louhy.

To master: archery: God: Apollo. **the cardinal points**: God: Sobek. **ego**: God: Hanuman. **the elements**: God: Sobek. **horses**: Neptune, Poseidon. **hunting**: Animal: cougar; God: Horned God. **an opponent**: God: Malah. **runes**: God: Odin. **a very strong woman**: God: Nergal.

Maturity

Full Moon/Water/West

Color: indigo; Animal: frog; Stone: kunzite; Goddess: the Crone, Hera, Prakriti; God: Marduk, Patrimpas.

Emotional maturity: Color: deep blue. **Mature elegance**: Plant: pomegranate. **Mature love**: Color: blue. **Mature vigor**: Summer.

To finally grow up: Goddess: Athena; Plant: bracken.

Immaturity

(See also: Childishness)

Color: coral, green; Evocation: Puck.

Premature baby: (See: Babies).

Meditation

Jupiter/Venus/Moon/Water

Tool: censer, pentacle; Charm: aromatherapy, mandala; Number: 3, 7; Color: blue, royal blue, gray, indigo, purple, silver, turquoise, violet, white; Stone: agate, banded agate, amethyst, ametrine, Apache tear, apophyllite, avalonite, aventurine, azurite, calcite, clear or yellow calcite, carnelian, celestite, chrysocolla, chrysoprase, diamond, emerald, blue fluorite, geode, hematite, jade, kunzite, labradorite, lapis lazuli, malachite, onyx, peridot, clear quartz crystal, sapphire, selenite, sodalite, tourmaline, turquoise; Metal: manganite; Oil: neroli; Plant: acacia, angelica, anise, ash, benzoin, bodhi tree, camphor, cannabis, catnip, cedar, chamomile, cinnamon, copal, elecampane (as incense), eyebright, frankincense, gotu kola, gum arabic, hawthorn, heather, heliotrope, ivy, jacaranda, jasmine, laurel, lemon balm, lily of the valley, lotus, magnolia, milkweed, myrrh, nutmeg, rosemary, rosewood, sage, sandalwood, sandalwood with cinnamon, spearmint, thyme, uva ursi, vanilla, wisteria, wood aloes, ylang-ylang; Goddess: Kukuri-Hime, Kwan Yin, Neith, Sarasvati; God: Krishna Yogini, Shiva, Tsuke-Yomi.

Complex meditation: Color: gray, silver. **Deep meditation**: Color: black, indigo; Stone: amethyst; Plant: myrrh; *to overcome fear of*: Stone: azurite, malachite. **Devotional meditation**: Color: light blue. **Focused meditation**: Animal: cat. **Inspirational meditation**: Color: light blue. **Personal meditation**: Plant: hawthorn berry (as incense). **Spiritual meditation**: Color: light blue; Plant: frankincense, jasmine; God: Vagisvara.

Meditative strength: Stone: turquoise.

Guidance in meditation: Animal: wolf. **Protection during meditation**: Stone: turquoise.

Memories

(See also: Memory)

Air/Water

Plant: aster, everlasting, evergreens, forget-me-not, periwinkle, rosemary; Goddess: Isis, Saga, Sesheta.

Ancestral memories: Pluto. **Childhood memories**: Plant: buttercup. **Good memories**: Goddess: Saga. **Happy memories**: Plant: rosemary. **Painful memories**: Plant: Adonis. **Past life memories**: *to awaken*: Plant: camphor, lemon balm; *to recall*: Plant: lilac. **Repressed memories**: *to release*: Plant: forget-me-not, rosemary. **Sad memories**: Plant: pheasant's eye, rue; *to ease*: Plant: sweetgrass. **Sweet memories**: Plant: periwinkle.

For help to remember something: Goddess: Glispa.

To remember: the dead: (See: The Dead). **dreams**: (See: Dreams). **lessons**: Plant: rosemary. **traditions**: God: Hu Gadarn. **your purpose**: Animal: spider; Stone: sugilite.

Memory

(See also: Memories)

Mercury/Air

Color: orange, yellow; Animal: elephant, orca, raven, whale; Stone: amber, carnelian, emerald, fossil, onyx; Oil: petitgrain; Plant: benzoin, eyebright, honeysuckle, lavender, lemon balm, marjoram, nutmeg, parsley, patchouli, rosemary, sage, very old trees; Goddess: Mnemosyne, Savitri; Evocation: Muninn.

Pleasures of memory: Plant: periwinkle.

Memory of great events: Goddess: Mnemosyne. **Memory in psychic work**: (See: Work).

To: improve memory: Color: orange; Stone: beryl, calcite, emerald, hematite, howlite, opal, pyrite; Plant: basil, blessed thistle, broom, caraway seed, clove, comfrey, eyebright, fig tree, forget-me-not, foti, ginseng, gotu kola, honeysuckle, lavender, lily of the valley, melilot, mint, onion, orchid, patchouli, periwinkle, rosemary, wintergreen. **not forget the past**: Animal: toad. **restore lost memory**: Stone: emerald. **stimulate memory**: Stone: andalusite; Plant: basil, forget-me-not, rosemary.

Men

(See also: The Body, Virility, Women, Yang)

Mars/Sun

God: Nergal.

Dead men: God: Osiris. **Evil men**: *to protect against*: Stone: ruby. **Young men**: God: Apollo, Liber; *compassion for*: God: Marduk; *to protect until they are fully grown*: Goddess: the Oceanids; *young manhood*: God: Apollo, Tezcatlipoca.

Men's lodges: *spirit of*: Evocation: Kmantah. **Lost manhood**: *to restore*: Charm: iron thumb ring; Metal: iron; Plant: acorn (carried), *Artemisia*, dill, evergreens, oat, snakeroot, yohimbine; God: Min.

Right eyes of men: Sun. **Right side of men**: Moon. **Secret rites of men**: God: Mithras. **Transition from boyhood to manhood**: God: Apollo.

For a man to: control a woman: Plant: woodruff. **enrapture a woman**: God: Pluto. **have a son**: Goddess: Sarasvati. **learn how to please a woman sexually**: God: Krishna.

To: arouse men: Plant: evergreens. **attract men**: Charm: orange flower water; Oil: neroli; Plant: lavender, orange blossom, orris root, vetiver; *attract love from a man*: Plant: lavender, orris root. **encourage love in men**: Plant: orris root. **improve conversational ability in men**: Stone: lodestone. **increase physical strength in men**: Goddess: Strenia. **initiate men into the Mysteries of sex**: Goddess: the Horae. **keep men faithful**: Plant: raspberry leaf (in bath). **love and leave a man**: Goddess: Aphrodite. **make men gracious**: Stone: lodestone. **make men perform sexually**: Plant: bistort root; Goddess: Maeve. **make men persuasive**: Stone: lodestone. **make men pleasant**: Stone: black agate with white veins. **protect men**: God: Lubangala, Min; Evocation: genius; *from witchcraft*: Plant: holly. **strengthen men**: Stone: black agate with white veins; *physically*: Goddess: Strenia.

Mercy

(See also: Compassion, Kindness)

Tool: wand; Color: red; Plant: tamarind; Goddess: Anath (Maiden Merciful, The Merciful), Astarte (Benignant and Merciful), Athena, Clementia, Eir, Holda (Merciful), Inanna (Merciful), Isis (The Merciful), Juno, Kali, Kwan Yin (Merciful Mother), Mary (Our Lady of Mercy, Our Lady of Pity, Mary of the Mercies), Mother Earth, Pandora, Tara, Yemaya; God:

Aguku, Ahura Mazda (The Merciful), Allah (The Merciful), Avalokiteshvara (Merciful Lord), Baal (God of Mercy), Baldur, El, Juchimen, Latipan (Compassionate God of Mercy), Obatala (The Pure and Merciful), Orunmila, Shiva, Ti-Tsang Wang, Wadd (The Merciful), Yahweh (The Merciful One, The Compassionate and Merciful), Zeus; Evocation: Gabriel, Metatron (Great Healer of Mercy), Raphael.

To beg for mercy: Goddess: Auge.

Messages

(See also: Communication, Contact, Omens, Oracles)

Mercury/Capricorn

Charm: wings; Animal: baboon, bat, cat, crocodile, crow, fox, hawk, hummingbird, owl, parakeet, carrier pigeon, raven, wren; Plant: dandelion, iris; Goddess: Iris, Pheme; God: Hermes, Legba, Mercury, Turms.

Angelic messages: Stone: angelite, obsidian; Plant: angelica; Evocation: angels; *to open to*: Plant: angelica. **Death messages**: Animal: owl; Goddess: Sekhmet (Lady of the Messengers of Death); God: Namtar, Thanatos; Evocation: Bean Sidhe. **Divine messages**: Charm: comet; Animal: crow, eland, hawk, owl, all birds; Goddess: Aruru, Fulla, Gna, Guantuava, Iris, Shapash, Shekinah; God: Aktab Kutbay, Hermes, Legba, Mercury, Ninurta, Paynal, Raja Indainda; Evocation: angels, Gabriel, Gapen, Hermod, Hlin, Matarisvan, Qadesh, Skirnir, Slava, Ugar, Valkyries. **Dream messages**: Animal: raven, wolf; Plant: marigold (under the pillow); God: Kalisia, Maximon; *via nightmares*: God: Pan. **Psychic messages**: Capricorn; *to send*: Color: red; Stone: garnet, ruby, red tourmaline. **Secret messages**: Animal: owl. **Spirit messages**: Animal: harrier hawk.

To: receive messages: Stone: red calcite; *from the Otherworld*: Animal: bat, white stag; God: Cromm Cruaich; *from the subconscious*: Animal: bat; *from the Underworld*: Animal: owl; God: Namtar. **send messages**: Animal: all birds; Stone: angelite, red calcite; Plant: dandelion (seed head, blown); God: Hermes, Legba, Mercury; *to higher powers*: Animal: cougar; *to the Otherworld*: Charm: ice water; God: Cromm Cruaich; *to the Underworld*: Animal: owl; God: Thoth. **speed messages**: Number: 8642 (written on instrument of transmission); Evocation: Baduh. **understand messages**: Plant: marigold.

The Mind

(See also: Concentration, Consciousness, Intelligence, Intellect, Thought)

Mercury/Air/Fire/East/Virgo

Color: blue, yellow; Animal: all white birds; Stone: hematite; Plant: honeysuckle, mace, oregano, rosemary; Goddess: Alaghom-Naom (Mother of Mind), Mens, Sarasvati, Vidya Lakshmi, Visahari; God: Khnum, Obatala.

Agile mind: Color: orange. **Alert mind**: Stone: aquamarine, carnelian; Oil: palmarosa; Plant: ginkgo, black pepper, rosemary. **Analytical mind**: Stone: fluorite. **Anguished mind**: Plant: marigold. **Beautiful mind**: Plant: clematis, kennedia, rosemary. **Calm mind**: Method: meditation; Stone: agate, blue lace agate, amethyst, bloodstone, emerald, smoky quartz, blue topaz; Plant: benzoin, red clover, cosmos, datura, madwort, nutmeg, pennyroyal, wild rose, sandalwood, mad dog scullcap, violet. **Clear mind**: Moon/Air; Color: yellow; Stone: amber, amethyst, aquamarine, aventurine, citrine, emerald, hematite, Herkimer diamond, yellow jasper, opal, blue quartz, clear quartz crystal, rhodonite, sodalite, tigereye, topaz; Oil: petitgrain;

Plant: basil, birch, blue bonnet, broom, caraway, cardamom, cedar, citronella, clove, clover, dill, fern, fig, balsam fir, goldenrod, gotu kola, grapevine, horehound, lemon, lemongrass, orchid, peppermint, rosemary, rue, sage, sandalwood, spikenard, thoroughwort, vanilla, violet; **Goddess:** Mary; *clarity of body/mind communication:* Plant: dandelion; *to clear the mind:* Method: meditation; Charm: silver balls (held in the hand); Metal: silver; Stone: amethyst; Plant: basil, clove, lilac, rue, smartweed; God and Goddess: Tsuki-Yomi. **Concrete mind:** Saturn. **Conscious mind:** Sun; Plant: caraway, coffee, lily of the valley, pennyroyal; *to quiet:* Plant: sandalwood; *to relax:* Plant: narcissus; *to unite with psychic mind:* Plant: marjoram. **Cosmic mind:** God: Brahma; *to contact:* Plant: birch. **Feeble mind:** *to improve:* Plant: broom. **Healthy mind:** Stone: turquoise. **Higher mind:** Jupiter. **Independent mind:** Number: 9; Stone: amethyst. **Level mind:** Stone: blue chalcedony. **Logical mind:** Animal: crane, heron. **Lucid mind:** Plant: lotus; Goddess: Sarasvati. **Open mind:** Stone: chrysoprase, citrine; Plant: apricot; God: Shiva. **Narrow mind:** *to open:* Plant: silverweed. **Psychic mind:** Stone: aquamarine, emerald; *to awaken:* Plant: lemongrass; *to unite the conscious mind with:* Plant: marjoram. **Rational mind:** Stone: jade. **Sharp/quick mind:** Color: yellow; Plant: birch, ginkgo, mint, peppermint, blue vervain. **Small minds:** *to battle:* God: Gwydion, Pan. **Still/quiet mind:** Stone: red agate, amethyst, anhydrite, sodalite; Plant: foxglove, sandalwood, Solomon's seal, violet. **Subconscious mind:** Goddess: Lilith. **Troubled mind:** *to help:* Stone: jasper; Plant: madwort, wolfsbane. **Unconscious mind:** Moon/Water; Color: black; Animal: lizard; *treasures of:* Animal: dragon. **Universal mind:** Plant: birch; God: Brahma. **Versatile mind:** Plant: saxifrage. **Vulgar mind:** Plant: African marigold. **Weak mind:** Plant: hemlock.

Constancy of mind: Stone: emerald; Plant: bunchberry. **Meeting of the minds:** Metal: zinc. **Peace of mind:** Color: blue; Stone: amethyst, anhydrite, chrysoprase, lapis lazuli, pearl, sapphire, turquoise; Plant: apple, benzoin, cow parsnip, patchouli, narcissus, olive, passion flower, tuberose, valerian, ylang-ylang; *for the mentally ill:* Plant: hyacinth. **Presence of mind:** God: Ganesha.

Absent-mindedness: Stone: carnelian. **Mindfulness:** Oil: palmarosa; Plant: basil, birch, costmary, hyssop, laurel, black pepper, peppermint, saffron, sage. **Mindlessness:** Goddess: Lethe. **Single-mindedness:** Animal: termite; God: Aegir.

To: activate the mind: Plant: thyme. **awaken the mind:** Stone: chrysoprase; Plant: benzoin, peppermint. **bind minds:** Color: yellow; Metal: gold; Stone: citrine, yellow diamond, yellow sapphire; God: Odin. **change your mind:** God: Ra. **comfort the mind:** Stone: chrysocolla. **change minds/attitudes/ways of thinking:** Color: green; Stone: kyanite, lepidolite; Plant: licorice, squill. **connect body/mind/emotions:** Stone: moonstone. **connect body/mind/spirit:** Charm: triangle; Number: 3. **free the mind:** Animal: dolphin, whale; Plant: sandalwood. **integrate mind/body:** Color: purple. **know your own mind:** Goddess: Britomartis, Gerd; *with respect to choosing a mate:* Goddess: Xoli Kaltes. **heal the mind:** Plant: borage. **improve the mind:** Color: yellow; Plant: dong quai. **protect the mind:** Stone: pyrite. **quiet the mind:** Plant: cassandra, Solomon's seal. **read minds:** Goddess: Kupala. **soothe the mind:** Stone: rhodochrosite; Plant: scullcap, violet. **train the mind:** God: Ganesha. **unbind minds:** God: Odin.

Mental ability: (See: Ability). **Mental action:** Wednesday; God: Baile. **Mental attunement:** Stone: clear quartz crystal. **Mental awareness:** Color: yellow; Stone:

yellow quartz; Plant: carnation. **Mental balance**: (See: Balance). **Mental barriers**: *to remove*: Animal: orca; Stone: pink tourmaline. **Mental blocks**: (See: Blockages). **Mental capacity**: Stone: pyrite. **Mental centering**: Plant: red clover. **Mental changes**: *to make*: Stone: lepidolite. **Mental confusion**: (See: Confusion). **Mental control**: Plant: Jacob's ladder. **Mental creativity**: (See: Creativity). **Mental dexterity**: Animal: monkey. **Mental discipline**: Method: meditation. **Mental energy**: Color: red; Stone: bloodstone, citrine, garnet, ruby, spinel, red tourmaline; Plant: basil, clove, lemon, ginseng, peppermint, rosemary. **Mental fatigue**: (See: Fatigue). **Mental flexibility**: (See: Flexibility). **Mental focus**: Stone: clear calcite, citrine; Plant: eucalyptus. **Mental freedom**: Plant: dandelion, sandalwood. **Mental health**: (See: Health). **Mental healing**: Stone: citrine. **Mental illness/the mentally ill**: (See: Illness). **Mental improvement**: Stone: fluorite; Plant: vanilla bean. **Mental laziness**: *to overcome*: Plant: peppermint. **Mental power(s)**: (See: Power). **Mental preparation for magick**: Plant: chamomile tea. **Mental problems**: (See: Problems). **Mental processes**: Stone: jasper, red jasper. **Mental progress**: Stone: fluorite. **Mental protection**: Plant: hyssop. **Mental purification**: (See: Purification). **Mental receptivity**: Plant: willow. **Mental relaxation**: (See: Relaxation). **Mental/spiritual connection**: Stone: pearl. **Mental steadiness/stability**: Stone: emerald; Plant: pennyroyal, wild rose, rosemary; *in psychic work*: Plant: chamomile and celery with rosemary. **Mental stimulation**: (See: Stimulation). **Mental strength**: (See: Strength). **Mental synthesis**: Plant: daisy. **Mental tonic**: Plant: ashwagandha, borage, ginseng, rosemary, sage. **Mental torture**: Evocation: the Rakshasas. **Mental vitality**: Stone: jasper; Plant: olive. **Mental well-being**: Stone: sugilite. **Mental work**: (See: Work).

Miscarriage
(See: Pregnancy)

Moderation
(See also: Control)

Saturn

Color: blue; Stone: amethyst; Plant: angelica, azalea, bergamot, hyssop, silverweed; Goddess: Artemis, Hokmah; God: Mithras; Evocation: Cassiel.

To become moderate: Goddess: Iris.

Immoderation
(See also: Diseases/Disorders: addiction)

Plant: coca, grape, opium poppy, tobacco.

Modesty
Dawn

Color: blue, violet, white; Number: 2; Animal: bluebird, panda; Stone: jade, jet, pearl; Plant: baby's breath, bamboo, chamomile, lily, madonna lily, violet; Goddess: Aedos, Astraea, Pudicitia, Vidya Lakshmi.

Modest beauty: Plant: painted trillium. **Modest genius**: Plant: cereus. **Modest worth**: Plant: primrose.

Money
(See also: Abundance, Finances, Poverty, Prosperity)

Jupiter/Mercury/Waxing Moon/Earth/Thursday/Taurus/Gemini

Tool: pentacle; Color: copper, gold, green, orange, silver; Charm: bread, coins, cowrie shell, green feather, money, shark tooth; Number: 6, 8; Animal: toad; Metal: brass, copper, gold, silver, tin; Stone: brown agate, moss agate, amethyst, aventurine, green aventurine, bloodstone, calcite, green calcite, chrysoprase, coal, emerald, Herkimer diamond, jacinth, jade, green jade, jasper, green jasper, lodestone, green lodestone, malachite, olivine, opal, fire opal, pearl, peridot, pyrite, salt, sapphire, spinel ruby, staurolite, tigereye, topaz, tourmaline, green tourmaline, turquoise, brown or green zircon; Plant: acacia, alfalfa, allspice, almond, aniseed, basil, bayberry, benzoin, bergamot, bistort, borage, bramble, bromeliad, bryony, buckwheat, cabbage, calamus, camellia, cascara sagrada, cashew, cedar, chamomile, horse chestnut, cinnamon, cinquefoil, clove, clover, black cohosh, comfrey, corn, cowslip, dill, dock, yellow dock, dragon's blood, all evergreens, fennel, fenugreek, fern, flax, fumitory, galangal, gardenia, ginger, goldenrod, goldenseal, gorse, grains of paradise, grapevine, heliotrope, High John, honesty, honeysuckle, horse chestnut, hyssop, blue flag iris, Irish moss, jasmine, kelp, laurel, lavender, lemon balm, lucky hand root, mace, maize, mandrake, maple, marjoram, mint, moneywort, moss, Irish moss, mountain grape, mustard seed, myrtle, nasturtium, nutmeg, oak, oats, onion, orange, parsley, patchouli, pea, pecan, peppermint, periwinkle, pine, pineapple, poplar, poppy seed, rattlesnake root, rice, saffron, sage, St. John's Wort, sarsaparilla, sassafras, sea kelp, sesame, snapdragon, spearmint, squill, storax, sunflower seed, black tea, thyme, tonka bean, trillium, valerian, vervain, vetiver, wheat, wintergreen, woodruff; Goddess: Abhijit, Aditi, Agathe Tyche, Ahurani, Aje, Artio, Ashiakle, Bona Eventus, Brigitte, Demeter, Dhanakshayanashini (Controller of Wealth Decrease), Hecate, Juno, Juno Moneta, Lakshmi (She of the Hundred Thousands), Minerva, Ninanna, Olwen, Ops, Oshun, Rosmerta, Sarasvati, Ushas, Yemaya Ataramagwa; God: Cernunnos, Chango Macho, Chao, the Dagda, Damuzi, Dhanya, Dionysus Plutodotes, Dis Pater, Enbilulu-Gugal, Ganesha, Hades, Hotei, Kuan Ti, Kubera, Math ap Mathonwy, Njord, Pluto, Tezcatlipoca, Volos, Zeus, Ziku; Evocation: Genii Cucullati.

Quick money: Color: gold, green; Plant: cinnamon. **Steady money**: Plant: Irish moss. **Money spells**: (See: Spells). **Money wishes**: Plant: cinnamon.

Good luck with money: Stone: amazonite, malachite; Plant: cinnamon, cinquefoil, Low John. **Growth of money**: Plant: mandrake root, thyme. **Power of money**: Stone: tigereye.

To: accumulate money: Earth; Color: brown. **always have money**: Charm: bread; Plant: heather. **attract money**: Color: brown, gold, green; Charm: coins, money; Metal: brass, copper, gold, silver; Stone: amazonite, green aventurine, bloodstone, green calcite, chrysoprase, green jade, lodestone, green lodestone, malachite, mother-of-pearl, fire opal, pearl, peridot, phantom, pyrite, tigereye, green tourmaline, turquoise; Plant: allspice, almond, basil, bayberry, bergamot, borage, cat's claw, cedar, chamomile, horse chestnut, cinnamon, clove, clover, black cohosh root, dandelion seed (caught in the air), ginger, ginseng, grapevine, heliotrope, High John, honeysuckle, horse chestnut, jasmine, lavender, lemon balm, lemon verbena, mint, myrtle, nutmeg, oakmoss, olive, patchouli, periwinkle, pine, poppy seed, sarsaparilla with cinnamon, tonka bean, vervain, vetiver; *to the home*: Charm: copper coin, vanilla extract (in wash water); Plant: bayberry, lavender, patchouli. **collect money/debts**: Color: green with black, purple, yellow; Stone: tigereye; Plant: allspice, clove, ginger, jasmine. **double your money**: Stone: calcite; Plant: mandrake root. **get a loan**: plant: alfalfa. **increase money**: Waxing Moon; Plant: four leaf clover, honeysuckle, horse chestnut, mandrake root, American mandrake; *power to manifest money*: Plant: lavender. **keep money**: Charm: honey, maple syrup; Plant: comfrey, fern seed, hand of Maryam, honeysuckle, rose of Jericho, thyme; Goddess: Dhanakshayanashini (Controller of Wealth Decrease). **obtain money**: Plant: cedar, rattlesnake root; *by chance/luck*: Goddess: Fortuna. **stretch money**: Plant: sassafras.

Monsters

Evocation: Echidna, Grendel, harpies, Lamia.

Earth monsters: Earth; Goddess: Coatlicue (Earth Monster); Evocation: Cipaxtli; *to battle*: God: Quetzalcoatl; Evocation: Born for Water and Monster Slayer (The Twin Brothers). **Sea monsters**: Water; Goddess: Sedna; God: Poseidon, Yamm; Evocation: Cetus, Charybdis, Hydra, Leviathan, Monster Killer Whale, Scylla, Yagis; *to rescue from*: Evocation: Perseus.

To: avert monsters: Plant: High John, moonwort; God: Glooskap. **battle monsters**: Goddess: Durga; God: Dionysus; Evocation: King Arthur, Beowolf, Cadhan, Gilgamesh, Hercules, Hidesato, Sigurd, Svyatogor. **create monsters**: Plant: scorpion weed. **protect against monsters**: Plant: garlic.

Mood

(See also: Anger, Emotions, Happiness, Sorrow, and so on.)

Moon/Cancer

Tool: censer; Method: color magick, lighting, music; Animal: chameleon; Stone: turquoise.

Bad mood: *to break*: Stone: black star sapphire. **Calm mood**: Goddess: Artemis, Kwan Yin. **Good mood**: Charm: rosewater; Stone: sapphire; Plant: cherry, cinnamon, rosemary, vanilla. **Ocean moods**: God: Aegir.

Male mood disorders: *to treat*: Plant: snake cereus. **Mood swings**: Mercury/Moon; Goddess: Erzulie; *to control*: Metal: silver; Plant: saffron; *to end*: Stone: moonstone; Plant: chamomile, sugar cane.

To: improve mood: Stone: amber, blue chalcedony, smoky quartz, topaz; Oil: neroil; Plant: bergamot, betel nut, chamomile, frankincense, mimosa, snake cereus, sweetgrass, ylang–ylang. **read others' moods**: Animal: squid.

Moodiness

Cancer

Color: dark blue; Number: 3; Plant: galangal, rye; God: Poseidon; Evocation: Pothos.

Morality

Sun

Color: pink, rose; Plant: mullein; Goddess: Ala, Durga; God: Hino, Jakomba, Mithras, Tarqeq, Varuna, Vishnu.

Moral balance: God: Vishnu. **Moral blindness**: Goddess: Ate. **Moral conduct**: Stone: jade. **Moral honesty**: Plant: mullein. **Moral judgment**: God: Shango. **Moral retribution**: God: Obaluaiye. **Moral strength**: Stone: onyx. **Moral victory**: Charm: crown of olive branches.

To test morals: God: Tezcatlipoca.

Amorality
God: Nergal, Zeus.

Immorality
Plant: amaranth.

Motivation
Waxing Moon/Fire/Saturday

Color: red; Stone: aventurine; Plant: cayenne, black pepper.

Motivation toward goals: Stone: sapphire.

Mourning
(See: Grief)

Movement
(See also: Action, Activity, Progress)

Sun/Moon/Air/Water/Fire

Color: yellow; Charm: wolf print; Animal: caribou, gibbon, all migrating animals; Metal: mercury (toxic, not recommended); Stone: meteorite, mother of pearl; Plant: hand of Maryam, tumbleweed.

Fluid movement: Animal: slug. **Physical movement**: *to manifest energy as*: Stone: celestite; God: Skan. **Orderly movement**: *of people at their normal tasks*: God: Janus. **Steady movement**: Animal: slug, tortoise.

Freedom of movement: Animal: crow, all birds; Stone: fluorite; Goddess: Epona; *to move freely in the afterlife*: Charm: tet amulet. **Power of movement**: Color: yellow; *power to move between moments*: Animal: hummingbird, praying mantis.

To move: forward: (See: Progress). **through time and space**: Animal: lynx. **upward**: Sun; Animal: eagle, all flying birds.

The Mysteries
Dark Moon

Number: 3; Animal: lynx, serpent; Goddess: Cybele, Demeter, Diana of the Mysteries, Hecate, Isis (Isis Mystis, Lady of the Mysteries), Mor, Morgen, Persephone, Rhea; God: Dionysus, Osiris of the Mysteries.

Deep mysteries: Animal: crane. **Earth Mysteries**: Earth; Charm: labyrinth, ley line; Animal: bison, mole, pig, snake; Goddess: Demeter, Ptè San Wi; God: Cernunnos, Hades, Osiris, Tatanka, Teutates, Ziku. **Lunar Mysteries**: Moon (all phases); Goddess: Blodeuwedd; God: Khonsu. **Male Mysteries**: Color: orange; Plant: rue; God: Cernunnos, Horned God, Mithras. **Night mysteries**: Night; Plant: jasmine, queen of the night. **Poetic Mysteries**: Goddess: the Graiae. **Toadstool Mysteries**: Fungus: fly agaric; God: Tlaloc; Evocation: Ladon. **Women's Mysteries**: Moon; Plant: bean, fig, flax, jasmine, rose, woad; Goddess: Agave, Hecate, Heqet, Libera, Phyllis, Yemaya; *to protect*: Goddess: Condwiramur, Stheino; *to celebrate agriculture as*: Plant: bean, flax; Goddess: Demeter, Ganija; *to initiate young women into childbearing*: Charm: flagellation with a pussy willow rod; Goddess: Libera; *mystery of baking bread*: Goddess: Fornax; *mystery of making linen*: Charm: linen cloth or thread, spindle; Plant: flax; Goddess: Calliope, Vaisgamta; Evocation: Harpatsch the Soot-faced Hag; *mystery of making dye from woad*: Color: blue; Plant: woad; *mystery of planting beans*: Plant: beans; *mystery of propagating figs*: Plant: fig.

Mystery of creation: God: Ptah. **Mysteries of love**: *initiation into*: Venus; Letter: O. **Mystery of magick**: God: Mithras. **Mysteries of time**: Water.

Doorway to the Mysteries: Plant: oak.

To: conceal Mysteries: Goddess: Isis. **initiate men into the Mysteries of sex**: Goddess: the Horae. **protect Mysteries**: Animal: vulture. **reveal Mysteries**: Goddess: Cailleach Bheara, Isis, Yemaya Olokun. **understand the Mysteries**: Goddess: the Crone, Nephthys.

The Mystical
Color: black; Number: 7, 9, 11, 22; Plant: alder, apple, frankincense; Goddess: Mary (Mystical Rose).

Mystical communication: Goddess: Vac. **Mystical insight**: Wednesday. **Mystical inspiration**: Pisces. **Mystical knowledge**: Goddess: Neith. **Mystic power/s**: Plant: mandrake; Goddess: Kali. **Mystical sleep**: Color: blue; Stone: blue opal. **Mystical wisdom**: Goddess: Ekadzati.

Mysticism

Scorpio

Color: purple, violet; Number: 7; Animal: blackbird; God: Shiva.

Chapter 14

Nature

(See also: Agriculture, Animals, Gardens, Land, Weather)

Earth

Color: green; Number: 2; Plant: all, but especially elder, forest trees, magnolia, patchouli; Goddess: Ah Wink Ir Masa, Ambika, Anima Mundi, Aphrodite, Artemis, Briah, Caera, Ce-Aed, Cerridwen, Cybele, Diana, the Duillae, Hecate (Great Goddess of Nature), Irpa, Isis (Green Goddess), Kwan Yin, Magog, Mother Nature, Nantosuelta, Pachamama, Prakiritia, South Daughter, Tana, Green Tara, Toci, Venus; God: Baal, Cernunnos, Dianus, Dionysus, Faunus, Herne, Horned God, Pan, Quetzalcoatl, Serapis, Silvanus, Tane; Evocation: Merlin, nature spirits, Orpheus.

Multifaceted Nature: Goddess: Vikruti. **Primal material Nature**: Goddess: Prakrta. **Untamed Nature**: Goddess: Artemis, Cybele; God: Green Man. **Nature spirits**: (See: Spirits).

Balance of Nature: Animal: wolf; *to maintain*: God: Cernunnos. **Cycles of Nature**: Goddess: Demeter. **Female principle of Nature**: Goddess: Anna Livia, Asherah, Isis. **Fertility of Nature**: Sun/Earth; Color: red; Plant: lotus; Goddess: Ashtoreth, Athtartu, Cybele, Gaia, Greine, Hou-Tu, Inanna, Mother Earth, Mother Nature, Mokosh, Pazardzik, Pidraya, Sheela-na-gig, Spendaramet, Talaya, Tellus Mater, Tonantzin; God: Osiris, Priapus; *to activate*: God: Krishna. **Flowering of Nature**: Goddess: Flora. **Force of Nature**: Goddess: Kali; God: Grand Bois; Evocation: elementals. **Love of Nature**: Plant: magnolia. **Order of Nature**: Goddess: Aditi, Estsanatlehi, the Horai; *to restore*: Goddess: Sedna. **Potency of Nature**: *female potency*: Animal: bee. **Power of Nature**: Animal: dragon; *creative power of*: Goddess: Hathor; *healing power of*: Goddess: Coatlicue; *productive power of*: Goddess: Ashtoreth. **Renewal/rebirth of Nature**: Spring; Color: spring green; Goddess: Chalchihuitlcue; God: Damuzi, Green Man, Osiris, Tammuz, Xipe Totec. **Verdancy of Nature**: Color: green; Goddess: Isis (The Green One), Kupole. **Wisdom of Nature**: Color: green; Stone: emerald, peridot, green tourmaline; Plant: pine, spruce, all evergreen trees.

Integration with Nature: God: Ganesha. **Professions which imitate Nature**: Goddess: Xochiquetzal.

To: appreciate Nature: Plant: reindeer moss. **ask forgiveness for unintentional slights against Nature**: God and Goddess: Pales. **connect with Nature**: Plant: petrified wood, pine. **encourage the fertility of Nature**: Goddess: Cybele. **maintain the balance of Nature**: God: Cernunnos. **protect Nature**: Animal: griffin; God: Helios. **understand the human place in Nature**: God: Sicun.

Need

Aries

Animal: all parasitic and symbiotic creatures; Plant: all creeping, climbing, parasitic and symbiotic plants.

Emotional needs: Stone: chalcedony; Plant: damiana, valerian. **Physical needs**: *to meet*: Color: orange; Animal: cow. **Sexual need**: Venus; Goddess: Anath, Medb; God: Shiva. **Needed changes**: (See: Changes). **Needed skills**: God: Itzamna. **Needs of others**: *sensitivity to*: Goddess: Walo; *to recognize*: Plant: linden. **Those in need**: *compassion for*: God: Shiva; *to bless*: Goddess: Lakshmi; God: Ganesha; *to help*: Goddess: Kwan Yin, Tara; God: Ellil, Obatala, Shiva; *to protect*: God: Shiva, Zeus; *to protect those in need of defense*: Goddess: Athena; *to protect women and children in need*: Goddess: Akinad; *to support*: God: Shiva. **Special needs children**: (See: Children). **Times of need**: *for help in*: Goddess: the Afliae, the Ahinehiae, the Ahueccaniae, the Alaferhviae, the Alagabiabus, the Alaisiagae, the Albiahenae, the Euthungae, the Friagabiae, the Gavasiae, the Hamavehae, Kwan Yin (Hearer of Cries), the Lanehiae, the Maluisae, the Marsacae, the Three Marys, the Seubis, Tara, the Xulsigiae; God: El, Pwyll Penn Annwn.

To: ask for what you need: Animal: slug. **bring rain needed for agriculture**: Goddess: Auxesia; God: Freyr. **distinguish between need and desire**: Stone: tigereye. **do only that which is needed**: Animal: elk. **get what you need**: (See: Acquisition). **overcome the need to control others**: Plant: bistort. **recognize what you no longer need**: Stone: snowflake obsidian. **release the need for attachments**: Plant: raspberry. **release the need to control**: Plant: horsetail. **release/discard that which is no longer needed**: Animal: earthworm; Stone: amethyst, moldovite, blue topaz; Plant:

dandelion, senna. **satisfy need**: Full Moon; Plant: papaya; Goddess: Diana, Hecate, Rhiannon. **use/take only what is needed**: Animal: squirrel.

Negativity

(See also: Anger, Destruction, Envy, Evil, Jealousy, Positiveness, and so on.)

Moon/Capricorn

Animal: dragon; Stone: onyx; Metal: lead, silver; Plant: blackthorn; Goddess: Cihuacoatl; God: Chernobog, Mot, Set; Evocation: Apep.

Negative actions: *to wash away*: Water; Goddess: Ganga. **Negative attachments**: (See: Attachments). **Negative attitude**: *to improve*: Plant: snowdrop, spider lily. **Negative beliefs**: *to release*: Animal: squirrel; Stone: sugilite. **Negative conditions/situations**: (See: Situations). **negative contacts**: (See: Contact). **negative cycle**: (See: Cycles, Uncrossing). **negative emotions**: (See: Emotions). **Negative energy**: (See: Energy). **Negative forces**: (See: Forces). **Negative influence**: (See: Influence). **Negative intentions**: *to avert*: Plant: cedar. **Negative omens**: (See: Omens). **Negative past life**: (See: Past Life Work). **Negative patterns**: *to end*: Stone: pearl; Oil: new mown hay; Plant: dragon's blood; *to overcome*: Plant: macadamia nut; *to release*: Stone: sugilite: Plant: columbine, tansy. **Negative people**: (See: People). **Negative relationships**: *to avert*: Stone: onyx. **Negative self image**: *to improve*: Stone: apatite, rose quartz. **Negative situations**: (See: Situations). **Negative thoughts**: (See: Thoughts). **Negative thought forms**: (See: Thought Forms). **Negative vibrations**: (See: Vibrations).

Negativity from past lives: *to heal*: Stone: hawk's eye. **Positive/negative balance**: (See: Positiveness). **Other people's negativity**: *to protect against*: Stone: black tourmaline; Plant: thyme.

To: **absorb negativity**: Color: black; Charm: black salt, eggs (disposed of or left at a crossroads for Hecate afterwards); Stone: garnet, lodestone, snowflake obsidian, clear quartz crystal, black tourmaline (purify stones in salt or salt water afterward); Plant: cumin, onions (disposed of or left at a crossroads for Hecate afterwards), violet. **avert negativity**: Saturday; Color: black; Charm: black salt; Animal: butterfly; Stone: garnet, lepidolite, black tourmaline; Plant: basil, burdock, clove, High John, laurel, nettle, patchouli, pennyroyal, peppermint, vetiver, yarrow; God: Ganesha; *from the home*: Charm: bells on the door; Plant: blueberry, ivy. **banish negativity**: Waning Moon; Tool: bell, gong; Color: black, dark blue, purple, silver; Charm: black salt, brimstone (as incense); Metal: silver; Stone: hematite, quartz crystal, smoky quartz; Plant: basil, cedar, cinnamon, clove, frankincense, High John, lavender, mullein, pine, rosemary, vervain. **break up/clear negativity**: Tool: bell, besom, rattle, sistrum; Charm: brimstone (as incense), egg, van van; Metal: silver; Stone: amethyst, ametrine, apatite, azurite, carnelian, citrine, black coral, geode, quartz crystal, cluster of quartz crystals, hematite, jade, jet, sea salt, sugilite; Plant: acacia, angelica, benzoin, camphor, cedar, clove, coltsfoot, cumin, dragon's blood, eucalyptus, frankincense, gum arabic, hawthorn, High John, hyssop, juniper, laurel, lemongrass, mistletoe, Spanish moss, myrrh, onion, patchouli, rosemary, rue, sandalwood, spikenard, tangerine (oil), yarrow. **Change a negative into a positive**: Color: orange, purple; Stone: unakite. **Consume negativity**: Goddess: Kali. **Deal with negativity**: Color: blue; Stone: turquoise; *deal with negative coworkers*: (See: Workers). **Deflect negativity**: Stone: black tourmaline; Metal: silver. **Destroy negativity**: Color: black.

Neutralize negativity: Plant: sage. **Overcome negativity**: Plant: ginseng. **Protect against negativity**: Metal: copper, steel. **Recognize negativity**: Stone: charoite. **Reduce negativity**: Stone: jade; Plant: ylang-ylang. **Release negativity**: Plant: copal, lovage. **Return negativity**: Charm: mirror; Stone: red jasper; Metal: brass; Plant: galangal.

Nervousness

(See also: Calm, Confidence)

Gemini

Color: light red; Animal: rabbit.

Nervous energy: *to end*: Plant: burdock. **Nervous system**: (See: The Body). **Nervous tension**: (See: Tension).

To: **ease nervousness**: Color: green, pink; Stone: alexandrite, amazonite, amber, amethyst, aquamarine, sapphire, turquoise; Metal: silver; Plant: angelica, bergamot, catnip, chamomile, lavender, lemon balm, nasturtium, parsley, pennyroyal, black pepper, rosemary, rue, sage, clary sage, sandalwood, tangerine (oil), valerian, vervain, vetiver, woodruff, ylang-ylang. **end nervousness**: Plant: garlic.

Neutrality

Color: beige, blue, brown, gray, indigo; Number: 3; Metal: pewter.

To **neutralize**: Color: gray, indigo, silver; Charm: celery salt. **an empowered object**: Stone: salt. **enemies**: Animal: dragon; Plant: dragon's blood. **evil**: Color: gray. **magick**: Color: indigo; *fairy magick*: Charm: turn your coat or cloak inside out. **negativity**: Stone: sard; Plant: sage; *negative energy*: Color: gray; *negative influences*: Color: gray, silver; Metal: silver. **smells**: Plant: parsley, summer savory. **venom**: God: Aker.

Nightmares

(See also: Dreams, Sleep)

Moon

Number: 9; Color: white; Plant: yew; Goddess: Albina, Hecate, Lamia, the Mare, the Morrigan, the Triple Goddess, the White Goddess; Evocation: Adekato, the alp, Leucippe (white mare), the lilitu, Queen Mab, the mahrt, Satan.

Dream messages via nightmares: God: Pan.

To: **avert nightmares**: Color: black; Charm: dream catcher, dream pillow; Metal: steel; Stone: carnelian (worn while sleeping), chalcedony (under the pillow), chrysoprase, citrine (worn while sleeping), diamond (worn while sleeping), Goddess rocks (tied to the bed), jet (worn while sleeping), lepidolite, onyx (worn while sleeping), ruby (worn while sleeping), blue topaz (worn while sleeping); Oil (from any of the following plants, to anoint dream pillows); Plant: aniseed (near bed, or in dream pillow), betony (as incense or under the pillow), cedar (rubbed on bed pillow), chamomile, daffodil (rubbed on bed pillow), eucalyptus (in a dream pillow), hyacinth (in a dream pillow), mullein (in a dream pillow), narcissus (under pillow), peony seeds, rosemary (under the pillow), rue, St. John's Wort (hung in the bedroom or taken as a supplement), thyme (in a dream pillow), lemon verbena, vervain (near the bed or in a dream pillow). **cause nightmares**: Potion: alcoholic beverages; Plant: clary sage. **clear nightmares**: Tool: besom; Plant (as incense): cedar, rosemary. **interpret nightmares**: Goddess: Geshtinanna. **prevent nocturnal attack or visitation**: (See: Aggression). **protect against nightmares**: Charm: castoreum; dream catcher; stop up the bedroom keyhole, turn the toes of your shoes to the door, and get into bed backwards; use a long piece of your hair to bind a poppet that represents the 'mare'; bottle your urine, leave it in the sun for three days, then throw it backwards into running water; put garlic under the pillow, hang a besom on the bedroom door, and use it to sweep away nightmares in the morning; musk; Stone: amethyst, carnelian, chalcedony, yellow chrysolite set in gold, chrysoprase, citrine, diamond, emerald, garnet, Goddess rocks, jasper, jet, lepidolite, peridot, ruby, blue topaz; Plant: aniseed, heavenly bamboo, betony (under pillow), catnip (conserve of young tips), cedar, chamomile, cinquefoil, daffodil, dill (hung in room), eucalyptus, hyacinth, lavender, mistletoe (hung over the doorway), mullein (in a dream pillow), peony root (worn on a necklace), peony seeds, periwinkle root, rosemary, rue (leaf or seed), thyme, St. John's Wort, lemon verbena, vervain, woodruff; Goddess: Niorun; *against recurring nightmares*: Color: blue; Stone: sapphire, blue tourmaline, blue topaz. **recover from a nightmare**: Charm: chamomile syrup, conserve of young catnip tips; Stone: amethyst, onyx, topaz; Potion: chamomile tea; Plant: heavenly bamboo (dream told to plant); *to help children recover from nightmares*: Charm: chamomile syrup. **transform a nightmare into good fortune**: Evocation: the Baku.

Nourishment

(See also: Agriculture, Hunting, Nurture)

Earth/Water

Color: green, yellow; Animal: cow; Stone: malachite, clear quartz crystal; Potion: milk; Plant: grain, linden, all food plants; Goddess: Aima, Allat, Ceres, Chicomecoatl, Demeter, Edusa, Gaia, Hathor, Ida, Isis, the Mother, Neith, Potina, Pushan (Nourisher), Sakambhari, Sekhmet (The One Who Creates all Nourishment), Uke-Mochi (She

Who Possesses Food); God: Alator (He Who Nourishes The People), Cinteotl, Hapy, Tsao-Chün (Lord of the Hearth), Varuna; Evocation: devas.

Proper nourishment: Plant: tiger lily. **Nourishing dew**: Water/Dawn/Summer; God: Baal. **Nourishing rain**: Water/Spring; Animal: frog, jaguar; God: Baal. **Nourishing warmth:** Plant: linden.

To nourish: **babies**: (See: Babies). **children**: Goddess: Edusa. **heart**: Color: red. **plants**: Sun/Water/Earth; *grain crops*: Goddess: Nissaba.

Nurture
Full Moon/Earth

Tool: chalice; Color: pink; Stone: jade, selenite; Plant: holy thorn, lady's slipper, orchid, spirea, tarragon, willow; Goddess: Isis, the Mother, Nokomis, Yemaya.

Self-nurture: Animal: bear; Stone: kunzite; Plant: cinquefoil, fireweed, mariposa lily, mullein. **Ability to nurture**: Plant: wild rose. **Nurturing relationships**: Earth; Color: pink.

To nurture: **animals**: *flock animals, herd animals*: Goddess: Pales. **passion**: Goddess: Urvasi. **skin**: Plant: carrot seed (also check with a health food store or vitamin shop about non magickal ways to use this). **the young**: Goddess: Demeter (Nurturer of Youth).

Chapter 15

Oaths

Earth

Goddess: Fides, Gaia, the Gavadiae, Mamitu, Vör; God: Hazzi, Horcus, Jupiter, Mithras, Ullr, Varuna, Veles, Volos.

Binding oath: God: Horcus. **Legal oaths**: Goddess: Zemlya; God: Njord. **Marriage oaths/vows**: Goddess: Vör; God: Hymen. **Devotion to an oath**: Goddess: Gaia, Pietas.

To: enforce oaths: Goddess: the Gavadiae, Isis, Vör, Zemlya; God: Horon, Zeus. **keep magickal vows**: Goddess: Aine. **punish oath breakers**: Goddess: Vör; God: Horon. **swear an oath**: Charm: tetractys; Goddess: Ala, Allat, Gaia, the Gavadiae, Vör, Zemlya; God: Apollo, Brianan, Jupiter, Njord, Perun, Tsui' Goab, Ullr, Varuna, Veles, Yahweh. **witness an oath**: Sun; Goddess: Iris; God: Helios.

Obsession

(See also: Fascination)

Scorpio

Color: violet; Goddess: Lilith; God: Apep; Evocation: elementals.

Obsessive behavior: *to ease*: Plant: hyacinth, nasturtium. **Obsessive love**: Goddess: Ishtar; Evocation: Dala Kumara, Merlin. **Freedom from obsessions**: Plant: frankincense.

To: end obsession: Tool: besom; Plant: broom, frankincense, fumitory. **reduce obsession**: Stone: bloodstone with rose quartz or quartz crystal; Plant: hyacinth, green rose.

Obstacles

(See also: Barriers, Blockages)

Saturn

Animal: caterpillar; Plant: restharrow; God: Ganesha (Lord of Obstacles), Vigneswara (Lord of All Obstacles).

Difficult obstacles: *to overcome*: Goddess: Oshun. **Future obstacles**: *to overcome*: God: Horus. **Large obstacles**: *to overcome*: God: Aganyu. **Personal obstacles**: *to overcome*: Goddess: Ekajata. **Unforeseen/unexpected obstacles**: God: Loki; Evocation: Satan.

To: avert obstacles: God: Ganesha. **break up obstructions**: Plant: yucca. **clear obstacles**: Animal: elephant; Stone: azurite, barite, malachite, moonstone, gray moonstone, opal, peridot; Plant: chicory, High John, vetiver; Goddess: Aditi, Kwan Yin; God: Ganesha (Remover of Obstacles), Ogun; *obstacles to goals*: Stone: malachite; God: Ogun; *obstacles to victory or success*: Plant: High John. **find a way around obstacles**: God: Enki. **open obstructions**: Plant: costmary. **overcome obstacles**: Waning Moon/South/Aries/Capricorn; Charm: bulldozer, Glory Water, machete, white elephant with six tusks; Animal: dragon, elephant; Stone: bloodstone; Oil: palmarosa; Plant: chicory, High

John, orris root, mistletoe; Goddess: Aditi, Ishtar, Oshun, Ritona, White Tara; God: Ganesha, Horus, Ogun; Evocation: Michael. **persevere despite obstacles**: Animal: ant; Plant: broom. **shatter obstacles**: Goddess: Kali.

Omens

(See also: Messages, Oracles, Prophecy)

Animal: blackbird, falcon, magpie, owl, raven; Goddess: Carmenta, Cihuacoatl, Danaë; God: Hermes, Phorcis, Zeus.

Death omens: Animal: deathwatch beetle, cricket (if found in the house); Goddess: Cyhiraeth (when she screams); *in a family*: Animal: owl (perched on the castle); Plant: parsley (transplanted); Evocation: Bean Sidhe; *of someone close*; Animal: snail (found indoors); *of a warrior*: Goddess: the Morrigan (seen before battle). **Evil omens**: *to remove threats from*: Goddess: Ereshkigal. **Family omens**: *negative omens for a family*: Evocation: Domovoi; *omen of bad times for a family*: Plant: ivy; *positive omens for a family*: Plant: ivy (growing on the walls of the house). **Happy omen**: Stone: jade; *of good news*: Animal: caterpillar, painted turtle. **Negative omen**: Animal: albatross, raven; Number: 2; Stone: emerald (if the stone falls from its setting), spilled salt; Incense: smoke not rising straight up; smoke flowing to the left; Plant: basil, laurel (if withered), mistletoe (if fallen from a tree); God: Kashku; *to avert*: Goddess: Lelwanis; *of disappointment*: Animal: sow (if it crosses your path); *of an enemy*: Animal: toad. **Positive omen**: Animal: pairs of fish, fly (in your drink), ladybug, robin, toad (crossing or near your path); Stone: alexandrite; Incense: smoke rising straight up; smoke flowing to the right; Plant: grain (if sprouted), holly; God: Hatsenas (Bird of Good Omen); *for harvests*: (See: Harvest); *at Yule*: Charm: sweetmeats of honey, figs and dates; Plant: branches of laurel and palm; *of a gift or surprise*: Animal: caterpillar.

Omen of the arrival of a letter with important news: Animal: moths (flying around you).

Opening

(See also: Activation, Awakening, Beginning, Openness)

Rising Sun/Dawn

Tool: wand; Charm: key; Stone: wulfenite; Plant: anemone, borage, butcher's broom, costmary, dandelion, grass of Parnassus, lemongrass, lotus, madder; Goddess: Alphito, Dilbah (She Who Opens the Heavens in Her Supremacy), Pandora, Zorya Utrenyaya; God: Anansi, Cernunnos (Opener of the Gates of Life and Death), Coyote, Geb, Kothar-wa-Khasis (The Opener), Ptah (The Opener), Ra (Opener of the Disk).

Inner opening: Metal: silver; Stone: green gypsum, moldovite, blue or green tourmaline. **Physical opening**: Plant: ripe mulberry. **Psychic opening**: Stone: amethyst, ametrine, iolite, kyanite, lapis lazuli, quartz crystal; Plant: clary sage, geranium, lemon, lotus, nutmeg. **Spiritual opening**: Plant: St. John's Wort.

To open: awareness: Plant: lady's slipper, lotus, reindeer moss. **blockages**: (See: Blockages). **the brain**: Plant: juniper, laurel. **breathing**: Air; Plant: eucalyptus, laurel. **a business or other enterprise**: (See: Business). **chakras**: (See: Chakras). **circulatory system**: Plant: mugwort. **communication**: (See: Communication). **consciousness**: (See: Consciousness). **creativity**: Stone: green tourmaline. **doors/gateways:** Stone: bloodstone, peridot; Plant: sesame; Goddess: Jana, Zorya Utrenyaya; God: Aker, Cernunnos (Opener of the Gates of Life and Death), Chango, the Horned God,

Legba; *to Earth*: God: Aker; *to the spirit world/realm*: (See: Spirits). **eyes**: Goddess: Shakti, Yhi. **flowers**: Goddess: Isis. **the heart**: (See: The Body). **the heavens**: Goddess: Dilbah. **intuition**: Stone: amethyst, sapphire. **joy**: Stone: kunzite; Plant: tangerine. **the liver**: (See: The Body). **locks**: Plant: chicory, lotus, martagon lily with mistletoe. **the heart**: (See: The Body). **the mouth**: (See: The Body). **a narrow mind**: Plant: silverweed. **obstructions**: Plant: costmary. **a pathway**: Stone: amethyst, clear quartz crystal; Plant: clary sage; God: Wepwawet. **possibilities**: Stone: alexandrite. **psychic gifts**: (See: Psychism). **self-expression**: Stone: blue lace agate. **sinuses**: Plant: eucalyptus, horseradish. **the spleen**: (See: The Body). **third eye**: (See: Chakras). **tombs**: Goddess: Vanth. **urinary system/tract**: Plant: couch grass, mugwort. **a way**: Color: orange; Stone: fluorite; Plant: clary sage; Goddess: Neith (Opener of the Ways), Sekhmet (Opener of Ways), Sheela-na-gig; God: Janus, Legba, Maximon, Wepwawet (Opener of the Ways); *for healing/psychological healing*: (See: Healing); *for seekers*: God: Legba; *for settling a disagreement*: God: Banaded; *to the Underworld*: God: Aker. **what is shut**: Goddess: Alphito, Cardea. **a window**: God: Kothar-wa-Khasis. **the womb/uterus**: (See: The Body). **yourself**: Stone: apatite; Plant: clary sage.

To open to: **angels/angelic messages**: Plant: angelica. **beauty**: Stone: blue apatite. **cosmic energy**: Plant: yarrow; Stone: moldovite. **fairies/fairyland/fairy magick, gifts, blessings**: Plant: forget-me-not, primrose. **the influence of stones**: Stone: fluorite (worn). **light**: (See: Light). **love**: (See: Love). **lunar energy/magick**: Moon; Plant: queen of the night. **other people**: Plant: anemone, holy thorn, toadflax. **peace**: Stone blue apatite. **pleasure**: Plant: mesquite. **the influence of stones**: Stone: fluorite. **yourself**: Plant: horsetail.

To: **keep your options open**: Goddess: Ceile De. **learn not to leave yourself open to treachery**: God: Baldur, Osiris. **shut what is open**: Goddess: Alphito, Cardea. **smash open**: Charm: hammer, thunderbolt; God: Thor.

Openness

Air

Color: clear, pink; Animal: emu; Stone: citrine; Plant: fig, honesty, wild rose, snowdrop, sycamore; Goddess: Empanada, Fama, Sheela-na-gig.

Open mind: (See: The Mind). **Open sky**: Goddess: Diana. **Open space**: God: Chaos. **Open sores**: Goddess: Alatonan. **Spiritual openness**: Plant: dandelion, lotus. **Openness in magick**: God: Thoth. **Openness to yourself and others**: Color: pink; Stone: kunzite, rose quartz, pink tourmaline.

Opportunity

Animal: butterfly, goldfish, jaguar; Number: 5; Stone: aventurine; Plant: laurel, palm, peony, sandalwood, sunflower, ylang-ylang; Goddess: Ami Seshet, Inanna, Isis. God: Legba.

Educational opportunities: Animal: elephant, owl. **New opportunities**: Animal: catbird, painted turtle; *to be alert to*: Animal: frog, jackal. **Unexpected opportunities**: Animal: cobra.

Opportunities to: achieve/succeed: Animal: carp. **learn life lessons**: God: Legba. **travel**: Plant: lucky hand root.

To: **make the most of an opportunity**: Animal: spider. **take advantage of an opportunity**: Animal: gibbon, moray eel, shark, toad, all ambush predators; Plant: African violet; Goddess: Ami-seshet (She Whose Opportunity Escapeth Her Not). **wait for an opportunity**: Goddess: the Pleiades.

Optimism

(See also: Positiveness)

Jupiter/New Moon/Aries

Color: orange, yellow; Number: 5, 7; Animal: camel, hummingbird; Metal: copper; Stone: beryl, chalcedony, garnet, hematite, rose quartz; Plant: bergamot, citronella, dahlia, heather, hyacinth, lily of the valley, orchid, persimmon, raspberry, snowdrop.

Pessimism

(See also: Negativity)

Color: black; Number: 7; Stone: jet, onyx.

To overcome pessimism: Plant: broom, orchid.

Oracles

(See also: Messages, Omens, Prophecy)

Method: I Ching; Charm: lightning; Animal: bull, cormorant, crow, dove, black dove, hare, hoopoe, raven, snake, wren; Stone: sapphire; Plant: acacia, beech, dandelion, laurel, oak, black poplar, reed, rowan; Goddess: Adraste, Akonadi, Carmenta, Diana Nemorensis, Dione, Egeria, Februata, Freya, Gaia, Hecate, Ida, Inanna, Ishtar (Source of Oracles of Prophecy), Namagiri, Nina, Oshun, Persephone, Qadesh, Shaushka, Sulis, Themis (Queen of the Oracles), Al-Uzzah, Vortumna, Zemlya; God: Amon, Apollo, Aristaeus, Baal Karmelos, Bel, Bran, Dionysus, Endouellicus, Enki, Faunus, Glaucus, Hoenir, Hubal, Jupiter, Mimir, Nebo, Nereus, Odin, Orunmila, Perun, Phoebus Apollo, Phorcys, Poseidon, Proteus, Ryangombe, Shamash, Ta'lab, Thor, Thoth, Tir, Tsuki-Yomi (considered a goddess in some traditions), Wamala, Zeus; Evocation: Bannik, Evander, Ladon, nereids, oceanids, Pharoneus, Pythia, Sibyl, Tiresias.

Dream oracles: Method: dream incubation; Goddess: Ishtar, Pasiphaë; *related to healing*: God: Asclepius. **Oracles of war and battle**: Goddess: Inanna. **Oracular communication**: God: Apollo. **Oracular inspiration**: Plant: laurel. **Oracular knowledge**: (See: Knowledge). **Oracular power**: (See: Power). **Oracular wisdom**: Goddess: Scathach.

To: learn to respect oracles: Goddess: Atalanta. **protect oracles**: Plant: alder. **read oracles**: Goddess: Delphine; Evocation: Pythia, Pythoness, Sibyl.

Order

Number: 1; Plant: laurel; Goddess: Aditi, Eunomia, Fura Chogue, Ishtar, Ma'at, Themis; God: Anu (Fountainhead of Order), Byelobog, Marduk, Ogoun Fer, Osiris, Ptah, Vishnu.

Cosmic order: Goddess: Durga, Estsanatlehi, Ma'at, Uma; God: Saturn, Shiva Nataraja, Thor, Thoth, Varuna; *to restore*: Goddess: Durga. **Cosmic law and order**: God: Varuna. **Divine order**: Stone: meteorite, moldovite; Goddess: Ma'at, Sekhmet (Divine Order); God: Varuna. **Domestic order**: Goddess: Hestia; *to put your house in order*: Goddess: Kikimora. **Law and order**: God: Enki, Igalima, Marduk (Guardian of Law and Order), Shamash, Thor, Tyr, Varuna; *cosmic law and order*: God: Varuna. **Martial order**: Goddess: Disciplina. **Proper order**: Goddess: the Kothirat, Themis. **Social order**: Saturn; Goddess: Aditi, Ala, Ma'at, Themis; God: Ptah. **world order**: Goddess: Kali; God: Enki.

Order of Nature: (See: Nature).

To: create order from chaos: God: Lugal-dim-erankia, Ptah, Spiniensis, Väinämöinen. **put your house in order**: Goddess: Kikimora. **sustain order**: God: Baal.

Disorder

(See: Chaos, Diseases/Disorders)

Orderliness

Taurus

Orderly change: God: Vertumnus (The Changer); *of the seasons*: God: the Dagda, Vertumnus. **Orderly conduct:** Goddess: Disciplina. **Orderly flow of time:** Goddess: Sesheta. **Orderly movement of people at their normal tasks:** God: Janus.

Organization

Crescent Moon/Air/Capricorn/Taurus

Color: blue, brown, orange; Number: 4, 8; Stone: bloodstone, red or leopardskin jasper, lepidolite; Plant: laurel; Goddess: Sesheta; God: Ea, Enki, Khnum, Muluku, Orunmila, Rama.

To organize your life: Charm: paua shell.

Otherworld

(See also: Afterlife, Death, Reincarnation, Underworld)

North

Color: gray, red; Charm: dew, gray feather; Animal: bull, crane, dog, pig; Plant: apple, hazel, willow; Goddess: Artemis, Badb, Cerridwen, Cliodna, Queen of Elphame, Rhiannon; God: Ailill, Arawn (King of Annwn, Lord of the Otherworld), Bran the Blessed, Cernunnos (Keeper of the Gates of the Otherworld), Esus, Gwynn ap Nudd (King of the Underworld), Hu, Mabon, Mac Da Tho, Math ap Mathonwy, Melwas, Mider, Pan, Pwyll, Tethra; Evocation: Breasal (High King of Earth and the Otherworld), fairies.

Guide to the Otherworld: Animal: cat, horse, gray horse, white stag; Goddess: Nair, Sheela-na-gig; God: Ogma. **Help in the Otherworld:** Animal: otter. **Messages from the Otherworld:** Animal: bat, white stag; God: Cromm Cruaich. **Messages to the Otherworld:** Charm: ice water; God: Cromm Cruaich. **Movement in the Otherworld:** Animal: lizard, horse; Evocation: Barinthus. **Transition to the Otherworld:** Animal: crane; Plant: apple; Goddess: Aoife, Cally Berry, Corra; God: Sucellos. **Wisdom of the Otherworld:** Plant: hazel nut.

Overcoming

(See also: Battle, Ending, Victory)

Goddess: Anahita, Venus Victrix (Conqueror); God: Baal, Quetzalcoatl.

To overcome: a false accusation: Goddess: Auge. **addictions:** (See: Diseases/ Disorders). **adversity:** (See: Adversity). **anxiety:** Goddess: Green Tara. **bad childhood:** Plant: valerian; Goddess: Atalanta. **bad habits:** (See: Habits). **base instincts:** God: Mithras. **brawling:** Stone: diamond. **confusion:** (See: Confusion). **creative blocks:** Moon; Plant: licorice. **danger:** (See: Danger). **darkness:** (See: Darkness). **death:** (See: Death). **debates:** Stone: green beryl. **demons:** (See: Demons). **desire for revenge:** Plant: canna lily. **a disability:** God: Llud. **ego:** Goddess: Durga, Kali. **emotional pain:** Goddess: Isis. **enchantment:** (See: Enchantment). **enemies:** (See: Enemies). **escapism:** Plant: birch. **evil:** Plant: mandrake root; God: Enki, Ra. **fatigue:** (See: Fatigue). **fear/s:** (See: Fear). **frigidity:** Plant: chicory. **greed:** Color: green, dark green; Plant: silverweed. **grief:** (See: Grief). **a handicap:** God: Llud. **hard feelings:** Plant: canna lily. **hexes:** (See: Hexes). **hopelessness:** Goddess: Nephthys. **ignorance:** Goddess: Kali; God: Shiva. **illusions:** (See: Illusion). **impotence:** Stone: lodestone; Plant: deerstongue, mandrake, oat. **indecision:**

(See: Decision/s). **inertia/lethargy**: Color: red; Plant: apple, cayenne, peppermint; God: Shiva. **infertility**: (See: Fertility). **invasion/invaders**: Animal: red dragon. **jealousy**: (See: Jealousy). **lawsuits**: Plant: celandine. **laziness**: (See: Laziness). **limitations**: (See: Limitation). **lust**: (See: Lust). **magick**: (See: Magick). **mental fatigue**: (See: Fatigue). **the need to control others**: Plant: bistort. **negativity**: (See: Negativity). **obstacles**: (See: Obstacles). **opponents/opposition**: Plant: High John, vervain, white oak bark; God: Sin. **pain**: Plant: mandavilla. **pessimism**: Plant: broom, orchid. **problems**: (See: Problems). **prudishness**: Goddess: Aeval. **self-consciousness**: Potion: elderberry wine; Plant: elder. **self-pity**: Plant: rowan. **sibling rivalry**: God: Poseidon. **sorrow**: (See: Sorrow). **speech problems**: (See: Speech). **spells**: (See: Spells). **sterility**: Plant: mandrake. **stress**: (See: Stress). **suffering**: Goddess: Tara. **victim consciousness**: Plant: everlasting. **water**: Earth. **wrongful punishment**: Goddess: Rhiannon.

Chapter 16

Pain

(See also: The Body, Diseases/Disorders, Illness)

[Note: All correspondences are given here as charms. Some of the plants are poisonous, and nothing is meant to be taken ingested. Magick is a supplement to medical care, not a substitute for it. In most cases, incense should not be burned near someone who is sick.]

Plant: fir; Goddess: Angerona, Devi; God: Thanatos; Evocation: Algos.

Abdominal pain: Plant: asoka tree, avens, Indian arnica, St. John's Wort, wild yam.

Aches and pains: *to avert*: Plant: horse chestnut; *to relieve*: Stone: Herkimer diamond; Potion: elderberry wine; Plant: asparagus, white bryony, catsfoot, chamomile, horse chestnut, elder, eucalyptus, fennel, ginger, ivy, mallow, rosemary, sunflower (in bath), lemon verbena, willow bark, yarrow.

Back pain: *to relieve* : Charm(*first patch test on skin)*: rubbing alcohol (in bath, or for massage), witch hazel (for massage); Stone: calcite, fluorite, lodestone, obsidian; Plant: alkanet, chamomile, horse chestnut, clove, American ginseng, lavender, logwood, marjoram, morning glory, spikenard, spindle tree, yarrow.

Bladder pain: *to relieve*: Plant: couch grass, dropwort, watermelon.

Bone pain: *to relieve*: Plant: heliotrope leaves, pennyroyal, rosemary.

Cancer pain: *to relieve*: Plant: opium poppy.

Chest pain: Plant: myrtle.

Earache: Charm: garlic vinegar; Stone: amber; Plant: basil, chamomile, fennel, feverfew, garlic, henbane, hops, cobweb houseleek, laurel, logwood, marjoram, horse mint, mullein, black mustard, narcissus, oregano, parsley, plantain, pulsatilla, tansy, willow.

Emotional pain: *to heal*: Stone: chrysocolla, jade, lapis lazuli, rose quartz; Plant: balm of Gilead, rosemary; *to overcome*: Goddess: Isis; *to release*: Stone: blue topaz; Plant: balsam, myrrh, sweetgale; *to relieve*: Stone: agate, morganite, rose quartz; Plant: coriander, lemon balm (See also: Grief, Heartbreak, Sorrow, and so on.).

Eye pain: *to protect against*: Plant: mugwort (especially a garland woven at Midsummer), rose of Provence.

Growing pains: *to relieve*: Plant: celery.

Headache: Jupiter; *to protect against*: Color: green; Stone: green aventurine, emerald, jet, peridot, green tourmaline, turquoise; Plant: mugwort, vervain; *to relieve*: Color: green; Stone: amber (held to forehead), amethyst, hematite, lodestone, moonstone (rubbed on temples), quartz crystal, rose quartz; Plant: aloe, wood anemone, angelica, Indian arnica, basil, beech nut, betony, blood root, bryony, castor bean, catnip, chamomile, cinnamon, damiana, endive, eucalyptus, feverfew, gotu kola, honeysuckle, lavender, lemon, mint, mulberry, passionflower, pennyroyal, peppermint, queen of the night, rosemary, rue, sage, spearmint, spikenard, star thistle, thyme, valerian, vervain, violet, walnut, willow, yucca. *migraines*: Mars; *to prevent*: Stone: green jasper; Plant: feverfew; *to relieve*: Charm: ivy juice (on forehead); Stone: amethyst, aventurine, iolite, rose quartz; Plant: basil, cannabis, cowslip (compress), darnel, feverfew, ginger, grapefruit (oil), laurel (on forehead), lavender, linden, masterwort, mint, mistletoe, peach, peppermint, rosemary, sage, snowdrop, thyme, valerian, lemon verbena, violet; *tension headache*: *to relieve*: Plant: rue.

Joint pain: Capricorn; *to relieve*: Charm: garlic vinegar (compress); Metal: copper; Stone: azurite, chrysoprase, hematite; Plant: asparagus, autumn crocus, birch, white bryony, garlic (paste), gentian, hemlock, henbane leaves (hot compress), horse chestnut (held), Indian arnica, lavender, great mullein, mustard (plaster), rue, silverweed, valerian, vetiver, wintergreen, wolfsbane, yarrow.

Karmic pain: *to relieve*: Stone: morganite.

Kidney pain: *to relieve*: Plant: cranberry, fennel.

Labor pain: *to relieve*: Plant: dittany, hyacinth, raspberry or strawberry leaves (clutched), trailing pearlwort (placed under the knee); Goddess: Heqet, Rauni, Taweret (See also: Childbirth).

Menstrual pain/cramps: Moon; *to relieve*: Color: yellow; Stone: jet, moonstone; Plant: angelica, aniseed, cayenne, chamomile, chamomile with ginger, blue cohosh, evening primrose, feverfew, holy thistle, hops, lavender, lemon balm, madonna lily, marigold, mugwort, pennyroyal, peppermint, pine, sage, clary sage, St. John's Wort, valerian.

Muscle pain: *to relieve*: Charm: witch hazel (for massage); Plant: balsam, birch, camellia, cayenne, chamomile, cinnamon, comfrey, daisy, eucalyptus, juniper, laurel (in bath), mallow, marigold (in bath), mugwort, oregano (in bath), pellitory of the wall, peppermint, pine, green pine cone (in bath), rosemary, sage, thyme, valerian (compress), willow bark, yarrow.

Neck pain: *to relieve*: Plant: daisy with mugwort (ointment).

Neurological pain: *to relieve*: Plant: feverfew, garlic, St. John's Wort.

Psychosomatic pain: *to relieve*: Stone: amethyst, tigereye.

Radiating pain: *to relieve*: Plant: barberry.

Sciatic pain: *to relieve*: Plant: autumn crocus, marjoram, compress of bruised rue, silverweed.

Sinus pain: Plant: black mustard.

Painful skin conditions: *to relieve*: Plant: eucalyptus.

Stomach pain/ache: *to protect against*: Plant: basil, rhubarb root, black spruce; *to relieve*: Plant: allspice, anise, basil, catnip, chamomile, gentian, ginger, gotu kola, melilot (poultice), peppermint, plum, sorghum, sorrel.

Teething pain: *to prevent*: Plant: daffodil; *to relieve*: Plant: marshmallow root (chewed).

Toothache: *to relieve*: Charm: garlic vinegar, wood from an oak that has been struck by lightning; Animal: mole; Stone: aquamarine, jet, malachite, clear quartz crystal; Plant: aspen, caraway, cayenne, chamomile, cinnamon, clove, coriander, darnel, date palm, garlic, ivy, marshmallow, mint, orris, pellitory root (held between the teeth), poplar, pulsatilla, tarragon, tarragon root (held between the teeth), willow, wormwood, yarrow; Goddess: Aibheaeg.

Freedom from pain: Goddess: Kwan Yin. **Painless death**: Goddess: Artemis. **Pain management**: Goddess: Achelois; God: Achelous. **Painful memories**: Plant: Adonis. **Pain and pleasure**: (See: Pleasure).

To: draw pain from the body: Stone: lodestone. **overcome pain**: Plant: mandavilla; Goddess: Isis. **protect against pain**: Plant: melilot. **release pain**: Stone: blue apatite, rose quartz; Plant: balm of Gilead, balsam, fireweed, forget-me-not, rowan; *the cause of pain*: Stone: azurite; *a painful experience*: Plant: fireweed. **relieve pain**: Color: indigo; Charm: compress with garlic vinegar or cool ginger tea; Metal: copper; Stone: amber, amethyst, aquamarine (worn or rubbed on body), blue aventurine (held), green calcite, red coral, hematite, jade, jasper, lapis lazuli, lodestone, moonstone, quartz crystal, ruby, sandstone, sapphire (rubbed on body), blue topaz; Plant: aloe vera, basil, belladonna, cannabis, cassia, greater celandine, chamomile, cinnamon, cowslip, datura, day lily petals, garlic (paste or compress), ginger (in bath), ginseng, hellebore, henbane, laurel, lavender, wild lettuce, lotus, mandrake, horsement, tropical myrtle, black nightshade, opium poppy, pulsatilla, rue, St. John's Wort, silverweed (applied topically), valerian, vervain, willow bark, wormwood; Goddess: Achelois (She Who Drives Away Pain), Kwan Yin, Panacea, Tara; God: Achelous (He Who Drives Away Pain), Hypnos, Somnus.

Partnership

(See also: Business, Marriage, Relationships, Union)

Venus/Friday

Color: pink; Number: 2; Animal: sea anemone, clam, wolf, all symbiotic creatures; Plant: all symbiotic plants.

New partnership: New Moon; God: Janus.

To strengthen a partnership: Plant: cardamom pod, stephanotis.

Passage

(See also: Birth, Death, Life, Movement, Transition)

Sun/Moon

Animal: bluebird; Goddess: Sheela-na-gig; God: Janus, Vagitanus.

Safe passage: Plant: cyclamen; Goddess: Alemona, Diana of the Crossways, Ellaman, Jizo, the Suleviae; God: Kamapua, the Michi-No-Kami, Tiberinus, Vagitanus, Wepwawet (Opener of the Way); *to the afterlife/Summerlands*: Plant: cypress; Goddess: Hathor; God: Februus (See also: Afterlife, transition to); *for children*: Goddess: Adeona; *for good people*: Goddess: Chalchihuitlcue; *over water*: Goddess: Anahita, Axona, Nehalennia; *through crocodile infested waters*: Goddess: Isis. **Secure passage**: God: Aker.

Life passages: Tool: pentacle; Charm: knot, spiral; Animal: guinea pig; Stone: garnet; Plant: cyclamen, cypress. **Rites of passage**: *to Crone*: Goddess: Tlachtga; *for girls/young women*: Goddess: Aphrodite, Athene, Ix Chel (See also: Initiation). **Passage of**: **the seasons**: God: the Dagda. **time**: Moon; God: Shiva, Sin. **To protect passages/passageways**: God: Janus.

Passion

(See also: Desire, Lust, Sex)

Mars/Venus/Fire/East/West/Aries/Taurus/Leo/Scorpio

Color: pink, red, rose, white, wine; Charm: ambergris, musk, nag champa; Number: 4, 5, 7; Animal: tiger, turtledove, wryneck; Stone: garnet, moonstone, rhodochrosite, ruby; Potion: passionflower juice; Plant: apricot, banana, bistort, caraway, cardamom, cayenne, cinnamon, coriander, cuckoo pint, cyclamen, dittany, dragon's blood, galangal, ginger, ginseng, heather, hibiscus, lavender, lemongrass, licorice, melon, mint, mustard seed, myrtle, passionflower, patchouli, pikaki, plumeria, rose, rosemary, saffron, sesame, turmeric, vanilla, vetiver, violet; Goddess: Anath, Aphrodite, Ashtart, Atalanta, Bast, Dahud, Druantia, Freya, Frigg, Ishtar (Lady of Passion and Desire), Isis, Lalita, Oreithita (She Who Rages Upon the Mountains), Parvati, Pasch, Psyche, Qedrin, Rati, Sapas, Sjofn, Unk, Urvasi, Venus; God: Anteros, Apollo, Cupid, Eros, Himeros, Krishna, Nergal, Pan, Shango, Shiva, Yarillo (The Uncontrolled); Evocation: Hanael, satyrs.

Animal passion: Animal: cat; Goddess: Bast. **Angry passion**: Mars; Letter: Z; God: Ares, Mars. **Cosmic passion**: God: Eros. **Creative passion**: God: Eros. **Emotional passion**: Mars/Aries; Color: red, purple. **Female passion**: Goddess: Arani. **Fleeting passion**: God: Eros. **Insane passion**: God: Dionysus; Evocation: Phaedra; *to treat*: Stone: topaz; Plant: Adam and Eve root (withered, in potion). **Male passion**: Plant: cardamom, cinnamon. **Physical/sensual passion**: Venus/Earth/Taurus; Color: red; Plant: lovage root, patchouli, rose; Goddess: Anath, Aphrodite, Dahud, Freya, Frigg, Ishtar (Lady of Passion and Desire), Lilith, Parvati, Rati, Semiramis, Venus; God: Nergal, Shiva. **Secret passion**: Animal: scorpion. **Sexual passion**: Charm: musk, nag champa; Letter: U; Plant: lovage root, myrtle, patchouli; Goddess: Anath, Aphrodite, Bast, Rati; God: Cupid; Evocation: satyrs; *to intensify*: Plant: damiana. **Strong passion**: Color: deep red; Plant: vetiver.

Passionate creativity: Waxing Moon. **Passionate ecstasy**: Goddess: Anath. **Passionate love**: (See: Love). **Passionate relationships**: Color: red. **Passionate zeal**: God: Zelus. **Crimes of passion**: Goddess: Inanna. **Passion as an end in itself**: Number: 7.

To: become passionate: Plant: licorice root (chewed). **cool passion**: West; Stone: onyx. **cure/heal passion**: West; Charm: candied borage flowers, lavender flower water; Plant: bistort, cinquefoil, hart's tongue, lavender; Goddess: Branwen. **excite passion**: Fire/East; Charm: ambergris, musk; Stone: bloodstone, garnet, ruby, red tourmaline; Plant: apricot, coriander seed, ginger, lavender, mandrake, melon; Goddess: Aphrodite, Urvasi; God: Eros, Paiva. **increase passion**: East; Plant: apricot; Goddess: Hathor. **make a lover more passionate**: Charm: ambergris; Plant: apricot, cardamom. **protect against passion**: Stone: amethyst; *against acts of passion*: Plant: white heather. **subdue/restrain passion**: West; Stone: amethyst, spinel ruby; Plant: love-lies-bleeding.

Past Life Work

(See also: Karma, Rebirth, Reincarnation)

Tool: crystal ball, scrying bowl, dish or mirror; Method: dream work, fire-gazing (especially with Fire of Azrael, kindled of cedar, juniper and sandalwood), hypnosis, meditation; Color: indigo; Animal: crane, crow, grosbeak; Stone: apatite, aquamarine, carnelian, fossils, garnet, kyanite, moonstone, opal, quartz crystal, selenite, tigereye; Plant: eucalyptus, silver fir, frankincense, lavender, lemon balm, lilac, myrrh, petrified wood, rosemary, sandalwood, thyme, yew; Goddess: Arianrhod, Cerridwen, Corchen, Frigg, Ituana, Macha, Postvorta, Sheela-na-gig, Urd; God: Llasar Llaesgyfnewid, Tuan.

Past life information: *to access*: Stone: carnelian; *to integrate*: Animal: crow; Plant: poppy, spruce; Goddess: Aditi, Frigg, the Norns, Prakriti; God: Proteus; Evocation:

Taliesin. **Past life issues**: *to work on*: Plant: canna lily, glory bush, yew; Goddess: Urd. **Past life memories**: (See: Memories).

To: **become free of a negative past life**: Plant: African tulip tree. **connect a past life with the current one**: Animal: spider. **examine how past lives impact the current one**: Animal: earthworm. **forget past lives**: Goddess: Meng-Po-Niang. **heal negativity from past lives**: Stone: hawk's eye. **protect against emotional upset from past life work**: Plant: eucalyptus. **see past lives**: Plant: sandalwood.

Pathworking

Sun

Goddess: Aoife.

Magickal path: Color: indigo. **Unique path**: Plant: walnut. **Endurance upon one's path**: Color: indigo; Animal: elk.

To: **clear a path**: Charm: machete; Animal: elephant; Stone: turquoise; Goddess: Oya; God: Ganesha, Ochosi, Ogun. **create your own path**: Animal: porcupine. **progress along your path**: Animal: goose; Stone: moonstone. **travel both male and female paths**: Animal: bass; God: Obatala; Evocation: Tiresias.

Patience

Earth/Water/Taurus

Number: 2, 4, 8; Color: blue, light blue, gray, rose; Animal: albatross, carp, cicada, elephant, hyena, jaguar, owl, pig, python, spider, all predators; Stone: amber, chrysoprase, garnet, morganite, onyx, rhodonite; Plant: adonis, azalea, chamomile, dock, impatiens, iris, pheasant's eye, stonecrop, sycamore; Goddess: Astraea, Prithivi, Rhiannon, Sesheta, Sigyn; Evocation: Arthur, Merlin, Morvran, Penelope.

Patient revenge: Animal: alligator, cat, crocodile. **Patient strength**: Plant: rose.

Patience in: **healing**: Animal: crane. **working toward goals**: Stone: garnet. **to become more patient**: Plant: chamomile, impatiens.

Impatience

Aries

Color: red; Number: 2; Plant: balsam, impatiens; Goddess: Ishtar.

Peace

(See also: Calm, Harmony, Tranquility)

Saturn/Moon/Earth/Water/Earth/Saturday

Color: blue, light blue, sky blue, gray, green, pink, rose, turquoise, violet, white; Charm: white, gray or blue feather; Number: 1, 7, 42; Animal: cat, dove, golden eagle, goldfish, kingfisher; Metal: silver; Stone: blue lace agate, black or red agate, amber, amethyst, Apache tear, blue apatite, aquamarine, aventurine, blue aventurine, calcite, carnelian, celestite, chalcedony, chrysocolla, diamond, blue diamond, Herkimer diamond, garnet, yellow jacinth, jade, jasper, kunzite, lapis lazuli, lepidolite, malachite, obsidian, white pearl, blue quartz, rose quartz, rhodochrosite, rhodonite, sapphire, sardonyx, sodalite, blue topaz, tourmaline, blue or brown tourmaline, zircon; Oil: neroli; Plant: almond, aloe, amber, angelica, apple blossom, ash, basil, bayberry bark, bergamot, bougainvillea, cassia, catnip, cedar, chamomile, cinnamon, cinquefoil, cherry blossom, cinnamon, coconut, coltsfoot, coriander seed, cypress, dragon's blood, dulse, eryngo, fir, gardenia, hawthorn, heather, hibiscus, High John, honeysuckle, jasmine, laurel, lavender, lemongrass, lilac, lily of the valley, loosestrife, lotus, magnolia, marjoram, meadowsweet, mistletoe, morning glory, motherwort, myrrh, myrtle, narcissus, olive (branch or oil), orange, palm, passionflower, patchouli, peace lily, pennyroyal, pine, primrose, rose, red rose, wild rose, rosemary, sage, scullcap, St. John's Wort, sunflower, tuberose, valerian, vanilla, lemon verbena, vervain, vetiver, violet, blue violet, winter bark (branches), witch grass, ylang-ylang; Goddess: Aerten, Allat, Amaterasu, Athena, Concordia, Eirene, Ertha, Harmonia, the Horai, Isis, Mary (Queen of Peace), Minerva, the Mother, Nerthus, Pax, Sekhmet, Shekinah, Sif, Turan; God: Baldur, Byelobog, Belun, Dazhbog, Eros, Freyr, Forseti, Frodi, Jesus (Prince of Peace), Kuan-Ti, Mannan, Mertus, Obatala (King of Peace, Bringer of Peace and Harmony), Mannan, Thoth, Volos, Vonir; Pantheon: the Vanir; Evocation: Deganiwada, Hiawatha.

Emotional peace: Plant: amber. **Inner peace**: Color: blue, indigo, light blue, dark blue; Stone: amethyst, anhydrite, aventurine, calcite, celestite, chrysoprase, apple coral, Herkimer diamond, jasper, leopardskin jasper, kunzite, lepidolite, rose quartz; Plant: white African violet, chamomile, coconut, lavender, myrrh, primrose, rosemary, sage.

Peacefulness: Animal: gorilla. **Peaceful communication**: (See: Communication). **Peaceful death**: Plant: wormwood. **Peaceful dreams**: (See: Dreams). **Peaceful family**: Plant: rose; Goddess: Chantico. **Peaceful feelings**: Stone: chalcedony; Plant: horsetail. **Peaceful home**: (See: The Home). **Peaceful intent**: Color: white; Plant: mistletoe. **Peaceful journey to the afterlife**: Plant: marjoram. **Peaceful life**: Stone: garnet, ruby. **Peaceful marriage**: Plant: violet (oil, in bath); Goddess: Lada. **Peaceful nature**: Stone: chalcedony; Goddess: Fair Maiden. **Peace offerings**: Tool: cauldron; Goddess: Anath. **Peaceful protection**: God: Mars Ollodius; Goddess: Sekhmet. **Peaceful relationships**: Stone: aquamarine; Plant: lavender. **Peaceful sleep**: (See: Sleep). **Peaceful workplace**: Charm: rosewater; Plant: rose.

Peace in death: Plant: cypress. **Peace of mind**: (See: Mind). **Peace and quiet**: (See: Quiet). **Peace between lovers**: Stone: sapphire.

To: attract peace: Color: deep blue; Stone: garnet, rose quartz; Plant: cinquefoil, lavender, rose, vervain. **encourage peace**: Color: aqua, blue, light blue, pink, red, white; Stone: red agate, aquamarine, carnelian, chalcedony, lapis lazuli, rhodochrosite, rhodonite, rose quartz, sapphire, blue topaz. **end a quarrel peacefully**: (See: Quarrels). **exist peacefully with natural forces**: Plant: reindeer moss. **express yourself peacefully**: Stone: blue lace agate. **find peace**: Plant: bergamot, enchanter's nightshade. **give someone peace**: Plant: cypress. **live in peace**: Charm: rainbow; Stone: garnet, white pearl; Goddess: Yhi; God: Coyote. **make peace**: Plant: olive branch, moneywort, verbena, vervain; God: Ba Neb Tetet, Nisien; Evocation: Deganiwada (Peacemaker), Hiawatha. **offer peace**: Color: white, blue; Stone: chrysocolla, blue opal, blue quartz, sapphire, blue tourmaline. **open to peace**: Stone blue apatite. **pacify**: Stone: sapphire.

People

(See also: Babies, Children, Family, Friends, Gossip, Lovers, Magicians, Marriage, Men, Relationships, The Social, Thieves, Travelers, Warriors, Witches, Women, Workers)

Annoying people: *to banish*: Plant: eucalyptus. **Blind people**: *to defend*: Goddess: Anahita. **Business people**: *bakers*: Goddess: Vesta; *businesswomen*: Goddess: Hathor, Hera; *curio dealers*: God: Kuan Kung; *distillers*: Goddess: Mary; *florists*: Goddess: Coatlicue; *mechanics*: God: Vulcan; Evocation: Hercules; *merchants*: God: Ek Chua, Ganesha, Inari, Manannan (Patron of Merchants), Mercury, Xaman Ek (Guide of Merchants); Evocation: Herakles Malkart; *to bless merchants/shopkeepers*: God: Mercury; *restauranteurs*: Goddess: Mary; *traders*: God: Mithras; Evocation: Hercules; *sea traders*: Goddess: Nehalennia; *tradespeople*: Goddess: Minerva. **Common people**: God: Thor. **Deaf people**: *to defend*: Goddess: Anahita. **Envious people**: (See: Envy). **Evil people**: *to avert*: Plant: arnica; *to protect against*: Plant: juniper; *against evil men*: Stone: ruby. **Good people**: *safe passage for*: Goddess: Chalchihuitlcue; *to protect*: Goddess: Sekhmet. **Harmful people**: *to avert from the family*: Plant: marjoram. **Helpful people**: Color: yellow. **Jealous people**: *to protect against*: Charm: van van; Plant: garlic, plantain. **Lost people**: *to locate*: Stone: ametrine, charoite, hematite, kyanite, moldovite, phenacite, tigereye; Goddess: Hannahannas. **Negative people**: *to avert*: Color: black; Stone: jet, obsidian, onyx; *to avert their negative intentions*: Plant: cedar, High John; *to banish*: Color: black; Charm: brimstone; *to clear from your life*: Color: black; Stone: aventurine, jade, petrified wood, clear quartz crystal; Plant: cedar, High John, lilac, patchouli, lemon verbena; *to deal with*: Stone: crystals (washed or purified after contact with negative people), smoky quartz; Plant: onion (peeled and placed in water to absorb their vibes, then discarded). **New people**: *to be selective in accepting*: Animal: wolf. **Other people**: *to deal with problems of*: Stone: apatite; *to open to*: Plant: anemone, holy thorn, toadflax; *to protect against the negativity of*: Stone: black tourmaline; Plant: thyme; *to protect against the negative thoughts of*: Plant: pennyroyal. **Powerful people**: *to gain favors from*: (See: Favors). **Working class people**: *to help*: Goddess: Acca Larentia. **Young people**: *good fortune for*: Plant: clover.

Guests: *to protect against*: God: Zeus. **Neighbors**: *good neighbor*: Color: green; *to deal with problem neighbors*: Charm: Four Thieves Vinegar (sprinkled on doorstep or poured along property line). **Troublemakers**: *to avert*: Plant: boldo leaf; *to disrupt*: Plant: black mustard seed; *to avert troublesome in-laws*: Plant: oregano. **Unwanted people**: *to avert*: Charm: Go Away Powder; *to banish*: Charm: Go Away Powder, Hot Foot Powder. **Visitors**: *to avert*: Charm: Go Away Powder; Plant: coriander, mugwort, all spiny, prickly or thorny plants.

The people's justice: Goddess: Laodice. **Orderly movement of people at their normal tasks**: God: Janus.

To: attract people: Plant: azalea, vanilla. **control people**: Plant: angelica, cubeb, iron weed, licorice root; *man to control a woman*: Plant: woodruff; *woman to control a man*: Plant: orris root. **dream of people**: God: Icelus. **not let people get too close to you**: Animal: lone wolf. **prevent people from speaking badly about you**: (See: Speech). **protect people**: (See: Amulets, Protection, Talismans). **render people who enter the home powerless to harm its residents**: Plant: High John (floor wash). **stop people**: Color: indigo; *from looking at or into things*: Plant: dragon's blood. **unite people**: Goddess: Aditi.

Perception

(See also: Awareness, Senses, Vision)

Sun/Day/Sunday

Color: purple, clear; Charm: Eye of Horus; Animal: eagle; Stone: labradorite, tigereye; Plant: alder, birch, eyebright, clary sage, orchid; Goddess: Tara; God: Kothar-wa-Khasis, Lugalucca, Sia.

Clear perception: Plant: alder, thoroughwort. **Emotional perception**: Water; Animal: starfish. **Exaggerated perception**: Plant: cannabis. **Higher perception**: Animal: basilisk. **Sensory perception**: God: Sif.

Spiritual perception: Animal: eagle, fox, macaw. **Subtle perceptions**: *to trust*: Animal: black widow spider. **Visual perception**: Goddess: Indrani; *to improve*: Plant: clary sage, eyebright.

To: change perception: Tool: censer; Charm: aromatherapy; Stone: meteorite, moldovite; Oil: arecoline; Plant: heather; *of time*: Plant: betel nut. **increase perception**: Animal: scarlet macaw; Stone: aquamarine, aventurine, green aventurine, garnet, clear quartz crystal; Plant: cannabis, eyebright, peppermint, yarrow. **stimulate perception**: Stone: emerald. **trust your perception**: Animal: cricket, scarlet macaw.

To perceive: **auras**: Animal: copperhead. **cold**: Plant: peppermint. **the cosmic**: (See: The Cosmic). **the future**: Animal: raven (See also: Foresight, Prophecy). **life**: Plant: cassandra. **others**: Plant: eyebright. **truth**: (See: Truth).

Perseverance
(See also: Persistence)

Capricorn/Taurus

Animal: aardvark, badger, boar, hyena, mussel, pig, polar bear, rat, sea turtle, wolf, wombat; Plant: broom, canary grass, couch grass, ground laurel, southernwood, yucca; Goddess: Cessair, Isis, Medb.

To persevere: **despite obstacles**: Animal: ant; Plant: broom. **To achieve goals**: Stone: garnet. **in your studies**: Animal: carp.

Persistence
(See also: Perseverance)

Animal: dingo, gazelle, nighthawk, salmon, shark; Stone: garnet; Goddess: Isis, Parvati.

Strength through persistence: Saturn.

Persuasion

Color: gold, yellow; Charm: honey, orange flower water; Animal: frog; Oil: palmarosa; Plant: mallow, orange blossom, slippery elm; Goddess: Gaia, Geshtinanna, Peitho, Suada, Uzumi; God: Baile of the Honeyed Speech, Coyote, Ea, Loki, Xipe Totec.

Gentle persuasion: Color: yellow; Number: 2. **Persuasive speech**: Goddess: Oya, Peitho; God: Baile.

The Physical
(See also: The Body, Senses, Sexuality)

Earth

Plant: beech

Physical action: (See: Action). **Physical affection**: Animal: cat, owl. **Physical balance**: (See: Balance). **Physical beauty**: (See: Beauty). **Physical body**: *to align*: Plant: ginger; *to align the aura with*: Stone: brown tourmaline; *to align the etheric body with*: Plant: amber; *to boost*: Plant: rosemary; *to have in the afterlife*: Charm: tet amulet. **Physical calm**: (See: Calm). **Physical change**: Plant: juniper berry. **Physical cleansing**: Plant: cedar. **Physical clearing**: Tool: besom; Plant mullein. **Physical danger**: (See: Danger). **Physical deformities**: Goddess: Akhushtal. **Physical disability**: *to have a good career despite*: God: Vulcan. **Physical endurance**: Plant: ginseng. **Physical energy**: (See: Energy). **Physical fatigue**: (See: Fatigue). **Physical fitness**: Goddess: Atalanta, Luaths Lurgann; *exercise*: God: Hermes Trismegistus. **Physical force**: Goddess: Macha. **Physical grounding**: Stone: obsidian; Plant: all trees. **Physical growth**: (See: Growth). **Physical harm**: *to protect against*: Plant: heliotrope; Goddess: Kwan Yin. **Physical healing**: (See: Healing). **Physical health**: (See: Health). **Physical immortality**: Goddess: Ameretat. **Physical**

joy: (See: Joy). **Physical love**: (See: Love). **Physical manifestation**: Earth; Number: 4. **Physical matter**: Goddess: Adamu. **Physical movement**: (See: Movement). **Physical needs**: *to meet*: Color: orange; Animal: cow. **Physical opening**: Plant: ripe mulberry. **Physical passion**: (See: Passion). **Physical plane**: *to link with higher planes*: Stone: opal; *to manifest spiritual qualities on*: Stone: turquoise. **Physical pleasure**: (See: Pleasure). **Physical power**: (See: Power). **Physical processes that sustain life**: Goddess: Carna. **Physical protection**: Stone: jasper, pyrite, ruby. **Physical reality**: (See: Reality) **Physical realm**: Earth; *spiritual penetration of*: Stone: meteorite; **Physical regeneration**: Stone: red calcite. **Physical relaxation**: (See: Relaxation). **Physical release**: (See: Releasing). **Physical revenge**: Plant: holly. **Physical self**: *to know*: Plant: patchouli. **Physical sensation**: Goddess: Sentia. **Physical skill/s**: Mars; Goddess: Emer; God: Lugh. **Physical spirituality**: (See: Spirituality). **Physical strength**: (See: Strength). **Physical tension**: (See: Tension). **Physical transformation**: (See: Transformation). **Physical vitality**: (See: Vitality). **The physical world**: Color: red; Number: 4; God: Poseidon.

🅿leasure

(See also: Ecstasy, Enjoyment, Satisfaction)

Venus/Friday

Color: orange; Number: 3; Animal: cat; Stone: amber, tigereye; Plant: amber, eglantine, valerian; Goddess: Athyr, Bast, Lakshmi, Tlazolteotl, Venus (Queen of Pleasure), Voluptas, Xochiquetzal; God: Frey.

Carnal pleasure: Charm: whip (hidden under a woman's bed); Goddess: Mamsapriya (Fond of Flesh). **Dangerous pleasures**: Plant: tuberose. **Delicate pleasures**: Plant: sweet pea. **Domestic pleasures**:

God: Bes. **Healthy pleasure**: Plant: marigold. **Human pleasures**: God: Bes. **Physical pleasure**: Goddess: Bast, Dahud, Fand, Liban, Sentia, Xochiquetzal, Venus, Volupta. **Sensual pleasure**: Goddess: Freya. **Sexual pleasure**: Goddess: Anath, Bast, Chuang-Mu, Hathor, the Kotharot, Maeve, Pertunda, Qadesh, Venus, Xochiquetzal; God: Coyote, Krishna, Shiva; *to increase*: Charm: musk; Plant: cannabis, damiana; *to learn how to please a woman sexually*: God: Krishna. **Simple pleasures**: Plant: silverweed. **Social pleasures**: Goddess: The Graces.

Ability to enjoy: Plant: daisy. **Pain and pleasure**: Plant: wild rose; Goddess: Aphrodite, Chantico. **Pleasures of memory**: Plant: periwinkle.

To: enjoy life: (See: Life). **enjoy your body**: (See: The Body). **open to pleasure**: Plant: mesquite. **teach pleasure**: Goddess: Oshun.

Displeasure

Plant: wormwood.

🅿lenty

(See: Abundance)

🅿olarity

(See also: Duality, Yang, Yin)

Number: 2; Animal: spider; Stone: tourmaline; Plant: holly; God: Shiva.

To balance polarity: Metal: copper.

🅿olitics

Jupiter/Tuesday/Capricorn

Goddess: Athena; God: Ammon, Ogun.

Political adroitness: Goddess: Isis. **Political alliances**: God: Jupiter. **Political stability**: God: Viracocha. **Political victory**: Jupiter; God: Jupiter, Jupiter Victor.

Popularity

Color: blue; Number: 3; Plant: angelica, grapevine, gum cistus, gravel root, lavender; God: Baldur.

Popular favor: Plant: rock rose.

To: attract popularity: Color: green; Plant: angelica, passionflower. **increase popularity:** Tool: pentacle; Plant: carnation, cinnamon, mandrake.

Positiveness

(See also: Goodness, Negativity, Optimism)

Sun

Number: 1; Animal: camel, dragon; Stone: amethyst, red jasper; Plant: orchid, clary sage, vervain; God: Byelobog.

Positive changes: (See: Changes). **Positive energy:** (See: Energy). **Positive reality:** Plant: willow. **Positive thinking:** Plant: moss agate. **Positive/negative balance:** (See: Balance). **Positive omen:** (See: Omens). **Positive vibrations:** (See: Vibrations).

To: be reincarnated in a positive situation: God: T'ai-Yüeh Ta-ti. **change a negative into a positive:** Color: blue, green, orange, red, purple, white, yellow; Stone: unakite. **create something positive from a negative situation:** Goddess: Atanea. **transform negative thought forms into positive ones:** Color: black; Stone: jet, obsidian, onyx. **transform negative emotions into positive ones:** Plant: juniper berry.

Possibility

(See also: Possibilities, Potential)

Number: 0.

To: make the impossible possible: Animal: dragon, firefly. **make it possible to create art:** God: Esizkur. **understand possible consequences of spells:** Goddess: Skuld.

Possibilities

(See also: Opportunity, Possibility)

Animal: caterpillar; God: Ea.

To: open possibilities: Stone: alexandrite. **realize possibilities:** God: Marduk.

Potential

(See also: Possibility)

Uranus/Water

Color: silver, white; Number: 1; Metal: mercury; Plant: acorn; Goddess: the Maiden; God: Ea.

Creative potential: Plant: milk thistle. **Human potential:** *to develop*: Goddess: Brigid. **Infinite potential:** Goddess: Nut. **Psychic potential:** *to develop*: Plant: galangal.

Potential danger: Goddess: Scylla; God: Silvanus, Yam. **Potential life:** Charm: scarab; Plant: all seeds; God: Kephera; *after death*: God: Osiris. **Potential of a new day:** *to activate*: Sun/Dawn; Goddess: Isis.

To: activate potential: Goddess: Tara. **manifest potential:** Earth/North; Goddess: Urd; **release one's potential:** Plant: enchanter's nightshade. **realize potential:** Stone: jade, rhodonite.

Poverty

(See also: Abundance, Adversity, Money, Prosperity)

Animal: rattlesnake, wolf; Plant: barley, basil, clematis, trailing evergreens, sycamore fig; Goddess: Nuzhda, Penia; God: Bimbogami.

To: end poverty: Color: green, white; Plant: alfalfa, clove, orange. **escape poverty:** Goddess: Acca Larentia. **inflict poverty:** Goddess: Fortuna; God: Sud. **overcome fear of poverty:** Plant: harebell. **protect against poverty:** Plant: alfalfa, carob.

Power

(See also: Authority, Empowerment, Energy, Strength)

Sun/Jupiter/Full Moon/Fire/North/Scorpio

Tool: pentacle, sword; Color: black, gold, orange, purple, royal purple, red, silver, violet, yellow; Charm: boar bristles, musk, torc, unicorn horn; Number: 8; Animal: bear, boar, bull, cougar, dragon, eagle, elephant, elk, horse, jaguar, komodo dragon, lion, panther, peacock, python, black widow spider, tiger; Metal: gold; Stone: moss agate, bloodstone, carnelian, coral, garnet, hematite, jacinth, lodestone, malachite, obsidian, opal, phantom, clear quartz crystal, rutilated quartz, ruby, sapphire; Plant: allspice, carnation, cayenne, cinnamon, cinquefoil, club moss, devil's shoestring, dragon's blood, ebony, frankincense, galangal, garden cress, gentian, ginger, ginseng, hemlock, High John, holly, honeysuckle, horehound, iris, laurel, loosestrife, lotus, mandrake, oak, palm, roots, rosemary, rowan, St. John's Wort, thyme, verbena; Goddess: the Afliae, Anath, Bia, Brigid, Dynë, Durga, Habondia, Hecate, Hecate Brimo, Inanna, Ishtar, Isis, Kadlu, Kali, Minerva, Modron, Oya, Parvati, Prithivi, Rauni, Sekhmet (The Powerful One), Spider Woman, Whaitiri, Yhi, Zemlya; God: Baal (Most Powerful), Camulos (powerful), Chango Macho, Cratos, Ganesha, Gonaqade't, Indra, Jumala, Jupiter, Kartikeya, Legba, Marduk, Odin, Ra, Shango, Taranis, Teutates, Tezcatlipoca, Thor, Zeus.

Absolute power: God: Odin. **Activating power**: Goddess: Shakti. **Astral power**: Stone: meteorite. **Community power**: Animal: ant, bee, goose. **Concentrated power**: Stone: geode. **Cosmic power**: Color: yellow, gold; God: Mithras. **Creative power**: Sun; Color: orange, yellow; Charm: scarab;

Animal: scarab beetle; Stone: amber, orange tourmaline; God: Anhur, Legba, Ra, Shiva Nataraja, Tane, Vishvakarman; *of Nature*: Goddess: Hathor; *female creative power*: Goddess: Juno; *male creative power*: Evocation: Genius. **Crone power**: Waning Moon; Goddess: Hecate. **Dark powers**: Plant: bat nut; Goddess: Kali; God: Set; Evocation: Pryderi, Satan (Prince of Darkness); *to battle*: God: Bishamon, Heimdall, Odin, Ra, Väinämöinen. **Destructive power**: God: Horned God; *of the ocean*: Water; Goddess: Scylla; God: Aegir; *of the Sun*: Sun; Goddess: Sekhmet; God: Menthu. **Distant power**: Goddess: Hecate. **Divine power**: Stone: rose quartz; Goddess: Durga; God: Great Spirit, Shiva, Tirwara-Atius; *god-power*: Sun; Metal: gold; Plant: cedar, oak; *goddess-power*: Moon; Metal: silver; Plant: elder, hazel, willow. **Double power**: Color: two colors used together; Stone: optical calcite, orange zircon set in gold. **Dragon power**: Animal: dragon; Goddess: Ishtar. **Elemental power**: Animal: dragon; Stone: fossils, staurolite; *Air power*: Air; Animal: eagle, falcon, hawk; Metal: aluminum; God: Aeolus, Gwydion, Llma, Lucifero (See also: wind power). *Earth power*: Earth; Animal: bull, cow, jaguar; Stone: all; Plant: all; Goddess: Demeter, Dewi Shri, Maka; God: Geush Urvan, Tekkeitsertok; *to release*: Charm: plow. *Fire power*: Fire; Animal: lion; Goddess: Brigid; *generative power of Fire*: God: Svarog; *power of Fire to free Earth from Water*: Plant: alder; *power over Fire*: Goddess: Brigit. *Water power*: Water; Charm: places where two bodies of water meet; Plant: ash; Goddess: Brigid; God: Enki, Viracocha (See also: sea power); *to activate the fertilizing power of water*: Goddess: Isis Ankhet; *numinous power resident in rivers, marshes, and rain*: God: Enki; *power of water to fertilize the Earth*: Goddess: Isis Ankhet; God: Enki, Osiris;

healing power of warm water: Goddess: Sulis; *of thermal springs*: Goddess: the Comedovae, Siron; God: Borvo; *power over Water*: Plant: sycamore; Goddess: Brigit. **Erotic power**: Fungus: fly agaric. **Established power**: Number: 12. **Executive power**: God: Baal. **Female power**: Moon; Color: red, silver, yellow; Animal: lioness, otter; Plant: angelica, gardenia; Goddess: Ambika, Arianrhod, Ceile De, Chuginadak, Emer, Fuji, Ishtar, Isis, Kali, Maeve, Masaya, Morgan le Fay, Oya, Sheela-na-gig, Yemaya; Evocation: Derdekea; *to understand*: Goddess: Condwiramur; *female sexual power*: Goddess: Qadesh; *to activate personal female power*: Goddess: Natilus. **Fertilizing power**: Goddess: Yemaya; God: Amun, Freyr, Min, Osiris; Evocation: nature spirits; *of sunlight*: (See: Light). **Foreign powers**: *to battle*: God: Teshub. **Generative power**: God: Amun, Geb, Shang Di. **Goddess power**: Color: silver; Goddess: Kali. **Government power**: God: Mars. **Healing power**: Sun/Moon/Waxing Moon/Scorpio; Animal: buffalo, macaw, owl; Stone: bloodstone, coral, hematite, jasper; Plant: elder, eucalyptus, ginger, mistletoe, herbs picked in August; Goddess: Aibheaog, Argante, Boannan, Coventina, Habetrot, Oenone; God: Borvo; *of drug-induced sleep*: (See: Sleep); *of laughter*: Goddess: Baubo, Chie, Uzume; *of Nature*: Goddess: Coatlicue; *of sound*: Animal: canary; *of water*: Goddess: Sulis; *inner healing power*: Plant: self-heal; *power that heals the world*: Goddess: Medicina Mundi; *to activate the healing powers of Coventina*: Charm: toss a shiny coin into a well. **Hidden power**: night Sunday Moon; Stone: geode; Goddess: Amauntet; God: Amun, Genius. **High power**: Color: magenta; God: Ard Greimme. **Higher power(s)**: Color: white; Plant: redwood; *to send messages to*: Animal: cougar. **Inner power**: Method: tantra;

Number: 8; Animal: dragon; Plant: bistort, dragon's blood, elder flower, High John, holly leaf or berry, laurel, lotus, mistletoe, oak leaf, rosemary, lemon verbena, vervain; *to manifest*: Stone: carnelian, citrine; *to protect*: Animal: cat; *inner healing power*: Plant: self-heal. **Intellectual power**: Color: purple; *to increase*: Plant: rosemary. **Intervening power**: Goddess: Isis. **Kundalini power**: Goddess: Kali, Kunkalini, Sekhmet, the Snake Mother. **Lunatic power**: Moon; Fungus: fly agaric. **Lunar power**: Moon/Full Moon/Monday; Plant: willow; Goddess: Hecate, Leucothea. **Magickal power/s**: Moon/Full Moon/Mercury/Fire/Scorpio; Charm: fetish; Color: purple, violet; Animal: boar, snake, thunderbird; Charm: menstrual blood, witch's burr; Metal: alloys, gold; Stone: bloodstone, citrine, clear quartz crystal, malachite, opal, ruby, sapphire; Plant: allspice, ash, carnation, centaury, cinnamon, clove, club moss, dragon's blood, elder, eye of Satan, fern seed, finger grass, ginger, Job's tears, laurel, logwood, mandrake, patchouli, rosemary, rowan (especially when found growing atop another plant: neither on Earth nor in heaven), tangerine (oil), vanilla, wall fern (especially if growing on oak trees), plants found growing on tamarind trees; Goddess: Frigg, Hecate, Isis, Pelé; God: Abraxas, the Dagda, Wakonda (Great Thunder Spirit); *of linen*: Goddess: Renenutet (Lady of the Robes); *of menstrual blood*: Charm: tet amulet; *to increase*: Color: crimson, purple, red; Stone: bloodstone, black opal, clear quartz crystal; Plant: carnation, cinnamon, dragon's blood, eye of Satan; *of amulets*: Plant: lemongrass; *of love amulets*: Plant: coltsfoot; *of charms*: Plant: High John, lemon verbena; *of a love charm*: Charm: van van; Plant: coltsfoot, meadowsweet; *of magickal herbs*: Plant: dragon's blood, High John; *of magical incense*: Plant: cinnamon, dragon's blood, frankincense, mastic, myrrh, sandalwood, tangerine (oil); *of healing incense*: Plant: mesquite; *of magickal oils*: Method: astrology; Charm: ambergris; Plant: bergamot, High John; *of a spell*: (See: Spells); *for disorders of magickal powers*: Plant: tamarisk; *to restore magickal powers*: Animal: bandicoot; *to transmit magickal power*: Method: breath work; Plant: galangal; *to learn to use magickal power wisely*: Goddess: Arianrhod. **Male power**: Stone: sapphire; God: Ogun, Somhlth; *to maintain*: Stone: sapphire; *male sexual power*: God: Amun, Maximón, Min, Pan; *to defy the male power structure*: Goddess: Eve, Lilith; Evocation: Jezebel, Vashti. **Manifest power**: Plant: red rose. **Martial power**: Goddess: Astarte, Athene; God: Mars, Ogun. **Mathematical power**: Number: 4; **Matriarchal power**: Metal: bronze. **Maximum power**: Full Moon. **Mental power(s)**: Color: yellow; Charm: van van; Metal: gold; Stone: amber, amethyst, aventurine, citrine, emerald, fluorite, Herkimer diamond, mother of pearl, selenite, sphene, topaz; Plant: caraway, celery, clove, clover, cypress, eyebright, grapevine, guarana seed, horehound, lemon, lily of the valley, mace, mustard, brown mustard seed, peppermint, periwinkle, rosemary, rue, spearmint, summer savory, tangerine (oil), tea tree, vanilla, blue vervain, walnut, wisteria; Goddess: Ceibhfhionn; God: Gwydion, Thoth; Evocation: Finvarra; *to increase/strengthen*: Stone: amethyst, aventurine, fluorite, rhodochrosite; Plant: benzoin, flax, laurel, mustard, spearmint. **Mobile power**: Charm: wheel; Animal; bull, horse. **Mystic power/s**: Plant: mandrake; Goddess: Kali. **Natural power**: Sun. **Nuclear power**: Pluto. **Occult power**: Mercury/Water; Color: dark blue; Charm: leftward spiraled conch shell; Stone: moonstone, peridot; Plant: mandrake, patchouli, woodrose; Goddess: the Khahdoma (Occult Ladies). **Oracular power**: Charm: lightning; God: Faunus; Evocation: Nereids. **Personal power**: your Zodiac sign; Color: red, yellow; Animal: cougar, horse; Stone: orange aventurine, carnelian, malachite, unakite; Plant: acacia (as incense), acorn, apple; Animal: horse; *to increase*: Metal: gold; Stone: peach aventurine, malachite; *to manifest*: Stone: citrine; *to not give away*: Goddess: Yemaya; *to release*: Color: red. **Physical power**: Animal: elephant, gorilla; Evocation: Cratus, Herakles/Hercules; *to activate*: Stone: chalcedony; *to maintain*: Stone: sapphire (See also: Strength); **Productive power**: *of Nature*: Goddess: Ashtoreth, Astarte; *of water*: Plant: lotus, myrtle. **Prophetic power**: Goddess: Cerridwen. **Protective power**: Animal: bear; Stone: meteorite; Plant: birch, fern, nettle. **Psychic power(s)**: Moon/Scorpio; Color: indigo, purple, yellow; Number: 7; Stone: amethyst, aquamarine, labradorite; Potion: absinthe (dangerous, not recommended); Plant: acacia, basil, bistort, borage, buchu, celery seed, cinnamon, citron, clove, coltsfoot, damiana, dandelion, deerstongue, ebony, elecampane, eyebright, flax, frankincense, galangal, gotu kola, grapefruit, grass, guarana seed, gum arabic, hibiscus, High John, hollyhock, honeysuckle, hyssop, kelp, laurel, lavender, lemongrass, mace, marigold, mallow, mastic, mugwort, nutmeg, peppermint, rose, rose hip, rosemary, rowan, saffron, sage, sandalwood, star anise, stillengia, sumbul, thyme, tuberose, wormwood, yarrow, yerba santa; Goddess: Amaunet, Bia; *to develop*: Color: silver; Animal: lynx; Stone: ametrine, azurite, howlite, lapis lazuli, opal, blue or yellow topaz; Plant: acacoa, aniseed, galangal, lemongrass, magnolia, tuberose, wormwood; Goddess: the Mother; *to increase*: Color: sky blue, purple, white; Stone: azurite, turquoise; Plant: acacia, camphor, cinnamon, eucalyptus, galangal, honeysuckle, juniper, laurel, lilac, lotus, mace, mastic, nutmeg, star anise, uva ursa, yarrow, yerba santa, celery seed with orris root; *to protect*: Plant: lotus, queen of the night; *to renew*: Plant: lovage (in bath); *to strengthen*: Stone: moonstone, azurite; Plant: camphor, cedar, cinnamon, elecampane (as incense), lotus, mugwort; *to use wisely*: Stone: labradorite. **Quiet power**: Color: black; Stone: black moss agate, coal, jet, onyx, black opal; Plant: camphor. **Raw power**: Animal: dragon. **Reproductive power**: *of herds*: God: Donn. **Royal power**: God: Baal; *pharaonic power*: Charm: crook and flail; God: Andjety, Sobek. **Sacred power**: Animal: jaguar. **Sea power**: Neptune; Stone: pearl; Plant: ash; Goddess: Isis; God: Llyr, Mannan, Neptune, Poseidon, Shoney, Triton; *power to calm or agitate waves*: God: Triton. **Secret power/s**: Stone: geode; Plant: ivy; Goddess: Hecate. **Serpent power**: Charm: shed skin or tooth of a snake; Animal: cobra, dragon, viper, all snakes; Stone: serpentary; Plant: bistort; Goddess: Coatlicue, Malinalxochi, the Snake Mother; God: Raja Naga, Tlaloc. **Sexual power**: Venus/Scorpio; Animal: goose, ram; God: Amun, Pan. **Shamanic power**: Animal: raven; Stone: fossil, clear quartz crystal, turquoise; Evocation: ancestral spirits. **Silent power**: Plant: laurel. **Solar power**: Sun/Sunday/Leo; Color: gold, yellow; Metal: gold; Animal: lion; Goddess: Sekhmet; God: Anhuret, Ra, Viracocha; *fertilizing power of sunlight*: God: Amun, Mithras, Ra; *power of the Sun to ripen grain*: Goddess: Bast. **Spiritual power**: Neptune; Color: purple, violet, white; Animal: condor, dragon, eagle; Plant: fennel, frankincense, iris, lotus; Goddess: Kupala, Lakshmi; *to strengthen*: Plant: laurel. **Steadfast power**: Earth; God: Zeus. **Supernatural powers**: Charm: crown of amaranth flowers; Animal: dragonfly, polar bear. **Supreme power**: God: Marduk. **Triple power**: Moon; Goddess:

Mariamne. **Unshakable power**: God: Poseidon. **Vocal power**: Goddess: Ambika. **Willpower**: (See: Will). **Wind power**: Air; *to understand*: Animal: cardinal, eagle.

Power animals: (See: Animals). **Powerful deeds**: Color: red. **Powerful emotions**: God: Eros. **Powerful experiences**: Stone: chrysocolla. **Powerful vibrations**: Color: magenta; Oil: palmarosa; Plant: rose geranium. **Ability to communicate powerfully**: Goddess: Oya. God: Bran.

Abuse of power: Number: 8; *to avoid*: Animal: horse. **Urge for power**: Sun. **Words of power**: Goddess: Isis; *power through the word that goes forth and comes into being*: Number: 3.

Power above: God: Wakonda (Great Thunder Spirit).

Power against enemies: God: Anhuret.

Power in: battle: Animal: eagle; Fungus: fly agaric. **darkness**: (See: Darkness).

Power of: belief: Animal: cricket. **breath**: Air; Goddess: Durga, Isis; God: the Dagda. **becoming fluid**: Metal: mercury (toxic, not recommended). **commitment**: Animal: elephant. **concentration**: Color: brown, violet, white, yellow. **cooperation**: Animal: beaver. **destiny**: Goddess: the Audrinehae (The Friendly Powers of Destiny). **divination**: (See: Divination). **enlightenment**: Goddess: Sapas. **giving**: Animal: deer, hart. **goodness**: God: Mithras. **healing**: Waxing Moon; Goddess: Hecate. **hearing**: God: Ve. **herbs**: *to strengthen*: Metal: gold (worn while harvesting); Evocation: Osain. **imagination**: Color: white. **intelligence**: Goddess: Sussistanako. **knowledge**: Tool: candle, grimoire; Method: candle magick. **life**: Animal: pair of birds. **life and death**: Goddess: Rhiannon; God: Reshep. **light/illumination**: (See: Light). **love**: (See: Love). **mobility**: Animal: bull, horse. **money**: Stone: tigereye. **movement**: (See:

Movement). **Nature:** Animal: dragon. **necessity:** Goddess: Ananke. **retribution:** Animal: cobra; God: Ra. **sexuality:** Goddess: Qadesh. **sight:** Plant: queen of the night; God: Ve. **silence:** North/Winter. **speech/voice:** (See: Voice). **stillness:** Animal: praying mantis. **stones:** *to strengthen*: Metal: gold; Stone: fluorite; *of protective stones*: Stone: antimony. **thought:** Color: yellow; God: Ptah. **transformation:** (See: Transformation). **trust:** Animal: butterfly. **wisdom:** *to overcome obstacles*: Charm: white elephant with six trunks. **words:** Plant: buttercup.

Power over: dangerous desert insects/animals: Goddess: Malinalxochi. **evil:** Goddess: Isis. **others:** Tool: scourge; Color: black; Plant: licorice root; God: Allah, Jehovah. **power that heals the world:** Goddess: Medicina Mundi.

Power to: be whole: Tool: chalice. **cause and cure disease/illness:** Goddess: Gula. **cure:** Animal: buffalo. **heal land:** Goddess: Ceres, Gaia. **impregnate:** God: Enki. **keep secrets:** North. **know:** East. **listen:** North. **manifest money:** Plant: lavender. **stop time:** Animal: hummingbird.

Lust for power: Evocation: Nimrod. **Words of power:** Air; Charm: lead tablet (inscribed with); Goddess: Isis. **Power resident in grapes:** Goddess: Geshtinanna. **Powers that be:** Jupiter; *to bring down those in power*: Goddess: Fortuna; *to gain favor with those in power*: (See: Favor); *to gain favors from powerful people*: (See: Favors).

To: accept power: Stone: tigereye. **attract power:** Charm: magnet; Stone: garnet, lodestone; Plant: wood aloes. **balance power:** Animal: cougar, mountain lion, puma. **battle foreign powers:** God: Teshub. **bestow power:** God: Kartikeya, Tirawa. **consolidate power:** Plant: birch. **enhance the power of a wish:** Plant: lemon verbena. **gain power:** Plant: heliotrope. **gain favor with those in power:** (See: Favor). **give up power:** Plant: willowherb; God: Geb. **ground power:** (See: Grounding). **hunger for power:** God: Horon, Poseidon. **increase power:** Method: invocation, meditation; Color: magenta; Charm: magick Circle; Plant: camphor, cinnamon, devil's shoestring, dragon's blood, ginger, mint; Evocation: elementals; *of divination tools*: (See: Divination); *of spells*: (See: Spells); *of spellcasters*: Plant: vervain; *of stones*: Stone: fluorite; *of visualization*: Color: yellow; Stone: yellow quartz.

learn not give your power away: Goddess: Erzulie, Yemaya. **raise power:** Sun/Moon; Tool: censer; Method: astral projection, binding, chanting, dancing, drumming, flagellation, Great Rite, intoxicants, invocation, meditation, trance; Metal: gold; Stone: clear quartz crystal; Incense: all; Plant: orange; Goddess: Arianrhod. **reclaim power:** Animal: jaguar. **send power:** Tool: wand; Metal: gold. **store power:** Tool: cord; Animal: horse; Stone: all, but especially quartz crystals. **use power:** Scorpio.

Powerlessness

To: make evil spirits powerless: Number: 5. **overcome feelings of powerlessness:** Plant: lime, thistle. **render people who enter the home powerless to harm its residents:** Plant: High John (floor wash). **render witches powerless:** Plant: elder, vervain.

Practicality

Earth/Taurus/Capricorn

Color: brown; Number: 4, 8; Stone: hematite, jade; Plant: cinnamon, maple; God: the Dagda.

Practical creativity: Color: green, brown. **Practical idealism:** Color: purple. **Practical inspiration:** God: Ptah. **Practical intuition:** Stone: labradorite. **Practical wisdom:** Goddess: Phronesia.

Prayer

East

Color: indigo, white, yellow; Charm: prayer beads, prayer wheel, rosary; Animal: buffalo; Stone: turquoise; Plant: cedar, frankincense, oak, rose, verbena; Goddess: Ida, Isis (Hearer of Prayers), the Litai, Sekhmet (She Who Listens to Prayers); God: Brihaspati (Lord of Prayer), Indra, Indra Brahamanaspati (Lord of Prayer), the Sadhyas, Savitri, Thoth; Evocation: Sandalphon.

Answered prayers: Goddess: Artemis, Ganga, Isis, Kwan Yin, the Litae; God: Apollo, Vishnu, Zeus. **Healing prayers**: Plant: hops (as incense). **Prayerfulness**: Goddess: Kwan Yin.

To: direct prayers: Plant: tuberose. **learn to pray**: Goddess: Pte San Wi. **send prayers**: Tool: censer; Charm: feathers (for wafting incense smoke upward); Plant: juniper berry.

Pregnancy

(See also: Babies, Childbirth, Conception, Fertility)

> [Note: No substance should be used or ingested by pregnant women, or by women who are trying to become pregnant, without medical advice.]

Moon/Full Moon/Water

Animal: cow, hippopotamus, burrowing owl, tadpole; Oil: newly mown hay; Plant: almond, black cohosh, hay, myrrh; Goddess: the Djanggawul Sisters, Hathor, Hesat, Ix Chel, Luperca, Taweret, Xochiquetzal; God: Chang Hsien.

Happy pregnancy: Plant: gooseberry, squash blossom, summer savory. **Successful pregnancy**: Potion: raspberry leaf tea; Goddess: Luperca.

Pregnant women: Goddess: Bast, Hathor, Xochiquetzal; *to protect*: Goddess: Hathor, Heset, Lilith, Taweret; God: Bes. **Unborn babies**: (See: Babies).

Endurance in pregnancy: Animal: elephant; Goddess: Luonnotar. **Help during pregnancy**: Goddess: Egeria, Kwan Yin; *help with stress of pregnancy*: Plant: watermelon.

To: bear magickal children: Goddess: Aine. **bear spiritual children**: Goddess: Kali. **handle emotions during pregnancy**: Plant: squash blossom, noni, watermelon. **have children**: Plant: watermelon; Goddess: Ahurani, Kwan Yin, Maha Lakshmi, Sinivali, Spenta Armaiti, Sung Tzu Niang-niang (The Lady Who Bestows Children); *have a son*: Goddess: Sarasvati (invoked by men who want sons), Tzu Sun, Niang-niang; God: Chang Hsien, Mitur. **learn the outcome of a pregnancy**: Goddess: Antevorta. **prevent pregnancy**: Plant: wild carrot seed. **protect pregnant women**: Goddess: Hathor, Heset, Lilith, Taweret; God: Acat, Bes. **treat morning sickness**: Plant: ginger.

Miscarriage

Color: red; Animal: dragon.

To: have something positive result from: Goddess: Atanea. **heal after**: Plant: dragon's blood. **prevent**: Stone: bloodstone, chrysoprase, lapis lazuli, ruby; Potion: raspberry leaf (tea), tansy. Plant: bisort, tansy.

Preservation

Color: red; Charm: alcohol, brine, honey, vinegar, wood smoke; Stone: emerald, salt; Potion: wine; Plant: benzoin (tincture), cedar, cinnamon, clove, coriander seed, cumin seed, frankincense, hops, myrrh, sugar cane, tansy; Goddess: Demeter, Eunomia, Kali, Prakriti; God: Vishnu (The Preserver).

To preserve: the dead: Stone: cinnabar; Plant: tansy; God: Anubis. **food**: Evocation: the Ovinniki. **health**: Stone: green beryl, garnet, fire garnet. **information**: Goddess: Sesheta. **life**: Sun; Animal: large fish; Plant: cinnamon; Goddess: Naste Estan. **love**: Stone: emerald; Plant: mistletoe, quassia (wood chips, burned with hair or finger nails); *married love*: Stone: green beryl. **a good marriage**: Plant: lemon verbena. **purity**: Stone: pearl. **virtue**: Stone: pearl. **youth**: (See: Youth).

Pride

Jupiter/Sun/North/South/Leo

Color: orange; Animal: lion, peacock; Number: 8; Plant: amaryllis, carnation, cedar, larkspur, rose, tiger lily; Evocation: High John the Conqueror.

Excessive pride: Animal: macaw; God: Vukub-Cakix; *to mitigate*: Color: yellow; Plant: toadflax; *to punish*: Goddess: Nemesis. **Misplaced pride**: God: Mider the Proud. **Parental pride**: Goddess: Sarasvati. **Personal pride**: Sun; Color: orange; Animal: cat, peacock; God: Balder.

Problems

(See also: Adversity, Uncrossing)

Behavior problems: *to end*: Plant: catnip, dragon's blood. **Emotional problems**: Plant: oleander; *compassion for*: Stone: green jasper; *freedom from*: Plant: lavender; *to calm*: Stone: amethyst, aquamarine; *to treat*: Plant: valerian. **Family problems**: *to end*: Plant: pennyroyal. **Health problems**: (See: Disease/Disorders, Illness); *to treat health problems caused by anger*: Stone: sodalite. **Hearing problems**: Stone: amethyst.

Legal problems: Jupiter; Color: orange; *to overcome*: Stone: brown chalcedony; Plant: galangal. **Marriage problems**: *to end*: Plant: pennyroyal, ylang-ylang. **Mechanical problems**: *to protect against*: Charm: cat's claw. **Mental problems**: *to overcome*: Stone: diamond (on left hand or arm); Plant: nettle, valerian; *depression*: (See: Depression, Illness: mental illness). **Relationship problems**: *to solve*: Stone: lodestone; Plant: balm of Gilead, fig. **Speech problems**: (See: Speech). **Vision problems**: *to treat*: Stone: sapphire. **Women's problems**: Stone: jade; Plant: lady's mantle.

Freedom from problems: Animal: ladybug; Goddess: Aditi (The Unfettered).

To: cause problems: Plant: chili pepper. **clear problems**: Charm: machete; God: Ogun. **deal with problems**: Plant: bergamot; *with other people's problems*: Stone: apatite; Plant: yarrow. **end problems**: Waning Moon; Plant: blackthorn; God: Lono. **get a new angle on a problem**: New Moon; Oil: new mown hay. **overcome problems**: Stone: agate, moonstone; Plant: birch, cottonwood, High John, poplar, valerian; Goddess: Inanna, Green Tara; God: Ganesha, Orunmila. **release problems**: Stone: lapis lazuli. **solve problems**: Full Moon; Stone: citrine; Plant: everlasting, High John, orange; Goddess: Aditi, Ashtart; *marital problems*: Plant: pennyroyal; *relationship problems*: Stone: lodestone; Plant: balm of Gilead, fig. **work on problems**: Stone: jade.

Productivity

Animal: ant, beaver, bee, bluebird, cow; Plant: pine; Goddess: Kupala, Macha, Ninhursaga; God: Kubera.

Male productivity: Animal: seahorse.

Productive energy: Charm: phallus; Plant: bamboo, all trees. **Productive fields**: Goddess: Sita (The Furrow); God: Eshara.

Productive labor: Goddess: Cihuacoatl. **Productive power**: (See: Power). **Cosmic productive urge**: Goddess: Prakrta. **Primal urge to produce**: Plant: pomegranate.

Productivity of: the Earth: Animal: jaguar. **farmland**: *to manage*: God: Enki.

Progress

Color: purple, red, violet; Charm: oar, spiral, wheel; Number: 3; Animal: gyrfalcon, kangaroo; Stone: labradorite; Plant: myrrh, sedum, spindle tree; Goddess: the Ratheihiae; God: Mithras, Ogun, Tob Tob.

Business progress: Color: royal blue, purple. **Career progress**: Goddess: Inanna. **Cultural progress**: Goddess: Isis; God: Osiris. **Mental progress**: Stone: fluorite. **Personal progress**: Goddess: Santoshi Ma. **Smooth progress**: Animal: sea turtle. **Spiritual progress**: Color: silver; Plant: African violet. **Unwise progress**: God: Baal.

Progress along one's path: Animal: goose; Stone: moonstone. **Progress of the seasons**: God: Vertumnus. **To make progress**: Animal: kangaroo.

Progressiveness

Sagittarius

Plant: fireweed.

Prophecy

(See also: Dreams, Foretelling, Omens, Oracles, Psychism)

Waning Moon/Water/Sagittarius

Tool: pendulum; Method: astrology, palmistry, runes, scrying, tarot; Color: purple; Animal: boar, crow, fox, hoopoe, magpie, owl, raven, toad, weasel, woodpecker, wren, all birds; Stone: amethyst, emerald, lapis lazuli, mother of pearl, tigereye; Fungus: fly agaric; Plant: alder, datura, dill, grapevine, laurel (as incense), lilac, marigold, sage, vervain, walnut, willow; Goddess: Adraste, Aeval, Albunea, Antevorta, Aricia, Astarte, Baba Yaga, Badb, Brigid, Brizo, Cardea, Carmenta, Cerridwen, Cethlion, Corra, Coventina, Danaë, Delphine, Demeter, Dione, Dubhlaing, Echidne, Egeria, Esther, Feithline, Gaia, Gefion, Goda, Gullveig, Gwendydd, Hecate, Hera, Heqet, Isa, Inanna, Ishtar (Source of Oracles of Prophecy), the Morrigan, Namagiri, Oenone, Phorcis, Rahab, Rhea, Sarah, Scathach, Shamash, Shapash, Shaushka, Sulis, Tamar, Themis, Tzu-Ku-Shen, the Vatviae, Völva; God: Ahura Mazda, Angus, Apollo, Arawn, Baal Zephon, Bran, the Dagda, Faunus, Hermes, Lugh, Mannan mac Lir, Marduk, Mimir, Nebo, Nereus, Nodens, Odin, Ogma, Orunmila, Phoebus Apollo, Phorcys, Picus, Proteus, Tatevali, Thoth; Evocation: the Ahueccaniae, Bannik, Calchas, Cassandra, Cathbad, Cethlion, Evander, Laocoon, Merlin, sirens, Taliesin, the Vatviae, the Vila, Zarathustra.

Prophetic dreams: (See: Dreams). **Prophetic knowledge**: (See: Knowledge). **Prophetic power**: Goddess: Cerridwen. **Prophetic secrets**: Animal: hoopoe. **Prophetic visions**: (See: Visions). **Prophetic wisdom**: Plant: almond branch.

Prosperity

(See also: Abundance, Finances, Money, Success)

Sun/Jupiter/Earth/Water/East/Thursday/December/Capricorn

Color: blue, green, gold, turquoise, yellowish green; Charm: beeswax candle, bread, coins, cornucopia, Eye of Horus, honey, money, musk, orange flower water, orange pomander, full purse; Animal: bee, boar, cow, dove, dragon, green dragon, eagle, fish, pair of fish, goldfish, kingfisher, leopard;

Metal: brass, copper, gold, silver, tin; Stone: agate, amethyst, aventurine, bloodstone, green calcite, Herkimer diamond, emerald, jade, jasper, malachite, mother of pearl, opal, pearl, peridot, pyrite, green quartz, ruby, salt, sapphire, tigereye, topaz, green tourmaline, turquoise; Potion: wassail; Plant: alfalfa, alkanet, allspice, almond, ash, banana, basil, bayberry, beech, benzoin (especially benzoin with basil, cedar, cinnamon or peony), bergamot, blue bonnet, bramble, bromeliad, broom (when flowering profusely), bryony, buckwheat, calamus, camellia, cascara sagrada, cassia, cashew, cat's claw, cedar, chamomile, cinnamon, cinquefoil, clove, clover, comfrey, cowslip, cumin, dill, dock, elder, all evergreens, fenugreek, fern, balsam fir, flax, fumitory, galangal, ginger, goldenrod, golden seal, gorse, grains of paradise, grapevine, hand of Maryam, harebell, heliotrope, High John, holy thistle, honesty, honeysuckle, horse chestnut, hyssop, blue iris, jade plant, jasmine, juniper, kelp, laurel, lucky hand, mandrake, American mandrake, maple, marjoram, mint, mistletoe, moss, Irish moss, myrrh, myrtle, nuts, nutmeg, oak, white oak bark, oats, onion, orange, patchouli, pea, pecan, periwinkle, pine, pine cone, pineapple, pomegranate, poplar, poppy seeds, rattlesnake root, rice, saffron, sage, sassafras, sesame, snakeroot, snapdragon, squill, black tea, tonka bean, trillium, tulip, verbena, vervain, blue vervain, vetiver, wheat, wisteria, wood aloes, woodruff; Goddess: Abundantia, Aditi, Aericura, Aine, Anath, Anumati, Apa, Artio, Aveta, Benzaiten, Bergusia, Bhasundara, Bo Dhu, Bo Find, Bonus Eventus, Bo Ruadh, Brigantia, Buddhi, Copia, Cuda, Danu, Demeter, Dhisana, Epona, Ertha, Fauna, Felicitas, Freya, Garmangabis, Gefion, Habondia, Hathor, Henwen, Ilmarinen, Inanna, Isis (Cornucopia of All Our Goods), Jara, Kupala, Lakshmi, Matangi, the Matronaea, the Mother, Nair, Nantosuelta, Ops, Qadesh, Radha, Rhiannon, Rosmerta (The Great Provider), Salus, Sasthi, Sequana, Sin, Sinivali, Sri-Devi, Vasudhara, Venus, Vidya-Lakshmi; God: Belenus, Bhaga, Borvo, Cernunnos, the Dagda, Daikoku, Easal, Freyr, Ganesha, Hades, the Hammer God, Ih P'en, Ilmarinen, Inari, Jupiter, Lu-Hsing, MacGreine, Marduk, Math ap Mathonwy, Maximon, Melkarth, Mercury, Mider, Mithras, Njord, Pluto, Porus, Ra, Reshep, Saturn, Sucellos, Svantovit, T'ai-Yueh-Ta-Ti, Teharon, Telepinu, Ubertas; Pantheon: the Vanir; Evocation: Genii Cucullati.

Agricultural prosperity: Goddess: Felicitas; God: Hapy; *of grain crops*: God: Neper. **Business prosperity**: Animal: goldfish; Plant: benzoin, sage, St. John's Wort; *in new endeavors*: God: Ganesha. **Family prosperity**: Charm: ash Yule log; Goddess: Maha Lakshmi; *of the family home*: Charm: ash Yule log; God: Majas Gars. **Material prosperity**: Goddess: Lakshmi; God: Pluto. **True prosperity**: Animal: buffalo.

Prosperous home: (See: The Home). **Prosperous marriage**: Plant: red clover; Goddess: Juno. **Prosperity visualization**: (See: Visualization). **Prosperity through war**: God: Bishamon. **Prosperity wishes**: Plant: chamomile, honeysuckle.

To: attract prosperity: Stone: aventurine, green calcite, citrine, dioptase, lodestone, green tourmaline; Plant: almond, amber, benzoin, bergamot, cedar, citronella, clove, ginger, High John, nutmeg, patchouli, sage, tangerine, vetiver, wisteria. **increase prosperity**: Plant: High John, honeysuckle, patchouli, pine. **manifest prosperity**: Plant: vetiver. **release prosperity**: Plant: snapdragon. **welcome prosperity**: God: Ganesha.

Protection

(See also: Amulets, Averting, Defense, Safety, Security, Talismans)

Neptune/Waxing Moon/Full Moon/Earth/ Fire/South

Tool: flint knife, pentacle/pentagram (especially an upward pointing silver one), sword, hazel wand; Method: common sense; Color: black, blue, bright blue, coral, gold, sea green, purple, red, silver, violet, white, yellow; Charm: amulet, ankh, blue bead, magick Circle, civet, door, Eye of Horus, fetish, Four Thieves Vinegar, hamsa hand, hand of Fatimah, lock, talisman, van van, white feather, witch hazel; Animal: angelfish, basilisk, condor, dog, elephant, griffin, jackal, lion, monkey, peacock, raven, scarab beetle, tiger, wolf, wolverine, your animal guide or totem animal; Metal: brass, copper, gold, iron, lead, silver, steel; Stone: agate (especially banded or black or red agate), alum, amber, amethyst, angelite, antimony, Apache tear, aquamarine, aventurine, peach aventurine, beryl, calcite, orange calcite, carnelian, chalcedony, chrysoprase, citrine, coral, diamond, emerald, flint, fossil, garnet, Goddess rock, hematite, Herkimer diamond, jade, jasper, red jasper, jet, lapis lazuli, lava, lepidolite, lodestone, malachite, marble, meteorite, mica, moonstone, mother-of-pearl, obsidian, olivine, onyx, pearl, peridot, pumice, clear quartz crystal, cluster of crystals, yellow quartz, ruby, salt, kosher salt, sea salt, sard, sardonyx, serpentine, staurolite, sulfur, sunstone, tanzanite, tigereye (especially when set in a silver ring), topaz, black or pink or red or green tourmaline, turquoise, zircon, red or clear zircon; Oil: niaouli, palmarosa; Plant: acacia, African violet, agrimony, alder, aloe, amaranth, amber, ambrosia, anemone, angelica, anise, arbutus, asafetida, ash, autumn crocus, avens, balm of Gilead, bamboo, barley, basil, bat nut, bayberry, beans, betony (especially at Midsummer), birch, bittersweet, blackthorn, bloodroot, blueberry, bodhi tree, bramble, broom, bryony, buckthorn, burdock, cactus, calamus, caraway seed, carnation, carob, cascara sagrada, cassia, cat's claw, cedar, celandine, chrysanthemum, cinnamon, cinquefoil, clove, red clover, club moss, coconut, black cohosh, coltsfoot, comfrey, copal, coriander, cotton, cowslip, cranberry, cumin, cyclamen, cypress, daisy, dandelion, datura, devil's bit scabious, devil's shoestring, dill, dogwood, dong quai, dragon's blood, ebony, Echinacea, elder, elecampane, eucalyptus, euphorbia, evergreens, eye of Satan, fennel, feverfew, figwort, fir, flax, fleabane, foxglove, galangal, garlic, gentian, red geranium, rose geranium, ginseng, gorse, gotu kola, grapefruit, grass, gum arabic, hawthorn, hazel, heather, High John, holly, hollyhock, holy thistle, honeysuckle, horehound, hyacinth, hyssop, Irish moss, ivy, jasmine, juniper, kava kava, kelp, ladies' slipper, larch, larkspur, laurel, lavender, leek, lemongrass, wild lettuce, lilac, lily of the valley, lime, linden, logwood, loosestrife, lotus, lucky hand root, madwort, maize, mandrake root, American mandrake, marigold, marjoram, mallow, marsh mallow, masterwort (carried), mimosa, mint, mistletoe, molukka, motherwort, mugwort, mulberry, mullein, mustard seed, myrrh, nettle, oak, oak moss, olive, onion, orris root, palm, papaya, papyrus, parsley, patchouli, pennyroyal, peony, black pepper, hot pepper, periwinkle, petrified wood, pilot weed, pimpernel, pine, plantain, primrose, purslane, putranjiva, quince, radish, raspberry branch, rattlesnake root, rhubarb, rice, red or yellow rose, rosemary, rowan, rue, sage, clary sage, sandalwood, slippery elm, snapdragon, Solomon seal, southernwood, Spanish moss, spearmint, squill, St. John's

Wort, sweetgrass, tamarisk, tangerine, tarragon, thistle, thorn, thyme, ti, toadflax, tomato, tormentil, trailing pearlwort, tuberose, tulip, unicorn root, valerian, Venus flytrap, lemon verbena, vervain, blue vervain, vetiver, violet, water lily, willow, wintergreen, wisteria, witch hazel, wolfsbane, woodruff, wormwood, yarrow, yerba santa, yew, yucca, all spiny or thorny plants; Goddess: Aditi, Aeval, Ala, Anahita, Anna Perenna, Aoife, Ariadne, Artemis, Athena, Auchimolgen, Bast, Brigid, Buto, Caireen, Cardea, Devi, Diana, Druantia, Frigg, Harimella, Hathor, Hera, Isis, Kali, Kupala, Kwan Yin, Mary, the Matronaea, Minerva, the Morrigan, Neith, Nut (Great Protectress), Ratis (The Fortress), Sarasvati, Securitas, Scathach, Sheela-na-gig, Sin, Tanith, Tsagaglalal (She Who Watches), Zvezda; God: Anubis, Ares, Atar, Bladud, Bolgois, Brennus, the Dagda, Elegua, Erh-Lang, Finn MacCool, Ganesha, Heimdall, Jupiter, Kutkhu, Mars, Mars Olloudius, Men-Shen, Morning Star, Neptune, Nuadh, Ochosi, Padmapani, Shui-Kwan, Sucellos, T'ai-Yueh-Ta-Ti, Terminus (Guardian of Boundaries), Teutates (Protector), Thor, Varuna, Vidar, Vishnu; Evocation: ancestors, angels, the Apacita, King Arthur, the Balam, Cuchulain, cherubim, gargoyles, the Manes, Merlin, Raphael, seraphim.

Divine protection: Plant: angelica, oak. *Aphrodite's protection*: Plant: fig wood; *Apollo's protection*: Charm: laurel branch wreathed in wool; *protection of Isis*: Charm: tet amulet, vulture amulet; *protection of Osiris*: Charm: carnelian heart amulet; *Ra's protection*: Charm: carnelian heart amulet. **Emotional protection**: Plant: rose; *to protect*: emotions: Stone: ruby; *against emotional drainage*: Stone: obsidian; Plant: garlic, yarrow; *against emotional upset from past life work*: Plant: eucalyptus. **Financial protection**: Animal: sand dollar; Stone: jet.

Gentle protection: God: Rudra. **Maternal protection**: Animal: alligator, bear, cat, crocodile. **Mental protection**: Plant: hyssop. **Peaceful protection**: God: Mars Ollodius; Goddess: Sekhmet. **Personal protection**: Oil: palmarosa; Plant: almond, cinnamon. **Physical protection**: Stone: jasper, pyrite, ruby; Plant: dragon's blood. **Psychic protection**: Tool: pentacle; Color: gray, silver; Charm: salt and water; Stone: angelite, calcite, salt, tigereye; Plant: aniseed, basil, benzoin, cedar, clove, dragon's blood, eye of Satan, frankincense, galangal, garlic, gotu kola, hyssop, mugwort, myrrh, nettle, patchouli, rosemary, sage, St. John's Wort, lemon verbena, yarrow; *to protect your thoughts against psychics*: Stone: carnelian. **Sacred protection**: Plant: sandalwood. **Spiritual protection**: Color: gray, lavender, silver, white; Stone: angelite, calcite, tiger's eye; Plant: aniseed, hyacinth, marigold, mistletoe, mullein, purslane, rosemary, thyme, ti, yarrow; Evocation: angels.

Protective energy: Earth; Stone: amethyst. **Protection wishes**: Plant: cinquefoil, horehound.

Protection at crossroads: (See: Crossroads). **Protection away from home**: Stone: lapis lazuli, moonstone. **Protection from without**: Stone: sodalite, tigereye.

Protection during: astral projection/travel: (See: The Astral). **inner work**: Plant: wolfsbane. **meditation**: Stone: turquoise. **sleep**: (See: Sleep). **thunderstorms**: (See: Storms). **the waning year**: Plant: holly; Evocation: Holly King. **the waxing year**: Plant: oak; Evocation: Oak King.

Protection in: the afterlife: Goddess: Aericura, Heretka. **battle**: (See: Battle). **confrontations**: Animal: cat. **court**: Color: purple. **darkness**: Stone: black moss agate, garnet. **the Underworld**: (See: Underworld). **wartime**: (See: War).

Protection while: traveling: Plant: Irish moss. **working defensive magick**: Stone: jade.

To: attract protection: Stone: garnet, malachite, moonstone, mother-of-pearl, pearl, clear quartz crystal, yellow quartz. **be protected by fairies**: Plant: rowan (planted near the house). **create a shield of protection**: New Moon; Method: visualization; Color: black; Stone: garnet, topaz; Plant: lime, pennyroyal. **encourage protection**: Plant: linden. **feel protected**: Stone: peridot; Plant: mullein. **find protection**: Plant: enchanter's nightshade.

Psychism

(See also: Clairaudience, Clairvoyance, Divination, Dreams, Foretelling, Intuition, Omens, Oracles, Prophecy)

Moon/Full Moon/Air/Water

Color: purple, yellow; Animal: cat, all insects with antennas; Metal: peacock ore, silver; Stone: amethyst, Apache tear, apatite, aquamarine, azurite, beryl, citrine, emerald, Goddess rock, jet, lapis lazuli, lepidolite, moldovite, moonstone, opal, clear quartz crystal, ruby, sapphire, sugilite; Plant: acacia, begonia, borage, buchu, celery, cinnamon, citron, coconut, elecampane, eyebright, flax, galangal, grass, gum arabic, honeysuckle, kelp, laurel, lemongrass, mace, mallow, marigold, mastic, mugwort, nutmeg, peppermint, rose, rowan, saffron, sandalwood, star anise, stillengia, sumbul, thyme, uva ursi, wormwood, yarrow, yerba santa; God: Odin, Woden.

Psychic ability: (See: Ability). **Psychic attack**: (See: Aggression). **Psychic awareness**: (See: Awareness). **Psychic balance**: Plant: red clover. **Psychic blocks**: *to open*: Stone: lapis lazuli. **Psychic bond**: *to bond psychically with a cat*: Plant: catnip. **Psychic closing**: Metal: iron. Psychic consciousness:

to connect with: Plant: marjoram. **Psychic dreams**: (See: Dreams). **Psychic energy**: (See: Energy). **Psychic exploration**: Stone: iolite. **Psychic fire**: Goddess: Pelé. **Psychic forces**: (See: Forces). **Psychic gifts**: *to open*: Plant: lotus, mimosa, mugwort, nutmeg, wisteria. **psychic growth**: (See: Growth). **Psychic guidance**: Stone: azurite. **Psychic healing**: (See: Healing). **Psychic increase**: Moon/Waxing Moon. **Psychic manifestation**: Color: purple, violet; Stone: blue lace agate. **Psychic messages**: (See: Messages). **Psychic mind**: (See: Mind). **Psychic opening**: (See: Opening. **Psychic potential**: *to develop*: Plant: galangal. **Psychic power(s)**: (See: Power). **Psychic protection**: (See: Protection). **Psychic purification**: Stone: clear quartz crystal; Plant: laurel. **Psychic purity**: Plant: iris. **Psychic radar**: Goddess: Angerboda. **Psychic release**: (See: Release). **Psychic sensitivity**: (See: Sensitivity). **Psychic shield**: *to create*: Method: visualization; *to disrupt*: Plant: eyebright. **Psychic strength**: Fir. **Psychic vision**: (See: Vision). **Psychic visions**: Stone: emerald; Plant: eyebright. **Psychic work**: (See: Work).

ESP: Stone: clear quartz crystal. **Psimagick**: (See: Magick). **Psychometry**: Animal: mole. **Telepathy**: Capricorn; Color: brown; Plant: comfrey, clary sage.

Purification

(See also: Clearing, Purity)

Saturn/Fire/Water/South/Tuesday/February/Virgo

[Note: Plants are listed as charms. None but foods and culinary herbs should be ingested.]

Tool: besom, censer; Method: asperging, smudging; Color: blue, violet, white, yellow; Charm: Beltane or Midsummer bonfire smoke, infusion of broom tops, egg, holy water, honey, hyssop water, lavender water, mandrake water, musk, orange flower water, rosewater, salt and water, white feather, wax; Animal: bee, frog, vulture, wren; Metal: gold, silver; Stone: amber, amethyst, aquamarine, blue aventurine, calcite, blue calcite, charoite, fluorite, green fluorite, garnet, lava, peridot, quartz crystal, smoky quartz, cluster of crystals, salt, sea salt, sapphire, schist, tigereye, blue topaz, tourmaline, turquoise; Potion: coconut milk; Plant: acacia, alkanet, aloe (juice), anise, anise with laurel, asafetida, ash, avens, azalea, basil, bayberry, benzoin, betony, birch, blackthorn, blood root, broom, burdock, burnet, cedar, centaury, chamomile, chili pepper, cinnamon, citronella, clove, coconut, coca leaf (as incense), copal, costmary, cumin, damiana, dill, dragon's blood, elder, elecampane, eucalyptus, euphorbia, evergreens, fennel, ferns, feverfew, fireweed, frankincense, garlic, grapefruit, gum arabic, hawthorn, heather, hawthorn, hemlock, holy thistle, horseradish, hyacinth, hyssop, iris, jasmine, juniper, juniper with cedar, laurel, lavender, lemon, lemongrass, lilac, lime, loosestrife, lotus, lovage, marjoram, mastic, mesquite, mimosa, mint, mugwort, mullein, mustard seed, myrrh, nettle, nightshade, oak leaf (as incense), olive, onion, orange, parsley, passionflower, patchouli, pennyroyal, pepper tree, peppermint, pine, rose, rosemary, rosemary with juniper berries, rue, sage, clary sage, sagebrush, sandalwood, shallot, St. John's Wort, soapwort, Solomon's seal, spearmint, spikenard, star anise, sweetgrass, tangerine, thistle, thyme, tulip, turmeric, uva ursi, valerian, lemon verbena, vervain, blue vervain, water lily, wintergreen, wood aloes, woodruff, wormwood, yarrow, yucca; Goddess: Adamisil Wedo, Adsullata, Anahita, Apa, Arnamentia, Chalchihuitlcue, Februa, Ganga, Hannahhannas, Hecate, Inanna, Ishtar, Isis, Juno, Kupala, Lady of the Lake, Meduna, Mehet-Weret, Nisaba, Sarasvati, Sedna, Sekhmet (The Great One in the Temple of Purification), Sequana, Sirona, Tlaelquarni, Tlazolteotl (Eater of Filth), Toci, Venus Cloacina (She Who Purifies with Myrtle); God: Agni (The Purifier), Apollo, Bel, Enki, Februus, Marduk, Mithras, Perun, Proteus, Tuku.

Emotional purification: Water; Plant: lotus, water hyacinth. **Inner purification:** Method: fasting; Plant: alkanet, blackberry, borage, broom, caper, centaury, chickweed, chicory, columbine, cucumber, dandelion root, devil's bit scabious, elder, fennel, fumitory, ginger, heather, black hellebore, plantain, plum, purslane, ragged robin, samphire, senna, smilax, soapwort, walnut. **Love purification:** Plant: valerian. **Magickal tools:** *to purify:* (See: Magick). **Mental purification:** Charm: lead crystal; Stone: hematite, lapis lazuli, malachite. **Psychic purification:** Stone: clear quartz crystal; Plant: laurel. **Ritual purification:** Method: bath, fasting; Charm: lustral water; Plant: hyssop, benzoin, frankincense, vervain, yucca root; *purification rituals*: Stone: blue calcite; Plant: benzoin, frankincense, hyssop, laurel, lavender, myrrh, sage, sweetgrass, yucca root; Goddess: Februlis, Nisaba; God: Apollo. **Spiritual purification:** Color: indigo; Stone: lapis lazuli, moonstone; Oil: petitgrain; Plant: cinnamon, garlic, laurel, juniper berry, laurel; God: Maximon.

Purification by: air: Air; Tool: censer. **fire:** Fire; Plant: betony (as incense); Goddess: Kali; God: Agni (The Purifier), Bel, Kagutsuchi, Nergal. **sweeping:** Tool: besom; Goddess: Devera; **transmutation:** God: Hermes. **water:** *purification baths*: Stone: salt, sea salt, rock salt; Plant: aniseed, dragon's blood, hyssop, laurel, lavender, lovage root, marjoram, pine, rosemary, thyme, vervain.

To purify: the air: Stone: clear quartz crystal; Plant: cedar, menthol crystals (as incense), pine, rosemary. **an altar**: Plant: hyssop, mullein, myrrh, spikenard, vervain. **the aura**: (See: Auras). **barns**: Plant: juniper (as incense). **blood**: (See: The Body). **breast milk**: Goddess: Anahita. **chakras**: (See: Chakras). **the dead**: (See: The Dead). **disease**: Plant: coca leaf (burned), Echinacea, tomato, yucca root. **disputes**: Goddess: Dike. **evil and negativity**: (See: Evil). **the heart**: Charm: Kananga Water; Plant: white lily. **the home**: Plant: allspice. **intestines**: (See: The Body). **objects**: Sun/Water; Charm: sunlight; Stone: salt; Plant: myrrh. **magickal tools**: Plant: mullein, rue. **sacred places**: Plant: vervain. **sacred space**: Plant: clove. **semen**: Goddess: Anahita. **stones/crystals**: Sun/Moon/Water; Charm: moonlight, salt water, sunlight; Stone: salt; Plant: copal. **the womb/uterus**: (See: The Body). **women**: Plant: myrrh. **yourself**: Tool: censer; Method: bath; Charm: shower in the rain; bathe in naturally running water such as a stream or waterfall; Plant: white clover.

To: purify after negative contacts: Plant: eucalyptus. **purify in preparation for magic**: (See: Magick).

Purity
(See also: Purification)

Fire/Water/North

Color: clear, silver, white; Animal: unicorn; Stone: amethyst, diamond, jade, pearl; Metal: silver; Plant: cedar, frankincense, hawthorn, lavender, madonna lily, lotus, magnolia, mistletoe, white rose, star of Bethlehem, white violet; Goddess: Astraea, Athena, Demeter (Pure One), Erzulie, Lakshmi, Mary, Nerthus, Sarasvati, Sekhmet (Pure One); God: Agni, Balder, Obatala (The Pure and Merciful).

Psychic purity: Plant: iris.

Pure affection: Plant: pink carnation. **Pure consciousness**: God: Shiva. **Pure joy**: Animal: hummingbird. **Pure love**: Plant: red carnation, rose, rosebud. **Pure spirit**: Sun; Plant: white jasmine. **Pure sweetness**: Goddess: Oshun;. **Pure water**: Goddess: the Pure Goddesses, Nammu, Nanshe, Tefnut.

Purity of: action: Plant: gardenia. **blood**: Stone: agate. **feeling**: Plant: primrose. **heart**: Plant: water lily. **purpose**: Animal: deer; Plant: gardenia.

To preserve purity: Stone: pearl.

Impurity
Animal: dog, donkey; Evocation: Nahema.

Impure thoughts: (See: Thoughts). **To: avert impurity**: Goddess: Cerridwen. **cleanse impurity**: Water; God: El.

Purpose
Earth/Fire

Stone: tigereye; Plant: camphor, cardamom, mullein; Goddess: Phronesia; God: Aegir.

Higher purpose: Plant: apple. **Purpose in life**: Plant: wintergreen; *to be true to*: Plant: daisy; *to find*: Color: deep blue; Stone: citrine; Plant: ladies tresses; *to know*: Color: blue; *to remember*: Animal: spider; Stone: sugilite.

Clarity of purpose: Plant: birch, broom. **Objectivity of purpose**: Stone: topaz. **Purity of purpose**: Animal: deer. **Strength of purpose**: Oil: palmarosa.

Chapter 17

Quarrels

(See also: Agreement, Discord, Enmity, Strife)

Mars/Aries/Leo

Charm: Four Thieves Vinegar; Stone: onyx, opal; Plant: broken straw, fig, vervain root; Goddess: Alecto, Discordia, Eris; God: Ares; Evocation: Agamemnon, Ajax, Makhai; Omen: cat fight, itchy nose, loaf of bread coming apart in someone's hands, spilled salt; *of a quarrel ending soon*: Plant: geranium.

Family quarrels: *to end/settle*: Goddess: Aerten; *to reduce*: Stone: blue lace agate; *to side with a sister during*: Goddess: Nephthys; *quarrels in marriage*: (See: Marriage). **Lovers' quarrels**: Stone: garnet; *to end*: Plant: geranium; *end peacefully*: Goddess: Juno; *to reconcile quarreling couples*: Stone: diamond; Plant: valerian root.

To: cause quarrels: Charm: putting bread into an oven together; Stone: onyx; Plant: vervain root (powdered); *between brothers*: Evocation: Efnisien; *between friends*: Stone: salt. **clear the air/clear negative energy after a quarrel**: Plant: copal, eucalyptus. **cool off after a quarrel**: Plant: mint, peppermint. **end quarrels**: Color: gray; Plant: slippery elm, valerian; Goddess: Conciliatrix; God: Forseti; *in relationships*: Stone: lodestone; *end a quarrel peacefully*: Goddess: Iris. **prevent quarrels**: Plant: moneywort. **protect against quarrels**: Plant: cat's claw. **reconcile after a quarrel**: Plant: valerian; God: Forseti. **restore good feelings after a quarrel**: Plant: bergamot, copal.

Quests

(See also: Travel)

West

Color: dark blue; Animal: gyrfalcon, white stag; Goddess: Geshtinanna, Isis; Evocation: King Arthur, Gilgamesh, Jason.

Magickal quest: Color: indigo. **Spiritual quest**: Plant: cinnamon, tiger lily; God: Odin. **Vision quest**: Method: fasting, meditation; Color: gray; Animal: polar bear, raven, snake; Stone: turquoise; Plant: birch, copal, sage.

Quickness

(See: Speed)

Quiet

(See also: Calm, Soothing)

Night/January

Color: blue, indigo; Animal: mourning dove, ferret, fox, mouse, owl, weasel; Plant: aster, lemongrass, lily, peach, queen of the night, Solomon's seal; Goddess: Nephthys; God: Mors, Thanatos.

Quiet home: Plant: dragon's blood, patchouli, peach. **Quiet life**: God: Hurukan. **Quiet mind**: (See: The Mind). **Quiet power**: (See: Power).

Inner quiet: Animal: buffalo. **Peace and quiet**: Libra; Plant: benzoin, dragon's blood, patchouli, peach; Goddess: Vesta.

To quiet: the brain: Stone: jacinth; Plant: lotus, wormwood. **coughing**: Plant: mullein. **emotions**: Stone: tigereye; Plant: borage, chamomile, jasmine, lemongrass, lily, passionflower. **the heart**: (See: The Body). **the mind**: Plant: cassandra, Solomon's seal; *conscious mind*: Plant: sandalwood. **nerves**: Plant: borage, chamomile, lemongrass. **nervous system**: Plant: sandalwood; Plant: passionflower, valerian. **a river**: God: Tiberinus. **sexual desire**: Stone: onyx; Plant: camphor, rue.

Chapter 18

Raising

(See also: Increase)

New Moon

To raise: **an army**: Goddess: Cymidei Cymeinfoll. **blood pressure**: (See: Diseases/Disorders). **chakras**: Stone: turquoise. **children**: (See: Children). **consciousness**: Plant: frankincense, passionflower. **the dead**: (See: The Dead). **energy**: Color: pink; Plant: cinnamon. **magick mists**: (See: Magick). **power**: (See: Power). **the spirit**: (See: Spirit). **storms**: (See: Storms). **vibrations**: Plant: peppermint. **winds**: Charm: whistle three times; Plant: alder, saffron.

Real Estate

(See also: Business, The Home, Land)

Saturn/Earth

God: Poseidon.

Farm estates: Goddess: Pherusa. **Landlords**: God: Aizen Myoo.

To: **acquire real estate**: Goddess: Acca Larentia, Gefion. **sell a property**: Charm: statue of St. Joseph (buried upside down in yard).

Realism

Taurus

Plant: mugwort, southernwood, tarragon, wormwood.

Reality

Earth

Plant: ash, gotu kola; Goddess: Allat.

Alternate reality: Tool: crystal ball; Stone: fluorite; Plant: honeysuckle. **Carnal reality**: Goddess: Carna. **Higher reality**: Stone: sugilite. **Physical/material reality**: Earth; Color: yellow; Goddess: Isis. **Positive reality**: Plant: willow. **Supreme reality**: Goddess: Allat; God: Brahma. **Ultimate reality**: Center.

To: **accept reality**: Stone: aragonite; Goddess: Luonnotar. **create reality**: Animal: spider. **distinguish between reality and illusion**: Plant: dill; Goddess: Ignis Fatuus. **face reality**: Animal: earthworm. **focus on reality**: Stone: hematite. **influence reality**: Goddess: the Norns; God: Anu. **know reality**: Stone: aquamarine, moonstone; God: Brahmavid (Knower of Reality). **return to reality**: Stone: blue chalcedony. **see beyond ordinary reality**: Plant: cannabis, datura, orchid. **turn an idea into reality**: Tool: wand. **understand reality**: Plant: frankincense. **view reality from a different perspective**: Animal: hawk; Plant: squill; Stone: hawk's eye, tigereye.

Realization

Color: white; Animal: butterfly; Stone: kyanite; Plant: birch, clary sage, gentian; Goddess: Canola, Luonnotar, Walo; God: Obatala, Odin.

Self-realization: Plant: everlasting; God: O-Kuni-Nushi.

To realize: **desires**: (See: Desires). **dreams**: Stone: turquoise. **possibilities**:

God: Marduk. **potential**: Stone: jade, rhodonite. **vision**: Plant: birch, laurel; *artistic vision*: Color: violet.

Reason

(See also: Intelligence,

Logic, Sense)

Sunday

Color: yellow, violet; Stone: aquamarine; Plant: citronella; Goddess: Athena, Mnemosyne, Moerae, Reason; God: Apollo, Vili.

Light of reason: Color: white.

Rebirth

(See also: Reincarnation, Past Life Work)

Pluto/Moon/Sun/New Moon/Waning Moon/ Water/East/South/Spring/ Scorpio

Tool: cauldron; Charm: necklace; Color: black, green, emerald green, spring green; Charm: shed skin of a snake; Animal: bat, benu bird, butterfly, chicken, cock, condor, fawn, frog, goat, horse, phoenix, polar bear, scarab beetle, snake, spider, stag, wolf; Stone: emerald, garnet; Plant: alder, almond tree, apple, ash, aspen, cypress, elder, holly, holy thorn, ivy, lotus, olive tree, pine, white poplar, vine, yew; Goddess: Badb, Cailleach, Coatlicue, Corchen, the Crone, Cybele, Damuzi, Epona, Estsanatlehi, Hera, Inanna, Ishtar, Isis, Mor, Morgen, Nantosuelta, Nehalennia, Neith, Nephthys, Ostara, Persephone, Queen of Elphame, Sedna, Sekhmet, Smashana-Kali, Taweret; God: Adonis, Angus, Attis, Baldur, Cernunnos, the Dagda, Dionysus Iacchos, Emma-O, Itzamna, Jesus, Mannan, Mathonwy, Osiris, Poseidon, Ptah-Seker-Osiris, Ra, Serapis, Shiva, Tammuz.

Emotional rebirth: Scorpio; Plant: calla lily. **Spiritual rebirth**: West; Plant: snowdrop. **Wisdom of rebirth**: Mercury.

Death and rebirth: Plant: cherry. **To assist rebirth**: Goddess: Nephthys.

Reconciliation

(See also: Relationships)

Water

Color: orange, red; Stone: calcite, diamond, Herkimer diamond, kunzite, moonstone, rose quartz, selenite; Plant: beans, damiana, eucalyptus, filbert, hazel, star of Bethlehem; Goddess: Psyche; God: Balder, Forseti.

Reconciliation in marriage: Stone: beryl, lodestone. **Reconciliation after a quarrel**: Plant: valerian; God: Forseti.

To reconcile: differences between friends: Stone: green beryl. **the ephemeral and the eternal**: Plant: evergreens. **estranged love**: Plant: balm of Gilead. **humans and deities**: Stone: sapphire. **lovers**: (See: Lovers). **lunar and solar time**: Number: 19. **quarreling couples**: Stone: diamond; Plant: valerian root.

Recovery

(See also: Healing)

Plant: daisy, foxglove, lemongrass, marigold, self-heal.

Emotional recovery: Stone: emerald.

To recover: lost property/objects: (See: Loss). **stolen property**: (See: Theft). **safe recovery of someone who has been kidnapped**: God: Hanuman.

To recover from: abuse: Plant: onion; Goddess: Rhiannon. **accidents**: Plant: catnip. **a bad childhood**: Color: pink; Stone: pink calcite, rose quartz. **a cold**: Metal: zinc; Potion: yarrow leaf tea with molasses and cayenne pepper; Plant: Echinacea. **a crisis**: Animal: otter. **domestic violence**: Plant: lemon balm, onion. **heartbreak**: Plant: yarrow. **illness**: (See: Healing, Illness). **infection**:

Plant: garlic. **nightmares**: (See: Nightmares). **sexual assault**: Plant: lemon balm. **surgery**: Stone: carnelian; Plant: cedar, lilac, pine, sandalwood. **trauma**: (See: Trauma). **travel**: Plant: gentian.

To speed recovery: Plant: carnation, cayenne; *after circumcision*: Goddess: Weri Kumbaba.

Regeneration

Sun/Pluto/Water/Scorpio

Tool: cauldron; Animal: lizard, octopus; Letter: L; Stone: sea salt; Plant: fennel, fireweed, lilac, loranthus, lotus, mistletoe growing on oak trees, olive tree, pine, plane tree, vetiver; Goddess: Airmid, Aphrodite, Baba Yaga, Cailleach, Cerridwen, Cessair, Corchen, Eileithyia, Hecate, Isis, Kali, Lady of the Lake, Lilith, Nut, Pelé, Persephone, Sheela-na-gig, Sirona, the Suleviae, Tara, Tsagaglalal, Yemaya; God: Amun, Arawn, Bran, Cernunnos, Cinteotl, the Dagda, Dian Cecht, El, the Horned God, Itzamna, Jesus, Legba, Nyambe, Osiris, Shiva.

Physical regeneration: Night; Color: red; Stone: red calcite, citrine, garnet, topaz; Oil: palmarosa; Plant: cedar. **Regenerative ecstasy**: Goddess: the Morrigan. **Regeneration through solitude**: Animal: ocelot.

To regenerate: **blood**: Plant: herb robert. **consciousness**: Stone: amethyst. **limbs**: Evocation: the Rakshasas. **losses**: Animal: lizard. **organs**: Stone: moonstone, peridot. **skin**: Oil: wheat germ; Plant: myrrh, patchouli, sandalwood. **spine**: Plant: lilac.

Regret

Color: black, purple; Plant: asphodel, bramble, hyacinth, raspberry, rue, purple verbena; Goddess: Oenone; Evocation: Aedon, Deianira, Midas.

To: **ease regret**: Stone: chalcedony; Goddess: Oenone. **release regrets**: Plant: rue.

Reincarnation

(See also: Karma, Past Life Work, Rebirth)

Saturn/Saturday

Tool: cauldron; Animal: butterfly, cricket, leopard, burrowing owl, snake; Plant: lilac. lotus, sandalwood; Goddess: Arianrhod, Blodeuwedd, Carravogue, Corchen, Cymidei Cymeinfoll, Ethniu, Greine, Hecate, Isis, Ituana, Kali, Nephthys, Ostara, Pana, Sheela-na-gig; God: Arawn, Cernunnos, the Dagda, the Horned God, Kephera, Lugh, Marduk, Ogma, Osiris, Ptah-Seker-Ausar, Shiva, T'ai-Yüeh Ta-ti, Thoth.

Cycle of reincarnation: *ignorance that causes*: Center; *to escape*: Evocation: the Buddha; *freedom from*: Goddess: Lakshmi. **Hope of reincarnation**: Plant: silver fir, white poplar; God: Osiris.

To: **be reincarnated in a positive situation**: God: T'ai-Yüeh Ta-ti. **prevent reincarnation as a donkey**: Charm: turquoise earring.

Rejuvenation

(See also: Rebirth, Regeneration, Renewal, Vitality, Youth)

New Moon/Spring

Tool: cauldron; Color: green; Animal: snake; Plant: benzoin, carrot seed, everlasting, fireweed, frankincense, jasmine, palm, patchouli, pine, rose, rosemary, snowdrop, sweetgrass, vanilla; Goddess: Aphrodite, Estsanatlehi, Hecate; God: Cernunnos, Mider, Sucellos.

To rejuvenate: **liver**: Plant: milk thistle. **the spirit**: Oil: petitgrain.

Relationships

(See also: Business, Family, Friendship, Love, Lovers, Marriage, Partnership, and so on.)

Venus/Full Moon

Color: green, red; Stone: moonstone, rhodochrosite; Plant: linden, maple; Goddess: Aphrodite; God: Puchan.

Committed relationship: Animal: dove, elephant. **Endangered relationship**: *to protect*: Goddess: Albina. **Estranged relationships**: (See: Reconciliation). **Family relations**: Stone: moonstone; *good family relations*: Goddess: Verplace. **Female/female relationships**: Goddess: Aphrodite Androphonos, Bast. **Good relationships**: Plant: corn; Goddess: Concordia. **Happy relationships**: Stone: aquamarine, rose quartz; Plant: hawthorn, patchouli. **Harmonious relationships**: Animal: goldfish; Oil: palmarosa; Plant: betony, corn, orris root, primrose, sea pink; Goddess: Concordia; God: Lu Pan; *with the Earth*: Animal: bison, buffalo; Plant: corn, reindeer moss. **Healthy relationships**: Oil: palmarosa; Plant: basil, gardenia, geranium; Goddess: Isis. **Improved relationships**: Animal: painted turtle. **International relations**: Goddess: Amphityonis. **Loving relationships**: Plant: maple; *to attract*: Color: pink. **Magickal relationship**: Animal: one's familiar. **Male/female relationships**: *good male/female relationships*: Stone: diamond; *healthy male/female relationships*: Plant: myrrh, wild strawberry, sweetgale. **Negative relationships**: *to avert*: Stone: onyx. **New relationships**: New Moon; Color: pink; Goddess: the Maiden; God: Janus. **Nurturing relationships**: Earth; Color: pink. **Parent/child relationships**: *to heal father/child relationship*: Stone: ruby; *to strengthen mother/child relationship*: (See: Children). **Passionate relationships**: Color: red. **Past**

relationships: *to understand*: Plant: geranium. **Peaceful relationships**: Stone: aquamarine; Plant: lavender. **Romantic relationship**: Color: rose; Plant: jasmine; *clarity in*: Plant: papaya; *to spice up*: Plant: chili pepper, ginger, paprika, black pepper; *to strengthen*: Plant: Adam and Eve root. **Social relationships**: Plant: sumac. **Troubled relationships**: God: Ares. **Unbalanced relationships**: Animal: flea, leech, tick, all parasites.

Relationship with the Earth: Earth; God: Manitou, Wakan Tonka. **Emotional healing after a relationship ends**: Plant: lemon balm, lily, rue. **Good communication in relationships**: Stone: blue lace agate; Plant: marigold, martagon lily. **Integrity in relationships**: Stone: lapis lazuli. **Truth in relationships**: *to protect*: Goddess: Aphrodite.

To: balance the emotions in a relationship: Stone: rose quartz. **cement a relationship**: Plant: spikenard (buried). **define relationships**: Animal: wolf. **end a relationship**: Waning Moon; Plant: African violet, turnip; Goddess: the Crone; *a toxic relationship*: Charm: brimstone. **end interference in a relationship**: Color: indigo; Stone: chrysocolla, moonstone, pyrite; Plant: frangipani, laurel, pine. **end quarrels in relationships**: Stone: lodestone. **enter into relationships**: Color: pink, red; Stone: lodestone; Plant: crown of thorns, jojoba. **get information about a relationship**: Method: tarot; Goddess: Vör. **have more relationships**: Animal: moth. **heal a relationship**: Plant: basil, geranium, sweetgale. **improve a relationship**: Color: pink, rose; Stone: agate, amethyst, aphrodite, lapis lazuli, morganite, prehnite, rose quartz, rhodonite; Plant: apple blossom, pink carnation, pink rose, sandalwood, yarrow; *improve sex in a relationship*: Plant: jasmine; *spice up a stale relationship*: Plant: pepper. **maintain a**

relationship: Potion: yerba maté (tea, drunk by both parties); Plant: chickweed. **maintain fidelity in a relationship**: Plant: magnolia. **make decisions about relationships**: Plant: apple. **resurrect a past relationship**: Plant: yew. **solve problems in relationships**: Stone: lodestone; Plant: balm of Gilead, fig. **strengthen relationships**: Animal: cockatoo.

Relaxation
(See also: Calm, Peace, Stress, Tension)

Venus/Water

Method: breath work, meditation; Color: blue, pink, violet; Charm: beeswax candle, honey, orange flower water; Animal: cat, koala; Stone: blue lace agate, citrine, kunzite; Oil: neroli; Plant: angelica, apple blossom, apricot, benzoin, birch, bougainvillea, catnip, cedar, chamomile, clary sage, black cohosh, cow parsnip, damiana, eucalyptus, honeysuckle, hops, hyacinth, hyssop, jasmine, kava kava, lavender, lemon balm, lotus, marjoram, marshmallow, myrrh, narcissus, orange, orange blossom, parsley, peppermint, primrose, rose, rosemary, sage, clary sage, sandalwood, scullcap, thyme, valerian, lemon verbena, vervain, vetiver, violet, woodrose, ylang-ylang; Goddess: Adsullata, Aphrodite, Bormana, Bricta, the Comedovae, Damona, the Griselicae, Ianuaria, Icovellauna, Ivilia, Nematona, Rosmerta, Sirona, Sulis, Venus, Vercana, Visuna; God: Apollo Grannus, Belenus, Borvo, Condatis, Damballa, Edovius, Leucetius, Luxovius.

Mental relaxation: Color: pink; Stone: pink diamond, kunzite, morganite, rose quartz, pink tourmaline; Plant: cedar, dandelion, narcissus, strawberry, ylang-ylang; *of the conscious mind*: Plant: narcissus. **Physical relaxation**: Stone: sodalite; Plant: chamomile, dandelion, tangerine, valerian, ylang-ylang (See also: The Body). **Relaxation in psychic work**: (See: Work).

To relax: **blood vessels**: Plant: linden, mistletoe, olive. **muscles**: (See: The Body). **pelvis**: Plant: Low John. **veins**: Plant: witch hazel.

Release
(See also: Freedom, Liberation)

Waning Moon/Air

Tool: censer, cord; Method: knot magick; Color: black, dark purple; Charm: balloon (let go), boiling water, potion, smoke, steam, votive boat (set adrift); Stone: kyanite; Plant: African violet, basil, beans, betony, birch, bunchberry, cedar, clove, comfrey, copal, cumin, cypress, dragon's blood, elder, fern, frankincense, garlic, iris, juniper, laurel, lavender, lilac, mint, mugwort, mullein, myrrh, myrtle, onion, patchouli, peach, peony, black pepper, peppermint, pine, rose, rosemary, rue, sandalwood, St. John's Wort, vervain, witch grass, yarrow; Goddess: Kali, Pandora; God: Anansi, Coyote, Dionysus, Ea, Ternan, Zeus; Evocation: Lyaeus (the Releaser).

Emotional release: Stone: agate, lapis lazuli, malachite, moonstone; Plant: fireweed, foxglove; *to release emotions*: (See: Emotions). **Psychic release**: *to release psychic abilities*: Plant: laurel (as incense); *to release psychic dreams*: Plant: heliotrope. **Physical release**: Stone: amethyst, blue topaz; Plant: potato. **Spiritual release**: Plant: snowdrop.

To release: **anger**: (See: Anger). **anxiety**: (See: Anxiety). **apathy**: Stone: carnelian. **attachments**: (See: Attachments). **blockages**: Plant: horsetail. **the bounty of the sea**: Goddess: Sedna. **captives**: Plant: myrtle; Goddess: Ceres, Corn Mother, Demeter; God: Apollo, Ea; Evocation: Odysseus. **creativity**: Plant: iris, especially wild iris. **a cycle**: Color: pink. **deadness of spirit**: Plant: sunflower. **discord**: Stone:

iolite; Plant: moneywort. **Earth spirits**: Charm: plow. **ego**: Goddess: Tara; Evocation: Buddha. **energy**: Stone: lava, lodestone, volcanic rock; Plant: grass of Parnassus. **envy**: Stone: carnelian. **evil**: Plant: myrrh. **fairy enchantment**: Plant: foxglove leaf. **fatigue**: Plant: marjoram. **fear**: (See: Fear). **grief**: Plant: Japanese maple. **guilt**: Stone: blue apatite, sugilite; Plant: sage. **guilt**: Stone: blue apatite. **healing**: Plant: elder, rosemary. **hexes**: Plant: basil, balsam, nutmeg. **illness**: God: Govannon. **illusions**: (See: Illusion). **intense emotions**: Method: breath work; Animal: dolphin. **issues**: Plant: ginger. **a lover**: Plant: camphor, sesame. **lust**: Plant: garlic. **magick**: Plant: enchanter's nightshade. **repressed memories**: Plant: forget-me-not, rosemary. **need**: (See: Need). **negativity**: (See: Negativity). **pain**: (See: Pain). **the past**: Plant: grass of Parnassus. **patterns**: Color: pink; Animal: bat; Stone: wulfenite; Plant: aster; *negative patterns*: Stone: sugilite; Plant: columbine, tansy. **power**: (See: Power). **one's potential**: Plant: enchanter's nightshade. **problems**: Stone: lapis lazuli. **prosperity**: Plant: snapdragon. **psychic dreams**: Plant: heliotrope. **recrimination**: Plant: pine. **regrets**: Plant: rue. **repressed emotions**: Plant: fuschia, onion. **resentment**: Plant: wormwood. **restrictions/constrictions**: Metal: copper; Stone: amethyst. **resentment**: Stone: sugilite; Plant: wormwood. **shame**: Stone: ruby. **sorrow**: (See: Sorrow). **spells**: Plant: elder, nutmeg. **spirituality**: Plant: myrrh, sandalwood. **stress**: Animal: lion; Stone: chalcanthite, hiddenite. **strife**: Stone: iolite; Plant: moneywort. **success**: Plant: clover. **subconscious tension**: Plant: corn, orange. **superstition**: Plant: blood root. **tension**: (See: Tension). **that which is no longer needed**: (See: Need). **toxins**: Stone: schist. **trauma**: Plant: fireweed, lady's tresses, orange. **truth**: Plant: Syrian rue. **wisdom**: Plant: rosemary.

Renewal

(See also: Rebirth, Regeneration, Rejuvenation)

New Moon/North/Spring/Scorpio

Tool: cauldron; Color: green, spring green; Charm: shed snake skin; Animal: serpent, snake; Plant: white African violet, elder, eucalyptus, reindeer moss, seeds and sprouts; Goddess: Athena, Hecate, Hokmah, Juno, Kali, the Maiden, Minerva, Ostara, Sekhmet, Tana, Venus; God: the Dagda, Mannan Mac Lir.

Emotional renewal: Plant: calla lily, carnation. **Self renewal**: Moon; Animal: bear; Plant: all perennial plants and deciduous trees; Goddess: Estsanatlehi. **Spiritual renewal**: God: Odin; *after an assault*: Goddess: Juturna.

Renewed hope: Plant: azalea, snowdrop; God: Mider.

Renewal of: an eon: Number: 432. **food supplies**: Goddess: Dea Nutrix; God: Mannan. **life**: Animal: dove, scarab beetle; Goddess: the Mother. **Nature**: (See: Nature). **Sacred places**: Plant: reindeer moss.

To renew: creation: God: Kalki. **energy**: (See: Energy). **interest in life**: Plant: wild rose. **life force**: Plant: gorse. **mental abilities**: Stone: turquoise. **psychic power(s)**: Plant: lovage (in bath). **sacred places**: (Plant: reindeer moss). **vitality**: (See: Vitality). **youth**: (See: Youth).

Repelling

(See: Averting)

Resilience

(See also: Flexibility, Strength)

Color: black; Stone: onyx, black opal; Plant: heather, snowdrop, sycamore, willow, yew. **emotional resilience**: Plant: dahlia.

Respect

Plant: gravel root; Goddess: Pietas.

Self-respect: Animal: skunk; Stone: pink calcite. **Respectful love**: Plant: lavender.

To: act with respect: Plant: linden. **gain the respect of others**: God: Bragi. **learn respect**: Goddess: Athena; *for your body*: Plant: marigold; *for boundaries*: Animal: elephant; *for dreams*: Animal: lizard; *for family members*: Plant: bloodroot; *for the opposite sex*: Plant: wild strawberry; *for oracles*: Goddess: Atalanta; *for trees*: Evocation: dryads, hamadryads.

Responsibility

Jupiter/Capricorn

Number: 6; Plant: devil's claw, lime.

To be responsible for: the consequences of your actions: Goddess: Greine. **yourself**: Goddess: Carravogue.

To: gain increased responsibility at work: Goddess: Inanna. **learn to hold your spouse responsible for an affair, not the third party**: Goddess: Greine. **meet responsibilities**: Goddess: Fides, Zorya; *meet family responsibilities*: Goddess: Pietas. **overcome fear of responsibility**: Animal: mountain lion. **take responsibility**: Plant: marigold.

Retribution

(See: Revenge)

Return

(See also: Reversal)

Sun/Moon/Venus/Water

Charm: boomerang; Animal: monarch butterfly, carrier pigeon, salmon, swallow; Goddess: Lada, Persephone; God: Baal, Damuzi, Helios, Osiris, Ra, Vishnu, Yarillo.

Safe return: Plant: mugwort; Goddess: Fortuna; *from a journey*: Goddess: Fortuna; *of a lost, stolen, or kidnapped child*: (See: Children).

Return of: affection: Color: orange; Plant: jonquil. **happiness**: Plant: lily of the valley. **joy**: Plant: calla lily, toadflax. **love**: Plant: ambrosia, toadflax; God: Anteros. **promise**: Plant: lily of the valley. **stolen goods**: Charm: magnet; Metal: iron; Stone: lodestone.

To: attract the return of a lover: Plant: damiana, dragon's blood, pineapple. **prevent the return of a spirit**: (See: Spirits). **refuse to return**: Goddess: Lilith; Evocation: Helen of Troy.

To return: evil to its sender/source: (See: Evil). **a hex**: (See: Hexes). **home**: Plant: mugwort; Goddess: Persephone; Evocation: Odysseus. **love**: Plant: ambrosia; God: Anteros. **magick to its sender**: Charm: mirror; Stone: red jasper. **negativity**: Charm: mirror; Stone: red jasper; Metal: brass; Plant: galangal. **negative energy to its sender**: Charm: mirror; Stone: red jasper, schist; Plant: pine. **peace to a home**: Charm: rosewater; Plant: rose. **psychic attack**: Charm: mirror; Stone: carnelian.

To return to: basics: Stone: agate. **life**: God: Deert. **reality**: Stone: blue chalcedony. **the sea**: Goddess: Bo Find; God: Dylan.

Revenge

Earth/Fire/Scorpio

Color: black; Animal: cobra, griffin, polar bear, wolverine; Plant: trefoil; Goddess: Alecto, Anath, Aphrodite, Arianrhod, Astarte, Circe, the Crone, Cybele, the Erinyes, Erzulie Dantor, the Furies, Hecate, Hera the Throttler, Holda, Itone, Kali, Lilith, Megaera, Melusine, the Morrigan, Nemesis, Poene, Praxidike, Sekhmet, Skadi, Tisiphone; God: Arawn, Chu Jung, Karttikeya, Lugh, Mars, Ra, Veive,

Wayland, Zeus Alastor; Evocation: Atreus, Clytemnestra, Cuchulain.

Divine vengeance: Goddess: Bast, the Erinyes, Nemesis, Sekhmet; God: Horus; Evocation: Auriel (Divine Avenger). **Karmic retribution**: Goddess: Nephthys. **Moral retribution**: God: Obaluaiye. **Patient revenge**: Animal: alligator, cat, crocodile; Evocation: Clytemnestra. **Physical revenge**: Plant: holly.

To avenge: **abuse**: Goddess: the Crone; God: Bran, Hephaestus. **broken oaths**: Goddess: Vör. **defiance of deities**: Goddess: Nemesis. **infidelity**: Goddess: Persephone, Propserine; God: Gwydion, Hephaestus. **insolence**: Goddess: Nemesis. **murder**: Goddess: the Crone, Tisiphone; God: Vali, Vidar. **seal hunting**: Evocation: selkies. **slighted love**: God: Anteros. **treachery**: God: Gwydion.

To: get revenge: Animal: jaguar. **judge the appropriateness of revenge**: Goddess: Melusine. **overcome desire for revenge**: Plant: canna lily. **protect against revenge**: Color: black.

Reversal

(See also: Return, Uncrossing)

Waning Moon

Charm: brimstone (as incense), mirror, wheel (revolving backwards); Color: black, red; Stone: red jasper, salt, sea salt; Plant: dragon's blood, rue, sage; Goddess: Cailleach; God: Zeus.

To reverse: **fortune**: Waning Moon. **hexes**: (See: Hexes). **bad luck**: God: Orunmila. **negative cycles**: Charm: van van. **negative energy**: Plant: pine; Stone: red jasper, schist. **spells**: (See: Spells). **negativity**: (See: Negativity).

Riches

(See: Wealth)

Romance

(See also: Affection, Love)

Venus/Full Moon/Dawn/May/Friday/ Pisces/Libra

Color: pink, red, rose; Number: 2; Animal: bee; Stone: pink diamond, rose quartz, pink tourmaline; Plant: apple, azalea, cherry, heather, jasmine, lavender, lovage root, pink rose, sandalwood, valerian, ylang-ylang; Goddess: Anath, Belili, Belit ilanit, Benzaiten, Cerridwen, Erzulie, Hathor, Ishtar, Isis (Lady of Romance), Urvasi, Venus; God: Amon-Ra, Angus, Cupid, Eros, Kama, Krishna.

Romantic love: (See: Love). **Romantic relationship**: (See: Relationships).

To attract romance: Color: orange; Stone: lodestone; Oil: blue sonata; Plant: orris root, tuberose; *from someone of the opposite sex*: Plant: lovage root.

Ruin

(See also: Destruction, Problems)

Animal: dragon; Goddess: Lilith, Mara, Pheme; God: Loki, Neepec.

Financial ruin: *to prevent*: Stone: tiger-eye. **Ruinous conduct**: Goddess: Ate.

To: call storms that ruin harvests: Goddess: Hecate. **escape ruin**: Evocation: Aeneas. **ruin a yard or lawn**: Plant: couch grass.

Rumors

(See: Gossip)

Chapter 19

The Sacred

Tool: cauldron, chalice; Color: red, yellow, white; Charm: barley cakes, anything struck by lightning; Number: 7, 8, 9, 13, 72, pi; Animal: boar, buffalo (especially white buffalo), cat, cow, crane, dog, white dog with red ears, black dove, golden eagle, elephant, falcon, horse, ibis, mouse, pheasant, slug, swan, wryneck; Metal: gold; Stone: yellow chrysolite, coral (especially red coral), emerald, garnet, jade, lapis lazuli, malachite, moonstone, salt, sapphire, turquoise, a circle of large standing stones; Fungus: fly agaric, mushroom, psilocybe mushroom; Plant: acacia, African marigold, alder, apple, ash, asoka, balsam, banyan, baobab, holy basil, birch, bodhi tree, cascara sagrada, cedar, deodar cedar, cedar of Lebanon, clover, crataeva, cypress, datura, dittany, dogwood, doum palm, dragon tree, elder, elm, fennel, fig, sacred fig tree, frangipani, frankincense, garlic, ginkgo, hawthorn, hazel, heliotrope, hellebore, hickory, hyssop, iroko, ivy, larch, laurel, lentil, lotus, blue lotus, marjoram, meadowsweet, mistletoe (especially when growing on oak), nettle, oak, olive tree, onion, moriche palm, susa palm, peach tree, primrose, pulsatilla, redwood, rose apple, rowan, sage, verbena, vervain, vine, willow, winter bark, wolfsbane, yarrow, yerba santa, yew, anything growing on an oak tree; God: Enki (Lord of the Sacred Eye).

Sacred affection: Plant: marigold. **Sacred buildings**: *to protect*: Color: coral.

Sacred dance: Animal: grouse; Goddess: Hathor; God: Shiva. **Sacred fire**: Plant: dittany, hazel, oak; Goddess: Hestia, Vesta; *to carry*: Plant: fennel stalk; *to kindle*: Stone: clear quartz crystal; Plant: oak fire drill. **Sacred flames**: Goddess: Brigid, Vesta. **Sacred gifts**: Animal: gyrfalcon. **Sacred groves**: Plant: acacia, apple, cedar, cypress, hazel, oak, olive, palm, plane, poplar, terebinth, willow; Goddess: Diana Nematona (Diana of the Sacred Grove), Nematona, Nemesis; God: Mars Rigonemetis (King of the Sacred Grove); *stewardship of*: Goddess: Arnamentia, Nematona; *to protect*: Goddess: Diana Nematona, Diana Nemorensi. **Sacred intoxicants**: Potion: kekyon, wine; Fungus: fly agaric, peyote, psilocybe mushroom; Plant: cannabis; God: Dionysus, Shiva. **Sacred kingship**: Color: crimson, purple; Number: 19; Charm: golden apple; Animal: horse; Plant: alder, barley; God: Dushares; Evocation: Curoi, Dyas, Hercules; *death of the sacred king*: Plant: oak, kerm oak; *by drowning*: Animal: all diving birds; *to decoy to*: Plant: apple. **Sacred knowledge**: North; Stone: lapis lazuli. **Sacred laws**: Goddess: Inanna. **Sacred magick**: (See: Magick). **Sacred marriage**: (See: Marriage). **Sacred mountains**: Goddess: Giriputri, Gunung Agaung, Sengen-Sama (Mt. Fujiyama); *spirit of*: Goddess: Yama-No-Kami. **Sacred places**: Goddess: Sekhmet (Most Holy of Places); *to protect*: Goddess: Nematona, Sheela-na-gig; *to purify*: Plant: vervain; *to renew*: Plant: reindeer moss. **Sacred poetry**: Goddess: Freya, Polyhymnia. **Sacred**

power: Animal: jaguar. **Sacred promiscuity**: Venus; Goddess: Anahita, Anath. **Sacred prostitutes**: Goddess: Athtart, Xochiquetzal. **Sacred prostitution**: Venus; Goddess: Acca Larentia, Aphrodite, Inanna, Ishtar, Kilili Mushritu (She Who Leans Out Invitingly), Qadesh, Teteoinnan, Tlazolteotl, Venus, White Shell Woman. **Sacred protection**: Plant: sandalwood. **Sacred records**: *to protect*: Animal: crow. **Sacred rites**: Plant: cinnamon, frankincense. **Sacred robes**: Plant: flax; Goddess: Amaterasu. **Sacred sex**: Plant: clary sage. **Sacred sexuality**: (See: Sexuality). **Sacred smoke**: Plant: tobacco; Goddess: Ptè San Wi. **Sacred songs**: Animal: bluebird, lark; Goddess: Polyhymnia. **Sacred space**: Color: white; Animal: baboon; Goddess: Nematona; *to create*: Tool: besom, censer, drum, gong; Method: music, asperging; Plant: broom, copal, frankincense, galbanum, myrrh, mullein, rue (for asperging with), vervain; Goddess: Isis, Ptè San Wi, Sheela-na-gig; God: Moccus, Mummu, Terminus; *to create outdoors*: Plant: pine bough (for sweeping); *to protect*: Goddess: Nematona, Vajravaraki; God: Dunatis; *to purify*: Plant: clove. **Sacred spells**: God: Kothar-wa-Khasis. **Sacred ways**: Goddess: Ptè San Wi. **Sacred wells**: Water; Goddess: Caedda, Sulis; *stewardship of*: Goddess: Sionnan; *to heal by poetic incantations at*: Goddess: Brigid; *to tend*: Goddess: Aibheaeg. **Sacred wisdom**: North; Goddess: Sophia. **Sacred words**: God: Kothar-wa-Khasis.

To: **enable communication between the sacred and the secular**: God: Legba. **understand that all/nothing is sacred**: Animal: coyote.

Sacrifice
Full Moon/Fire/East/South

Tool: censer; Method: bonfire; Color: black, red; Charm: barley cake, blood, image of human or animal; Animal: bull, chicken, cow, eland, goat, ox, pig, ram, rooster, sheep, sparrow; Stone: pink tourmaline; Plant: ash, barley, cedar, coca leaf, all flowers, frankincense, garlic, grain, hyssop, lavender (as incense), myrrh, oak, rice, rose, vervain, an apple or fig stuck with sticks to represent an animal, all incense; Goddess: Anath, Garbh Ogh, Tlachtga; God: Cernunnos, Chac, Cromm Cruiach, Holly King, Jesus, Mabon, Oak King, Odin, Ysbadadden; Evocation: John Barleycorn.

Animal sacrifice: God: Rudra. **Blood sacrifice**: Goddess: Artemis. **Bloodless sacrifice**: Goddess: Venus. **Loving sacrifice**: Plant: hyssop, marigold. **Ritual sacrifice**: Goddess: Anath. **Self-sacrifice**: Charm: Eye of Horus; Animal: coyote, lizard, pelican; Goddess: Enekpe; God: Horned God, Horus, Kamapua, Nanautzin, Odin, Ptah, Shiva, Tyr; *to learn not to sacrifice yourself*: Plant: tarragon, witch hazel.

To: **sacrifice beauty**: Goddess: Triduana. **sacrifice for the greater good**: Animal: deer; God: Nanautzin. **understand sacrifice**: Plant: cypress.

Sadness
(See: Sorrow)

Safety
(See also: Protection, Security)
Day

Color: gold; Charm: anchor; Stone: ruby, tanzanite; Plant: birch, holly, sage, spearmint, vervain; Goddess: Securitas, Soteria; God: Asaruludu, Jizo Bosatsu.

Public safety: Goddess: Salus.
Safe childbirth: (See: Childbirth). **Safe haven**: God: Nari lugal-dimmankia. **Safe home**: Goddess: Demeter; *safe house for battered women*: Goddess: Juno. **Safe landing**: Animal: cat. **Safe passage**: (See: Passage). **Safe place/space**: Color: blue, green, white, yellow; Animal: cat; Plant: calla lily,

catnip. **Safe recovery of someone who has been kidnapped:** God: Hanuman. **Safe return:** (See: Return). **Safe sleep:** Plant: laurel. **Safe transition to the afterlife:** (See: Afterlife). **Safe travel:** (See: Travel). **Safe astral travel:** Plant: cinnamon.

Safety and rescue: Goddess: Belat. **Safety at: night:** Goddess: Ratri. **sea:** God: Thor. **safety in the afterlife:** God: Bes.

To: balance risk and safety: Animal: coyote. **feel safe:** Stone: sandstone. **find safety:** Plant: enchanter's nightshade. **help a child find his/her way safely home:** Goddess: Persephone, Prosperina. **leave safety:** Animal: butterfly. **let infants drink safely:** Goddess: Potnia. **make safe:** Color: blue; Stone: sapphire.

Satisfaction

(See also: Contentment, Happiness, Success)

Color: peach; Animal: bluebird, hawk, silkmoth; Plant: violet; Goddess: Habondia, Unk, Voluptas.

Sexual satisfaction: Plant: patchouli roots (under the bed); Goddess: Achtland, Aeval, Ishtar, Kilili Mushritu, Pelé; *to seek*: Goddess: Eos, Lilith, Luonnotar. **Spiritual satisfaction:** Goddess: Lakshmi.

Satisfying honeymoon: Goddess: Juno Cioxia.

To satisfy: appetites: Animal: wolverine. **desires:** (See: Desires). **lust:** Venus; Plant: peach. **need:** (See: Need).

Secrecy

Pluto/Moon/North/Scorpio/Cancer

Animal: bobcat, cat, crane, heron, mouse, owl; Number: 7, 8; Charm: full-blown rose over two rosebuds; Plant: fig, rose; Goddess: Angerona, Diana, the Dark Goddess, Isis, Guhya Kali (Secret Kali), Umbria, Yemaya

(Mother of Dreams and Secrets); God: Amon, Harpocrates, Mithras, Orunmila (Father of Secrets), Sin.

Alphabetic secrets: Animal: crane, swan. **Betrayed secrets:** Plant: caraway. **Deep secrets:** Waning Moon; Goddess: Yemaya. **Fairy secrets:** *to learn*: Plant: cowslip, forget-me-not. **Hidden secrets:** Color: black; Charm: black feather; *revealed*: Plant: honeysuckle. **Inner secrets:** Stone: geode; *to discover*: Waning Moon. **Magickal secrets:** Goddess: Diana. **Ocean secrets:** Goddess: Yemaya. **Poetic secrets:** Animal: crane. **Prophetic secrets:** Animal: hoopoe.

Secret hope: Metal: tin. **Secret joy:** Stone: geode; Plant: crimson rose. **Secret knowledge:** (See: Knowledge). **Secret love:** (See: Love). **Secret messages:** Animal: owl. **Secret plans:** God: Consus. **Secret power:** Stone: geode; Plant: ivy; Goddess: Hecate. **Secret rites:** Goddess: Agave, Demeter; *of men*: God: Mithras; *of women*: Goddess: Bona Dea, Ceres, Fauna; Plant: flax. **Secret societies:** God: Kuan Kung. **Secret teachings:** *to protect*: Goddess: Senge Dongma. **Secret wisdom:** God: Nereus, Thoth. **Secret worship:** Goddess: Aradia. **Secret properties of plants:** God: Loco. **Secrets taken to the grave:** Goddess: Nephthys.

To: encourage revelation of secrets: Animal: horned owl; Plant: frangipani; Goddess: Blodeuwedd, Isis. **disguise a secret:** Animal: lapwing (black plover). **find out/discover secrets:** Animal: all birds; Goddess: Isis, Vör; Evocation: Cuchulain. **find your secret magickal name:** Goddess: Angerona; God: Arawn. **get someone to reveal a secret:** Goddess: Blodeuwedd; Evocation: Delilah. **hide secrets:** Animal: roebuck. **keep secrets:** North; Animal: dog, lynx; Stone: unbroken geode; Plant: juniper berry, lavender, white oak, rose, sage; Goddess: Angerona, Frigg, Geshtinanna, Umbria; God: Amon-Ra; *keep one's true* *religion a secret*: Goddess: Isis Amenti. **learn the secret language of trees**: Goddess: Kupala. **protect secrets**: Animal: bobwhite, dog; Plant: rose. **reveal secrets**: Color: white. Plant: honeysuckle.

Secretiveness

Scorpio

Color: black, gray; Animal: mandrill, platypus; Stone: geode.

Security

(See also: Amulets, Protection, Safety, Talismans)

Taurus

Animal: turtle; Metal: silver; Plant: apple, coriander, oak, olive, rice; Goddess: Chantico, Hestia, Securitas, Vesta; God: Gilma.

Business security: Plant: olive; *to protect a business from hexes*: Plant: marjoram. **Calm security**: Color: pink. **Emotional security**: Number: 2; *to increase*: Stone: malachite; *to increase in children*: Charm: teddy bear; Plant: chamomile (tea or syrup). **Home security**: Animal: chicken, pigeon; Plant: spearmint; Goddess: Demeter. **To avert**: *black magick from the home*: Plant: dill seed; *burglars/thieves from the home*: (See: Thieves); *evil from the home*: Plant: dogwood (rubbed on doorknobs), fennel (hung over doorways), garlic, nettle, papaya twigs (over the door), pomegranate tree (grown outside the door), rosemary (grown in the yard or near the door); *negativity from the home*: Charm: bells on the door; Plant: blueberry, ivy; *burglars/thieves from the home*: Plant: mustard seed; *to prevent evil spirits from entering the house*: Plant: fennel leaves (stuffed in the bedroom keyhole), hawthorn, black hellebore (planted by the door).

To protect the home: Color: purple, violet; Charm: bells (hung on or over door), brass amulet, right handprint (on outside wall), horseshoe (over the door), iron fence, iron nails (buried on property), Kananga Water, witch's bottle (buried on property or secreted in front closet); Animal: cat, dog; Metal: brass, iron; Stone: alum, lodestone; Plant: acacia, avens, bat nut (above doors and windows), betony, chamomile, cinquefoil, coriander, dragon's blood, elder, fennel (grown near house), fern, figwort, garlic, pink geranium, gum arabic, holly, houseleek, ivy (growing on house), laurel, lemon, lilac, lemon, mandrake, American mandrake (root, hung high indoors), marjoram, mimosa, mistletoe, morning glory, mustard seed (sprinkled across or buried beneath doorway), oak, periwinkle, raspberry branches (hung over doors and at windows), rosemary (grown near door), rowan, St. John's Wort, vetiver; Goddess: Bast, Juno, Lakshmi; God: Anubis, Legba, Syen, Zeus Herkios; *from black magick*: Plant: marjoram, St. John's Wort; *from danger*: (See: Danger); *from evil*: Plant: asphodel (planted near the entrance to the property), avens, holy basil, birch tree (planted in the yard), white daffodils (planted in the yard), yellow daffodils (grown indoors), ferns (grown near the house), hemlock (planted in the yard), holly (grown in the yard), ivy (grown on or near the house), pomegranate tree (planted near the door), rosemary (grown in yard), rowan branches, yucca; God: Men Shen; *from evil spirits*: Charm: vervain-water (sprinkled); Animal: cricket; *from negative influences*: Plant: coriander, cypress, meadowsweet garland (hung indoors); *from intruders/visitors*: Plant: coriander, juniper, spearmint; *from lightning*: (See: Lightning); *from outsiders*: Goddess: Athena; *from storms/storm damage*: Plant: ferns (as house plants), laurel (planted in the yard), St. John's Wort (hung in window); Goddess: Fulgora; *from thieves*: Color: black; Plant: bat nut (above doors or on window sills), garlic (hung up), juniper (grown near house), black pepper (sprinkled across doorways and window sills); *to protect the household*: Animal: dog; Plant: aloe, hazel, laurel, marjoram, pomegranate grown near door, rosemary grown near door; Goddess: Astarte, Bastet, Frigg, Hestia, Nephthys, Vesta; God: Anubis, Asuha-No-Kami, Kunado-No-Kami, Lar, Zeus Herkeios; Evocation: the Lares; *from illness*: Plant: eucalyptus, mandrake.

Inner security: Potion: raspberry leaf tea; God: Brahma. **Material security**: Charm: square.

Secure emotional commitment: Number: 2. **Secure family**: Plant: olive. **Secure footing**: Animal: mountain goat, llama. **Secure love**: Stone: emerald; Plant: olive. **Secure operation of world systems**: God: Varuna. **Secure passage**: God: Aker.

To: attract security: Plant: cinnamon, vetiver. **feel secure**: Stone: avalonite, tigereye; Plant: mullein; *false sense of security*: Animal: wolf.

Insecurity

Cancer

To: confront your innermost fears and insecurities: Goddess: Kupala. **reduce insecurity**: Color: coral; Stone: jasper, kunzite; Plant: garlic, mallow.

Selfishness

(See also: Greed)

Aries

Number: 1.

Selfish lust: Plant: African marigold.

To: improve selfishness: Stone: moonstone; Plant: benzoin; Plant: apple. **punish selfishness**: God: Akongo.

Unselfishness

(See also: Charity, Generosity, Hospitality)

Color: pink, rose; Number: 9; Stone: moonstone; Plant: tarragon; Goddess: Ma'at; God: Hanuman.

Sense

(See also: Intelligence, Senses)

God: Sentinus.

Common sense: Color: brown; Metal: gold; Stone: hematite; Plant: rosemary.

Sense of: connection with others: Stone: ruby. **freedom**: Stone: ruby, sugilite; Plant: geranium; God: Hermes. **humor**: Aquarius; God: Bes. **identity**: Animal: wolf. **responsibility**: *to ease*: Plant: valerian. **security**: *false sense*: Animal: wolf. **well-being**: Plant: coca leaf, masterwort, poppy. **wonder**: Animal: butterfly, hummingbird, sea horse.

Senses

(See also: Perception, Vision)

Taurus

Color: blue, green, red, white, yellow; Number: 5; God: Shiva (Lord of the Senses), Ve.

Acute senses: God: Purusha. **Physical sensation**: Goddess: Sentia. **Sensory awareness**: Stone: hematite, ruby. **Sensory perception**: God: Sif.

To: control the senses: Stone: chrysocolla; Plant: aspen, rowan. **restore lost senses**: Stone: lignite, wonderstone; Plant: lemon balm, melilot, rosemary; God: Odin. **strengthen senses**: Animal: fox, jackal, wolf; Plant: cinquefoil, sage. **trust your senses**: Animal: electric eel, ferret, sea turtle.

Hearing

Air/Ether; Color: blue; Animal: bear, chipmunk, frog, sea turtle; Stone: amethyst; Goddess: Tashnit; God: Al-Sham'ah.

Divine hearing: Goddess: Fama, Isis (Hearer of Prayers, All-Hearing), Kwan Yin (Hearer of Cries), Sekhmet (She Who Listens to Prayers). **Inner hearing**: Stone: anhydrite, Herkimer diamond, clear quartz crystal; Plant: bougainvillea, mullein.

Power of hearing: God: Ve. **Hearing problems**: Stone: amethyst.

Listening: Animal: deer, raven; Plant: patchouli, pine; *attentive listening*: Plant: marigold; *power to listen*: North; *to be listened to*: Color: purple; *to listen to your higher self*: Stone: angelite; Plant: angelica; *to learn to listen to your inner voice*: Stone: labradorite; Plant: pine; *to listen to others*: God: Bres.

To hear: both sides in a disagreement: God: Forseti. **cries for help**: Goddess: Kwan Yin. **grievances**: God: Forseti. **prayers**: Goddess: Isis (Hearer of Prayers), Sekhmet (She Who Listens to Prayers). **truth**: Plant: pine.

To: improve hearing: Plant: garlic, ginkgo. **learn not to believe everything you hear**: Goddess: Ailinn. **trust what sounds right to you**: Animal: muskrat.

Sight

Fire; Color: green, white; Animal: cheetah, condor, eagle, hawk, lynx, owl, black vulture; Stone: Apache tear, aventurine, emerald, malachite, opal, tigereye; Goddess: Ophthalmitis.

Clear sight: Color: clear, indigo; Plant: birch. **Divine sight**: Sun; Goddess: Isis (All-Seeing), Sekhmet (Eye of Ra), Sulis (Seeing Eye); God: Ra, Shamash, Sol, Varuna. **First sight**: *love at*: Charm: lightning bolt; God: Zeus; *lust at*: God: Zeus. **Good eyesight**: Animal: eagle, macaw; Plant: vervain. **Inner sight**: Color: indigo; Stone: Apache tear. **Power of sight**: Plant: queen of the night; God: Ve.

Ability to see: the big picture: Animal: elephant. **both sides of an issue**: Animal: coyote. **inner beauty**: Goddess: Psyche. **into the future**: Stone: lapis lazuli. **what others miss**: Animal: owl. **what troubled you**: Stone: apatite.

To: improve sight: Stone: Goddess rock (look through hole), opal; Plant: birch, clove. **restore sight**: Stone: rhodochrosite; Plant: eyebright, fennel, rue; Goddess: Eos, Hathor; God: Al Ruyah, Bugid Y Aiba, Sobek. **safeguard eyesight of newborns**: Goddess: Lucina. **strengthen sight**: Color: green; Stone: green aventurine, chrysoprase, emerald, lapis lazuli, lodestone (set in silver), peridot, turquoise; Plant: caraway seed, clove, eyebright, juniper berry. **trust what you see**: Animal: vulture; Metal: peacock ore.

To see: beyond ordinary reality: Plant: cannabis, datura, orchid. **beyond yourself**: Plant: birch. **the big picture**: Plant: silver fir. **both sides of an issue**: Animal: coyote. **in darkness**: (See: Darkness). **fairies**: (See: Fairies). **the future**: Tool: crystal ball, scrying dish or mirror; Stone: emerald, lapis lazuli. **the heart of the matter**: Animal: hawk. **magickal creatures**: Plant: marigold. **the past**: Tool: crystal ball, scrying dish or mirror; *past lives*: Plant: sandalwood. **spirits**: (See: Spirits). **the truth**: (See: Truth). **winds**: Animal: goat, pig. **yourself**: Tool: mirror; Animal: coyote; Goddess: Amaterasu; Evocation: Narcissus.

Smell

Air/Earth; Tool: censer; Color: yellow; Animal: aardvark, bear, dingo, dog (especially bloodhound), ferret, hyena, moth, pig, shark, starfish, turkey vulture; Charm: sachet; Plant: asafetida, basil, cinnamon, clove, lemon, garlic, mint, pine, rosemary, tansy, soapwort, vetiver; all scented flowers, incense, strong-smelling plants and pungent spices.

To: **neutralize smells**: Plant: parsley, summer savory. **restore the sense of smell**: Plant: cat thyme, soapwort. **trust what smells right to you**: Animal: shark.

Taste

Water; Animal: carp, catfish, all bottom-dwelling marine life; Color: red; Plant: all edible plants with intense flavors.

Touch

Earth/Air/Taurus; Charm: magickal powder; Animal: flamingo, leopard, mole, spider, starfish, all primates; Plant: avocado, bistort, calamus, primrose; Goddess: Hathor.

Gentle touch: Animal: deer; Plant: ladies slipper. **Healing touch**: Scorpio.

To trust what you feel: Animal: mole, spider.

Sensitivity

(See also: Emotions)

Neptune/Libra/Pisces

Color: blue, lavender, purple, violet; Number: 2; Animal: crab, deer, panda, rabbit, swan; Plant: ash, aspen, hibiscus, mimosa, orange, rosemary, valerian, violet; God: Apollo.

Domestic sensitivity: Cancer. **Emotional sensitivity**: Animal: starfish. **Hidden sensitivity**: Animal: crab. **Physical sensitivity**: Animal: mole; Oil: neroli. **Psychic sensitivity**: Moon/Water/Cancer/Aquarius; Plant: clove, violet.

Sensitivity in communication: Animal: catfish; Plant: marigold.

Sensitivity to: auras: Animal: rattlesnake. **cold**: Plant: chamomile, cucumber, lavender, peppermint, rock rose. **environment**: Animal: salamander. **light**: Plant: St. John's Wort. **natural cycles**: Stone: moonstone. **others**: Animal: copperhead; *feelings of others*: Stone: moonstone; *needs of others*: Goddess: Walo. **vibrations**: Animal: mole.

To: awaken sensitivity: Animal: cricket. **increase sensitivity**: Animal: canary; Stone: moonstone, pink tourmaline; Plant: eyebright, rosemary. **stimulate sensitivity**: Charm: sea shell.

Insensitivity

Fire

Oversensitivity

Color: pink, violet; Number: 9; Animal: chimera.

To reduce oversensitivity: Plant: chamomile, daisy, germander, jojoba, cat thyme, valerian, wolfsbane, zinnia.

Sensuality

Venus/Waxing Moon/Earth/Water/Taurus/Libra

Color: pink, yellow; Animal: cat, tiger; Plant: amber, damiana, hibiscus, jasmine, mustard seed, patchouli, queen of the night, sandalwood, strawberry, turmeric; Goddess: Aphrodite, Freya, Hathor, Inanna, Indrani, Itzpapalotl, Kali, Sentia, Volupta, Xochiquetzal; God: Hrishikesha, Indra.

Female sensuality: *to increase*: Plant: juniper berry. **Sensual love**: Taurus; Color: scarlet; Goddess: Sarasvati. **Sensual passion**: (See: Passion). **Sensual pleasure**: Goddess: Freya.

To awaken sensuality: Plant: rose, vetiver.

Serenity

(See: Tranquility)

Service

Color: pink; Number: 6; Animal: horse; Plant: rowan, sweet pea; Goddess: Hebe, Iris, Ninsubur; Evocation: Ganymede.

Public service: Aquarius; Plant: lime; *to protect public servants*: God: Emperor Kuan. **Military service**: *to avoid*: Plant: four-leaf clover. **guidance in service**: Goddess: Frigg.

To serve the Goddess with the altar of your body: Goddess: Yolkai Estsan.

Sex

(See also: Libido, Lovers, Lust, Passion, Sexuality)

Venus/Mars/Fire/Friday/Aries/Taurus/Scorpio

Color: red; Charm: musk; Stone: ruby; Animal: rabbit; Plant: jasmine, patchouli; Goddess: Aeval, Anath, Aphrodite, Astarte, Artemis, Ashtoreth, Bast, Druantia, Erzulie, Freya, Ishtar (Great Lover), Kupala, Lilith, the Morrigan, Oshun, P'an Chin-Lien, Tlazolteotl, Venus, Xochiquetzal; God: Agni, Coyote, Dosojin, Eros, Ghede, Pan, Tunkan Ingan. Evocation: satyrs.

Good sex: Plant: lemongrass. **Rough sex**: Goddess: Eos; God: Nergal. **Sacred sex**: Plant: clary sage; Goddess: Anahita, Anath, Qadesh. **Violent sex**: Goddess: Ishtar.

Sex act: Goddess: Aphrodite, Druantia; God: Eros; *cunnilingus*: Goddess: Bast; *orgies*: Goddess: Ops; *voyeurism*: Goddess: Peeping Aphrodite. **Sex crimes**: *to escape*: Goddess: Akycha, Atalanta; Evocation: Asteria, Cyparissus, Daphne, Pitys, Syrinx; *to punish*: Goddess: Aine; *to recover from*: Plant: lemon balm; *to report*: Goddess: Alcippe. **Sex drive**: (See: Libido). **Sex magick**: (See: Magick). **Sex organs**: (See: The Body: reproductive system).

Sexual ability: Goddess: Anath, Maeve; God: Fergus, Herne. **Sexual activity**: Animal: moth. **Sexual advances**: Mars/Venus; Plant: betony, rose hips; *to make*: Goddess: Carna, Greine, Inanna, Ishtar, the Morrigan;

God: Azacca, El, Enki, Pan, Ravana, Zeus; Evocation: Peleus, satyrs; *to refuse*: Goddess: Asherah, Rhiannon, Sita, Thetis, Triduana, Uttu; Evocation: Cuchulain, Gilgamesh, nymphs, Penelope. **Sexual aggressiveness**: Goddess: Isis, Kali. **Sexual appetite**: (See: Libido). **Sexual arousal**: Stone: sunstone. **Sexual assault**: *to recover from*: Plant: lemon balm; *assault of males by females*: Plant: flax. **Sexual attention**: *to attract*: Charm: musk; Plant: High John, rose hip; Goddess: Aphrodite, Nimuë/Vivienne; God: Krishna. **Sexual attraction**: Plant: orris root; God: Krishna; *mutual*: Plant: magnolia. **Sexual attractiveness**: *female*: Plant: rose hips; *male*: Plant: acorn. **Sexual blocks**: (See: Blockages). **Sexual boundaries**: *to transcend*: God: Dionysus, Hermes, Pan. **Sexual chakra**: (See: Chakras). **Sexual confusion**: *to overcome*: Plant: coconut. **Sexual creativity**: (See: Creativity). **Sexual desire**: (See: Desire, Lust). **Sexual disorders**: (See: Diseases/Disorders). **Sexual ecstasy**: Goddess: Anath. **Sexual encounters**: Plant: saw palmetto; Goddess: Anahita, Aphrodite; God: Krishna; *anonymous*: Goddess: Artemis; *homosexual*: Plant: safflower. **Sexual empowerment**: Stone: lava. **Sexual energy**: (See: Energy). **Sexual excess**: God: Shiva; *to treat*: Stone: topaz. **Sexual excitement**: Plant: violet. **Sexual expertise**: God: Krishna. **Sexual expression**: Plant: apple. **Sexual extravagance**: Goddess: Erzulie, Flora. **Sexual freedom**: (See: Freedom). **Sexual grounding**: Plant: sandalwood. **Sexual guilt**: *to cleanse*: Goddess: Tlazolteotl. **Sexual harmony**: Stone: garnet. **Sexual healing**: Venus; Color: red; Goddess: Kilili-Mushritu. **Sexual intrigue**: Goddess: Venus. **Sexual inventiveness**: God: P'an Chin-Lien. **Sexual issues**: *to deal with*: Plant: basil. **Sexual joy**: (See: Joy). **Sexual liberation**: (See: Liberation). **Sexual love**: (See: Love). **Sexual need**: Venus; Goddess: Anath, Medb; God: Shiva. **Sexual** passion: (See: Passion). **Sexual pleasure**: (See: Pleasure). **Sexual potency**: Color: red; Plant: dragon's blood; *male sexual potency*: Plant: ginseng, oak, mistletoe; God: Maximon, Min. **Sexual power**: (See: Power). **Sexual prowess**: Plant: aloe, saffron; Goddess: Anath, Arani, Astarte, Maeve; God: Fergus, Herne, Min, Nergal; *male sexual prowess*: Plant: High John root (carried by a man below his waist). **Sexual revelry**: Goddess: Vacuna. **Sexual satisfaction**: (See: Satisfaction). **Sexual tension**: (See: Tension). **Sexual union**: (See: Union). **Sexual vibrations**: (See: Vibrations). **Sexual vigor**: God: Shiva. **Sexual virility**: Animal: goat. **Sexual vitality**: (See: Vitality). **Sexual weakness**: *to strengthen*: Plant: black cohosh. **Sexual well being**: Stone: aventurine. **Sexual wishes**: Goddess: Aeval, Maeve.

Sex in the afterlife: (See: Afterlife). **Sex in the morning**: Goddess: Eos. **Healthy sex life**: Goddess: Parvati; God: Bes.

To: **initiate men into the Mysteries of sex**: Goddess: the Horae. **improve sex**: Stone: smoky quartz; *in a relationship*: Plant: jasmine. **increase sex**: Plant: mint. **make men perform sexually**: Plant: bistort root; Goddess: Maeve. **protect sex within marriage**: Goddess: Cloacina. **resolve sexual issues**: Stone: prase. **use sex to get what you want**: Goddess: Freya.

Ⓢexuality

(See also: Sex)

Venus/Full Moon/Fire/Scorpio/Sagittarius

Charm: civet, musk; Animal: clam, oyster, rabbit, snake, turtle; Stone: garnet; Plant: hibiscus, mastic, mint, vanilla; Goddess: Aeval, Aideen, Ailinn, Aphrodite, Asherah, Astarte, Ayida, Bast, Branwen, Dahut, Dubhlaing, Hathor, Inanna, Ishtar (Goddess of Sighing), Macha, Medb, Mylitta, Naamah, Nephthys, Oshun, Pertunda, Tara, Teteoinnan, Tlazolteotl, Ushas, Xochiquetzal; God: Cernunnos, Damballah, Krishna, Min, Yarillo; Evocation: Agrat Bat Mahalat, 'Aisha Quandisha.

Bisexuality: God: Ptah. **Earthy sexuality**: Taurus; Plant: patchouli, vetiver; God: Hermes. **Female sexuality**: Charm: sea shell, open shell; Plant: hawthorn; Goddess: Akka, Aphrodite, Qadesh; *to contact*: Plant: hibiscus. **Frank sexuality**: God: Pan. **Free sexuality**: Stone: onyx. **Homosexuality**: *male*: God: Set; *homosexual love*: (See: Love). **Male sexuality**: Animal: eel; God: Backlum Chaam, Horned God, Pan, Pluto, Priapus, Sarudahiko. **Sacred sexuality**: Goddess: Kilili-Mushritu, Qadesh; God: Shiva; *to awaken*: Plant: sandalwood; *sacredness of sexuality*: Goddess: Qadesh. **Spiritual sexuality**: Method: tantra; Plant: lavender, rose; *sexuality as a road to spiritual illumination*: Method: tantra; Goddess: Tara. **Uncompromising sexuality**: Goddess: Kali. **Wanton sexuality**: Number: 5; Plant: primrose.

Power of sexuality: Goddess: Qadesh. **Sexuality as a road to spiritual illumination**: Method: tantra; Goddess: Tara.

To: **accept your sexuality**: Stone: ruby. **awaken sexuality**: Plant: ylang-ylang. **control sexuality**: Virgo; Color: white; Charm: orange flower water, witch hazel; Stone: amethyst, jasper, clear quartz crystal, sapphire; Plant: acacia, cactus, camphor, coconut, cucumber, fleabane, hawthorn, lavender, lettuce, orange blossom, pineapple, sweet pea, vervain, witch hazel; Other; orange flower water, witch hazel; Goddess: Artemis, Diana, Emer, Matronit, Sita; God: Mithras; *control female sexuality*: Stone: emerald. **enhance sexuality**: Plant: cannabis, mint with savory. **free sexuality**: Stone: onyx. **own your own sexuality**: Goddess: Ashtoreth, Atalanta. **unblock sexuality**: Plant: hibiscus.

Shapeshifting
(See also: Change, Transformation, Transmutation)

Air/Water

Method: dancing, drumming; Charm: shape-changing water; Animal: coyote, crow, fox, hare, jaguar, owl, merlin, raven, salmon, squid, swan, wolf, gray wolf; Metal: mercury (toxic, not recommended); Plant: catnip, yucca (twisted into a circle that is then stepped into); Goddess: Annis, Artemis, Banba, Benzaiten, Cerridwen, Coatlicue, Dechtere, Demeter, Diana, Epona, Eriu, Estsanatlehi, Flidais, Freya, Frigg, Gefion, Goda, Greine, Hecate, Inari, Iris, Isis, Lilith, Melusine, Morgen, the Morrigan, Nemain, Otter Woman, Pelé, Philyra, Pte San Wi, Scylla, Tatsuta-Hima, Thetis, Ushas, Vedma, Visahari; God: Achelous, Angus, Arawn, Cernunnos, Cian, Cuchulain, Cu Roi, Damuzi, Dionysus, Eshu, Fintan, Gucumatz, Gwion, Kamapua, Llew Llaw, Loki, Mannan, Michabo (Great Hare), Nakki, Odin, Poseidon, Proteus, Pwyll, Quikinn A'Qu (Big Raven), Svarog, Vainamoinen, Vertumnus, Zagreus, Zeus, Zeus Atabyrius; Evocation: the hu hsien, Merlin, Periclymenus, Seryï Volk (Gray Wolf), Taliesin, Vila, the vodonoi, water spirits and elementals.

Shyness
Color: yellow; Animal: crab, mandrill, mouse, wolf; Stone: lepidolite; Plant: vetch, violet, wallflower; Goddess: Parvati, Sarasvati.

To: overcome shyness: Stone: apatite; Plant: ambrosia, black cohosh, cosmos, mallow. **strengthen courage in a shy person**: Stone: orange calcite, carnelian.

Sickness
(See: Diseases/Disorders, Healing, Illness)

Simplicity
Number: 1; Stone: manganite; Metal: gold; Plant: chickweed, briar rose, single rose, wild rose, silverweed, spikenard, violet.

Innocent simplicity: Plant: chickweed. **Simple joy**: Plant: silverweed. **Simple life**: Waning Moon; Color: purple. **Simple pleasures**: Plant: silverweed.

Sincerity
Color: blue, navy blue, white; Stone: amethyst, onyx, pearl; Plant: chervil, fern.

Insincerity
Plant: foxglove.

Situations
(See also: Adversity, Life, Problems)

Difficult/stressful situations: *to cope in*: Animal: horse; Goddess: Isis; *to deal with*: Stone: banded agate. **Negative situations**: *to banish*: Color: black; Charm: brimstone; *to clear from your life*: Color: black; Stone: aventurine, jade, petrified wood, clear quartz crystal; Plant: cedar, High John, lilac, patchouli, lemon verbena; *to clear long-standing negative situations*: Stone: hematite; *to create something positive from*: Goddess: Atanea; *to end*: Metal: silver; Plant: celandine, High John; Goddess: Sekhmet; *to escape*: Plant: celandine, ephedra; *to make the best of*: Goddess: Turrean; *to relieve*: Stone: sodalite. **Scary situations**: *courage to face*: Plant: thistle. **Strange situations**: *to help deal with*: Plant: dill, High John. **Troubled situations**: *to calm*: God: Njord. **Unfair situations**: *to endure*: Goddess: Rhiannon; *to escape*: Plant: celandine.

Situational depression: (See: Depression).

To: accept situations: Color: brown; Stone: agate, sard; Plant: gardenia, orange, rose. **be reincarnated into a positive situation**: God: T'ai-Yüeh Ta-ti. **change a situation**: Stone: malachite, turquoise; Plant: cayenne. **control a situation**: Color: orange; Stone: carnelian; Plant: bayberry, calamus root. **feel comfortable in a situation**: Stone: staurolite. **see beyond a situation**: Plant: orchid. **stop situations**: Color: indigo. **understand situations**: Color: light blue; Plant: dill. **watch what you say in situations**: Stone: chrysocolla.

Skills
(See also: Ability, Talent)

Animal: spider, wolf, all birds; Plant: jasmine, spider plant, willow; Goddess: Athena, Brigid, the Kotharat; God: the Dagda (Lord of Skill), Gwydion, Hephaestus, Imhotep, Kothar-wa Khasis (Skillful and Wise, Deft with Both Hands), Lugh (Lord of Skills, Master of All Arts), Mannan Mac Lir, Ptah; Evocation: Daedalus, elves.

Artistic skills: Goddess: Athena. **Battle skills**: Goddess: Aoife, Scathach, Uathach; God: Odin. **Communication skills**: *to improve*: Plant: papyrus. **Equestrian skills**: Goddess: Epona, Xatel-Ekwa. **Hunting skill**: God: Parashurama. **Magickal skill**: Animal: serpent; Stone: amethyst; Plant: yew; Goddess: Freya; God: Math ap Mathonwy. **Management skills**: God: Enki. **Navigation skills**: *to improve*: Plant: papyrus. **Needed skills**: God: Itzamna. **Negotiating skills**: *to improve*: Plant: papyrus. **Oral skills**: Color: blue; God: Ogma. **Physical skills**: Mars; Goddess: Emer; God: Lugh. **Social skills**: Animal: wolf; Plant: narcissus; *to strengthen*: Plant: wolfsbane. **Survival skills**: Animal: sea turtle; God: the Horned God. **Tracking skills**: Charm: footprints, hoof prints, paw prints, and so on; Animal: dog. **Warrior skills**: Animal: wolf; God: Llew Llaw; Evocation: Conla, Cuchulain; *with weapons*: God: Ishum, Lugh.

To: teach skills: Goddess: Ptè San Wi. **use skills**: Animal: kite, toad.

Sleep
(See also: Dreams, Nightmares)

Water/Winter/Night

Color: blue, green; Charm: dream pillow, potion; Number: 5; Animal: bear, lizard, all hibernating animals; Stone: amber, amethyst, diamond, Herkimer diamond, lodestone, malachite, opal, moonstone, peridot, blue tourmaline, zircon; Plant: aniseed, apple, butterbur, cannabis, catnip, celery seed, chamomile, cinquefoil, datura, dandelion, dill, elder, elm, eucalyptus, hops, jasmine, juniper, kava kava, lady's mantle (under the pillow), laurel, lavender, lettuce, linden, linden with lavender, mandrake, motherwort, holly, lotus, marjoram, mugwort, nutmeg, passionflower, peppermint, poppy, opium poppy, purslane, rose, rosemary, shower of gold, thyme, valerian, lemon verbena, vervain, vetiver, violet; Goddess: Caer, Erzulie, Evaki, Isis, Persephone, Yhi; God: Angus, Ea, Hypnos, Morpheus, Somnus, Vishnu.

Children's sleep: Goddess: Cuba. **Deep sleep**: Plant: agrimony (in dream pillow). **Enchanted sleep**: Plant: field of bluebells, yew; Evocation: fairies. **Eternal sleep**: Evocation: Endymion. **Good sleep**: Stone: citrine, blue topaz; Plant: anise, chamomile, rosemary (under the pillow). **Mystical sleep**: Color: blue; Stone: blue opal. **Peaceful sleep**: Color: blue; Animal: swan; Stone: amethyst, diamond, jet, malachite, sapphire, blue topaz, blue tourmaline; Plant: anise, bergamot, birch, chamomile, heather, jasmine, lavender, narcissus, poppy, valerian; Goddess: Caer; God: Angus. **Restful sleep**: Stone: green jasper, lodestone; Oil: neroli; Potion: apple juice; Plant: apple, crab apple, catnip, chamomile, hops, lemon balm, mistletoe, peach, thyme with basil, valerian; God:

Tuku. **Safe sleep**: Plant: laurel. **Twilight sleep**: Fungus: fly agaric; Plant: henbane.

Sleep disorders: (See: Diseases/ Disorders). **Sleep potions**: Goddess: Greine. **Healing power of drug-induced sleep**: Plant: poppy; Goddess: Spes; God: Morpheus. **Protection during sleep**: Charm: dream catcher; Plant: coriander, eye of Satan, garlic, mandrake, rosemary, spearmint; Goddess: Isis, Urmya; God: Bes.

To protect: **sleep**: Goddess: Urmya. **sleeping children**: (See: Children).

Sleeplessness

Animal: shark.

Sobriety

(See also: Diseases/Disorders: addiction, Habits)

Stone: amethyst; Goddess: Anahita (Mother of Sobriety), Sheela-na-gig.

The Social

(See also: Friendship, People, Relationships)

Venus/Thursday

Color: orange; Animal: hornet, parakeet, starling, all hive creatures; Plant: lemon balm; Goddess: the Graces, Hathor, Themis.

Social awareness: Uranus. **Social change**: Goddess: Dakini. **Social class**: *to disregard*: God: Agni. **Social climbing**: Capricorn; Goddess: Copper Woman (See also: Status). **Social cohesion**: Plant: mallow; Goddess: Themis. **Social consciousness**: Number: 6. **Social contracts**: Goddess: Themis. **Social conventions**: Goddess: Themis. **Social cooperation**: Animal: bee, wolf. **Social graces**: Libra. **Social justice**: Goddess: Aradia. **Social order**: Saturn; Goddess: Aditi, Ala, Ma'at, Themis; God:

Ptah. **Social pleasures**: Color: emerald green; Goddess: the Graces. **Social respectability**: Capricorn. **Social situations**: *to feel more comfortable in*: Plant: clove, corn, mallow. **Social skills**: Animal: wolf; *to strengthen*: Plant: wolfsbane. **Social unity**: Plant: mallow. **Social virtue**: Goddess: Liberalitas.

Sociability: Air/Gemini; Color: red; Animal: butterfly, cockatoo, parrot; *to increase*: Plant: mallow. **Unsociability**: Color: blue.

Solutions

Clever solutions: Goddess: Ambika, Goda; God: Hephaestus, Thoth, Vishnu; Evocation: Asteria, Odysseus, Zipporah. **Wise solutions**: Plant: violet.

To solve problems: (See: Problems).

Soothing

(See also: Calm, Comfort, Quiet, Relaxation)

Method: bath; Charm: electuary; Color: blue, lavender, light blue, pink, violet; Stone: amethyst, aquamarine, avalonite, blue lace agate, hematite, lapis lazuli, malachite, rose quartz, selenite; Oil: neroli; Plant: almond, apple, balsam, bergamot, birch, catnip, cedar, chamomile, cherry, chickweed, clary sage, cowslip, cypress, evergreens, hollyhock, honeysuckle, hops, hyssop, lavender, lemon balm, lemongrass, lilac, mallow, marigold, marjoram myrrh, narcissus, orange, peach, rose, rue, tangerine, tea tree, thyme, violet, ylang-ylang; Goddess: Yemaya.

To soothe: **body**: Stone: rhodochrosite; Plant: flax. **cough**: Plant: coltsfoot. **digestive system**: Plant: oregano. **emotions**: Plant: aster, birch. **eyes**: Color: green; Plant: anise, potato. **heart**: Stone: aquamarine. **inflammation**: (See: The Body). **liver**: Plant:

licorice. **irritation**: Plant: acacia, aloe vera. **mind**: Stone: rhodochrosite; Plant: scullcap, violet. **muscles**: Plant: eucalyptus, paprika. **nerves**: (See: The Body). **the ocean**: God: Poseidon. **pancreas**: Plant: licorice. **skin**: (See: The Body). **urinary system/tract**: (See: The Body).

Sorrow

(See also: Depression, Emotions, Grief, Happiness, Heartbreak, Loss)

Moon/Sunset/Water/Autumn/Winter

Color: black, gray, purple, violet; Charm: inverted torch; Animal: lone wolf; Stone: onyx with white veins; Plant: aloe, cypress, elder, myrtle, primrose, rue, willow, yew; Goddess: Demeter, Ishtar (Lady of Sorrows), Isis, Mary (Mater Dolorosa, Sorrowful Mother, Our Lady of Sorrow, Queen of Sorrows, Our Lady of Seven Sorrows), Melusine, Nedolya, Nephthys; God: Cautopates, Ponos; Evocation: Achall, Deirdre of the Sorrows.

Unexpected sorrow: God: Ueuecoyotl. **Sorrowful love**: Plant: basil. **Sad dreams**: *to banish*: Plant: peony seeds. **Sorrowful love**: Plant: basil. **Sad memories**: (See: Memories). **Sad songs**: Evocation: Echo. **Sad story**: *to fall for*: Pisces.

To: avert sorrow: Stone: diamond, ruby. **balance joys and sorrows**: (See: Joy). **banish sorrow**: Color: pink; Charm: water in which Maximon's image has been washed; Stone: carnelian, chalcedony, ruby; Plant: marjoram, thyme; *banish sad dreams*: Plant: peony seeds. **ease sorrow**: Stone: chrysoprase, opal, rose quartz; Potion: borage tips in red wine, lemon balm tea; Oil: palmarosa; Plant: balm of Gilead, borage, bougainvillea, cypress, rose geranium, hawthorn, pitcher plant, snowdrop, sunflower, viper's bugloss, willow; God: El. **heal sorrow**: Goddess: Tara. **overcome sorrow**:

Plant: benzoin, cypress, hyacinth, lemon balm, marjoram, myrrh, rose, sandalwood, sweetgrass; Goddess: Isis, Yhi. **release sorrow**: Color: black, fuchsia; Stone: carnelian; Plant: basil, fuchsia. **share someone's sorrow**: Plant: rose. **understand sorrow**: Plant: myrrh. **wash away sorrow**: Water; Plant: marjoram, thyme; Goddess: Yemaya.

Speech

(See also: Communication, Eloquence, Expression, Voice)

Mercury/Air

Color: blue, orange; Animal: dolphin, parrot, trumpeter swan, whale, all birds; Metal: silver; Plant: all trumpet-shaped flowers; Goddess: Sarasvati, Vac; God: Al Lisan (The Tongue), Baile, Bran, Nabu, Ogma Cermait, Thoth, Vagisvara (Lord of Speech), Ve.

Clear speech: Stone: celestite; Plant: laurel. **Flattering speech**: Charm: blarney stone; God: Baile of the Honey Speech. **Inspirational speech**: Plant: trumpet vine. **Persuasive speech**: Goddess: Oya, Peitho; God: Baile of the Honey Speech. **Public speaking**: Color: blue; Stone: blue lace agate, angelite, azurite, celestite; Plant: cosmos; *to overcome fear of*: Stone: carnelian; Plant: trumpet vine. **Rapid speech**: Mars/Moon. **Unkind speech**: Animal: snapping turtle.

Speech problems: *to overcome*: Animal: dolphin; Stone: chrysoprase, blue tigereye; Plant: snapdragon; God: Thoth. **Power of speech/voice**: (See: Voice).

To: improve speech: Animal: dolphin; Metal: silver. **know what not to say**: North. **learn to think before you speak**: Goddess: Providentia. **make yourself heard**: God: Manco Capac. **prevent people from speaking badly about you**: Charm: wolf's tooth and heliotrope blossom wrapped in a laurel leaf (carried); Plant: slippery elm. **speak in the afterlife**: (See: Afterlife). **speak the truth**: Earth; Plant: aster; God: Osiris Un-Nefer. **speak well in court**: Plant: black pepper. **teach children to speak**: God: Fabulinus. **unite speech with communication**: God: Al-Shafi.

Speed
Mercury

Color: magenta; Animal: boar, cheetah, cobra, cougar, deer, eagle, eland, gazelle, greyhound, horse, owl, roadrunner, squid, swift, wolf; Stone: meteorite; Plant: cassia, speedwell; Goddess: Atalanta, Epona, the Harpies, Luaths Lurgann, Medb, Rhiannon, Satis; God: Glooskap, Hanuman, Hermes, Legba; Evocation: Antilochus, Hugi.

Fast abundance: Plant: honeysuckle. **Fast action**: Color: magenta; Animal: cobra, komodo dragon; Plant: cinnamon. **Fast childbirth**: Plant: columbine, juniper berry, laurel, madonna lily. **Quick death**: Goddess: Artemis. **Quick decisions**: Animal: cobra, komodo dragon; Stone: jade . **Rapid growth**: Sun/South; Plant: bugle, flame tree, loosestrife, spearmint, thyme. **Fast healing**: Plant: cinnamon. **Fast luck**: (See: Luck). **Quick mind**: (See: The Mind). **Quick money**: Color: gold, green; Plant: cinnamon. **Fast movement**: Metal: mercury (toxic, not recommended). **Fast response**: Animal: chameleon, eland, gazelle. **Quick thinking**: (See: Thought). **Fast speech**: Mars/Moon/Gemini. **Quick wits**: Plant: forget-me-not, peppermint; God: Loki.

To: **make time seem to pass quickly**: Animal: cheetah; Plant: betel nut, thyme.

To speed: **digestion**: Plant: fennel. **enlightenment**: Plant: lotus. **healing**: (See: Healing). **manifestation**: Stone: garnet. **messages**: (See: Messages). **recovery**: Plant: carnation, cayenne; Goddess: Oya.

Spells
(See also: Hexes, Magick, Witchcraft)

[Note: For any type of spell, see the correspondences for that subject, such as Beauty for beauty spells, Happiness for happiness spells, Healing for healing spells, Travel for travel spells, and so on.]

Moon

Charm: graveyard dust (powdered mullein or patchouli leaves); Number: 9; Stone: lodestone; Plant: basil, bayberry, cedar, cinquefoil, coriander seed, datura, dragon's blood, eye of Satan, galangal, hawthorn, holy thistle, iris, lavender, lemon, mandrake root, mistletoe berries, mullein, black pepper, peppermint, rosemary, rowan, rue, sandalwood, tormentil, uva ursi, vervain, blue vervain, witch hazel, wormwood, yarrow, ylang-ylang; Goddess: Adsagsona (Weaver of Spells), Arianrhod, Cardea, Carman, Cerridwen, Circe, Freya, Habetrot, Hecate, Isis (Lady of Spells), Kamrusepas (Goddess of Spells), Luna, Oshun, Selene, Tara; God: Arawn, Ea, Kothar-wa-Khasis, Marduk, Odin, Ogma, Ra; Evocation: fairies, Merlin, Pressine.

Air spells: (See: Elements). **Cauldron spells**: Moon/Water; Tool: cauldron; Number: 9; Goddess: Brigid, Cerridwen, Cymidei Cymeinfoll, Gonlod, Hecate; God: Arawn, the Dagda. **Evil spells**: (See: Hexes). **Fairy spells**: Plant: rose petals, violet; *to break*: Plant: four leaf clover; *to make more powerful*: Plant: mistletoe (on Midsummer Eve); *to protect against*: Plant: rowan, St. John's Wort (See also: Fairies). **Fire spells**: (See: Elements). **Healing image spells**: Color: blue; Charm: poppet; Plant: potato, rosemary. **In drinking spells**: Color: black. **Justice/legal spells**: *to bind*: Charm: bright or dark blue thread; Plant: nettles, vine (See also: Court, Justice). **Love spells**:

Plant: apple, carnation, dragon's blood, High John, rose, vervain; Goddess: Hecate; *to bind*: Charm: red thread; Stone: red lodestone; *to break*: Plant: lily, nuts, pistachio; Goddess: Tana; *to increase power of*: Plant: coltsfoot, meadowsweet; *gay love spells*: Plant: morning glory, pansy, vetiver; God: Eros; *to overcome love enchantments*: Plant: poppy; *to overcome love hexes*: Plant: dill, rose petals (See also: Love). **Money/financial spells**: Taurus; Tool: pentacle; Plant: cinquefoil, dragon's blood, galangal, High John, vervain; *to bind*: Charm: green thread; Stone: green lodestone; *to counter those worked against you*: Plant: alkanet (See also: Finances, Money, Prosperity). **Protection spells**: (See: Amulets, Protection, Talismans) **Rain spells**: Water; Method: chanting, dancing, sympathetic magick; Charm: rain sticks; Plant: fern, pansy. **Reversing spells**: (See: Return, Reversal). **River spells**: Water; Goddess: Adsulatta, Aeron, the Ahinehiae, Anahita, Anna Livia, Axona, Briant, Chairmé, Clairmeziné, Clota, Devona, Ganga, Icauna, Ina, Ituana, Jumna, Logia, Naitienae, Nantosuelta, Oya, Rosmerta, Sarasvati, Sequana, Sionnan (pronounced 'shannon'), Souconna, Vaga; God: Dylan, Inachos, Khnum, Lugal-id or Lugal-idak, Osiris, Sucellos, Tiberinus. **Sacred spells**: God: Kothar-wa-Khasis. **Sea spells**: Moon/Water; Color: aqua, blue, gray, sea green; Charm: ambergris, beach glass, fish oil, sand, sea shell, shark tooth, starfish; Animal: fish, whale, dolphin, all marine life and sea birds; Stone: amber, aquamarine, coral, pearl, mother-of-pearl, sea salt; Plant: driftwood, gray dulse, kelp, rosemary; Goddess: Agwe, Amberella, Amphitrite, Aphrodite, Ashiakle, Asima Si, Ashtoreth, Athirat, Acuecueyotl, Benzaiten, Brizo, Domnu, Doris, Dubh Lacha, Fand, Jurata, Mari, Huruing Wuhti, Idliragijenget, Ina, Ishtar, Isis, Jamaina, Jandira, Mama Cocha, Mami Wata, Mamlambo, Mary, Mater Matuta, Mor, Muireartach, Nehalennia, the Pleiades, Ran, Salacia (Lady of the Salt Sea), Al-Sarah, Sedna, the Sirens, Thetis, Una-Kuagsak, Vellamo, Venus, Verbeia, Yemaya, Yum; God: Aegir, Dagon, Ea, Llyr, Lugal-apsu or Lugal-abzuak, Melkarth, Neptune, Nereus, Nuadh, the Oannes, Oceanus, Poseidon, Raja Naga; Evocation: merfolk, nereids, oceanids, sea fairies. **Sleep spells**: (See: Dreams, Sleep, Nightmares). **Water spells**: (See: Elements). **Wind spells**: Air; Tool: whistle; Plant: anemone, aspen, broom, saffron, kelp; Goddess: Cardea (Queen of Winds), Delphine, Gna, Kajsa, Oya, Urania (Queen of Winds); God: Aeolus (Warden of the Winds), Aquilo, Astraeus, Auster, Boreas, Ellil, Enlil, Eurus, Favonius, Mercury, Njord (Lord of the Winds), Notus, Ophion, Quetzalcoatl, Skan, Tate, Volturnus, Zephyrus; *to command winds*: God: Lugal-dim-er-ankia.

To: activate spells: Color: yellow. **avert spells**: Color: silver; Charm: mirror; *evil spells*: Stone: jet; Plant: hellebore, rue. **bind spells**: Charm: linen thread; Charm: rhymes; Number: 3; Plant: bindweed, dragon's blood, grapevine, periwinkle vine; Goddess: Isis, Linda. **break spells**: Color: orange; Stone: salt, tigereye; Plant: bamboo, basil, benzoin, cascara sagrada, clove, coconut, comfrey, copal, frankincense, galangal, iris, mint, mustard seed, myrrh, nettle, nutmeg, oak moss, orris root, patchouli, rue, sassafras, St. John's Wort, slippery elm, turmeric, lemon verbena, yarrow. **counter spells**: Plant: angelica, chili pepper, datura, lily of the valley, squill, thistle, wintergreen. **create spells**: God: Kothar-wa-Khasis. **defeat spells**: Plant: bloodroot, rue, vetiver. **destroy spells**: Plant: juniper. **empower spells**: Full Moon; Charm: witches burr; Plant: dragon's blood, ginger; Goddess: Oshun. **increase the power/effectiveness of spells**: Full Moon; Tool: candle; Color: orange, white; Charm: van van, Method: work barefoot; Stone: amber, bloodstone, calcite, fluorite, rutilated quartz; Plant: carnation, cinnamon, copal, damiana, dragon's blood, Echinacea, eye of Satan, frankincense, galangal, gotu kola, High John, kelp, patchouli, St. John's Wort, lemon verbena, yarrow; Goddess: Isis, Oshun; *of spell-casters*: Plant: vervain. **increase the success of spells**: Plant: benzoin, clove. **make a spell last a long time**: (See: Longevity). **make things happen**: Plant: High John. **overcome spells**: Plant: vetiver. **protect against spells**: Charm: witch ball; Plant: angelica, bamboo, black hellebore, chili pepper, datura, holy thistle, horehound, squill, thistle, toadflax, wintergreen; *protect a crib or cradle against spells*: Stone: dark green malachite. **release spells**: Plant: elder, nutmeg. **remove spells**: Plant: angelica, nightshade. **reverse spells**: Plant: mandrake root, papaya leaf, sage; *upon their makers*: Tool: mirror; Stone: diamond, red jasper; Plant: agrimony (burned), galangal, Low John, nettle, nutmeg; *to reverse a hex*: (See: Hexes). **stabilize spells**: Plant: elm. **strengthen spells**: Color: black; Stone: amber, lodestone; Plant: Echinacea. **understand possible consequences of spells**: Goddess: Skuld. **write spells**: God: Thoth.

Spirit

(See also: Depression, Mood)

Fire/Center

Color: violet, white; Charm: white circle, black oval, spiral; Number: 3; Stone: amethyst, green stone set in gold, jade, meteorite; Plant: wild rose, tulip.

Free spirit: Air; Animal: bird; Plant: fennel, juniper berry. **Good humor/spirits**: Plant: cherry blossom. **Pure spirit**: Sun; Plant: white jasmine. **Deadness of spirit**: *to release*: Plant: sunflower.

To: connect the spirit: (See: Connection). **cultivate the spirit**: Stone: morganite. **clear the spirit**: Plant: butterbur. **diagnose problems with the spirit**: Stone: malachite. **heal the spirit**: Color: pink, white; Animal: crane, swan; Stone: amethyst, jade, pearl, unakite; Goddess: Yemaya. **quicken the spirit**: Charm: rosewater; Plant: burnet, mustard, dead nettle, red rose, rosemary, saffron. **raise the spirit**: Color: yellow; Animal: your familiar; Stone: garnet, lapis lazuli; Oil: neroli, palmarosa, petitgrain; Plant: apple blossom, bergamot, crab apple, basil, borage, clove, copal, dragon's blood, elecampane, eucalyptus, frankincense, grapefruit, honeysuckle, hyacinth, jasmine, lemon, lemon balm, lemongrass, lime, linden flower, mandarin orange, orange, papaya, patchouli, peony, peppermint, pine, rose, rosemary, rosewood, rue, saffron, sage, savory, Spanish moss, tea tree, orange, mandarin orange, verbena, ylang-ylang, zinnia. **relieve the spirit**: Plant: lemon balm, sundew. **restore the spirit**: Plant: strawberry. **strengthen the spirit**: Color: gold; Plant: ginger, quince, rose. **sustain the spirit**: Plant: elecampane.

Spirits

(See also: The Dead)

Animal: jellyfish, burrowing owl, black snail; Plant: rosemary; Goddess: Chalchihuitlcue, Hecate, Manea, Nephthys; God: Gauna; Evocation: Genii Cucullati (hooded spirits), Genius, Holy Spirit, the Manes.

Ancestral spirits: Charm: ancestral altar; Plant: yam; Evocation: the Lars Familiaris. **Angry spirits**: *to placate*: Plant: rice, sesame seeds. **Animal spirits**: *flow of*:

Stone: sapphire; *to comfort*: Metal: silver; *fox spirits*: Metal: silver; Evocation: the hu hsien. **Animal spirit guides**: (See: Guidance). **Benevolent spirits**: Plant: ash; Evocation: the Lamas; *to attract*: Tool: censer; Color: white, lilac; Plant: catnip, gardenia, jasmine, lemon, lilac, marshmallow, mastic, mint, wisteria. **Death spirits**: Animal: birds; Evocation: Guédé, Harpies, the Manes, upyr, Valkyries, the Vanths. **Earth spirits**: Earth; Plant: harebell, wheat; Goddess: Khon Ma; Evocation: Aktunowihio, gnomes, pchuvushi, Zam; *to release*: Tool: plow. **Earthbound spirits**: Earth; *to help to reach the light*: Tool: censer; Method: smudging; Animal: leopard; Plant: sage, sweetgrass. **Evil spirits**: Fungus: stinkhorn; Evocation: Dogai, Sta-au, Towiscara; *to appease*: Animal: guinea pig; Plant: rice, sesame seeds; *to attract*: Tool: Ouija Board (dangerous, not recommended); Plant: valerian root; *to avert*: Charm: blue water; Stone: jacinth, ruby, zircon; Plant: arnica, avens, birch twig, cinquefoil, eye of Satan, fennel leaf, ginseng, juniper berry, laurel, lemon balm, mandrake root, onion, parsley (chaplet), periwinkle, rosemary, rue (chaplet), St. John's Wort (hung over the doors and windows, especially at Midsummer); Goddess: Auchimolgen, Ushas; God: Bes; *to avert from new mothers*: Goddess: Intercidona; *to banish*: Tool: bell, besom, rattle, sistrum; Method: asperging, smudging; Color: white; Charm: a piece of coral with silver bells; Stone: coral, emerald, zircon; Plant: agrimony, black beans (spit at them), birch twig, blackberry leaf, dandelion root, fern, juniper, lemon balm, mistletoe, mullein, rosemary, sandalwood, St. John's Wort, spurge seed, wild olive, peach branches; Goddess: Hathor, Vajravaraki; God: Erh-Lang, Hanuman; *to battle*: Plant: fennel stalk; *to control*: Goddess: Kupala; *to destroy*: Plant: asafetida; *to expose*: God: Sin; *to help to*

reach the light: Goddess: Yhi; *to immobilize*: Plant: rowan, walnut; *to make powerless*: Number: 5; *to overcome*: Goddess: Yhi; *to prevent from entering the house*: (See: The Home); *to protect against*: Stone: emerald, jacinth; Plant: Aaron's rod, angelica, anise leaves, avens, betony, birch, blueberry, caraway, coca leaves (as incense), dill, black hellebore, laurel, lemon balm, mistletoe, mugwort, mullein, oak (hung over doors and windows), wild olive, peony root, periwinkle, rosemary, St. John's Wort, spurge seeds; Goddess: Auchimolgen, Bast, Hecate, Kupala; God: Bes, Kuan Ti; *against the influence of*: Plant: laurel; *against possession by*: Plant: daffodil (carried in a clean napkin); *to protect babies from*: Charm: birch wood cradle; *to protect children from*: Charm: dill; *to protect the dead from*: Plant: elder branches (buried or cremated with them); *to protect the home from*: Charm: vervain-water. **Fire spirits**: Animal: salamander; God: Kagutsuchi, Wakonda; Evocation: Tcolawitze. **Great Spirit**: Goddess: Geezhigo-Quae; God: Airsekui, Ha Wen Neyu, Kagutsuchi, Wakonda; *to offer to*: Plant: Echinacea. **Guardian spirits**: Plant: ash. **Holy Spirit**: Air/Spirit/Fire; Charm: flame; Animal: dove; Plant: angelica, columbine; Goddess: Hokmah, Sophia. **Harvest spirit**: Evocation: Parthanan. **Household spirits**: Evocation: brownies, the Domoviye, Kikimora, the Penates; *barn spirits*: Evocation: the Ovinniki; *bathhouse/sauna spirits*: Evocation: the Banniki; *stable spirits*: Evocation: the Vazily; *storehouse spirits*: Evocation: the Gumeniki; *yard spirits*: Evocation: the Dvorovoi. **Nature spirits**: Earth; Color: green; Animal: oriole; Plant: evergreens, pine, reindeer moss; Goddess: Parvati; Evocation: the Apsaras; *to capture*: God: Anansi; *to protect*: Animal: griffin; *field/pasture spirits*: Evocation: the Poleviki; *flower spirits*: *peach blossoms*: Evocation: T'ao Hua Hsiennui (Peach Blossom Girl); *forest/ sylvan spirits*: Plant: evergreens, fir, holly, oakmoss; God: Silvanus; Evocation: Dames Vertes, dryads, Hiisi, the Meliae, Metsik, Musail (Forest Tzar), Poluvirica, Sicksa; *meadow spirit*: Evocation: Lugovik; *mountain spirits*: Goddess: Rauni; *of sacred mountains*: Goddess: Yama-No-Kami; *tree spirits*: Evocation: Pfingstgl, Vanadevatas, the vili; *apple tree*: Evocation: Le Grand Mondard; *ash tree*: Evocation: the Meliae; *oak tree*: Animal: bull; Evocation: Mess (Timber Knots); *peach tree*: Goddess: T'ao Hua Hsiennui (Peach Blossom Girl); *pine tree*: Evocation: Akoya. **Night spirits**: Waning Moon/Night; Goddess: Manea. **Protective spirits**: Animal: snail; Evocation: the disir, Tsagaglalal (She Who Watches); *to channel*: God: 'Ngai. **Strong spirits**: *to attract*: Plant: lotus root. **Vegetation/plant spirits**: Earth; Color: green; Goddess: Nana; God: Adonis, Attis, Damuzi, Dionysus, Green Man, Jesus, Osiris, Tammuz; Evocation: Alakhani, Carnevale, devas, Grass King, Kostroma, Little May Rose, May King, May Queen, Metsik, Pfingstl, Straw Man, Wild Man; *of beans*: Evocation: the Deohako; *of flax*: Evocation: Linos; *of gourds*: Evocation: the Deohako; *of grain*: Animal: bear, cat, cattle, cock, deer, dog, white or red dog, donkey, fox, goose, goat, hare, hen, horse, kite, mouse, ox, rabbit, roe, sheep, stag, steer, stork, swan, swine, wolf; Evocation: Carline, Corn Baby, Corn Cat, Corn Mother, Corn Spirit, Corn Wolf, Harvest Child, Ivy Girl, Kern Baby, Linus, Lityerses, Maid, Maiden, Maneros, Mother, Old Man, Old Woman, Straw Goat, Witch; *of barley*: Goddess: Barley Mother; Evocation: Barley Horse, Barley Wolf; *of maize*: Evocation: the Deohako; *of rice*: Evocation: Kelah; *of rye*: Evocation: Rye Wolf; *of sorghum*: Evocation: Morkul Kua Luan (Spirit of the Long Grass); *of wheat*: Goddess: Onatha; *of grass*: Evocation: Grass Long, Morkul Kua Luan (Spirit of the Long Grass);

of herbs: God: Osain; *of madder*: Evocation: Madder Spirit; *of peas*: Evocation: the Pea Mother, Peas Pug; *of rowan*: Goddess: Raini; *of squash*: Goddess: the Deohako; *of herbs*: God: Osain (See also: Nature spirits). **Unborn spirits**: Plant: loranthus, mistletoe. **Water spirits**: Water; Goddess: Oshun; Evocation: the Ahueccaniae, Chahuru, Liban, Naaki, the Vodonoi, water nymphs, Water King; *evil water spirits*: Evocation: the Rusalki, the Zazavavindrano; *bog spirits*: Evocation: Bolotny; *fog/mist spirits*: Evocation: Yina'mna'ut (Fog Woman), Yina'mtilan (Fog Man); *sea spirits*: Evocation: Adaro, nercids, oceanids; *spring spirits*: Evocation: Glanis; *well spirits*: Goddess: Sionnan; Evocation: Nechtain. **Wind spirits**: Air; Evocation: Hoturu, the lilitu, Takuskanskan, Takuskanskan, Valkyries.

Spirit guides: (See: Guidance). **Spirit work**: (See: Work). **Spirit world/realm**: Color: clear, gray, white; Plant: almond tree in bloom, mastic, mistletoe; Goddess: Hecate; God: Arawn, Nagi; *to contact*: Method: trance; Color: purple; Animal: wolverine; *to open to*: Animal: lemur; *to open a door/gateway to*: Tool: Ouija Board (dangerous, not recommended), mirror; Method: séance; God: Legba.

Spirit/s of: the dead: (See: The Dead). **disease**: (See: Disease). **men's lodges**: Evocation: Kmantah. **motion**: God: Skan. **sexuality**: Evocation: Agrat Bat Mahalat, 'Aisha Quandisha. **thunder**: God: Shango, Wakonda (Great Thunder Spirit), Wakinyan. **the Wheel of the Year**: *New Year*: Evocation: Robin Redbreast; *Old Year*: Evocation: Gold Crest Wren; *to drive out the spirit of the old year*: Plant: birch, wild olive; *Samhain*: Goddess: Carline; *waning year*: Evocation: Holly King; *waxing year*: Evocation: Oak King; *winter*: Evocation: Gahone, Jack Frost, Old Man Winter, Thorri.

To: **attract spirits**: Tool: Ouija Board (dangerous, not recommended), pentacle; Color: white; Charm: nag champa with myrrh; Stone: jade; Plant: anise, dandelion, elecampane, lemon, lemongrass, lotus, mullein (as incense), myrrh, rowan, sandalwood with lavender, sweetgrass, wormwood (as incense). **banish spirits**: Tool: bell, gong; Plant: black beans (thrown or spit), daffodil, sage, Solomon's seal, sweetgrass; God: Ishana, Perun; *from a business/workplace*: Plant: oak with mistletoe. **bar ghosts and spirits**: Charm: garlic and rosemary with sea salt. **clear spirits**: Tool: bell, censer; Method: smudging; Color: black, silver, white; Charm: brimstone, rosewater; Stone: agate, bloodstone, clear quartz crystal, sea salt; Plant: black beans (to spit at them), frankincense, garlic, myrrh, patchouli, rosemary, sage, spurge seed, sweetgrass, vervain, vetiver, yarrow. **comfort spirits**: Plant: yew. **communicate with spirits**: Animal: eland, lemur. **connect with spirits**: Animal: cougar. **contact spirits**: Tool: mirror, Ouija Board (dangerous, not recommended), pentacle; Method: seance, trance; Color: indigo, purple, violet, yellow; Animal: condor; Stone: amethyst, emerald, labradorite, moonstone, sugilite; Plant: dandelion, frankincense, ginkgo, lavender, lemongrass, lotus, myrrh, wormwood, yarrow; Goddess: Arianrhod, Cliodna; God: Arawn; Evocation: Witch of Endor; *via dreams*: Charm: ice water (under the bed, with a letter in it); Plant: cowslip (under the pillow); *to prevent confusion from spirit contact*: Color: black. **control spirits**: Goddess: Inanna; God: Ishana. **counter spirits**: Metal: iron. **feed spirits**: Plant: apple, corn pollen. **make offerings to spirits**: Fire; Tool: censer; Charm: Kananga Water. **manifest/conjure spirits**: Waning Moon; Method: whistling; Plant: dittany (thrown into fire), heather, masterwort (sprinkled), sandalwood, willow bark with sandalwood, wormwood. **prevent the return of a spirit**: Plant: African tulip tree (leaves and flowers, buried with body), rowan (stake, through the heart). **protect against spirits**: Metal: iron; Plant: violet, wormwood (as incense); Goddess: the Crone, Sheela-na-gig. **seduce spirits**: Goddess: Lilith. **see spirits**: Animal: cat; Plant (as incense): mugwort, wormwood. **summon spirits to battle**: Plant: rowan (bonfire). **unmanifest spirits**: Plant: asafetida (thrown into fire).

🄢pirituality

Jupiter/Moon/Waning Moon/Air/Water/ Scorpio

Tool: censer; Method: meditation; Color: blue, light blue, clear, purple, violet, white; Number: 5, 7, 8, 11; Charm: circle, holy water, pyramid, white feather; Animal: cat, all birds, white birds, pairs of birds, jaguar, swan; Metal: copper; Stone: blue lace agate, amber, amethyst, bloodstone, calcite, clear calcite, celestite, diamond, Herkimer diamond, lepidolite, clear quartz crystal, sapphire, sugilite; Oil: palmarosa; Plant: acacia, allspice, arnica, bodhi tree, African violet, cassia, cedar, cinnamon, copal, elder, frankincense, gardenia, rose geranium, gum Arabic, heather, heliotrope, jasmine, juniper berry, lady's mantle, lotus, myrrh, primrose, rose, sage, sandalwood, sweetgrass, green tea, wisteria, wood aloes, yarrow, yerba santa; Goddess: Hokmah, Isis, Kwan-Yin, Lakshmi, Sophia, Tara; God: Niyan, Obatala, Quetzalcoatl, Shiva, Vagisvara.

Deep spirituality: Color: black, purple. **Physical spirituality**: Plant: clary sage; *physical/spiritual balance*: Stone: black moss agate, apophyllite, malachite; *physical/spiritual connection*: Animal: cat, ocelot, swan; Stone: jet; *physical/spiritual life*: *to harmonize*: Charm: ankh.

Spiritual ability: Stone: pyrite; Plant: frankincense. **Spiritual assistance**: (See: Assistance). **Spiritual attraction**: Plant: sweetgrass. **Spiritual attunement**: Stone: turquoise; Plant: sweetgrass. **Spiritual authority**: (See: Authority). **Spiritual awakening**: (See: Awakening). **Spiritual awareness**: (See: Awareness). **Spiritual balance**: (See: Balance). **Spiritual beauty**: Plant: cherry blossom. **Spiritual beginnings**: Stone: iolite. **Spiritual blessings**: (See: Blessings). **Spiritual blocks**: (See: Blockages). **Spiritual challenges**: Night Sun; Animal: jaguar. **Spiritual children**: *to bear*: Goddess: Kali. **Spiritual clarity**: Stone: malachite. **Spiritual cleansing**: Charm: Kananga Water; Plant: dragon's blood. **Spiritual confidence**: Plant: passionflower, reed. **Spiritual connection**: (See: Connection). **Spiritual consciousness**: Plant: sage. **Spiritual darkness**: *to overcome*: God: Vishnu. **Spiritual destiny**: God: Jesus, Osiris. **Spiritual depth**: Animal: scarlet macaw. **Spiritual development**: Charm: vulture crown; *to protect*: Deities: the Dharmapatat. **Spiritual direction**: Plant: mugwort; Goddess: the Mother. **Spiritual discipline**: Method: chanting, dance, meditation, yoga. **Spiritual ecstasy**: Stone: diamond; Goddess: the Great Mother. **Spiritual endurance**: Plant: poplar. **Spiritual energy**: (See: Energy). **Spiritual enlightenment**: Color: white; God: Hurukan. **Spiritual evolution**: Animal: swan; Stone: malachite. **Spiritual expression**: Plant: fir, laurel, pine, sunflower. **Spiritual fire**: God: Xiuhtecuhtli. **Spiritual food**: Plant: corn pollen. **Spiritual gifts**: *to awaken*: Animal: firefly. **Spiritual growth**: (See: Growth). **Spiritual guidance**: (See: Guidance). **Spiritual harm**: *to protect against*: Goddess: Kwan Yin. **Spiritual harmony**: Plant: lotus. **Spiritual healing**: (See: Healing). **Spiritual healers**: *to protect*: Stone: moldovite. **Spiritual home**: Charm: altar; Plant: African violet.

Spiritual illumination: (See: Illumination). **Spiritual immortality**: Goddess: Ameretat. **Spiritual initiation**: Plant: snowdrop. **Spiritual insight**: Goddess: Kwan Yin. **Spiritual inspiration**: Pisces. **Spiritual integrity**: Plant: plumeria; Goddess: Haurvatat. **Spiritual journey**: Animal: eel. **Spiritual knowledge**: Animal: wolf. **Spiritual life**: Color: blue; Stone: turquoise. **Spiritual love**: (See: Love). **Spiritual magick**: Plant: cinnamon, frankincense. **Spiritual manifestation**: Color: blue; Stone: blue agate, turquoise. **Spiritual meditation**: (See: Meditation). **Spiritual opening**: Plant: St. John's Wort. **Spiritual openness**: Plant: dandelion, lotus. **Spiritual perception**: Animal: eagle, fox. **Spiritual perfection**: Plant: lotus. **Spiritual penetration**: *of the physical realm*: Stone: meteorite. **Spiritual power**: (See: Power). **Spiritual progress**: Color: silver; Plant: African violet. **Spiritual protection**: (See: Protection). **Spiritual purification**: (See: Purification). **Spiritual quests**: (See: Quests). **Spiritual rebirth**: West; Plant: snowdrop. **Spiritual redemption**: God: Dionysus. **Spiritual release**: Plant: snowdrop. **Spiritual renewal**: (See: Renewal). **Spiritual satisfaction**: Goddess: Lakshmi. **Spiritual sexuality**: (See: Sexuality). **Spiritual stimulation**: Stone: amethyst. **Spiritual strength**: (See: Strength). **Spiritual support**: Plant: angelica; Evocation: angels. **Spiritual teachings**: (See: Teachings). **Spiritual transcendence**: Animal: swan. **Spiritual transformation**: (See: Transformation). **Spiritual travel**: Stone: amethyst, phenacite. **Spiritual truth**: Animal: eagle. **Spiritual understanding**: (See: Understanding). **Spiritual unity**: Plant: lotus. **Spiritual vibrations**: (See: Vibrations). **Spiritual virtue**: Goddess: Lakshmi. **Spiritual vision/perception**: (See: Vision). **Spiritual will**: Color: clear, white. **Spiritual wisdom**: Color: indigo; God: Krishna, Odin. **Spiritual work**: Stone: brown jasper.

To: **accept spirituality**: Plant: Jacob's ladder. **increase spirituality**: Color: white; Stone: obsidian; Plant: cinnamon, frankincense, lilac, myrrh. **manifest spirituality**: Stone: turquoise. **release spirituality**: Plant: myrrh, sandalwood. **stimulate spirituality**: Stone: amethyst.

Stability
(See also: Balance, Constancy)

Saturn/Sun/New Moon/Earth/Center/
Taurus/Capricorn

Color: brown, gray, silver, neutral colors; Charm: square, tet amulet; Number: 4, 8; Animal: centipede, millipede, wolf; Stone: amazonite, amethyst, chrysocolla, hematite, jasper, red jasper, black onyx, sphene; Plant: amber, angelica, birch, garden cress, lavender, oak, passionflower, sea pink, spikenard; Goddess: Holda, Ma'at, Securita, Vesta; God: Ogun Fer, Ptah.

Emotional stability: Color: brown; Stone: angelite, black tourmaline; Plant: geranium, passionflower. **Inner stability**; Plant: wild rose (See also: Centering). **National stability**: Goddess: Isis; God: Horus; Evocation: King Arthur. **Political stability**: God: Viracocha. **Stabilizing influence**: Charm: a well tended hearth fire. **Stable marriage**: Goddess: Vesta.

To stabilize: **anything**: Stone: ametrine, calcite, celestite, hematite, Herkimer diamond, jasper, red jasper, lava, onyx, rhodochrosite; Plant: sea pink. **menstruation**: Plant: sage. **root chakra**: Stone: black obsidian. **spells**: Plant: elm.

Instability
Water

Stone: opal; Plant: dahlia.

Stamina
(See also: Endurance, Strength)

Animal: bear, camel, elk, gazelle, horse; Plant: betel nut, garlic, onion, parsley, black pepper, sow thistle.

Emotional stamina: Charm: musk; Plant: dahlia. **Sexual stamina**: Plant: jasmine, vanilla.

Starting
(See: Beginning)

Status

Animal: baboon, wolf; Metal: gold, platinum; Stone: diamond, emerald, ruby; Plant: High John; Goddess: Inanna; God: Lü-hsing (Star of Status), Tai-yue da-di.

To reach a higher position: Stone: sardonyx.

Steadfastness
(See: Constancy)

Stimulation
Sun/Fire

Color: orange, red, yellow; Charm: orange flower water; Stone: tigereye; Plant: bayberry, calamus, carnation, cherry, chili pepper, cinnamon, coriander, ephedra, eucalyptus, fennel seed, frangipani, galangal, garlic, ginger, ginseng, goldenseal, gravel root, holy thistle, jasmine, lavender, lemon, lemongrass, lime, nutmeg, orange, oregano, pennyroyal, peppermint, pine, rosemary, rue, sage, sandalwood, savory, sesame seed, spearmint, thyme, yarrow; Goddess: Sarasvati (Stimulator).

Intellectual stimulation: Method: books, chess, computers, puzzles; Stone: apatite, danburite, smoky quartz; Plant: clove, lemon. **Mental stimulation**: Metal: aluminum; Stone: olivine, peridot, clear quartz crystal, topaz; Plant: basil, clove, gotu kola, lavender, lemon, peppermint, rosemary. **Spiritual stimulation**: Stone: amethyst.

To stimulate: anything: (See: correspondences above, or for that thing). **awareness**: Plant: freesia. **appetite**: (See: The Body). **bile**: (See: The Body). **brain**: Plant: ginseng, mint, peppermint, saffron. **chakras**: (See: Chakras). **circulation**: (See: The Body). **clear thinking**: (See: Thought). **creativity**: (See: Creativity). **desire**: (See: Desire). **digestion**: (See: The Body). **psychic dreams**: Plant: ash leaves (under the pillow). **energy**: (See: Energy). **female hormones**: Plant: sage. **glands**: Plant: anise, barberry. **growth**: *of skin*: Plant: comfrey; *physical growth in humans*: Charm: dinosaur bone. **happiness**: Stone: amber, garnet. **healing**: Stone: bloodstone, iolite, lapis lazuli. **heart**: Plant: adonis, foxglove, ginseng, St. John's Wort. **immune system**: (See: The Body). **intuition**: Charm: sea shell; Stone: apophyllite. **kidneys**: Plant: angelica, goldenrod, marsh mallow. **liver**: Plant: goldenrod. **love**: (See: Love). **memory**: (See: Memory). **menstruation**: (See: The Body). **metabolism**: Plant: calamus, ginseng, pansy, St. John's Wort. **nerves**: Plant: peppermint. **nervous system**: Plant: ginseng, rosemary, wolfsbane. **pancreas**: Plant: cassia. **passion**: Plant: coriander seed. **perception**: Stone: emerald. **psychic ability**: (See: Ability); **psychic awareness**: (See: Awareness). **sensitivity**: Stone: sea shell. **spirituality**: (See: Spirituality). **thyroid**: Plant: ginseng. **urinary system/tract**: (See: The Body). **womb/uterus**: Plant: broom, goldenseal, senna; *contractions in*: Plant: broom, cotton, pennyroyal. **yin**: Stone: pearl; Plant: patchouli.

Over-stimulation

To reduce over-stimulation: Plant: lavender.

Storms

(See also: Lightning, Weather)

Air/Water/February

Goddess: Bardaichila, Begoe, Chalchihuitlcue, Coatrischie, Feng-Po-Po, Guabancex, Hecate (Goddess of Storms), Isis, Ix Chel, Mary, Oya, Pallas, Ratu Lara Kidul, Rodasi, Rudrani, Sekhmet, Tempestes; God: Adad, Alignak, Apep, Baal, Baal-Hadad, Chernobog, Dagan, Donar, El (God of Storms), Ellil, Enlil (Lord of the Storm), Dagon, Huitzilopochtli, Hurukan, Ilyap'a, Indra, Khuno, Leucetios, Mannan Mac Lir, Perun, Pillan, Rudra, Shango, Shiva, Stribog, Summanus, Susa-no-wa, Taranis, Thor, Tupan, Ukko, Zeus. **Angry storms**: God: Aegir. **Desert storms**: God: Set. **Hailstorms**: Animal: squirrel; God: Perun. **Hurricanes**: God: Hurukan. **Lightning storms**: (See: Lightning). **Monsoons**: Animal: snake; God: Indra. **Ocean storms**: Goddess: Atlacamani, Ran; God: Aegir, Mannan Mac Lir, Poseidon, Yamm; Evocation: the Maruts; *to call*: God: Poseidon; *to protect against*: Charm: wren feather; Stone: beryl; Plant: garland of ti leaves (worn); Goddess: Amphitrite; *to calm stormy seas*: Plant: ginger; Goddess: Amphitrite; *to protect against*: Charm: wren feather; Stone: beryl; Goddess: Amphitrite. **Rainstorms**: Goddess: Isis (Master of Rainstorms); God: Agilma (Bringer of Rain); *violent rainstorms*: Goddess: Oya; God: Adad; *winter rainstorms*: God: Baal. **Sand storms**: God: Set. **Snowstorms**: God: Khuno. **Tempests**: Goddess: Tempestes; God: Ares; *to protect against*: Stone: coral. **Thunderstorms**: Air/Fire/Water; God: Adad, Addu, Baal, Chernobog (Thunderer), Hurukan, Indra, Jupiter, Jupiter Fulgurator, Leucetius, Marduk, Perun, Ryujin Fulgurator, Summanus, Susa-no-wa, Taranis, Thor, Zeus; *for protection during*: Charm: Midsummer pine garland (burned in fireplace); *to call*: God: Vahagn; *to protect against*: Stone: agate, coral, jet; Plant: St. John's Wort. **Tornados**: Goddess: Oya. **Tropical** storms: Goddess: Ix Chel. **Violent storms**: Goddess: the Harpies; God: Adad, the Maruts. **Wild storms**: God: Baal, Zeus Maimaktes. **Winter rainstorms**: God: Baal.

Storm clouds: God: Enki. **Stormy weather**: God: Agwe. **Calm after a storm**: Charm: rainbow; Goddess: Rauni.

To: avert storms: Stone: agate (burned); Goddess: Alcyone (the Queen Who Wards Off Storms), Mary; God: Perun. **call/summon storms**: Goddess: Chalchihuitlcue, Cybele, Oya; God: Ambisagrus, Shiva, Summanus, Thor; *storms that ruin harvests*: Goddess: Hecate. **calm storms**: Animal: kingfisher; Stone: coral; Goddess: Chalchihuitlcue; God: Krishna; *calm storms at sea*: Charm: menstruating woman expose her genitals to the sea; *calm stormy seas*: Plant: ginger; Goddess: Amphitrite. **clear storms**: God: Vayu. **control storms**: God: Mabon. **predict storms**: Animal: crane; Goddess: Cally Berry. **protect against storms**: Goddess: Alcyone (the Queen Who Wards Off Storms); God: Perun; *against storm damage*: Plant: fern, hawthorn. **protect crops from storms**: *from heavy storms*: Goddess: Diana; *from thunderstorms*: Charm: powdered coral mixed with seeds at planting. **protect a home from storms/storm damage**: (See: Security). **raise storms**: Goddess: Cybele; God: Aeolus, Summanus; Evocation: selkies.

Strength

(See also: Endurance, Energy, Fatigue, Intensity, Power, Stamina)

Mars/Sun/Earth/Fire/South/West/Taurus

Color: gold, orange, red; Charm: boar bristle, dinosaur bone, eye of Horus, musk, red feather, paua shell; Number: 8; Metal: gold, iron, manganite, steel; Animal: bear, boar, buffalo, bull, condor, cougar, dragon, eagle, elephant, elk, gorilla, horse, hyena, lion, mountain lion, ox, panda, puma, wolverine; Stone: agate, black agate with white veins, leopardskin agate, amazonite, amber, amethyst, aquamarine, bloodstone, chalcedonyx, chrysocolla, diamond, garnet, hematite, lapis lazuli, lodestone, clear quartz crystal, ruby, topaz, red tourmaline; Plant: allspice, balm of Gilead, bamboo, basil, blue bonnet, carnation, catnip, cedar, cinnamon, cinquefoil, black cohosh root, dragon's blood, evergreens, fennel, frankincense, galangal, garlic, goldenseal, High John, holly, juniper (wood, bark or berry), lavender, lemongrass, lime, linden, lotus root, masterwort (carried), mugwort, mulberry, mustard seed, myrrh, nutmeg, oak, onion, opoponax, peach, pennyroyal, black pepper, peppermint, pine, rosemary, saffron, sage, sassafras, St. John's Wort, sweet pea, black tea, thistle, thyme, turmeric, vetiver, willow, yerba santa; Goddess: Anath, Artio, Athena, Athtartu (The Strong One), Bellona, Cessair, Cymidei Cymeinfoll, Diana, Durga, Hathor, Hokmah, Ishtar (Bestower of Strength), Isis, Kali, Maeve, Morgan, Pallas, Qadesh, Romë, Savasi, Sekhmet (Strength of Life, Mistress of Strength), Sin, Sita, Strenua, Suwa, Uathach, Urjani, Ushas, Zorya; God: Apollo, Ares, Atlas, the Dagda, El, Gwynn ap Nudd, Hanuman, Horus, Lisa, Llasar Llaesgyfnewid, Lugallanna, Mabon, Mars, Mithras, Odin, Ogma, Ogun, Perun, Ra, Shakuru, Shiva, Sobek, Telesphorus, Thor, Wachabe (Black Bear), Zeus; Evocation: Achilles, amazons, Cratos, Cuchulain, Gabriel (Strength of Divinity), Hercules/Herakles, Hrungnir, Orion, Perseus.

Artistic strength: Animal: hippopotamus. **Astral strength**: Plant: frankincense, myrrh. **Athletic strength**: Plant: mistletoe. **Emotional strength**: Stone: opal; Plant: amaryllis, dahlia, yarrow. **Female strength**: Plant: angelica, motherwort; Goddess:

Anath, Hecate, Isis, Kali, Lilith, Oya, Pombagira. **Gentle strength**: Color: peach; Animal: bear, panda; Stone: pink diamond; Goddess: Isis (Gentle Lady). **Inner strength**: Animal: gorilla, toad; Stone: chrysocolla, chrysoprase, red jasper, labradorite, turquoise; Plant: apple, benzoin, daisy, snowdrop; *to access*: Stone: green aventurine; Plant: sycamore; *to increase*: Charm: paua shell; Stone: labradorite; *to maintain*: Plant: dill. **Magickal strength**: Stone: amber; Plant: ash. **Male strength**: Stone: black agate with white veins; Plant: melon, mistletoe; Goddess: Strenia. **Meditative strength**: Stone: turquoise. **mental strength**: Plant: dill, mint, vanilla; *to strengthen the mind*: Stone: jacinth, jade, malachite, zircon; Plant: honeysuckle. **Moral strength**: Stone: onyx. **Muscular strength**: Animal: boa constrictor, python. **Patient strength**: Plant: rose. **Personal strength**: Color: orange; God: Thor. **Physical strength**: Tuesday; Color: red; Metal: iron; Stone: agate, amazonite, amber, bloodstone, chalcedony, garnet, Herkimer diamond, quartz crystal, rhodochrosite; Plant: carnation, garlic, honeysuckle; God: Balarama, Magni, Ninegal (Strong-armed Lord), Ogma, Tajika-no mikoto, Thor, Zulummar; Evocation: Hercules/Herakles, Lugh, Samson; *to increase*: Stone: bloodstone, diamond; *in men*: Goddess: Strenia; *for sports*: Taillte. **Primal strength**: Animal: crocodile, musk ox. **Psychic strength**: Fire. **Spiritual strength**: Color: royal blue, white; Number: 8; Plant: grapefruit, oak, poplar, yerba maté, ylang-ylang. **Vegetative strength**: God: Cernunnos, Green Man. **Vital strength**: *to balance*: Plant: morning glory. **Warrior strength**: Animal: boar.

Strong character: Color: red; Animal: wolf. **Strong children**: Plant: hazel nut. **Strong decisions**: Goddess: Lilith. **Strong faith**: Color: green. **Strong family**: Animal: lion; Plant: bloodroot. **Strong passion**: Color: deep red; Plant: vetiver; *to protect against*: Stone: amethyst. **Strong spirits**: *to attract*: Plant: lotus root. **Strong will**: (See: Will). **Strong woman**: *to marry*: God: Nergal.

Ador of strength: Fire. **Strength after loss**: Plant: cypress. **Strength against enemies**: Stone: diamond.

Strength in: adversity: (See: Adversity). **conflict**: Tuesday. **times of danger**: God: Vidar.

Strength of: conviction: Stone: tigereye. **expression**: Stone: chrysocolla; Goddess: Isis. **fate**: Plant: blackthorn. **life**: Goddess: Anath, Sekhmet. **purpose**: Oil: palmarosa. **resolve**: Goddess: Alfhild. **will**: (See: Willpower).

Strength to: heal: Plant: broom. **see something through to the end**: Full Moon; Goddess: the Mother.

Strength through persistence and endurance: Saturn.

To: become stronger: Animal: wren; Stone: garnet; Plant: garlic, onion, thistle. **express yourself strongly**: Plant: sunflower. **increase strength**: Stone: agate, leopard skin agate, amber; Plant: chrysanthemum, horehound, sow thistle. **know when to reserve your strength**: Animal: bear; Goddess: Artio. **manifest strength**: Plant: agave.

To strengthen: Waxing Moon. **anger**: Color: red. **the aura**: Stone: garnet, iolite; Plant: vetiver. **bladder**: Stone: jasper. **blood**: (See: The Body). **bones**: (See: The Body). **bone marrow**: Stone: black onyx. **brain**: (See: The Body). **capillaries**: Plant: rose hips. **circulatory system**: Stone: pyrite. **character**: Plant: rosemary. **convictions**: Stone: labradorite. **courage**: (See: Courage). **digestive system**: Plant: garlic mustard. **energy**: Plant: gum tragacanth, yarrow.

etheric body: Stone: hematite. eyes: (See: The Body). eyesight: (See: Senses). family relations: Plant: bloodroot. human fertility: Metal: copper. friendship: Stone: emerald; Plant: macadamia nut; God: Arawn. gallbladder: Stone: jasper. health: Plant: geranium. healing herbs: Charm: harvest them in August; Stone: sunstone. the heart: (See: The Body). immune system: Stone: jade, ruby; Plant: Echinacea, tea tree, thyme. inner eye: Stone: malachite. joints: Stone: aventurine; Plant: horsetail. kidneys: (See: The Body). life force: Plant: citronella. limbs: Plant: juniper with laurel; God: Khnemu. liver: (See: The Body). love: (See: Love). loyalty: (See: Loyalty). lungs: Plant: hazelnut, thyme. magickal incense mixtures: Plant: dragon's blood, frankincense. magical workings: Stone: garnet. memory: Stone: emerald. the mother/child bond: (See: Children). muscles: Plant: spearmint. nerves/nervous system: Stone: chrysocolla; Plant: comfrey, cowslip, spearmint. organs: Stone: angelite, peridot. pancreas: Stone: azurite, malachite. powers(s): (See: Power). romantic relationships: Plant: Adam and Eve root. senses: (See: Senses). sex organs: Plant: quince. sexual weakness: Plant: black cohosh. shoulders: Plant: juniper with laurel. sight: (See: Sight). social skills: Plant: wolfsbane. spells: (See: Spells). spine: Stone: selenite. spirit: (See: Spirit). spleen: Stone: azurite, malachite; Plant: black alder. stomach: Stone: jasper; Plant: lavender, quince. teeth: Stone: fluorite. unions and partnerships: Plant: cardamom pod. virility: Stone: lodestone; Plant: Echinacea root. voice: Stone: carnelian. womb: Plant: feverfew, mugwort.

Stress

(See also: Adversity, Anxiety, Problems, Relaxation, Tension)

Emotional stress: *to relieve*: Stone: blue lace agate, amethyst, carnelian, celestite, dioptase, Herkimer diamond, tigereye; Plant: dahlia, lavender, nettle, valerian. **Stressful situations**: (See: Situations).

To: **balance stress**: Stone: jasper; Plant: orchid, vanilla. **deal with stress**: Water; Color: purple, violet; Animal: wolf; Stone: blue lace agate, amethyst, angelite, apophyllite, barite, Herkimer diamond, red jasper, onyx, sunstone, yellow topaz; Plant: dill, fennel, lavender, rose hips, clary sage, sycamore; *of aging*: Plant: mallow, sage; *of air travel*: Stone: hematite; *of extremes*: Plant: dill, Labrador tea; *of family*: Plant: rose; *of life*: Plant: geranium; *of pregnancy*: Plant: watermelon; *of situations*: Stone: banded agate; *of urban life*: Plant: dill. **increase resistance to stress**: Stone: hematite. **overcome stress**: Stone: sodalite; Plant: asafetida, kava kava, rosemary, scullcap, valerian. **protect against stress**: Stone: lepidolite; Plant: ginseng. **release stress**: Animal: lion; Stone: chalcanthite, hiddenite. **relieve stress**: Method: meditation, yoga; Animal: cat; Metal: gold, silver; Stone: alabaster, agate, banded agate, amber, amethyst, ametrine, argonite, azurite, carnelian, chrysocolla, chrysoprase, dioptase, hematite, Herkimer diamond, howlite, red jasper, kunzite, labradorite, lepidolite, malachite, onyx, peridot, rhodochrosite, rhodonite, rose quartz, staurolite, sugilite, sunstone, blue tourmaline, turquoise' Oil: neroli, petitgrain; Plant: amber, balm of Gilead, basil, birch, cedar, chamomile, cypress, dong quai, fennel, geranium, ginseng, lavender, lemon, lotus, rose hips, rosemary, sage, clary sage, sycamore, spruce, tangerine, valerian, vervain, vetiver, woodrose.

Strife

(See: Discord)

Structure

Saturn

Charm: square; Animal: beaver; Number: 4; God: Odin.

Study

(See also: Concentration, Focus, Memory, Intelligence, Knowledge, Learning, Tests)

Mercury/Air/Capricorn

Color: brown, yellow; Stone: beryl, green tourmaline; Plant: air fern, comfrey, peppermint, rosemary; God: Brahma, Ogma, Thoth.

To: **begin a course of study**: God: Ganesha. **to persevere in your studies**: Animal: carp.

To study: **agronomy**: Goddess: Agrona. **medicine**: Stone: galena. **the collective unconscious**: Method: study mythology.

Success

(See also: Overcoming, Victory)

Jupiter/Sun/Earth/Thursday/Sunday/ Capricorn/Scorpio

Color: brown, gold, green (any shade), indigo, orange, purple, silver, violet; Charm: orange feather; Number: 7, 8; Animal: carp, eagle, monkey, silkworm moth, nighthawk, wolf; Metal: gold; Stone: black or brown agate, amazonite, aventurine, chalcedony, chrysoprase, pyrite, lodestone, malachite, marble, rose quartz, sunstone, tourmaline, green tourmaline, turquoise; Plant: allspice, aloe, amber, apple blossom, basil, bergamot, cassia, cedar, chamomile, cinnamon, cinquefoil, clover, red clover, frankincense, galangal, geranium, ginger, High John, lemon balm, lucky hand root, mistletoe, mustard seed, myrrh, oak, orange blossom, patchouli, rowan, sandalwood, shamrock, Solomon's seal, spindle tree, vanilla, lemon verbena, winter bark, woodruff, yarrow; Goddess: Badb, Devana, Durga Siddhi, Korraval, Lakshmi, Nike, Rosmerta, Sarvakaryasiddhi Pradayika (Granter of Success in All Attempts), Victoria, Vijaya; God: Al Yusif, Apollo, Belenus, Bonus Eventus, Fu-Hsing, Ganesha, Janus, Osiris, Saturn, Sucellos, T'ai-Yueh-Ta-Ti, Thoth, Zeus; Evocation: Hercules.

Business success: Virgo; Color: green, violet; Stone: green aventurine, bloodstone, citrine, fluorite, garnet, lodestone, malachite, tiger's eye, blue or green tourmaline, zircon, yellow zircon; Plant: bayberry, benzoin, cinnamon, clove, dock, ginger, kelp, marigold, peony, vetiver, violet; God: Inari, Maximon, Mercury; *to increase*: Stone: malachite; *safe, successful business trip*: Goddess: Fortuna. **Financial success**: Stone: jasper; Color: brown, green; Animal: cowrie shells; Plant: benzoin; *to attract*: Color: brown; *to increase*: Color: brown; Plant: hyssop (See also: Prosperity). **Intellectual success**: Plant: benzoin. **Magickal success**: Plant: benzoin, ginger. **Total success**: Sun; Stone: pyrite. **Worldly success**: God: Al Yazid, Maximon.

Good luck with success: Stone: fluorite.

Successful childbirth: Goddess: Bride, Egeria. **Successful completion of a cycle**: Animal: wolf. **Successful life**: Stone: coral; Plant: High John, sandalwood. **Successful pregnancy**: Potion: raspberry leaf tea; Goddess: Luperca. **Successful transition**: God: Janus; *to the afterlife*: Goddess: Corra. **Successful voyage**: Goddess: Nehalennia; *to determine*: God: Njord.

Success at/in/with: **artistic careers**: Plant: vervain. **future battles**: Goddess: Aeron. **competitions**: Stone: black agate. **court**: (See: Court). **financial transactions**: Stone: tiger's eye. **gambling**: (See:

Gambling). **games of chance**: Stone: lodestone; Plant: laurel. **hunting**: (See: Hunting). **long range plans**: Color: purple; Stone: amethyst. **love**: (See: Love). **magick**: (See: Magick). **petitions**: Goddess: Anath, Athirat; God: Baal. **new undertakings**: Stone: chrysoprase. **work**: Plant: hawthorn, rowan.

Success through: **abilities**: Animal: toad. **perseverance**: Animal: cicada, tortoise, sea turtle.

To: **attract success**: Stone: amazonite, orange aventurine, labradorite, lodestone, green tourmaline; Plant: cinnamon, dragon's blood, High John. **clear obstacles to success**: Animal: elephant; Plant: High John. **increase success**: Stone: tourmaline; *of spells*: Plant: benzoin, clove. **release success**: Plant: clover. **understand success**: Color: gold; Animal: monkey.

Summerland

(See: Otherworld)

Summoning

Tool: bell; Method: candle magick, evocation, invocation; Color: red; Animal: owl.

To summon: **the dead**: Plant: wormwood. **deities**: Tool: athame; Method: invocation; **rain**: Stone: turquoise (thrown in river). **spirits**: Tool: bell, censer; Plant: dandelion, wormwood; *to battle*: Plant: rowan (bonfire). **storms**: (See: Storms). **winds**: Charm: white clay whistle.

Support

(See also: Assistance)

Charm: pillar, tet amulet; Metal: steel; Stone: apatite; Plant: aloe, banyan tree, mullein, self-heal, wolfsbane; Goddess: Agiscchanak, Aponibolinayen, Onatha;

God: the Bacabs, Ea, Imana, Inyan, Ngendei (Supporter of the World); Evocation: Akupera, Atlas, Kujara.

Emotional support: Cancer; Stone: obsidian; *emotional self support*: Plant: mullein. **Magical support**: Color: black. **Maternal support**: Plant: birch. **Self-support**: Plant: aloe, mullein, self heal. **Spiritual support**: Plant: angelica; Evocation: angels.

Support in times of danger: God: Vidar. **Support when your family objects to your choice of mate**: Goddess: Lofn. **To support**: **the needy**: God: Shiva. **outcasts**: God: Shiva.

Survival

Animal: alligator, blue jay, camel, cockroach, dingo, polar bear, shark, wolf; Charm: alligator tooth, shark tooth, image of the sphinx; Stone: black tourmaline; Plant: ginkgo, yellow stonecrop; Goddess: Carna, Cessair, Danaë, Gullveig, Isis, Liban, Rhiannon, Walutahanga, Xochiquetzal; God: Hoenir, Horned God, Vali; Evocation: Aeneas, fairies, Lif, Lifthrasir, Magni, Manawydan, Modi, Noah, Pryderi, Talos, Ukko, Utnapashtim, Vidar, Zaltyz.

Survival instincts: Animal: komodo dragon. **Survival skills**: Animal: sea turtle; God: the Horned God.

Ability to survive: Animal: polar bear. **Failure to survive**: Animal: dinosaur, dodo; Plant: black mulberry.

To survive: **a false accusation**: Goddess: Rhiannon. **by one's wits**: Animal: coyote. **flood**: Evocation: Dayang-Raca, Noah, Parnapishtim. **incest**: Goddess: Arianrhod, Ushas; God: Horus. **kidnapping**: God: Mabon, Pryderi. **loss of a spouse**: Goddess: Isis. **marriage to an unsuitable mate**: Goddess: Aphrodite, Venus. **a mastectomy**: Goddess: Lakshmi. **mental illness**: Goddess: Goleuddydd; God: Dionysus. **a natural disaster**: Goddess: Liban, Pyrrha,

Xochiquetzal; Evocation: Deucalion, Manu, Noah, Utnapishtim. **transitions**: (See: Transitions). **in the wilderness**: Goddess: Atalanta, Isis.

Sympathy
(See also: Compassion, Empathy)

Moon/Water/Aquarius

Color: green, pink; Number: 6; Stone: pink tourmaline; Plant: basil, elder flower, jonquil, lemon balm, briar rose, light pink rose, thrift; Goddess: Iyatiku; God: Barashakushu.

Sympathetic judge: Plant: carnation, galangal.

Chapter 20

Talent

(See also: Ability. Skill/s)

Stone: bloodstone; Plant: white carnation; Goddess: Benzaiten; God: Apollo, Kusor, Samildanach.

Artistic talent: Plant: carnation; God: Lu Pan.

To: **discover talent**: Animal: hawk. **share talent**: Plant: laurel.

Talismans

(See also: Amulets, Protection, Security)

To protect: **abdomen**: Goddess: Oshun. **agriculture**: (See: Agriculture). **animals**: (See: Animals). **the aura**: (See: Auras). **babies**: (See: Babies). **beauty**: Stone: jasper. **beekeepers**: God: Aristaios. **boats**: Goddess: Ma-Tzu; *fishing vessels*: God: Hung Sheng. **body**: Stone: ruby, turquoise; Plant: clove. **boundaries**: Animal: porcupine. **brain**: Plant: lemon balm. **the brave**: Goddess: Athena. **caravans**: God: Sai' Al Qaum, Aktab al-Kutbay. **cars**: Plant: eye of Satan (in trunk). **chastity**: Stone: emerald. **children**: (See: Children). **cities**: Goddess: Athena, Athene Polias (Protector of the City), Baalat, Cybele, Pallas Athene (Goddess of the City), Salus, Tanith, Tyche; God: Ch'eng-huang, Huitzilopochtli, Zeus Polieus; *Athens*: Goddess: Athena; *London*: God: Lugh; *New York City*: Goddess: Lady Liberty. **the courageous**: Goddess: Athena. **crops**: (See: Agriculture). **the dead**: (See: The Dead). **the defenseless**: Goddess:

Demeter. **deities**: God: Brihaspati, Indra; Evocation: Michael. **personal destiny**: Goddess: Enekpe. **domestic life**: Goddess: Neith. **doorways**: God: Janus. **the downward direction**: Invoke: Sambha; Sambharaj. **dreams**: God: Morpheus. **the Earth**: God: Heimdall (Earth Watcher). **Egypt**: Goddess: Amauntet, Edjo (Lower Egypt), Nekhebet (Upper Egypt). **emotions**: Animal: snail; Stone: ruby. **an endangered relationship**: Goddess: Albina. **one's energy**: Plant: tuberose, violet. **England/Great Britain**: God: Bran; Evocation: King Arthur, Merlin; *British royal family*: God: Bran; *Isle of Man*: God: Mannan. **the enlightened**: Evocation: Ista Devata. **entrances and exits**: Goddess: Patadharini; God: Bhairava, Janus (Guardian of Doors), Ksetrapala, Kushi-Iwa-Mado-No-Mikoto, the Menshen, Portunus, Wei Ch'eng. **explorers**: Evocation: Breasal. **fairies**: Plant: elder. **family**: (See: Family). **family life**: Goddess: Cardea. **fatherhood**: Plant: holly. **fidelity**: Stone: emerald. **fields**: God: Svantovit. **fisher folk**: Goddess: Hatmehyt, Ma-Tzu. **forests**: Goddess: Durga, Faun; God: Cocidius, Faunus, Green Man, Sucellos. **fortifications**: Goddess: Ratis. **freedom**: Goddess: Lady Liberty; God: Zeus Eluetherious. **freed slaves**: Goddess: Feronia. **fugitives**: God: Zeus (Preserver of Fugitives). **gallbladder**: God: Qebsennuf. **gamblers**: Evocation: the Apsaras. **a garden**: (See: Gardening). **gardeners**: Goddess: Pomona; God: Vertumnus. **good people**: Goddess: Sekhmet. **grasslands**: Goddess:

Ve'ai (Grass Woman). **groves**: *olive groves*: Goddess: Athene; *sacred groves*: Goddess: Diana Nematona, Diana Nemorensis. **harbors**: God: Portunus. **hard workers**: God: Saturn. **harvest**: Goddess: Ala; God: Lugh. **health**: (See: Health). **heart**: God: Duamutef. **herbalists**: Goddess: Artemis, Diana. **home**: (See: Security). **hospitality**: God: Zeus Xenios. **hospitals**: Invoke: Dhanvantari, Kantatman (Guardian of Hospitals). **household**: Goddess: Frigg. **humankind**: Goddess: Kwan Yin; God: Indra, Jizo Bosatsu, T'ai-Yueh-Ta-Ti. **hunters**: Goddess: Hastseyalti; God: Rudra. **ideas**: Animal: badger. **independence**: Stone: jade. **initiates**: God: Oshosi. **inner child**: Animal: slug, snail; Stone: coral. **inner power**: Animal: cat; *inner healing power*: Plant: self-heal. **intestines**: (See: The Body). **land**: (See: Land). **Ireland**: God: Mannan. **lepers**: God: Zeus of the White Poplar. **life**: Plant: holly. **a life in danger**: Goddess: Hlin. **liver**: (See: The Body). **the lonely**: God: Shiva. **love**: (See: Love). **lovers**: (See: Lovers). **lungs**: God: Duamutef. **luggage** (from theft): Plant: comfrey. **magick circle**: Animal: musk ox; Plant: turmeric (sprinkled). **marriage**: (See: Marriage). **men**: (See: Men). **the mind**: Stone: pyrite. **mines**: God: Min. **miners**: Animal: canary; Evocation: the karzelek. **mountains/mountain-dwellers**: Goddess: Tork. **Nature**: God: Helios. **the needy**: (See: Need). **nursery**: Goddess: Cunina, Volumna. **oceans**: Evocation: nereids. **oracles**: Plant: alder. **organs**: Goddess: Carna. **orphans**: God: Zeus. **passages/passageways**: God: Janus. **paper (from vermin)**: Plant wormwood. **paper houses**: God: Ho Masubi. **pilgrims**: Goddess: Kwan Yin. **places of death**: (See: Death). **places where goodness is taught**: God: the Celestial Kings. **poets**: Goddess: Brigit. **the poor**: Goddess: Aradia; God: Shamash, Zeus. **personal property**: Animal: badger; God: Kokola, Terminus, Zeus Ktesios. **poets**:

Goddess: Cerridwen. **poetry**: God: Bran. **princes**: Evocation: Ouestucati. **procreators**: God: Prajapati. **prostitutes**: Goddess: Inanna, Lupa, Sheng-Mu. **psychic power**: Plant: lotus, queen of the night. **records**: Animal: whale; Goddess: Sesheta; *sacred records*: Animal: crow. **religious ceremonies**: Goddess: Aizan. **the righteous**: Goddess: Sekhmet. **rivers**: Invoke: Aha. **roads**: God: Chimata-no-kami, Dosojin, Min. **sacred buildings**: Color: coral. **sacred space/places**: Tool: besom; Plant: broom (for sweeping), myrrh; Goddess: Nematona; God: Dunatis. **seafarers**: Stone: aquamarine, moonstone; Goddess: Amphitrite, Aphrodite, Elen, Kwan-Yin, Leucothea, Miao-shan, Nehalennia; God: Castor and Pollux, Faivarongo (Grandsire of the Ocean), Kuanyin of the Southern Sea, the Munakata-No-Kami, Sirsir. **ships**: God: Njord. **secret teachings**: Goddess: Senge Dong-ma. **sexual organs**: (See: The Body). **shepherds**: God: Aristaeus. **sleep**: Goddess: Uma, Urmya. **sleepers**: God: Bes. **soldiers**: Stone: amethyst; *military expeditions*: God: Meness. **soul/s**: Stone: turquoise. **spiritual healers**: Stone: moldovite. **the state**: Goddess: Amauntet, Athena; Evocation: Emperor Kuan. **stomach**: God: Imsety. **storehouses/warehouses**: Goddess: Inanna; God: Mi-Kura-Tana-No-Kami. **strangers**: God: Zeus Xenios. **suppliants**: God: Zeus Hikesios. **tents**: God: Mahakala. **territory**: Animal: blue jay, gibbon. **thieves**: Charm: four thieves vinegar. **towns/villages**: Plant: angelica; God: the Lares, Lubangala. **traders**: God: Hermes. **trails**: God: Chimata-no-kami. **travelers**: (See: Travelers). **treasure**: Animal: dragon; Evocation: Andvari (Guardian of Treasure), Fafnir. **trees**: God/dess: Medeine of the Trees; Evocation: dryads, hamadryads, tree spirits. **the unborn**: Goddess: Alemona. **the Universe**: (See: The Universe). **the upward direction**: Goddess: Usnisa. **vegetation**:

Goddess: the Duillae, Venus; *medicinal plants*: Goddess: Airmid. **virginity**: Goddess: Diana. **warriors**: (See: Warriors). **the weak**: Goddess: Diana; God: Lugh, Zeus. **wealth**: Stone: tiger's eye. **wilderness**: Goddess: Diana. **wild things**: Goddess: Artemis. **witches**: (See: Witches). **womb/uterus**: Goddess: Oshun. **women**: (See: Women. **the wronged**: God: Shamash. **young couples**: Invoke: Ya'halan. **yourself**: Charm: silver pentacle; Animal: crab, toad; Plant: bergamot, clove, yerba santa; Goddess: Isis; God: Anubis; Evocation: guardian angel. **youth**: God: Iovantucarus.

Teaching

(See also: Education, Learning)

Mercury/North

Color: green; Animal: gorilla, polar bear, raven, spider, wolf; Stone: kyanite, lapis lazuli, sodalite; Plant: coconut (broken), lavender, pine; Goddess: Aoife, Hokmah, Ishtar, Luaths Lurgann, Namagiri, Sarasvati, Scathach, Sekhmet (Beloved Teacher), Tara; God: Brahma, the Dagda, Guruttam (Greatest Teacher), Heimdall, Nebo, Orunmila; Evocation: animal guides, Gabriel.

To find a teacher: Stone: meteorite.

To teach: **by example**: God: Osiris. **charity**: Goddess: Nzambi; God: Odin. **children**: (See: Children). **dancing**: Ahnt Kai'. **magick**: (See: Magick). **martial arts**: Goddess: Aoife. **parenting**: Animals: cat, coyote, kangaroo; Goddess: Athena. **pleasure**: Goddess: Oshun. **singing**: Ahnt Kai'. **to speak**: God: Fabulinus. **yoga**: Animal: cat.

Teachings

Color: green.

Teachings from Water: Animal: dolphin. **ancient teachings**: Animal: crane.

hidden teachings: Animal: rabbit. **secret teachings**: *to protect*: Goddess: Senge Dongma. **spiritual teachings**: Goddess: Demeter; *to understand*: God: Niyan.

Temperance

(See: Moderation)

Tension

(See also: Calm, Relaxation, Stress)

Color: purple, violet; Charm: knot.

Emotional tension: *to protect against*: Plant: yarrow; *to release*: Stone: moonstone; Plant: balm of Gilead, chamomile, dandelion, foxglove, myrrh, sweetgale. **Nervous tension**: *to release*: Plant: comfrey, corn, marjoram; *to relieve*: Plant: cedar, lavender, scullcap, passionflower, valerian, wood rose, ylang-ylang. **Physical tension**: *to release*: Stone: geode; Plant: dandelion, forget-me-not, marjoram, passionflower, rowan, rue, zinnia; *to relieve*: Plant: cannabis, dandelion, squash blossom. **sexual tension**: Goddess: Luonnotar, Parvati; *to release*: Plant: balm of Gilead, fuchsia. **subconscious tension**: *to release*: Plant: comfrey, corn, orange; Plant: comfrey, orange.

Tension headache: (See: Pain). **freedom from tension**: Plant: dandelion, fireweed, passionfruit.

To: **release tension**: Plant: garlic, rowan, zinnia. **relieve tension**: Method: massage, meditation; Stone: amber, amethyst, chrysoprase, coral, Herkimer diamond, lepidolite, rose quartz, smoky quartz, rhodochrosite, rhodonite; Oil: neroli; Plant: aster, bergamot, birch, comfrey, cranberry, dandelion, fennel, forget-me-not, garlic, geranium, jasmine, lavender, mallow, pine, clary sage, spruce, tangerine, valerian, vervain, wormwood, ylang-ylang. **resolve tension**: God: Shiva.

Terror
(See also: Fear, Nightmares, Terrorism)

Animal: lion, sow, all mammals who eat their own young; Plant: snakeroot; Goddess: Bhairavi, Inanna, Sekhmet (Mistress of Terror), Timores, Tursa; God: Arawn, Pan, Phobos, Shango, Varuna (Lord of Terror).

To inspire terror: Goddess: Cybele.

Terrorism
(See also: Battle, War)

Mars

Goddess: Kali; God: Allah, Ares.

To: battle terrorism: Goddess: Isis, Kali. **protect against terrorism**: Goddess: Mary.

Tests
(See also: Study)

Fire

God: Chung-Kuei.

For: energy when taking tests: Plant: lovage. **insight in tests**: God: K'uei Hsing.

To: pass tests: Plant: honeysuckle, peach, sycamore, wintergreen, wisteria; God: K'uei Hsing. **test endurance**: Plant: wormwood. **test morals**: God: Tezcatlipoca.

Thankfulness/Thanksgiving
(See: Gratitude)

Theft
(See also: Security, Thieves)

Moon/Night/Monday

Color: gray; God: Balor, Cacus, Hermes, Loki, Maui, Mercury; Evocation: fairies, Cuchulain, Jason.

Stolen children: (See: Children). **Stolen goods/property**: *to recover*: Method:

footprint magick; Charm: magnet; Metal: iron; Stone: lodestone; Plant: marigold; God: Cian, Punarvasu, Thor; *to replace*: Goddess: Sif. **Stolen innocence**: Evocation: Shamhat. **Stolen knowledge**: Goddess: Aoife. **Stolen love**: God: Angus; Evocation: Paris.

To learn: that it isn't worth it to acquire things via theft: Goddess: Maeve. **your lesson about stealing vehicles**: Evocation: Phaethon.

To: protect against theft/thieves: Mercury; Animal: dog; Stone: amethyst, coral, garnet; Plant: aspen, caraway seed, garlic, juniper, larch, black pepper (sprinkled), vetiver; Goddess: Durga, Kwan Yin, Tara, Urmya; God: Fudo-Myoo. **steal in order to benefit others**: Evocation: Prometheus, Robin Hood.

Thieves
(See also: Security, Theft)

Mercury

Goddess: Furina; God: Hermes, Mercury.

To: avert burglars/thieves: Plant: bat nut (placed above door or on window sill), fern, garlic, mustard seed. **bring a thief to justice**: Method: footprint magick. **protect thieves**: Charm: Four Thieves Vinegar. **protect against thieves**: Plant: plantain leaf. **uncover a thief**: Charm: key (used as a pendulum, or spun); Metal: mercury (toxic, not recommended); Plant: galangal, hazel, poke root, vetiver.

Thought
(See also: Logic, The Mind, Reason)

Mercury/Air

Color: indigo, white, yellow; Animal: wolf, all bird; Plant: pansy; Goddess: Alaghom-Naom (Mother of Mind), Minerva, Sussistanako; God: Jen-Shen, Ptah.

Analytical thinking: Virgo. **Clear thinking**: Stone: aquamarine, carnelian, celestite, fluorite, moonstone (rubbed on temples), tigereye, tourmaline, clear zircon; Plant: daffodil, dill, jasmine, lavender, lemon, lotus root, magnolia, peppermint, petunia, rosemary; God: Baile, Llma; *to stimulate*: Plant: jasmine. **Creative thinking**: Stone: topaz; Plant: broom, garlic; Goddess: Sesheta. **New thinking**: Number: 5. **Positive thinking**: Plant: moss agate. **Precise thinking**: Virgo. **Quick thinking**: Aquarius; Animal: rabbit; Plant: honeysuckle, horehound; God: Baile. **Strategic thinking**: Animal: chimpanzee.

Thought patterns: *to release*: Plant: birch; *to break negative thought patterns*: Oil: new mown hay. **Power of thought**: Color: yellow; God: Ptah.

To: change ways of thinking: Color: green; Stone: kyanite, lepidolite; Plant: licorice, squill; *make needed changes in thinking*: Stone: lepidolite. **encourage someone to think about you**: Plant: clover. **expand thinking**: Stone: tourmaline. **focus thought**: Plant: orchid. **improve thinking**: Stone: amazonite, tiger's eye; Plant: foxglove, peppermint. **learn to think before you act or speak**: Goddess: Providentia. **stop thinking about someone/something**: Plant: fumitory.

Thought Forms

Air

Negative thought forms: *to avert*: Color: black; Plant: geranium; *to clear*: Tool: besom, censer; Color: black; Charm: Florida Water, Kananga Water, salt water; Metal: silver; Plant: eye of Satan; *to transform into positive ones*: Color: black; Stone: jet, obsidian, onyx.

Thoughtfulness

(See also: Graciousness)

Taurus

Color: blue; Plant: agrimony; God: Ganesha.

Thoughts

(See also: Ideas, Memories)

Air

Plant: pansy.

Bitter thoughts: Plant: deadly nightshade. **Dark thoughts**: Color: black; Plant: nightshade. **Envious thoughts**: *to stop*: Stone: agate. **Evil thoughts**: Moon; *to avert*: Stone: amethyst, ruby; *to protect against*: Stone: amethyst, carnelian, ruby, zircon. **Foolish thoughts**: *to avert*: Stone: ruby. **Happy/pleasant thoughts**: Plant: lotus root, pansy. **Impure thoughts**: *to prevent*: Stone: sapphire; Plant: juniper berry. **Lustful thoughts**: *to stop*: Plant: hemlock. **Negative thoughts**: *to banish*: Color: black; Charm: brimstone (as incense); *to improve*: Stone: sapphire; *to protect against those of other people*: Plant: pennyroyal. **Unpleasant thoughts**: *to forget*: Potion: cool drinks with leafy tips of borage. **Unwanted thoughts**: *to banish*: Stone: sapphire; Evocation: Addanc; *to protect against*: Plant: juniper berry. **Wise thoughts**: Plant: sunflower.

To: control your thoughts: Metal: silver. **exchange thoughts**: Color: yellow; Plant: juniper berry (See also: Communication). **manifest thoughts**: Plant: Turk's cap lily; Goddess: Yhi; God: Io. **Protect thoughts against psychics**: Stone: carnelian. **Read thoughts**: Plant: fern.

Time

(See also: Longevity)

Saturn/Moon

Color: black; Charm: calendar, chronometer, circle, clock, hourglass, pyramid, spiral, sundial; Animal: dinosaur, sphinx; Stone: amber, fossil, meteorite, moldovite;

Plant: sequoia; Goddess: Aditi, Ariadne, Arianrhod, At-Em, Coventina, Emer, Juno, Kali (Black Time, Mighty Time), Kefa (Mother of Time), Manat, Savitri, Sekhmet (Time, Devourer of Time), Sesheta (Minister of Time), Ushas (Mistress of Time); God: Amon (Lord of Time), Angus, Cronos, El (Father of Time, Master of Time), Kala, Mahakala (Great Time), Ra, Saturn (Father Time, Old Father Time), Shiva, Sin, Tai sui-xing, Thoth, Zurvan; Evocation: Father Time.

Ceaseless time: Animal: serpent. **Circular time**: Moon; Animal: jaguar, praying mantis. **Dreamtime**: Animal: lizard; Goddess: Yhi; God: Gidja; Evocation: Kutjara, Wati. **Infinite time**: Goddess: Nitya-Kali (Endless Time); God: Zurvan (Boundless Time). **Linear time**: Animal: crow. **Orderly flow of time**: Goddess: Sesheta.

Time management: Animal: tiger; Plant: morning glory; God: Thoth. **Measurement of time**: Moon; God: Thoth (Reckoner of Time and Seasons), Tsuki-Yomi. **Mysteries of time**: Water. **Passage of time**: Moon; God: Shiva, Sin. **Power to stop time**: Animal: hummingbird. **Recording of time**: God: Thoth.

To: affect time: Animal: hummingbird, praying mantis; Goddess: Kali (Conqueror of Time); *make time seem to pass quickly*: (See: Speed); *make a spell last a long time*: (See: Longevity). **change perception of time**: Plant: betel nut. **move through time and space**: Animal: lynx. **reconcile lunar/solar time**: Number: 19.

Timelessness

Spirit

Tolerance

Animal: donkey; Stone: chrysoprase; Plant: beech, impatiens, lime; God: Apollo.

Intolerance

Number: 2; God: Allah, Jehovah.

Trade

(See: Business)

Trance

Tool: censer; Method: chanting, dance, drugs (dangerous, not recommended), drumming, fasting, mantra, meditation, sensory deprivation (dangerous without special training), spirit possession; Charm: blindfold, prayer beads; Plant: bistort, cannabis, datura, dragon's blood, ginger, ginseng, laurel (as incense), wild lettuce, mandrake, maravilla, myrrh, nutmeg (as incense), peyote, saffron (tea or incense), spearmint, tangerine, ylang-ylang, cannabis with laurel and barley (as incense); Goddess: Freya, the Crone, Lilith, Urd; God: Odin, Shiva, Tlaloc; Evocation: fairies.

Trance possession: God: Legba. **Divination in trance work**: Plant: nutmeg (as incense).

To revive someone from a trance state: Charm: aromatherapy; Potion: cold water; Stone: jet (burned as incense).

Tranquility

(See also: Calm, Harmony, Peace)

Moon/Water

Color: aqua, blue, light blue, white; Number: 1; Metal: silver; Stone: blue lace agate, aquamarine, aventurine, chrysoprase, jade, leopardskin jasper, kunzite, larimar, moonstone, blue or rose quartz, sapphire; Metal: maganite; Potion: apple juice, passion flower juice; Plant: acacia, bayberry, benzoin, bergamot, burdock, chamomile, red clover, coconut, coltsfoot, coriander, cypress, blue hyacinth, lavender, linden, lotus, myrrh, passion flower, peach, rose, sage, clary sage, stonecrop, valerian, white water lily, willow, wisteria, yarrow; Goddess: Alcyone, Isis, Kwan Yin, Mary, Quies, Sarasvati; God: Shiva.

Domestic tranquility: Method: hearth magick; Color: light blue; Plant: bayberry, rose, peach; Goddess: Chantico, Hestia, Vesta; Evocation: the domovoi.

To tranquilize: Color: emerald green; Stone: amethyst, emerald, chrysoprase, lepidolite, onyx; Plant: apple, crab apple, belladonna, calamus, feverfew, hawthorn, black hellebore, henbane, hops, lady's mantle, St. John's Wort.

Transcendence

Color: black, blue, green, red, white, yellow; Animal: swan; Plant: lotus, snowdrop; Goddess: Hathor, Isis, Kali.

Spiritual transcendence: Animal: swan. **Transcendent intuition**: Goddess: Prajnaparamita. **Transcendental knowledge**: Goddess: Corra, Rajarajesvari. **Transcendental wisdom**: Goddess: Prajnaparamita (Lady of Wisdom). **All that transcends form or measurement**: Goddess: Aditi. **To transcend boundaries**: (See: Limitation).

Transformation

(See also: Change, Shapeshifting, Transmutation)

Moon/Full Moon/Waning Moon/Pluto/Fire/Water/Autumn/Scorpio

Tool: cauldron, censer; Method: alchemy, dance; Color: orange, purple, red; Charm: shape-changing water, shed skin of a snake; Animal: butterfly, caterpillar, dragon, eel, frog, moth, newt, snake, polar bear, rattlesnake, salamander, scarab beetle, scorpion, swine, vulture, water birds, all amphibians; Metal: mercury (toxic); Stone: amber, amethyst, charoite, Goddess rock, malachite, obsidian, onyx, sodalite, sugilite, topaz, torbenite, tourmaline, unakite; Plant: calla lily, cayenne, flax, frankincense, grain, grape, lotus, myrrh, orange blossom, rosemary, violet, wormwood; Goddess: Annapurna, Artemis, Butterfly Maiden, Caer, Carravogue, Cerridwen, Chicomecoatl, Estsanatlehi, Greine, Hecate, Ho Hsien-Ku, Isis, Kali, Melusine, Oya, Parvati, Pombagira, Pressina, Sekhmet (Lady of Transformations); God: Horus (Mighty One of Transformations), Kephera, Odin, Poseidon, Sin, Zeus; Evocation: Fuamnach, Gwydion, Salmon Boy.

Conscious transformation: Stone: smoky quartz. **Dynamic transformation**: Fire; Animal: scorpion. **Emotional transformation**: Stone: obsidian. **Inner transformation**: Stone: sugilite; Plant: marigold; Goddess: Cyhiraeth. **Personal transformation**: Fire; Stone: coral, black onyx; Plant: cayenne, fireweed, self-heal, stonecrop; Goddess: Ambika, Cailleach, Cerridwen, Coatlicue, Cyhiraeth, Ho Hsien-Ku, Inari, Kali; God: Amaethon, Angus, Cernunnos. **Physical transformation**: Goddess: Aetna, Chuginadak, Fuji, Pelé; God: Thomagata, Zeus (See also: Shapeshifting). **Self-transformation**: Goddess: Ambika, Inari; God: Angus, Odin. **Spiritual transformation**: Stone: blue lace agate; Plant: juniper berry; Goddess: Hokmah, Isis, Tara.

Power of transformation: Fire/Water; Animal: butterfly, frog, dragon, snake, pig; Charm: shape-changing water; Stone: obsidian; Goddess: Aetna, Fuji, Pele. **Transformation from death to life**: God: Osiris. **Transformation through love**: Plant: holy thorn; Goddess: Latis. **Transformation through travel**: Animal: eel.

To: accept transformation: Plant: mallow. **achieve true transformation**: Stone: staurolite. **ease transformation**: Plant: sweetgrass.

To transform: anger into wisdom: Color: blue. **attachment into discernment**: Color: red. **consciousness**: Goddess: Tara. **energy**: (See: Energy). **hatred into compassion**: Color: black. **jealousy into accomplishment**: Color: green. **negative emotions into positive emotions**: Plant: juniper berry. **negative thought forms into positive ones**: Color: black; Stone: jet, obsidian, onyx. **a nightmare into good fortune**: Evocation: the Baku. **substance into energy**: Goddess: Annapurna.

Transition
(See also: Change, Passage)

Color: purple, violet; Charm: rainbow; Animal: bluebird; Plant: cyclamen, stonecrop; Goddess: Nut, Sarasvat; God: Janus.

Successful transition: God: Janus. **Transition to the afterlife**: (See: Afterlife). **Transition to the Otherworld**: (See: Otherworld). **Transition between life stages**: Animal: guinea pig; *from boyhood to manhood*: God: Apollo.

To: ease transition: Color: black, blue, white; Animal: swan; Stone: chiastolite, staurolite; Plant: butterwort, cypress, walnut. **survive transition**: Goddess: Brigid, Cihuacoatl, Mokosh, Oshun, Sarasvati, Yemaya; God: Legba, Ogun.

Transmutation
(See also: Alchemy, Shapeshifting)

Animal: caterpillar, snake; Stone: moldovite, obsidian; Plant: linden, yucca; Goddess: Aetna, Artemis, Athene, Chuginadak, Fuji, Isis, Pelé; God: Quetzalcoatl.

Purification through transmutation: God: Hermes.

Trauma
(See also: Accidents)

Emotional trauma: *to heal*: Stone: azurite; Plant: fireweed, lemon balm.

To: recover from trauma: Stone: aventurine, chrysoprase, diopside, rose quartz, rhodochrosite, rhodonite; Oil: petitgrain; Plant: calla lily, chamomile, comfrey, daisy, dragon's blood, fireweed, geranium, lady's slipper, ladies' tresses, lavender, lemon, lemon balm, mace, onion, clary sage, scallion, thyme; *help children to recover*: Plant: sweet potato. **release trauma**: Plant: fireweed, lady's tresses, orange.

Travel
(See also: Quests, Travelers)

Mercury/Sun/Moon/Air/West/Wednesday/Sagittarius

Color: brown, orange, yellowish green; Number: 5, 7; Animal: monarch butterfly, camel, caribou, horse, sea gull, all migrating birds; Metal: aluminum, silver; Stone: aquamarine, amethyst, yellow carnelian, chalcedony, Herkimer diamond, jet, malachite, moonstone, tigereye, orange zircon; Plant: driftwood, mint, tumbleweed; God: Ek Chua, Ganesha, Hasammelis, Hermes, Janus, Legba, Mercury.

Air travel: Air; Animal: all flying birds; Plant: dandelion seed head, mustard seed; Goddess: Freya; God: Lugaldurmah; *to help deal with the stress of*: Stone: hematite. **Astral travel**: (See: The Astral). **Business travel**: Sagittarius; Goddess: Fortuna; God: Yacatecuhtli; *safe, successful business trip*: Goddess: Fortuna. **Forest travel**: Earth; God: Byelobog. **Night travel**: Moon/Sun/Night; Goddess: Hecate; God: Ra. **Road travel**: Earth; God: Janus, Kunado. **Safe travel**: Charm: turquoise ring; Stone: malachite; Plant: cinquefoil, comfrey, eye of

Satan, Irish moss, olive; *over water*: Animal: dolphin, porpoise; Stone: moonstone; Goddess: the Ahinehiae, the Ahueccaniae, the Matronaea, the Xulsigiae; *safe return*: Goddess: Fortuna. **Sea travel**: Water; Goddess: Isis, Mater Matuta, Nehalennia; God: Njord; *good sea voyage*: Goddess: Aphrodite Euploia. **Space travel**: Air; Stone: meteorite, moldovite, tektite; God: Lugaldurmah, Nwyvre. **spiritual travel**: Stone: amethyst, phenacite. **Water travel**: Moon/Water; Stone: chalcedony; Plant: bat nut, driftwood; Goddess: Akaru-Hime, Coventina; God: Glaucus.

Good health during travel: Plant: comfrey root. **Luck during travel**: Plant: lucky hand root, sea holly.

To: begin a journey: God: Frey, Ganesha. **get the opportunity to travel**: Plant: lucky hand root. **protect luggage from theft**: Plant: comfrey. **recover from travel**: Plant: gentian. **travel both male and female paths**: Animal: bass; God: Obatala; Evocation: Tiresias. **travel to new places**: Animal: eagle.

ravelers

(See also: Travel)

Stone: aquamarine, leopardskin jasper; Goddess: Isis, Mary; God: Ekahau, Hermes, Ilmarinen, Mercury, Pushan, Tayon al-Kutbay.

Air travelers: *to protect*: Stone: aquamarine; Metal: aluminum. **Business travelers**: God: Ek Chua, Hermes, Mercury; *to guide*: God: Yacatecuhtli. **Forest travelers**: *to confuse*: Evocation: dame vertes; *to frighten*: God: Pan, Silvanus; *to help*: God: Byelobog. **Sea travelers**; *to protect*: Animal: cat; Metal: silver; Goddess: Amphitrite, Aphrodite, Athirat, Kwan Yin, Miao Shan, Nehalennia; God: the Dioscuri, Faivarongo, Hung Sheng, Kuan-yin, the Munakata-No-Kami, Poseidon, Sirsir.

To: confuse travelers: Evocation: Pooka. **guide travelers**: God: Puchan. **protect travelers**: Animal: jackal; Metal: silver; Stone: jet, malachite, moonstone, tiger's eye, orange zircon; Plant: comfrey, Irish moss, morning glory, mugwort (in shoes), sea holly; Goddess: Pravasarakshika (Protectress of Travelers); God: Aktab al-Kutbay, Apollo, Breasal, Chung-kuei, Dosojin, Hasamelis, Hermes, Ilmarinen, Kshitigarbha, the Kumado-No-Kami, the Lares, Meness, Min, Mullo, Pusan, Shamash, Tayon al-Kutbay, Zeus; *while sailing*: Stone: aquamarine, beryl; Goddess: Nehalennia; *explorers*: God: Breasal; *military expeditions*: God: Meness.

reachery

(See also: Deceit)

Color: olive green; Charm: blood; Plant: bilberry, red rose, wolfsbane; Goddess: Fraud; God: Loki, Set.

To: avenge treachery: God: Gwydion. **learn to detect treachery**: Stone: emerald (grows pale or changes color), sapphire; Goddess: Fraud. **learn not to leave yourself open to treachery**: God: Balder, Osiris.

rust

North/South

Color: green; Stone: aphrodite, chrysoprase; Animal: butterfly, dolphin, swan; Plant: basil, bistort, cowslip, mallow, mint, wild rose; God: Fides.

Perfect trust: God: Marduk. **Power of trust**: Animal: butterfly.

To: attract trust: Plant: frangipani. **determine whom to trust**: Animal: hyena. **learn to trust**: Stone: flint; Plant: bistort, horsetail, thistle; *inner knowledge*: Plant: heather, pine; *intuition*: Animal: gazelle; Plant: pine. **learn not to be too trusting**: God: Osiris.

To trust: in truth: Animal: coyote. **inner wisdom**: Plant: saguaro cactus. **your instincts**: Animal: cobra, goshawk, jaguar, vulture. **your perception**: Animal: cricket, scarlet macaw. **yourself**: Animal: wolf; Plant: day lily, raspberry, rose, Syrian rue. **your senses**: (See: Senses).

Distrust

Plant: apricot, lavender.

Truth

(See also: Deceit, Honesty)

Fire/Monday

Color: blue, dark blue, white, violet; Charm: white ostrich feather; Animal: chickadee, owl; Number: 7; Stone: agate, moss agate, diamond, dioptase, garnet, lapis lazuli, smoky quartz, sapphire; Plant: bluebell, white chrysanthemum, cyclamen, nightshade, redwood; Goddess: Aleitheia, Asase Yaa, Astraea, Bast, the Erinyes, Fila Vocis, Isis, Kukuri-Hime, Ma'at (Feather of Truth, Witness of Truth in All Things), Mati Syra Zemlya, rDo-rje-rnal hbyor-ma (Lady Truth), Rhiannon, Sin (Guardian of Truth), Syn, Veritas; God: Ahura Mazda, Anubis, Apollo, Aten (Who Lives in Truth), Chango, Forseti, Gibil, Ida-Ten, Jupiter Fidus, Mabon, Marduk, Misharu, Mitra, Mithras, Nereus, Ningizzida (Lord of the Tree of Truth), Nusku, Obatala, Orunmila, Osiris (Establisher of Right and Truth Throughout the World), Ra (King of Truth, Lord of Right and Truth), Shamash, Sin, Thoth (Judge of Right and Truth), Tyr, Varuna (Lord of Truth).

Bitter truth: Plant: savory. **Cosmic truth**: Goddess: Kali. **Divine truth**: Plant: lotus. **Higher truths**: Animal: eagle; Plant: alder. **Highest truth**: Plant: wintergreen. **Inner truth**: Color: blue, white; Charm: musk; Stone: blue topaz, blue tourmaline; *to reveal*: Stone: lapis lazuli, blue tourmaline. **Personal truth**: Animal: whale. **Spiritual truth**: Animal: eagle. **Ultimate truth/s**: Number: 7.

Truthfulness: Sagittarius; Charm: Eye of Horus; Stone: jasper, lapis lazuli; God: Mithras. **True affection**: Plant: parsley wreath. **True appreciation**: Plant: valerian. **True friendship**: (See: Friendship). **True friends**: God: Thor. **True love**: (See: Love). **True prosperity**: Animal: buffalo. **True religion**: *to keep one's true religion secret*: Goddess: Isis Amenti (The Hidden One). **True self**: (See: Inner Work). **True transformation**: (See: Transformation).

To: be true to your purpose in life: Plant: daisy. **face the truth**: Stone: aragonite. **hear/recognize truth**: Plant: pine. **know if your lover is telling the truth**: Stone: emerald. **learn/discover the truth**: Color: dark brown, purple; Animal: owl, wolf; Stone: agate, chrysoprase, geode, tiger's eye; Plant: carnation, clove, cypress, eyebright, sage, sandalwood, Syrian rue, tuberose; *about yourself*: Stone: smoky quartz. **release truth**: Plant: Syrian rue. **see/recognize/perceive truth**: Sagittarius; Plant: bladderwort, clary sage, eyebright, orchid. **seek truth**: Tuesday; Color: red, white; Animal: chickadee. **tell the truth**: Color: blue; Stone: moss agate, lapis lazuli; Plant: aster, devil's club, snapdragon, Syrian rue; God: Osiris Un-Nefer, Zeus. **truly know yourself**: Goddess: Demeter. **trust in truth**: Animal: coyote.

Chapter 21

Uncrossing

(See also: Adversity, Cycles, Hexes, Negativity, Problems, Protection, Return, Reversal)

Wednesday

Color: black, blue, gray, purple, red, white; Number: 7; Animal: rat; Charm: ammonia, lemon ammonia, broken chain, black cat hair, Florida Water, Kananga Water, van van, witch hazel; Metal: iron; Stone: amethyst, lodestone, obsidian, onyx, clear quartz crystal, salt, rock salt, sea salt; Plant: ague weed, angelica, basil, bergamot, betony, carnation, cassia, cedar, chamomile, cinnamon, cinquefoil, citronella, clove, black cohosh, copal, dill, dragon's blood, eye of Satan, galangal, gardenia, ginger, hazel, High John, High John with trillium, hyssop, jasmine, laurel, lavender, lemon, lemongrass, lilac, lily of the valley, lotus, mimosa, myrrh, orris root, patchouli, black pepper, peppermint, pine, rosemary, sandalwood, spindle tree bark, tonka bean, lemon verbena, vervain, vetiver, wintergreen, wisteria, witch grass, witch hazel, wormwood.

To uncross love: Plant: dill.

Understanding

(See also: Wisdom)

Sun/Full Moon/Wednesday/Friday/Saturday

Method: meditation; Color: blue, light blue, gold, green, yellow; Number: 6, 9; Animal: owl, raven; Stone: amethyst, Apache tear, azurite, green beryl, dioptase, emerald, lapis lazuli, meteorite, blue opal, rhodochrosite, ruby, sapphire, tigereye, topaz, blue topaz, blue or pink tourmaline, turquoise; Plant: apple tree, corn, horsetail, queen of the night, rose, sage, Solomon seal; Goddess: Airmid, Binah, Hokmah; God: Brahma, Ea, Fugen Bosatsu, Hanuman, Thoth; Evocation: Donn.

Conscious understanding: *of life experiences*: Stone: ruby. **Group understanding**: Aquarius; Animal: hyena. **Intuitive understanding**: Plant: marigold. **Magickal understanding**: Color: violet. **Spiritual understanding**: Charm: Celtic knot; Stone: ruby, sapphire, sugilite; Plant: sage.

To awaken understanding: Sun.

To understand: **abilities**: Plant: tamarack. **animals**: (See: Animals). **changes**: Stone: peridot. **chaos**: Animal: jaguar. **cooperation**: Animal: ant, hyena. **death**: Plant: cypress. **deceit**: Animal: alligator, crocodile. **destiny**: Stone: moonstone. **divine will**: Goddess: Themis. **emotions**: Plant: fuchsia. **energy**: Animal: mole. **ethics**: Animal: crow, puma. **female power**: Goddess: Condwiramur. **fluxes**: Animal: mole. **grief**: Plant: cypress. **growth as a part of the cycle of life**: (See: Life). **the human place in Nature**: God: Sicun. **influence**: Method: astrology. **inner signals**:

Animal: hawk. **the interconnectedness of everything**: God: Tob Tob (Bear). **jealousy**: God: Abarta. **life**: (See: Life). **life lessons**: Charm: dinosaur bone; Stone: charoite. **love**: Stone: green gypsum, rubiolite. **magick**: Stone: sugilite; Plant: dill. **messages**: Plant: marigold. **misfortune**: God: Horus. **the Mysteries**: Goddess: the Crone, Nephthys. **past relationships**: Plant: geranium. **possible consequences of spells**: Goddess: Skuld. **reality**: Plant: frankincense. **rocks/stones**: Color: purple; Stone: amethyst. **sacrifice**: Plant: cypress. **situations**: Color: light blue; Plant: dill; **sorrow**: Plant: myrrh. **spirit guides**: Stone: morganite. **spiritual teachings**: God: Niyan. **success**: Color: gold; Animal: monkey. **that all/nothing is sacred**: Animal: coyote. **things that are felt**: Stone: amethyst. **weather**: Animal: crocodile. **the wheel of the year**: Goddess: Latis. **wind power**: Animal: cardinal, eagle. **what is necessary to survive**: Animal: deer. **your dark side**: Color: black.

Misunderstanding

Charm: Tower of Babel (ziggurat); Animal: hedgehog; Plant: lavender; God: Al Balal.

Underworld

(See also: Afterlife, Death, Otherworld)

Pluto/Waning Moon/Earth/Scorpio

Color: black, white; Charm: tet amulet; Animal: white dog with red ears, burrowing owl, pig, raven, scorpion, snake; Plant: apple, aspen, asphodel, white carnation, copal, cypress, lily, mint, myrtle, pomegranate, white rose; Goddess: Adsagsona, Ahemait, Allat (Queen of the Underworld), Amenti, Antaboga, Ataecina, Bebhionn, Belit-Seri, Culsa, Demeter, Dewi Shri, Don, Echidne, Eo-Anu, Ereshkigal (The Great Below, Queen of the Underworld), Eve, Freya (Queen of the Underworld), Geshtinanna, Hathor, Hecate (Lady of the Underworld), Hel (Queen of the Underworld), Ishhara, Isis (Great Goddess of the Underworld), Kalma, Lada, Malophoros, Mania, Mictlantecuhtli, Nephthys, Nijole, Papa, Persephone, Prosperine, Rhiannon, Schathach, Sedna, Tara, Tefnut, Thenenet, Ulupi, Umbria, Xochiquetzal, Yambe-akka; God: Aed, Aericura, An, Anubis, Arawn (Lord of the Underworld), Arcurius, Auf, Baron Samedi, Beli, Camazotz, Cernunnos (Lord of the Underworld), Charun, Chernobog, Consus, Cumhau, Cythrawl, Damuzi, Dionysus of the Underworld, Dis Pater, Don (Lord of the Underworld), Dumash, Endukugga, Enmesharra, Erragal, Februus, Guana, Gwynn ap Nudd (Lord of the Underworld), Hades, Khnum, Mahiuki (Ruler of the Underworld), Mictlantecuhtli, Mider (King of the Underworld), Mixcoatl, Ndara, Nedu, Neheb-kau, Nergal, Ningizzia, Nyame, Osiris (Bull of the Underworld), Pikuolis, Pluto, Pwyll Pen Annwn, Ra, Rati-mbati ndua, Reshep, Rod, Sobek, South Star, Sumugan, Supay (Lord of the Underworld), Tammuz, Thoth, Triglav, Tuoni, Ukur, Varuna, Veles, Yama, Zeus Katachthonios (Zeus of the Underworld); Other Deities: the Anunnaki, theoi khthonioi, the Vanths; Evocation: the Manes, nagas.

Underworld entities: *underworld demons*: Goddess: Sedna; Evocation: Satan, the utukki; **Underworld ocean**: God: Abzu.

Protection in the Underworld: Goddess: Sekhmet (Protectress from the Perils of the Underworld), Shapash.

To: enter the Underworld: Animal: dolphin, mole; Plant: apple (blossoms, fruit or branch with buds), mistletoe; God: Aker, Anguta, Charun, Mercury, Sucellos; Evocation: Charon; **open the way to the Underworld**: God: Aker. **open to the Underworld**: Animal: kite. **receive messages**

from the Underworld: Animal: owl; God: Namtar. **send messages to the Underworld**: Animal: owl; God: Thoth.

Union

(See also: Connection, Marriage, Partnership, Relationships, Unity)

Water/Libra/Pisces

Method: tantra; Charm: beryl engraved with a crow that has a crab beneath it, black and white feather; Animal: carp; Metal: copper; Plant: straw, verbena; Goddess: Aditi, Branwen, Lada, Parvati, Shakti.

Conjugal union: (See: Marriage). **Divine union**: Goddess: Parvati. **Family union**: Animal: lion; Plant: garlic, nettle, pink verbena; Goddess: Athena, Durga, Hestia. **Male/female union**: Tool: besom, broomstick, chalice or cauldron and sword or wand; Method: Great Rite; Charm: lance and grail; Plant: ginger. **Neighborly union**: God: Apollo. **Sexual union**: Venus; Method: Great Rite; Stone: lapis lazuli; Plant: apple, pear; Goddess: Kali, Lilith; *to bless*: Goddess: Shekinah.

To unite: against evil: Plant: scarlet verbena; **chakras**: Stone: rose quartz, smoky quartz; Plant: hibiscus. **conscious mind/psychic mind**: Plant: marjoram. **cosmic forces**: God: Min. **the human/the divine**: Number: 3. **opposites/contrasts**: Charm: cross, 6-pointed star; Goddess: Ometeotl. **people**: Goddess: Aditi. **speech/communication**: God: Al-Shafi. **with collective consciousness**: Plant: lime.

Unions

(See also: Marriage, Partnership, Relationships, Union)

Illicit/forbidden unions: Goddess: Lofn.

To strengthen unions: Plant: cardamom pod.

Unity

(See also: Union)

Color: pink, white, yellow; Number: 3; Stone: zircon; Metal: manganite; Plant: nettle, red and white roses (together), trefoil.

Cultural unity: Goddess: Amaterasu. **Family unity**: Animal: lion, kangaroo; Goddess: Athena. **Group unity**: Plant: mullein. **Social unity**: Plant: mallow. **Spiritual unity**: Plant: lotus.

United hearts: Plant: phlox. **Unity with life**: Stone: amazonite; Plant: enchanter's nightshade.

The Universe

Color: black; Charm: black veil studded with beads, sequins, pearls, crystals, or anything else that can be used to represent stars; Animal: buffalo; Stone: meteorite; Plant: lotus, onion; Goddess: Eurynome (Queen of the Circling Universe), the Goddess, Hera, Inanna (Queen of the Universe), Isis (Queen of the Universe), Juno, Parvati, Savasi, Shakti; God: Jupiter (Lord of the Universe), Marduk, Odin (Lord of the Universe), Perun, Ptah, Shiva, Vishnu, Zeus (Lord of the Universe).

Physical Universe: God: Poseidon. **Sacred laws of the Universe**: Goddess: Inanna. **Order of the Universe**: Goddess: Ma'at; God: Saturn, Thoth, Vishnu; *natural order of the Universe*: Goddess: Estsanatlehi.

To: get assistance from the Universe: Plant: High John with galangal. **maintain the Universe**: God: Guienapun, Janus (Custodian of the Universe), Ukko; *maintain its balance*: God: Orunmila. **protect the Universe**: Animal: dragon; Goddess: Devi, Zorya; Other Deities: the Lokapalas (World Protectors). **request help from the Universe**: Plant: High John with galangal. **unravel the secrets of the Universe**: God Orunmila.

The Universal

Plant: lotus; Goddess: Tana.

Universal compassion: Goddess: Tara. **Universal consciousness**: Goddess: Isis. **Universal energy**: (See: Energy). **Universal friendship**: Aquarius. **Universal healing force**: *to get in touch with*: Aquarius. **Universal knowledge**: Stone: lapis lazuli, clear quartz crystal. **Universal law**: Goddess: Nisaba; *to communicate*: Stone: azurite. **Universal love**: (See: Love). **Universal mind**: Plant: birch; God: Brahma. **Universal passion**: God: Eros.

Chapter 22

Vanquishing
(See: Overcoming, Victory)

Vengeance
(See: Revenge)

Vibrations
(See also: Energy)

Color: magenta, purple, violet; Stone: amethyst, leopardskin jasper, phenacite, scolecite; Plant: myrrh, ylang-ylang.

Angry vibrations: *to clear*: Stone: jet; Plant: elecampane. **Good/positive vibrations**: Tool: bell, rattle, sistrum; Plant: frankincense, myrrh, peppermint, wisteria; Goddess: Hathor. **Healing vibrations**: Color: blue, green; Plant: ash, eucalyptus, horehound, rosemary. **High vibrations**: Color: violet; Plant: cinnamon, myrrh; *to attract*: Charm: dove's blood. **Loving vibrations**: Stone: rhodochrosite, rose quartz; Plant: rose. **Negative vibrations**: God: Set; *to attract*: Metal: iron; *to clear*: Tool: pentacle; Method: asperging, smudging; Color: black, blue, silver; Charm: brimstone, Florida Water, salt water; Stone: agate, bloodstone, onyx, obsidian, clear quartz crystals, salt; Plant: camphor, frankincense, ginger root, myrrh, onion bulb, patchouli, vetiver, yarrow; *to protect food from*: Plant: garlic; *to protect against*: Stone: antimony; *against negative vibrations of mourners*: Plant: cypress. **Powerful vibrations**: Color: magenta; Oil: palmarosa; Plant: rose geranium. **Sexual vibrations**: Color: pink; Stone: rose quartz, all pink stones; Plant: cubeb, vanilla. **Sound vibrations**: Air, Water (See also: Senses: hearing). **Spiritual vibrations**: Plant: acacia, cinnamon, clove, heliotrope, lotus, sandalwood, wood aloes; *to attract*: Plant: saffron (as incense), wood aloes; *to raise*: Plant: cinnamon, jasmine.

Vibrational energy: (See: Energy). **Sensitivity to vibrations**: Animal: mole.

To: clear vibrations: Tool: besom; *of violence*: Stone: jet; Plant: elecampane. **raise vibrations**: Plant: peppermint.

Victory
(See also: Defeat, Overcoming, Success)

Color: red, silver; Charm: crown, garland; Animal: lion; Metal: gold, silver; Stone: alabaster, bloodstone, diamond; Plant: cherry, High John, ivy, laurel, fennel, wild olive, palm tree, parsley, peony, woodruff; Goddess: Anahita, Anath (The Victorious Goddess), Andarta, Andraste, Aparajita (the Unconquered), Aphrodite, Astarte, Brigantia, Brigid, Devana, Devi, Diiwica, Hecate, Ishtar (Lady of Victory), Isis, Isis-Nike, Isis Victrix (Ever-Victorious), Korraval, Nike, Pallas Athene, Scathach Buanand (Victorious), Sekhmet, Venus Victrix, Victoria, Vijaya; God: Baal, Horus, Ida-Ten, Jupiter Victor, Marduk, Mars Segomo, Mithras, Odin (Father of Victory), Perun, Savitri, Segomo (The Victorious), Shiva, Sigtyr, Teshub, Vahagn; Evocation: Boudicca, Coyote, Hercules, Nicippe, Paeon.

Fair victory: God: Ares. **Futile/pyrrhic victory**: Evocation: King Arthur. **Military victory**: Charm: conch shell; Goddess: Andraste, Arinna, Badb, Victoria; Evocation: Boudicca. **Moral victory**: Charm: crown of olive branches. **Political victory**: Jupiter; God: Jupiter, Jupiter Victor.

Victory in: battle: (See: Battle). **court**: (See: Court). **sports competitions**: Goddess: Nike; God: Apollo, Zeus; *horse races*: Evocation: Nicippe (Victorious Mare). **war**: (See: War).

Victory of: light over darkness: Animal: rooster; God: Ra.

Victory over: adversaries: Stone: opal; Goddess: Aerten; God: Gizh-numun-ab. **enemies**: Stone: amethyst. **evil**: God: Ioskeha. **passion**: Stone: amethyst.

To overcome obstacles to victory: Plant: High John.

Vigor

(See also: Strength, Vitality)

Earth

Color: red; Charm: Eye of Horus; Number: 16; Animal: bull, horse; Stone: garnet, sapphire; Plant: apple, ginger, laurel, lemongrass, oak, peppermint, pine; Goddess: Anahita, Eostre, Strenua; God: Ahura Mazda, Baal, Chango, Horus, Thor; Evocation: Fergus.

Male vigor: Stone: sapphire; Plant: ginseng; *in battle*: Plant: holly. **Mature vigor**: Summer. **Sexual vigor**: God: Shiva. **Youthful vigor**: Color: green; Goddess: Hebe; God: Angus, Thor.

To restore vigor: Stone: sapphire; Plant: mint; Goddess: Hebe.

Violence

(See also: Abuse, Aggression, Battle, War)

Mars/Fire/Aries

Color: red; Goddess: Anath, Badb, Bia, Chalchihuitlcue, Ereshkigal, Erzulie, the Morrigan, Sekhmet, Yemaya Oqqutte; God: Erra, Nergal, Set; Evocation: Bia, Dian.

Constructive violence: God: Poseidon. **Destructive violence**: Goddess: Hathor. **Domestic violence**: *to: protect against*: Goddess: Erzulie, Kali; *protect women from*: Goddess: Hera, Juno, Kali, Sekhmet; *punish*: Goddess: Kali; *recover from*: Plant: lemon balm, onion. **Male violence**: *to deal with the threat of*: Goddess: Danu; *to treat*: Plant: saffron; *to punish male violence towards women*: Goddess: Amaterasu; *safe house for battered women*: Goddess: Juno. **Nonviolence**: Goddess: Kwan Yin.

Capacity for violence: Taurus.

Violent accidents: *to protect against*: Stone: coral. **Violent dancing**: God: Shiva. **Violent death**: (See: Death). **Violent grief**: Goddess: Anath. **Violent rites**: Goddess: Bellona, Cybele, Kali; God: Dionysus. **Violent seas**: Goddess: Scylla. **Violent sex/ violently physical love**: Goddess: Ishtar. **Violent storms**: (See: Storms). **Violent temper**: Mars/Sagittarius; Goddess: Ereshkigal; God: Zaka; *to calm*: Plant: chamomile, honeysuckle, saffron.

To: clear vibrations of violence: Stone: jet; Plant: elecampane. **enlighten a violent person**: Goddess: Diana. **protect against violence**: God: Agayu; *protect a woman in imminent danger of violence*: Goddess: Kali Ma. **punish the violent**: God: Pu'gu. **stop violence**: Plant: lavender.

Vision

(See also: Perception, Senses: Sight)

Neptune/Air/North/West

Color: blue, clear; Number: 2, 22; Animal: peacock; Stone: optical calcite, lapis lazuli, sapphire; Plant: cinquefoil, clove, ephedra, fennel, lavender, magnolia; Goddess: Idunn, Ishtar (Lady of Vision); God: Odin.

Aerial vision: Animal: eagle, hawk, all high-flying birds; Stone: hawk's eye. **Artistic vision**: *to realize*: Color: violet. **Astral vision**: Stone: carnelian, clear quartz crystal. **Auric vision**: Animal: copperhead. **Clear vision**: Color: indigo, violet, white; Animal: eagle, hawk, ocelot; Stone: hawk's eye, leopardskin jasper, sodalite; Plant: birch, indigo, eyebright, fennel, fir, goldenrod, lavender, clary sage, sandalwood. **Creative vision**: Goddess: Turan, Vac; God: Zeus. **Inner vision**: Color: indigo; Animal: basilisk; Stone: labradorite; Plant: citronella, clary sage, indigo, willow, wolfsbane; *inner eye*: Stone: malachite; *to strengthen*: Stone: malachite; *inner eye of wisdom*: Moon. **Intuitive vision**: Animal: cobra. **Lost vision**: *to restore*: Plant: fennel, masterwort. **Night vision**: Animal: bat, cat, firefly, owl; Plant: willow; Goddess: Hecate; *to improve*: Plant: bilberry. **Poetic vision**: Neptune; God: Odin. **Psychic vision**: Tool: mirror, scrying bowl; Animal: jaguar; Plant: cascarilla, laurel; God: Odin; *to strengthen*: Stone: opal. **Spiritual vision**: Color: clear, purple; Animal: condor, eagle, fox, gyrfalcon; Stone: clear calcite; Plant: birch, bougainvillea.

Visual images: Water. **Visual perception**: (See: Perception). **Vision problems**: *to treat*: Stone: sapphire. **Vision quest**: (See: Quests).

To: **make the invisible visible**: Plant: primrose. **protect against the visible**: Stone: jade. **realize vision**: Plant: birch, laurel.

Visions

Neptune/Air

Tool: censer, crystal ball, mirror, scrying bowl; Color: purple, white, yellow; Animal: polar bear; Stone: lapis lazuli, tanzanite, tourmaline; Fungus: fly agaric; Plant: acacia, angelica, autumn crocus, bistort, cannabis, cinnamon, clove, coltsfoot, damiana, datura, dittany, eyebright, frankincense, hyssop, jasmine, jurema, kava kava, laurel, lavender, lemongrass, lotus, marigold, mugwort, nutmeg, peppermint, rowan, clary sage, strawberry, vervain, wormwood, yarrow, yew, juniper with thyme; Goddess: Jubbu-jang-sangne, Lucina, Luna; God: Tlaloc.

Accurate visions: Stone: iolite. **Angelic visions**: Plant: angelica, angel's trumpet. **Dream visions**: Plant: poppy; Goddess: Niorun; *prophetic dream visions*: Plant: laurel. **Magickal visions**: Stone: green beryl, jasper. **Night visions**: Goddess: Hecate, Niorun; *to protect against*: Stone: chalcedony. **Prophetic visions**: Plant: laurel; Goddess: Anna Perenna; *in remote places*: Goddess: Aricia. **Psychic visions**: Stone: emerald; Plant: eyebright. **Terrible visions**: Stone: onyx; Goddess: the Furies; *to prevent*: Plant: betony, chamomile, rosemary.

Visionary imagination: Goddess: Turan. **Visionary insight**: Animal: gazelle.

To: **communicate visions**: Stone: tanzanite. **have a vision of your future spouse**: Tool: mirror (for gazing into at midnight on Samhain); Plant: hemp seeds (planted at midnight on Samhain). **protect against visions**: Plant: nettles with yarrow, rosemary.

Visualization

Air

Tool: pentagram; Color: black, blue, pale green, violet, white, yellow; Charm: mandala; Stone: avalonite, azurite, blue chalcedony, yellow carnelian, iolite, lapis lazuli, clear quartz crystal, yellow quartz, selenite, tigereye, topaz, green tourmaline; Plant: anise, bergamot, chamomile, juniper, mugwort, black pepper, rose, sandalwood, skullcap, tangerine, ylang-ylang.

Visualization for: **healing**: Color: deep blue; Stone: lapis lazuli. **Prosperity**: Plant: bergamot, cinnamon.

Energy for visualization: Plant: ginseng.

To increase the power of visualization: Color: yellow; Stone: yellow quartz.

Vitality
(See also: Life, Longevity, Vigor)

Sun/Fire/Water/Earth/West/Tuesday/Leo

Color: orange, red; Charm: ankh, musk; Animal: boar, cardinal, snake, all animals; Stone: garnet, red jasper, lava, pyrite, clear quartz crystal, turquoise; Plant: allspice, red carnation, comfrey, ginseng, gorse, morning glory, rosemary, snakeroot, vanilla; Goddess: Chalchihuitlcue, Frigg, Ishtar, Kupala, the Maiden, Sekhmet; God: Enlil, Fufluns, Ogun; Evocation: devas, elementals, sylphs.

Agricultural vitality: Earth; Color: green; *of crops*: God: Lactanus; *of soil*: God: Geb. **Inner vitality**: Stone: azurite, malachite. **Family vitality**: Goddess: Frigg; *of a royal family*: God: Telepinu. **Male vitality**: Animal: ram; Plant: cardamom, damiana, ginger, ginseng, gum tragacanth, licorice, sarsaparilla, saw palmetto, peony root, black pepper; God: Amun. **Mental vitality**: Stone: jasper; Plant: olive. **Physical vitality**: Color: red; Metal: iron; Stone: chrysocolla, red zircon; Plant: angelica, cypress, olive; *to increase*: Stone: black tourmaline; Plant: cayenne. **Sexual vitality**: Method: night magick; Plant: damiana, morinda root; Goddess: Astarte; *to reduce*: Plant: chaste tree. **Youthful vitality**: Animal: lamb.

Vital energy: *flow of*: Charm: shell, spiral. **Vital force**: Goddess: Ishtar. **Vital strength**: *to balance*: Plant: morning glory. **Vitality in old age**: Plant: chinaberry.

To: increase vitality: Method: breath work, feng shui; Charm: gold ball (held in the palm); Metal: gold; Stone: agate, aventurine, bloodstone, orange calcite, diamond, garnet, hematite, rose quartz, sugilite, sunstone; Plant: Adam and Eve root, ginseng, juniper berry, nasturtium. **renew vitality**: Spring; Stone: rose quartz, topaz; Plant: allspice, aloe, butterbur, chili pepper, elder, gorse, lime, morning glory, olive; Goddess: Inanna, Isis; God: Damuzi, Osiris, Tammuz.

Voice
(See also: Communication, Eloquence, Speech)

Air

Animal: lark.

Beautiful voice: Taurus; Color: gold; Charm: honey; Goddess: Calliope, Yhi; Evocation: sirens, the vila. **Fairy voices**: Air; Plant: willow (the sound of wind in). **Inner voice**: Air; Animal: seal, whale; Plant: mullein; *to tune in to*: Color: blue; Animal: whale; Stone: Herkimer diamond, rose quartz; Plant: mullein, Scotch pine; *to learn to listen to*: Stone: labradorite; Plant: pine. **Powerful voice**: Goddess: Nut; God: Baal, Phan Ku; Evocation: Connla.

Voice magick: (See: Magick). **Vocal power**: Goddess: Ambika. **Power of voice/ speech**: Animal: lark; Goddess: Isis, Vac; God: the Dagda, Odin, Ptah, Ve; *to restore*: Stone: chalcedony; Plant: agrimony, heliotrope, lavender, mustard; God: Odin; *words of power*: Goddess: Isis; God: Thoth.

To strengthen the voice: Stone: carnelian.

Vows
(See: Oaths)

Chapter 23

War

(See also: Aggression, Battle, Battlefields, Peace, Terrorism, Warfare, Warriors)

Mars/Tuesday

Tool: sword; Charm: arrow, bow, spear, trumpet; Animal: crow, large dog (such as mastiff), raven, wolf; Goddess: Aeron, Agasaya, Agrona, Alaisiagae, Anahita, Anath, Andraste, Ankt, Anouke, Aphrodite, Aphrodite Areia, Arinna, Astarte, Athena, Athtart, Bast, Badb, Bellona, Cathubodua, Chun Ti, Crove Dairg, Cymidei Cymeinfoll, Discordia, Durga, Enyo, Eshara, Estiu, Fea, Freya, Inanna, Ishtar (Lady of Battle, Leader of Hosts, Great Goddess of Love and War, Queen of Attack and Hand-to-Hand Fighting), Isis (Terrible One, Queen of War), Litavis, Lot, Macha, Maeve, Medb, Minerva, the Morrigan (Supreme War Goddess), Neith, Nemain, Nematona, Nina, Oya, Rhiannon, Sekhmet (The Warrior, Lady of the Bloodbath), Tara, Vacuna; God: Ah Cun Can, Ah Kin Xoc, Ahulane, Aliy the Warrior, Arawn, Ares (Throng of War), Ashur, Astabis, Baal (Mightiest of Warriors, Conqueror of Warriors), Belatucadros, Bishamon, Bran, Brenos, Camulos, Cariociecus, Chernobog, Cit Chac Coh, Cocidius, Condatis, Ek Chua, Freyr, Gwyn ap Nud, Hachiman, Hoa-Tapu, Huitzilopochtli, Ictinike, Indra, Jarovit, Karttikeya, Kibuka, Kovas, Ku, Kuan-ti, Kuklikimoku, Laran, Luchtain, Lugh, Mars, Mars Camulos, Masauwu, Menthu, Nacon, Nanna, Nayenezgani, Neith, Nergal, Ninurta, Nuadh, Odin, Ogun, Oro, Perun, Quirinus, Reshep, Segomo, Semnocosus, Smertrios, Sumannus, Svantovit, Taran, Teutates, Tezcatlipoca, Thor, Tiwaz, Tobadzistsini, Tu, Tyr, Volos, Yahweh, Zaba, Zamama

Clan wars: *outcome of*: Goddess: Aeron. **War horses**: Goddess: Ishtar. **Accurate aim in war**: Stone: turquoise. **Brutality of war**: God: Ares. **Death in war**: Goddess: the Morrigan; God: Nergal, Reshep. **Declaration of war**: Plant: tansy; Goddess: Bellona. **Ecstasy of war**: Goddess: Anath. **Fortunes of war**: God: Nergal. **Omen of war**: Goddess: Badb (as a giant), Cihuacoatl (when she roars). **Oracles of war**: Goddess: Inanna. **Prosperity through war**: God: Bishamon. **Protection in wartime**: Charm: shield; Goddess: Cybele, Macha, Sangramarakshika (Protectress in War); God: Janus, Teutates; *of property*: Goddess: Neith. **Sage advice in wartime**: Goddess: Athena. **Victory in war**: Stone: diamond; Goddess: Andraste (The Invincible One), Apadeva (The Unconquered), Aparajita, Durga, Sangramajayaprada (Granter of Victory in War), Sekhmet (Invincible One, She Who Prevails, Victorious One, She Who Overcomes All Enemies), Victoria; God: Zeus. **Weapons of war**: God: Ullr.

To: **end war**: Tool: cauldron; Color: white; God: Kuan Ti. **find/make peace during war**: Goddess: Bellona. **protect against**

war: Goddess: Kwan Yin; God: Kuan Ti. **start a war**: Goddess: Coatlicue, Eris (Nurse of War).

Warding

(See: Protection)

Warding off

(See: Averting)

Warfare

(See also: Battle, War)

Mars

Goddess: Aoife, Athene, Brigid, Durga, Ishtar, Minerva, Neith, Al-Uzza; God: Ares, Nuada, Ogun, Yggr.

   Tactical warfare: God: Odin.

Warriors

North

Animal: boar, hawk; Stone: bloodstone; Plant: dragon's blood; Goddess: Chantico, Freya, the Morrigan, Sin, Zorya; God: Bishamon, Cernunnos, the Dagda, Gwydion, Mithras, Odin, Perun, Svantovit.

   Brave battle-slain warriors: God: Idi; *to guide*: Goddess: the Morrigan (Choosers of the Slain); God: Odin; Evocation: Valkyries; *to protect*: God: Tonatiuh; Evocation: Valkyries. **Dead warriors**: God: Gwyn ap Nudd, Odin, Teoyaomqui; Evocation: Valkyries; *to escort*: Goddess: Niamh; *to restore*: Goddess: Cymidei Cymeinfoll; God: Dian Cecht, Llasar Llaesyfnewid. **Spiritual warriors**: Plant: holly.

   Female warrior energy: (See: Yin). **Warrior skills**: Animal: wolf. **Warrior strength**: Animal: boar. **Omen of a warrior's death**: Goddess: the Morrigan (seen before battle).

To: **help warriors escape enemies**: Plant: vervain. **protect warriors**: Animal: boar; Goddess: Freya, Zorya; God: Bo, Freyr, Reshep; Evocation: Donn of Culnge. **reward gallantry, bravery, or success**: Charm: crown of oak leaves. **train warriors**: Goddess: Aoife, Cailleach, Scathach, Uathach.

Warmth

Sun/Fire/Earth/South/Summer/Leo

Charm: fire pit, fireplace, hearth; Color: orange, pink, red, yellow; Animal: buffalo, cat; Stone: coal, salt; Metal: copper; Plant: cactus, clary sage, clove, coriander seed, fennel seed, feverfew, frankincense, ginger, hibiscus, indigo, linden, Japanese maple, marigold, marjoram, mesquite, myrrh, oak, orange, rhododendron, rosemary, sage, black tea; Goddess: Allat, Amaterasu, Bast, Brigid, Chantico, the Heliades, Hestia, Isis (Lady of Warmth), Saule, Summer Daughter, Unelanuhi, Vesta, Yhi; God: Amun, Apollo, Coyote, Dazhbog, Ra, Sol.

   Hidden warmth: Plant: coriander seed. **Inner warmth**: South/Fire; Plant: fireweed, Japanese maple. **Warm feelings**: Plant: peppermint, spearmint. **Warm friendship**: Plant: basil. **Warm water**: God: Borvo; *healing power of*: (See: Power).

Wealth

(See also: Abundance, Finances, Money, Prosperity)

Jupiter/Mercury/Pluto/Earth

Color: gold, green, yellow; Charm: money, musk, sea shell; Animal: bat, bear, boar, cattle, dragon, goldfinch, horse, swine; Metal: gold; Stone: brown, green, moss or tree agate, amethyst, aventurine, bloodstone, calcite, citrine, emerald, all gems, Herkimer diamond, jacinth, jade, jasper, green jasper, malachite, mother-of-pearl,

pearl, peridot, ruby, salt, tigereye, topaz, green tourmaline, turquoise (especially when received as a gift), brown or green zircon; Plant: almond tree, apple, avocado, basil, bayberry, benzoin, bergamot, blackberry, buttercup, camellia, cedar, chamomile, cinquefoil, cinnamon, clove, clover, four leaf clover, dill, elder, fern, galangal, ginger, goldenrod, grain, hand of Maryam, heliotrope, High John, honeysuckle, hyssop, jasmine, lucky hand root, mace, maize, mint, moonwort, moss, Irish moss, myrrh, myrtle, nutmeg, oak, olive, orange, patchouli, pepperwort, periwinkle, pimpernel, pine, pomegranate, rice, rose of Jericho, saffron, sage, sassafras, snapdragon, black tea, teak, tonka bean, vervain, blue vervain, vetiver, wheat, woodruff; Goddess: Abundantia, Aje, Anumati, Apa, Ashiakle, Benzaiten, Chantico, Copia, Copper Woman, Demeter, Dhisani, Eirene, Erzulie, Fortuna, Freya, Gaia, Ganga, Hecate, Isis, Isis Ploutodotai (Giver of Riches), Juno, Lakshmi, Lennaxidaq, Lupa, Mary, Moneta, Prithivi, Purandhi, Pushti (Owner of All Wealth), Rosmerta, Sarasvati, Saule, Sekhmet, Sri-Devi, Al 'Uzza, Ushas, Yemaya, Yemaya Olokun (Natural Wealth); God: Bhaga, Cernunnos, Chango Macho, Daikoku, Dhanya (Giver of Wealth), Dis Pater, Dyaus, Enbilulu-Gugal, Ganesha, Hades, Horned God, Ih P'en, Jupiter, Kubera, Lu-hsing, Maximon, Njord (Giver of Wealth), Nodens, Nuadha (Wealth Bringer), Odin, Olokun, Pluto (Lord of Riches), Pushan, Rudra, Tai-yue da-di, Teutates, Tezcatlipoca, Veles, Volos, Yum Caaz, Ziku.

Agricultural wealth: Goddess: Ubertas. **Earned wealth**: God: Lu-hsing. **Impending wealth**: Animal: rat; Plant: marigold. **Lost wealth**: *to restore*: Stone: tigereye. **Material wealth**: Color: purple; Goddess: Lupa. **Mineral wealth**: Earth; Goddess: Califia; God: Pluto. **Wealth of the Earth**: Earth; Animal: cow; Goddess: Gaia; *to attract*: Stone: citrine.

To: acquire wealth: Stone: citrine, turquoise; Plant: avocado, fern, marigold; Goddess: Dhisani, Purandhi, Raka, Tyche; God: Dhanya (Giver of Wealth), Helios, Njord (Giver of Wealth). **attract wealth**: Stone: moss agate, bloodstone, emerald, lodestone, mother-of-pearl, peridot, pyrite, staurolite, tigereye; Plant: basil, benzoin, bistort, clove, dragon's blood, heliotrope, High John, horse chestnut, nutmeg, patchouli, blue vervain. **increase wealth**: Stone: tigereye, red zircon; Goddess: Anahita; God: Math. **learn to share wealth**: Goddess: Nemesis. **maintain/manage wealth**: Goddess: Dhanakshayanashini (Controller of Wealth Decrease), Dike, Eirene, Eunomia. **manifest wealth**: Plant: cactus. **protect wealth**: Stone: tigereye. **refuse to marry for wealth**: Goddess: Kwan Yin.

Weather
(See also: Lightning, Storms)

Earth/Air/Water/Fire

Animal: dragon; Stone: jade; Plant: yarrow; Goddess: Alcyone, Anahita, Asiaq, Atlacamani, Ayauhteotl, Begoe, Cailleach, Chalchihuitlcue, Fulgora, Gaia, Guabancex, the Horae, Inanna, Isis, Kadlu, Kali, Mama Cocha, Mari, Mother Earth, Mother Nature, Nut, Rainha Barba, Ran, Rauni, Shapash, Tamar, Tasimmet; God: Adad, Ambisagrus, Apep, Aplu, Baal, the Dagda, Dagon, Eacus, El, Enlil, Frey, Ilmarinen, Ilyap'a, Indra, Jupiter, Leucetios, Leza, Litavis, Perkunas, Perun, Pillan, Ryujin, Shammanus, Shango, Shapash, Sol Invictus, Stribog, Summanus, Taranis, Taru, Teshub, Tethra, Thor, Tlaloc, Tupan, Ubumo, Ukko, Vahagn, Viracocha, Yggr, Zahrim

(Lord of Lightning), Zeus; Evocation: Ardat Lili, the Dama, Hreidmar, Sila.

Bad weather: *to avert*: Plant: clove, garlic (hung up outdoors); *to protect against*: Charm: charred embers from the Midsummer bonfire; Plant: garlic; Goddess: Alcyone (The Queen Who Wards Off Storms); *against drought*: Goddess: Raksha-Kali; *against lightning*: (See: Lightning); *against storms*: (See: Security, Storms). **Dry weather**: God: Shapash, Mot. **Cold weather**: Evocation: Negafok. **Hot weather**: God: Mot. **Nice weather**: Plant: garlic; Goddess: Sao-ch'ing Niang; God: Ilmarinen. **Sea weather**: Water; God: Mannan. **Stormy weather**: God: Agwe.

Weather changes: Plant: yarrow. **Weather divination**: Plant: yarrow. **Weather forecasting**: Plant: yarrow; Goddess: Cally Berry; God: Mannan.

To: bind weather: God: Baal. **change weather**: God: Perun. **control weather**: Stone: jade; Goddess: Cailleach Bheara, Kali; God: Ilmarinen. **forecast weather**: Animal: wooly caterpillar, woodpecker. **protect land from weather**: (See: Land). **understand weather**: Animal: crocodile.

Weddings

(See also: Marriage)

New Moon/Thursday/June

Tool: bell, besom, broomstick, chalice, cord; Charm: musk, orange flower water; Animal: dove; Stone: diamond, jade, moonstone; Metal: gold, platinum, silver; Potion: champagne, mead; Oil: palmarosa; Plant: Adam and Eve roots, almond, broom, gardenia, hawthorn, hemp seed, jasmine, lavender, myrtle, nuts, orange blossom, orris root, pikaki, rice, rose, rosemary, verbena, yarrow, yohimbine; Goddess: the Graces, Hera, Juno Interduca, the Kotharot, Venus; God: Hymen.

Wedding anointment: Goddess: Unxia. **Wedding bouquet/chaplet/wreath**: Plant: hawthorn, myrtle, rose, rosemary. **Wedding cake**: Plant: laurel (as a bed or garnish, or one leaf baked in the cake as a charm for the fortunate one who gets that slice). **Wedding feast**: God: Hymen.

To: bless a wedding ceremony: Charm: orange flower water. Animal: dove, entwined snakes. Goddess: Aphrodite, Arianrhod, Gaia, Venus. **Encourage a wedding**: Plant: honeysuckle, orange blossom; Goddess: Hera.

Well-being

(See also: Health)

Sun/Waxing Moon

Method: candle magick, massage; Color: green; Charm: aromatherapy; Animal: ladybug; Stone: aventurine, emerald, geode, jade, peridot, sugilite; Plant: bayberry, clary sage, coca leaf, masterwort, mistletoe, poppy, tarragon; Goddess: Athirat, Brigid, Eir, Gula, Hestia, Hygeia, Kamrusepas, Kwan Yin, Liban, Qadesh, Salus, Saukhyada (Bestower of Well-Being); God: Al-Hanishah, Apollo, Ascelpius, Dian Cecht, Eshmun, Tien-Kuan.

Emotional well-being: Moon; Color: yellow; Stone: aventurine, rhodochrosite, **Mental well-being**: Stone: sugilite. **Sexual well-being**: Stone: aventurine.

Well-being of: the Earth: Goddess: Gaia, Mother Earth, Mother Nature. **family**: Goddess: Frigg; God: the Penates. **home**: Animal: toad. **household**: Goddess: Saule. **tribe**: Animal: birds, cattle, boar, fish, herd animals, serpent; Goddess: Frigg, the Matronaea.

Sense of well-being: Plant: coca leaf, masterwort, poppy. **To attract well-being**: Plant: sage.

Will

(See also: Control, Determination, Discipline)

Mars/Sun/Fire/South/Saturday/Leo

Color: black, yellow; Number: 1; Animal: tiger; Metal: gold; Stone: hematite, lodestone, rhodochrosite, tigereye; Plant: dill, laurel, vervain; Goddess: Durga, Inanna; God: Paiva, Vili.

Divine will: Plant: sundew; Goddess: Themis; God: Apollo; *receptivity to*: Plant: gladiola. *to implement*: Goddess: Dike, Themis; *to obey*: Plant: apple; *to understand*: Goddess: Themis. **Evolutionary will**: Goddess: Shakti. **Free will**: Air; Color: yellow; Plant: willow; Goddess: Ishtar. **Good will**: (See: Positiveness). **Ill will**: (See: Negativity). **Spiritual will**: Color: clear, white. **Strong will**: Animal: cougar, mountain lion, puma; Stone: lodestone, pyrite, green tourmaline; Plant: garlic, snapdragon; Goddess: Creiddylad, Inanna, Isis, Maeve, Volumna; God: Mars.

To: **activate will**: Plant: ephedra. **balance will/emotion**: Color: gold, yellow. **direct will**: Stone: green tourmaline. **hinder will**: Plant: vervain and dill. **manifest will**: Stone: tanzanite. **strengthen will**: Color: orange; Animal: cougar; Stone: citrine, lodestone, pyrite, rainbow pyrite, green tourmaline; Plant: cayenne, dill, masterwort, rosemary, St. John's Wort. **use will effectively/properly**: Full Moon; Color: yellow; Stone: citrine; Plant: apple, willowherb.

Willfulness

Number: 1; Animal: magpie; Goddess: Erzulie, Inanna; God: Zeus; Evocation: fairies.

To lessen willfulness: Plant: cypress.

Willingness

Metal: copper; Goddess: Astarte.

Willingness to: **change**: (See: Change). **fight for something**: Color: red. **heal**: Plant: eucalyptus. **take risks**: Goddess: Oya.

Willpower

Fire/Earth

Color: red; Animal: polar bear; Metal: gold; Stone: chrysoprase, lodestone, onyx, tigereye; Plant: allspice, apple, cypress, dragon's blood, elm, heliotrope, iris, rosemary, St. John's Wort, vervain; Goddess: the Vasita, Volumna; God: Shiva.

Wisdom

(See also: Enlightenment, Ignorance, Illumination, Intelligence, Knowledge)

Jupiter/Mercury/Moon/Full Moon/Waning Moon/Earth/Water/Air/East/North/Wednesday

Tool: cauldron; Method: yoga; Color: black, blue, dark blue, gray, green, emerald green, purple, red, turquoise, violet, yellow; Charm: Eye of Horus, pyramid, well; Number: 0, 7; Animal: crane, dolphin, dove, eagle, eel, elephant, griffin, owl, peacock, porpoise, salmon, serpent, wolf, gray wolf; Metal: gold; Stone: blue lace or tree agate, amethyst, carnelian, chrysocolla, coral, garnet, jacinth, jade, jasper, lapis lazuli, snowflake obsidian, quartz crystal, ruby, sodalite, sugilite, tanzanite, turquoise, zircon; Potion: mead; Plant: acacia, acorn, almond tree, benzoin, birch, bodhi tree, broom, cypress, dragon's gall, elder, fig, hazel, iris, laurel, lotus, magnolia, white mulberry, nut trees, papyrus, peach, pine, redwood, rosemary, rowan, rue, sage, clary sage, Solomon's seal, black spruce, sunflower; Goddess: Alcmene, Amaterasu, Anahita, Armaiti,

Asherah, Astarte, Athena, Badb, Benzaiten, Blodeuwedd, Brigid, Cailleach, Caolainn, Car, Carmenta (Revealer of Wisdom), Ceibhfhionn, Ceres, Cerridwen, Chantico, the Crone, Cunneware (Female Wisdom), Danu, Druantia, Egeria, Eve, Frigg, Gasmu, Greine, Gwenhwyfar, Hannahhannas, Heh, Hera, Hecate, Heqet, Hokmah, Kono-hana sakuya-hime, Kwan Yin, Lilith, Macha, Mens, Metis, Minerva, Neith, Ninsun, Pandora, Persephone, Prajnaparamita (Lady of Wisdom), Reason, Sarasvati, Sarpanitum, Sekhmet, Shekinah, Snotra, Sophia (The Holy Wisdom), Spider Woman, Sulis, Tara, Uma, Ushas, Vör, Yemaya; Gods: Ahura Mazda (Wise Lord), Apollo, Aranunna (Giver of Wisdom), Astalluhi, Atri, Bacchus, Balder, Beag, Bragi, the Dagda (Mighty One of Knowledge), Dainichi, Damballah, Ea (Lord of Wisdom), Ebisu, Enki (Lord of Wisdom), Finn MacCool, Fugen Bosatsu, Fukurokuju, Fukurojuku, Ganesha, Glooskap, Guan Di, Hanuman, Hephaestus, Hermes, Ifa, Imhotep, Itzamna, Jupiter, Legba, Manannan Mac Lir, Mimir, Mithra, Nabu (Wise God of Wednesday), Neptune, Oannes, Obatala, Odin, Ogma, Orunmila, Proteus, Purusha, Quetzalcoatl, Shaka (the Silent Sage), Sin, Tages, Tao-de tian zong, Thoth, Tyr, Väinämöinen (The Eternal Sage), Zeus; Evocation: Amergin, Buddha, Chiron, Genetaska, Hervor (The Wise), Kvasir, Merlin, Prometheus, Seryï Volk, Taliesin, Vasilisa (The Wise).

All-accomplishing wisdom: North. **Ancient wisdom**: Animal: elephant; Stone: amber, celestite, fossil, quartz crystal; Plant: pine, Solomon's seal; Goddess: Yemaya. **Applied wisdom**: Animal: nuthatch. **Cosmic wisdom**: Animal: whale. **Deep wisdom**: Color: silvery blue; Stone: opal. **Divine wisdom**: Color: blue, clear, white; Goddess: Lakshmi, Sophia, Tara. **Female wisdom**: Charm: snakes in the hair;

Goddess: Athena, Cunneware (Female Wisdom), Medusa. **Gentle wisdom**: God: Nereus. **Hidden/occult wisdom**: Plant: hazel; Goddess: Ekadzati; God: Odin, Thoth. **Higher wisdom**: Plant: ash; Stone: lapis lazuli. **Infinite wisdom**: Stone: aquamarine. **Inner wisdom**: Moon/Full Moon; Color: yellow; Plant: birch; God: Enki; *to share*: Metal: peacock ore; *to trust*: Plant: saguaro cactus; *inner eye of wisdom*: Moon. **Intuitive wisdom**: Plant: Solomon seal root. **Lunar wisdom**: Moon; Number: 9; Goddess: Hecate. **Maternal wisdom**: Animal: bear, mandrill; Goddess: Isis. **Mystical wisdom**: Goddess: Ekadzati. **Occult wisdom**: God: Odin. **Oracular wisdom**: Goddess: Scathach. **Practical wisdom**: Goddess: Phronesia. **Prophetic wisdom**: Plant: almond branch. **Sacred wisdom**: North; Goddess: Sophia. **Secret wisdom**: God: Nereus, Thoth. **Silent wisdom**: Animal: owl. **Spiritual wisdom**: Color: indigo; God: Krishna, Odin. **Transcendental wisdom**: Goddess: Prajnaparamita (Perfection of Wisdom). **Tricky wisdom**: Animal: crow.

Wisdom beyond wisdom: Goddess: Hannahhannas. **Wisdom leading to illumination**: Crescent Moon. **Wisdom through experience**: Saturn; Stone: tektite; Goddess: Vajravarahi. **Clarity leading to wisdom**: New Moon. **Immortality through wisdom**: Plant: apple. **Wisdom**: Goddess: Parvati. **Power of wisdom to overcome obstacles**: Charm: white elephant with six trunks. **Pursuit of wisdom**: Plant: plane tree.

Wisdom of: discernment: Color: red. **the dream world**: Animal: owl. **the Earth**: Stone: turquoise; Goddess: Ceres. **the Otherworld**: Plant: hazel nut. **rebirth**: Mercury.

Wise counsel: Goddess: Athena, Minerva, Themis; God: Mimir; Evocation: Merlin. **Wise decisions**: (See: Decision/s). **Wise judgment**: Stone: tigereye; Goddess: Aeval. **Wise leadership**: Animal: cougar, lion.

To: **attract wisdom**: Stone: sodalite; Plant: hyacinth. **acquire wisdom**: Color: deep blue; Stone: amethyst, jade, pearl, turquoise; Plant: African violet, goldenseal, hazel; Goddess: Emer, Ereshkigal, Eve; God: Odin. **delegate authority wisely**: God: Enki. **learn to use magickal power wisely**: Goddess: Arianrhod. **release wisdom**: Plant: rosemary. **store wisdom**: Animal: polar bear, whale; Plant: all old trees. **transform anger into wisdom**: Color: blue. **use energy wisely**: Animal: elk. **use psychic powers wisely**: Stone: labradorite. **use wisdom to transform hatred into compassion**: Color: black.

Wishes

Tool: birthday candle, willow wand; Charm: shooting star, wishing well; Color: red, yellow; Stone: carnelian, emerald; Plant: balm of Gilead, bamboo, bayberry, beech, buckthorn, chestnut, dandelion (seed head), dogwood, fairy wand, garlic, ginseng, hawthorn, hazel, holly, Job's tears, juniper, laurel, lavender, peach, pomegranate, sage, sandalwood, sunflower, tonka bean, violet, walnut, willow; Goddess: Allat, Amaterasu, Anahita, Asherah, Caolainn, Coventina, Ishtar, Lakshmi, the Litae, Sarasvati, Tara, Varada (Granter of Boons), Yemaya; God: Danvendra, Ganesha, Glooskap, Helios, Indra, Leucetius, Leza, Maximon, Ptah, Shiva Varada, Shoney, Zeus.

Best wishes: Plant: basil. **Fertility wishes**: (See: Fertility). **Financial wishes**: (See: Finances). **Good wishes**: Plant: basil. **Health wishes**: Plant: cinquefoil. **Love wishes**: (See: Love). **Luck wishes**: Plant: hazel. **Money wishes**: Plant: cinnamon. **Prosperity wishes**: Plant: chamomile, honeysuckle. **Protection wishes**: Plant: cinquefoil, horehound. **Sexual wishes**: Goddess: Aeval, Maeve. **Strength wishes**: Plant: horehound.

To: **enhance the power of a wish**: Plant: lemon verbena. **help wishes come true**: Animal: ladybug; Plant: balm of Gilead, dandelion, Job's tears, tonka bean, willow; God: Glooskap. **learn to be careful what you wish for**: Goddess: Caolainn, White Buffalo Woman.

Witchcraft

(See also: Enchantment, Magick, Spells, Witches)

Moon

Color: black; Animal: baboon, bat, cat, black cat, hooded crow, stoat, hare, hyena, owl, weasel; Fungus: dung mushroom, toadstool; Plant: African tulip tree, alder, basil, blackthorn, couch grass, elder, enchanter's nightshade, harebell, hawthorn, hellebore, mandrake, mugwort, parsley, rowan, willow, witch grass, wolfsbane, yarrow, yew; Goddess: Airmid, Angitia, Artemis, Baba Yaga, Bast, Brigid, Chantico, Chlaus Haistic, Circe, Diana, Ertha, Freya, Gullveig (the Heig Witch), Habondia, Helice, Isis (Witch in the Stone Boat), Krtya, Lamia Tres (the Three Witches), Morgen, Nerthus, Oya, Teteoinnan, Tlazolteotl (Lady of Witches), Unial, Zobiana; God: Tagni.

Evil witchcraft: (See: Hexes). **Kitchen witchcraft**: Goddess: Ayabe, Chantico, Chiconahui, Ertha, Fornax, Hestia, Vesta; Evocation: the Kikimora. **White witchcraft**: Goddess: Nerthus.

To: **avert witchcraft**: Plant: dill seed. **counter witchcraft**: Plant: snapdragon. **defeat witchcraft**: Plant: ash leaves (burned), benzoin, betony (burned in fire or added to incense), hellebore, holly, rue, tormentil, woody nightshade. **prevent witchcraft**: Plant: fennel seeds (carried), St. John's Wort; *prevent suffering from witchcraft*: Plant: elder berries (gathered on Beltane eve). **protect against witchcraft**: Charm: hex sign, witch ball, water in which the clothes from an image of the god Maximón have been washed; Stone: marble, staurolite; Plant: betony, dill (hung over doorway), dill seed, flax flower, garlic, marjoram, mistletoe, rowan branch (hung over the doorway), rue, St. John's Wort (placed in windows), snapdragon, vervain; *against diseases caused by witchcraft*: Plant: willow; God: Hayenezgani; *protect children against witchcraft*: Stone: amber; *protect men from witchcraft*: Plant: holly.

Witches

(See also: Magicians, Witchcraft)

Moon

Plant: alder, beans, blackthorn, rowan, rue, willow, witch hazel, wolfsbane, yew; Fungus: stinkhorn, toadstool; Goddess: Aradia (Queen of the Witches), Artemis, Cailleach, Diana (Queen of Witches), Elphame, Ertha, Habondia, Hecate (Queen of Witches), Helice (Matron of Witches), Kali, Lilith, Morgan le Fey, Morgen, the Morrigan (Queen of Witches), Nicneven, Nostiluca, Tlazolteotl (Lady of Witches), Yemaya (Queen of Witches); God: Cernunnos, Horned God, Ocasta.

Witch's besoms/broomsticks: Plant: ash, birch, broom, willow (for binding together). **Witches' gatherings**: Goddess: Coventina, Thekla. **Witches' necklaces**: Stone: amber, jet.

Good luck for witches: Number: 13; Animal: spider. **Incantations against witches**: Plant: rue.

To: avert witches: Plant: broom, cinquefoil, rowan branch (hung over doorway), sow thistle, vervain; God: Janus; *from children*: Plant: caraway seeds (under bed). **banish witches**: Plant: St. John's Wort. **be invisible to witches**: Plant: sow thistle. **be**

invulnerable to witches: Plant: ash tree buds (eaten or burned on Beltane eve). **defeat witches' charms**: Plant: rowan. **detect a witch**: Plant: agrimony, maidenhair fern. **enhance witchiness**: Charm: witch hazel; Plant: witch hazel. **evade a witch**: Method: cross running water. **protect witches**: Plant: carnation; Goddess: Aradia, Hecate; *from capture*: Plant: carnation. **protect against witches**: Charm: ashes from a Beltane bonfire that was kindled with a huge fire by 9 (3 × 3) people or 27 (3 × 9) people; Plant: angelica, beans, gorse, juniper, laurel, mistletoe, rosemary, rowan, rue, walnut; *protect children from witches*: Plant: caraway seeds (under the bed). **render witches powerless**: Plant: elder, vervain.

Women

(See also: The Body, Childbirth, Men, People, Pregnancy, Yin)

Venus/Moon

Animal: cat, otter; Goddess: Hathor, Hera, Ishtar, Juno.

Abused/battered women: God: Mars; Evocation: Matholwch; *to protect women from abuse*: Goddess: Erzulie Dantor, Juno, Kali, Sekhmet; Evocation: the Domovoi; *safe house for*: Goddess: Juno. **Businesswomen**: Goddess: Hathor, Hera. **Dead women**: Goddess: Hathor; *who die in labor*: Cihuacoatl; *to reward the courage of women who die bravely in childbirth*: God: Tonatiuh; *justice for women who die of knife wounds*: Goddess: Ma Kiela. **Lesbians**: Goddess: Aphrodite Androphonos, Bast, Diana. **Maidens**: Waxing Moon; Goddess: the Maiden; *to protect*: Goddess: Chasca, Holda. **Married women**: Goddess: Frigg; *to protect*: Goddess: Hera, Juno, Mama Quilla. **Mothers**: Full Moon; Goddess: the Mother; *to protect*: Goddess: Kwan Yin, Lilith, Nekhebet, Sheng Mu; *to protect new* *mothers*: Goddess: Pi-Hsai Yuan Chin; *to protect nursing mothers*: Goddess: Hesat. **Old/post-menopausal women**: Waning Moon; Goddess: the Crone. **Other women**: *to protect against*: Plant: scullcap. **Pregnant women**: (See: Pregnancy). **Strong woman**: *to marry*: God: Nergal. **Young women**: Waxing Moon; Goddess: the Maiden; *rites of passage for*: Goddess: Aphrodite, Athene, Ix Chel; *to protect*: Goddess: Diana.

Cycle of a woman's life: Number: 3. **Left eyes of women**: Sun. **Left side of women**: Moon.

Good fortune in marriage for women: God: Bhaga.

Women's health: Goddess: Eir. **Women's lives**: Goddess: Diana. **Woman's love**: Plant: pink carnation; Goddess: Aphrodite. **Women's Mysteries**: (See: The Mysteries). **Women's problems**: Stone: jade; Plant: lady's mantle. **Women's rights**: Goddess: Atalanta. **Women's work**: Moon. **Secret rites of women**: Goddess: Bona Dea, Ceres, Fauna; Plant: flax.

For women to: dominate the home: Plant: rosemary. **gain favors**: Goddess: Kwan Yin.

To: attract women: Plant: dill, High John, holly leaves and berries (carried), laurel, patchouli, tuberose; *to attract love/lust from females*: Plant: henbane, High John. **comfort women in distress**: Stone: jasper. **defend women**: Goddess: Boldogasszony. **protect women**: Plant: motherwort; Goddess: Akonadi, Artemis, Bast, Boldogasszony, Fauna, Hathor, Hera, Juno, Neith, Taweret; *from domestic violence*: (See: Violence); *in childbirth*: (See: Childbirth); *in imminent danger of violence*: Goddess: Kali Ma; *in need*: Goddess: Akinad. **punish male violence towards**: Goddess: Amaterasu. **purify women**: Plant: myrrh.

Work

(See also: Career, Employment, Job, Pathworking, Workplace)

Sun

Goddess: Hebe.

Astral work: Plant: frankincense, galangal, rowan. **Breath work**: Air; Animal: dolphin, swallow-tailed kite. **Community work**: Goddess: Ala. **Computer work**: Goddess: Sesheta. **Creative work**: Color: yellow; Stone: angelite; Plant: cinnamon, ginseng, lavender, laurel, myrtle; *to inspire*: the Muses; *to protect*: Stone: coral. **Detail-oriented work**: Goddess: Sesheta. **Dream work**: Method: journaling; Charm: dream pillow; Stone: amethyst, citrine, jade, red jasper, kyanite, labradorite, lapis lazuli, marble, opal, clear quartz crystal, rose quartz, ruby; Plant: yarrow; Goddess: Canola, Estsanatlehi, Kali, Rhiannon; God: Angus, Oneicopompus. **Evil human handiwork**: *to avert*: Plant: cinquefoil. **Good works**: Stone: sapphire. **Healing work**: (See: Healing). **Housework**: Plant: flax, houseleek; Goddess: Hebe, Holda, Mokosh; Evocation: Kikimora. **Inner work**: (See: Inner Work). **Karmic work**: Saturn/Saturday; Color: indigo; Plant: frankincense; Goddess: Kali, Kwan Yin, Urd. **Magickal workings**: (See: Magick). **Mental work**: Gemini/Libra/Aquarius; Color: yellow; Goddess: Ceibhfhionn, Vac; God: Baile, Brahma, Sicun. **Overwork**: Stone: amethyst; Plant: rosemary, wood rose. **Past life work**: (See: Past Life Work). **Pathworking**: (See: Pathworking). **Psychic work**: Air/Water/Cancer/Pisces; Stone: amethyst, brown jasper, clear quartz crystal; Plant: bistort, cedar, cinnamon, mugwort, patchouli, saffron, wisteria, wormwood, yarrow; Goddess: Carmenta, Cybele, Fortuna, Freya, Hecate, Nanshe, Nephthys, Tana; God: Ahura Mazda, Bhalanetra, Glaucus, Math, Nereus,

Phorcys, Poseidon, Proteus, Thoth; *concentration in*: Oil: petitgrain; Plant: eyebright, lemon balm, marjoram, nutmeg, parsley, rosemary, sage; *energy in*: Plant: ginseng, yerba maté; *memory in*: Oil: petitgrain; Plant: eyebright, lemon balm, marjoram, nutmeg, orange, parsley, rosemary, sage; *mental steadiness in*: Plant: chamomile and celery with rosemary; *relaxation in*: Plant: anise, catnip, chamomile, clover, dandelion, hops, lavender, linden, mint, nutmeg, parsley, sage, savory, tarragon, wild thyme, valerian, vervain; *to induce dreams for*: Plant: wild lettuce; Goddess: Nephthys; *to stay grounded during*: Animal: harrier hawk. **Spellwork**: (See correspondences for: Magick, Spells). **Spirit work**: Goddess: Niamh; God: Arawn, Esus, Gwynn ap Nudd, Legba, Lugalucca, Pwyll. **Spiritual work**: Stone: brown jasper. **Soul work**: Animal: jaguar. **Teamwork**: Animal: ant, beaver, bee; Plant: mullein; God: Abarta, Aegir. **Trance work**: Plant: bistort; *divination in*: Plant: nutmeg (as incense) (See also correspondences for: Trance).

Work ethic: Animal: ant, beaver, bee. **Success at work**: Plant: hawthorn, rowan.

Patience in working toward goals: Stone: garnet. **Reward for hard work**: God: Degei. **Success at work**: Plant: hawthorn, rowan. **Work for small children**: (See: Children).

To: balance work and family life: Plant: pomegranate. **enjoy work**: Animal: wolf. **gain increased responsibility at work**: Goddess: Inanna. **make decisions about work**: Plant: apple. **work with the energies of light and darkness**: (See: Light). **work magick**: (See: Magick). **work toward goals**: (See: Goals).

To work on: past life issues: (See: Past Life Work). **problems**: Stone: jade.

To work with: angels: Air; Color: pastels, white; Stone: angelite; Plant: angelica. **animals**: (See: Animals). **energy**: (See: Energy). **fairies**: (See: Fairies). **the Goddess**: Full Moon; Stone: azurite. **spirit guides**: (See: Guidance).

orkers

Coworkers: *to deal with negativity of*: Color: purple; Plant: garlic, iron weed. **Disabled workers**: God: Vulcan. **Hard workers**: Color: blue; Plant: valerian; *to protect*: God: Saturn. **Workaholics**: Taurus.

To: help working class people: Goddess: Acca Larentia. **gain increased responsibility at work**: Goddess: Inanna.

orkplace

Harmony in the workplace: Animal: beaver; Plant: chamomile. **peaceful workplace**: Plant: rose.

To: banish spirits from a workplace: Plant: oak with mistletoe. **deal with negative coworkers**: Color: purple; Plant: garlic, iron weed.

orry

(See: Anxiety)

Chapter 24

Yang

(See also: Men, Yin)

Sun/Mars/Fire/Air/South/Summer/Aries/ Capricorn/Leo

Tool: athame, staff, sword, wand; Color: black, blue, gold, gray, green, orange, purple, red, white, yellow; Charm: phallus; Animal: copperhead, dragon, sheep; Number: odd numbers; Metal: gold, mercury; Stone: bright red carbuncle, Herkimer diamond, light blue sapphire; Fungus: fly agaric; Plant: allspice, almond, angelica, anise, asafetida, ash, aspen, bamboo, basil, benzoin, betony, cactus, caraway, carnation, carrot, cashew, cattail, cedar, celandine, celery, chamomile, chestnut, chicory, chili pepper, chrysanthemum, cinnamon, cinquefoil, clove, clover, coriander, cumin, cypress, dandelion, dill, dragon's blood, elecampane, elm, eye of Satan, eyebright, fennel, fern, fig leaf, frankincense, galangal, garlic, gentian, ginger, ginseng, hawthorn, hazel, heliotrope, High John, holly, hops, horehound, horseradish, hyssop, ivy, Jacob's ladder, juniper, laurel, lavender, leek, lemon, lily of the valley, lime, laurel, lovage, mace, male fern, white mandrake root, maple, marigold, marjoram, melon, mint, mistletoe, mullein, mustard, nettle, nutmeg, oak, olive, onion, orange, parsley, patchouli, pennyroyal, peony, pepper, peppermint, pimpernel, pine, Japanese black pine, pineapple, radish, rosemary, rowan, rue, saffron, sage, sassafras, sesame, spearmint, spruce, sunflower, tea, thistle, tobacco, vanilla, walnut, witch hazel, wolfsbane, wormwood, yohimbine, yucca; God: Horned God, Ogun, Somhlth, Zeus.

Yang problems: *to heal*: Plant: burdock root.

Male anger: (See: Anger). **Male attractiveness**: (See: Attractiveness). **Male beauty**: (See: Beauty). **Male bladder problems**: Plant: avens, parsley. **Male creativity**: Animal: sea horse; Metal: gold. **Male ego**: *to improve*: Plant: sunflower. **Male energy**: *male creative energy*: Metal: gold; *male sexual energy*: God: Hermes; *to balance*: Plant: banana; *to restore*: Plant: horny goatweed, yohimbine; *to synchronize*: Plant: balm of Gilead; *to unblock*: Plant: wild oat, yohimbine; God: Min. **Male/ female balance**: Animal: bass, slug, snail. **Male/female union**: (See: Union). **Male fertility/infertility**: (See: Fertility). **Male fidelity**: (See: Fidelity). **Male genitals**: Mars/Pluto. **Male inner healing**: Charm: musk. **Male initiation**: (See: Initiation). **Male liberation**: God: Soma; *male sexual liberation*: God: Pan. **Male libido**: (See: Libido). **Male lust**: (See: Lust). **Male magick**: (See: Magick). **Male mood disorders**: *to treat*: Plant: snake cereus. **Male Mysteries**: (See: The Mysteries). **Male passion**: Plant: cardamom, cinnamon. **Male potency**: Plant: hawthorn; *sexual potency*: (See: Sex). **Male principle**: Color: red. **Male problems**: *to treat*: Plant: snake cereus (See also: Diseases/Disorders). **Male productivity**: Animal: sea horse. **Male sexuality**: (See: Sex, Sexuality). **Male

sexual disorders: *to treat*: Metal: gold; Stone: lodestone. **Male sex magick**: (See: Magick). **Male strength**: (See: Strength). **Male vigor**: (See: Vigor). **Male violence**: (See: Violence). **Male vitality**: (See: Vitality). **Male wellness**: Plant: paprika, rosemary, saffron. **Yin/yang balance**: (See: Balance).

Good luck for males: Plant: holly.

To: attract yang: Sun; Metal: gold; Plant: dragon's blood. **balance yang**: Plant: banana, holly, sunflower. **get in touch with your inner male or female self**: God: Ometeotl. **stimulate yang**: Plant: cardamom, celery, cinnamon, ginseng, holly, lettuce, myrrh, yohimbine.

Yearning

(See: Desire, Wishes)

Yin

(See also: Women, Yang)

Venus/Moon/Earth/Water/North/West/Winter/Aquarius/Pisces/Scorpio/Virgo/Taurus

Tool: cauldron, chalice, drum, pentacle; Color: blue, brown, gray, green, pink, rose, silver, white; Charm: cowrie shell, yoni; Animal: swift, tiger, white tiger; Number: 2, even numbers; Metal: mercury, platinum, silver; Stone: blue lace agate, dull red carbuncle, chrysocolla, Herkimer diamond, moonstone, mother-of pearl, pearl, dark blue sapphire; Fungus: mushroom; Plant: aloe, amaranth, apple, avocado, balm of Gilead, barley, beech, belladonna, birch, blackberry, buckwheat, cabbage, camellia, camphor, cannabis, cardamom, catnip, cherry, coconut, comfrey, corn, cotton, cowslip, cucumber, cypress, daffodil, daisy, date palm, datura, dittany of Crete, *Dracena*, elder, eucalyptus, fern, fig, foxglove, fumitory, gardenia, geranium, grapevine, hellebore, hemlock, henbane, hibiscus, honeysuckle, hyacinth, iris, ivy, jasmine, kava kava, lemon, lemon balm, licorice, lilac, lily, linden, lotus, magnolia, maidenhair fern, black mandrake root, meadowsweet, mimosa, mistletoe, morning glory, mugwort, mulberry, myrrh, myrtle, nutmeg, oats, oleander (poisonous, not recommended), orange, orris root, papaya, papyrus, passionflower, patchouli, pea, peach, pear, pennyroyal, periwinkle, Japanese red pine, pomegranate, poplar, poppy, potato, primrose, pumpkin, queen of the night, quince, raspberry, rose, rose geranium, rye, sandalwood, scullcap, slippery elm, spearmint, strawberry, sweet pea, tamarind, tamarisk, tansy, thyme, tomato, trillium, tulip, valerian, vanilla, lemon verbena, vervain, violet, watermelon, wheat, willow, wintergreen, wood aloes, yarrow, yew; Goddess: Aphrodite, Ashtoreth, Astarte, Hera, Isis, Lakshmi, Maka, Neith, Prajnaparamita, Shakti, Suwa, Tara, Triple Goddess, Weiwobo, Xi Wang Mu, Yemaya.

Female ambition: Plant: white hollyhock; Goddess: Durga. **Female attractiveness**: (See: Attractiveness). **Female beauty**: (See: Beauty). **Female creativity**: (See: Creativity. **Female distress**: *to comfort*: Stone: jasper (worn). **Female enchantment**: Number: 7; Letter: S. **Female energy**: Goddess: Weiwobo, Xi Wang Mu; *female cosmic energy*: Goddess: Jagad-Yoni, Lilith, Shakti; *female creative energy*: Metal: silver; *female sexual energy*: *to unblock*: Plant: hibiscus, queen of the night, rose with hibiscus; *female warrior energy*: Animal: leopard, praying mantis; Goddess: Anath, Badb, the Morrigan. **Female fertility/infertility**: (See: Fertility). **Female fidelity**: Animal: emu; Plant: veronica. **Female freedom**: Goddess: Minerva, Yemaya. **Female genitals**: Venus/Moon. **Female hormones**: (See: The Body). **Female inconstancy**: Plant: hellebore. **Female independence**: (See: Independence). **Female initiation into**

motherhood: Plant: pussy willow; Goddess: Libera. **Female leadership**: Goddess: Cessair, Oya. **Female liberation**: Goddess: Lilith. **Female libido**: Goddess: Anath, Maeve. **Female lust**: (See: Lust). **Female magick**: (See: Magick). **Female/women's Mysteries**: (See: The Mysteries). **Female passion**: Goddess: Arani. **Female potency of Nature**: Animal: bee. **Female power**: (See: Power). **Female principle**: Color: blue; Animal: vulture; Metal: mercury; Goddess: Shakti, Suwa; *of Nature*: Goddess: Anna Livia, Asherah, Isis. **Female problems**: *to treat*: Plant: motherwort (See also: Diseases/Disorders). **Female prowess**: Goddess: Aphrodite. **Female reproductive system**: (See: The Body, Diseases/Disorders). **Female scent**: Plant: hawthorn. **Female sensuality**: *to increase*: Plant: juniper berry. **Female sex magick**: (See: Magick). **Female sexuality**: (See: Sex, Sexuality). **Female strength**: (See: Strength). **Female virtue**: Stone: pearl. **Female wellness**: Plant: marsh mallow. **Female wisdom**: (See: Wisdom).

Male/female balance: Animal: bass, slug, snail. **Male/female union**: (See: Union).

Good luck for females: Metal: silver; Stone: green aventurine; Plant: ivy. **Traditional female roles**: *to refuse to be bound by*: Goddess: Arianrhod. **Yin/yang balance**: (See: Balance).

To: activate yin: Plant: rose. **attract yin**: Moon; Metal: silver. **balance yin**: Plant: patchouli, quince. **get in touch with your inner male or female self**: God: Ometeotl. **stimulate yin**: Stone: moonstone, pearl; Plant: damiana, patchouli, saw palmetto.

Youth

(See also: Childhood, Children, Longevity)

Rising Sun/Spring

Color: green, pink, rose; Stone: moonstone; Plant: acorn, anise, apple, clover, cowslip, daisy, myrtle, primrose, rosemary, lemon verbena, vervain, wisteria; Goddess: Chalchihuitlcue, Flora, Freya, Ganymede, Hebe, Idunn, Juventas, the Maiden, Morgen, Mylitta, Renpet, Green Tara; God: Angus (Son of the Young), Cinteotl, Horus, Mabon (Divine Youth), Nodens, Yarillo (Young Lord).

Eternal youth: Color: green; Stone: aquamarine, emerald; Plant: bergamot, fern; Goddess: Idunn, Juventas; God: Eros. **Innocent youth**: Plant: white lilac, white lily; God: Mabon. **Lost youth**: *to restore*: Plant: anise.

Young animals: Goddess: Diana. **Young children**: (See: Children). **Young couples**: *to protect*: Invoke: Ya'halan. **Young love**: (See: Love). **Young men**: (See: Men). **Young people**: (See: People).

Good fortune for the young: Plant: clover.

Youthfulness: Plant: elder. **Youthful activity**: Goddess: Juventas. **Youthful appearance**: Stone: moonstone, tigereye; Plant: acorn, rosemary. **Youthful beauty**: (See: Beauty). **Youthful happiness**: Plant: spring crocus. **Youthful vigor**: (See: Vigor). **Youthful vitality**: Animal: lamb.

To: maintain youth: Plant: rosemary. **nurture the young**: Goddess: Demeter (Nurturer of Youth). **preserve youth**: Plant: acorn, myrtle wood, patchouli, rosemary. **protect youth**: God: Iovantucarus. **renew youth**: Plant: lemon balm, masterwort; Goddess: Cailleach, Hebe, Waldmichen; God: Dazbog (See also: Rejuvenation). **retain youth**: Plant: rosemary.

Chapter 25

Zeal

(See also: Passion)

Fire

Color: red; Number: 3, 11; Animal: crane; Plant: basil, cardamom, cayenne pepper, elder, ginger, gorse, pine, sycamore; Evocation: Zelus.

Passionate zeal: God: Zelus. **Religious zeal**: God: Dionysus.

Zodiac

Aquarius

Uranus/Saturn/Fixed Air/Saturday/January 21 to February 20/Winter

Color: blue (all shades), green, indigo, silver, turquoise, violet, pale yellow, multicolors; Charm: star, water bearer, water jar; Number: 11; Animal: otter; Metal: aluminum, lead, silver, uranium; Stone: amber, amethyst, aquamarine, chalcedonyx, white coral, garnet, jacinth, onyx, pearl, clear quartz crystal, sapphire, zircon; Plant: acacia, almond, anise, ash, aspen, benzoin, bittersweet, citron, cypress, dandelion, foxglove, frankincense, galbanum, iris, lavender, mace, Madagascar periwinkle, mastic, mimosa, myrrh, pansy, patchouli, peppermint, pine, pitcher plant, rosemary, rowan, sage, sandalwood, snowdrop, lemon verbena, violet, water violet; Goddess: Astarte, Hebe, Ishtar, Isis, Juno, Juno Februa, Nut; God: Ea, Hapy, Ouranos, Uranus, Varuna; Evocation: Deucalon, Ganymede, Uriel, Utnapishtim.

Aries

Mars/Cardinal Fire/Tuesday/March 21 to April 20/Spring

Color: pink, red, white, yellow; Charm: musk; Animal: ram, red-tailed hawk; Number: 1; Metal: gold, iron, steel; Stone: bloodstone, carnelian, coral, diamond, garnet, red jasper, fire opal, quartz crystal, ruby, sard; Plant: alder, allspice, angelica, basil, betony, bramble, carnation, cayenne, cedar, cinnamon, clove, copal, cowslip, cumin, dandelion, deerstongue, dragon's blood, frankincense, garlic, ginger, gorse, hemp, fennel, galangal, holy thistle, juniper, marjoram, mustard, onion, pepper, peppermint, pine, rosemary, wild thyme, willow; Goddess: Anath, Badb, Belat, Cybele, Durga, Hecate, Hestia, Ishtar, Macha, Minerva, the Morrigan, Neith, Nemain, Oya, Pallas Athene, Sekhmet, Seret, Tiamat; God: Ammon, Amun-Ra, Ares, Bel, Bel Marduk, Indra, Khnum, Marduk, Mars, Nergal, Pallas, Surya; Evocation: Gilgamesh, Machidiel, Malahidael, Samael.

Cancer

Moon/Cardinal Water/Monday/June 22 to July 23/Summer

Color: blue, pale blue, smoke gray, green, sea green, dark green, pink, silver, white; Charm: ambergris; Animal: crab, scarab beetle, turtle; Metal: silver; Stone: agate, amber, carnelian, chalcedony, emerald, jacinth, moonstone, opal, pearl, quartz crystal, rose quartz, ruby, sapphire; Plant: adder's tongue, agrimony, aloe, apple, balm, calamus, catnip, chamomile, daisy, eucalyptus, gardenia, geranium, holly, honeysuckle, hyssop, jasmine, lemon, lemon balm, lettuce, loosestrife, lotus, marigold, marsh woundwort, mimosa, moonwort, myrrh, oak, pansy, poppy, rose, wild rose, sandalwood, sundew, lemon verbena, violet, water lily; Goddess: Artemis, Ceres, Demeter, Diana, Isis, Juno Luna, Kwan Yin; God: Heimdall, Kephera, Mercury, Nzambi, Toko'yoto; Evocation: Charon, Gabriel, Muriel.

Capricorn

Saturn/Cardinal Earth/December 22 to January 21/Winter

Color: black, blue, royal blue, brown, dark brown, gray, dark green, indigo, red, russet, white; Animal: goat, snow goose; Metal: coal, lead, silver; Charm: civet, musk; Stone: amethyst, azurite, beryl, bloodstone, carnelian, garnet, all gems, jet, lapis lazuli, malachite, onyx, white-banded onyx, ruby, obsidian, quartz crystal, rose quartz, smoky quartz, ruby, sapphire, green tourmaline, turquoise, yellow zircon; Plant: birch, Brussels sprout, cabbage, comfrey, cypress, elder, holly, honeysuckle, horsetail, jasmine, kale, nightshade, magnolia, mimosa, mint, oakmoss, patchouli, poppy, rue, sassafras, slippery elm, thyme, vervain, vetiver, woodruff; Goddess: Amalthea, Amba, Aphrodite of the Goats, Freya, Gaia, Hecate, Juno Caprotina, Mylitta, Olwen, Virgo Caelestis; God: Aegipan, Agni, Baal Gad, Dionysus, Ea, Enki, Faunus, Freyr, the Horned God, Leshy, Oannes, Pan, Perun, Priapus, Saturn, Thor; Evocation: Azazel, Cambiel, Cassiel, Gabriel, Ganymede, Satan, satyrs.

Gemini

Mercury/Mutable Air/Wednesday/May 22 to June 22/Summer

Color: blue, green, orange, pink, red, silver, turquoise, violet, white, yellow, iridescent shades, multi-colors; Number: 2; Charm: twins; Animal: deer; Metal: mercury (toxic); Stone: agate, moss agate, alexandrite, aquamarine, carbuncle, emerald, moonstone, pearl, quartz crystal, tigereye, topaz, bicolored and variegated stones; Plant: almond, anise, bergamot, caraway, citron, clover, dill, eyebright, fennel, hawthorn, horehound, iris, lavender, lemongrass, lily, mace, mandrake, marjoram, mastic, mugwort, oak, parsley, pear, peppermint, sea holly, snapdragon, lemon verbena, vervain, wormwood, yam, yarrow; Goddess: Artemis, Inanna, Sheela-na-gig, Tefnut; God: the Alci, Apollo, the Asvins, Damuzi, the Dioscuri (Castor and Pollux), Enki, Hermes, Janus, Kokopeli, Krishna, Legba, Maximon, Mercury, Odin, Shu, Thoth, Tinira, Vali, Vidar; Evocation: Ambriel, Odysseus, Raphael, Romulus and Remus.

Leo

Sun/Fixed Fire/Sunday/July 23 to August 23/Summer

Color: green, gold, orange, red, yellow; Number: 1, 4; Charm: musk; Animal: lion, sphinx, sturgeon; Metal: gold, iron; Stone: amber, chrysolite, garnet, onyx, peridot, ruby, sapphire, sardonyx, tigereye, topaz; Plant: acacia, angelica, anise, benzoin, borage, celandine, chicory, cinnamon, clove, copal, dill, eyebright, frankincense, goldenseal, hazel, heliotrope, holly, juniper, laurel, marigold, mint, motherwort, nutmeg, oak, orange, peony, raspberry, rosemary, rue, saffron, sandalwood, St. John's Wort, sunflower; Goddess: Anath, Atalanta, Athirat, Bast, Cybele, Devi, Diana, Durga,

Freya, Hathor, Hera, Inanna, Ishtar, Juno, Libya, Nana, Omphale, Qadesh, Sekhmet, Sesheta, Smyrna, Sphinx, Tefnut, Al-Uzza; God: Aker, Aton, Atum, Helios, Ishkur, Mithras, Nergal, Ra, Vagisvara, Vishnu; Evocation: Hercules, Michael, Verchiel.

Libra
Venus/Cardinal Air/Friday/September 23 to October 23/Autumn

Color: black, blue, royal blue, brown, green, pink, yellow, pastels; Charm: scales, sword; Animal: raven; Metal: copper; Stone: aquamarine, beryl, coral, chrysolite, diamond, emerald, jacinth, jade, jasper, lapis lazuli, malachite, opal, sapphire, tourmaline; Plant: apple blossom, catnip, galbanum, *Justicia*, kidneywort, lilac, magnolia, marjoram, mugwort, mullein, orchid, passion flower, pennyroyal, persimmon, plumeria, rose, spearmint, sugar cane, sweet pea, thyme, vanilla, lemon verbena, violet, vine; Goddess: Astraea, Athena, Dike, Isis, Justicia, Libra, Ma'at, Minerva, Nemesis, Psyche, Themis, Unk, Venus, Yemaya; God: Cernunnos, Hephaestus, Horned God, Inyan, Mithras, Nagi, Njord, Orunmila, Shango, Shiva, Thoth, Orunmila, Vishnu, Vulca; Evocation: Anael, Uriel, Zuriel.

Pisces
Neptune/Jupiter/Mutable Water/Thursday/ February 20 to March 21/Winter

Color: aqua, green, sea green, pale blue, indigo, lavender, violet, white, light yellow; Animal: fish; Charm: ambergris, fish oil, two fish chained together; Metal: tin, platinum, alloys; Stone: amethyst, aquamarine, bloodstone, coral, diamond, jade, jasper, moonstone, mother of pearl, pearl, sapphire; Plant: alder, aloe, anise, ash, calamus, catnip, clove, cotton, eucalyptus, gardenia, heliotrope, honeysuckle, hyacinth, Irish moss, jasmine, laurel, lavender, lemon, lovage, mimosa, Norfolk Island pine, nutmeg, opium poppy, orris, rue, sage, sandalwood, sarsaparilla, star anise, sweet pea, willow; Goddesses: Aphrodite the Fish, Atargatis, Atargatis Derketo, Athirat, Dea Syria, Derceto, Diana, Mari, Mary, Nehalennia, Nina, Saga, Sedna, Urania, Venus, Yemaya; God: Cupid, Dylan, Ea, Enki, Eros, Jesus, Neptune, Poseidon, Tethra, Varuna, Vishnu.

Sagittarius
Jupiter/Mutable Fire/Thursday/November 23 to December 22/Autumn

Color: black, dark blue, gold, purple (all shades), red, yellow, patterns; Charm: archer, centaur; Animal: horse, elk; Metal: tin; Stone: amethyst, jacinth, lapis lazuli, obsidian, opal, sapphire, yellow sapphire, sodalite, sugilite, topaz, turquoise, zircon; Plant: anise, burdock, carnation, cedar, clove, red clover, copal, deerstongue, dragon's blood, elder, fig, frankincense, ginger, holly, honeysuckle, hyssop, juniper, mugwort, myrtle, nutmeg, orange, reed, rose, rosemary, sage, St. John's Wort, sassafras, black spruce, star anise, vervain, wood aloes; Goddess: Anath, Artemis, Atalanta, Athene Hippia, Cassandra, Diana, Epona, Isis, Rhiannon, Rigantona, Satis; God: Cronos, Hades, Jove, Jupiter, Mars, Nergal; Evocation: Amazons, Antiope, centaurs, Chiron, Crotus, Okyale, Pandarus, Sachiel, Teucer, Troxaris.

Scorpio
Pluto/Mars/Fixed Water/Tuesday/October 23 to November 23/Autumn

Color: black, brown, gray, maroon, orange, red, dark red; Charm: ambergris; Number: 0, 9; Animal: phoenix, scorpion, snake, dog, eagle, hawk, vulture; Metal: iron, steel, plutonium, copper; Stone: agate, aquamarine, beryl, bloodstone, citrine, coral, garnet, geode, malachite, obsidian, opal, pearl, rutilated quartz, ruby, topaz; Plant: allspice, ash, basil, benzoin, chrysanthemum, clove, cumin, deerstongue, dill, galangal, gardenia, ginger, heather, honeysuckle, hops, horehound, ivy, myrrh, nettle, opoponax, patchouli, pine, pomegranate, reed, saffron, sarsaparilla, thistle, vanilla, violet; Goddess: Ereshkigal, Hecate, Hel, Ishhara, Isis, Lilith, Persephone, Proserpina, Prosymna, Selqet; God: Ahriman, Anubis, Mars, Njord, Osiris, Pluto, Set; Evocation: Azrael, Barbiel.

Taurus

Venus/Fixed Earth/Friday/Midnight/April 20 to May 21/Spring

Color: blue, green, pink, red, yellow, pastels; Animal: bull, cow, ox, beaver, white tiger; Metal: bronze, copper, brass; Stone: moss agate, carnelian, chrysoprase, coral, red coral, diamond, emerald, jade, malachite, opal, pyrite, sapphire, topaz, golden topaz; Plant: apple, apricot, benzoin, bramble, cardamom, cedar, cherry, coltsfoot, daisy, dandelion, figwort, hawthorn, heather, hibiscus, honeysuckle, lilac, lily of the valley, lovage, magnolia, mugwort, oakmoss, orchid, patchouli, plumeria, raspberry, rose, sage, storax, thyme, tonka bean, vanilla, violet, willow; Goddess: Acca Larentia, Aditi, Aphrodite, Asherah, Astarte, Bast, Fatima, Flora, Frigg, Gaia, Hathor, Io, Ishtar, Isis, Lakshmi, Maia, Ninsûna, Skadi, Tanith, Al-Uzza, Vacca, Venus, Yaoji; God: Baal, Bacchus, Cernunnos, Dionysus, Horus, Indra, Jupiter, Krishna, Marduk, Min, Mithras, Serapis, Osiris, Poseidon, Ptah, Zeus; Evocation: Anael, Apis bull, Asmodel, Guinevere, Maid Marian, Minotaur, Perseus, Robin Hood.

Virgo

Mercury/Mutable Earth/Wednesday/August 23 to September 22/Summer

Animal: brown bear; Color: black, navy blue, brown, gold, gray, green, pink, purple, tan, violet, white, yellow; Metal: platinum, mercury (toxic, not recommended), nickel; Stone: agate, moss agate, amethyst, apatite, aquamarine, aventurine, carnelian, diamond, emerald, jacinth, green jade, jasper, pink jasper, lapis lazuli, marble, opal, peridot, sapphire, sardonyx, turquoise, zircon; Plant: almond, bergamot, caraway, cornflower, cypress, dill, eyebright, fennel, hazel, honeysuckle, horehound, hyacinth, lavender, lily, lily of the valley, mace, marjoram, moss, narcissus, patchouli, peppermint, rosemary, savory, scullcap, valerian, violet, vine; Goddess: Anath, Artemis, Ashtoreth, Astraea, Atalanta, Daphne, Demeter, Diana, Dike, Erigone, Frimla, Hestia, Ilmatar, Inanna, Iris, Ishtar, Isis, Kore, Mary, Nana, Narisah, Neith, Pallas Athene, Athena Parthenos, Persephone, Proserpina, Specifera Virgo Ceres, Tyche, Vesta; God: Forseti; Evocation: Hamaliel, Raphael.

Selected Bibliography

Al Ahram Weekly. Cairo: Al Ahram Publishing, 1993–1994.

Andrews, Ted. Animal Speak: The Spiritual and Magical Powers of Creatures Great and Small. St. Paul, Minn: Llewellyn, 2003.

_____. Animal Wise: The Spirit Language and Signs of Nature. Jacksonville, Tenn: Dragonhawk Publishing, 1999.

Aristotle (attributed to). Secretum Secretorum. Sami Salman al-A'War, trans. Beirut: Dar al-'Arabiyah lil-Tibaàh, 1995.

Best, Michael R. and Frank H. Brightman The Book of Secrets of Albertus Magnus of the Virtues of Herbs, Stones and Certain Beasts. York Beach, Maine: Samuel Weiser, 1999.

Betz, Hans Deiter (editor). The Greek Magical Papyri in Translation, Including the Demotic Spells. Chicago: University of Chicago Press, 1992.

Bircher, Warda H. Gardens of Hesperides: A Book on Old and New Plants for Egypt and Similar Climes. Cairo: The Anglo-Egyptian Bookshop, 1960.

Boericke, William, M.D. Materia Medica with Repertory. Santa Rosa, Calif: Boericke & Tafel Inc., 1927.

Boulos, Loutfy and el-Hadidi, Nabil M. The Weed Flora of Egypt. Cairo: The American University in Cairo Press, 1984.

Buckland, Raymond. Color Magick. St. Paul, Minn: Llewellyn Publications, 2002.

Budge, Sir E.A. Wallis. Egyptian Magic. New York: Dover Publications, 1971.

_____. Egyptian Book of the Dead: The Papyrus of Ani. New York: Dover Publications, 1967.

_____. Egyptian Religion. New York: Gramercy Books, 1959.

_____. Gods of the Egyptians. New York: Dover Publications, 1969.

Bulfinch, Thomas. Bulfinch's Mythology. New York: Modern Library, 1988.

Campbell, Joseph. The Masks of God (4 volumes). New York: Viking Press, 1975.

Cotterell, Arthur. The Encyclopedia of Mythology. New York: Southmark, 1996.

_____. A Dictionary of World Mythology. New York: Oxford University Press, 1990.

Culpepper Nicholas. Culpepper's Complete Herbal and English Physician. Glenwood, Ill: Meyerbooks, 1990.

Cunningham, Scott. *Cunningham's Encyclopedia of Magical Herbs*. St. Paul, Minn: Llewellyn, 1999.

Davidson, Gustav. *A Dictionary of Angels: Including the Fallen Angels*. New York: The Free Press, 1967.

Farb, Peter. *The Land, Wildlife and Peoples of the Bible*. New York: Harper & Row, 1967.

Fernie, M.D. William T., *Precious Stones: For Curative Wear, Other Remedial Uses and Likewise the Nobler Metals*. Kila, Mont: Kessinger Publications, LLC.

Fischer-Schreiber, Ingrid et al. *The Encyclopedia of Eastern Philosophy and Religion*. Boston: Shambhala, 1994.

Folkard, Richard. *Plant Lore, Legends and Lyrics: Myths, Traditions, Superstitions, and Folk-lore of the Plant Kingdom*. London: Sampson Low, Marston & Company, Ltd., 1892.

Forty, Jo. *Mythology: A Visual Encyclopedia*. London: PRC Publishing, 1999.

Frazer, Sir James G. *The Golden Bough: A Study in Magic and Religion*. New York: The MacMillan Company, 1953.

Gimbutas, Marija. *The Living Goddesses*. Berkeley, Calif.: University of California Press, 1999.

_____. *The Goddesses and Gods of Old Europe: Myths and Cult Images, 6500-3500* B.C. Berkeley, Calif.: University of California Press, 1996.

Goodrich, Norma Lorre. *Ancient Myths*. New York: Meridien Books, 1994.

Graf, Alfred Byrd. *Exotic Plant Manual*. East Rutherford, NJ: Roehrs Company, 1970.

Grant, Michael and Litzel, John. *Who's Who—Classical Mythology*. Routledge Who's Who Series. London: Routledge, 1995.

Graves, Robert. *The Greek Myths*, Volumes I and II. Baltimore, Md.: Penguin Books, 1955.

_____. *The White Goddess*. New York: Farrar, Straus and Giroux, 1966.

Graves, Robert and Patai, Raphael. *Hebrew Myths: The Book of Genesis*. Garden City, N.Y.: Doubleday & Company, Inc., 1963.

Grieve, Mrs. M. *A Modern Herbal*. http://www.botanical.com.

Grigson, Geoffrey. *The Goddess of Love: The Birth, Triumph, Death and Rebirth of Aphrodite*. London: Constable, 1976.

Hamilton, Edith. *Mythology*. Boston, Mass.: Little, Brown and Company, 1942.

Hart, George. *A Dictionary of Egyptian Gods and Goddesses*. Routledge, Kegan & Pack, 1986.

Ions, Veronica. *Egyptian Mythology*. New York: Peter Bedrick, 1983.

Jacobsen, Thorkild. *The Treasures of Darkness: A History of Mesopotamian Religion*. New Haven and London: Yale University Press, 1976.

Jordan, Michael. *Encyclopedia of Gods*. New York: Facts On File, 1993.

Kibby, Geoffrey. *Mushrooms and Toadstools*. Secaucus, N.J.: Chartwell/Octopus, 1977.

Kinsley, Davis. *Hindu Goddesses: Visions of the Divine Feminine in the Hindu Religious Tradition*. Berkley, Calif: University of California Press, 1998.

Lewis, James R. and Evelyn Dorothy Oliver. *Angels A to Z*. New York: Gale Research, 1996.

MacLennan, Bruce. *Biblioteca Arcana.* http://www.cs.utk.edu/~mclennan/ OM/BA/.

Miller, Richard Alan. *The Magical and Ritual Use of Herbs.* New York: Destiny Books, 1983.

Monaghan, Patricia. *The Book of Goddesses and Heroines.* New York: E. P. Dutton, 1981.

Noble, Vicki. *Motherpeace: A Way to the Goddess Through Myth, Art and Tarot.* St. Paul, Minn.: Llewellyn, 1997.

Osborn, Harold. *South American Mythology.* New York: Peter Bedrick Books, 1986.

Perry, Frances. *Flowers of the World.* London: Optimum Books, 1972.

Phillips, Roger and Foy, Nicky. *The Random House Book of Herbs.* New York: Random House, 1990.

Regula, DeTraci. *The Mysteries of Isis: Her Worship and Magick.* St. Paul, Minn.: Llewellyn, 1999.

Rosenberg, Donna. *World Mythology: An Anthology of the Great Myths and Legends.* Lincolnwood, Ill.: NTC Publishing Group, 1993.

Sargent, Denny. *Global Ritualism: Myth and Magic Around the World.* St. Paul, Minn.: Llewellyn, 1994.

Sharman-Burke, Juliet and Greene, Liz. *The Mythic Tarot.* NY: Simon & Schuster, 1986.

Shearer, Alastair. *The Hindu Vision: Forms of the Formless.* New York: Thames & Hudson, 1993.

Slater, Herman. *Magickal Formulary Spellbook, Books I & II.* Magickal Childe: New York, 1987.

Spence, Lewis. *An Encyclopaedia of Occultism.* Secaucus, N.J.: Citadel Press, 1993.

_____. *The History and Origins of Druidism.* N. Hollywood, Calif.: Newcastle Publishing Co., 1995.

Spretnak, Charlene. *Lost Goddesses of Early Greece: A Collection of Pre-Hellenic Myths.* Boston, Mass.: Beacon Press, 1992.

Starhawk (Miriam Simos). *The Spiral Dance: A Rebirth of the Ancient Religion of the Great Goddess.* San Francisco, Calif.: HarperSanFrancisco, 1989.

Stewart, R.J. *Celtic Gods, Celtic Goddesses.* London: Blandford, 1996.

Stone, Merlin. *When God Was a Woman.* New York: Harcourt Brace & Company, 1976.

Stuckey, Maggie. *The Complete Herb Book.* New York: Berkley Publishing Group, 2001.

Sykes, Egerton. *Who's Who: Non-Classical Mythology.* New York: Oxford University Press, 1993.

Tackholm, Vivi. *Students' Flora of Egypt.* Cairo: Anglo-Egyptian Bookshop, 1956.

Tarostar. *Witch's Formulary and Spellbook.* Tarostar Enterprises: Bronx, N.Y., 1997.

Turner, Patricia and Coulter, Charles Russell. *Dictionary of Ancient Deities.* New York: Oxford University Press, 2000.

Watterson, Barbara. *The Gods of Ancient Egypt.* London: B. T. Batsford, 1984.

Weiser, Francis X. *Handbook of Christian Feasts and Customs.* New York: Harcourt, Brace and World, Inc., 1958.

Yronwode, Catherine. *Hoodoo Herb and Root Magic: A Materia Magica of African-American Conjure.* Forestville, Calif.: 1992.

About the Author

Eileen Holland is a Wiccan priestess, a solitary eclectic Witch who writes books about witchcraft. She is also the Webmaster of Open, Sesame (*www.open-sesame.com*), a popular Wiccan Website. She began writing this book a long time ago because she needed such a book, but found that it didn't exist.

Eileen lives quietly in upstate New York with her husband and son.

Notes: